OUT OF
OUR PAST

*The Forces That Shaped
Modern America*

OUT OF
OUR PAST

The Forces That Shaped
Modern America

REVISED EDITION

CARL N. DEGLER

Harper & Row, Publishers
New York and Evanston

LIBRARY OF CONGRESS CATALOG CARD NUMBER: 77-88637

To Catherine,
who endlessly read it,
and to Paul and Suzanne,
who endlessly heard about it.

"Nor for the past alone—for meanings to the future."

WALT WHITMAN

Contents

Preface to the First Edition

WHEN the historian sits down to write about the past, there are always several approaches open to him. The one most commonly taken might be called descriptive history, in which the story of what happened in the past is told as accurately and minutely as research, literary style, and the space available will permit. Insofar as it is possible, the events of the past are presented as they took place; small effort is made to distinguish between those events which have relevance to the present and those which have little. The primary purpose is to recreate the past as nearly as possible, not to draw morals or to uncover guides for the present.

That is not the approach taken here. To put it simply, this book seeks an answer to the question "How did Americans get to be the way they are in the middle of the twentieth century?" In other words, the multitudinous events of the American past are here seen through the lens of the present. Admittedly, much of the material usually included in the story of America is missing in such an approach. Readers should be warned that they will find nothing here on the Presidential administrations between 1868 and 1901, no mention of the American Indians or the settlement of the seventeenth-century colonies; the War of 1812 is touched upon only in a footnote.

History viewed through the eyes of the present is understandably different from history written from the standpoint of the past. Persons and events which in other treatments might remain unnoticed or unappreciated now spring into focus. Therefore, in this book events and developments usually ignored or subordinated in standard accounts of American history now move to the center of the stage. For example, the history of the Negro in America figures prominently in three chapters, the rise and influence of the city dominate two, and the beginnings of American nationality in the colonial period come in for extended discussion.

All written history, no matter how slow its pace or numerous its

xiii

pages, is a selection from the infinite number of facts in the past. A history of a whole nation in one volume, like this, is of necessity even more selective. Therefore, in addition to confining myself to those aspects of the past which bear on the present, I have also limited myself to the history of Americans as a people. There is little in this book about great men or individual genius, except where such men embody the values and aspirations of the whole people. The work and thought of many American thinkers, artists, scientists, and statesmen are therefore ignored, not because they are unimportant, but because to have included them would have made this something other than a history of the shaping of the American people.

In current historical writing it is fashionable to look to economic and social forces for the explanation of the movement and direction of history. Certainly this approach is more sophisticated than attributing the course of history to the actions of a few great men. But at the same time it seems to ignore a force in history which this book seeks to emphasize—the role of ideas. And by ideas I mean the beliefs, assumptions, and values of the people rather than the great ideas of thinkers which form the basis of formal intellectual history. Because, for example, Americans cherished ideas like freedom, equality, and Christian justice, they acted to realize them; in doing so, they changed the course of their history.

Karl Marx and other writers of the nineteenth century made a luminous contribution to the understanding of human history when they were able to show that men's ideas bore a close relation to the socioeconomic context in which they flourished; that, for example, the poetry of a pastoral people is filled with pastoral imagery, that an industrial society extols free labor. But this insight is often betrayed by the careless conclusions drawn from it. It is one thing to see connections between ideas and the economy and quite another to assume that all ideas must necessarily be but pale reflections of economic interests and the mode of production. One cardinal assumption in this book is that ideas have a life of their own, regardless of their origin. And by "a life of their own" I mean that men defend or oppose ideas for reasons not always related to their immediate self-interest, or to the socioeconomic character of their society.

The truth of this, it seems to me, arises out of the nature of man himself. Admittedly, men are animals and, in common with other beasts, have powerful drives toward food, self-preservation, and sex, none of which can be easily denied or sublimated. On these indubitable facts rests the materialist conception of history. But man is more than an animal. He surrounds himself with ritual, ideal, and prejudice to such an extent that the essentials of life, like food-gathering, sexual satisfaction, and the urge to know the universe, are unnecessarily hedged about with obstacles to immediate gratification. No other animal is guilty of such illogicality. No other animal, for example, exposes himself to death in defense of vague, indefinable conceptions like national honor or the nature of God. Ideas are live forces in human history; often they are more powerful than the elemental drives. On an individual basis and in psychoanalytical language, this is to say that the superego can and does override the id.

Sometimes ideals derived from one social context are still vital in another. An example of this is the Progressive period, when Americans attempted to retain the ideology of Jefferson in the face of economic and social forces which ran counter to it. The ideology was not overwhelmed, however; for though economic and social pressure are potent, ideals are tenacious.

This toughness of men's ideals is part and parcel of the human condition. By nature man is moral; on all levels of culture and through all recorded time, men have labeled things as good or evil. And so long as men divide their world into good and bad, they will strive to make the world and themselves conform to their ideal of the good. Of course, they do not and will not always succeed. For, as this book tries to show, though Americans at times successfully imposed their ideals on the society, at other times they permitted the social relations they evolved to dictate what was morally good and bad. But wherever men have striven to realize their moral visions, they have demonstrated that ideas, as well as economic forces, can change the direction of history.

Recently, in *The Power Elite,* C. Wright Mills, the sociologist and critic of modern American society, called historians "the celebrants of the present." Perhaps this book places me in what Mr. Mills obviously intended to be an uncomfortable and unenviable category. By the standards of those who believe that criticism is synonymous with denigration, this book will indeed seem to celebrate the American past as well as the present. To those who are frustrated by and discontented with the state of American culture, the criticisms of that culture contained in this book will appear tepid and mild. In reply I can only say that this is not an arraignment of American society, but neither is it a panegyric. At the outset I freely admit that I am somewhat awed by the 350-year history of the American people. For even when one has discounted all the blessings bestowed upon Americans by their fortunate separation from the turmoil and destruction of Europe's wars and by the bounty of nature in the soil, the achievement of Americans is still worthy of being ranked with that of any people.

This is true, it seems to me, whether one measures that achievement in the scales of material wealth or in the balance of spiritual values. Noble ideals like equality, opportunity, and democratic government are as American as big, flashy automobiles or indoor plumbing. Moreover, the ideal of a wide distribution of wealth that America has long represented and come closer to achieving than any other people in the history of the world is something more than dollar-chasing; it is truly one of the great humanitarian visions of mankind. One basic assumption of this book is that one can stress the positive achievements of America without descending into the swamp of sycophancy or the desert of chauvinism. Only the reader can judge whether this purpose is gained.

Another assumption upon which this book rests is that Americans are different from other people, that their culture is unique. Undoubtedly, in the long perspective of world history, the United States is but one of several variants of western European civilization. But within the framework of that civilization, I believe, the Americans are distinct and even unique. From time to time within these pages these similarities and differences are a part of our story, for in them can be discerned the outline of the American national character. Indeed, this book might well be called "An Exploration into the Origins of the American Character." The word "exploration" is important. For, considering the magnitude of the subject, this venture cannot be a definitive chart of American social topography; it can be only exploratory. It is in that spirit that it is offered.

More than most books, this one is indebted to many people. In this instance, they are not so much librarians and friends, though they too figured in its making, but the scores of writers on American society, past and present, who have quarried the material which alone has made it possible to write a broad-swinging venture like this. Today it is no longer possible to write an interpretation of American history directly from the sources; the documentation is too vast for one or even a dozen men to encompass in a lifetime. Hence, the great bulk of the material I have used in writing this book was first dug out of the sources by a myriad of scholars. Occasionally I have done some of the digging myself in order to try to get answers to questions which I thought vital to my story but which I could not find in the published literature. But it would be untrue to the facts if I left the impression that this book is a work of original research.

The Critical Bibliographical Essay at the end of the book attempts to discharge partially my overwhelming indebtedness to my fellow workers in the field of American culture. Needless to say, none of these writers is responsible for what I have written in this book since I have not always agreed with their individual interpretations, nor have I always used their facts as they did. For that reason the weaknesses and mistakes which inevitably must be found in this book are all due to me; the valuable things are largely the result of the work of those many scholars from whom I have shamelessly borrowed.

In common with all authors, I am deeply indebted in a variety of ways to a number of people who helped me write this book. Mildred Campbell, John Dydo, Clyde Griffen, and Charles C. Griffin of the Vassar faculty read several of the chapters and graciously gave me the benefit of their knowledge and criticism. Needless to say, they are in no way responsible for what here appears, though they often saved me from errors of fact and interpretation. John Appleton and Evan Thomas of Harper's gave me not only the benefit of their substantial editorial skills but, even more precious to any writer, that indispensable commodity—encouragement.

Though individuals are usually thanked in this place, an institution—Vassar College—also richly deserves mention. Though a small college, Vassar has given more than lip service to the ideal of encouraging scholarship and writing by its faculty. For a whole year, while I worked on this book, I was supported by a Vassar Faculty Fellowship in the style to which I was accustomed. No greater faith can a college display in its faculty.

I am also indebted to the several scores of students with whom, over the years, I discussed these ideas in History 265. With their criticisms and insights they helped me to hammer out the substance of this book. I should also like to thank Miss Sandra Suits for her careful checking of the Bibliography and Mrs. J. R. Churchill for her conscientious and accurate typing of the manuscript.

As is traditional, my wife, Catherine Grady Degler, appears last, but not least. Although she did none of the typing for which wives are usually commended, her assistance was of the kind none but a wife dare offer. Because she was impatient with vagueness, scornful of pomposity, and ruthless with verbiage, I am greatly indebted to her; and so will the reader be.

C. N. D.

Poughkeepsie, New York

Preface to the Revised Edition

THE purpose of this brief preface is to acquaint the reader who may be familiar with the original edition with the extent of the revisions here. In one sense, this revised edition is complete. I have gone over the entire text, line by line, measuring its content against what I have learned about the nature of the American experience in the decade since the original book appeared. Where I have found that I no longer agree with the earlier version, I have made appropriate changes in the text. Occasionally I have deleted material that I now believe to be erroneous or misleading, as, for example, in regard to the comparison between Latin American and United States slavery in Chapter I, or in relating the social attitudes of the 1950's to those of the 1930's. In a number of other places I have added information or interpretations that seem warranted by recent scholarship.

In another sense, this revision is not thorough, for I have not set out to write a new book, as I probably would if I rethought the whole project. The approach and the main outlines of the original book are the same here, except for the addition of an entirely new chapter on foreign policy. In that chapter I have tried to do for the complicated and lengthy subject of foreign policy what I sought to do for domestic history in the book as a whole, that is, to account for how the United States got to where it is today. Thus, the new chapter makes no pretense to being a survey of foreign affairs, though I hope not to have slighted important steps in the transition of the United States from a minor to a prime power in the world.

Finally, it is worth pointing out here that the bibliography has been brought up to date in a manner described more specifically in a headnote that precedes it.

I would also like to take this opportunity to thank those friends and readers who have taken the trouble to call to my attention errors of fact or of interpretation and thereby have helped me in this revision. I am particularly indebted to Thomas A. Bailey, Henry F.

Preface to the Revised Edition

Graff, Kirk Jeffrey, Jr., Joseph Jeppson, C. Gordon Post, and Donald Raichle. Special thanks go to Stephanie Saunders who did a careful and efficient job in helping me bring up to date the bibliography and to Catherine Grady Degler who, as always, gave me the benefit of a critical and careful reading of my prose in the new chapter on foreign policy. I am also deeply indebted to Charles Lofgren for his close and thoughtful reading of that same chapter, permitting me to draw upon his broad knowledge of the history of United States foreign policy. Needless to say he bears no responsibility for any errors that may appear in that chapter. Probably to my detriment, I did not always take his advice.

Stanford, California   CARL N. DEGLER

OUT OF
OUR PAST

*The Forces That Shaped
Modern America*

CHAPTER I

The Beginnings

IN MORE ways than is often recognized, the one hundred years after the death of Elizabeth I in 1603 comprise the first century of the modern world. A number of developments peculiar to modern European thought cluster within these years: the true beginnings of modern science in the work of Galileo and Newton, Harvey and Boyle; the first expression of modern democratic ideas by the Levelers and in the Army Debates of the English Civil Wars; the decisive break in a millennium of religious dominance with the end of the wars of religion and the acceptance of the principle of religious tolerance; the achievement of lasting constitutional and representative government in England with the Glorious Revolution of 1688. It was also the time of the first permanent settlement of English colonists.

For America, its origin in this first century of the modern era was filled with meaning. In the New World, the future was still fluid. Europe's ways, both the new and the old, could be planted in America free of the choking weeds of outmoded habits. America would be a testing ground, but it would be difficult to predict what would happen. Some of the European ways would wither; some would strike root; still others would change and adapt to the new environment. For a good part of the century this plasticity was characteristic. But then, by the end of the century, the mold had hardened. In a number of ways what Americans would be for generations to come was settled in the course of those first hundred years.

1. CAPITALISM CAME IN THE FIRST SHIPS

To men coming from the "tight little isle" the vast land of America, though untamed and dense with forest, was remarkably like the old, both in the flora that covered it and in the crops that it would yield. Although in a region like New England settlers would soon discover the soil to be thin and unfertile compared with that of the more southern colonies, it was not a desert, and from the beginning a well-organized group like the Massachusetts Bay people were able to wring a comfortable, if not opulent, living from the lean and rocky soil. The Chesapeake colonies had better soil and, as it turned out, a climate conducive to the production of a staple of world-wide appeal—the infamous weed, tobacco.

A land endowed with such promise could not fail to attract a continuous stream of men and women from the shops and farms of Europe. For centuries the problem in Europe had been that of securing enough land for the people, but in the New World the elements in the equation were reversed. "I hear . . . that servants would be more advantageous to you than any commodity," wrote a Londoner to a Virginian in 1648. For over three centuries, through wars and revolutions, through economic disaster and plague, the underlying, insistent theme of American history was the peopling of a continent.

Though the pervasive influence which Frederick Jackson Turner attributed to the frontier in the shaping of the American character can be overestimated, the possibility of exaggeration should not hide the undeniable fact that in early America, and through most of the nineteenth century, too, land was available to an extent that could appear only fabulous to land-starved Europeans. From the outset, as a result, the American who worked with his hands had an advantage over his European counterpart. For persistent as employers and rulers in America might be in holding to Old World conceptions of the proper subordination of labor, such ideas were always being undercut by the fact that labor was scarcer than land.

The imagination of men was stretched by the availability of land in America. Though land was not free for the taking, it was nearly so. In seventeenth-century New England there were very few landless people, and in the Chesapeake colonies it was not unusual for an indentured servant, upon the completion of his term, to be granted a piece of land. Thus, thanks to the bounty of America, it was possible for an Englishman of the most constricted economic horizon to make successive jumps from servant to freeman, from freeman to freeholder, and, perhaps in a little more time, to wealthy speculator in lands farther west. Not all men were successful in America, to be sure, but, as the emigration literature reveals, enough were to encourage most men in the new land to strive hard for wealth and success.

In America the availability of land rendered precarious, if not untenable, those European institutions which were dependent upon scarcity of land. Efforts to establish feudal or manorial reproductions in the New World came to nothing. The Dutch, for example, tried to set up an ambitious system of patroons, or great landowners, whose broad acres along the Hudson were intended to be worked by tenants. In keeping with the manorial practices common in Europe, the patroon was to dispense justice and administer in his own right the government of his little kingdom. But contrary to the popular tradition that sees these patroonships carrying over into the period of English rule after 1664, only two of the Dutch grants outlasted New Netherland, and of them, only one was in existence ten years later. Under English rule only Rensselaer retained his original grant; all the others returned or forfeited them to the Dutch West Indies Company. It is significant that the other land-granting policy of the Dutch, that of individual small holdings, was much more successful.

At the beginning, Lord Baltimore's attempt to erect manors in Maryland and to create a feudal aristocracy enjoyed more success than that of the Dutch. Some sixty manors were established in the province during the seventeenth century, the lords of which constituted a kind of new Catholic aristocracy. On at least one of these manors, that of St. Clement, manorial courts-leet (for tenants) and baron (for freeholders) were actually held, private justice being dispensed by the lord. But here too the experiment of transplanting European social ways to the free and open lands of America was to prove futile. Slavery and the plantation were much more efficient ways for utilizing land than the outmoded manor; moreover, tenants were restive in the face of free lands to the west.

The failure in New York and Maryland to reconstitute the manors of Europe did not prevent the founders of the Carolinas from making one more attempt. In the Fundamental Constitutions of 1669 provisions were included for "leet-men" who would not be able "to go off from the land of their particular lord" without permission. Moreover, it was decreed that "all children of leet-men shall be leet-men, and so to all generations." Atop this lowest stratum of hereditary tenants was erected a quasi-feudal hierarchy of caciques and

landgraves, capped by a palatine. It seems hardly necessary to add
that this design, so carefully worked out in Europe, was implemented
in America only to the extent of conferring titles upon the ersatz
nobility; the leetmen, so far as the records show, never materialized.
Indeed, the Fundamental Constitutions caused much friction between
the settlers and the proprietors. Even though the hereditary nature
of leetmen was discarded in 1698, the popular assembly never accepted the revised Constitutions. By the opening years of the eighteenth century, the baronies which had been taken up ceased to exist,
having become simply estates or farms, none of which enjoyed the
anticipated array of tenants.

Thus in those areas where an attempt was made to perpetuate the
social system of Europe, it was frustrated almost from the beginning.
Quite early in the colonial period, great disparities of wealth appeared in the agricultural South, as elsewhere, but this was stratification resting initially and finally upon wealth, not upon honorific
or hereditary conceptions derived from Europe. As such, the upper
class in America was one into which others might move when they
had acquired the requisite wealth. And so long as wealth accumulation was open to all, the class structure would be correspondingly
flexible.

In New England there was no experimentation with feudal or
manorial trappings at all. The early history of that region is a deliberate repudiation of European social as well as religious practices.
As early as 1623, for example, William Bradford wrote that com-
munal property arrangements had failed in Plymouth and that as a
consequence the governing officials divided the land on an individual
basis. Individual ownership of land, so typical of American land tenure ever since, was thus symbolically begun. The larger colony of
Massachusetts Bay, in its first codification of laws, the Body of
Liberties of 1641, made explicit its departure from feudal and manorial incidents upon landholding. "All our lands and heritages shall
be free from all fines and licenses upon Alienations, and from all
hariotts, wardships, Liveries, Primerseisins, yeare day and wast, Es-
cheates and forfeitures. . . ."[1]

---

[1] Not all of the legal incidents and limitations on landholding then in practice in England were absent in America. Primogeniture, for example, obtained
in the southern colonies and entail prevailed in all the English settlements.
But it is also a fact that both institutions, all through the colonial period,
were viewed as foreign to the tendency of American social development, to

The failure of America to inherit a feudal aristocracy carried implications for the future which transcended the mere matter of land tenure. The very character of the society was affected. As we have seen already, it meant that wealth, rather than family or tradition, would be the primary determinant of social stratification. Furthermore, the absence of a feudal past in America has meant that there are no classes which have a vested interest in the social forms of an earlier age. American society, as a consequence, has never split into perpetually warring camps of reactionaries and radicals in the way, for example, French society has been riven ever since the Great Revolution. Moreover, without a feudal past America offers only the thinnest of soils into which a conservatism of the European variety can sink its roots. Almost all Americans, regardless of class, have shared a common ideology of Lockean or Whig liberalism. The so-called conservatives of the American past have been only more cautious liberals. There has been in America no widely held tradition analogous to the conservatism of Edmund Burke. Burke's considerable doubts about the hopefulness of progress, the efficacy of reason, and the value of revolution have found few sympathetic ears in America. Only some ante-bellum Southerners like Thomas Dew and George Fitzhugh showed any signs of a Burkean conservative outlook. And those murmurings were killed off with the end of slavery. The conservativism of a Senator Barry Goldwater today is really only a species of nineteenth-century liberalism, as his emphasis upon laissez faire and individualism make clear.

There are economic as well as political consequences which flow from the fact that America was born free of the medieval tradition of aristocracy. These are seen in purest form if we contrast the attitudes of French and American businessmen of today. (It is not so true of Englishmen because participation in trade never carried the taint it did in France.) Recruitment into management has often been hampered in France, John Sawyer has shown, because of the tradi-

---

be abandoned completely by the end of the eighteenth century. "By the time of the Revolution, although much land throughout Colonial America was still held in fee tail estates, the practice of holding land in fee simple estates was widespread. Great strides had been made in barring fee tail estates by provisions in original grants to private parties, by private action in the making of wills, and by special acts of the colonial assemblies on behalf of individual cases." Marshall Harris, *Origin of the Land Tenure System in the United States* (Ames, Iowa, 1953), p. 373. By way of contrast, it might be recalled that primogeniture was not finally relinquished in England until 1926.

tion of family enterprises. Businesses, as a result, were confined to a limited group of potential entrepreneurs and managers, "much like hereditary fiefs." Instead of being able to draw upon the population at large for the best men available, French business enterprises have often been handicapped by adherence to a feudal-like familism. Morover, a feudally derived aristocratic disdain for trade and business still permeates French thought. As a consequence, the French businessman, unlike the American, is beset by a nagging feeling that success in business carries little prestige, and is perhaps a sign of unfashionable materialism. Hence he does not drive to expand his business or to make a lot of money; he is satisfied with a comfortable, gentlemanly living. As Sawyer concluded, "the French businessman has *himself* been unable to slough off the anti-capitalist sentiment in his social inheritance." Devoid of such an inheritance, America was also free of such inhibitory attitudes; from the beginning, to paraphrase a President of the United States, the main business of America has been business.

In place of medieval and aristocratic notions about the degrading nature of trade and business, seventeenth-century Englishmen brought to America two forms of that bourgeois spirit which Max Weber has called the Protestant ethic: Puritanism and Quakerism. It is possible to overemphasize the extent to which Puritanism departed from medieval conceptions of a just price, prohibitions on interest, and so forth, for such restrictions on unfettered capitalism also formed a part of Puritan economic practice in Massachusetts. But the general loosening of economic restraints which Puritanism unquestionably condoned, and its strong accent on work and wealth accumulation, bestowed religious sanction upon business enterprise. The backward-looking and forward-looking economic attitudes of Puritanism are both apparent in a Massachusetts statute of 1633. The first part of the law, in keeping with medieval practices, prescribed the proper wages for bricklayers, wheelwrights, and other skilled craftsmen, while the second part of the statute ordered "that noe person, hawseholder or other, shall spend his time idely or unprofflably, under paine of such punishment as the Court shall thinke meet to inflicte. . . ." The close connection the Puritans saw between godliness and worldly success is implied in a story told by Governor Winthrop in his *History*. The story concerns one Mansfield who arrived in Massachusetts poor but "godly." With the help of a local rich man, "this Mansfield grew suddenly rich, and then lost his godliness, and his wealth soon after."

The calling or occupation of a Christian was an important conception in Puritan thought; it also serves as an illuminating instance of the tight linkage between religion and economics. To the Puritan, a Christian's work was a part of his offering to God. "As soon as ever a man begins to look toward God and the way of his Grace," the Reverend John Cotton taught, "he will not rest til he find out some warrantable calling and employment." No matter what the calling, "though it be but of a day laborer," yet he will make of it what he can, for "God would not have a man receive five talents and gain but two; He would have his best gifts improved to the best advantage." To work hard is to please God. As Cotton Mather, the grandson of Cotton, said at the end of the century, "Would a man *Rise* by his Business? I say, then let him Rise to his Business. . . . Let your *Business* ingross the most of your time."

Important, but often overlooked in the Puritan conception of the calling, was the idea of social obligation. For a calling to be "warrantable," John Cotton emphasized, a Christian "would see that his calling should tend to public good." Moreover, he continued, "we live by faith in our vocations, in that faith, in serving God, serves man, and in serving man, serves God." Cotton Mather at the end of the century put it even more succinctly. One should have a calling "so he may Glorify God by doing Good for *Others,* and getting of *Good* for himself." It was this cementing of social conscience to thoroughgoing individualism which saved Puritanism from degenerating into a mere defense of economic exploitation.

If the earliest New England divines, like John Cotton, had some doubts about the trader because—as the medieval schoolmen had contended—he bought cheap and sold dear, later Puritans easily accepted the new economic order. Cotton Mather, in good Calvinist fashion, argued that there "is every sort of law, except the Popish, to justify a regulated *usury.* 'Tis justified by the law of necessity and utility; humane society, as now circumstanced, would sink, if all *usury* were impracticable." By the end of the century the bulging warehouses, the numerous ships in Boston Harbor, and the well-appointed mansions of the merchants bore ample testimony to the compatibility of Puritanism and wealth-getting.

Widely recognized as the dominance of Puritan economic ideals may be in New England, it is less often acknowledged that the thriving commercial center of Philadelphia owed much of its drive to a similar ethic among the Quakers. It was William Penn, not John Winthrop, who advised his children to "cast up your income and live on half; if you can, one third; reserving the rest for casualties, charities portions." Simple living, as the bewigged Cotton Mather reminds us, was more a trait of Quakers in the seventeenth and eighteenth century than of Puritans. Indeed, so concerned were the Friends over the vices of ostentation and vanity that they would not permit portraits to be painted of themselves. The only concessions to the ego were black silhouettes. "Be plain in clothes, furniture and food, but clean," William Penn told his children, "and the coarser the better; the rest is folly and a snare." Furthermore, he counseled, diligence "is the Way to Wealth: *the diligent Hand makes Rich.* . . . *Frugality* is a Virtue too, and not of little Use in Life, the better Way to be Rich, for it has less Toil and Temptation."

As early as the seventeenth century, "the legend of the Quaker as Businessman" was widely accepted. This view, which was very close to the truth, pictured the Friends as shrewd, canny traders, "singularly industrious, sparing no Labour or Pains to increase their Wealth," as one seventeenth-century observer put it. Much like the Puritans, the Quakers were eminently successful in the counting-house, preaching and practicing that doctrine of the calling which united religion and bourgeois economic virtues in happy and fruitful marriage.

As New Englanders fanned out into the upper Middle West in the late eighteenth and early nineteenth centuries, the seed of Puritanism, now stripped of its theological skin, was planted across America. Furthermore, if one recognizes that the doctrine of the calling was Calvinist before it was Puritan, then the numbers of people imbibing that economic precept with their religious milk swells to impressive proportions. At the time of the Revolution, Ralph Barton Perry has calculated, one out of every two white Americans was a Calvinist of some persuasion.

Though no longer clothed in theological vestments, the virtue of work and wealth has remained with Americans. As Max Weber pointed out, the advice of Franklin's Poor Richard is but the Puritan ethic shorn of its theology; in Franklin the Puritan has become the Yankee. No longer anxious about unearthly salvation, but keenly concerned about a good bargain, the American still carries the telltale brand of Puritanism.

2. WERE THE PURITANS "PURITANICAL"?

To most Americans—and to most Europeans, for that matter—the core of the Puritan social heritage has been summed up in Macaulay's well-known witticism that the Puritans prohibited bearbaiting not because of torture to the bear, but because of the pleasure it afforded the spectators.[2] And as late as 1925, H. L. Mencken defined Puritanism as "the haunting fear that someone, somewhere, may be happy." Before this chapter is out, much will be said about the somber and even grim nature of the Puritan view of life, but quips like those of Macaulay and Mencken distort rather than illumine the essential character of the Puritans. Simply because the word "Puritan" has become encrusted with a good many barnacles, it is worth while to try to scrape them off if we wish to gain an understanding of the Puritan heritage. Though this process is essentially a negative one, sometimes it is clarifying to set forth what an influence is *not* as well as what it is.

Fundamental to any appreciation of the Puritan mind on matters of pleasure must be the recognition that the typical, godly Puritan was a worker in the world. Puritanism, like Protestantism in general, resolutely and definitely rejected the ascetic and monastic ideals of medieval Catholicism. Pleasures of the body were not to be eschewed by the Puritan, for, as Calvin reasoned, God "intended to provide not only for our necessity, but likewise for our pleasure and delight." It is obvious, he wrote in his famous *Institutes,* that "the Lord have endowed flowers with such beauty . . . with such sweetness of smell" in order to impress our senses; therefore, to enjoy them is not contrary to God's intentions. "In a word," he concluded, "hath He not made many things worthy of our estimation independent of any necessary use?"

It was against excess of enjoyment that the Puritans cautioned and legislated. "The wine is from God," Increase Mather warned, "but the Drunkard is from the Devil." The Cambridge Platform of the

[2] Joseph Crouch, in his *Puritanism and Art* (London, 1910), p. 350 n., attempted to even the score with Macaulay by quoting from the Puritan Stubbes, who wrote against bearbaiting in 1583: "What Christian heart can take pleasure to see one poor beast to rend, tear and kill another, and all for his foolish pleasure? . . . So, love God, love his creatures." And Increase Mather, father of Cotton Mather, condemned cockfighting by saying that "to delight in tormenting dumb creatures, and to make sport of their miseries, is a great inhumanity and scandalous Violation of the 6th Commandment."

Church of 1680 prohibited games of cards or dice because of the amount of time they consumed and the encouragement they offered to idleness, but the ministers of Boston in 1699 found no difficulty in condoning public lotteries. They were like a public tax, the ministers said, since they took only what the "government might have demanded, with a more *general imposition* . . . and it employes for the welfare of the publick, all that is raised by the *lottery*." Though Cotton Mather at the end of the century condemned mixed dancing, he did not object to dancing as such; and his grandfather, John Cotton, at the beginning saw little to object to in dancing between the sexes so long as it did not become lascivious. It was this same John Cotton, incidentally, who successfully contended against Roger Williams' argument that women should wear veils in church.

In matters of dress, it is true that the Massachusetts colony endeavored to restrict the wearing of "some new and immodest fashions" that were coming in from England, but often these efforts were frustrated by the pillars of the church themselves. Winthrop reported in his *History,* for example, that though the General Court instructed the elders of the various churches to reduce the ostentation in dress by "urging it upon the consciences of their people," little change was effected, "for divers of the elders' wives, etc., were in some measure partners in this general disorder."

We also know now that Puritan dress—not that made "historical" by Saint-Gaudens' celebrated statue—was the opposite of severe, being rather in the English Renaissance style. Most restrictions on dress that were imposed were for purposes of class differentiation rather than for ascetic reasons. Thus long hair was acceptable on an upper-class Puritan like Cromwell or Winthrop, but on the head of a person of lower social status it was a sign of vanity. In 1651 the legislature of Massachusetts called attention to that "excess in Apparell" which has "crept in upon us, and especially amongst people of mean condition, to the dishonor of God, the scandall of our profession, the consumption of Estates, and altogether unsuitable to our poverty." The law declared "our utter detestation and dislike, that men or women of mean condition, should take upon them the garb of Gentlemen, by wearing Gold or Silver Lace, or Buttons, or Points at their knees, or to walk in great Boots; or Women of the same rank to wear Silk or Tiffany hoods, or Scarfes, which tho allowable to persons of greater Estates, or more liberal education, is intolerable in people of low condition." By implication, this law affords a clear description of what the well-dressed Puritan of good estate would wear.

If the Puritans are to be saved from the canard of severity of dress, it is also worth while to soften the charge that they were opposed to music and art. It is perfectly true that the Puritans insisted that organs be removed from the churches and that in England some church organs were smashed by zealots. But it was not music or organs as such which they opposed, only music in the meetinghouse. Well-known American and English Puritans, like Samuel Sewell, John Milton, and Cromwell, were sincere lovers of music. Moreover, it should be remembered that it was under Puritan rule that opera was introduced into England—and without protest, either. The first English dramatic production entirely in music—*The Siege of Rhodes*—was presented in 1656, four years before the Restoration. Just before the end of Puritan rule, John Evelyn noted in his diary that he went "to see a new opera, after the Italian way, in recitative music and scenes. . . ." Furthermore, as Percy Scholes points out, in all the voluminous contemporary literature attacking the Puritans for every conceivable narrow-mindedness, none asserts that they opposed music, so long as it was performed outside the church.

The weight of the evidence is much the same in the realm of art. Though King Charles' art collection was dispersed by the incoming Commonwealth, it is significant that Cromwell and other Puritans bought several of the items. We also know that the Protector's garden at Hampton Court was beautified by nude statues. Furthermore, it is now possible to say that the Puritan closing of the theaters was as much a matter of objection to their degenerate lewdness by the 1640's as an objection to the drama as such. As far as American Puritans are concerned, it is not possible to say very much about their interest in art since there was so little in the seventeenth century. At least it can be said that the Puritans, unlike the Quakers, had no objection to portrait painting.

Some modern writers have professed to find in Puritanism, particularly the New England brand, evidence of sexual repression and inhibition. Though it would certainly be false to suggest that the Puritans did not subscribe to the canon of simple chastity, it is equally erroneous to think that their sexual lives were crabbed or that sex was abhorrent to them. Marriage to the Puritan was something more than an alternative to "burning," as the Pauline doctrine of the Catholic Church would have it. Marriage was enjoined upon the righteous

Christian; celibacy was not a sign of merit. With unconcealed disapprobation, John Cotton told a recently married couple the story of a pair "who immediately upon marriage, without ever approaching the *Nuptial* Bed," agreed to live apart from the rest of the world, "and afterwards from one another, too. . . ." But, Cotton advised, such behavior was "no other than an effort of blind zeal, for they are the dictates of a blind mind they follow therein and not of the Holy Spirit which saith, *It is not good that man should be alone.*" Cotton set himself against not only Catholic asceticism but also the view that women were the "unclean vessel," the tempters of men. Women, rather than being "a necessary Evil are a necessary Good," he wrote. "Without them there is no comfortable Living for Man. . . ."

Because, as another divine said, "the Use of the Marriage Bed" is "founded in man's Nature" the realistic Puritans required that married men unaccompanied by wives should leave the colony or bring their wives over forthwith. The Puritan settlements encouraged marriages satisfactory to the participants by permitting divorces for those whose spouses were impotent, too long absent, or cruel. Indeed, the divorce laws of New England were the easiest in Christendom at a time when the eloquence of a Milton was unable to loosen the bonds of matrimony in England.

Samuel Eliot Morison in his history of Harvard has collected a number of examples of the healthy interest of Puritan boys in the opposite sex. Commonplace books, for example, indicate that Herrick's poem beginning "Gather ye rosebuds while ye may" and amorous lines from Shakespeare, as well as more erotic and even scatological verse, were esteemed by young Puritan men. For a gentleman to present his affianced with a pair of garters, one letter of a Harvard graduate tells us, was considered neither immoral nor improper.

It is also difficult to reconcile the usual view of the stuffiness of Puritans with the literally hundreds of confessions to premarital sexual relations in the extant church records. It should be understood, moreover, that these confessions were made by the saints or saints-to-be, not by the unregenerate. That the common practice of the congregation was to accept such sinners into church membership without further punishment is in itself revealing. The civil law, it is true, punished such transgressions when detected among the regenerate or among the nonchurch members, but this was also true of contemporary non-Puritan Virginia. "It will be seen," writes historian

Philip A. Bruce regarding Virginia, "from the various instances given relating to the profanation of Sunday, drunkenness, swearing, defamation, and sexual immorality, that, not only were the grand juries and vestries extremely vigilant in reporting these offences, but the courts were equally prompt in inflicting punishment; and that the penalty ranged from a heavy fine to a shameful exposure in the stocks . . . and from such an exposure to a very severe flogging at the county whipping post." In short, strict moral surveillance by the public authorities was a seventeenth-century rather than a Puritan attitude.

Relations between the sexes in Puritan society were often much more loving and tender than the mythmakers would have us believe. Since it was the Puritan view that marriage was eminently desirable in the sight of God and man, it is not difficult to find evidence of deep and abiding love between a husband and wife. John Cotton, it is true, sometimes used the Biblical phrase "comfortable yoke mate" in addressing his wife, but other Puritan husbands come closer to our romantic conventions. Certainly John Winthrop's letters to his beloved Margaret indicate the depth of attachment of which the good Puritan was capable. "My good wife . . . My sweet wife," he called her. Anticipating his return home, he writes, "So . . . we shall now enjoy each other again, as we desire. . . . It is now bed time; but I must lie alone; therefore I make less haste. Yet I must kiss my sweet wife; and so, with my blessing to our children . . . I commend thee to the grace and blessing of the lord, and rest. . . ."

Anne Bradstreet wrote a number of poems devoted to her love for her husband in which the sentiments and figures are distinctly romantic.

> To my Dear and loving Husband
> I prize thy love more than whole Mines of gold
> Or all the riches that the East doth hold.
> My love is such that Rivers cannot quench,
> Nor aught but love from thee give recompense.

In another poem her spouse is apostrophized as

> My head, my heart, mine Eyes, my life, nay more
> My joy, my Magazine of earthly store

and she asks:

> If two be one, as surely thou and I,
> How stayest thou there, whilst I at Ipswich lye?

Addressing John as "my most sweet Husband," Margaret Winthrop perhaps epitomized the Puritan marital ideal when she wrote,
"I have many reasons to make me love thee, whereof I will name
two: First, because thou lovest God and, secondly, because thou lovest me. If these two were wanting," she added, "all the rest would be
eclipsed."

It would be a mistake, however, to try to make these serious,[3]
dedicated men and women into rakes of the Renaissance. They were
sober if human folk, deeply concerned about their ultimate salvation
and intent upon living up to God's commands as they understood
them, despite their acknowledgment of complete depravity and un-
worthiness. "God sent you not into this world as a Play-House, but
a Work-house," one minister told his congregation. To the Puritan
this was a world drenched in evil, and, because it truly is, they were
essentially realistic in their judgments. Because the Puritan expected
nothing, Perry Miller has remarked, a disillusioned one was almost
impossible to find. This is probably an exaggeration, for they were
also human beings; when the Commonwealth fell, it was a Puritan,
after all, who said, "God has spit in our faces." But Professor Miller's generalization has much truth in it. Only a man convinced of
the inevitable and eternal character of evil could fight it so hard and
so unceasingly.

The Puritan at his best, Ralph Barton Perry has said, was a
"moral athlete." More than most men, the Puritan strove with himself and with his fellow man to attain a moral standard higher than
was rightfully to be expected of so depraved a creature. Hence the
diaries and autobiographies of Puritans are filled with the most tor-
turous probing of the soul and inward seeking. Convinced of the
utter desirability of salvation on the one hand, and equally cognizant
of the total depravity of man's nature on the other, the Puritan was
caught in an impossible dilemma which permitted him no rest short
of the grave. Yet with such a spring coiled within him, the Puritan

---

[3] Winthrop provides an example of the rather trivial lengths to which this
serious view of life could lead an otherwise worldly-wise Puritan. Early in his
life in America he gave up toasting the health of fellow drinkers—though,
significantly, not the drinking. Starting from the premise that "Every empty
and ineffectual representation of serious things is a way of Vanity," Winthrop
was led to the conclusion that toasting was vain. For it holds "forth love and
wishes of health, which are serious things, by drinking, which neither in the
nature, nor use, it is able to effect. . . ."

drove himself and his society to tremendous heights of achievement both material and spiritual.

Such intense concern for the actualization of the will of God had a less pleasant side to it, also. If the belief that "I am my brother's keeper" is the breeding ground of heightened social conscience and expresses itself in the reform movements so indigenous to Boston and its environs, it also could and did lead to self-righteousness, intolerance and narrow-mindedness, as exemplified in another product of Boston: Anthony Comstock. But this fruit of the loins of Puritanism is less typical of the earthy seventeenth-century New Englander than H. L. Mencken would have us think. The Sabbatarian,[4] antiliquor, and antisex attitudes usually attributed to the Puritans are a nineteenth-century addition to the much more moderate and essentially wholesome view of life's evils held by the early settlers of New England.

To realize how different Puritans could be, one needs only to contrast Roger Williams and his unwearying opponent John Cotton. But despite the range of differences among Puritans, they all were linked by at least one characteristic. That was their belief in themselves, in their morality and in their mission to the world. For this reason, Puritanism was intellectual and social dynamite in the seventeenth century; its power disrupted churches, defied tyrants, overthrew governments, and beheaded kings.

The Reformation laid an awesome burden on the souls of those who broke with the Roman Church. Proclaiming the priesthood of all believers, Protestantism made each man's relationship to God his own terrifying responsibility. No one else could save him; therefore no one must presume to try. More concerned about his salvation

---

[4] It is true that the Puritans insisted on proper behavior during the Sabbath, but so did other seventeenth-century communities. The law in Virginia, like the law in Massachusetts, compelled church attendance. Moreover, the records of seventeenth-century Virginia are filled with examples of indictments and convictions for breaking the decorum of the Sabbath. P. A. Bruce lists the following as examples of such infractions of Sunday in Virginia: shelling corn, hiring out a horse, carrying a gun, fishing, killing a deer, getting drunk, going on a journey, stripping tobacco, selling cider, driving a cart, fiddling and dancing, swearing, carrying wheat, and fighting. The greater rigidity of the Victorian age regarding the Sabbath is indicated by the nineteenth-century editor's comments on Winthrop's traveling on the Sabbath. "His example would justify the many others," wrote editor Savage in 1854. "Such instances are now almost unknown."

than about any mundane matter, the Puritan was compelled, for the
sake of his immortal soul, to be a fearless individualist.

It was the force of this conviction which produced the Great Migration of 1630–40 and made Massachusetts a flourishing colony in
the span of a decade. It was also, ironically, the force which impelled
Roger Williams to threaten the very legal and social foundations of
the Puritan Commonwealth in Massachusetts because he thought the
oligarchy wrong and himself right. And so it would always be. For
try as the rulers of Massachusetts might to make men conform to
their dogma, their own rebellious example always stood as a guide
to those who felt the truth was being denied. Such individualism, we
would call it today, was flesh and bone of the religion which the
Puritans passed on. Though the theocracy soon withered and died,
its harsh voice softened down to the balmy breath of Unitarianism,
the belief in self and the dogged resistance to suppression or untruth
which Puritanism taught never died. Insofar as Americans today can
be said to be individualistic, it is to the Puritan heritage that we must
look for one of the principal sources.

In his ceaseless striving for signs of salvation and knowledge of
God's intentions for man, the Puritan placed great reliance upon the
human intellect, even though for him, as for all Christians, faith was
the bedrock of his belief. "Faith doth not relinquish or cast out reason," wrote the American Puritan Samuel Willard, "for there is nothing in Religion contrary to it, tho' there are many things that do
transcend and must captivate it." Richard Baxter, the English Puritan, insisted that "the *most Religious,* are the *most* truly, and *nobly
rational.*" Religion and reason were complementary to the Puritan,
not antithetical as they were to many evangelical sects of the time.

Always the mere emotion of religion was to be controlled by reason. Because of this, the university-trained Puritan clergy prided
themselves on the lucidity and rationality of their sermons.[5] Almost
rigorously their sermons followed the logical sequence of "doctrine,"

[5] One of the persistent myths about the Puritans is the assertion that they
preached "hell-fire and damnation." The original source for this myth is undoubtedly Jonathan Edwards' timeworn sermon at Enfield, "A Sinner in the
Hands of an Angry God." This sermon, however, is not only unrepresentative
of the seventeenth-century Puritans—it was delivered in 1739—but it is extreme for Edwards himself. As a deliberate effort to ignite a revival in Enfield
during the Great Awakening, it reflected neither Edwards' usual style of
preaching nor the closely reasoned, decidedly unemotional sermons which
were the usual fare of Puritan congregations in the seventeenth century.

"reasons," and "uses." Conscientiously they shunned the meandering and rhetorical flourishes so beloved by Laudian preachers like John Donne, and in the process facilitated the taking of notes by their eager listeners. One of the unforgivable crimes of Mistress Anne Hutchinson was her assertion that one could "feel" one's salvation, that one was "filled with God" after conversion, that it was unnecessary, in order to be saved, to be learned in the Bible or in the Puritan writers. It was not that the Puritans were cold to the Word—far from it. A saint was required to testify to an intense religious experience —almost by definition emotional in character—before he could attain full membership in the Church. But it was always important to the Puritans that mere emotion—whether it be the anarchistic activities of the Anabaptists or the quaking of the Friends—should not be mistaken for righteousness or proper religious conduct. Here, as in so many things, the Puritans attempted to walk the middle path —in this instance, between the excessive legalism and formalism of the Catholics and Episcopalians and the flaming, intuitive evangelism of the Baptists and Quakers.

Convinced of reason's great worth, it was natural that the Puritans should also value education. "Ignorance is the mother (not of Devotion but) of Heresy," one Puritan divine declared. And a remarkably well-educated ministry testified to the Puritan belief that learning and scholarship were necessary for a proper understanding of the Word of God. More than a hundred graduates of Cambridge and Oxford Universities settled in New England before 1640, most of them ministers. At the same date not five men in all of Virginia could lay claim to such an educational background. Since Cambridge University, situated on the edge of Puritan East Anglia, supplied most of the graduates in America, it was natural that Newtown, the site of New England's own college, would soon be renamed in honor of the Alma Mater. "After God had carried us safe to New-England," said a well-known tract, some of its words now immortalized in metal in Harvard Yard, "one of the next things we longed and looked after, was to advance learning, and perpetuate it to posterity; dreading to leave an illiterate ministry to the churches, when the present ministers shall lie in the dust." "The College," founded in 1636, soon to be named Harvard, was destined to remain the only institution of higher learning in America during almost all the years of the seventeenth century. Though it attracted students from as far away as Virginia, it remained, as it began, the fountainhead of Puritan learning in the New World.

Doubt as one may Samuel Eliot Morison's claims for the secular origins of Harvard, his evidence of the typically Renaissance secular education which was available at the Puritan college in New England is both impressive and convincing. The Latin and Greek secular writers of antiquity dominated the curriculum, for this was a liberal arts training such as the leaders had received at Cambridge in England. To the Puritans the education of ministers could be nothing less than the best learning of the day. So important did education at Harvard seem to the New Haven colony in 1644 that the legislature ordered each town to appoint two men to be responsible for the collection of contributions from each family for "the mayntenaunce of scolars at Cambridge. . . ."

If there was to be a college, preparatory schools had to be provided for the training of those who were expected to enter the university. Furthermore, in a society dedicated to the reading of the Bible, elementary education was indispensable. "It being one chief project of that old deluder Satan to keep men from the knowledge of the Scriptures" began the first school laws of Massachusetts (1647) and Connecticut (1650). But the Puritans supported education for secular as well as religious reasons. The Massachusetts Code of 1648, for instance, required children to be taught to read inasmuch "as the good education of children is of singular behoof and benefit to any Common-wealth."

The early New England school laws provided that each town of fifty families or more was to hire a teacher for the instruction of its young; towns of one hundred families or more were also directed to provide grammar schools, "the master thereof being able to instruct youths so far as they may be fitted for the University." Though parents were not obliged to send their children to these schools, if they did not they were required to teach their children to read. From the evidence of court cases and the high level of literacy in seventeenth-century New England, it would appear that these first attempts at public-supported and public-controlled education were both enforced and fruitful.

No other colony in the seventeenth century imposed such a high educational standard upon its simple farming people as the Puritans did. It is true, of course, that Old England in this period could boast of grammar schools, some of which were free. But primary schools were almost nonexistent there, and toward the end of the seventeenth century the free schools in England became increasingly tuition schools. Moreover, it was not until well into the nineteenth century that the English government did anything to support schools. Primary and secondary education in England, in contrast with the New England example, was a private or church affair.

Unlike the Puritans, the Quakers exhibited little impulse toward popular education in the seventeenth and early eighteenth centuries. Because of their accent on the Inner Light and the doctrine of universal salvation, the religious motivation of the Puritans for learning was wanting. Furthermore, the Quakers did not look to education, as such, with the same reverence as the Puritans. William Penn, for example, advised his children that "reading many books is but a taking off the mind too much from meditation." No Puritan would have said that.

Virginia in the seventeenth century, it should be said, was also interested in education. Several times in the course of the century, plans were well advanced for establishing a university in the colony. Free schools also existed in Virginia during the seventeenth century, though the lack of village communities made them inaccessible for any great numbers of children. But, in contrast with New England, there were no publicly supported schools in Virginia; the funds for the field schools of Virginia, like those for free schools in contemporary England, came from private or ecclesiastical endowment. Nor was Virginia able to bring its several plans for a college into reality until William and Mary was founded at the very end of the century.

Though the line which runs from the early New England schools to the distinctly American system of free public schools today is not always progressively upward or uniformly clear, the connection is undeniable. The Puritan innovation of public support and control on a local level was the American prototype of a proper system of popular education.

American higher education in particular owes much to religion, for out of the various churches' concern for their faiths sprang a number of colleges, after the example of the Puritans' founding of Harvard. At the time of the Revolution, there were eight colleges besides Harvard in the English colonies, of which all but one were founded under the auspices of a church. William and Mary (1693) and King's College, later Columbia (1754), were the work of the Episcopalians; Yale (1701) and Dartmouth (1769) were set up by orthodox Congregationalists dissatisfied with Harvard; the College of New Jersey, later Princeton (1747), was founded by the Presbyterians; Queens College, later Rutgers (1766), by the Dutch Reformed Church; the College of Rhode Island, later Brown (1764), by the Baptists. Only the Academy of Philadelphia, later the University of Pennsylvania (1749), was secular in origin.

The overwhelming importance of the churches in the expansion of American higher education during the colonial period set a pattern which continued well into the nineteenth century and to a limited extent is still followed. Well-known colleges like Oberlin, Wesleyan, Haverford, Wittenberg, Moravian, Muhlenberg, and Notre Dame were all founded by churches in the years before the Civil War. By providing a large number of colleges (recall that England did not enjoy a third university until the nineteenth century), the religious impulses and diversity of the American people very early encouraged that peculiarly American faith in the efficacy and desirability of education for all.

When dwelling on the seminal qualities of the seventeenth century, it is tempting to locate the source of the later American doctrine of the separation of Church and State and religious freedom in the writings of Roger Williams and in the practices of provinces like New York, Maryland and Pennsylvania. Actually, however, such a line of development is illusory. At the time of the Revolution all the colonies, including Rhode Island, imposed restrictions and disabilities upon some sects, thus practicing at best only a limited form of toleration, not freedom of religion—much less separation of Church and State. Moreover, Roger Williams' cogent and prophetic arguments in behalf of religious freedom were forgotten in the eighteenth century; they could not exert any influence on those who finally worked out the doctrine of religious freedom enshrined in the national Constitution. In any case, it would have been exceedingly difficult for Williams to have spoken to Jefferson and the other Virginians who fought for religious freedom. To Williams the Puritan, the great justification for freedom of religion was the preservation of the purity of the Church; to the deistic Virginians, the important goal was the removal of a religious threat to the purity and freedom of the State.

3. RIGHTS OF ENGLISHMEN

For one who cherishes American political institutions, the manner in which representative government began in the seventeenth century might well make him shudder as well as wonder. The process was largely "accidental," arbitrary and hardly to be anticipated from the nature of things. This is especially true of Virginia, where the whole precedent of self-government in America was first worked out. When in 1619 the Virginia Company suggested that the colonists "might have a hande in the governinge of themselves," there was, as Charles Andrews has pointed out, "no sufficient reason, legal or other, why a popular assembly should be set up in Virginia." It was all that casual.

The precarious existence of this first representative assembly in America was emphasized in 1624, when the Crown, for various reasons, revoked the Company's charter, the King declaring that "the Government of the Colonies of Virginia shall immediately depend upon Our Selfe." Thus was terminated the legal authority for an assembly. Three times between 1625 and 1629 the planters held "conventions" for specific purposes, but these were neither regular nor legitimate assemblies. Beginning in 1630, however, and each year thereafter, without any encouragement from the Crown, the Virginians held an Assembly and presumed to legislate. Interestingly enough, in the light of the later Revolution, among their earliest laws was a prohibition upon the Governor and the Council—both of whom were appointed by the Crown—to "lay any taxes or impositions, upon the colony, theire land or commodities, otherwise then [sic] by the authoritie of the Grand Assembly." The legal authority for the Assembly, however, was still in doubt, for the King had not assented to its existence, and no one disputed his final and complete authority. Then in 1637 the royal instructions to the Governor contained a call for an Assembly, but the failure to provide for annual sessions indicated that the Crown was still undecided on the matter. Finally, the Governor's instructions in 1639 made it clear that the King had responded favorably to the colony's persistent requests for a continuing representative assembly.

The importance of this decision as a precedent can hardly be exaggerated. Virginia was the first English settlement to fall under the direct control of the Crown, and its forms of government could not fail to influence, if not determine, those of subsequent royal colonies —and, it should be remembered, in time all but four of the thirteen colonies would be royal.

The evolution of Massachusetts' government was somewhat different; the fact that the charter was brought with the settlers insured that events in America would be the determining factors. The narrow limits of the charter, which was intended for the running of a corporation, not a community, came under attack in the first year, when over a hundred settlers applied for the rights of freemen. At that point the decision was made to open the coveted rank to "such as are members of some of the churches within the lymitts of" the colony. This broadening of the franchise signalized the transformation of the corporation into a true commonwealth, composed of citizens with rights and duties. In practice, confining citizenship to church members was not as restrictive as might at first be supposed, for this was, after all, a Puritan venture. There were towns like Roxbury in 1638–40, for example, which consisted of sixty-nine householders, of whom fifty-nine were church members and voters.

For the first four years Massachusetts was governed by the magistrates, who, in turn, were elected by the whole body of freemen; there being no representative assembly, the magistrates made the laws. It is more than coincidental, however, that at about the same time the Virginia Assembly was putting itself on record as opposing taxation by the executive, a similar remonstrance was afoot in Massachusetts. Early in 1632, Winthrop tells us, a group of ministers and elders of Watertown "delivered their opinion, that it was not safe to pay moneys" levied upon the people by the Governor and the assistants, "for fear of bringing themselves and posterity into bondage." The coincidence, of course, is not accidental, for it simply underscores the common English origins of the two widely separated colonies. For centuries Englishmen had jealously guarded their right to levy their taxes locally; they continued to do so in the New World. Moreover, in the first part of the seventeenth century the issue of taxation and representative government was before the eyes of the whole nation as King and Parliament carried on their struggle for supremacy. It was to be expected that history and current events would both be reflected in the two English colonies in America.

As the number of settlers in Massachusetts increased, thereby rendering it more and more difficult for all freemen to meet together, it became necessary either to abandon the meeting of freemen, a step which men like Governor Winthrop apparently urged, or else to elect deputies or proxies who would act for the general body of freemen. At the insistence of the freemen, the latter method was accepted at the same time that it was agreed that taxes would be levied only by the legislature. Thus, in May, 1634, the first representative assembly met in Boston, with each town sending three deputies. It was understood that they "shall have full power and voice of all and said freemen," except for the election of the magistrates.

The history of constitutional development in both Massachusetts and Virginia makes it quite apparent that the ordinary man's dogged insistence upon self-government in America was perhaps the most important single factor in the establishment of the representative government we esteem today. Even an opponent of popular government, John Winthrop, expressed grudging admiration for the people's ingenious if illogical pursuit of their own governance. Noting their appeal to the patent or charter in a recent dispute with the magistrates, Winthrop wryly commented that it "may be observed how strictly the people would seem to stick to their patent, where they think it makes for their advantage, but are content to decline it, where it will not warrant such liberties as they have taken up without warrant from thence."

If representative government can be said to have triumphed in the seventeenth century, it can also be said that the idea of democracy, defined as government by the consent of all the governed, was born in that century. The line to the present, however, is more tenuous, the traces fainter; not until the nineteenth century was democracy in full flower. But the beginnings of the democratic idea are already to be found in the Puritans' conception of the covenant. The idea of an agreement between the ruler and the ruled as the basis for government was very well understood in seventeenth-century Protestant America, not only because of the contemporary theological use of it, but because the extensive and close reading of the Bible among all classes made the idea common coin. The covenants with Adam, with Noah, and with Abraham were well-known Biblical agreements between God and men. Only by the agreement of all concerned, read the Cambridge Church Platform of 1648, could "we see . . . how members can have Church-power over one another mutually." It was natural that this religious or Biblical example should be extended to civil affairs,[6] especially in a new land where the usual sanctions for government were wanting. Thomas Hooker of Connecticut fame, for example, applied the covenant idea directly to government when he

---

[6] It is hardly accidental that the most democratic political document of the seventeenth century, the Agreement of the People, originated in the turmoil of the Puritan revolution in England. The very title of the document suggests the debt to the covenant idea, and its contents set forth a conception of popular participation in government which was not realized in any country before the nineteenth century.

wrote, "there must of necessity be a mutual agreement . . . before, by any rule of God," men "have any right or power, or can exercise either, each toward the other."

Since the Church, according to Puritan thought, could be brought into existence only by the action of the whole membership, and the minister was called and ordained by the congregation, it was hardly to be expected that the state would long remain outside such popular participation. It was this germ of democracy which never ceased to ferment within the hard shell of Puritan government. In a very real sense, Puritanism, with its doctrines of individualism and the covenant, contained the seeds of its own destruction as an authoritarian government.

"Nothing is more striking to a European traveler in the United States than the absence of what we term the government, or the administration," wrote Alexis de Tocqueville after his tour of the United States in the 1830's. "Written laws exist in America, and one sees the daily execution of them; but although everything moves regularly, the mover can nowhere be discovered." The reason for this, Tocqueville concluded, was the great importance and strength of local government in America. Over a century later local self-rule still means much to Americans, as the appeals to its principles by modern conservatives and opponents of centralized government make evident.

It is not to be doubted that the strength of local government in America derives from the English heritage of the first settlers. Immigrants brought with them a long experience in local self-rule in the shires and towns of old England. But the distribution of the two primary forms of local government in the United States—the town of New England and the county of Virginia—is largely the result of geography and the motivations of the people who settled in the two sections of English America. When the Puritans landed in Massachusetts, they laid out their settlements in a form that best secured the object of their coming—that is, the practice of their religion. Instead of the spreading out over the land in individual farms—a procedure which would have hampered church attendance and hindered control over the religious and moral life of the people—the seventeenth-century settlements took the shape of compact villages, with the farming land stretching around the periphery. Though such a nucleated village was similar to those in England and on the Continent, the fact that settlers in Virginia evolved a much different scheme of settlement makes it clear that religious and social aims, not the European inheritance, were the controlling factors.

The Englishmen who settled in Virginia, once the dangers of Indian attacks and starvation had been surmounted, spread themselves out on individual farms, forsaking the village settlement so familiar to many of them in England. (It is true that in the western part of England, especially in Devon, whence some settlers came to Virginia, separate farmsteads were well known, but even there the nucleated village was common.) The settlers in Virginia quickly found that large plantations situated along the great rivers of the tidewater were best suited to the growing of tobacco. These widely separated plantations became so typical of the colony that by the end of the century Virginian historian Robert Beverley was regretting they had ever gotten started. "This Liberty of taking up Land and the Ambition each Man had of being Lord of a vast, tho' unimproved Territory, together with the Advantage of many Rivers, which afforded a commodious Road for shipping at every Man's Door, has made the Country fall into . . . an unhappy Settlement and course of Trade." As a result, he continued, "to this Day they have not any one place of Cohabitation among them, that may reasonably bear the Name of a Town."

The forms of local government adopted in both Virginia and New England reflected the configuration of the settlements. With population spread thin by the centrifugal forces of geography and economy, the county, with its sheriffs, justices of the peace, and county court, all inherited from England, became the Virginian, and by extension, the southern form of local government. In New England, geographical forces were largely neutral—there were no navigable rivers to encourage the spreading out of population—while religion acted as a powerful cohesive force. Though as early as 1650 a Connecticut law spoke of the "great abuse of buying and purchasing home lots and laying them together, by means, whereof great depopulations are like to follow," the village or town, clustering around the all-important meetinghouse, was the typical New England form of local government, with town meeting and selectmen.

Since the church was self-governing in New England, it was to be anticipated that the town meeting, which was in some seventeenth-century towns indistinguishable in membership from the church, should be also. Indeed, it might be said with justice that the town meeting, so peculiar to New England and so remarkable to Tocqueville, was the natural offspring of the religion and geography of New England. In practice the town meeting was one of the most democratic features of seventeenth-century life. All residents of the Massachusetts town, whether they were church members or not, could speak at meeting, though before 1647 only "saints" could vote.[7] After that date and at the instance of the freemen, it was provided that all male residents over twenty-three could vote, be elected to town offices, and serve on juries, regardless of church membership. Recent investigations make it clear that all through the Puritan era most men in Massachusetts could participate in town government if they wished to. The New England town was truly a training ground for responsible and democratic government.

From what has been said up to now regarding the political institutions of the seventeenth-century colonists, it is apparent that they were formative for modern Americans. But the adaptation of English political ways to America, especially the representative assembly, exercised a further influence upon the course of American history. The very rhetoric and framework within which the revolutionary crisis of 1765–76 was carried out stemmed from the political forms which Americans had evolved in the wilderness. Indeed, without this particular development of representative assembly, local government, and political freedom, the Revolution, if it took place at all, would have had different goals and different slogans. For this reason, if for no other, this haphazard, often accidental, transfer of English political ways to America is suffused with a significance which origins otherwise rarely enjoy.

4. BLACK MEN IN A WHITE MEN'S COUNTRY

As the germ of the Revolution is to be detected in the political history of the seventeenth century, so the genesis of the Civil War is implicit in its social history. In late August, 1619, said John Rolfe, a Dutch ship dropped off "twenty Negars" at Jamestown. But, contrary to popular history, the American race problem did not begin then. It would be another half century before slavery, as it was to be known later, was clearly established in America. As late as 1671 the

---

[7] That the tendency of these town governments was more democratic in practice than in law is shown by a statute of the New Haven colony in 1656. After calling attention to the fact that only freemen could vote in the towns, the General Court went on to observe that in some towns "others besides freemen have had liberties to vote in things of weightie trust and concernment."

Governor of Virginia estimated that Negroes made up less than 5 per cent of the population.

For most of the seventeenth century, Virginia society consisted largely of small, independent, landowning farmers; slave plantations as they would be known in the eighteenth century were not only few in number but their owners were relatively insignificant politically and socially.

Not until the opening years of the eighteenth century were land-holding yeomanry and indentured servants displaced to any appreciable degree by Negro slaves. Whereas in 1671, 5 per cent of the population was Negro, in 1715 the figure was up to 24 per cent, and by 1756 Negro slaves accounted for over 40 per cent of the population. (By 1724, Negro slaves outnumbered whites more than two to one in South Carolina.) As slavery grew in importance, so did the great planter; by the end of the seventeenth century, the landed squire with his scores of slaves had superseded the sturdy yeoman in the political and social affairs of Virginia. The causes for this sharp shift in class power in the province do not concern us here. The reason for discussing it at all is in order to make clear that for most of the century neither the institution of slavery nor the Negro was an important part of the life of Virginians.

Yet it must be said that slavery and racial discrimination began in the seventeenth century. Over a century ago, that most perspicacious student of America, Alexis de Tocqueville, pointed to slavery as the origin of the American prejudice toward the black man. Contrary to the situation in antiquity, he remarked, "among the moderns the abstract and transient fact of slavery is fatally united with the physical and permanent fact of color." Furthermore, he added, in the North "slavery recedes, but the prejudice to which it has given birth is immovable." More modern historians have also stressed this causal connection between the institution of slavery and the color prejudice of Americans. And it is patent to anyone conversant with the nature of American slavery, especially as it functioned in the nineteenth century, that the impress of bondage upon the character and future of the black man in this country has been deep and enduring.

But if one examines the early history of slavery in the English colonies and the reaction of Englishmen toward black men, it becomes evident that the assumption that slavery is responsible for the low social status of Negroes is open to question. For one thing, the institution of slavery as it was to be delineated in law by the end of the seventeenth century, apparently did not prevail when the first Negroes came to Jamestown. Or at least it did not appear in the statute books of Virginia until 1660. Indeed, it is this late appearance of the status of slavery in law that has led some historians to argue that prior to the 1660's Negroes enjoyed a status equal to that of white indentured servants. To historians of that persuasion slavery was the force that dragged down the Negro to social inferiority and discrimination. Unfortunately for this view, the recent scholarship of Winthrop Jordan concludes that the exact status of Negroes during the first decades in America cannot be known for certain, given the available sources. One reason that the status cannot be surely known is that there is some cause to believe that Negroes were discriminated against long before the institution of slavery appeared in the law. In short, if one is seeking to uncover the roots of racial prejudice and discrimination against the Negro in America, the soundest procedure would be to abandon the idea that slavery was the causal factor. In place of it, one ought to work on the assumption that discrimination preceded slavery and by so doing helped to reinforce it. Under this assumption American race prejudice originated in the discriminatory social atmosphere of the early seventeenth century, long before slavery was written into law. When slavery did appear in the statutes, it could not help but be shaped by the folk bias within which it grew. Thus legal slavery in the English colonies reinforced and helped to perpetuate the discrimination against the black man that had prevailed from the beginning of settlement.

Simply because the Negro differed from the Englishman in a number of ways, it was unlikely that men of the seventeenth century would accord the black man an equal status with Englishmen. Even Irishmen, who were white, Christian, and European, were held to be literally "beyond the Pale," and some were even referred to as "slaves." The African, after all, was a heathen at a time when "Christian" was a title of import. Moreover, he was black and culturally different. As one sixteenth-century English observer of Africans phrased it, "although the people were blacke and naked, yet they were civill." In Shakespeare's play, Brabantio's horror at his daughter's elopement with the black Othello reflects the seventeenth-century Englishman's consciousness of the Negro's differences. "Damned as thou art, thou hast enchanted her," exclaims the outraged father, ignoring the fact of Othello's Christianity. Only in a betwitched state, he argues, would his daughter shun "the wealthy curled darlings of our nation . . . to incur a general mock" and leave her family in order to seek "the sooty bosom of such a thing as thou." Desdemona herself admitted that she perceived the Moor's "visage in his mind" —an acknowledgment that his difference in countenance would have been a serious obstacle to a love less profound than hers. In *Titus Andronicus* Tamora is reviled by Bassianus for loving the Moor Aaron. "Believe me, queen, your swarth Cimerian doth make your honour of his body's hue, spotted, detested and abominable." Why, he asks her, are you wandering in the forest "with a barbarous Moor"?

But a feeling that Englishmen and Negroes were different did not depend upon vague impressions gained from chance or occasional contact with black men or Moors in England. The fact that Negroes arrived in English America as the cargo of the international slave trade unquestionably fostered a sense of superiority among Englishmen. If the noble and commanding Othello could be stigmatized as a "thing," how much more likely it was that degrading terms be applied to those wretches newly spilled out of the slave ships! It was to be anticipated that from the beginning a special inferior position would be assigned black men.

Such, indeed, was the fact even though the Virginia and Maryland records in the years between 1620 and 1660 rarely refer to "slaves" but speak mainly of "Negroes." The failure to use the term slave should not blind us to the real possibility that the status for which it stood was already in being. The legal definition of the inferior status which Englishmen in America—both in New England and in the Chesapeake colonies—were building for Negroes was imprecise in those early years. But that an inferior status was in the process of being worked out seems undoubted. Moreover, the treatment accorded another dark-skinned heathen people, the Indians, offers further evidence that enslavement was early the lot reserved for Negroes. Indian slavery was practiced in all the English settlements almost from the beginning; rarely were any distinctions made between Indians and Negroes when discriminatory legislation was enacted. But let us now turn to the beginnings of slavery in the English colonies.

The colonies of Virginia and New England had ample opportunity to learn of discriminatory practices against Negroes from island settlements of Englishmen like Bermuda and New Providence in the Caribbean. As early as the 1620's and 1630's these colonies provided a discriminatory or outright slave status for Negroes. In 1623, for example, the Assembly of Bermuda passed an act restraining "the insolencies of the Negroes," limiting the black man's freedom of movement and participation in trade, and denying him the right to bear arms. The Puritan venture of New Providence Island in the western Caribbean was notorious for its pirating of Negro slaves from the Spanish colonies in order to sell them or use them on its plantations. By the 1640's, according to the contemporary historian Richard Ligon, Barbados, another Caribbean English settlement, was using Negroes as outright slaves.

There is evidence as early as the 1630's and 1640's that Virginia and Maryland were singling out Negroes for discriminatory treatment as compared with white indentured servants. One Hugh Davis in Virginia in 1630 was "soundly whipped before an assembly of Negroes and others for abusing himself to the dishonor of God and the shame of Christians, by defiling his body in lying with a Negro." An act passed in Maryland in 1639 enumerated the rights of "all Christian inhabitants (slaves excepted)." The slaves referred to could have been only Indians or Negroes since all white servants were Christians. Negroes were specifically denied the right to bear arms in Virginia in 1640 and in Maryland in 1648, though no such prohibition was put upon white servants; indeed, in statutes that prohibited Negroes from being armed, masters were directed to arm the white servants.

It is significant that though both Maryland and Virginia passed statutes to fix limits to the terms for indentured servitude for those who came without written contracts, Negroes were never included in such protective provisions. The first of such statutes were enacted in 1639 in Maryland and in 1643 in Virginia. Three times before 1660 —in 1643, 1644, and 1658—the Virginia Assembly included Negro and Indian women among the "tithables," though white women were never included in such a category. The discrimination was a recognition of the fact that Negro and Indian women worked in the fields, whereas white women, servants or no, usually did not.

Two cases for the punishment of runaway servants in Virginia throw some light on the status of Negroes by 1640. The first case concerned three runaways, of whom two were white men and the third a Negro. All three were given thirty lashes, and the white men had the terms owed their masters extended a year, at the completion of which they were to work for the colony for three more years. The other, "being a Negro named *John Punch* shall serve his said master or his assigns for the time of his natural Life here or elsewhere." It is obvious that the Negro's punishment was the most severe and that his penalty, in effect, was reduction to slavery, though it is also clear that up until his sentencing he must have had the status of a servant.

The second case, also of 1640, suggests that by that date some Negroes were already slaves. This one also involved six white men and a Negro who had plotted to run away. The punishments meted out varied, but Christopher Miller, "a dutchman (a prince agent in the business)," was given the harshest treatment of all: thirty stripes, burned with an "R" on the cheek, a shackle on his leg for a year "and longer if said master shall see cause," and seven years of service for the colony upon completion of his time due his master. The only other one of the plotters to receive the stripes, the shackle, and the burning of the "R" was the Negro Emanuel, but, significantly, he did not receive any sentence of work for the colony. Apparently he was already serving his master for a lifetime—i.e., he was a slave.

From a proceeding before the House of Burgesses in 1666 it appears that as early as 1644 that body was being called upon to determine who was a slave. In 1666 the records of the House report that in 1644 the Assembly "adjudged" a certain mulatto "no slave" even though he had been bought "as a Slave for Ever." No reasons are given as to why he was freed, but we do know that his master was surprised, for he petitioned for recompense. The Assembly refused the request, however, contending that it was not a public obligation to relieve those buyers who made poor purchases. In any case, it is clear that even this Negro served a term the length of which —twenty-one years—was unheard of for a "Christian servant."

In early seventeenth-century inventories of estates there are two distinctions which appear in the reckoning of the value of servants and Negroes. Uniformly, the Negroes are more valuable, even as children, than any white servant. Secondly, the naming of a servant is usually followed by the number of years yet remaining to his service; for the Negroes no such notation appears. Thus, in an inventory in Virginia in 1643, a twenty-two-year-old white servant, with eight years still to serve, was valued at 1,000 pounds of tobacco, while a "Negro boy" was rated at 3,000 pounds; a white boy with seven years to serve was listed as worth 700 pounds. An eight-year-old Negro girl was calculated to be worth 2,000 pounds. On another inventory in 1655, two good men servants with four years to serve were rated at 1,300 pounds of tobacco, and a woman servant with only two years to go was valued at 800 pounds. But two Negro boys, who had no limit set to their terms, were evaluated at 4,100 pounds apiece, and a Negro girl was said to be worth 5,500 pounds.

Such wide differences in the valuation of Negro and white "servants" strongly suggest, as does the failure to indicate term of service for Negroes, that the latter were slaves. Beyond a question, there was some service which these blacks were rendering which enhanced their value—a service moreover, which was not or could not be exacted from the whites. Furthermore, a Maryland deed of 1649 suggests slave status not only of lifetime term but also of inheritance. Three Negroes "and all their issue both male and female" were deeded.

More positive evidence of true slavery is afforded by the court records of the 1640's and 1650's. In 1646, for example, a Negro woman and a Negro boy were sold to Stephen Charlton to be of use to him and "his heyers etc. for ever." A Negro girl was sold in 1652 to one H. Armsteadinger "and his heyers . . . forever with all her increase both male and female." One investigator, Susie Ames, describes the case of two Negroes brought into the eastern shore of Virginia in 1635. Over twenty years later, in 1656, the widow of the master was bequeathing the child of one of the original Negroes and the other Negro and her children. This was more than mere servitude—the term was longer than twenty years and apparently the status was inheritable.

It is true that, concurrently with these examples of onerous service or actual slavery exacted from Negroes, some black men did gain their freedom. But such instances do not deny the existence of discrimination or slave status; they simply testify to the unsteady evolution of a status for the Negro. Indeed, the tangential manner in which recognition of Negro slavery first appeared in the Virginia statutes strengthens the supposition that the practice long preceded the law. In 1660, in a statute dealing with punishments for runaway servants, only casual reference was made to "those Negroes who are incapable of makeing satisfaction by addition of time." Apparently, everyone at the time knew what was meant by the circumlocution.

But as legal questions of status arose from time to time, clarification of the Negroes' position had to be written into law. Thus in 1662 Virginia declared that the status of offspring would follow that of the mother in the event of a white man getting a Negro with child. When Maryland in 1664 prescribed service for Negroes *durante vita* and included hereditary status through the *father,* it also prohibited unions between the races. The preamble of the statute offers a clue as to the motives behind this separation of the races. Prohibition of intermarriage is necessary because "divers free born *English* women, forgetful of their free condition, and to the disgrace of our nation, do intermarry with Negro slaves," from which fact questions of status of issue have arisen. Therefore, the law was enacted in order to prevent harm to masters and "for deterring such free-born women from such shameful matches. . . ." Interestingly enough, the South Carolinian slave code of 1712 justified special legislation for Negroes on grounds of cultural difference. "The Negroes and other slaves brought unto the people of this province . . . are of barbarous, wild, savage natures, and such as renders them wholly unqualified to be governed by the laws, customs, and practices of this province. . . ."

Regardless of the reasoning behind the singling out of Negroes, as early as 1669 the law in Virginia implicitly viewed Negroes as property. An act of that year assured masters that they would not be held responsible for the accidental death of a slave as a result of punishment because it should be presumed that no man would "destroy his owne estate." But it still would be a long while before the legal status of slave property would be finally settled. In 1705, for example, Virginia law declared slaves to be real estate, though with many exceptions. Similarly, in South Carolina slaves were first denominated real estate in 1690 and then chattels in 1740. By 1750, the law in the southern colonies settled on chattels as the proper designation of slave property.

The important point is not the evolution of the legal status of the slave, but the fact that discriminatory legislation regarding the Negro long preceded any legal definition of slavery. Equally important, in view of the commonly held view that numbers of Negroes determined the inferior status imposed upon the black, is the evidence of discrimination long before numbers were large. In 1680 Virginia enacted a series of regulations which were very close to the later slave codes in restricting the movement of Negroes, prohibiting their bearing arms, and providing capital punishment for those who ran away or offered resistance to whites. Yet it would be another twenty years before the Negroes would make up even a fifth of the total population of Virginia. In short, long before slavery was an important part of the labor system of the South, the Negroes had been fitted into a special and inferior status.

The same process whereby the white man's sense of difference regarding the Negro shaped the status of the black man can be traced in the northern colonies. Englishmen there, like their countrymen in the southern colonies, inherited no legal basis for slavery; yet a slave status and an inferior position for the black man developed in New England, even though there the economic need for black labor was considerably less than in the South.

So few Negroes were imported into New England during the seventeenth century that references to their status are scattered, but those pieces of evidence which are available suggest that from the earliest years an especially low status, if not slavery itself, was reserved for the Negro. One source of 1639, for example, tells of a Negro woman being held as a slave on Noddles Island in Boston Harbor. Her master sought to mate her with another Negro, but, the chronicler reported, she kicked her prospective lover out of bed, saying that such behavior was "beyond her slavery." It is also well known that the first Massachusetts legal code, the Body of Liberties of 1641, permitted enslavement of those who are "sold to us," which would apply to Negroes brought by the slave ships.

Nor was the use of Negroes as slaves unknown or undesirable to the Puritans. One correspondent of John Winthrop in 1645, for instance, talked of the desirability of war against the Indians, so that captives might be taken who could be exchanged "for Moores [Negroes], which will be more gayneful pilladge for us then [*sic*] wee conceive, for I doe not see how wee can thrive untill wee get into a stock of slaves sufficient to doe all our business, for our children's children will hardly see this great Continent filled with people. . . ." Moreover, he went on, "servants" will not stay but "for verie great wages. And I suppose you know verie well how we shall maynteyne 20 Moores cheaper than one English servant." The following year the United Colonies (Massachusetts, Plymouth, New Haven, and Connecticut colonies) decreed, in order to save prison costs, that contumacious Indians would be delivered up to those they had injured or "be shipped out and exchanged for Negroes" as the case might justify. That enslavement of Negroes was well known in New England by the early 1650's is evident from the preamble of a Rhode Island statute of 1652. It was said that it "is a common course practised amongst Englishmen to buy Negers, to that end they may have them for service or slaves forever. . . ."

Though the number of Negroes in New England was exceedingly small, the colonies of that region followed the same path as the southern provinces in denying arms to the blacks in their midst. In 1652, Massachusetts had provided that Indians and Negroes should train in the militia the same as whites. But this ruling apparently caused friction, for in 1656 the earlier law was countermanded by the words "henceforth no Negroes or Indians, although servants of the English, shalbe armed or permitted to trayne." Connecticut in 1660 also excluded Indians and "Negar servants" from the militia and "Watch and Ward," although as late as 1680 it was officially reported to London that there were no more than thirty "slaves" in the colony.

Edward Randolph as commissioner of the Crown reported in 1676 that there were a few indentured servants in Massachusetts, "and not above two hundred slaves in the colony," by which he meant Negroes, for he said they "were brought from Guinea and Madagascar." Yet not until 1698 did the phrase "Negro slave" appear in the Massachusetts statutes. Practice was preceding law in New England just as it had in the South. In 1690, discrimination against the few Negroes in Connecticut reached the point where all Negroes were forbidden to be found outside the town bounds without "a ticket or a pass" from either master or the authorities, the restriction applying equally to free Negroes and slaves. Furthermore, it was provided that ferrymen would be fined if they permitted Negroes without passes to use their ferries. And though as early as 1680 official reports to London were distinguishing between slaves and servants, statute law barely defined the institution of slavery. In 1704, for example, the Governor gave it as his opinion that all children born of "Negro bondwomen are themselves in like condition, i.e. born in servitude," but he admitted that no law had so provided. Legislation, he said, was "needless, because of the constant practice by which they are held as such. . . ." In 1703, Massachusetts provided that "molatto and Negro slaves" could be set free only if security was given that they would not be a charge on the community, and two years later a prohibition against sexual relations between Negroes and whites was enacted. In 1717, Negroes were barred from holding land in Connecticut.

Thus, like the southern colonists, the New Englanders enacted into law, in the absence of any prior English law of slavery, their recognition of Negroes as different in race, religion, and culture. It should be especially noted that in many instances discriminations were made against all Negroes, whether slave or free—a fact which reinforces the argument that the discrimination preceded slavery and was not simply a consequence. Unquestionably, the coincidence of slavery with discrimination fastened still more firmly the stigma of inferiority upon the Negro, but slavery must be absolved of starting the cycle.

Once the sense of difference between the two peoples was embodied in law, the logic of the law widened the differences. All through the early eighteenth century, judges and legislatures in all the colonies elaborated the law along the discriminatory lines laid down from the beginning. In this, of course, especially in the South, they had the added incentive of perpetuating and securing a labor system which had become indispensable to the economy. As a consequence, the cleavage between the races was deepened and hardened.

In time the correspondence between the black man and slavery would be so perfect that it would be difficult to realize that the Negro was not always and everywhere in a degraded status. Thus began in the seventeenth century the Negro's life in America. With it commenced a moral problem for all Americans which still besets us in the middle of the twentieth century. Though started casually, thoughtlessly, and without any preconceived goal, the web became so interwoven, so complex, so tightly meshed, that John C. Calhoun could say, in 1850, slavery "has grown with our growth, and strengthened with our strength."

The full social implications of American slavery, however, were not apparent until the expansion and elaboration of the institution in the nineteenth century. For that reason our discussion of its import for the future of America should wait while we now consider the contributions of the eighteenth century to the making of the social patterns of modern America.

CHAPTER II

The Awakening of
American Nationality

THE first half of the eighteenth century, as Thomas Wertenbaker has said, was a golden age for American culture; elegance was replacing mere comfort in the homes of the rich, comfort was supplanting privation in the houses of the not-so-rich; farmers and merchants, planters and craftsmen, were building a prosperous and productive economy. A new society, often graceful and cultivated, following the model of western European culture, was being firmly established on the edge of the North American wilderness. At the middle of the eighteenth century towns like Boston, New York, Charleston, and Philadelphia were already miniature Londons; the frontier of forests and Indians was now a hundred miles to the west.

But within the European civilization transplanted to the New World the seeds of a new civilization were sprouting. Paradoxically enough, Europe's colonizing experience in the New World was doomed by its success; in the act of flourishing, the English colonies were also ceasing to be European. This budding of American consciousness was already in evidence before 1763; under the forcing frame of the Revolutionary era, it would burst into flower.

1. COUNTRY COUSINS

To probe for signs of cultural independence among the arts of colonial America—even in the 1750's—is to take on an unrewarding task. As Franklin remarked in 1763, "After the first Cares for the Necessaries of Life are over we shall come to think of the Embellish-

37

ments." America was too new, too raw, too poor to be able to train, to teach, or to afford artists in anything like the style achieved in contemporary Europe. Though Franklin said, "Already some of our young geniuses begin to lisp Attempts at Painting, Poetry and Musick," he would have been the first to admit that these "geniuses" were attempting little more than the transplanting of European culture to America. They hardly dared express the spirit of their own land in artistic forms. Such cultural independence could come only with the self-confidence of years.

The limited possibilities for great art imposed by the rude environment of America are suggested by a comparison of the primitive techniques of the best colonial artists—men like Feke and Copley— with the finished and polished performances of English contemporaries like Gainsborough, Hogarth, and Reynolds. To an even greater degree the same was true in musical composition and performance. Literature, too, despite a solitary oak like Franklin, was still in the sapling stage when compared with Richardson, Addison, Steele, Johnson, and Boswell, to name only the most obvious in contemporary England. The absence of a long, cultivated tradition, of schools of art, of artistic and literary communities for the exchange of learning and ideas, relegated the English colonies to the backwash of European artistic and cultural achievement.[1]

Even in architecture, where the demands of living compelled the Americans to engage in its pursuit, the European influence was overwhelming; the American emulation of English models bordered on the abject. Though the climate and weather of America were different from England's and one might have expected, therefore, some significant modifications in structure of dwellings, there was surprisingly little. Georgian architectural forms, which enjoyed enormous vogue in England, duplicated their triumph in the colonies almost without alteration. In the extant homes of the colonial gentry, like Mount Vernon, one can still see the faithful reproductions of Palladian windows prescribed in the contemporary English architectural

[1] In a new field of intellectual endeavor like natural science, the Americans were not at such a decided disadvantage. The work of Franklin in electricity, for example, stands out as one of the foremost achievements of science in the first half of the eighteenth century; it was on a par with any work then being done in Europe in the field of experimental physics. In older departments of natural science, like botany and zoology, although Americans made contributions, they largely "depended upon the intellectual stimulus they received from Europe," writes Brook Hindle, *The Pursuit of Science in Revolutionary America* (New York, 1956), p. 58.

handbooks. Similarly, in the homes of the wealthy colonials, the ornate Georgian fireplaces are of a design which might have been copied without change from a country house in Old England. In time the American environment would work its alchemy upon European forms brought to the new country, but that day was still in the future.

There were aspects of colonial life, however, in which American consciousness of self was growing and where the future was more than implicit. Two criteria can be utilized to throw into relief the beginnings of a sense of Americanism or nationalism in the pre-Revolutionary years; both will be employed in this chapter as they were implicitly used in the last. First of all, we shall notice those divergencies of American theory and practice from European models, for in this we catch the first glimmerings of an emergent American people. Secondly, we shall direct our attention to those elements in colonial society which have persisted down into our own time; in these we first see the outlines of modern American civilization.

2. MATERIAL FOUNDATIONS

"The economic history of the United States," one scholar has written, "is the history of the rise and development of the capitalistic system." The colonists of the eighteenth century pushed forward what those of the seventeenth century had begun: the expansion and elaboration of an economy born in the great age of capitalist expansion. The economic life of the vast majority of the million and a half people in the colonies of the mid-eighteenth century, was still dominated, as in the seventeenth, by the rhythm of agriculture. But now a sizable merchant class thrived in a half dozen seaboard cities, its trading operations being one of the great sources of the new wealth which distinguished the eighteenth-century economy from the seventeenth.

At mid-century the continental colonies were England's most valuable possession. *"America* has become the fountain of our riches," it was said in the widely circulated *Gentleman's Magazine* in January, 1755, "for with *America* our greatest trade is carried on." The entry bills "at the Custom-House of *London* only, shew the great quantities of our manufactures which they consume." For Americans themselves, the economic growth of their provinces betokened a general prosperity which was the envy of Europe.

The great bulk of the accumulated wealth of America, as distinguished from that which was consumed, was derived either directly or indirectly from trade. Though some manufacturing existed, its role in the accumulation of capital was negligible. A merchant class of opulent proportions was already visible in Boston, New York, Philadelphia, Newport, and Charleston, its wealth the obvious consequence of shrewd and resourceful management of the carrying trade. Even the rich planters of tidewater Virginia and the rice coast of South Carolina finally depended for their genteel way of life upon the ships and merchants who sold their tobacco and rice in the markets of Europe. As colonial production rose and trade expanded, a business community emerged in the colonies, linking the provinces by lines of trade and identity of interest.

The needs of business and trade compelled the colonies—and to some extent the mother country—to improve the means of intercolonial communication in the early decades of the eighteenth century. By 1740, for example, there was a complete series of post roads running from Portsmouth, New Hampshire, to Charleston. Moreover, old Indian trails into the interior were gradually being turned into roads, penetrating the hinterlands of New York, Pennsylvania, and even newly opened Georgia. Indicative of the improvement in the possibilities for travel was the publication of the first guidebook for America in 1732. Packet ships, running on schedule, linked the major ports of the colonies, greatly facilitating the movement of goods and people in an age when land travel was everywhere the most uncomfortable mode. In the first part of the century the colonial postal service was so haphazard as to be almost worthless, but once Benjamin Franklin got a chance to work his organizing abilities upon it— that is, after 1753—it became an efficient agency for the transacting of business and served to pull the spread-out colonies closer together. Travel between some of the larger towns was sufficiently important to justify the running of stage coaches on schedule. The best known of such attempts at rapid means of communication was the "flying machine," which raced the one hundred miles between New York and Philadelphia in the unprecedented time of two days.

More important than the actual physical means of communication, which must always appear to the twentieth century as inexpressibly primitive, was the fact that as people moved along these lines of travel, meeting their fellow colonists, they could not help noticing the characteristics they held in common. "I found but little difference in the manners and character of the people in the different provinces I passed thro," commented Dr. Alexander Hamilton at the end of his tour of the colonies in 1744.

There were less tangible, but nonetheless significant, ways in which the accumulation of wealth and the improvement of communication served to bind the disparate colonials together. The upper classes of the several provinces, for instance, were joined together by ties of family. The Wendells of New York were related to the Quincys, Sewalls, and Hancocks of Massachusetts. Benjamin Smith of South Carolina was related to Abigail Smith, the wife of John Adams. When the Bayards of Philadelphia journeyed north, they were welcomed in the homes of Bayards in New York and in Boston. The socially and politically prominent De Lanceys of New York were intermarried with the equally distinguished Allens of Philadelphia. The spread of the Masonic Order, among all levels of society, in the early decades of the century also provided a medium for increased intercolonial connection. Masonic lodges were established in half of the provinces of English America by 1741. Traveling Masons were always welcomed by their brethren, and the functions of the order often brought together men who might otherwise not leave their own bailiwicks.

As business expanded, so did the lawyers. Prominent ones like John Kempe and James Alexander of New York and Andrew Hamilton of Philadelphia often had clients outside their own provinces, thereby functioning as links between provinces. Jared Ingersoll, after he assumed his seat as judge of vice-admiralty in Philadelphia, continued to maintain his widespread professional connections in his native Connecticut. Leaders of the bar like Kempe, Hamilton, and others often served as instructors of young lawyers from other provinces, thus giving a unity of outlook to the provincial bars not otherwise to be expected.

Erstwhile businessmen like Franklin of Philadelphia and Cadwallader Colden of New York maintained close communication through their common interest in the science of the day. In 1745, as an outgrowth of this interest, the American Philosophical Society was born. As its name suggests, the Society brought together those men of the American colonies who were working and thinking about things philosophical, which at that time included all of human inquiry.

It was the eighteenth century which saw the first solid beginnings of the colonial periodical press; some twenty-two weekly newspapers were started in 1713–45 in seven of the thirteen colonies. Though circulation was always small and the viewpoint strongly English, these papers served to link together the ruling circles in the various colonies. Other periodicals, aside from newspapers, also made their appearance in the thirty years prior to the Revolution. The publication of books in America was a thriving business in the late colonial era; in number of books printed, Boston was second only to London among all the cities of the British Empire. By the middle of the century, in brief, interested colonials enjoyed ample intellectual fare for their mutual enlightenment and interchange of ideas.

Quantitatively, of course, and especially when compared with modern means of mass communication, the opportunities for the transmission of ideas in the colonial era were limited and narrow. But this was equally true of Europe at this time, though we often casually assume a body of public opinion in countries like England and France. Though the American colonies were more spread out than any European country, the upper classes in the provinces in America were small and therefore easily reached by limited means of communication. Because the small upper classes set the tone of public opinion in America as they did in Europe, the means of intellectual interchange did not have to be attuned to a mass audience or to be of spectacular proportions to create a sense of unity. "Socially and spiritually, as well as in trade and politics," Carl Bridenbaugh has written in his study of the biggest eighteenth-century colonial cities, "the gentlefolk of all five cities came to know one another better, to exchange amenities and to sense their common bonds in the leadership of an American society."

3. A POOR MAN'S COUNTRY

An expanding economy meant increasing opportunities for economic advancement, as many Americans were quick to tell the land-hungry people of old Europe. Benjamin Franklin, America's best-known booster, wrote in 1751 that land was plentiful "and so cheap . . . that a laboring man that understands husbandry can in a short time save money enough to purchase a piece of land sufficient for a plantation. . . ." Nor, Franklin went on, need the enterprising young man worry about providing for the future of his children, for he will soon see "that more land is to be had at rates equally easy, all circumstances considered." It was the boast of another colonial that

"You may depend upon it that this is one of the best poor man's Countrys in the World." Cadwallader Colden of New York thought that the opportunity for any man to set himself up as a farmer was so good in this country that little manufacturing could be expected "because of the dearness of Labor and want of hands. . . ." More than the future of manufacturing was involved; the status of the laborer was also affected. What a difference there was, Crèvecoeur observed, between the hiring of workers in England and in America. "When we hire any of these people we rather pray and entreat them. You must give them what they ask. . . . They must be at your table and feed . . . on the best you have." In the colonies, a British official concluded in 1760, "a plentiful subsistence may be . . . gained by very moderate labour, and even opulence acquired from no other stock then [*sic*] is to be found in industry and economy only. . . ."

The clearest evidence of the broad opportunities available in America, even though the economic situation was not everywhere and at all times as roseate as some commentators made out, was the remarkably wide distribution of property, especially land. Thomas Hutchinson, Royal Governor of Massachusetts, said in 1764 that in all the colonies not more than 2 per cent of the tillers of the soil were tenants. "This is the ruling passion to be a freeholder," he remarked. At another time he asserted, "Property is more equally distributed in the colonies, especially those to the northward of Maryland than in any nation in Europe." In 1755 the General Court of Massachusetts gave as its opinion that land was so abundant that any young man who wanted to could start a family without venturing a farthing—an opportunity, the legislature pointed out, which could not be matched in any country in Europe. More recently, Jackson Turner Main in a path-breaking investigation of property distribution in the late colonial period concluded "that revolutionary America produced enough wealth to save even its poor from suffering, to permit the great majority to live adequately, even in comfort, and to enable a few to live in real luxury." Less than thirty per cent of the society, he determined, held no property, and in that group were included slaves and indentured servants.

A broadly based property-holding class, regardless of whether it primarily held land, as in the colonial era, or chattels and real estate, as in the nineteenth and twentieth centuries, has always been the principal and ultimate shield of capitalism in America. With property widely distributed from the very beginning, American political and social institutions have been conservative about it; but in doing so they have accurately reflected the people's direct interest in private property. Indeed, as the Revolution was to make clear, Americans defined liberty as the right to control their property. A twisted echo of the principle was still heard in the 1960's, in objections to laws that would prohibit discrimination against Negroes in housing.

Even in a new society with broad economic opportunities, the eighteenth-century colonial was actually aware of status, if only because he was a child of class-conscious Europe. One Anglican clergyman who knew American urban society and English life equally well called attention to the class demarcations visible in the colonial towns. Despite the absence of a nobility or orders of gentry, he said, "you might see a proof [of] how necessarily some difference of rank, some inequality must and ought to grow up in every society, and how Eutopian and ridiculous the contrary idea and attempt is." All through the literature of the period one finds references to "the Better Sort," the "Middle Sort," and the "meaner sort" of people.

Although it was true that breeding, ancestry, occupation, and learning played their parts in determining which "sort" one was, the final arbiter in the eighteenth century as in the seventeenth was wealth. "The only principle of Life propagated among the young People," complained Cadwallader Colden in 1748, "is to get Money and men are only esteemed according to . . . the Money they are possessed of." With property as a social escalator, the acquisition of wealth became the object of the many. "The hopes of having land of their own and becoming independent Landlords," Colden said, "is what chiefly induces peoples into America." Men purchased land as quickly as possible after their arrival, Colden continued, even though a few more years as laborers would have made life easier, "but such is the desire of being independent and of leaving a certain estate to their children that it overcomes all other Considerations."

Underlying the drive for wealth among Americans was the widespread opportunity which the new land afforded. In America, Franklin wrote, "no man continues long a journeyman to a trade, but goes among those new settlers and sets up for himself." A Philadelphia newspaper in 1776 summed up both the wide distribution of property and the rapidity of social advancement. "Is not one half of the property in the city . . . owned by men who wear *Leather Aprons?*" the paper asked. "Does not the other half belong to men whose fathers or grandfathers wore Leather Aprons?"

The fluidity of class lines in colonial America can be further illustrated in the lives of men who rose from lowly status to high rank within their communities. Most spectacular, perhaps, is the history of Anthony Lamb. In 1742 he was awaiting execution at Tyburn, England, when a last-minute commutation of his sentence sent him to Virginia as an indentured prisoner. After his service he worked in a number of occupations, eventually ending up in New York City as a respected citizen and the owner of an instrument maker's shop. His son John, also an instrument maker, ultimately rose to be included among the leading gentry of the city. He entered history as one of the leading Sons of Liberty who sparked the Revolutionary movement in New York. Or one might cite the case of Adino Paddock of Harwich, Massachusetts, who came to Boston in 1736 as an apprentice to a carriage maker. In 1758 he owned his own shop and was prominent in the Masonic Order. By 1769 he was serving on the important Committee on the State of Public Affairs for Boston; he was appending "esquire" to his name in 1772. At the time of the evacuation of Boston by the British in 1776, Paddock left the country as a Tory, with property valued at over £3,000 sterling.

Even the well-known painter John Singleton Copley experienced in his lifetime a quick ascent from low social origins. Born the son of an immigrant tobacconist in 1738, Copley by 1769 was earning 300 guineas a year from his painting—enough to permit him to marry the fashionable Susannah Clarke. Though his marriage undoubtedly was a factor in catapulting him into the upper reaches of Boston society, it was his earnings, not his marriage, which permitted him to build a sumptuous mansion on Boston's Beacon Hill appropriate to his new status.

Historical studies of social mobility in the colonial years bear out the contemporary views. A study of the town of Kent, Connecticut, between 1740 and 1777, for example, reveals that of the men in the town who did not migrate, some 77 per cent acquired land in the course of their lifetimes. A similar rate of social mobility apparently obtained in southern communities. In Lunenberg County in western Virginia, for instance, of 150 men without land in 1764, three-quarters owned land by 1782. This proportion, however, goes down, Jackson Turner Main found, when examination is made of older, more settled areas. Thus Main discovered that only 38 per cent of the landless in an eastern Virginia county acquired land between 1764 and 1782. The frontier was not the only area of mobility.

About 60 per cent of New York merchants and 70 per cent of Boston merchants, Main has shown, began as poor men. In Main's judgment, the towns of colonial America would be second only to the frontier as areas for rapid social mobility in these years.

The relative ease with which wealth could be accumulated stimulated a materialistic drive among even those in the lower ranks of society who would probably never live on Beacon Hill or lower Broadway. That most Americans, whether of high or low estate, should display this avidity for wealth was, as we have seen, clearly a disappointment to aristocratic Cadwallader Colden. Even the usually sanguine and democratic Crèvecoeur was disturbed by the obvious scramble for money among the colonials. "If it is not 'bellum omnium contra omnes,' " he wrote, " 'tis a general mass of keenness and sagacious acting against another mass of equal sagacity; 'tis caution against caution. Happy when it does not degenerate into fraud against fraud!" The ambitious American, intent on his own success, Crèvecoeur sadly noted, was harsh and even fraudulent in his dealings with the new arrivals. The American, he wrote, appears "litigious, overbearing, purse-proud." After 1740, when the wars with the French provided wider and more frequent opportunities for the piling up of wealth and the perpetrating of highly profitable, if dubious, commercial deals, colonial incomes and avarice scaled new heights. While British and colonial soldiers and seamen were dying fighting the French and Indians in the forests of the West and on the high seas, other colonials were lucratively trading with the enemy.

Although, in a general way, society in the colonies was pyramidal as it was in Europe, there were differences in more than detail. For one thing, the absence of a hereditary nobility and royalty in America meant that the social pyramid was truncated rather than pointed. But, further than this, the wide dispersion of property brought the top and bottom levels of society much closer together than in Europe. Though it is true that the pretensions of the upper classes in colonial society seemed almost without limit, the highest stratum of society was in fact quite "middle class" by European standards. Nicholas Cresswell, who was familiar with English society, thought that George Washington's father was no more than "a creditable Virginia Tobacco Planter (which I suppose may, in point of rank, be equal to the better sort of Yeomanry in England)." It was indicative of the narrow distance—by European measures—between the base and the summit of society that colonial craftsmen were to be found on every level of society, from slaves to gentry. A further measure of the middling nature of colonial society was John Witherspoon's observation that the common man in the colonies spoke better English on the average than his counterpart in England, but that the speech of the educated colonial was inferior to that of the educated Briton. Carl and Jessica Bridenbaugh, in discussing the society of Philadelphia, concluded that though the "aristocracy" of the city were "members of a privileged oligarchy, none of them could have said, with Catherine of Russia, 'Je suis aristocrate; c'est mon métier.' "

It was to be expected that egalitarian sentiments would be rife in a society in which large numbers of men possessed property and in which almost all men could read and write.[2] "The people of this Province," commented a writer in the *Pennsylvania Journal* in 1756, "are generally of the middling Sort, and at present pretty much upon a Level. They are chiefly industrious Farmers, Artificers or Men in Trade; they enjoy and are fond of Freedom, and the *meanest among them* thinks he has a right to Civility from the greatest." With manifest distaste, Comptroller Weare, a British official, observed in 1760 that in America "under forms of a democratical government, all mortifying distinctions of rank are lost in common equality; and . . . the ways of wealth and preferment are alike open to all men. . . ." He might have noted that it was likely that the "common equality" prevailed because "the ways of wealth were open."

Philip Fithian noticed in the 1760's that the trend toward social equality permeated even the upper classes. Among the people of his native province of New Jersey, Fithian saw "the Level" at work. "Hence, we see Gentlemen, when they are not actually engaged in the publick service, on their farms, setting a laborious example to their Domesticks, and on the other hand we see labourers at the Tables and in the Parlours of their Betters enjoying the advantage, and honour of their society and conversation." Even in Virginia, where Fithian served as a tutor on the plantation of the aristocratic Robert Carter, he was seated daily at table with the family, and, in the absence of the master, the lowly teacher was accepted as the man of the house for ceremonials like carving and serving at meals.

Thus, in the midst of a hierarchical social pattern, there were forces at work which not only modified the pattern as compared with

[2] "A native American who cannot read or write is as rare an appearance as a Jacobite or a Roman Catholic, that is, as rare as a comet or an earthquake," wrote John Adams in 1765.

European models, but which led directly to an egalitarian social structure in the future. In short, the stage was already set in the colonial period for that assertion of equality which is usually associated only with the Jacksonian movement of the early nineteenth century. The Revolution would add its impetus to this gathering egalitarian sentiment which, in the first half of the eighteenth century, Europeans already recognized as one of the distinctive characteristics of American society.

4. NOT ALL COLONIALS WERE ENGLISHMEN

It is a cliché to say that all Americans are descendants of immigrants; the truly striking thing about the American population is its ethnic diversity. This diversity began in the eighteenth century. Prior to the last decade of the seventeenth century, the vast majority of those who came to America—with the exception, of course, of the Dutch living in New York and the small colonies of Swedes and Finns in the Delaware River region—were of English stock.

Toward the end of the seventeenth century, however, a trickle of non-English nationalities, impelled by the hard times in their homelands, encouraged by the English authorities, and drawn by the magnet of American economic opportunity, began to come into the colonies. The signs of this movement are still upon the land. Occasional town names like New Rochelle and New Paltz in New York and New Bordeaux in South Carolina, as well as well-known family names like Revere, Ravenal, Legaré, Faneuil, Jay, and De Lancey, still bear witness to the French Huguenots who came in the years after the revocation of the Edict of Nantes in 1685. New Bern in North Carolina and Swedesboro and Finns Point in New Jersey are memorials of other tiny groups of continental Europeans who settled in the English colonies. The exquisite eighteenth-century synagogue built by Peter Harrison in Newport and the still extant Portuguese cemetery in New York recall the small but thriving Spanish and Portuguese Jewish communities of the colonial era, just as ancient Sephardic names like Cardozo, Lopez, and de Sola Pool still remind us of their continuing influence.

The great influx of non-English immigration came in the eighteenth century with the Scots, Scots-Irish, and Germans. The latter two groups arrived in large numbers in the opening decades of the century, while the Scots were most prominent after 1750. Unlike the two larger contingents, the Scots were especially noticeable in trade. Virginia planters in the 1750's and 1760's filled their letters with complaints against the Scottish factors to whom they sold their tobacco and from whom they bought European manufactures. By the time of the Revolution, Scottish immigration was well in excess of 25,000 for the century. Surprisingly enough, considering their age-long struggle against the English, the Scots in America proved to be stanch supporters of the Crown at the time of the Revolution. However, two of the best-known patriots, James Wilson of Pennsylvania and John Witherspoon, president of the College of New Jersey and a signer of the Declaration, were both born and bred in Scotland.

The Scots-Irish came from Ireland, but, unlike the later Irish, they were overwhelmingly Protestant—Presbyterians from the counties of the north. Their ancestors had been transplanted from their native Scotland in the early years of the seventeenth century by James I in an effort to secure the Emerald Isle for Protestantism. In place names like Ulster and Orange counties (New York), Orange (New Jersey), and Donegal (Pennsylvania), the Irish origins of the first settlers are still in evidence. But the importance of the Scots-Irish in America far exceeded the few towns and counties to which they gave names reminiscent of their European origins. Pennsylvania west of the Susquehanna was thickly seeded with Protestant Irish; so was the Great Valley in Virginia and the Carolina piedmont. Seeming to strike for the westernmost frontier as a plant pushes toward the sun, these hardy, God-fearing Calvinists made themselves into a veritable human shield of colonial civilization. With one hand, as it were, they battled the irate landlords on whose lands they unceremoniously squatted, while with the other they killed Indians and pushed back the forest. From the loins of this people have sprung some of the most eminent names in American political history: Andrew Jackson, John C. Calhoun, James K. Polk, and the greatest covenanter of them all, Woodrow Wilson.

While the spirited Scots-Irish were war-whooping it on the frontier, the less dramatic but numerous Germans were also spreading through the English colonies. Their line of settlement can be followed in the Germanic town names: Rhinebeck and Newburgh, New York; Germantown, Pennsylvania; German Valley, New Jersey; Hagerstown and Fredericktown, Maryland; Strasburg, Harpers Ferry and Germantown, Virginia; Mecklenburg, North Carolina; Orangeburg and Saxe-Gotha, South Carolina. The greatest concentration of Germans,

of course, was in southeastern Pennsylvania, where the so-called
Pennsylvania Dutch still offer visible testimony to the migration.

The Germans were so numerous in Pennsylvania in the middle of
the eighteenth century that Franklin doubted they would ever fit into
the life of an English colony. "Why should the Palatine boors be
suffered to swarm into our settlements, and, by herding together,
establish their language and manners, to the exclusion of ours?" he
asked in 1751. Their numbers—they constituted about a third of
the population of the province—caused him to wonder why "Pennsylvania, founded by the English," should "become a colony of aliens,
who will shortly be so numerous as to Germanize us, instead of our
Anglifying them? . . ." In Franklin's irritation are the first signs of a
recurring anxiety in the history of immigration to America—the
native-born's fear of the growing number of strangers in his midst.
Nativism, along with diversified immigration, began in the eighteenth
century.

If the Germans constituted one great block of people in America
who did not speak the language of England, the Dutch in New York
were another. Almost ninety years after the English took over in
New Amsterdam, Peter Kalm the Swedish traveler, visiting Albany,
reported that although all the citizenry dressed like Englishmen,
"rarely is an English word heard." About the same time, in 1743,
Dr. Alexander Hamilton (no relative of the later Secretary of the
Treasury) took a trip up the Hudson from New York to Albany
and found that the large number of Dutch-speaking people on board
ship almost precluded his finding a companion.

The diversity of language and custom in the colonies was held
responsible by one British official for the intractable spirit of the
Americans under English rule. Comptroller Weare wrote in 1760
that it was not surprising there were so many controversies between
the officials of the Crown and the colonials "considering how many
of the subjects of alien states are settled here, without that reverence
for British government, or partiality to British interest which can be
derived only from education. . . ." Because they tend to settle in
their own national communities, Weare continued, "one sees and
hears the religions, languages and manners of Germany, spoken and
professed in the British plantations by subjects born under British
government."

Thanks to the massive influx of immigrants from non-English
countries, the ethnic character of the colonies was markedly altered

in the course of the four or five decades before the Revolution. It has
been calculated that by 1776 as much as one half and perhaps more
of the population was of non-English origin. This represented more
than just the beginning of a long history of diverse immigration into
America; it marked the establishment of an ethnic pattern which
then, as now, has set America off from England and other European
countries.

As Comptroller Weare implied, this first great wave of European
—as distinguished from English—immigration added to the diversity
of American life in still another fashion. Each of these new peoples
brought a new religion with them. It is to the Scots and Scots-Irish
that Presbyterians owe their numerical importance in early America;
the Germans introduced into America a host of Protestant sects
—Moravians, Lutherans, Mennonites, Amish, Schwenkfelders, and
Dunkers. Though most of the French who came to America were
Protestants fleeing the bigotry of Louis XIV, some were Catholics,
and the bishops of the Roman Church in early America were sometimes French.

By the middle of the eighteenth century, religious diversity was
already recognized as peculiarly American. To an unsympathetic
visitor like Gottlieb Mittelberger, Pennsylvania in 1750 was simply
a chaos of religious sects, "which cannot all be enumerated." James
Reed, a missionary of the Anglican Society for the Propagation of
the Gospel in North Carolina, wrote to London in 1760 that he was
astounded by the "great number of dissenters of all denominations
. . . particularly Anabaptists, Methodists, Quakers and Presbyterians." For a European this spectrum of religions and the numerical
weakness of the Established Church were new experiences and, then
as now, they served to differentiate American civilization from European.

During the eighteenth century, religion in America underwent another change which carried implications for the future. Actually, the
change was twofold and, in a sense, paradoxical. One aspect of this
dual change was the decided trend toward secularization, toward the
playing down of the place of religion and the Church in the lives of
the people. The most obvious form of this alteration was the decline
of Puritanism in New England, but the growing lack of interest in
religion was wider than that. Though Mittelberger was shocked at
the diversity of sects in Pennsylvania, he was thoroughly horrified by
the irreligion of many of the people. There are "many hundreds of

adult persons," he wrote, "who have not been and do not even wish to be baptized. . . . Many do not even believe that there is a true God and Devil, a Heaven and a hell, salvation and damnation, a resurrection of the dead, a judgment and an eternal life; they believe that all one can see is natural."

In the back country of the Carolinas in the 1760's, earnest Charles Woodmason, an itinerant Anglican preacher, plodded many a weary mile looking for settlers willing to hear the word of Christ. After preaching one day to a hundred people, he reported that not a single person stepped forward to accept his offer to baptize children. "Do not find but one religious person among this Great Multitude," he wrote. The unconcern of these backwoods people for conventional church morality was implicit in one of his journal entries: "Married a couple—for the 1st Time—Woman very bigg."

By the time of the Revolution, actual church attendance probably touched one of the lowest points it has ever reached in American history, or at least since the first years of settlement. Edwin Scott Gaustad has estimated that in 1800 there were 1,122 persons for each church in the United States; in 1950 he finds the ratio to be 528 to one.

Though it is accurate to see a contraction in the popular influence of the Church during the last years of the colonial period, it should not be assumed that the intensity of religious interest fell off. Indeed, it might be said that just the opposite occurred: while the number of churchgoing people declined, the religious feelings of those who remained with the Church were actually intensified. This revitalization of the religious spirit and of the churches in the eighteenth century is the Great Awakening. As its name implies, the Great Awakening was a rebirth of emotion in religion; sometimes the emotion bordered on hysteria or uncontrolled ecstasy, but in general it was a recognition that religion was an emotional as well as an intellectual experience. This elementary fact had often been forgotten in the late seventeenth century as religion became increasingly rigid in its dogma, ritual, and message; the Great Awakening was a direct challenge, as it was a response, to the dry, formal, and heavily intellectual religion of the earlier period. Like a pillar of fire this rebirth of emotional intensity in religion swept through church after church from New England to Georgia in the 1740's and 1750's, its progress and heat stimulated by the impassioned evangelical preaching of men like George Whitefield, Theodore Frelinghuysen, Jonathan Edwards, and, somewhat later, John Wesley. The sermons of such preachers, by skillfully blending hell-fire and damnation oratory with a wide knowledge of Biblical literature, fired the hearts and seared the souls of those who came within listening distance.

One farmer in Middletown, Connecticut, in 1740 has left an account of what it meant to him. Farmer Nathan Cole had anxiously awaited word of the great Whitefield's coming to town. When news came that the evangelist had finally come to Middletown, Cole dropped his work, grabbed his horse and wife, and with scarcely a breath to spare raced the thirteen miles to town. There the Coles were engulfed in a crowd of several thousand equally eager farmers literally panting (from their exertions) to hear the melancholy diagnosis of the state of their souls which Whitefield was sure to make. Whitefield did not disappoint Nathan Cole, for "he looked as if he was clothed with authority from the Great God, and a sweet solemnity sat upon his brow, and my hearing him preach gave me a heart wound." Since the purpose of the evangelist was to awaken in his hearers a consciousness of sin, Whitefield achieved his purpose within Nathan Cole. "By God's blessing," Cole admitted afterward, "my old foundation was broken up, and I saw that my righteousness would not save me."

Even canny, unemotional Benjamin Franklin was not secure against Whitefield's preaching. In his *Autobiography* he tells of attending a sermon delivered by Whitefield in behalf of an orphanage in Georgia, a project of which Franklin disapproved. Because of his objections, even though he knew Whitefield would be asking for money, Franklin resolved not to contribute a copper penny. But as Whitefield "proceeded I began to soften, and concluded to give the coppers. Another stroke of his oratory made me asham'd of that, and determin'd me to give the silver; and he finished so admirably, that I empty'd my pocket wholly into the collector's dish, gold and all."

Churches were split asunder by the conflict between the new "enthusiastic" approach to religion and the staid and more thoughtful forms which had been once so characteristic of colonial Protestantism. To some old-timers, emotionalism in religion was anti-intellectual, a reversion to the sectarian chaos of the early Reformation. To the "new-lights," as they were called, the injection of feeling and emotion into religion was to revivify what had been lifeless, dull, and essentially without meaning. As Whitefield said, "How can dead Men beget living children?" Though for a while extremists on both sides seemed incapable of working out a synthesis of the two views, gradually the new view began to prevail. Religion in America lost the theological and formal cast so characteristic of the seventeenth century and regained an emotional significance for the individual reminiscent of the early Church and the Reformation. Furthermore, in the years after the middle of the century, new sects like Baptists and Methodists, because of active participation in the new movement, expanded their membership. Thus the once despised "enthusiastic" sects, as the seventeenth-century Puritans called them, took their places as major churches in America.

The Great Awakening was only the first of several great religious revivals which would wash over large areas of rural America from time to time. As a result of these periodic waves of religious emotionalism, Christian ideals and a strong moral sense were freshened and refreshened in the minds of Americans, never to be completely effaced even in the dark years of deistic questioning in the eighteenth century or of materialistic cynicism in the nineteenth. Puritanism certainly bequeathed to later generations, as we have seen, a penchant for moralism which is typically, if sometimes unfortunately, American, but the dissemination of this among the masses down through the years is as much the work of the revivals as it is of the original Puritans.

5. A PARADISE FOR WOMEN

Women in America, commented an Austrian traveler in the 1870's, are surrounded "with privileges and attentions unknown in the Old World." European wives of returning American soldiers after World War II often made the same observations upon their arrival in the United States. The origins of this special place for women in America are buried deep in the colonial era.

If the empty land of the New World acted as a magnet for the land-hungry, it was also a barrier to the delicate. Because of the hardships inherent in the settling of a wilderness, men tended to predominate over women among the passengers on the immigrant ships of the seventeenth and eighteenth centuries. For example, in a group of 10,000 indentured servants who left Bristol, England, between 1654 and 1686, there were 338 males for every 100 women. A Maryland census as late as 1755 showed that the sex ratio for whites was 113 males to every 100 females. The ratio in South Carolina in

1708 was 148 males to 100 females. Indeed, all through the colonial period, except in New England in the eighteenth century, the excess of males in America is an inescapable demographic fact. The sexes had not always been in balance in Europe, but rarely if ever had there been excesses of men. Wars, the daily occupational dangers to which men were exposed, and the weaker survival power of males biologically had combined to keep women more numerous than men. In colonial America, these social and biological forces could not operate fully since the population was heavily augmented by immigration and the rigors of the primitive life tended to keep the number of women immigrants considerably below the men. In this difference in sex ratios in Europe and America are the beginnings, at least, of the differing attitudes toward women in the old country and the new. Simply put, women in America commanded influence and prestige because they were scarce.

That the position of the colonial woman was better than that of her European sister all visitors recognized. Gottlieb Mittelberger, who was no admirer of America, commented in 1750 on the fact that "the women enjoy . . . great liberties and privileges" in Pennsylvania. He told of a servant girl who had been made pregnant by her master, but had succeeded in compelling him to marry her. The court, much to Mittelberger's surprise, took the side of the girl against her superior by offering the master the choice of marriage or a heavy fine. The German traveler was further impressed by the knowledge that in Philadelphia the "English servant women" were "as elegantly dressed as an aristocratic lady in Germany." Englishman Nicholas Cresswell dryly observed that America was a paradise for women because the chances for marriage were so good. Though on the frontier women undoubtedly worked as hard or harder than most urban women in Europe, the poorer women in America were usually much better off than their counterparts in the old country. Usually they did less outdoor work—even female indentured servants in Virginia were not expected to work in the fields—and, as Mittelberger observed, they dressed better than European women. From the beginning, the social freedom of young women, which is still in marked contrast with custom in some European countries today, was evident in America. Chaperons were too delicate a refinement for the frontier and were not taken seriously in the cities. Indeed, just because the country was raw and undeveloped, women were clothed in new importance. The wife and mother in the rude settlement on or near the frontier was more than a housekeeper; she was an indispensable part of the apparatus of survival. Since the whole family was dependent upon her for a score of necessities like clothes, spices, soap, candles, lard, vegetables, medicines, and perhaps even protection when the husband was absent, a woman was a person of value.

Even in the cities, the scarcity of labor gave an advantage to women in America; there were more jobs for women outside the home.[3] In 1733 the New York *Weekly Journal* carried an advertisement which told in a few words both the stuff of which some women in colonial America were made and the fact that they were economically important. "We, the widdows of this city," it read, protest the failure to invite us to "court." "We are House Keepers, Pay our Taxes, carry on Trade, and most of us are she Merchants. . . . We have the Vanity to think we can be full as Entertaining, and make as brave a Defense in Case of Invasion and perhaps not turn Taile as soon as" some of the men. On the basis of an admittedly small sample, but one nevertheless suggestive, one authority has computed that there were proportionately more "she merchants" in the 1770's in America than in 1900. Enough records from the colonial period still survive to show that it was not an uncommon event for a widow to take over the business of her deceased husband. This was especially true of taverns, boarding houses, and shops not requiring a skilled craftsman.

Nor was it unknown for women to act for their husbands, not only in an economic or business capacity, but in a legal one as well. Many women exercised power of attorney for their spouses and were sole executrices of estates. The most renowned example of the latter is Margaret Brent of Maryland, who in 1647 acted as the sole executor of Governor Leonard Calvert's substantial estate. As all this suggests, in the eyes of colonial law the rights of women were a decided cut

[3] One must not, of course, overemphasize the opportunities for women to work in the colonial period. Professions like medicine, the ministry, the law, were totally closed to them; most crafts were also; even teaching, which later was to become the mainstay of female professional employment, was largely in the hands of men, though a few women did run the so-called dames' schools. Mrs. Spruill, in her study of *Women's Life and Work in the Southern Colonies* (Chapel Hill, 1938), pp. 241–42, writes that "the eighteenth century saw a decline in the vigor and self-reliance of women in wealthier families and a lessening of their influence in public matters. Because of the rural character of their lives and the general influence of the frontier, American ladies were less idle and artificial than those of England, but compared with the daring and independent matrons of the preceding century, they appear somewhat effeminate and timid."

above those accorded to the sex under the common law of England. Women, for example, whether married or not, sued and were sued in colonial courts.

There were significant differences in the legal rights of married women in America and England. The conception of marriage in Richardson's *Pamela*—that it was a "kind of state of humiliation for women"—may have been true of eighteenth-century England, Richard Morris has commented, but "it would not be applicable to the American colonies." The American environment, for one reason or another, produced important changes in the rights of women. For example, though the common law of England took no notice of a woman's right to her property once she was married, by the end of the colonial period it was rather well established in America that a woman's property could be disposed of by her husband only with her consent and acknowledgment.[4] Under the common law of England married women retained no capacity to make contracts, a disability which followed from their being incompetent to hold property. In the colonies, however, because married women did possess property rights, the law granted them contractual capacity as well. As a result, wives often transacted business for their husbands when the latter were absent.

On occasion the colonial law seemed to overstretch itself to grant rights to the wife to protect her against her husband—an approach to the conjugal relationship which neither the English common law nor its noted expositor, Blackstone, would have countenanced. The common law, for instance, working on the assumption that "their interests are absolutely the same," would not permit a wife to testify against her husband. In some colonial courts, on the other hand, such testimony was permitted in both civil and criminal proceedings. Instances are known, moreover, where colonial courts and legislatures sought to protect widows whose husbands had not treated them properly in wills. Thus in 1714 a New Hampshire statute provided that

---

[4] On the other hand, it should be said, women were not able to control their property completely. Husbands, for instance, frequently sued for the value of their working wives' services, and collected. Richard B. Morris, *Studies in the History of American Law* (New York, 1930), p. 126, notes that the institution of marriage in America was strongly influenced, through the Calvinist sects, by the continental and Radical Protestant tradition which taught that marriage was a contract and not a sacrament of the Church. As a consequence, "the notion of mutuability in the civil marriage lay at the root of the substantial advance in the position of the wife in seventeenth century American law."

where a husband's will proved to work an injury upon the wife, the widow should receive such proportion of her husband's estate "as if he had dyed intestate."

The superior position of women in colonial America derives from a number of circumstances. Certainly, the fact that English women enjoyed more freedom than those on the Continent has something to do with it. But it would seem that the more compelling reasons arose out of the American environment: the greater number of men than women, and the demands and opportunities of a frontier society. Taken together, these circumstances could not help but enhance the value of women in the eyes of men and hence in the view of society at large.

6. AMERICANS HAVE NEW RIGHTS

"It is . . . to England that we owe this elevated rank we possess," remarked Crèvecoeur, "these noble appellations of freemen, freeholders, citizens; yes it is to that wise people we owe our freedom. Had we been planted by some great monarchy, we should have been mean slaves of some distant monarch." It was for sound historical reasons that during the Revolutionary crisis the colonials stoutly asserted their claims to the "rights of Englishmen." Yet despite the English substance at the core of colonial political forms, the colonists departed in a number of ways from the example of the mother country. Frequently these deviations were merely novel twists given to English institutions; sometimes they were new institutions called into being by the new conditions in America. But whatever the nature of the changes, by the middle of the eighteenth century the forsaking of English practices was in evidence and the American constitutional system of the future was visible.

A common political vocabulary can certainly serve to bind together a colony and a mother country. But when the meaning behind the words is different, then the stage is set for misunderstanding, recrimination, and conflict. During the 1850's the North and the South found themselves in this dangerous position; the colonists and the English in the years immediately preceding the American Revolution also fell into this predicament. Steeped as they were in the English political language, the colonials spoke in what they thought was the common intellectual coin of the Empire, neglecting to observe that the American experience had given the words a content quite different from that accepted by the Englishmen with whom they debated. That Americans and Britons were saying different things when they employed the same words did not become apparent until after 1765, but the actual differences in political and constitutional practices of the two peoples were there long before the Stamp Act.

It is true, of course, as Crèvecoeur implied, that in many respects the political institutions of England were reproduced in close detail in the colonies. By the middle of the eighteenth century, for instance, all of the mainland colonies except four were headed by a Royal Governor, appointed by the King and therefore bearing a relation to the people of the colony similar to that of the King to the British people. Moreover, each of the thirteen colonies enjoyed a representative assembly, which was consciously modeled, in powers and practices, after the British Parliament. The resemblance to the English example was carried still further in the division of the colonial assemblies into upper and lower houses in emulation of the House of Commons and the House of Lords. In both England and the colonies, furthermore, the suffrage was exercised only by property holders; in all the colonies, as in England, it was an axiom, as an act of South Carolina put it in 1716, that "none but such persons who have an interest in this Province shall be capable to elect or be elected."

Though in the letter the English and colonial constitutions were similar, in the spirit they were moving in different directions. For example, English constitutional development from the earliest years of the seventeenth century had been sometimes drifting, sometimes driving, but always moving in pursuit of the absolute power of Parliament. The most unmistakable sign of this tendency was the assertion that the King was under the law, as exemplified in the Petition of Right in 1628, the judgment and execution of Charles I in 1649, and finally the *de facto* deposition of James II in 1689. Together with this resolute denial of the divine right of kings went the assertion that Parliament was unlimited in its power; that it could change even the Constitution by its ordinary acts of legislation, just as it had created the Constitution by its past acts. By the eighteenth century, as today, the British accepted the idea that the representatives of the people were omnipotent; that, as the aphorism has it, "Parliament can do anything except change a man into a woman and a woman into a man."

The colonials did not look upon the English Parliament with such

fond eyes, nor—equally important for the future—did they concede
that their own assemblies possessed such wide powers. There were
good historical reasons for this. Though to the English the word
"Constitution" meant nothing more nor less than the whole body of
law and custom from the beginning of the kingdom, to the colonials
it meant a written document, enumerating specific powers. This distinction in meaning is to be traced to the fact that the foundations of
government in the various colonies were written charters granted by
the Crown. These express authorizations to govern were tangible,
definite things. Over the years the colonials had often repaired to
the timeless phrases and sonorous periods in their charters to justify
themselves in the struggle against rapacious Governors or tyrannical
officials of the Crown. More than a century of government under
written constitutions convinced the colonists of the necessity for and
efficacy of protecting their liberties against government encroachment
by explicitly defining all governmental powers in a document.

Even before the Stamp Act was passed, James Otis of Massachusetts articulated the striking difference between the colonial and
British conceptions of Parliamentary power and the nature of
constitutions. "To say the Parliament is absolute and arbitrary is a
contradiction," he asserted. Parliament cannot alter the supreme law
of the nation because "the Constitution is fixed; and . . . the supreme legislative . . . cannot overlap the Bounds of it without destroying its own foundation." Here, long before the Revolution, was
a succinct expression of what was to become the cardinal principle
of American constitutionalism, clearly setting it off from the English
in both practice and theory.

It is worth emphasizing that it was English practice which was
moving away from colonial. Earlier in the seventeenth century, in
the minds of jurists like Sir Edward Coke, Otis's arguments would
have carried much weight, but now the mutability of the Constitution
was widely accepted in England. The colonials in the middle of the
eighteenth century, as we shall have occasion to notice during the
Revolutionary crisis, were following the old-fashioned and more conservative line.

There was another way in which English and colonial constitutional developments were drifting apart. The intimate relation between the executive and Parliament, so characteristic of English and
continental democracies today, was already taking shape in the middle of the eighteenth century. The executive was the cabinet of min-

isters, who were drawn from the Parliament itself; as a result there was no separation of powers, the executive and legislative branches being merely different manifestations of the same body. This development, however, did not take place in America. The existence, for one thing, of a royally appointed Governor made such a development impossible; he could not be readily supplanted by a cabinet or ministerial council. Moreover, by having written constitutions or charters, the colonies were limited to the forms provided in earlier days. Under such circumstances it is not surprising that the colonial leaders entirely overlooked what was happening in England. From their distance they remained convinced that the King—like their own Royal Governors—was the real executive. Thus, because of the peculiarly American experience, the colonists were committed to a conception of government quite at variance with the English.

An important corollary to the English doctrine of parliamentary absolutism was the assumption that the colonies were subject to the legislative power of that body. For most of the seventeenth century the doctrine was no more than an assumption, and so the colonies did not feel it. This was partly because parliamentary supremacy was achieved late in the century—in 1689—and partly because the British government, embroiled in successive wars with Holland and France, did not seek to test its authority with the colonies.

This practice of "salutary neglect," as Burke named it, provided a long period during which the colonies developed self-reliance and their own ideas of government. The representative assembly in each of the provinces was widely viewed as the focus of government, peculiarly American, and constitutionally competent for all internal legislative purposes. The sole political tie of any consequence between the colonies and England was through the Royal Governor, and in four of the thirteen provinces there was not even this connection. It was to be expected, therefore, that the colonies should grow to think of their little assemblies as bearing the same relation to the Crown as the Parliament of Great Britain. Such a conception of colonial equality with England, however, ran counter not only to the strong current of parliamentary absolutism we have already noticed; it also flew in the face of a growing movement to centralize the government of the Empire in London.

There is irony in the growing divergence between England and the colonies regarding the power of representative assemblies. No institution introduced into the New World was probably more English than the representative assembly; yet it was this very political form, transformed by the American experience, which, more than anything else, served to bring about a break between the colonies and the Mother of Parliaments.

With the franchise, as with the parliamentary power, the colonists took a typically English institution and remade it into a wedge which drove the two peoples apart. Though both England and the colonies based the franchise on property holding, in the mother country this practice produced a small electorate. In America, however, the same requirement resulted in a quite different effect. Since property was widely distributed, even the use of property qualifications identical with those in England resulted in the colonies in a large electorate, occasionally even approaching universal manhood suffrage. The studies of Robert Brown in the history of colonial Massachusetts, for example, have made it clear that in both provincial and town elections well over a majority of men—perhaps 80 per cent—could vote. When Thomas Hutchinson was defeated in Boston in 1749 he said of the 200 votes he received: "they were the principal inhabitants, but you know we are governed not by weight but by numbers." At another time Hutchinson remarked with obvious distaste: "The town of Boston is an absolute democracy. . . ." Even allowing for some exaggeration on the part of a defeated politician, these statements of a contemporary indicate that large numbers of men could vote in colonial Massachusetts.

Though some of the other colonies probably could not boast as wide a franchise as Massachusetts or other New England provinces, the franchise in the eighteenth century in all the colonies was considerably wider than is often supposed.[5] Richard McCormick, for example, has shown that in New Jersey the property qualifications were quite easy for the great majority of the adult males to meet. Indeed, he has uncovered instances where the regulations at the polls

---

[5] Contrary to the usual belief that the political rights of the common man have been steadily improving through the years, it should be pointed out that the franchise in the seventeenth-century colonies was generally wider than in the eighteenth. In the early years of the Virginia colony, for example, except for Negroes, virtually universal manhood suffrage prevailed. Down to 1716, voters in South Carolina were required to possess only £10 in property at a time when a house and a few farm animals would easily surpass this value. As late as 1715 any white male who paid taxes could vote in North Carolina. Before 1702, £20 in property granted the vote to a resident of Connecticut. During the seventeenth century all freemen—a rank awarded to all who applied—possessed the franchise in Rhode Island.

were so lax that women, boys, and even Negroes voted. Milton Klein has shown that in New York as many as 55 per cent of the adult white males actually voted, suggesting that the eligible actually reached proportions close to 100 per cent. In Pennsylvania, Albert McKinley has estimated, at least one half of the males in a farming area outside Philadelphia could vote, though the figure would be lower in the city itself. Robert and Katherine Brown have found a wide participation in elections in Virginia, often taken as an aristocratically inclined province in the colonial period and after. In a general survey of the colonial suffrage, Chilton Williamson has found that in virtually all areas, where figures are available, the proportion of adult white males who could vote was at least 50 per cent. In some places, as we have seen, it reached 75 per cent. Furthermore, unlike Virginians and other colonists, South Carolina voters also enjoyed the democratic device of the secret ballot. In short, the forms of political democracy were already beginning to appear in the colonial period.

To many observers it seemed that the spirit of democracy or republicanism was also evident in the colonies, thereby setting the colonials further apart from the English. "The New England Governments are all formed on Republican Principles and those Principles are zealously inculcated in the Minds of their Youth in opposition to the Principles of the Constitution of Great Britain," complained Cadwallader Colden to the Board of Trade in 1763. Comptroller Weare, in offering advice on the keeping of the colonies in due subordination, argued in 1760 that even in the royal colonies, where the King appointed the Governor and the Council, "the authority of the Crown is not sufficiently supported against the licentiousness of a republican spirit in the people, whose extreme jealousy of any power not immediately derived from themselves," and whose lack of true affection for England "dispose them generally to send as representatives the most artful and factious amongst them."

Already in the colonial period the ordinary citizen participated in government to an extent far beyond anything in contemporary England. As we have seen, Europeans and Americans alike conceived of colonial politics as essentially popular and quite different from English in this regard. It is also apparent that in this strong tendency toward political democracy in the colonies lay the genesis of the movement for universal manhood suffrage, which was to be characteristic of the United States in the nineteenth century.

It is somewhat paradoxical that the United States, with a long tradition of universal suffrage, also has an equally strong tradition of an appointed Supreme Court charged with the responsibility of passing upon the constitutionality of legislation enacted by the elected representatives of the people. This peculiarly American doctrine of judicial review has its roots in the colonial period. In one sense, of course, the power of the courts to declare a piece of legislation null and void when it conflicts with the Constitution is deducible, as Chief Justice Marshall pointed out in *Marbury* v. *Madison,* from the conception of a written Constitution. It stems from the belief, widely held in the colonies, that no legislative or executive power could extend beyond the authority set forth in the charter or Constitution. As James Otis phrased it in 1761, "An Act against the Constitution is void."

But there was another colonial source from which the uniquely American doctrine of judicial review of legislation was drawn. All through the eighteenth century the Privy Council in England acted as a final court of appeals for the colonies. Early in that century, in 1728, in the case of *Winthrop* v. *Lechmere* the Council declared an act of Connecticut contrary to the law of England and therefore null and void.[6] This case and two subsequent ones in 1738 and 1745 make it clear that the Privy Council was serving as a court for reviewing colonial legislation in the light of the "higher law" of the English Constitution. From start to finish the procedure in these cases was judicial and therefore an exact precedent for the later American procedure of judicial review, which is also exclusively judicial. It might not be too farfetched to perceive in this central court of the Privy Council the germ of the later United States Supreme Court. Both the eighteenth-century English and nineteenth-century American tribunals sought to bring a variety of local legal systems into conformity with a larger constitutional framework, yet neither aimed to destroy the individual provincial or state jurisdictions.

[6] It is of interest here that this decision was itself evoked by the differences between colonial and English legal practices. The case revolved around the fact that Connecticut, in common with other New England colonies, did not practice primogeniture. Because partible inheritance was contrary to the English common law, the Privy Council declared null and void a Connecticut statute which assumed there was no primogeniture. Though for a while it seemed that the decision would overturn hundreds of land titles in the colony, the Council modified its position in a subsequent case, *Clark* v. *Toucey,* and the matter was not pressed in the colonies by the Crown.

Related to both the political and constitutional innovations of the colonials was their defense of freedom of the press against the arbitrary power of government. The trial of John Peter Zenger in New York in 1735 is justly considered a landmark in the history of freedom. Under the English and colonial law of that time, the sole responsibility of a jury in a trial for seditious libel was to determine whether the accused had in fact written the alleged libel. Whether the material was in fact libelous was left up to the judge to decide. Since, in Zenger's case, Judge De Lancey was a creature of the Governor against whom the alleged libel was directed, the results of the trial seemed a foregone conclusion. This high probability was further enhanced when Zenger and his attorneys announced that they conceded Zenger's responsibility for writing and printing the article in question.

The drama and long-range significance of the case, however, turns upon the action of Andrew Hamilton, who assumed the leadership of the defense. Contending that the truth of Zenger's charges was the crux of the case, Hamilton argued that a press, unfettered by official control, was indispensable in a society claiming to be free. Truth, he said, was a legitimate, nay, a necessary defense in a libel suit. Almost casually he conceded Zenger's authorship of the offending piece. But then he turned to the jury and, in a masterful presentation, urged upon the jurors a new course. Disregarding the law and appealing to their love of liberty, Hamilton challenged the jurors to decide the larger question of whether the charges Zenger levied against the Governor were true or not. If they were, Hamilton advised, then the jury should acquit the printer. Despite its sure knowledge that it was affronting a powerful and partisan judge, the jury nobly matched Hamilton's boldness and found Zenger not guilty.

It is true that censorship of the press, particularly by the assemblies, and even trial for libel in which truth was not accepted as a defense, occurred after the Zenger case. But there were no more trials for seditious libel in New York for the rest of the colonial period. Moreover, the trial and its outcome produced repercussions in England. Radicals and Whigs, won over by the brilliant colonial innovation in behalf of a free press, began a campaign in support of American liberty which was to reach its full power at the time of the Revolution in the voices of Burke, Fox, John Wilkes, Dr. Price, and Colonel Barré.

The principle inherent in the Zenger decision was not quickly implemented in America, as Leonard Levy has pointed out. It was not until 1798, during the Jeffersonians' powerful attacks upon the theory of the Sedition Act that the modern view of freedom of the press was worked out. Heretofore, all sides to the question, including the Jeffersonians themselves, had accepted the idea that a government had a right to suppress statements critical of its officials. The new view, going beyond that set forth in Zenger, asserted that if a society was to be considered free it could not suppress criticism under the old rubrics of "seditious libel" or "a licentious press." In fact, the crime of seditious libel, *i.e.,* bringing government into disrepute by attacking its officials, was abandoned. The concept that truth was a defense in a libel suit—the central principle in the Zenger case—was established in New York law in the case of Henry Coswell in 1804 through the joint efforts of Alexander Hamilton and James Kent. The doctrine was reinforced by legislative act in 1805 and inserted, for good measure, in the state constitutions of 1821 and 1846. It was not until 1791, however, with Fox's Act, that English juries were granted the right to determine whether the writing in question was libelous or not, and it was not until 1843 that truth was accepted as a defense in a libel suit under English law.

7. "ALL OF US AMERICANS"

In the course of the Zenger trial Andrew Hamilton had chided the attorney general for his constant citing of English precedent. "What strange doctrine is it to press everything for law here which is so in England," the clever Philadelphian exclaimed. Hamilton knew full well that the law of England prevailed in the colonies, but he was playing upon the colonials' growing pride of country.

In the years after 1740 the colonials became increasingly conscious of themselves as Americans. To be sure, there were very few outright demands for independence. It would take a good number of years, during which a consciousness of kind was only dawning, before the idea of independence would be thought of, much less advocated. Nevertheless, for two decades or more before the Revolutionary crisis of the late 1760's, Americans were expressing the feeling that they were different from Europeans, that they had a destiny of their own.

Ironically enough, the most obvious manifestations of this budding sense of Americanism appear in the course of the wars with France in the 1740's and 1750's, when colonials fought side by side with the English. During most of the century-long struggle against France in the seventeenth and eighteenth centuries, Britain had not demanded that the American colonies contribute anything more than the defense of their home areas and perhaps an occasional foray into adjacent French-held Canada. But beginning with the so-called War of Jenkins' Ear in 1739, which was first waged against Spain and then (as King George's War) against France, Britain stepped up her expectations of colonial military support. In 1741 the home government succeeded in goading the colonials to assist in the mounting of an offensive against Cartagena, the great port of the Spanish Main.

In part because the enterprise was a colossal fiasco, but largely because American and European soldiers were thrown together under novel circumstances, the differences between Americans and Europeans were sharply illuminated for both sides. Admiral Vernon, the British commander of the expedition, for example, consistently referred to the colonials as "Americans." The colonials, in turn, referred to their supposed blood brothers, the English, as "Europeans." The words, of course, had been used before, but never so generally or consistently as at this time. The failure of the Cartagena expedition added its bit to the splitting apart of the two national groups. The Americans came away convinced that the English were callous and cruel in their treatment of colonials, and the English soldiery and officers were disgusted with what they stigmatized as the cowardice and ineffectiveness of the colonial soldier.

When the New Englanders under Sir William Pepperell succeeded in capturing the French fortress at Louisbourg in the St. Lawrence in 1745, the colonials' incipient pride of country burst forth. To some it seemed to prove, as one bit of doggerel put it, that in valor

> . . . the British Breed
> In Western Climes their Grandsires far exceed
> and that New England Schemes the Old Surpass,
>   As much as Gold does tinkling Brass;
> And that a Pepp'rell's and a Warren's Name,
> May vie with Marlb'rough and a Blake for Fame.

With the fall of Quebec in 1759, there was loosed a flood of prophecies that the star of American destiny was in the ascendant. "A new world has arisen," exulted the *New American Magazine,* "and will exceed the old!" It is noteworthy, considering its nationalistic name, that the magazine was then in its first year of publication. One scholar, Richard Merritt, in examining the colonial press of the mid-eighteenth century, found a remarkable increase in the early 1760's in references to "America" and "Americans" at the same time that there was a falling off in references to the connection with England. He finds, in short, a rise in American self-awareness prior to the catalyst of the Stamp Act crisis in 1765.

Meanwhile a developing American nationality was evident—perhaps less spectacularly, but nonetheless profoundly—in other ways. Under the influences of distance and the new environment, the mother tongue of the colonists was undergoing change. New words from the Dutch and Indian languages, for example, were constantly being added to the speech of the English in America; words like "boss," "stoop," "cruller," "crib," "scow," and "spook" came from the Dutch. The Indian names were all over the land, and they made America exotic for Englishmen as they still do for Europeans.

Americans also made up words, some of which reflected the new environment. "Back country" and "backwoods" were designed to describe the novelty of the frontier. Bullfrog, canvasback, lightning bug, razorback, groundhog, potato bug, peanut, and eggplant are similar colonial name tags for new natural phenomena.

Familiar English words sometimes assumed new meanings in America. "Lumber" in eighteenth-century England meant unused furniture, but in the colonies it was applied to the raw wood—and so it has remained. "Pie" in England, to this day, means a meat pie, but in the colonies that was a "potpie"; "pie" was reserved for fruit pastry. Dry goods in England included all nonliquids, like corn or wheat; the colonials, however, changed the meaning to textiles only. The same alteration took place with the word "rock," which in England denoted a large mass; in America as early as 1712 it was being applied to a stone of any size. "Pond" was an English word meaning an artificial pool, but in unkempt America it came to mean any small lake. Certain words obviously attached to the English environment were lost in America, where their referents did not exist: fen, heath, moor, wold, bracken, and downs. It is not to be wondered, therefore, that in 1756 lexicographer Samuel Johnson was talking of an American dialect.

The burgeoning sense of Americanism was reflected also in the colonials' image of themselves. When Eliza Pinckney of South Carolina was presented at King George's Court in 1750, she insisted upon being introduced as an "American." That same year an advertisement in a Boston paper advertised beer as "American" and urged that Bostonians should "no longer be beholden to Foreigners for a Credible [*sic*] Liquor, which may be as successfully manufactured in this country." It is not the self-interest which is important here, but the fact that the advertiser obviously felt he could gain by making an appeal to a sense of American pride among his potential customers. This feeling among Americans that they were different from Europeans was put forth explicitly by a Carolinian in 1762. Speaking about the question of sending young colonials to England for their education, he said it would be most surprising if a British education should suit Americans, "because the Genius of our People, their Way of Life, their circumstances in Point of Fortunes, and Customs, and Manners and Humours of the Country, difference us in so many important Respects from Europeans. . . ." Such an education could not be expected to fit Americans, he went on, any more "than an Almanac, calculated for the Latitude of London, would that of Williamsburg."

As relations between the colonies and the mother country worsened after 1765, expressions of Americanism became more explicit and sometimes belligerent. Colonial students at Edinburgh University before 1765 commonly designated themselves as from the various provinces, but at the time of the Stamp Act, Samuel Bard wrote, he and several others began to style themselves "Americans" and the precedent was followed by many in subsequent years. About the same time Ezra Stiles of New Haven drew up a plan for an "American Academy of Science," which was designed, he said, "for the Honor of American Literature, contemned by Europeans." He stipulated that only native-born Americans should be members. And at the Stamp Act Congress, Christopher Gadsden of South Carolina urged the gathered colonial leaders to take cognizance of their common nationality. "There ought to be no New England man, no New Yorker, known on the Continent," he advised, "but all of us Americans. . . ."

The magic of the moment and the atmosphere in the new country were so potent that John Morgan, newly arrived at Philadelphia from London in 1765, declared, only a year later, "I consider myself at once as a Briton and an American." Such an ambivalent attitude must have been common among colonials in the early stage of the crisis between the colonies and the mother country. But regardless of Morgan's own ambiguous feelings, his work in helping to establish the new medical school at Philadelphia was hailed by Benjamin Rush as an aid to the growing self-consciousness of the people of America. Pointedly calling Britain an alien land, Rush wrote Morgan that no longer would the colonial student have to tear "himself from every tender engagement" and brave the dangers of the sea "in pursuit of knowledge in a foreign country."

One of the most curious but very clear manifestations of a growing American awareness of differences between the peoples of the Old and New Worlds was the widespread belief that English society was morally inferior, even decadent, when compared with the social character of the colonies. As early as 1735 Lewis Morris, visiting England, wrote in his diary that he and his party "wish'd ourselves in our own Country, far from the deceits of a court." London appeared to Ebenezer Hazard as at once a wonderful "little World" and a "Sink of Sin." In 1767, English social conditions appeared shocking to William S. Johnson, who found the extremes of wealth and misery "equally amazing on the one hand and disgusting on the other." Benjamin Rush wrote from Edinburgh in 1767 that "every native of Philadelphia should be sent abroad for a few years if it was only to teach him to prize his native country above all places in the world."

Standing out against the decadence of England in the minds of colonials and of some Englishmen was the example of America as the hope of the world. In 1771, John Penn, who was certainly no radical, wrote that he considered Great Britain "as an Old Man, who has received several strokes of the Palsy, and tottering upon the brink of the Grave, whereas America was growing daily toward perfection." In 1745 a writer in the *Gentleman's Magazine* drew the lesson from the American success at the siege of Louisbourg that the colonials were truly in the classical tradition so dear to the men of the eighteenth century. He saw the colonists in "the great image of the ancient Romans leaving the plow for the field of battles, and retiring after their conquests to the plow again." For many Englishmen, America seemed to be utopia in actuality. But it was the Americans who above all were convinced of the moral superiority of their society. Colonials returned from Europe overflowing with tales of the iniquities they had witnessed in London or commenting on the manifest corruption of British politics. As early as 1748, Josiah Quincy was saying he was fearful that the venality of English political life would ruin the country. The self-righteousness of Americans toward Britain in the 1750's and 1760's reminds one of nothing so much as an adolescent's indignant strictures against his parent's time-worn but now suddenly recognized foibles. The American people were coming of age.

Along with adolescent carping, assertions of moral superiority, and self-righteousness in the years before 1765, there were also a few strong hints that independence was coming. The war against the French in Canada prompted some Americans to anticipate separation from England. Peter Kalm, for example, traveling through the colonies in 1748, was told that after the French were expelled from the western borders of the colonies, independence would come in a matter of thirty to fifty years. Once the "Gallicks" are removed, John Adams thought in 1755, the colonies would be able to go it alone. "The only way to keep us from setting up for ourselves," he wrote, "is to disunite us."

In 1760 and after, when the British government was wrestling with the question of whether or not the French should be expelled completely from the North American continent, there was much speculation as to the effect such expulsion would have upon the restive colonies. Though the canny Franklin blandly assured Parliament that the removal of the French would bind the colonies still closer to Britain, less suspect parties, like Comptroller Weare, pointed out that never before in history had an industrious and favored people like the Americans hesitated to break away from their mother country when they had the power to do so. It is highly likely, he added, "that a thousand leagues distance from eye and strength of government" would suggest just that *"to a people accustomed to more than British liberty."* Also of this opinion was a correspondent of the *Gentleman's Magazine* in 1760. "If the people of our colonies find no check from Canada, they will extend themselves, almost without bounds into the inland parts. . . . What the consequences will be," he added ominously and prophetically, "to have a numerous, hardy, independent people possessed of a strong country, communicating little, or not at all with England, I leave to your own reflections."

There was more behind the thought of independence than the removal of the French threat. There was the coming to climax of the whole history of a geographically separate and different people in America. English traveler Andrew Burnaby noticed it in 1759 when he pointed out that the growing cities of the coast were already turning their citizens into "great republicans" and that the farm dwellers too had "fallen into the same errors in their ideas of independency."

In a vague cultural sense, the colonies were ready for the parting of the ways with Britain. What still remained was something which would cleanly and definitely cut the political ties connecting the two peoples. The occasion would come after 1763 when Britain sought to find a new basis for its relations with the continental colonies, for then the differences between the two peoples would be translated into political terms. That is the story of the coming of the American Revolution.

CHAPTER III

A New Kind of Revolution

ON AT least two scores, the American Revolution was something new under the sun. Although most of the major powers of Europe boasted overseas colonial empires, never before had a colonial people successfully rebelled against the mother country. But once it was done by the United States, the example was not ignored. Within a century after the Revolution, France, Spain, and Portugal lost portions or all of their New World empires through colonial rebellion. Nor have the echoes yet ceased. In 1945, one sour Englishman in Batavia during the rebellion of the Indonesians against the Dutch remarked, "That damned American Revolution . . . is still giving us trouble."

Despite its precedent-setting character, however, the American revolt is noteworthy because it made no serious interruption in the smooth flow of American development. Both in intention and in fact the American Revolution conserved the past rather than repudiated it. And in preserving the colonial experience, the men of the first quarter century of the Republic's history set the scenery and wrote the script for the drama of American politics for years to come.

1. CAUSES WERE CONSEQUENCES

Though the colonists had long been drifting away from their allegiance to the mother country, the chain of events which led to the Revolutionary crisis was set in motion by external factors. The shattering victory of the Anglo-American forces over the French in the Great War for the Empire (1754–63), as Lawrence Gipson has rechristened the French and Indian War, suddenly revealed how wide the gulf between colonists and mother country had become. The very fact that the feared French were once and for all expelled from the colonial backdoor meant that another cohesive, if negative, force was gone. At least one friend of Britain, looking back from the fateful days of 1776, thought that "had Canada remained in the hands of the French, the colonies would have remained dutiful subjects. Their fears for themselves in that case," he reasoned, "would have supplied the place of the pretended affection for this nation. . . ." What actual effect the removal of the French produced upon the thinking of the colonists is hard to weigh, but there can be little doubt that the Great War for the Empire opened a new era in the relations between the colonies and the mother country.

Great Britain emerged from the war as the supreme power in European affairs: her armies had swept the once-vaunted French authority from two continents; her navy now indisputably commanded the seven seas. A symbol of this new power was that Britain's ambassadors now outranked those of France and Spain in the protocol of Europe's courts. But the cost and continuing responsibilities of that victory were staggering for the little island kingdom. Before the war the annual expenditures for troops in America and the British West Indies amounted to £110,000; now three times that sum was needed to protect the western frontier, suppress Indian revolts and maintain order. Furthermore, the signing of the peace found Britain saddled with a debt of £130 million, the annual charges of which ran to another £4 million. Faced with such obligations, the British government was compelled to reassess its old ways of running an empire, particularly in regard to the raising of new revenues.

Before the war, the administration and cost of the Empire were primarily, if not completely, a British affair. Imperial defense on the high seas was in the hands of the Royal Navy, and though the colonies were called upon from time to time to assist in the war with France, the bulk of the fighting was sustained by British troops. In return, the colonies had acquiesced in the regulation of their trade through a series of so-called Navigation Acts, which were enacted and enforced by the British authority; no revenues, however, except those collected as import or export duties, were taken from the colonies by Britain.

Under the pressure of the new responsibilities, the British authorities began to cast about for a new theory and practice of imperial administration into which the colonies might be fitted as actively contributing members. Prior to the war the government had been willing to protect the West Indian sugar interests at the expense of the rest of the Empire. But now, in the interest of increased revenue, the old protective duty, which was much too high to bring any return, was cut in half, thus permitting French molasses to compete with British West Indian in the English and colonial markets. In 1766, this molasses duty, in a further effort to increase revenue, was cut to two thirds of what it had been before the war. In short, the need for imperial revenues, not private interests, was now dictating legislation. The Stamp Act of 1765 and the Townshend duties of two years later were similar efforts to spread the financial burdens of the Empire among the beneficiaries of the British triumph over the French.

It seemed only simple justice to London officialdom that the colonies should share in the costs as well as the benefits to be derived from the defeat of the ancient enemy. At no time, it should be noticed, were the colonies asked to contribute more than a portion of the price of their own frontier defense. The stamp duty, for instance, was envisioned as returning no more than a third of the total military expenditures in America; the remainder would be borne by the home government. And because the colonists had difficulty scraping together the specie with which to pay such duties, the British government agreed to spend all the revenue obtained from the stamp tax in the colonies in order to avoid depleting the scanty colonial money supply. Nor were Americans heavily taxed; it was well known that their fiscal burden was unique in its lightness. In 1775 Lord North told the House of Commons that the per capita tax payments of Britons were fifty times those of the Americans. It was not injustice or the economic incidence of the taxes which prompted the colonial protests; it was rather the novelty of the British demands.

The new imperial policies of the British government caught the Americans off guard. Reveling in the victory over the French, the colonists confidently expected a return to the lax, uninterested administration of the prewar years and especially to their old freedom from any obligation to support the imperial defenses. Therefore, when the first of the new measures, the Sugar Act of 1764, became law, the Americans protested, but on a variety of grounds and without sufficient unity to command respect.[1] By the time of the Stamp Act in the following year, however, the colonists were ready.

---

[1] For example, although the preamble of the Sugar Act explicitly cited revenue as one of the objects of the law, only two of the colonies, North Carolina and New York, denied the right of Parliament to tax them. The rest of the colonial protests were on other, nonconstitutional grounds.

The essential colonial defense, from which the colonies never deviated,[2] was a denial that the British Parliament had any right in law or custom to lay taxes upon the colonies for revenue purposes. Such taxes, the colonials insisted, could only be levied by the colonial legislatures. Actually, this expression of the colonial constitutional position was as novel as the imperial policy. Never before had there been an occasion for such an assertion simply because England had heretofore confined her colonial legislation to the regulation of trade. It is true that the Pennsylvania Charter of 1681 specifically reserved to the British Parliament the right to tax the colony; but since Parliament had never used this power, the colonists had a case when they said the new British taxes were historically unknown and therefore unconstitutional. The details of this controversy, in which merit is by no means the exclusive possession of either side, do not concern us here. The important fact is not whether the Americans or the British were right in their respective readings of imperial constitutional history, but that the colonials believed they were right and acted accordingly. Regardless of the constitutional niceties involved, it is patent that the English had waited too long to assert their authority. Too many Americans had grown accustomed to their untrammeled political life to submit now to new English controls. In brief, the colonists suddenly realized that they were no longer wards of Britain, but a separate people, capable of forging their own destiny.

This conviction runs all through the polemics of the Revolutionary crisis. For underlying the constitutional verbiage which Englishmen and Americans exchanged were two quite different assumptions about the nature of the British Empire and the character of the American people. Whereas Englishmen saw America as a part of an Empire in which all elements were subordinate to Britain, the Americans, drawing upon their actual history, saw only a loose confederation of peoples in which there were Britons and Americans, neither one of whom could presume to dictate to the other. The colonials,

---

[2] American history books have long expressed the view that the American constitutional argument, as described above, was not finally arrived at until after the Townshend Acts. The implication is that the colonists shifted their arguments to meet new demands from the British. However, since the publication of Edmund S. Morgan's "Colonial Ideas of Parliamentary Power, 1764–1766," *William and Mary Quarterly*, 3rd Series, V (July, 1948), such a view is no longer tenable. He has shown quite conclusively that during the Stamp Act crisis the colonial leaders already reached, in one step, their ultimate position—namely, no taxes, except duties for trade regulation, could be levied upon the colonists by the British Parliament.

in effect, now felt themselves Americans, not displaced, subordinate Englishmen. Jefferson suggested this to the King himself when he wrote in his *Summary View of the Rights of British America:* "You are surrounded by British counsellors. . . . You have no minister for American affairs, because you have none taken from us." Furthermore, even after 1776 many a Loyalist exiled in Britain found the English annoying and strange—evidence of the fact that residence in America had worked its influence even upon those loyal to the Crown. "It piques my pride, I must confess," wrote one expatriated Loyalist, "to hear us called 'our colonies, our plantations,' in such terms and with such airs as if our property and persons were absolutely theirs, like the 'villains' in their cottages in the old feudal system."

The imperial view so confidently advanced by Grenville and others of the British administration came too late; the Americans were not interested in making a more efficient Empire to be manipulated from Whitehall. Because of this basic conflict in assumptions, American demands continued to leapfrog ahead of British concessions right up to the Carlisle Peace Mission in the midst of the Revolutionary War. Even ministerial assurances in 1769 that there would be no further imperially imposed taxes[3] failed to divert the colonial drive toward equality with Britain. The child was truly asserting himself, and, as so often happens, the parent was reluctant to strike him down.

Measured against the age of Hitler and Stalin, the British overlords of the eighteenth century appear remarkably benign in their dealings with the colonies in the years after 1763. For it is a fact that the colonies were in revolt against a potential tyrant, not an actual one. Much more fearsome in the eyes of the politically sensitive colonials was the direction in which the British measures tended rather than the explicit content of the acts. As Bernard Bailyn has pointed out after a survey of some 400 tracts of the Revolutionary era, Americans were convinced that a conspiracy was afoot in Britain to deprive them of their liberties, though historians can find little basis for such political paranoia. But that such fear was a source of revolutionary fervor, Bailyn has no doubt. Furthermore, Englishmen

---

[3] In May, Lord Hillsborough officially informed the colonial governments that the Cabinet "entertained no design to propose to Parliament to lay any further taxes on America for the purpose of raising revenue." At about this time, however, the British people were paying per capita taxes of 25*s.*, though Americans paid only 6*d.*, according to the estimate of Lord North.

could never bring themselves to enforce, with all the power at their command, what they believed was the true nature of the Empire, that is, the subordinate position of the colonies. More than once General Thomas Gage, commanding the British troops in America, reported that his forces were too scattered to preserve proper order and government in the colonies. "I am concerned to find in your Lordship's letters," he wrote from New York in 1768, "that irresolution still prevails in our Councils; it is time to come to some determination about the disposition of the troops in this Country."

Part of this irresolution was born of British confusion as to what should be the government's purpose, as the hasty repeals of the stamp and Townshend duties testify on the one hand, and the remarkably inept Tea Act reveals on the other. Part of it stemmed from the fact that within their own house, so to speak, were Americans: at times Lord Chatham himself, at all times Edmund Burke, Colonel Isaac Barré, John Wilkes, and Dr. Price, who insisted that Americans possessed the rights of Englishmen. "The seditious spirit of the colonies," George Grenville wryly complained on the floor of Commons in 1776, "owes its birth to the factions in this House."

Divided as to aims and devoid of strong leadership, the British permitted the much more united colonists, who were blessed with superb and daring leadership, to seize and hold the initiative. Not until the very end—after the destruction of the tea at Boston Harbor in 1773—did the patience of the British ministry run dry. By then, however, the years of acrimony, suspicion, and growing awareness of the differences between the two peoples had done their work, and the harsh coercive measures taken against Massachusetts only provoked counterviolence from all the colonies. Lexington and Concord, Bunker Hill and Independence Hall, were then not far behind.

By implication, the interpretation of the coming of the Revolution given here greatly subordinates the role of economic factors. Since the economic restrictions imposed upon the colonies have traditionally played a large role in most discussions of the causes of the Revolution, they deserve some comment here. Those who advance an economic explanation for the Revolution argue that the series of economic measures enacted by Britain in the century before 1750 actually operated to confine, if not stifle, the colonial economy. Therefore, it is said, the colonies revolted against Britain in an effort to break through these artificial and externally imposed limits. On the

surface and from the assumptions of twentieth-century economic
life, the mercantilistic system appears severe and crippling and worthy of strong colonial opposition. But before such speculative conclusions can be accepted, they deserve to be checked against the
facts.

Several historians have sought to measure quantitatively the restrictive effects of English mercantilism upon the colonial economy.
Their conclusions, it can be said at the outset, are generally in the
negative. For example, take the three major British limitations on
colonial manufactures. On the statute books the Iron Act of 1750
appears to halt the erection of additional slitting mills in the colonies,
but the fact is that many were set up after that date, regardless of
the act's prohibitions, and to such an extent that by 1776 there were
probably more such mills in America than in England. Nor, Lawrence Harper tells us, did the Woolens Act of 1699, designed to
prevent colonial competition with a major English industry, actually
inhibit American endeavors in the field, since few Americans cared
to engage in the industry. True, Harper concluded that the colonial
beaver-hat industry suffered from the restrictions of the Hat Act of
1732, but, as he adds, that branch of economic activity could hardly
be considered an important segment of the economy. And those are
the three major British efforts to "stifle" American manufacturing.

Nor can the restrictions on the settlement of the West be viewed,
as some historians have asserted, as a significant motive for the Revolution. For one thing, movement into the West was never absolutely
halted, and as early as 1764 the Proclamation Line of the previous
year was being moved westward to permit settlement beyond the
mountains. Furthermore, as Thomas Abernathy has shown, the Virginia gentry—often cited as heavily involved in western land speculation and therefore concerned with restrictions on the West—were
not vitally interested in the matter economically, though the religious
and political implications of the later Quebec Act, for example, did
arouse them. All in all, it would appear that the western land question may have been an irritating factor, but, in view of the changing
and indecisive English policy, hardly a revolution-making force.

Perhaps the most that can be said quantitatively about the burden
of the whole navigation or mercantilist system in which England encased the colonies is that the regulations concerning the routing of
trade added between $2.6 million and $7 million to the cost of doing

business in the colonies.[4] Over against this, however, must be placed the fact that the system did not seem a burden to the colonies. Very few objections to the navigation system appear in the voluminous literature of the crisis. In fact, so acceptable did it appear to that jealous American, Benjamin Franklin, that in 1774 he suggested to Lord Chatham that all the basic Navigation Laws be re-enacted by the colonial legislatures as an earnest of colonial loyalty. Furthermore, in October of that year, the first Continental Congress publicly declared the colonies willing to "cheerfully consent to the operation of such acts of the British Parliament, as are bona fide, restrained to the regulation of our external commerce, for the purpose of securing the commercial advantages of the whole empire to the mother country, and the commercial benefits of its respective members. . . ." In short, the navigation system was acceptable. Certainly laws the repressive nature of which no one was disturbed about can hardly be accepted as the grounds for a revolution.

No better economic argument can be made for taxation as a cause for the Revolution. Despite the tradition of oppressive taxation which the myth of the Revolution has spawned, the actual tax burden of the colonies was much heavier in the seventeenth century than in the years immediately before the conflict. On a per capita basis, taxes were five times greater in 1698 than they were in 1773. The lightness of the British taxes in the pre-Revolutionary period is also shown by the fact that the duty on molasses in 1766 was only a penny a gallon, or less than the duty the federal government imposed in 1791. As Lord North pointed out in 1775, taxation of the Americans was neither excessive nor oppressive.

From the unconvincing character of the economic explanations for the coming of the Revolution, it would appear, therefore, that the underlying force impelling the break was the growing national self-consciousness of the Americans. "The Revolution was effected before the war commenced," John Adams remarked years afterward. "The Revolution was in the minds and hearts of the people. . . ." The origins of the "principles and feelings" which made the Revolution, Adams thought, "ought to be traced back . . . and sought in

---

[4] Douglass C. North, *Growth and Welfare in the American Past* (Englewood Cliffs, 1966), pp. 43–49, summarizes research critical of Harper's method. But North's conclusion is that the burden of British mercantilism on the colonies was even less than that calculated by Harper, though North does not put his estimate into figures.

the history of the country from the first plantations in America."
For a century and a half the Americans had been growing up and
now they had finally come of age. Precisely because the Revolution
was the breaking away of a young people from a parent, the substance of the Revolution was political. The argument concerned the
question of parental authority, because that is the precise point at
which tension appears as the child approaches maturity and seeks to
assert his independence. Unfortunately for Britain, but like so many
modern parents, the mother country had long before conveniently
provided the best arguments in favor of freedom. And the colonists
had learned the arguments well. For this reason, the rhetoric of the
Revolutionary argument was in the language of the British political
and constitutional tradition.

As children enjoying a long history of freedom from interference
from their parent, the Americans might well have continued in their
loose relationship, even in maturity, for they were conservative as
well as precocious. History, however, decreed otherwise. Britain's
triumph in the Great War for the Empire put a new strain on the
family relationship, and so intense was the pressure that Americans
could not fail to see, as the argument increased in acrimony, that
they were no longer members of the English family, but rather a new
people, with their own separate destiny. Some Americans saw it earlier than others;[5] a good many saw it by 1776. John Penn, while in
England in 1773, was struck by the English ignorance "with respect
to *our* part of the world (for I consider myself more American than
English). . . ." To South Carolinian Henry Laurens, the Boston
Port Act hit at "the liberty of all Americans," not just at that of the
people of Massachusetts. Once they were convinced of their essential
difference as a people and that British obduracy would not melt,
Americans could not accept the old familiar arrangements. Anything
less than their independence as a people was unacceptable; it would
take Englishmen another generation to realize that the disagreement
was as deep as that.

---

[5] As early as 1768 Benjamin Franklin voiced the opinion that England
would have to treat the colonies as equal with herself or forgo any connection. England, he said, was supreme in everything or in nothing insofar as the
colonies were concerned. He thought it was supreme in nothing. In which
case, he said, "the colonies would then be so many separate states, only subject to the same king, as England and Scotland were before the Union." John
Adams and Lord Camden, the English statesman, also came to this view in the
course of the crisis.

At no time during the ten-year crisis, however, were most Americans spoiling for a rupture with England merely for the sake of a break. Indeed, no one can run through the constitutional arguments of that day without being struck with the reluctance—almost misgivings—with which Americans reached the conclusion of independence. After attending the Continental Congress in 1774, Washington, for example, was "well satisfied that" independence was not "desired by any thinking man in all North America." And, as late as July 6, 1775—over two months after the embattled farmers made their stand at the "rude bridge"—Congress denied any "designs of separation from Great Britain and establishing independent states."

This was no heedless, impetuous overthrow of an oppressor; rather it was a slowly germinating determination on the part of Americans to counter and thwart a change in their hitherto established and accepted ways of governing. Except for the long-deferred assertion of independence, the whole corpus of Revolutionary rhetoric—and nothing lends itself more to radicalism than words—was conservative, expressive of the wish to retain the old ways. The demands made upon Britain were actually pleas for a return to the old relationship: repeal the Stamp Act, the Townshend Acts, the Mutiny Acts; restore trial by jury as abrogated by the expanded admiralty courts; remove the restrictions recently placed upon western migration. One needs only to run through that famous list of grievances in the Declaration of Independence to be forcefully reminded that what these revolutionaries wanted was nothing but the *status quo ante bellum.*

"We have taken up arms," the Continental Congress carefully explained in July, 1775, two months after Lexington, "in defense of the freedom that is our birth-right, and which we ever enjoyed til the late violation of it. . . ." These men had been satisfied with their existence, they were not disgruntled agitators or frustrated politicians; they were a strange new breed—contented revolutionaries.

2. NEW GOVERNMENTS IN OLD CHARTERS

"You and I, my dear friend," exulted John Adams to Richard Lee in 1776, "have been sent into life at a time when the greatest lawgivers of antiquity would have wished to live. How few of the human race have ever enjoyed an opportunity of making an election of government . . . for themselves or their children!" Actually, of course, the new nation was not born, like a Venus fresh from the sea, unencumbered by history. But John Adams was not exaggerating when he referred to the novelty of the opportunity. And insofar as posterity is concerned, the governments which were erected by the Revolutionary states expose, better than any treatise can, the prevailing political and constitutional views of the Revolutionary Fathers. Even more important is the fact that these early conceptions of what constituted just government continued to be accepted, in subsequent years, as the basic assumptions and ideals of American political philosophy, the economic and historical realism of John C. Calhoun to the contrary notwithstanding.

When the allegiance to the British Crown, which heretofore had been the juridical source of governmental authority in America, was dissolved, a new legal basis for government was needed. The search for one, however, was not long or difficult since it lay conveniently at hand in the familiar political philosophy of John Locke, the English theorist of the seventeenth century. In his works, the Americans had earlier found the justification for their Revolution, a version of which Jefferson had elegantly embodied in the Declaration of Independence. The Lockean conception which the Americans now borrowed was that the true origin of government was a compact among the governed. Unlike Europeans, eighteenth-century Americans can be pardoned for their ready acceptance of the Lockean theory as historically valid, since all around them they witnessed governments coming into being by virtue of agreement. The Mayflower Compact, formed at the settlement of Plymouth, was only the most formal variety of innumerable compacts by which Americans agreed to live together in the forbidding wilderness.

During the Revolutionary era, therefore, when Americans were compelled to lay down a new juridical basis for their government, they naturally turned to the compact. The Maryland Convention of 1776 could speak for almost all the states when it asserted "that all government of right originates from the people, is founded in compact only, and instituted solely for the good of the whole." For most modern Americans, the just powers of government still derive from the compact of the people.

The actual making of a compact among the people of a whole state, however, was not feasible in the eighteenth century, so the

Americans introduced a political device which met the requirements of the compact theory and still made it possible to write a constitution: the constitutional convention. Today, Americans, along with most of the western world, accept the convention as a part of the natural political order, but its inception dates only from those early days of the Revolution. In Massachusetts and New Hampshire, the institution actually contained the two essential elements of the modern convention. The body was convened for the sole purpose of constitution-making, and the product of its labors was submitted to popular ratification—the people of New Hampshire requiring three versions before they were satisfied! Most of the other states insisted only on the separation of the legislative and constitution-making functions, but this was the essence of the convention principle. The reason for the insistence on separation of authority was best expressed by the town meeting of Concord, Massachusetts, in 1776: "The same body that forms a Constitution have of consequence a power to alter it, and a Constitution alterable by the legislature is no security at all to the individual."

The content of the constitutions which the new states adopted reveals a remarkable continuity with the colonial experience. That the organic law was a written document was itself a hangover from the colonial charter. Connecticut and Rhode Island did not even feel it necessary to write new constitutions; they merely dropped a few words from their Crown-granted charters and continued to be governed under them. Usually, the new constitutions included bills of rights, or guarantees of the individual against the power of government. These too had their roots in English history and the colonial experience with tyrannical and rapacious agents of the Crown. As a whole the constitutions and the bills of rights were symptomatic of that exaggerated faith of the eighteenth century in the power of documents and words to insure free government. As true children of the Enlightenment in which their country was born, Americans still exhibit enormous faith in written documents as protections of the liberties of the citizen.

During the colonial period, as we have seen, the belief had been growing that only through a separation of the powers of the three branches of government were freedom and good government to be secured. The conservatism of the American political thinkers would not permit the new state constitutions to bestow plenary power upon the legislatures—the creatures of the "people"—but neither would the memory of the recent struggles with the Royal Governors allow the executive to dominate. As Fisher Ames recalled years later in connection with the circumscribed powers of the executive: "we looked for danger on the same side where we had been used to look. . . ." Similarly, the Crown's efforts to dominate the judiciary decreed that, under the new governments, the courts, like the executive and the legislature, would be independent. Though the separation of powers, so carefully built into these first constitutions, and in the Federal Constitution of 1787, has been challenged at times, notably during Reconstruction, as a principle it remains today perhaps the most characteristically American element in our constitutional system.

Probably nothing reveals more accurately the cautious, conservative political habits of these Americans than the franchise qualifications which were included in the new constitutions. Possession of real property had been a universal requirement for voting during the colonial eighteenth century, the assumption being that only propertied citizens had a "stake in society." Though, as we have seen in the last chapter, this principle was not as restrictive in practice as it sounds, it still resulted in the barring of a substantial number of people from the suffrage. Significantly enough, the colonial suffrage pattern was barely disturbed by the Revolution. As late as 1800 only two of the sixteen states of the Union had removed all property and taxpaying qualifications for voting. Furthermore, property qualifications for officeholding, which had been common in the colonial period, were retained in all but one of the thirteen original states after the Revolution. All of the states, for example, required representatives to hold some property, while five of them also demanded that the governor possess some minimum of property, usually land.[6] Not until well into the nineteenth century would the property basis for the suffrage and officeholding give way before the modern, democratic view that manhood was sufficient.

[6] It is true, of course, that some states like Pennsylvania, New York, Georgia, and South Carolina lifted their restrictions on disfranchised religious sects, notably Catholics and Jews, but such an expansion of the suffrage was numerically insignificant, though the liberal principle embodied in the enfranchisement was important. Chilton Williamson, *American Suffrage from Property to Democracy, 1760–1860* (Princeton, 1960), p. 116, argues that the "stake in society" principle was abandoned during the Revolution. It may have been in the writings of political thinkers, but in the actual law of suffrage, it remained until the nineteenth century.

3. REVOLUTIONARIES CAN BE CONSERVATIVE

In the historical literature dealing with the years between 1775 and 1800, two words—"radical" and "conservative"—seem to be indispensable for describing or analyzing the political events and men of the period. Tom Paine, it is said, was a radical; James Wilson and George Washington were conservatives; James Madison was a conservative in 1787, but a Jeffersonian radical in 1794; Alexander Hamilton a conservative all the time, and so on. But it is clear that these words do not always describe the same individual all the time, and especially is this true of those who are called radicals before 1776, but conservatives after the Revolution. Everyone knows, for example, that John Adams of Massachusetts was a "radical" in 1775, as it is also known that he was a "conservative" in 1790. Such a switch suggests that either he was inconstant in his views or that the terms are inadequate to deal with the factual situation. A knowledge of Adams would strongly suggest that the latter is the more likely of the two explanations.

If, however, we try to see what the terms really meant in each of three periods—the early 1770's, the 1780's, and the 1790's—then perhaps the continuity which runs through all three will stand out as it does not if we think of radical and conservative as having constant meanings. Before 1776 the term radical designated anyone who advocated a hard policy toward Britain, even looking toward independence, if necessary. People like Sam Adams, Tom Paine, and John Adams would fall into this category. Conservatives, on the other hand, included those who wished to conciliate Britain as much as possible, to work out some accommodation whereby independence could be avoided, if possible. Robert Morris, John Dickinson, and Joseph Galloway, the last of whom remained to the end a Loyalist, were representatives of this group. Once the colonial connection was broken, however, there was a new alignment; many so-called radicals found themselves facing former comrades across ideological barricades. Tom Paine and John Adams, both at one time in hot pursuit of independence, are classic examples of this, the years after 1776 bringing a progressively frigid atmosphere to their relationship.

Such a shift in ideological allegiances after the Revolution makes it plain that rather than being a united party, as appeared superficially, the so-called radicals before 1776 were actually of two persuasions in regard to their opposition to Britain. Though both factions of the radicals opposed the Crown's efforts at imperial centralization in London, their reasons for doing so were quite different. To one wing, which we might call the radicals, centralization endangered local control and thereby threatened colonial freedom; to the other wing, which we will call the conservatives, centralization was objectionable primarily because British and not American authorities undertook it. Before 1776 this divergence in motivation was largely obscured or ignored under the pressure of events and the obvious need for a united front against Britain. Once independence was declared, however, the conflict split the Revolutionary party into two factions—radicals and conservatives—who now clashed over the large question of the purpose of the Revolution and the direction in which the newly freed nation was to move.[7]

In the final analysis, the central issue between the conservatives and the radicals in the period of the 1780's was still the matter of where supreme authority was to be lodged. Now, however, it took the form of the states versus an American central authority instead of the colonies versus London. Take, for example, the attitudes of the two factions toward the question of a union of the emergent states. The Articles of Confederation, as adopted in 1781, embodied the radical position, as the Constitution of 1787 represented the conservative. The Articles of Confederation, really the first constitution of the United States, baldly exalted local government: "Each state," the second article warned, "retains its sovereignty, freedom and independence." Limiting the states almost not at all, the article established a deliberately weak government, hobbled by a plural executive and emasculated by the denial of any direct power to tax the people or the states over which it presumed to rule. To radicals like Thomas Burke of North Carolina or George Clinton of New York, such a central government was precisely that for which they had fought the Revolution. To them free government inhered in local control and the supremacy of the states.

The triumph of the radicals, however, was short-lived, for the Constitutional Convention of 1787 was dominated by conservatives.

---

[7] Looked at from this viewpoint, the shift from radicalism before independence to conservatism after, as happened in the case of men like John Adams, William Floyd of New York, and Thomas McKean of Delaware, to mention some of the Signers, is easily understood. Basically they were not radical at all; they were merely opponents of British centralization, or conservatives.

The Constitution which was produced there reflected the conservatives' belief in a central government which could support itself, enforce order, and command respect at home and abroad. In the dexterous hands of the conservatives, the weak position of the central government under the Articles of Confederation was dramatically reversed. The new Constitution provided that the "Constitution and Laws of the United States, which shall be made in Pursuance thereof . . . shall be the supreme Law of the Land . . . the Constitution or Laws of any States to the Contrary notwithstanding." Considering the boldness of the reversal, it is not surprising that when old radical Sam Adams read the new Constitution, he said, "As I enter the building I stumble on the threshold. I meet with a National Government instead of a Federal Union of Sovereign States."

And it truly was a national government. The ability of the new central government directly to tax individuals within the states and to bring them to its own system of courts was completely unknown under the old Articles. Simultaneously with the increased powers of the national government, the states were being severely restricted in their authority. No state, for example, could erect tariff barriers, issue money, enact stay laws for the relief of debtors, or deal directly with any foreign power.

The contrast in the energy of the central authorities under the old Confederation and under the new Constitution was painfully apparent in the area of military power. In 1787, Shays' Rebellion in Massachusetts was just too tricky a matter and too threatening for the Congress to aid in its suppression, though it was obviously a danger to the peace of the Union. But when the Whisky Rebellion of 1794 broke out in western Pennsylvania, the central government under the new Constitution quickly snuffed it out with overwhelming military power.[8]

---

[8] The dangers of employing terms like radical and conservative to cover what actually amount to congeries of ideas instead of a single attitude are most apparent in this matter of centralization. Insofar as the so-called conservatives worked for a strong central government, they were, in reality, not conserving anything; central government was unknown in the colonies. Rather it was the so-called radicals, with their accent on local government, who were conserving. Those who pushed for a strong central government were, in actuality, completing the Revolution which George Grenville had begun in 1765, for the stamp tax he offered was but an earlier version of what later would be the federal taxing power contained in the Constitution. The power was acceptable, of course, because it was carried out by Americans and not by Englishmen.

Deep as their fear of strong government ran, the radicals, once the new Constitution was ratified, fell into line behind the new government. Even passionate defenders of the sovereignty of the several states like Patrick Henry and George Clinton bowed to the decisions of the ratifying conventions. By shunning the temptation of continued opposition, the radicals added their voices to the growing veneration of the Constitution and the beginning of a long tradition of political stability. Since those days radicals and conservatives alike have accepted the Constitution as beyond debate; no party or movement of significance has advocated scrapping it. Even on the eve of secession in 1860–61, southern leaders did no more than accuse the North of deliberately misinterpreting a fundamentally sound instrument of government, and they closely followed it in writing the Constitution of the Confederacy.

Though they were certainly defeated in their attempt to maintain the supremacy of the states, the radicals in the 1790's did not change the substance of their disagreement with the conservatives. The argument still concerned the proper locus of power in a free government. And, as in the days before 1776, the question which divided the two groups was still local versus foreign rule, only now "foreign" meant Philadelphia and Washington instead of London. Though unable to secure the kind of weak central government they preferred, the radicals were still free to do their utmost to prevent the new government from being any more powerful than was literally spelled out in the Constitution. For this reason the radical Jeffersonians of the 1790's filled their quiver of arguments with arrows marked "strict construction," or a literal interpretation of the Constitution.

Fisher Ames, an uncompromising Federalist from Massachusetts, was both amused and exasperated by this new stage of the old argument. "We have near twenty *antis* [former opponents of the Constitution], dragons watching the tree of liberty," he complained from Congress in 1792, "and who consider every strong measure and almost every ordinary one, as an attempt to rob the tree of its fair fruit. We hear incessantly, from the old foes of the Constitution,

---

The labels "conservative" and "radical" became twisted and misapplied in this confusing fashion because historians and contemporaries focused their attentions on other aspects of their several beliefs, like the suffrage, paper money, credit, and so forth, overlooking the anomaly of denominating strong Federalists as conservatives, when their view of the central government's proper power was probably the most radical innovation in American political life at that time.

'this is unconstitutional, and that is': and indeed, what is not? I scarce know a point which has not produced this cry, not excepting a motion for adjourning."

Though this was the Jeffersonian position as seen through rather clouded glasses, it was reasonably accurate; for to the Jeffersonians of the 1790's, the federal government should be rarely heard and even more rarely seen. And how reminiscent it was of those "radicals" who had said the same about English rule in the days before '76.

When weighed in the scales of such a constitutional philosophy the economic program of Alexander Hamilton quite naturally became another point of difference between radicals and conservatives. Inasmuch as the Hamiltonian plan envisioned a national bank, the assumption of a great debt to buttress the national credit, and a protective tariff to encourage manufacturing, the Jeffersonians could not fail to oppose this enhancement of the federal authority.

Moreover, the Hamiltonian program touched the sensitive nerve of the radicals' self-interest, revealing the hitherto concealed material divergence of interest which separated the two camps. Since the radicals were largely drawn from the agricultural class, they took a jaundiced view of Hamilton's ambitious efforts to expand credit, create a banking system, and encourage manufacturing through the power of the federal government. To the Jeffersonians such machinations smacked of favors paid for by the taxes of the "honest, hard-working part of the community," as Representative Jackson of Georgia complained, in order to "promote the ease and luxury of men of wealth." After a debate in the Senate over the Bank of the United States, radical Senator Maclay from Pennsylvania wrote that he made no secret, in the course of the debate, that "I was no advocate of the banking system; that I considered them as machines for promoting the profits of unproductive men."

Convinced of the evil intent of the Federalist approach to government and its favoritism to business, the Jeffersonians fought the Hamiltonian program as they would the Devil. Hamilton and his fellow Federalists, however, were no more devils than they were saints. Hamilton himself was inspired by the noble vision of a durable, wealthy, and powerful United States, the actualization of which, he was convinced, depended upon bold and imaginative measures to support the public credit, encourage manufacturing, and secure the allegiance of the wealthy and commercial classes. Almost all of the Hamiltonian program was enacted in the early 1790's and, from the vantage point of retrospect, this was most fortunate; for of the two contending economic programs, the Federalists' was the more far-sighted. The laissez-faire Arcadia of Jefferson would have been nei-ther a strong nor a prosperous nation for long.

If the Hamiltonians won in the sense that their vision of a com-mercial and industrial America was gradually made fact, the Jeffer-sonians did not lose, either. Their ideology of opposition to business has remained as bright as the new nickels which bear the leader's head and home. The Jeffersonian platform of suspicion of business, of antimonopoly, and of opposition to government favors to the spe-cial interests has become a seemingly inexhaustible reservoir of ideals and rhetoric upon which numerous radical and democratic groups have drawn. Jacksonian Democracy, Greenbackism, Populism, the Progressive Movement, the New and Fair Deals, and Kennedy's New Frontier are only the best known of such beneficiaries of the Jeffersonian economic tradition. To a great degree the tension be-tween the Jeffersonian ideology and the Hamiltonian facts of eco-nomic life accounts for the seemingly inconsistent history of the rela-tion between government and the economy in America.

Tradition and the parlance of the times have it that these two parties, symbolized by the rivalry between Jefferson and Hamilton, held views separated by a wide and virtually impassable gulf. In some respects, as we have seen, this is true. Certainly, for example, in sentiment the Jeffersonians placed a larger measure of trust in the "Great Beast" of the people, as Hamilton is supposed to have de-scribed them, than did the wary and pessimistic Federalists. However, it would be well to point out that their areas of agreement were larger and perhaps more important than either side was willing to admit in the heat and joy of political rivalry.

When the Jeffersonians captured the national government in 1800, and the confusing dust of conflict had settled, the new President admitted that the area of agreement was indeed great. For, as he observed, "every difference of opinion is not a difference of principle. We have called by different names brethren of the same principle. We are all Republicans, we are all Federalists." And in office Thomas Jefferson showed that he practiced his dictum. His administration retained the hated Bank, paid off the fearsome debt, embargoed the states in the interest of a national policy, and doubled the territory of the Union in the face of the President's and the party's doubts as to constitutionality.

In 1805, like a delayed echo to Jefferson's assertion of agreement on fundamentals, aristocratic, high-Federalist Fisher Ames of Massachusetts extended what looked suspiciously like the warm hand of conversion: "I have never yet met with an American of any party," he emphasized, "who seemed willing to exclude the people from their temperate and well-regulated share of concern in the government. Indeed," he went on, "it is notorious that there was scarcely an advocate for the Federal Constitution who was not anxious, from the first, to hazard the experiment of an unprecedented and almost unqualified proportion of democracy, both in constructing and administering the government, and who did not rely with confidence, if not blind presumption on its success." In short, the conflict over the rule of the people was less a matter of principle than of method. "This is certain," Ames concluded, "the body of the federalists were always, and yet are, essentially democratic in their political notions."

That these were more than rhetorical flourishes is suggested by the record. Ames was correct when he observed that no Federalist envisioned government in the United States without popular participation; even the imperious Hamilton, it is worth remembering, advocated universal manhood suffrage for the election of the lower house of a federal Congress. Moreover, one can exaggerate the Jeffersonian Republicans' belief in the uncontrolled will of the people; both Republicans and Federalists were in fundamental accord on the necessity of restraints upon the people and the state in the interests of order and liberty.

Economically, the war between them concerned rather peripheral issues like banks and debts and never touched basic assumptions like private property or freedom of enterprise. "The soul [*sic*] end of Government," the ultraradical farmer William Manning wrote, "is the protection of life, Liberty and property." Government, he continued, has only to be evenhanded; "the poor man's shilling ought to be as much the care of government as the rich man's pound."

Seen through the lenses of a century and a half, the divergencies of the Hamiltonians and the Jeffersonians are more a matter of tone or temperament than of hard substance. The Jeffersonians leaned toward the agrarians and the mass of people, but they were no enemies of what the Federalists liked to call sound money, sound credit, and the commercial classes. Similarly, the Federalists were aristo-cratically inclined, but they also stood for popular elections, republican institutions, and a free and open society in America. The best government, Federalist John Adams had written in 1776 in his hand-book for conservative constitutions, *Thoughts on Government,* is "the form of government which communicates . . . happiness to the greatest numbers of persons, and in the greatest degree. . . ." No Jeffersonian Republican, or Benthamite Radical for that matter, wanted to go any further.

One measure of the essential agreement of the two early parties was the harmonious consequences of their furious and often vitu-perative battles. Contrary to the fears of both sides, the Constitu-tion proved to be a government of the people and a bulwark of indi-vidual liberty at the same time that it was a stable and energetic national government capable of sustaining itself and the economy of the country.

The vigorous party battles of those stirring days also forged weap-ons which would henceforth occupy a prominent place in the armory of American politics. The states' rights doctrine of the Jeffersonians is today a respectable doctrine, historically associated with the Dem-ocratic party, but actually employed by all—including Republicans— who distrust, fear, or hate Washington, regardless of their opinions of those embattled agrarians who originally enunciated its virtues. Sim-ilarly, the glory, dignity, and essential supremacy of the national au-thority—the hallmark of Federalists, Whigs, and Republicans—has found acceptance in all camps from Populists to New Dealers to advocates of the Great Society of Lyndon Johnson. Thus, in the proc-ess of determining the significance of their Revolution and the es-sence of free government, that first generation of Americans defined the intellectual framework within which the subsequent politics of the country has been carried on.

4. CONSERVATIVES CAN BE INNOVATORS

Like fabled genii grown too big to be imprisoned in their bottles, wars and revolutions frequently take on a life of their own irrespec-tive of their first purposes. The overarching considerations of sur-vival or victory distort or enlarge the narrow and limited aims for which the conflict was begun. The American War for Independence was such an event. Begun for only limited political and constitutional purposes, the war released social forces which few of the leaders ever anticipated, but which have helped to mold the American tradition.

One such unforeseen result was the rapid and final disestablishment of the Anglican Church, heretofore the state-supported religion in all of the colonies south of Mason and Dixon's Line and in parts of New York and New Jersey as well.[9] In knocking out the props of the State from beneath the Anglican Church, the states provided the occasion for wider and more fundamental innovations. Virginia in 1786, in disestablishing the Anglican Church, put no other church in its place and instead passed a law guaranteeing religious freedom. This law, with which Madison and Jefferson had so much to do, prepared the ground for the ultimate triumph of the American doctrine of separation of Church and State.

The ratification of the federal Constitution in 1788 constituted the first step in the acceptance of the principle that a man's religion was irrelevant to government, for the Constitution forbade all religious tests for officeholding.[10] Then in 1791, when the first ten amendments were added, Congress was enjoined from legislating in any manner "respecting an establishment of religion or prohibiting the free exercise thereof." These legalistic and now commonplace phrases had centuries of man's religious history packed within them; upon their implementation western Christendom reached a milestone in its

[9] This is not to say, however, that disestablishment of all churches was brought about by the Revolution. All of the New England states, with the exception of Rhode Island—still loyal to Roger Williams in this respect—continued to support the Congregational Church.

[10] Just because the so-called conservatives dominated the Constitutional Convention, such religious indifference was possible. Generally the radicals during the Revolutionary era were in favor of state support or recognition of some religion. Thus in the states where the radicals dominated, religious tests were part of the Constitution: Georgia (all members of the legislature had to be Protestants); North Carolina (no one could hold office who denied "God or the truth of the Protestant religion"); and Pennsylvania (the test oath demanded a belief in one God and his rewarding and punishing, and the acknowledgment that the Old and New Testaments were "given by Divine Inspiration"). The contrast with the Constitutional Convention of 1787 is striking. The Continental Congress, which had been dominated by the radicals, always opened its deliberations with chaplain-led prayers; the Convention of 1787, however, failed to have either a chaplain or prayers, though Franklin made an eloquent plea for both. He wrote later that "the Convention except three or four persons thought Prayers unnecessary." Whereas the Declaration of Independence refers to "God" and "Divine Providence," such words are completely absent from the "conservative" Constitution—much to the mystification of modern conservatives.

long quest for a viable accommodation between man's religious conscience and *raison d'état*.

For millennia a man's religion had been either a passport or a barrier to his freedom and the opportunity to serve his State; it had always mattered how a man worshiped God. Since Emperor Theodosius in the fourth century of the Christian era, religious orthodoxy had been considered necessary for good citizenship and for service to the state. All this weighty precedence was boldly overthrown by Americans in 1789–91 when they erected a government wherein "a man's religious tenets will not forfeit the protection of the Laws nor deprive him of the right of attaining and holding the highest offices that are known in the United States," as George Washington said.

In the course of the early nineteenth century, the federal example of a strict divorce of State and Church was emulated by the individual states. At the time of the Revolution many states had demanded Christian and often Protestant affiliations for officeholding, and some had even retained a state-supported Church. Gradually, however, and voluntarily—Massachusetts was last in 1833—all the states abandoned whatever connections they might have had with the churches. The doctrine of separation has been more deeply implanted in our tradition in the twentieth century by the Supreme Court, which has declared that separation is a freedom guaranteed by the Fourteenth Amendment to the Constitution and therefore obligatory upon the states as well as the federal government. Thus the two extremes of the American political spectrum—the popular state governments and the august Supreme Court—have joined in sanctioning this doctrine born out of the Revolution by the liberalism of the Enlightenment.

It was a remarkably novel and even unique approach to the question of the relation between the State and religion. Although the doctrine repudiates any connection between the State and the Church, the American version has little in common with the practice in countries like revolutionary France and Mexico and atheistic Soviet Russia, where separation has been so hostile to religion as to interfere, at times, with freedom of worship. The American conception is not antireligious at all. Our Presidents invoke the Deity and offer Thanksgiving prayers, our armies and legislatures maintain chaplains, and the state and federal governments encourage religion through the remission of taxes. In America the State was declared to be secular, but it continued to reflect the people's concern with religion. The popular interest in religion was still evident in 1962 and 1963 when the Supreme Court invoked the principle of separation of church and state to ban prayers and Bible-reading from the public schools. In both Congress and the public press there was loud protest against such a close and allegedly antireligious interpretation of the principle. But efforts to amend the Constitution in order to circumvent the Supreme Court's interpretation failed.

In the eighteenth century the American principle of separation of Church and State was indeed an audacious experiment. Never before had a national state been prepared to dispense with an official religion as a prop to its authority and never before had a church been set adrift without the support of the state. Throughout most of American history the doctrine has provided freedom for religious development while keeping politics free of religion. And that, apparently, had been the intention of the Founding Fathers.

As the principle of the separation of Church and State was a kind of social side effect of the Revolution, so also was the assertion in the Declaration of Independence that "all men are created equal." These five words have been sneered at as idealistic, refuted as manifestly inaccurate, and denied as preposterous, but they have, nonetheless, always been capable of calling forth deep emotional response from Americans. Even in the Revolutionary era, their power was evident. In 1781 the Supreme Judicial Court of Massachusetts declared slavery at an end in that state because it "is inconsistent with our own conduct and Constitution" which "set out with declaring that all men are born free and equal. . . ." The Reverend Samuel Hopkins told the Continental Congress that it was illogical to "be holding so many hundreds of blacks in slavery . . . while we are maintaining this struggle for our own and our Children's liberty." In 1782 William Binford of Henrico County, Virginia, set free twelve slaves because he was "fully persuaded that freedom is the natural right of all mankind." Another Virginian, a few years later, freed all his slaves which had been "born after the Declaration of Independence." Such efforts to reconcile the theory of the Declaration with the practices of life represent only the beginnings of the disquieting echoes of the celebrated phrase.

It is wrong to assume, however, that the mere inclusion of that phrase in the Declaration worked the mighty influence implied in the foregoing examples; social values are not created so deliberately or so easily. Like so much else in the Declaration, this sentence was actually the distillation of a cherished popular sentiment into a ringing phrase, allegiance to which stemmed from its prior acceptance rather than from its eloquence. The passionate belief in social equality which commentators and travelers in Jacksonian America would later find so powerful was already emergent in this earlier period. Indeed, we have already seen its lineaments during the colonial period. After 1776 the conviction was reinforced by the success of the Revolution and by the words of the great Declaration itself.

It was also supported by the facts of American social life. Despite the lowly position accorded the Negro, wrote the French traveler Brissot in 1788, it still must be admitted "that the Americans more than any other people are convinced that all men are born free and equal." Moreover, he added, "we must acknowledge, that they direct themselves generally by this principle of equality." German traveler Johann Schoepf noticed that in Philadelphia "rank of birth is not recognized, is resisted with a total force. . . . People think, act, and speak here precisely as it prompts them. . . ."[11] And in the privacy of the Federal Convention of 1787, Charles Pinckney of South Carolina urged his fellow delegates to recognize the uniqueness of their country. "There is more equality of rank and fortune in America than in any other country under the sun," he told them.

There were other signs of what an earlier generation would have stigmatized as "leveling tendencies" in the new post-Revolutionary society. The attacks made by the Democratic-Republican societies upon the privileged Order of the Cincinnati, because it was secret and confined to Revolutionary officers and their descendants, were obviously inspired by a growing egalitarian sentiment. French traveler Moreau de Saint-Méry recalled with disgust how Americans proudly told him that the hotel custom of putting strange travelers together in the same bed was "a proof of liberty." By the end of the century old social distinctions like rank-seating in churches and the differentiating title of esquire were fast passing out of vogue. On an economic level, this abiding American faith was translated as equality of opportunity, and here dour Federalist Fisher Ames could lock arms

---

[11] Schoepf, interestingly enough, discovered in the economic opportunities available in America the source of the social equality. "Riches make no positive material difference," he wrote concerning Philadelphia society, "because in this regard every man expects at one time or another to be on a footing with his rich neighbor, and in this expectation shows him no knavish reverence, but treats him with an open, but seemly familiarity."

with his Republican opponents when he averred that "all cannot be rich, but all have a right to make the attempt."

Though economic grievances seem to have played a negligible role in bringing on the Revolution, this is not to say that there were no economic consequences. The economic stimulus afforded by the war demands and the freedom from English mercantilistic restrictions which victory made permanent provided adventuresome American merchants and entrepreneurs with wide opportunities for gaining new markets and new sources of profit. The expansion of the American economy, which was to be characteristic all through the nineteenth century, was thus begun.

But even when one has added together the new constitutions, the enlightened religious innovations, and the stimulus to equality, it is quickly apparent that the social consequences of the Revolution were meager indeed. In both purpose and implementation they were not to be equated with the massive social changes which shook France and Russia in later years. For the most part, the society of post-Revolutionary America was but the working out of social forces which were already evident in the colonial period.

It is significant, for example, that no new social class came to power through the door of the American Revolution. The men who engineered the revolt were largely members of the colonial ruling class. Peyton Randolph and Patrick Henry were well-to-do members of the Virginia Assembly; Washington, reputed to be the richest man in America, was an officer in the Virginia militia. The New York leaders John Morin Scott and Robert Livingston were judges on the Supreme Court of the colony, while William Drayton, a fire-eating radical of South Carolina, was a nephew of the lieutenant governor of the province, and himself a member of the Governor's Council until his anti-British activities forced his removal. Certainly Benjamin Franklin, citizen of the Empire, celebrated scientist, and long retired, well-to-do printer, was no submerged member of Philadelphia's society—or London's for that matter. Moreover, Franklin's natural son, William, was a Royal Governor at the outbreak of the Revolution. Hancock of Boston and Christopher Gadsden of Charleston were only two of the many respected and wealthy merchants who lent their support to the patriot cause. In fact, speaking of wealth, the Revolution in Virginia was made and led by the great landed class, and its members remained to reap the benefits. Farther down the social scale, in the backwoods of Massachusetts, it has been shown that the chief revolutionists in the western counties were the old leaders, so that no major shift in leadership took place there either, as a result of the Revolution.

This emphasis on position and wealth among the Revolutionary leaders should not be taken as a denial that many men of wealth and brains left the colonies in the exodus of the Loyalists. Certainly few patriots were the peers of Jared Ingersoll in the law, Jonathan Boucher in the Church, and Thomas Hutchinson and James Galloway in government. But the Loyalist departure did not decapitate the colonial social structure, as some have suggested—it only removed those most attached to the mother country.[12] A large part of the governing class remained to guide the Revolution and reap its favors. It is true that in the states of Georgia and Pennsylvania, where the radical democrats held sway in the early years of the Revolution, new men seemed to occupy positions of power. But these men were still unknowns on the periphery of government and business, and generally remained there; they cannot be compared with the Robespierres and the Dantons, the Lenins and the Trotskys, of the great continental eruptions.

A convenient gauge of the essential continuity of the governing class in America before and after the Revolution is to be found in an examination of the careers of the signers of the Declaration of Independence. Surely these fifty-five men are important patriot leaders and presumably among the chief beneficiaries of the Revolution they advocated. Yet they were by no means a disadvantaged lot. Fully 40 per cent of them attended college or one of the Inns of Court in England at a time when such a privilege was a rarity. An additional 21 per cent of them came from important families of their respective colonies, or, like Robert Morris and Joseph Hewes, were men of acquired wealth. Over 69 per cent of them held office under the colonial regimes, 29 per cent alone holding some office within the executive branch; truly these were not men held at arm's length from the plums of office.

Most striking about the careers of these men is the fact that so many of them held office before and after the dividing line of the Revolution. Of those who held an office under the state governments

---

[12] William Nelson, *American Tory* (Oxford, 1961), suggests in his last chapter that America lost an organic or conservative view of society with the departure of the Loyalists. Insofar as that is true, it would reinforce the liberal bias that has been so characteristic of American political and social thought.

after the Revolution, 75 per cent had occupied offices before 1774, proving, if need be, that service in the colonial governments before the Revolution was no obstacle to political preferment for a patriot afterward. If those who held no office before 1774 are not counted—and several might be considered too young to be expected to have held office—then the continuity shows up even more clearly. Eighty-nine per cent of those who filled an office before the Revolution also occupied an office under one of the new state governments. And if federal office after 1789 is included, then the proportion rises to 95 per cent. Add to this the fact that other leaders, not included in the group of signers, had similarly good social backgrounds—men like Washington, Robert Livingston, Gouverneur Morris, Philip Schuyler, and a dozen more—and the conclusion that the Revolution was a thoroughly upper-middle-class affair in leadership and aim is inescapable.

A further and perhaps more important conclusion should be drawn from this analysis of the political careers of the signers after the Revolution. These conservative, upper-class leaders who proclaimed the Revolution suffered no repudiation in the course of the struggle; no mass from the bottom rose and seized control of the Revolutionary situation to direct the struggle into new channels. Rather these men merely shifted, as it were, from their favored status under the colonial regimes to comparable, if not improved, positions after the Revolution.

As a colonial revolt against an alien power, such a development is not surprising. But certainly—for better or for worse—the continuity brought a degree of social and political stability to the new nation rarely associated with the word "revolution" and serves, once again, to illustrate the truly conservative nature of the American revolt.

Similarly, in the redistribution of land, which played such a crucial role in France and Russia, the American Revolution set no example of social motivation or consequence. The Crown's lands, it is true, were confiscated, and—of greater import—so were the lands of the proprietors and those of the literally thousands of Tories. But the disposition of these lands hardly constitutes a social revolution of major proportions. One can collect, of course, examples of the breakup of great estates, like the De Lancey manor in New York, which was sold to 275 individuals, or the 40,000-acre estate in North Carolina which was carved into scores of plots averaging 200 acres apiece, or the vast 21,000,000-acre proprietary lands of the Penns. But the more significant question to be answered is who got the land. And, from the studies which have been made, it would appear that most often the land went to speculators or men already possessing substantial acreage, not to the landless or even to the small holder. To be sure, much Tory land which first fell under the auctioneer's hammer to a speculator ultimately found its way into the hands of a yeoman, but such a procedure is a rather slow and orderly process of social revolution.

Furthermore, it is obvious from the Confiscation Acts in the several states and the commissioners who operated pursuant to them that the motive behind the acquisition of Tory lands was enhancement of the state revenues—as, indeed, the original resolution from Congress had suggested. Under such circumstances, pecuniary motives, not democratic theories of society, determined the configuration distribution would take. And it is here that we begin to touch upon the fundamental reason why the confiscation of the royal, proprietary, and Loyalist lands never assumed crucial social importance. Land was just too plentiful in America for these acres to matter. Speculators were loaded down with it; most men who wanted it already possessed it, or were on the way toward possession. One recent investigator of the confiscations in New York, for example, has pointed out that land there could be bought cheaper from speculators than from a former Tory estate.

Even the abolition of primogeniture in all the southern states by 1791 cannot be taken as a significant example of the Revolution's economic influence. The fact of the matter is that primogeniture had never appreciably affected land distribution, since it came into play only when the owner died intestate. Considering the notorious litigiousness of eighteenth-century Americans, it is hardly to be doubted that partible inheritance was the practice, if not the theory, long before primogeniture was wiped from the statute books. Furthermore, in almost half of the country—New Jersey, Pennsylvania, and all of the New England states—primogeniture never prevailed anyway.

As for the abolition of entail, it was frequently welcomed by owners of entailed estates, as was the case in Jefferson's Virginia, since it would permit the sale of otherwise frozen assets. These laws had not created a landed aristocracy in America and their repeal made no significant alteration in the social landscape.

Instead of being an abrupt break, the Revolution was a natural

and even expected event in the history of a colonial people who had
come of age. It is true that social and political changes accompanied
the Revolution, some of which were destined to work great influence
upon American institutions in the future, but these had been implicit in the pre-Revolutionary society. Moreover, important social
institutions were left untouched by the Revolution: the class structure, the distribution of property, the capitalistic economy, the ideas
of the people concerning government.

This lack of profound and widespread social and economic change
is not surprising. These Americans, for all their talk, had been a contented and prosperous people under the British Crown and they were,
therefore, contented revolutionaries who wanted nothing more than
to be undisturbed in their accustomed ways. They are in no wise to
be compared with the disgruntled lawyers, the frustrated bourgeois,
the tyrannized workers, and the land-hungry peasants of the *anciens
régimes* of France and Russia.

Yet, in conclusion, it is perhaps fitting to recall that America was
born in revolution, for this fact has become embedded in our folk
and sophisticated traditions alike. It was apparent in the self-conscious, often naïve enthusiasm displayed by American statesmen and
people in support of the colonial rebellions in South America and
Greece in the early years of the nineteenth century. Revolutionaries
of the middle of the century, like Louis Kossuth and Garibaldi, garnered moral and material benefits from this continuing American
friendship for rebellion. European exiles and revolutionaries of 1848
were entertained at the London residence of United States Minister
James Buchanan. And it is still apparent today. The declarations of
independence of Ho Chi Minh's Democratic Republic of (North)
Vietnam in 1945 and Ian Smith's Rhodesia in 1965 both begin with
quotations from the United States Declaration of Independence! And
Nasser of Egypt, at the time of the United States intervention in
Lebanon in July, 1958, taunted Americans with their revolutionary
tradition. "How can the United States, which pushed off British colonialism many years ago, forget its history?" he shouted to a crowd
in Damascus.

An anticolonial tradition of such weight could not fail to leave
its stamp upon American attitudes. As we shall see in a later chapter, it was invoked again and again in debates over American foreign policy, and its continuing influence is evident in the movement

of former colonies like Hawaii and Alaska into statehood and the Philippines into independence.

Long before, in the era of the Revolution, American leaders, profiting from the lessons of Britain's imperial problems, agreed in the Ordinance of 1787 and the Constitution that newly acquired territories could attain, in the natural course of events, equal constitutional status with the original thirteen states. Thus, in a single stroke, Americans sidestepped the tensions and divisions attendant upon a colonial empire and laid the enduring foundations for an expanding and united country.

Constitutional devices, however, no matter how clever or farsighted, cannot of themselves create a new people. The forces of economics and geography can wreak havoc with the best laid plans of Founding Fathers. Whether Americans would retain their independence and become a truly united people was to be determined only by time and the people themselves.

CHAPTER IV

To Make a More Perfect Union

BETWEEN the War of 1812 and the Spanish-American War in 1898, the great events which agitated American life were almost exclusively internal and domestic. One of the objects of this inward concentration was the taming and settling of the vast geographical reaches of the new country. This task, which was not completed until the end of the century, was not thrust upon Americans; rather it was one which they eagerly undertook. The conquest of a continent with ax, plow, and factory was at once an expression and a determinant of the American character.

Land, however, does not make a people. Indeed, when the land is of great extent, as it was in the United States, it poses serious problems for a young Republic seeking to become a united nation. In the course of the years between 1812 and the Civil War, the economic bonds and sinews of the Union were created. So well did the Americans of those years build that the Union was able to withstand the disruptive force of a rebellion of unprecedented proportions.

1. AGRARIAN IMPERIALISM

In 1800 the United States stretched no farther inland than the Mississippi River and, though its northern border was very much as it is today, on the south the American flag did not anywhere touch the Gulf of Mexico: Florida, which then extended along the coast to the Mississippi, was still in the hands of Spain—and so was New Orleans at the mouth of the river. Within the lifetime of a middle-aged man—that is, within less than fifty-five years—the United States exploded to its present size, an increase in area of some 300 per cent.

In no case was the acquisition of new land dictated by the elemental need for *Lebensraum;* Americans always had access to more land within the United States than they could utilize. In 1820, for instance, when Americans were already moving into Louisiana, Mississippi, and Illinois—states which at that date were "western"—the density of population in Georgia was still less than two persons per square mile. County after county in north-central Pennsylvania, which later would support thousands of people, was largely unsettled. There were still great areas of South and North Carolina which averaged no more than eighteen persons per square mile. And in 1840, when the nation was eyeing the territories of Mexico stretching beyond the Louisiana Purchase, large parts of central Illinois, southern Georgia, and western Virginia were still only at the frontier stage.

It was the West which drew them on, the West which was free for the taking, the West which was a challenge and a terror all in one. Free land, unencumbered by speculator's high prices or landlord's rents, was an irresistible magnet to native American and displaced European alike. As the world was to find out, there was nothing that could stem this drive short of the sea itself.[1]

Early in the history of the Republic, abundant land was placed at the disposal of the people long before they felt any need for it. The Louisiana Purchase, as is well known, was an accident—another of those instances where Europe's distress was America's gain. President Jefferson would have been content to buy the port of New Orleans from Napoleon, but the needs of the French ruler made it possible for the American ministers to purchase half the land between the Mississippi River and the Rocky Mountains. Though the Purchase doubled the size of the Republic with a few strokes of the pen—and for a mere $15 million—it was only the beginning of that lust for real estate which would bring the American people face to face with salt

---

[1] Illustrative of the process whereby Americans before 1860 filled up the West was the migration of Thomas Lincoln, small farmer and father of the President. Born in western Virginia, Thomas Lincoln moved as a small boy, with his father, to central Kentucky. When he married, he settled on a farm in Hardin County in the western part of the same state, where Abraham was born in 1809. When the son was only seven the family moved to Spencer County in southwestern Indiana. By the time the future President reached his majority, Thomas was on the move again—this time to Macon County in central Illinois. Though the frequency of Thomas' moves is somewhat unusual, the shortness of the jumps is quite in keeping with frontier practice. Aside from the European immigrants, very few westering people made a dramatic leap from the East to the farthermost fringes of civilization.

water within a generation after Jefferson's death. As the English traveler Harriet Martineau observed in the 1830's, "The possession of
land is the aim of all action, generally speaking, and the cure for all
social ills, among men in the United States. If a man is disappointed
in politics or love, he goes and buys land. If he disgraces himself, he
betakes himself to a lot in the West."

Sometimes this hunger for land, for settlement, for speculation,
for temporary squatting, for isolation—all these motives were operative—was so strong as to run ahead of the boundaries of the nation.
Even though the United States had only recently acquired the enormous and empty expanse of the Louisiana Purchase, a number of
Americans in the early years of the century pushed into the scantily
populated lands of Spain along the Gulf of Mexico. By 1810 these
hardy souls had effected a revolution against Spain in the territory
then called West Florida and now included in southern Louisiana
and Mississippi. With almost studied casualness, these settlers offered this generous slice of Spanish territory to the United States; and,
with less reason for naïveté, President Madison accepted—but not
before the administration deliberately misdated documents to cover
up American governmental complicity in the *coup d'état*. Apparently
swayed by the success of such intrigues against the "effete Spaniard,"
the President looked forward to a similar coup in the rest of West
Florida—that is, as far east as Mobile. His hopes, however, garnered
no fruit. Not until the War of 1812, in which Spain was conveniently
the ally of Great Britain, was the United States able to wrest Mobile
from Spanish Florida. The process of rounding out the southeastern
border of the nation was completed in 1819, when John Quincy
Adams succeeded in negotiating the purchase of the rest of what is
now the State of Florida.[2]

This was only the springtime of American territorial ambitions;
summer was still to come. But it was about this time that Adams, as
Secretary of State, told a private Cabinet meeting that "the world
shall be familiarized with the idea of considering our proper domain
to be the continent of North America." Ever since we gained our

---

[2] The confident air which surrounded American thoughts on the matter of
the proper borders for the country is strikingly illustrated in a quotation from
a newspaper in 1819, when the purchase of Florida was being discussed. "Any
man . . . must have seen that the Floridas would certainly pass into the possession of the United States. They as naturally belong to us as the county of
Cornwall does to England."

independence, he said, "it was as much a law of nature that this should become our pretension as that the Mississippi should flow to the sea." Before long, Americans would be saying such things in public.

During the 1820's and 1830's large numbers of Americans moved into the northern portion of Mexico, and by 1835 these new settlers were strong enough to carry out a successful revolt against Mexican authority. Once again the restless, vigorous, and expansive spirit of Americans on the move and on the make proved overwhelming for a people whose ancestors had been the suzerains of Europe and the conquistadors of the New World.

The American infiltration of Texas was more than simply a revolt against Mexico; it provided the occasion for the war between the United States and Mexico in 1846.[3] The Texan Revolution, which Harriet Martineau called "the most high-handed theft of modern times," had not ended in a clear-cut victory for the Texans because Mexico refused to acknowledge the independence of the newly declared Republic even though the Mexican government was powerless to exercise control over its erstwhile subjects. This, however, did not prevent the Texans from negotiating for annexation to the United States. In 1845, as inclusion of Texas in the United States came closer to reality, Mexico agreed to full recognition of the Republic of Texas on the condition that annexation to the United States would not take place. In the light of history, Mexico had good reason to fear that annexation was merely a prelude to further encroachments upon Mexican territory. Neither the United States nor the Texans, however, permitted the Mexican concern to impede annexation. When Texas was incorporated into the American Union, the stage was set for war between the United States and Mexico.

[3] This was not the first time that "agrarian cupidity" had helped to push the United States into war with its neighbors. Before 1812 it was the Westerners who clamored for war against Canada and Spanish Florida in order to gain access to the lands of those colonies. The famous War Hawks of the period were almost entirely congressmen from the western states. It was in the course of the fateful Twelfth Congress (1811–12) that John Randolph of Roanoke made his celebrated attack upon the war party. "Sir, if you go to war it will not be for the protection of, or defence of your maritime rights," he said. "Gentlemen from the north have been taken up into some high mountain and shown all the kingdoms of the earth; and Canada seems tempting in their sight. That rich vein of Genesee land, which is said to be even better on the right side of the lake than on this. Agrarian cupidity, not maritime right, urges the war."

One thorn which had long irritated Texan-Mexican relations had been the determination of the southern border of Texas. Mexico argued that the boundary was the Nueces River; Texas, and now the United States, claimed it was the Rio Grande, the mouth of which was over a hundred miles south of that of the Nueces—the distance between Corpus Christi and Brownsville. As was to be anticipated, soon after the annexation of Texas, the armed forces of the United States and Mexico clashed in the disputed area. For this and other reasons, President Polk called upon an expansion-minded Congress to declare war against Mexico.

Though once held to be a gigantic slaveholders' conspiracy to extend the area open to slavery, the Mexican War is today likely to be viewed by historians as part of that feeling of Manifest Destiny[4] which eventually planted the American flag on the shores of the Pacific. The irresistible territorial ambitions and sense of mission which gripped Americans in this era are only credible in the language of the time. Listen to this speaker at a Democratic state convention in 1844. "Make way, I say, for the young American Buffalo—he has not yet got land enough; he wants more land as his cool shelter in summer—he wants more land for his beautiful pasture grounds. I tell you, we will give him Oregon for his summer shade, and the region of Texas as his winter pasture. Like all of his race, he wants salt, too. Well, he shall have the use of two oceans—the mighty Pacific and turbulent Atlantic shall be his. . . . He shall not stop his career until he slakes his thirst in the frozen ocean." Except for the implied interest in the acquisition of Canada, which was real enough, the future was to fulfill the orator's prophecy.

Convinced as they were of their virtues and hungry for the unused lands of the Mexican-held Southwest, Americans could not resist, when the cost seemed so slight, taking what they craved. One journal in 1845 spoke of the American people as "the most independent, intelligent, moral and happy people on the face of the earth." And Caleb Cushing asked, in affirming the annexation of territory after

[4] Historians usually credit John L. O'Sullivan, spread-eagle nationalist editor of the Jacksonian-Democratic organ *United States Magazine and Democratic Review*, for originating the phrase. In an article in 1845, justifying American claims to the Oregon territory, O'Sullivan asserted that the American claim "is by right of our manifest destiny to overspread and to possess the whole of the Continent which Providence has given us for the development of the great experiment of liberty and federated self-government entrusted to us."

the Mexican War, "Is not the occupation of any portion of the earth by those competent to hold and till it, a providential law of national life?" The victory over Mexico added territory to the Union from which were created the states of California, Nevada, New Mexico, Arizona, Utah, and Texas.

While the troubles with Mexico were deteriorating into war, President Polk successfully carried through negotiations with Great Britain concerning our northwestern boundary with Canada. Unable to sustain against powerful Britain the highly inflated claims blown up by the winds of Manifest Destiny, the American government resorted to compromise. The 49th parallel, which was already the northern boundary of the Louisiana Purchase, was simply extended from the Great Lakes to the Pacific. (The original American demand of 54 degrees and 40 minutes north latitude would have set the border just below the present southern tip of Alaska!) As a consequence of the agreement with Britain and the concluding of peace with Mexico, when James K. Polk left office in March, 1849, the map of the United States looked as it does today, with the exception of a little slice of southern Arizona and New Mexico—the so-called Gadsden Purchase, which was acquired in 1854.

The incorporation within the United States of the immense trans-Mississippi region by the peaceful Louisiana Purchase and the violent war with Mexico opened up a treasure chest of natural resources. In that territory were to be found some of the richest wheat- and breadstuff-producing lands of the New World; pasture lands of fabulous extent which would one day support a great cattle industry; almost endless forests of superb timber; deposits of copper, zinc, lead, silver, and gold sufficient to quench the greed of a Spanish conquistador. The future triumph of American industrial power was largely foreshadowed in those gifts of nature and the westward movement.

A gargantuan territory, however, also presented problems. From a political standpoint alone, the new lands, long before they were even settled, were responsible for the sharpening of the conflict between North and South. It was over the question of the extension of slavery into the trans-Mississippi region that the long-bubbling issue of slavery finally boiled up into secession and civil war. As the West had lain at the center of the constellation of forces which brought on the Mexican War, so it lay like a smoldering fuse among the powder kegs of North-South suspicions and animosities.

2. MORE THAN SENTIMENT

But this is getting ahead of our story. Long before it presented itself as an issue in politics, the West was an economic problem. Moreover, before there was a trans-Mississippi West there was an earlier West—the land between the Appalachians and the Mississippi —and its challenge to the new nation was both early and real.

Even before the Louisiana Purchase in 1803, the United States far exceeded in extent every country in Europe with the exception of the multinational empires of Russia and Austria-Hungary. As a result and in view of the scattered character of the settlements west of the Appalachians, the problems of communication alone were at once enormous and vital if the new nation was to stay together. At the time of the Revolution, Europeans had freely predicted that no country of such dimensions could long remain united. And when one contemplates the travel facilities of the time, the predictions have the ominous ring of truth: one and a half weeks at best to make the trip from New York to Pittsburgh in 1800; four days from New York to Washington; four weeks for the trip from New Orleans to New York. Moreover, it should be remembered that news could travel no faster in those days than a man.

Such great distances carried economic as well as political implications. It meant that surplus goods would have only local, and therefore limited, markets unless the interior was provided with improved communications. And so long as the market was restricted, there would be restraints on the expansion of production and the accumulation of wealth. In short, in the absence of adequate transportation facilities, the new nation would be held down—or at least large segments of its population would be held down to a subsistence level of production and consumption. Politically, the geography of the country was a source of disunity. After the Revolution, thousands of Americans climbed the Appalachians to seek out the untouched territories of the West. With only primitive and tedious communications to connect them with the East, the allegiance of these Westerners was both tested and eroded by the elemental facts of topography.

As early as the 1780's and 1790's disaffection among the transmontane settlements in Kentucky and Tennessee was acute; the people of these areas found their most expeditious routes for exporting surpluses to be the great rivers of the region: the Cumberland, the Tennessee, the Ohio, the Green, and the Kentucky, all of which ultimately drained into the Mississippi and thence to the Spanish-held port of New Orleans. The leaders of the young nation, however, well aware of such dangers to national unity, took several steps to forestall the separation of the West. The climactic stroke was the purchase, in 1803, of New Orleans and its hinterland for a thousand miles to the north.

Nor were such precautions premature. Several conspiracies to detach from the Union the men and lands of the West punctuated the history of the early years of the Republic. General James Wilkinson had been active all during the 1780's and 1790's in behalf of the Spanish power; and in 1804–6 Vice-President Aaron Burr was engaging in shadowy schemes with Wilkinson and former English and Spanish agents, all of which boded ill for the territorial integrity of the country.

Though the assorted separatist conspiracies failed, there was nothing inherent in the vastness of the new country to weld it into a nation. Only improved means of communication and transport could do that, for only when a people know one another and their common land do they begin to experience that quickening of emotion and consciousness of kind called national feeling. The material foundation for the growth of a national consciousness, laid down in the first half of the nineteenth century, has come to be called the Transportation Revolution.

Historians are wary, and rightly so, of the word "revolution" when applied to social and economic change, for rarely do such alterations come rapidly and dramatically enough to justify the term. But sometimes, when the word is applied to changes measured against a long previous history, it is appropriate. Despite the fact that fifty years were required for the completion of this Transportation Revolution, those years are telescoped to but an instant of time when compared with the preceding two or three millennia during which no comparable improvements in communication were made.

The Transportation Revolution began in the last years of the eighteenth and first decades of the nineteenth centuries with the construction of improved roads and turnpikes.[5] State and local govern-

[5] The word "turnpike," which in the automobile age signifies a superhighway, did not, of course, have any such meaning in the early years of the Republic. It merely stood for a road upon which tolls were paid at stated intervals. When the toll was paid, the pike, which had been placed across the road, was turned—hence the name—and the traveler permitted to proceed. It is,

ments and private companies were responsible for the building of roads westward into the interior and north and south. The national government made its contribution in the form of a major east-west artery which ultimately connected Cumberland, Maryland, with central Illinois.

Prior to the coming of the railroad, land transport, regardless of the quality and quantity of roads, was held down to the low efficiency of animal power. Because of this, beginning in the 1820's with New York's spectacularly successful Erie Canal, the construction of canals was undertaken to link the rivers and lakes of the interior and to connect them with seaboard ports. Down to 1816 there were no more than one hundred miles of canals in the United States, but by 1840, when the canal-building era was at its zenith, there were over 3,300 miles in being. By water the bulky farm products of the interior could be cheaply shipped to distant markets, with consequent stimulus to the economic growth of the newly opened lands.

The Erie Canal, running almost 400 miles into the West and connecting the Hudson River with Lake Erie, providing an incredibly cheap means of transportation between the Great Lakes states and New York City, was an outstanding example of the potentialities of the inland waterway. (Francis Lieber said that it was also "a clamp by which the west of this Union is tightly fastened to the east and north.") Between 1817 and the 1850's the Erie Canal cut the cost of transportation between Buffalo and New York City 95 per cent. Feeder canals north and south extended the benefit of the waterway to the widely scattered farmers of western and northern New York.

Canals in Indiana, Ohio, and Illinois linked the settlers of the interior with oceanic ports, either to the north, through the Lakes and the Erie Canal, or to the south, through the Ohio-Mississippi rivers. The Wabash and Erie Canal, which ran between Toledo on the Lakes to Evansville, Indiana, on the Ohio River, when completed in 1856 exceeded even the Erie Canal in length; it was over 450 miles.

States other than those along the Lakes found that canals provided a desperately needed answer to the problems of settlement and economic expansion. Pennsylvania, for instance, attempting to duplicate New York's success, built a combined canal, railroad, and sys-

---

of course, the payment for travel which has caused the word to be revived in the middle of the twentieth century.

tem of inclined planes to stretch from Philadelphia to Pittsburgh. The geographical obstacles in Pennsylvania were too great for that effort to be as successful as the Erie—there was no low pass through the Alleghenies such as the Mohawk River provided in New York— but parts of it were links between ports, markets, and the back country. Other canals were built north and south, following the Susquehanna River, thus providing the northern and southern parts of Pennsylvania with outlets for goods. Maryland constructed the Chesapeake and Ohio Canal, which ran beside the Potomac River into the interior of the state. The cities of Richmond and Lynchburg, on the James River in Virginia, were joined by a canal. New Jersey mixed the waters of the Delaware River and the Atlantic Ocean by digging the Delaware and Raritan Canal in 1838. With the opening of the "Soo" Canal, between Huron and Superior, in 1855, the Great Lakes themselves were turned into a gigantic inland waterway usable by large ships. Though England had built canals with success in the eighteenth century and even the Romans had constructed shipping canals almost two millennia earlier, the extensive canal building in the United States, compressed as it was into a mere generation, is accurately called a minor revolution in transportation.[6]

Cheap as canal transportation was, its speed was still tied to the plodding gait of the mule, just as the movement of goods overland was held down to the speed and power of the horse. The adaptation of steam power to inland water transportation was, therefore, one of the liberating innovations of the early nineteenth century. Considering the immense distances within the United States and the large number of navigable rivers in the interior, it is not surprising that the river boat was an American invention. Though originating in the East, the steamboat figured most prominently on the rivers and in the economy of the West.

The western steamboat was quite a different craft from the eastern. As a study in technological adaptation to environment, the steamboat of the West is eminently instructive. Compelled to sail upon rivers which were notorious for their shallow depth (the Mississippi above St. Louis averages less than five feet), the river boats

---

[6] Nor has the canal lost its usefulness in the age of the railroad and the truck. Some of the canals built in the early nineteenth century still function, notably the Erie and several in Ohio and Illinois. The Erie, now the New York State Barge Canal, regularly carries about 4.5 million tons of goods each year.

were designed to carry everything, including the engines, above the waterline—hence their characteristic pile of superstructure. Charles Dickens likened them to "a child's Noah's Ark in form, with the machinery on the top of the roof." In order to deal with the treacherous currents and innumerable snags and bars, the boats had to have great power—hence the constant danger of explosion.

It was not until the years 1815–17 that the full potential of the steamboat on western waters was recognized. Within these years a number of long trips up the Mississippi demonstrated the enormous economic value of the western rivers. Henry Shreve, who helped to break Robert Fulton's monopoly on steamboat construction, sailed the *Enterprise* (1815) and the *Washington* (1817)—the latter being the biggest boat on the river at the time—from New Orleans to Louisville in the unheard-of time of twenty-five days. Within these same years, one of Fulton's boats, the *Aetna,* made four such long and rapid trips.

Prior to the introduction of steam in navigation, the western rivers had been usable, of course, on a downstream trip, but as arteries of trade they were almost totally useless upstream, short of a back-breaking and costly poling against the current. For this reason the arrival of the towering river boat at a town was more than a picturesque social event—though it was usually that, too. The river boat, like the later railroad, was a symbol of the great importance of machine technology in the making of the United States. The steamboat could, like the later railroad, make or break an ambitious community. The fact that Cincinnati was known as Porkopolis— because of its large shipments of hog meat—is largely attributable to the steamboat. In the same way, cities like St. Louis, Cairo, Memphis, Natchez, and Louisville were almost the creations of the river boats.

Probably the technological device in transportation which most truly merits the appellation "revolutionary" is the railroad. Introduced into the country at the end of the 1820's it found a secure niche in American economic life almost from the outset; by 1860, over 30,000 miles of track had been laid and, as events would prove, this was only the beginning.

The economic and social consequences of the railroad can scarcely be exaggerated. It was the first land transport vehicle in history which could carry bulk goods in competition with water routes. Louis Hunter, seeking to compare costs of transportation during the years

1831–58, offers some figures on rates which also serve to sum up statistically the economics of the Transportation Revolution. Roughly comparable rates in cents per ton-mile were: by road, 11.66; by canal, 2.37; by railroad, 2.25; by steamboat, 1.14. Though railroad rates were often higher than those of river boat or barge, the greater speed and adaptability to topography of the railroad easily made up the difference. In many sections of the country the coming of the railroad blackened the future as well as the sky over the canal barge. Considering the fact that a farmer in 1810 was still sending his goods to market by the same means as a farmer in the days of Julius Caesar, the advent and expansion of the railroad was a revolutionary event in the economic life of the American people—as it has proved to be for any people into whose lives it has been introduced. Emerson wrote at the time, "Railroad iron is a magician's rod in its power to evoke the sleeping energies of land and water."

A measure of the importance the American people attached to canals and railroads was the support which their governments gave to such enterprises. From the work of a number of scholars in recent years it has become increasingly clear that financial assistance from state and local government was often crucial in the building of lines of transport. The best-known example, of course, was the Erie Canal, which was entirely state-built. Two other ventures in which the state assumed full responsibility for construction when private enterprise had neither the heart nor the resources for it were the Blue Ridge Railroad of Virginia and the Western and Atlantic of Georgia.

But the commonest mode of public assistance to internal improvements was the so-called mixed enterprise, in which public and private funds were pooled. For some forty years before the Civil War, Virginia employed the mixed corporation in the building of internal improvements. Three fifths of the capital in such corporations was contributed by private persons and two fifths by the state, the latter naming a proportionate number of directors, but receiving its dividends last. Between 1816 and 1861, the State of Virginia invested about $41 million in such projects.

Other states also encouraged transportation construction in concrete ways. The Missouri Constitution of 1821, for instance, explicitly stated that "internal improvements shall forever be encouraged by the government of this State," and by 1860 something like $23 million had been pledged by the state to such improvements, despite the fact that the figure was twenty-five times the state's average annual income. Pennsylvania invested over $6 million of state funds in some 150 mixed corporations, while Massachusetts spent $8 million on eight railroads in the years before 1860. The latter state continued its interest in public aid to transportation after the Civil War, building the Hoosac Railroad Tunnel at a cost of almost $20 million. Well over half of the cost of construction of the railroads of the South before 1860 came from public funds, one authority has calculated. A study of canal building throughout the nation reveals that 60 per cent of the almost $200 million invested in canals between 1815 and 1860 came from public funds.

Local communities were as vitally interested as the states in the support of railroad construction. Between 1826 and 1875, it has been estimated, some 315 New York cities and towns pledged almost $37 million to railroad building in the state. The city of Baltimore alone invested $20 million between 1827 and 1866, while Cincinnati topped even that figure. Towns and cities contributed almost a third of the $144 million in public aid to railroads in the South before 1860.

In the 1830's Mrs. Trollope, so critical of America in many ways, was moved to say that nothing in the American character "commands so much respect as the boldness and energy with which public works are undertaken and carried through." In this historical context, Lincoln's dictum that the "legitimate object of government" is to do for the people what they "cannot do at all or cannot do so well for themselves in their separate or individual capacities" takes on a meaning more friendly to government enterprises than usually supposed.

Apart from the improvement in internal communication, public assistance to economic enterprise during the first half of the nineteenth century has important implications. It suggests that government aids like land grants to railroads after the Civil War and even the much later Tennessee Valley Authority and the communications satellite (Comsat) are quite within a long American tradition of fruitful union between public and private enterprise. More concerned about getting the job done than about dogmatic conceptions of the relations between government and the economy, the Americans of the pre-Civil War era amply demonstrated the practical streak in their economic thought.

In the building of an American nation, the transportation net was of tremendous importance. Emerson observed that "the rage of road building" was "beneficent for America . . . inasmuch as the great political promise" of internal improvements was "to hold the Union staunch" against "the tedious distances of land and water." But of all the various improvements in transportation, the railroad was the most important. Canals, roads, and steamboats, for all their advantages, were, if nothing else, severely limited in their efficiency and usefulness. Canals required water to fill them, and despite the steamboat captain's boastful jest that his light-draft ship could sail anywhere so long as there was a heavy dew, rivers were his only roads. Simply because of this limitation, if for no other, large areas of the back country never heard the deep-throated whistle or saw the tall black stacks of the river boat. The railroad, however, with its magic rails, could leap over the most desolate areas almost as easily as it followed the gentle roadbed of the river valley.

The cohesive power of transport and particularly of the railroad is dramatically evident in the years leading up to the disruption of the Union in 1861. Because settlement in Ohio, Indiana, and Illinois prior to 1825 was primarily in the southern portions, along the Ohio and Mississippi rivers, goods and people tended to flow south and north, following the natural trade artery of the rivers. When the Erie Canal was opened in 1825, the northern portions of these western states grew rapidly by shipping their goods and receiving immigrants via the New York canal and the Lakes. But even though the eastern pull of the canal was strong, it could not eliminate the powerful southward attraction of the Mississippi-Ohio route. As late as 1850, the southern-flowing rivers were carrying 2.4 million bushels of corn compared with 3.6 million bushels traveling eastward. While only 300,000 barrels of western pork were being sold in the East, 1.2 million barrels were being shipped in 1850 down the rivers to the South.

For this reason, southern leaders in the late 1840's and early 1850's looked with confidence to the West for support in the political struggle with the Northeast over the questions of the nature of the Union and slavery. Economic self-interest, they felt, would compel the West to side with the South or at least remain neutral in the event of a showdown between the sections. The southern leaders, however, reckoned without the influence of the railroad. By 1860 and secession, when the South sought to capitalize upon its control of the Mississippi, several thousand miles of railroad track between Chicago and the East had effectively weakened the once-powerful trade monopoly of the Mississippi-Ohio system. In that year over 19 million bushels of corn went to the East as compared with a mere 4.8 million to the South; pork from the West to the East was three times what it had been in 1850, while that to the South was only a half of the figure ten years earlier. The railroads built during the decade thus helped to create that united front which the North and the West presented to the secession of the South. Moreover, by knitting together the industry of the Northeast and the breadbasket of the West, the railroads forged a crucial economic link in the chain of northern victory in the ensuing war; for the winning of the Civil War was as much a matter of logistics and supply as it was of men and military ardor.

Beside the marching tracks of the railroad swung the wires of another invention which helped to bring about the revolution in communications in the first half of the nineteenth century. Soon after its successful trial in 1844, the telegraph of Samuel F. B. Morse began to weave its slim web across the nation, building markets, carrying news, and helping to create a new people.

3. THE FACTORY COMES

A natural outgrowth of the extension of transportation and communication lines was the expansion of manufacturing; the two went hand in hand. To be sure, during the colonial period there had been manufacturing in America, but the so-called Industrial Revolution cannot be said to have come to the United States until the second decade of the nineteenth century. Before then the factory and the industrial worker were novelties in the economy. Though no single year can be properly singled out as the beginning of industrialization in the United States, 1816 has a better claim than most; the first frankly protective tariff was passed in that year. During the War of 1812, American capital and labor had been attracted into manufacturing because the hostilities cut off the usual imports from Great Britain. In effect, the wartime interruption of trade acted as protection for the development of new industry. With the cessation of the war in 1815, however, American manufacturers were threatened with extinction by a flood of cheaper British goods. As a result, a strong movement for a protective tariff quickly got under way.

The sponsors of the tariff ranged in motivation from the narrow self-interest of a manufacturer to the broadly patriotic concern of a publicist like Hezekiah Niles, who hoped to render the national economy independent of British exports. The truly great breadth of the protariff forces is revealed by the fact that even old Jeffersonians like President Madison acceded to this departure from the ancient faith that once had sanctioned a tariff only for revenue. Measured against subsequent protective tariffs of the post-Civil War years, the act which was passed in 1816 was modest indeed, but it stands, nevertheless, as a convenient and accurate bench mark in the rise of American industry. From this date on, there was a growing pressure for the protection of American industry against foreign competition.

By the decade of the 1830's the factory, with its disciplined workers, its whirring machines, and its prodigious production, was sufficiently widespread to allow one to speak of the onset of industrialization. Most noticed by foreign and native observers alike were the textile mills of eastern Massachusetts, where the celebrated girl workers astounded visitors by their intelligence, their poetry reading while tending the looms, and their distinctly unproletarian appearance. The records of the period, however, make it quite clear that the girls at Lowell were exceptional both in their intellectual surroundings and in their contentment. (Realistic Herman Melville described a factory of women operatives as "the Tartarus of Maids.") Actually, most manufacturing in the United States was carried on in urban centers under conditions of low wages, stale air, poor light, atrocious housing, and tediously long hours of work under the rigorous tempo and discipline of a machine.

There was more aborning in those early years of industrialization than the slow spreading of the factory through the land. Very early in the history of the new Republic, the fundamental principle of manufacture from which would develop the mass-production techniques of modern industrialism was set forth. In 1798 a young Connecticut Yankee and former schoolteacher, who had recently revolutionized agriculture in the southern United States, contracted with the federal government to turn out 10,000 muskets in the short space of two years. Probably because Eli Whitney was well known to Vice-President Jefferson and to Secretary of the Treasury Oliver Wolcott, the government agreed to his ambitious undertaking. But whatever the reason for the government's accepting him at his word, at the end of the contract period, no more than 500 muskets had been produced. Nevertheless, when Whitney demonstrated to his sponsors the innovation he had introduced into the manufacture of guns, instead of annoyance, additional money was forthcoming.

Whitney's new process was nothing less than the principle of the interchangeability of parts, the fundamental idea in mass production. The principle was described by President Jefferson, who realized from the outset the tremendous industrial implications of the innovation. "He has invented moulds and machines for making all pieces of his locks, so exactly equal," the President explained, "that take 100 locks to pieces and mingle their parts and the hundred locks may be put together as well by taking the first pieces which come to hand. This is of importance in repairing," Jefferson went on, "because out of 10 locks, e.g., disabled for want of different pieces, 9 good locks may be put together without employing a smith." The President might have added that the principle considerably cheapened the cost of production and, furthermore, enabled unskilled workers to manufacture items like guns, which heretofore could only be turned out by highly skilled men. It is important to observe that only machines, with their unvarying cutting of shapes and sizes, could make interchangeable parts; the most skilled mechanic depending on eye and hand could not make each piece precisely alike. Whitney, it might be added, invented not only the machinery but the production processes used in the new method as well.

For a society chronically short of labor and skills, the interchangeability of parts was a tremendous fillip to the expansion of manufacturers. Producers of goods like clocks, watches, hardware, and sewing machines, which used a number of parts in their manufacture, appreciated the advantages of the procedure and adopted it. Though a century would pass before one could talk of mass production on the scale popularized by Henry Ford and well known today, the basic technique and some good approximations of the later quantity of production were already in evidence as the nineteenth century moved into its second half.

Manufacturing, by the decade of the fifties, had spread far beyond New England; Pennsylvania and New York both led Massachusetts in goods produced and capital invested. The Census of 1860 revealed that well over half a million men and women were working in some 53,000 manufacturing establishments in the Middle Atlantic states alone, and the value of manufactured goods produced in the nation as a whole was almost $2 billion. On the eve of the Civil War, an urban working class was already in existence; it would be only a matter of time before the dominance of the farmer in American society would be seriously challenged by the urban wage earner, the by-product of the new factory.

That the shift away from agriculture was beginning as early as the 1850's is apparent from the fact that in 1860 less than 60 per cent of the labor force was still in agriculture. (Twelve per cent was in manufacturing, the remainder in services and trade.) The movement away from farming and toward industry would accelerate after the Civil War, but as recent scholars like Douglass North and Stuart Bruchey have emphasized, the economic growth of the 1850's provided the springboard for the great industrialization of the post-Civil War era.

The South, however, did not share proportionately in this prewar upsurge in industrial activity. Of the 140,000 manufacturing establishments in the nation in 1860, only 21,000, or fifteen per cent, were in the southern states, though that region contained a third of the population. Furthermore, southern production of manufactured commodities was only one tenth of the national total when the war began. In what proved to be the first of modern wars, industrial power occupied a prominent place in the balance of forces between the sections. The dire poverty of the Confederacy in the last years of the war and the poor quality of its military equipment bear ample testimony to the high price the South paid for failing to develop its industry in step with that of the North. The South could boast of having Lee and Jackson, but the North had railroads, iron mills, machine shops, clothing factories, and shipyards—as well as U. S. Grant. The Civil War, it is true, was neither won nor lost by material forces alone. But insofar as its outcome was affected by the difference between the industrial capacities of North and South, then the dogged and heroic defense of the Confederacy takes on many of the aspects of a cause that was lost from the beginning.

4. DOES LAND MAKE A PEOPLE?

"So vast is the Territory of North America," prophesied Benjamin Franklin in 1751, "that it will require many Ages to settle it fully; and, till it is fully settled, Labour will never be cheap here, where no Man continues long a Labourer for others, but gets a Plantation of his own. . . ." Franklin's observations on the impact of empty land upon Americans was echoed by many another American in his time and later: Jefferson, Hamilton, Emerson, and Henry George are only some of the older ones. The conviction that the roots of the American character are to be found in the frontier experience has long since passed into the folk wisdom of the nation, and in our own century it has been a stock in trade of historical scholars as well.

In the waning years of the nineteenth century, the vague belief that, in some fashion or other, the frontier was a formative factor in the history of the United States was boldly cast into an academic hypothesis by a young historian from the West. The study of American history has not been the same since Frederick Jackson Turner made that presentation before the American Historical Association in 1893; only Charles A. Beard has exercised a comparable influence upon the writing of American history.

This influence has stemmed primarily from Turner's broad, but highly suggestive and challenging thesis, running all through his writings, that the settling of a new land did more to mold the character of the American people and institutions than the European heritage. "American democracy was born of no theorist's dream," he argued in one essay, "it was not carried in the *Susan Constant* to Virginia, nor in the *Mayflower* to Plymouth. It came out of the American forest, and it gained new strength each time it touched a new frontier. Not the constitution," he asserted, "but free land, and an abundance of natural resources open to a fit people, made the democratic type of society in America. . . ." Furthermore, something more than democracy issued from the forest; "the frontier," he contended, "is productive of individualism" in the American character. In his first and most famous frontier essay, he concluded "that to the frontier the American intellect owes its striking characteristics."

As a number of scholars have subsequently pointed out, Turner was generous in attributing a variety of American traits to the frontier, but it is not always clear what he meant by the frontier. Sometimes, in Turner's writings, it is an area—that is, the zone where civilization and forest meet; at other times the frontier is little more than the western part of the United States, although it is obvious that Illinois in 1850 is hardly a zone of contact between civilization and savagery. At still other places in his writings Turner is apparently thinking of the frontier as a process—a way of life for those actually participating in the settling of vacant lands. Then, at another time, he will write of the frontier as an abundance of natural resources. As analytical tools for explaining the origins of Americans, these four definitions are of quite different orders. To lump them under the single heading of the "influence of the frontier" is to obscure rather than to clarify. "As an analytical device," Richard Hofstadter has said, the frontier thesis "was a blunt instrument." If the frontier is the cutting edge of civilization, then it clearly cannot also be the western part of the United States at a later stage of social evolution; and if it is natural resources, then it is not the process of settlement, for men may wrestle with the problems of subduing a wilderness but enjoy only a paucity of natural resources. In short, these four definitions of the same term are not only different; they are sometimes mutually exclusive.

Turner never tired of reiterating that the frontier remade the Europeans who entered it. "The wilderness masters the colonist," he explained. "It finds him a European in dress, industries, tools, modes of travel, and thought. . . . It strips off the garments of civilization and arrays him in the hunting shirt and the moccasin. It puts him in the log cabin of the Cherokee and Iroquois and runs an Indian palisade around him. . . . In short, at the frontier the environment is at first too strong for the man." But after the first adjustment, the pioneer begins to change. "Little by little he transforms the wilderness, but the outcome is not the old Europe. . . . The fact is, that here is a new product that is American." This was a most persuasive argument, but Turner was so imbued with a belief in the influence of environment that he underestimated the tough conservative character of men's cultural patterns.

Sixty years before Turner, Alexis de Tocqueville believed, much the same as Turner, that in America one could actually witness the successive stages of social evolution.[7] Upon visiting the actual frontier of Michigan, however, Tocqueville found that his assumption required serious modification. "Of all the countries of the world America is the least fitted to furnish the spectacle I came there to seek," he noted in his diary. "In America, even more than in Europe there is only one society. . . . The plane of a uniform civilization has passed over it. The man you left behind in New-York you find again in almost impenetrable solitudes: same clothes, same attitude,

---

[7] Turner wrote in his first essay on the frontier: "The United States lies like a huge page in the history of society. Line by line as we read this continental page from West to East we find the record of social evolution. It begins with the Indian and the hunter" and goes down through the various stages of development.

same language, same habits, same pleasures." To factors like widespread education, "the spirit of equality," and the very recent contact with civilized living Tocqueville attributed the "universal civilization" in America. The settlers on the Michigan frontier, he wrote, "have come with the customs, the ideas, the needs of civilization. They only yield to savagery that which the imperious necessity of things exacts from them. . . ." Tocqueville then described a cabin, deep in the virtually untouched forest, at which he visited. But, he said, if you think you are entering the abode of the American peasant, you are wrong. "You enter this cabin which seems the asylum of all the miseries, but the owner wears the same clothes as you, he speaks the language of the cities. On his rude table are books and newspapers"; he asks about events in Europe. In fact, "the wood cabin is only a temporary refuge for the American, a temporary concession made to the exigencies of the situation." As soon as possible he will reproduce his civilized life as he knew it, right in the midst of the wilderness.

Tocqueville, the observer, is a better guide to the cultural impact of the frontier than Turner, the historian. Instead of recapitulating the cultural history of the race, men on the frontier did their best to reproduce the civilization as quickly as they could when they came. More recently, Louis B. Wright, in his book *Culture on the Moving Frontier,* has shown in some detail how this was done through the seventeenth, eighteenth, and nineteenth centuries.

The most widely accepted part of Turner's frontier hypothesis is that American democracy is a unique product of the struggle with the wilderness. One of the favorite means for substantiating this point has been to point to the democratic features of the western state constitutions. Universal manhood suffrage, elected officials, and so forth, it is argued, first appeared in the western states and then spread to the rest of America. Actually, however, as one of Turner's disciples, John Barnhart, has shown, the constitutions of Kentucky and Tennessee—the first transmontane states to enter the Union— were both modeled after the Pennsylvania Constitution of 1790—a document which was considerably more conservative than the 1776 organic law of that state! Rarely, as Barnhart demonstrates, did these western states, for all their supposed democratic propensities, make a novel contribution to government; they merely copied from the eastern states.

From his investigations of the provisions of the state constitutions of the Ohio-Mississippi region—the so-called "Valley of Democracy" —Barnhart found only a handful of clauses whch could be called original with the West. In Ohio's first constitutions, for example, out of 106 clauses, only eleven were counted as original, while fifty were very much like those in Tennessee's and nineteen like those in Pennsylvania's. Lest this be thought to be an instance of one "advanced democratic" western state copying from another, it should be noted that forty-seven of Tennessee's clauses were taken from the constitution of Pennsylvania and nineteen from North Carolina's.

To be sure, as one looks over the constitutions of the states in the first half of the nineteenth century, it is clear that democratic forms came earlier, on the average, to the new states than to the old. But since it can also be shown that an old state like Pennsylvania in 1776 wrote a constitution more radically democratic than those of most western states in subsequent years, it does not appear that democracy is uniquely a product of the West, much less of the forest.

Moreover, if we broaden our perspective a little, we cannot escape noticing that the most democratic ideas expressed anywhere in European civilization before the nineteenth century were those of the Levellers in seventeenth-century England. No one has argued, however, that their demand for universal manhood suffrage and a written constitution to protect the people against arbitrary government was a result of the frontier.

But the failure of the Levellers to gain their democratic objectives, while the pioneers in the American forest secured theirs, suggests that the influence of the frontier lay not in its evocation of democratic ideas, but in the providing of an opportunity for them to be put into practice regardless of their place or occasion of origin. This would explain why democratic forms seemed to come more slowly to eastern states than to western; the latter had a clean slate on which to write new ideas. Though Turner seems to have underestimated the conservative streak which makes men strive to perpetuate the old in the midst of the new environment, he nevertheless grasped the important fact that ideas and innovations unable to get a trial in the older states often were put into practice in the communities abuilding in the West.

Such a function of the frontier, though not as formative as Turner asserted, is still important. Free land offered a chance for political and social experiment by peaceful means, and this opportunity unquestionably aided the rapid triumph of democratic ideals in America. But to repeat, the availability of opportunity should not be confused with the origination of democratic ideas. Later, by looking at the experiences of other peoples who were confronted with frontiers of empty land, we shall see that empty land does not always produce democracy or liberty.

But there is more to be said about the democratic influence of the frontier. Two scholars, Eric McKitrick and Stanley Elkins, have suggested that Turner's accent on the frontier as the molder of American democracy has been not so much misplaced as merely inexpertly elucidated. They decry, to begin with, the excessive emphasis by Turner's critics upon formal definitions of democracy, such as suffrage qualifications, constitutional provisions, and the like. McKitrick and Elkins would substitute a functional definition of American democracy in which the essence is taken to be concern with political problems and the active participation in community affairs on the part of large numbers of citizens. Under this definition, they point out, the newness of the land, the necessity of establishing brand-new communities in the wilderness, demanded greater participation in political activity than was true in Europe. Therefore, they say, the empty land may be said to have contributed to the making of a peculiarly American variety of democracy.

Moreover, with so much to be done in the raw communities of the West, there simply were not enough trained and traditionally accepted leaders to organize and manage the new settlements. Hence ordinary people, Everyman, had to come forward and pitch in. As this procedure was repeated across the face of the land, the habit of community problem solving, to use the phraseology of McKitrick and Elkins, became fixed in the American character. From this, they think, stemmed the American propensity for associative activity, committee forming, writing of petitions, and the general recourse to political and group action. This conception of the frontier is close to Turner's; but because it does not suffer from his confusion of definitions for the frontier, it is much more convincing.

The participation of many people in the affairs of government, McKitrick and Elkins further point out, inevitably reinforces self-confidence and self-reliance—qualities usually associated with the frontier and the American. How the new land did this economically was illustrated by Karl Marx in the latter part of the nineteenth century. Marx's example was a letter written by a French worker who went to California. "I never could have believed," the worker wrote, "that I was capable of working at the various occupations I was employed on in California. I was firmly convinced that I was fit for nothing but letter press printing. . . ." But once "in the midst of this world of adventurers, who change their occupation as often as they do their shirt, egad, I did as the others. As mining did not turn out remunerative enough, I left it for the town, where in succession I became a typographer, a slater, plumber, etc. In consequence of thus finding out that I am fit for any sort of work, I feel less of a mollusk and more of a man."

One must be careful, however, not to romanticize the opportunities of the free land to the point of unreality. Both Turner and his followers, for example, have written of the West as a safety valve for the unsuccessful and discontented of the East. So plausible has this hypothesis appeared that laymen and academic historians alike talk of the significance for American society of the "closing" of the frontier in 1890.

But, suggestive as the safety-valve theory is, it, too, like the thesis of the frontier origins of American democracy, suffers when subjected to close analysis. For example, of the large number of historians who have undertaken concrete examinations of the validity of this thesis, almost none has found evidence that discontented and poor urban workers of the East could find a second chance in the West of the nineteenth century. Two economic historians tried to uncover examples of workers who left an industrial town like Fall River, Massachusetts, for new opportunities in the West; but, though they combed newspaper after newspaper, they found no evidence of emigrating workers. Another historian demonstrated that the cost of starting a farm in the West in the nineteenth century was in excess of a year and a half's income of the average urban worker if he was fortunate enough to work all year. Confirmation of the urban worker's inability to finance his own movement to the West was forthcoming in another study which reported that, during the 1850's in New York City, societies were formed to assist workers to make the trip to the hinterland. By implication this was evidence that few workers were in a position to leave for the West on their own. Finally, in what he called a "post-mortem" on the safety-valve thesis, Fred Shannon noted that the census, especially after the Civil War, clearly showed that the largest migration of Americans was from the country to the city, and not the other way around, as the safety-valve hypothesis would have it.

Yet, despite the avalanche of attack, adverse evidence, and the paucity of defensive data, something is still to be salvaged from this much-mauled thesis of Turner. Shannon, resting his case on the census data, has vehemently argued that, rather than the country's being a safety valve for the discontent of the city, the urban centers were outlets for farm discontent. Such an argument goes too far to be convincing. The very existence of an empty frontier, which in the course of the years was gradually populated, makes it obvious that pressure on the city was reduced to the extent that many people—especially impoverished farmers and new immigrants—went to western farming areas instead of to the cities. In this indirect sense, one is justified in talking about the ameliorative effect of the frontier on urban crowding and in preserving opportunities for city workers. Nor should it be forgotten, though little research has been done on this aspect of the problem, that the West—though not the frontier—contained cities; many craftsmen and small shop owners must have migrated from the highly competitive and overcrowded cities of the East to seek new opportunities in the towns of the West. Furthermore, several economic historians in seeking to explain the higher wages that prevailed in the United States during the nineteenth century, as compared with those in Europe, have turned to the empty West as the principal explanation. They argue that because the agricultural sector of the economy was expanding along with the industrial sector, the former could not help but have an upward effect upon wages in the latter. The American situation, in short, was quite different from the English, where the agricultural sector of the economy at the time of the industrial expansion was static and thus did not compete with industry for labor. In sum, as Ellen von Nardoff has written, the frontier certainly did not provide an actual outlet for discontented urban workers as such, but its existence as part of an expanding agriculture had the effect of improving the wage levels of urban workers nonetheless.

An important secondary effect for American development follows from the fact that wages were higher in the United States. Relatively high wages had the effect of encouraging American employers to use machines, which, in turn, increased productivity, both industrial and agricultural. One English economic historian has traced to the high wages in the United States, as consequence of the frontier, the greater tendency toward acceptance of technological innovation here than in England during the nineteenth century.

Finally, in looking at reevaluations of Turner's thesis[8] mention ought to be made of David M. Potter's *People of Plenty*—an imaginative examination of the American character. In that book Potter concedes that the frontier hypothesis is a special case of his own argument that abundance has helped to make the American people what they are today. Abundant land—Turner's principal explanatory force—has been superseded, Potter argues, by industrially produced plenty, but the American character has been molded by both forms of abundance.

To concentrate our analysis of the impact of the West on America to measurable or economic matters is to miss the tremendous psychological import of the safety-valve conception. All through the nineteenth century, Americans believed that the West was a haven for the oppressed and a cornucopia for the ambitious. This was the underlying reason for the liberalizing of the land laws in the course of the century. George Henry Evans and his Land Reformers, Thomas Hart Benton and his Pre-emption Act, and the Republican party's Homestead Act, all epitomized the belief that if the lands of the West were made easy of acquisition, "every worker will be enabled to hew out for his family a home from the virgin soil of the Great West," as Horace Greeley put it in 1859. A form of this conviction lay behind the efforts on the part of businessmen and philanthropists in the 1850's to organize societies to help defray the expenses of the unemployed in traveling to the western lands. During the Panic of 1857, newspapers constantly urged the unemployed to go West for work. "It should be known to females out of employment," counseled a Philadelphia newspaper in 1857, "that throughout the West, there are thousands of homes and liberal pay awaiting any reputable persons who are willing to engage themselves for domestic duties." The Children's Aid Society of New York, under the imaginative and energetic leadership of Charles Loring Brace, undertook a continuous program of sending homeless children to the West. Between 1853 and 1872 some twenty thousand New York City children were placed in homes in the West. The Association for the Improvement of the Condition of the Poor, in 1858, though hostile to the idea of aided

---

[8] Even George Pierson, one of the earliest and severest critics of Turner's frontier thesis, has come, by the back door of mobility, to see some merit in Turner's amorphous if persistent explanation for the American character. See his "The M-Factor in American History," *American Quarterly*, XIV (Summer, 1962 Supplement), 275–89.

emigration for urban workers, nevertheless conceded that "The relief of our overburdened city of its pauperism, by migration to the country is a very popular idea. . . ."

And precisely because it was *believed* to be a safety valve, regardless of what it was in fact, the western frontier worked an influence upon the attitudes of Americans. It left its mark in the optimism, the belief in progress, the promise of the future and the second chance—all of which have been deeply embedded in the American character.

The influence of the doctrine is seen also in the widespread acceptance of the corollary that the closing of the frontier meant the end of an older America. "Our last frontier has long since been reached," Franklin Roosevelt said in 1932, "and there is practically no more free land. . . . There is no safety valve in the form of a western prairies to which those thrown out of work by the eastern machines can go for a new start." The view that the ending of the frontier posed new problems for the American economy found easy acceptance among a group of prominent and influential economists in the 1930's. For them the economy had lost its motive power when the frontier closed. "The Bogy of Economic Maturity," as one of their opponents phrased it, gripped a whole generation of depression economists, of whom Alvin Hansen of Harvard was the chief. These men found in the depression the final confirmation of the effects of the end of the frontier in 1890. They asked, as Hansen put it in the title of one of his books, "Stagnation or Recovery?" Only through government investment, they argued, could the natural stagnation of the economy now be overcome.

Generally, of course, these economists drew upon John Maynard Keynes for their economics, but their historical frame of reference was the work of Frederick Jackson Turner. In the remarkably widespread acceptance of the frontier hypothesis among men of affairs and humble citizens alike is a striking vindication of Lord Keynes' remark that ideas, whether right or wrong, can exert enormous social influence.[9] As a psychological force the frontier has not yet lost its power;

[9] Keynes wrote that "the ideas of economists and political philosophers, both when they are right and when they are wrong, are more powerful than is commonly understood. Indeed the world is ruled by little else. Practical men, who believe themselves to be quite exempt from any intellectual influences, are usually the slaves of some defunct economist. Mad men in authority, who hear voices in the air, are distilling their frenzy from some academic scribbler of a few years back. I am sure that the power of vested interests is

it is still common coin in American thought. Certainly while the frontier was in being, it was powerful in fostering the belief that the American was unique and different from the European. And insofar as he believed so, he was.

Underlying most of the criticisms of Turner is the assumption that the frontier influence is in reality passive rather than active. When Turner's thesis, which is essentially a geographical interpretation of history, is cut to its marrow, it stands forth as the simple assertion that when people move into a new geographical setting they alter their mores. This proposition has been amply documented and repeatedly demonstrated for a variety of environments. An especially convincing example is *The Great Plains,* by Walter Prescott Webb, a follower of Turner. But even in Webb's study it is apparent that geography is less a creator of culture and more a selector of existent cultural patterns. Men found it difficult to continue to be wheat farmers when climatic and soil conditions were more suited to cattle raising. But the cattle business did not spring forth for the first time on the Great Plains— it merely flourished there after being introduced from other areas. Climate and soil prevented New England from being a cotton-producing area, but they did not dictate that Maine should grow potatoes. Geography may set the limits within which men must live, but it does not determine which of several alternatives available to man's cultural versatility actually will be pursued.

The best proof of this generalization in regard to the frontier theory can be found in an examination of the effects of empty land upon peoples other than Americans. Several peoples of the world, both in the remote and recent past, have had to wrestle with the challenge of a raw frontier. In the twelfth century, the area east of the Elbe River constituted a nearly empty frontier land for the restless Saxons of north Germany. The movement of Germans into this region was one of the great colonizing efforts of the Middle Ages; and in some respects, this frontier wrought changes in the customs of the Saxons who settled on the vacant lands. The form of village settlement, for example, changed strikingly. Serfdom declined and its burdens were considerably lightened as lords were compelled to recognize that the peasants had access to more land and opportunity to the east. Though undoubtedly there were changes in cultural patterns, they were al-

---

vastly exaggerated compared with the gradual encroachment of ideas." *General Theory of Employment, Money and Interest* (New York, 1938), p. 383.

ready implicit in the old ways; they merely awaited an opportunity for expression, just as the liberalizing of franchise requirements in the western United States waited upon the opportunity of a new land for realization. In sum, the empty land in Germany determined neither the direction the changes would take nor the character of them.

This is illustrated even more clearly if one compares the alleged effects of the frontier upon the character of Americans and the South African Boers. The history of both peoples is dominated by the movement into open land. There can be no question of the fierce individualism and the hatred of outside control which characterize the typical cattle-raising Boer, but his almost fanatical conservatism in matters of religion, science, education, and government are in sharp contrast with the belief in progress, education, science and liberal government which has always stood out in the complex of American national traits. Both peoples struggled with the demands of the empty lands in which they settled, but the resulting traits and cultural patterns were strikingly different because each brought its own cultural baggage into the more or less neutral frontier. New land denies vitality to certain cultural patterns, but it creates no particular ones.

One other frontier experience might be mentioned. Like the Americans, the Russians of the eighteenth and nineteenth centuries were a people constantly in contact with a frontier. While the Americans were moving west, the Russians were striking east across Russia and Siberia. Both peoples reached their respective Pacific shores about the same time. Here, however, the similarity stops; movement into the steppes of southern Russia and into Siberia by a people governed by an autocrat brought no liberalization of the regime, nor did it prepare the ground for a democratic society. The Cossacks of the lower Don, it is true, came into being as a people in the seventeenth century while in direct contact with the free lands of the region, and enjoyed for a while a primitive democratic military organization. But it was not long, despite the frontier, before an oligarchy emerged, slowly but ineluctably changing the Cossacks into the most reactionary arm of the czarist regime. It is hard to find among the Cossacks any signs of the frontier influence of democracy and individualism as Turner spoke of it in America. Once again the cultural patterns of each people remained largely unchanged even though both peoples moved into an area of empty land.

Old cultural traits persisted on the American frontier. One scholar has found that when Germans in colonial America moved into Pennsylvania, Maryland, and Virginia, they differed markedly from the English colonists in farming methods, crops, and labor system. The Germans selected clay loams in heavily wooded areas, while the English chose light, sandy uplands. Whereas the English girdled trees and farmed among the stumps, the fastidious Germans cleared the land completely and plowed deeply. The English, on the other hand, merely scratched the soil and were appalled to see it run away in the rains. Tidewater Virginians let their stock roam freely, but the careful Germans actually built their barns before they built homes. Unlike the English, the conservative Germans did not take to tobacco cultivation, but stuck to the familiar wheat; nor did they become slaveholders as avidly as the English. Both peoples were on the same frontier, but the vacant land did little more than provide them with a canvas upon which each depicted the old familiar cultural patterns. In his enthusiastic conception of the frontier as a democratizing force, Turner ignored the new lease on life given to slavery by the free land of the West. Though the new southern states in the early years of the nineteenth century accurately reflected in their constitutions the national trend toward greater popular participation in government, these same constitutions were conspicuous for their complete acceptance of human slavery at the very time the institution was more and more viewed as contrary to the democratic spirit.

It is apparent from any survey of frontiers throughout the world that free land offers opportunities for social advancement and wealth accumulation. But whether men will seize these opportunities often depends more upon the cultural attitudes they bring with them than upon the free land. The land, in and of itself, will not do it. The history of the Indians and the Spaniards on the American frontier is a case in point here. The availability of free land and natural resources did not spur them on to new forms of production because their cultural heritage did not include the traits which fostered such activity. But bring into this empty land the work-conscious Puritan, for instance, and then the free land takes on a different aspect; it now becomes a spur, a veritable goad to economic activity and hard work. Similarly, a people with a vigorous conception of self-government, moving into new lands, finds it natural to expand popular participation in government, as McKitrick and Elkins have shown occurred on the American frontier. But it is important to recognize that it is not the land which makes the difference; it is the cultural attitudes of the people. The frontier, rather than being the key to American development, is merely one among a number of influences which have gone into the shaping of Americans.

One of the manifestations of the western influence upon Americans was Andrew Jackson and the Democracy for which he spoke. Jackson was proudly a Westerner, and in many respects the West's *beau idéal* for most of the years between the War of 1812, in which he played so conspicuous a role, and the election of 1860, when his beloved Union was split asunder. He was also, however, more than a western figure, for he gathered to himself, almost like the symbol of Uncle Sam itself, the democratic aspirations and hopes of Americans for their country and their future. For this reason the Era of Jackson was also the Age of the Great Experiment.

CHAPTER V

The Great Experiment

EVEN before the first settlers had arrived, America was an object of curiosity to Europeans; but in the thirties, forties, and fifties of the nineteenth century the United States was as interesting to Europeans as Soviet Russia was to the world a hundred years later. Scores of foreign travelers made the Grand Tour of America in those years, dutifully recording their impressions for the edification of their less fortunate, but no less curious, fellow Europeans. This was the era of Tocqueville, Mrs. Trollope, Charles Dickens, Harriet Martineau, Charles Lyell, Fredrika Bremer, and Captain Hall. And whatever else America may have been in the writings of visitors, all seemed agreed that the United States was the great experiment in democracy. To English Chartists, struggling to democratize English government, the United States appeared as "the bright luminary of the western hemisphere whose radiance will extend across the Atlantic's broad expanse and light the whole world to freedom and happiness."

It was in the course of these years that the Democratic Dogma, as Brooks Adams was to call it later, was pushed to its outer limits. The common people came into their own as political arbiters and participants; majority rule was invested with a kind of sanctity. By the time the era was over, new, popular colors had been added to the bare outline of American politics inherited from the Revolutionary Fathers. The modern party system was in being, the Presidency bore the indelible marks of Andrew Jackson and James K. Polk, and the principle of a people's administration of government had been permanently implanted in American political thought.

1. "LET THE PEOPLE RULE"

Even during the eighteenth century, as we have noticed, more people could vote, proportionately, in the United States than in England and other European countries. But in the years after 1815, Americans deliberately expanded the suffrage in order to rest their governments upon the consent of all the governed.

By the decades of the 1830's and 1840's this movement reached flood tide, as the states altered their constitutions in conformity with the principle that manhood, not property, was the most just basis for political rights. This was a new view, one which constituted a sharp departure from colonial and early republican theory and practice. "The pretense has been that none but the rich have a stake in society," James Fenimore Cooper wrote. But this is wrong, he insisted. "Every man who has wants, feelings, affections and character, has a stake in society." Hence he is entitled to vote. It was precisely this abandonment of the traditional assumptions regarding the suffrage which renders this period significant; goodly numbers of people had always voted in America, where property was widely distributed. Now, however, even property was removed as a limitation. Once it was conceded that the basis for the suffrage was mere citizenship, then it was possible for any group or class to advance a claim to participation in government. The floodgates of democracy were open. In due time, on this basis, women, Negroes, and eighteen-year-old youths would be accepted as voters.

The shift in practice away from the stake-in-society conception of politics was dramatic because it was accomplished so rapidly. The abandonment of the theory of a stake-in-society had begun, as we have noted, at the time of the Revolution. In 1800, only three of the fifteen states of the Union granted the vote to all white men, regardless of property; by 1860, in a Union of thirty states, all but seven states extended the ballot to all white men,[1] rich and poor alike. Property holding as a test of fitness to hold office was also discarded. Most of the new states in the early years of the century entered the Union without such requirements, while the original states gradually dropped theirs: Maryland began in 1810, Pennsylvania followed in 1838, then New Jersey in 1844, and so on.

---

[1] It is revealing that during the very period that the suffrage was being extended to new economic levels of the white population, it was being withdrawn from Negroes. At least three southern states—North Carolina, Maryland, and Tennessee—withdrew the ballot from free persons of color during this period. And New York, in 1821, when property qualifications for voting were removed for white men, deliberately retained such requirements for the Negro voter. Since the new states did not extend the suffrage to Negroes at all, there was no need to withdraw it.

The suffrage was only one of the several governmental innovations which embodied the upsurge in democratic ideals. Governors, for example, were now popularly elected instead of being chosen by the legislature. Maryland in 1837, North Carolina in 1835, New Jersey in 1844, and Virginia in 1850 all made changes in this direction. A large number of other offices were also made elective; indeed, it might be said that during this period the "long ballot" came into being, for a host of minor and middling offices were newly opened to election on the state and local level.

Most striking as a measure of the belief in the validity and value of a wide suffrage was the subjection of the judiciary to popular election. Between 1846 and 1853, thirteen states made various of their judges subject to the direct pleasure of the people—an extension of the democratic ideal which probably none of the Founding Fathers would have sanctioned.

The democratic faith was also extended to the making of the state constitutions. At the time of the Revolution only two states had found it necessary to submit their constitutions to the people for ratification; by the Age of Jackson, however, such a procedure was the usual practice; only an occasional state failed to seek the people's judgment on a constitution. The principle that just government derives from the consent of the governed was taken literally in this democratic age.

Faith in the infallibility of the people's judgment was the sun around which American political thought now revolved. Andrew Jackson, for example, upon retiring from the Presidency in 1837, told the people in his Farewell Address that they should "Never for a moment believe that the great body of the citizens of any State can deliberately intend to do wrong." It is true, he confessed, that they may be misled, "but in a community so enlightened and patriotic as the people of the United States, argument will soon make them sensible of their errors" and they will therefore rectify them. Martin Van Buren, Jackson's successor, was widely known for his dictum that "the sober second thought of the people is never wrong." And George Bancroft, Democratic theoretician, historian, and politician, contended that "true political science does indeed venerate the masses. . . . Individuals are of limited sagacity; the common mind is infinite in its experience. . . . Individuals are time-serving; the masses are fearless." To Bancroft the new democratic upsurge meant that "the day of the multitude is now dawned." "Democracy is the cause of Humanity," proclaimed the first number of the radical Democratic organ *The United States Magazine and Democratic Review.* "It has faith in human nature. It believes in its essential equality and fundamental goodness. It respects, with a solemn reverence to which the proudest artificial institutions and distinctions of society have no claim, the human soul. It is the cause of philanthropy." The virtues of the common man as a class were often said to be superior. At the New York Constitutional Convention of 1821, for example, it was asserted that "more integrity and more patriotism are generally found in the labouring class of the community than in the higher orders."

Such a deeply held belief in the people's wisdom was something new in conservative America; neither Thomas Jefferson nor even Tom Paine would have gone to such extremes, for both these advocates of the people saw the flaws as well as the beauty in humankind. To be sure, there still were many who would not accept the newfound democratic oracle; the Whig party in general for a while stood against such doctrine. But by the election of 1840 even the Whigs, at least publicly, were throwing their money and their oratory in the same direction as the Jacksonians—that is, in outright flattery of the people. After 1840 no political party would again dare to doubt the wisdom of the people as the Federalists and even some of the Whigs had done in earlier years. Charles Francis Adams, for example, while editing his grandfather's works in 1851, bemoaned the fact that candid political criticism was no longer possible in America. ". . . The fact is certain," he wrote, "that no leading political man" since John Adams' day "has been known to express a serious doubt of the immaculate nature of the government established by the majority." America was now committed to the dubious dogma that wisdom in politics was in direct proportion to the participation of the people.

The people did not need politicians to bolster their self-esteem; they demanded not only the ballot but access to appointive office as well. Even before Jackson's administration there was popular demand for a rotation of officers among the people. Jackson, however, gave the movement intellectual footing when, in his first annual message to Congress, he justified the removal of many old civil servants. "I cannot but believe," the new President wrote, "that more is lost by the long continuance of men in office than is generally gained from their experience." And it was true that many officeholders were superannuated in both mind and body. (Not insignificant in Jackson's motivation was the patent fact that a good number of the officeholders thought "the wild man from the West" a real danger in the White House after the incumbency of cultivated John Quincy Adams.) Moreover, many of them had come to think of their offices as a species of personal property—as Englishmen were wont to do in the eighteenth century. "In a country where offices are created solely for the benefit of the people," Jackson argued in lofty democratic tones, "no one man has any more intrinsic right to official station than another. Offices were not established to give support to particular men at the public expense."

Though the rotation of public office among the people opened the gates for an increasingly vicious spoils system, it also faithfully mirrored the American democratic philosophy that any citizen could adequately perform the work of government. Nor was this rather naïve conception of governmental work without truth. While today the tasks of government bureaus are infinitely complex and technical, in the early years of the Republic the bulk of the employees were little more than clerks, postmasters, and the like. The vast proportion of the jobs of the government could be effectively and efficiently carried on by the average citizen.

Jackson's deliberate removal of the old and the partisan from the offices of his administration brought forth a flood of aspirants for the vacancies. Thus was initiated the burden of the patronage system, the weight of which, in the course of subsequent years, has almost borne down the Presidency. Whig Daniel Webster said in 1835: "No one can deny that office of every kind is now sought with extraordinary avidity. . . ." Convinced that theirs was a people's government, the people were not hesitant in demanding their places. The policy initiated under the Democrats was continued by the Whigs in 1841, the faithful rushing "pell-mell to Washington, every man with a raccoon's tail in his hat" to identify himself as a supporter of William Henry Harrison. Such men, John Quincy Adams wrote with distaste in 1842, were "wolves of the antechamber, prowling for offices." President after President struggled hopelessly and unendingly with the "wolves" until the murder of a Chief Executive in 1881 by an alleged disappointed office-seeker startled the American people from their unconcern. It was only then that civil service reform got an opportunity to lighten the crushing burden of the patronage.

Though the rotation system unquestionably wasted much of the Presidents' time and threatened to reduce officeholding to the work of party hacks,[2] something of value, nevertheless, came out of it. Principally this was democratization of administration on both the federal and state levels. There would never grow up in America any remote civil service which was divorced from the people or which conceived of itself as a superior caste or class, outside or above the main body of the citizenry, as, for example, occurred in Germany to the detriment of the democratic Weimar Republic. Americans made sure, in this period, that their government, like the society at large, reflected their firm belief in the equality of men. Undoubtedly, a democratic administrative structure has been a prop and a succor to the whole democratic way of life in America.

At first glance it appears incongruous that in this very period when popular control of government was at its height, the office of the President, occupied as it is by a single person, should also attain new strength and prestige. This consequence is largely the result of two men's influence upon the people and upon the office. It is true that George Washington, as the first President, did more than any other incumbent to create the mold from which the Chief Magistracy of the Republic would thereafter be cast. But if the austere and essentially aristocratic Washington bequeathed dignity, independence, and high prestige to the Presidency, it remained for Andrew Jackson and James K. Polk to make it also an expression of the democratic spirit of the American people.

It was Jackson, for instance, who first declared that "the President is the direct representative of the people" and no less capable of speaking for the people than the Congress. In practice, Jackson did not hesitate to appeal to the people to sustain policies which the Congress opposed, as, for example, when he vetoed the Bank recharter bill in 1832. Polk, who with reason was often called "Young Hickory," made no secret of following Jackson's conception of the President as the Tribune of the People. "The President," Polk wrote, "represents in the executive department the whole people of the

---

[2] Graft, "voluntary" political contributions, and assessments of government employees for the support of the party in power, as well as the placing of incompetents in posts for party reasons, all followed naturally, if undesignedly, from the Jacksonian theory and practice. It is necessary to emphasize, however, that Jackson himself was no spoilsman in the sense of using patronage as a naked device for building the party. He hated "honest" graft, assessments, and other devices which converted rotation into a party-building subterfuge. His political adviser, Amos Kendall, as Fourth Auditor of the Treasury, set forth the first—and in some respects the most stringent—rules pertaining to the work habits and standards of behavior expected of government employees.

United States, as each member of the legislative department represents portions of them." As early as 1824, ardently democratic Senator Thomas Hart Benton advocated changes which would bring the President closer to the people than the cautious Founding Fathers had intended. Stigmatizing indirect election through the Electoral College as a "favorite institution of aristocratic republics," Benton urged that the people be able to vote directly for the Chief Magistrate. Jackson himself, in his first annual message, also urged the amending of the Constitution in order to permit the people to elect the President directly. Though nothing came of either Benton's or Jackson's proposals regarding election, the nomination of the President was democratized in the early 1830's. The Anti-Masonic party[3] held the first Presidential nominating convention in the United States in 1831; within a few years the two major parties abandoned the old caucus system in favor of the more popular convention.

It was Jackson who conclusively established the right of a President to control his Cabinet, even though the Congress may have legislated otherwise. At the time of his war against the Bank of the United States in 1832–33, Jackson, despite Congress' deliberate effort to make the Secretary of the Treasury responsible to the legislature, successfully compelled two Secretaries of the Treasury to resign because they would not implement his policies. Congress protested vehemently and the Senate, in an extraordinary procedure, formally censured the President. But Jackson was vindicated and the President's power enhanced when a more friendly Senate later, in a dramatic ceremony, expunged the censure from its records. Since that time all Presidents, with the exception of the befuddled Grant, have been encouraged by the example of Jackson to fight vigorously against any congressional efforts to control the Cabinet.

It was left to James Polk to explore the immense reservoir of power inherent in the President as Commander in Chief of the armed forces. The Mexican War, as Leonard White has pointed out, was

[3] This party began in New York State in the late 1820's, but coalesced with the Whigs in 1836. As its name suggests, its *raison d'être* was opposition to the influence of the Masonic Order after the lodges of upper New York State were implicated in the mysterious disappearance of William Morgan, a former Mason who had revealed the secrets of the order. The party easily became an anti-Jackson force, since many high Democrats, including Jackson, were Masons. In the political history of the United States, the Anti-Masonic party is noteworthy as the first third party and the first political party to set forth a platform.

really fought from the White House: Polk named the generals, set forth the grand strategy which won the war, cajoled and bullied the Congress into granting the necessary credits and support, and finally drew up the peace terms. All this was achieved with a minimum of consultation with or dependence upon Congress. When faced with a much greater military challenge, Abraham Lincoln would find encouraging precedent in Polk's use of the Presidential power.

Under imaginative handling by Jackson and Polk, even an essentially negative power like the veto was made to strengthen the authority and prestige of the Presidency. For the first forty years of the Republic it was more or less assumed, from the precedent set by Washington, that the veto was merely a check on unconstitutional legislation and not a weapon which the President could use to enforce his own views. All the Presidents prior to 1829 used their negatives so sparingly that Jackson's vetoes numbered more than all those of his predecessors combined. More important, Jackson made no effort to conceal the fact that the motives behind his vetoes were at best a compound of constitutional scruple and expediency. It is true that he said he doubted the constitutionality of the Bank when he vetoed the recharter bill. But a perusal of his veto message made it clear to everyone that his opposition stemmed from his distrust of the Bank as such and not from any questions of constitutional niceties concerning an institution which, after all, had functioned in one form or another for almost forty years.

The new Democratic view of the veto power was not discarded by John Tyler, the first Whig President. And even though Tyler was threatened with impeachment for daring to veto legislation which Congress considered constitutional, the Jacksonian conception of the veto prevailed then and later. In vetoing a river and harbors bill Polk did not find it necessary to offer any justification for his act other than his mere disapproval. The power and prestige which the Jacksonian veto added to the arsenal of the President is best appreciated when it is recognized that no veto of a major piece of legislation was overridden by Congress until 1866.

Such an accretion of Presidential power was possible only after the President had been transformed into the Tribune of the People. Prior to that time, the unlimited exercise of the veto smacked of the royal prerogative and of the flouting of the will of the people's representatives. But once the President was accepted as a representative of the people, then the augmentation of his power, even during a period of expanding popular participation in politics, was quite possible and in conformity with democratic ideals.

Indeed, it might be said that the expansion of Presidential power during these years, as well as the increasingly popular character of the office, bear testimony to the realistic political judgment of the American people. Rather than being jealous of the power of the executive, the people seemed to recognize the vital role which strong executive leadership must occupy in any democratic polity which seeks to avoid the deadly paralysis of factionalism.[4] As a result, twentieth-century Americans enjoy an executive unparalleled in its independence and power, yet one responsive to the people's will.

2. "ALL MEN ARE CREATED EQUAL"

The democratization of politics and government was only one of the signs spelling out the Rise of the Common Man; the new democratic spirit was apparent throughout society. Dixon Ryan Fox went so far as to entitle his history of these years *The Decline of Aristocracy*. But that is a phrase which almost sacrifices accuracy to neatness. For as we have seen, it is doubtful that an aristocracy, as the term has meaning in European history, ever existed in America, much less declined. Any ruling class which may have existed in this country has always been tempered by the fact that it could lay no claim to a long tradition of wealth and power such as European aristocracies enjoyed and which is the true soil of an aristocracy.

But even if Fox's phrase somewhat overstates the situation, it does serve to accentuate the fact that in the years between 1820 and 1860, Americans made it quite clear that theirs was to be an equalitarian and open society. Earlier expressions of this sentiment had been sporadic and moderate; in the Age of Jackson it was blatantly and continuously proclaimed. "The equality of Man is, to this moment," wrote British traveler Alexander Mackay in 1842, the "cornerstone" of American society. Earlier Alexis de Tocqueville concluded that democratic societies like America were "ardent, insatiable, incessant and invincible" in their passion for equality. "They will endure poverty, servitude, barbarism, but they will not endure aristocracy."

---

[4] The example of Jackson and Polk on the federal level was not lost upon the states. A number of states during these years lengthened the term of office of their governors, or otherwise strengthened the hand of the executive, thereby bringing to the division of powers more balance than the fears born of the colonial experience had heretofore permitted.

A symptomatic expression of this strong distaste for privilege was evident in the attacks upon West Point during the mid-1830's. Tennessee, for example, in a resolution of the legislature, stigmatized the Military Academy as "this aristocratical institution." And the Ohio legislature declared that West Point was "wholly inconsistent with the spirit and genius of our liberal institutions." And so sure were Americans of their "liberal institutions," wrote Mrs. Trollope, that she "once got so heartily scolded for saying that I did not think all American citizens were equally eligible" for the Presidency "that I shall never again venture to doubt it."

The source from which the reservoir of American faith in equality was constantly being replenished was opportunity. "The United States are certainly the land of promise for the labouring class," wrote Michel Chevalier in 1834. "After landing in New York, I thought every day was Sunday, for the whole population that throngs Broadway seemed to be arrayed in their Sunday's best." Even prickly Mrs. Trollope bore witness to the opportunities of the new country. "Any man's son may become the equal of any other Man's son," she admitted, "and the consciousness of this is certainly a spur to exertion." Harriet Martineau thought she saw unlimited horizons for the lowly in America: "an artisan may attain to be governor of the state, member of Congress, even President," she said. "It is extremely seldom," Englishman Alexander Mackay observed, "that the willing hand in America is in want of employment."

The opportunities open to Americans were reflected in how well the average citizen lived. "I saw no table spread, in the lowest order of houses," Harriet Martineau recalled, "that had not meat and bread on it. Every factory child carried its umbrella; and pig-drivers wear spectacles." Michel Chevalier related the story of a newly arrived Irishman who showed his employer a letter he wrote to his family in the old country. " 'But Patrick,' said his master, 'why do you say that you have meat three times a week, when you have it three times a day?' 'Why is it?' replied Pat; 'it is because they wouldn't believe me, if I told them so.' " Other observers remarked on the notable absence of beggars. There were poor in America, to be sure, for while some men prospered others slipped and fell. And already the tenements of the burgeoning cities were open for inspection and the slum was no longer a European monopoly. But even with such qualifications, and especially when compared with European social conditions, this country opened new economic vistas for Everyman. As Emerson said, "America is another word for opportunity."

One immediate consequence of the breadth of opportunity was the looseness of class lines. We have noticed already a tendency in this direction all through American history; during the first half of the nineteenth century, however, this blurring of classes was a fact and a boast. "We have no different estates," Erastus Root told the New York Constitutional Convention of 1821, "having different interests, necessary to be guarded from encroachment by the watchful eye of jealousy. We are all of the same estate—commoners. . . ." New citizen Achille Murat said that "the lines which divide" Americans "are so delicate that they melt into each other; and that . . . there are neither castes nor ranks." European social patterns do not fit in the United States, German immigrant Francis Lieber wrote home. "In America there is no peasant. . . . He is a farmer, and may be rich or poor; that is all the difference."

In a country in which most men possessed "a competence," as Alexander Mackay put it, property was in no danger. Where acquisition of property is relatively easy, as it was in America, the demand for equality of holdings is rarely heard. It is significant that at no time, insofar as the great majority of Americans was concerned, did "equality" signify an equal division of wealth; too many men owned wealth, or soon expected to, to become involved in schemes or theories which might someday be fashioned into weapons with which to wrest from them their tangible goods. "There will be no attack on property in the United States," Harriet Martineau correctly prophesied. Because property was distributed throughout the various levels of society, no philosophy or organization fundamentally opposed to private property, be it Brook Farm or "agrarianism," was able to win the support of the American people.

3. JACKSONIAN LIBERALISM

For many Americans of the early nineteenth century the belief that the opportunities of their country were almost unlimited was most often embodied in the figure of Andrew Jackson. Born into a poor Carolina back-country family, Jackson rose to be a heroic general, an astute politician, a wealthy planter, and an exceptionally popular President of the United States. In some respects, as John

Ward has pointed out, Andrew Jackson was as much a symbol of his age as he was a molding force. The people saw themselves and their aspirations reflected in him and his fabulous career. In an article entitled "The Poorest Boy May Be President," the St. Louis *Argus,* in 1837, called attention to the low social origins of Jackson. The conclusion was that the Presidency itself was "within reach of the humblest urchin that roams the streets of our villages. . . . *Liberty and Equality* is the glorious motto of our republic." Jackson's life, the popular portraits of him, the songs about him, the very cartoons which praised and ridiculed him, were suffused with the people's conception of what the leader of the rising American democracy should be. Understandably, therefore, the popular image of his personality and career was shot through with paradox. He was the gruff War Hero who struggled unflaggingly to keep the nation at peace; the Man of Iron Determination and Inflexible Purpose who loved children; the Unschooled Backwoodsman who could match wits and wield power in competition with eastern bankers and great merchants. There was enough of the Walter Mitty in most Americans to find themselves in Jackson.

Of course, he was more than this. He was the first President who was not from the establishment: the first from beyond the mountains, the first from a state other than Virginia or Massachusetts, and the first who had not been either a Vice-President or a Secretary of State. He was also the first President to capture the imagination of the common people and to evoke from them unquestioning devotion while drawing almost unreasoning hatred from his opponents. (Jackson was also the first President on whom an assassination attempt was made.) An archconservative like wealthy Philip Hone of New York bore witness to both kinds of responses evoked by Jackson. "The President is certainly the most popular man we have ever known," he wrote in his diary in 1833. "Talk of him as the second Washington! It won't do now. Washington was only the first Jackson." The following year Hone told of meeting some friends while traveling on board ship. We talked, he said, "as is the fashion nowadays—abusing General Jackson and marveling at the undeserved popularity he still enjoys. . . ." Old Chancellor Kent of New York wrote Justice Story, "I look upon Jackson as a detestable, ignorant, reckless, vain and malignant tyrannt." Cultivated Philip Hone was also convinced that Jackson was a threat to the nation. "If the people continue to support him in his unwarrantable assumption of power," he wrote in his diary, "it will be idle to talk about the republican principles on which the government is founded." On the other hand, his supporters could be ecstatic about him. In 1839 a sonnet appeared in the *United States Magazine and Democratic Review* in which Jackson was portrayed as more than man-sized. The sonnet began:

> Come, stand the nearest to the country's sire,
> Thou fearless man of uncorrupted heart!
> . . . Raised by the voice of freemen to a height
> Sublimer far than Kings by birth may claim,
> Thy stern, unselfish spirit dared the right. . . .

Given the tremendous appeal of Jackson, it is no accident that during his tenure the President became the leader of his party. To some extent this had been true in Jefferson's day, but then the parties were much less organized and disciplined than they were after 1828. Thus, during the 1830's, began the modern party system, both in structure and mass character.

Jackson was more than a man who occupied the Presidency and helped to mold its character; he was also a spokesman and symbol of a philosophy of government and economics which soon came to dominate America. It is difficult, if not foolhardy, to try to fit into a neat pattern so diverse a group of interests as those which went to make up the Jacksonian movement. Some, for example, like the radically eccentric Loco-Focos of New York, in their philosophy were really throwbacks to the Jeffersonian agrarians, although their habitat was urban. Others, like many businessmen of the eastern cities and towns who were pushing for the main chance, were harbingers of the future. Still others of the Jacksonian coalition were farmers in the old American tradition of the farmer-speculator, covetously eyeing the vacant lands of the West. Yet, amid such diversity of interests, there does seem to be a common attribute which deserves to be called the Jacksonian Principle. This was the belief in economic freedom.

When the Jacksonians talked of economic freedom, they meant freedom of opportunity. Even radicals like the Loco-Focos and William Leggett, the outspoken editor of the Jacksonian New York *Evening Post,* had this in mind when they used their favorite slogan of "equal rights." Indeed, the official name of the radical Jacksonian Loco-Focos was the Equal Rights party. Equal rights, however, did not mean that government should guarantee rights to all equally; rather it meant that no one should obtain rights or privileges from government which no one else enjoyed. In practice this meant that the state should not favor one class or individual over any other. If government, said Andrew Jackson, "would confine itself to equal protection, and, as heaven does its rains, shower its favors alike on the high and the low, the rich and the poor, it would be an unqualified blessing."

In Jacksonian thought, special legislation in behalf of only a portion of the community came under the heading of "monopoly." The Bank of the United States, for example, was a monopoly, not because it cornered the banking business, which it did not, but because it enjoyed a federal charter that endowed it with privileges no other bank possessed. Another example of Jacksonian reasoning was evident in Chief Justice Taney's decision in the Charles River Bridge Case of 1837.

When appointed to the Supreme Court by Jackson in 1835, Roger Taney was already notorious as an ardent supporter of the President. He had been amply tested and retested in the hottest fires of controversy, the most notable example of which was the unprecedented rejection of his appointment as Secretary of the Treasury by the Senate in 1834. It was to be expected that he would not follow in the judicial footsteps of his illustrious but Federalist predecessor, Chief Justice John Marshall.

For almost a third of a century John Marshall had used his position on the Supreme Court to build impregnable protections for property against the onslaughts of the state legislatures. Especially noteworthy were the cases of *Fletcher* v. *Peck* and *Dartmouth* v. *Woodward,* in which it was made clear that a charter or a grant by a state to a private individual or corporation was a contract within the meaning of the constitutional clause which prohibited the states from impairing contracts. Even if the grant was fraudulently obtained, *Fletcher* v. *Peck* held it was still valid and to be honored by the state which entered into it.

It was from behind this sturdy bulwark of law erected by Marshall that the Charles River Bridge Company challenged the issuance of a charter by the State of Massachusetts to a rival bridge company. Because the new bridge had, in point of fact, deprived the old bridge of much traffic and thereby virtually destroyed its value, it was asserted that the state was guilty of breaching the original contract with the Charles River Bridge Company. The property value of the old bridge was one of the rights protected by the federal Constitution, it was argued; therefore no state could impair it. It was this argument which Justice Joseph Story, Marshall's aptest pupil on the Court, followed in his dissent.

The Court under Taney, however, executed a decided modification of the Marshall-Story approach. The sanctity of private property was not impaired, despite the assertions of contemporary alarmists, but its pre-eminence as a judicial desideratum was considerably reduced. With Taney writing the decision, the Court found in favor of the new bridge and enunciated the doctrine that whenever there is some doubt as to the precise privileges granted in a charter, the benefit must be awarded to the state. "While the rights of property are sacredly guarded," Taney pointed out, "we must not forget that the community also have rights. . . ."

Taney was not unmindful of the economic importance of this principle in an age when new means of transportation were challenging old ones and legal flexibility was crucial if the expansion of the economy was to continue. "The whole community are interested in this inquiry," the Chief Justice noticed, "and they have a right to require that the power of promoting their comfort and convenience, and of advancing the public prosperity," by new methods and devices "shall not be construed to have been surrendered or diminished by the States, unless it shall appear by plain words that it was intended to be done. . . ." In this sentence were summed up the basic economic and political assumptions of Jacksonian Americans.

A later age would characterize the Jacksonian approach to economic activity as simply one of "laissez faire," citing as evidence Jackson's veto of the bill for a feeder line to the National Road in Kentucky. Though Polk's vetoes of internal improvements show that the attitude was persistent, the evidence of the Maysville veto of Jackson tends to oversimplify the Jacksonian conception of the government's role in the economy. We have already noticed, for instance, that during the 1830's and 1840's most of the states, many of which were dominated by good Jacksonian Democrats, were busily supplying funds for internal improvements. Moreover, it should not be forgotten that the federal government, under Jackson, appropriated far more money for roads and canals than did the previous administration of John Quincy Adams, though the earlier President was easily the nation's most ardent exponent of the principle that the federal government should underwrite economic growth. Even from the standpoint of theory, there was a body of Jacksonian opinion which encouraged governmental support of internal improvements. Improvements, wrote John Vethake, a New York Jacksonian of prominence, "like the Great Erie and Champlain Canal . . . should be paid for out of the common purse for the common benefit of all." He then went on to echo the classic Jacksonian division of constitutional labor: "If national in character, these works should be constructed by the general government; if local, by the state, county, or town to which their benefits are more especially confined. . . ." The Jacksonians certainly entertained serious doubts as to the wisdom of restrictions by the states upon business, but governmental assistance *to* business in opening up the country did not fall under such a ban. After all, it was a later Jacksonian, Stephen A. Douglas, who championed the first federal land grants to railroads.

To governmental interference in the competitive system the Jacksonians were unalterably opposed. No one, said the *United States Magazine and Democratic Review,* should be artificially assisted by government to a position of superiority over his fellow men. Men of talent, it asserted, can make their own way without such aid. Moreover, society benefits most from such abilities when they are permitted to function within "a perfectly free democratic system, which will abolish all artificial distinctions," thereby permitting "the free development of every germ of talent wherever it may exist, whether on the proud mountain summit, in the humble valley or by the wayside of common life."

This principle of free competition and individualism was followed to its logical conclusion by the radical Jacksonian editor William Cullen Bryant in his attack on the usury laws. Instead of such "fetters" on "the trade in money," he argued, there was "no reason why the laws of supply and demand, which regulate the value of all other articles," should be suspended in the case of money "and their place supplied by the clumsy substitute of feudal ignorance and worse than feudal tyranny." This was laissez faire of the purest sort. Such a pristine doctrine is no longer in fashion; indeed, it is almost subversive; but in the context of the early nineteenth century, laissez faire was both progressive and necessary.

For decades, business in America, and more so in England, had been enmeshed in government regulation and privilege-mongering of one sort or another. The common practice of dispensing favors and privileges to special interests had long ceased to be an effective device for expanding business enterprise; instead, it became a bar to the enterprising who often could not secure the favor of government. The most obvious examples of this kind of discrimination were acts of incorporation. Prior to 1837, incorporations were special acts of the state legislatures, a procedure which made businessmen who desired to take advantage of the corporate form dependent upon the pleasure and honesty of a large body of men. After that date, however, spurred by the new views then coming forward, state after state began to enact general incorporation laws. These statutes permitted anyone to enjoy the legal advantages of incorporation simply by compliance with certain administrative procedures. The corporation was thus made into a vehicle for the future expansion of the economy; in time, the corporate form would dominate American business. In sum, the historic function of Jacksonian laissez faire was to free private enterprise of those governmental restrictions left over from the age of mercantilism; at the time it was liberating and progressive, but it also cleared the field for what V. L. Parrington called the "Great Barbecue" after the Civil War.

Business was not the only beneficiary of the new spirit of freedom of Jacksonian America; workingmen stood to gain as well. Government has always been on the side of wealth, complained William Leggett, the radical New York Jacksonian. "It was never wielded in behalf of the community. . . . Thus it will be seen that the sole reliance of the labouring classes, who constitute a vast majority of every people on the earth, is the great principle of Equal Rights; that their only safeguard against oppression is a system of legislation which leaves all to the free exercise of their talents and industry, within the limits of the General Law," which bestows upon no class or group "rights or privileges not equally enjoyed by the great aggregate of the body politic." As Theophilus Fisk, another Jacksonian, declared in behalf of labor: "We ask no protection; we simply desire *to be let alone.*"

It must be admitted that these remarks sound more like modern strictures of the National Association of Manufacturers against government interference than utterances of labor spokesmen. But in the early nineteenth century, laissez faire could be sound doctrine for workingmen.

Up until the 1830's, at least, the courts and the common law in America were openly hostile to labor organization. Usually any attempt on the part of workers to organize or to strike or to bargain collectively was interpreted by the state courts as a conspiracy in restraint of trade and punishable under the common law. Under this doctrine, strike after strike was broken by the jailing or fining of leaders. In 1836, for example, twenty-one tailors were fined a total of $1,150 by a New York court for having "perniciously" formed and united "into an unlawful club or combination to injure trade" and for having gone on strike. (A good annual wage for a worker employed all year round was no more than $600.)

The impact of the rising labor movement and the new accent on freedom in economic affairs were reflected in Chief Justice Lemuel Shaw's decision in *Commonwealth of Massachusetts* v. *Hunt* in 1842. Labor unions, the Chief Justice of Massachusetts announced, were legal organizations and therefore could not be construed as conspiracies or combinations in restraint of trade. That public and judicial opinion in the nation was ready for such a declaration is evident from the fact that courts in the rest of the states thereafter generally ceased to hold labor organizations contrary to the common law. Workers, like other men, were thereafter free to join together in pursuit of their economic ends. Shaw's decision and its acceptance throughout the nation constituted the legal foundation of the American labor movement; the unions, however, would have to wait another generation before social and economic conditions were such that they could strike root and grow.

4. ON THE ROAD TO DAMASCUS

Although many in Jackson's America concentrated their attention upon the economic and political sides of the Great Experiment, there were others whose horizons were wider. Indeed, sometimes it appeared that nothing except the dogmas of democracy and equality were left unchallenged throughout the length and breadth of society. The whole period was one of change. The steamboats and canals, the revolutionary railroads, the new factories, the growing cities were at once causes and symptoms of the upheaval through which the old order was passing. The very intellectual underpinnings of the eighteenth-century Enlightenment were being knocked out. The ideals of that previous age—urbanity, precision, reason—were under attack from the Romantic cult of the natural, the simple, and the ordinary. Nathaniel Hawthorne,[5] Herman Melville, Walt Whitman, and the

[5] Hawthorne, in the introduction of his novel *The Marble Faun,* gave expression to some of the problems of a Romantic writer in America; his words are worth repeating here for what they reveal about America in the 1850's.

Hudson River school of painters were but the New World counter-parts of more celebrated European Romantics who were revolting against the optimistic and reasonable assumptions of the Enlightenment.

In the face of so much change and ferment, it was inevitable that the basic institutions of society should be called into question and challenged to justify themselves. "Education, labor, politics, debt, war, dress, health, family life, church, prisons, the poor, the crippled and the unfortunate," as Russell Nye has said, were all tumbled together as fit subjects for scrutiny by a host of eager reformers. It is not our purpose here to get involved with Amelia Bloomer and her improvements in women's clothing or to explore the interesting if strange customs of the Oneida Community, or to discuss the merits of prisons which held their inmates incommunicado. Yet the fact that reforms and reformers were so numerous and so diverse in this period throws not a little light on the ingredients which went into the formation of the American character.

The very act of being a reformer reveals something of one's assumption about the world. To work for reform implies a belief in the efficacy of making the world over, even if only in a small corner. To Americans tomorrow always looked better than today, not because today was so miserable, but because it was so good. As one writer in the southern magazine *De Bow's Review* put it, "To him who has watched the progress of discovery and invention in the different countries of Europe and America, scarcely anything now will appear to be impossible." To be convinced that the future is unlimited, "it is sufficient to contemplate what man has done." Nor was there much doubt that men, along with conditions, could be changed for the better. "I have faith," wrote Horace Mann, the great educational reformer, "in the improvability of the race—in their accelerating improvability." A workingman's newspaper in 1830 dwelt on the immense capabilities of the human mind. The railroads, canals, and other inventions of the age, the paper said, "dwindle into insignificance—into mere child's play—when brought into comparison with the intellectual and moral improvement of the people." The Ameri-

---

"No author, without a trial," he wrote, "can conceive of the difficulty of writing a romance about a country where there is no shadow, no antiquity, no mystery, no picturesque and gloomy wrong, nor anything but a commonplace prosperity, in broad and simple daylight, as is happily the case with my dear native land. . . . Romance and poetry, ivy, lichens, and wall-flowers need ruin to make them grow."

can commitment to simple progress was a source of real irritation to Mrs. Trollope. Of all the strictures of the Americans against the English, she remembered, "the favorite, the constant, the universal sneer that met me everywhere, was on our old-fashioned attachment to things obsolete."

It is true, of course, that belief in progress and perfectibility of man is as much an eighteenth-century article of faith as it is nineteenth. Reformers of the nineteenth century, almost by definition, were believers in natural law, natural rights, and the application of reason to human institutions (just as the men of the Enlightenment had been. As Merle Curti has noticed, the austere rationalism of English utilitarianism was well exemplified in America's Age of Reform. But in practice, nineteenth-century reform exhibited at least two important additions to that of the Enlightenment. For one thing, in the earlier period interest in reform was usually confined to a relatively small class of people who were quite divorced from the mass of the population. If the eighteenth century was an age of Enlightenment, the masses rarely shared in the glow. The reforming spirit of the nineteenth century, however, as befitted a self-consciously democratic people, penetrated the lower levels of society, as foreign observers soon discovered.

The second difference between the two periods of reform was to be found in the motivation behind the impulse. By and large the reformers of the Enlightenment were moved by reason; they attacked institutions because they were irrational, useless, or inefficient. Slavery was evil, for example, for the man of the eighteenth century, more because it was a denial of natural and economic law than because it was cruel. The abolitionist of the nineteenth century, however, opposed slavery because of its inhumanity as often as for its denial of abstract rights to the slave. Impatience with irrationality and prejudice was the animating force in most gentlemen of the Enlightenment; pity for the hungry, the oppressed, the mistreated was often the mainspring of the nineteenth-century reformer. Pity was a conspicuous element among the reformers. At best it was manifested as a compassionate humanitarianism which included within its circle of concern all mankind, high and low, white and black; at worst it was an uncritical sentimentality which would equate animal vivisection with human torture. Modern American reform has never lost that broad strain of humanitarianism which burst forth with such energy in the Era of Jackson.

In the twentieth century American faith in progress and the perfectibility of man has been tempered by realistic psychology and unpleasant economics. But deep inside himself, the modern American still feels the optimism which animated the nineteenth-century reformer. His self-confidence may be reduced, but there are still very few Americans in the mid-twentieth century who are not convinced that the United States is the model for the world. There may be almost continuous crises in the perilous world of today, but the old optimism, the familiar belief in a better tomorrow, Americans have not lost.

Indeed, so confident have Americans been regarding the future that they have willingly borne a mission in the world. The Puritan who said God "sifted a whole nation that he might send choice grain over to this Wilderness" was convinced of it. The leaders of the Revolution were sure it would mark a turning point in the history of free men. By the Age of Jackson, Americans were convinced that their country was the model for the world. "The old and motheaten systems of Europe have had their day," wrote Walt Whitman in the Brooklyn *Eagle. "Here* we have planted the standard of freedom, and here we will test the capacities of men for self-government." Even normally hardheaded John C. Calhoun subscribed to the proposition that America was unique. "We are charged by Providence," he declared, "not only with the happiness of this great people, but . . . with that of the human race." If the American experiment should succeed, he continued, "it will be the commencement of a new era in human affairs. All civilized governments must in the course of time conform to this principle." Herman Melville summed up the attitude when he said Americans are "the peculiar chosen people, the Israel of our time."

Central to American belief in progress was the conviction that through the door of education the better world would be reached. To Americans of the first half of the nineteenth century, education was the key to everything: to a successful democracy, to progress, and to individual enrichment. Education, said the educator Horace Mann, is "the great equalizer of men. . . . It does better than to disarm the poor of their hostility towards the rich, it prevents being poor." "Free schools," an Ohio educator wrote in 1822, "lessen the distinction, which fortune makes, between the children of the rich and the poor. . . ." But important as educational reform seemed then, to modern Americans the significance of those years lies in the fact that it was then that the essential outline of the present school system in America took shape.

As enterprising Europeans who emigrated to a new and empty land, Americans have always been intensely concerned about the transmission of their values to their children. The Puritans of the seventeenth century, as we have seen, made a significant educational innovation with their town-supported schools; the eighteenth century also contributed its bit to the modern educational pattern in America by the proliferation of collegiate institutions of learning. But during the latter portion of the eighteenth and first decades of the nineteenth centuries, the enunciation of a strong belief in the value of education far exceeded the performance. Schools were permitted to decline for lack of funds and repairs; little effort was even made to insure that children would receive the rudiments of reading and writing; nothing was done to secure qualified teachers or even to provide adequate training schools for their recruitment, though the number of children was mounting.

One of the first fruits of the reforming spirit of the 1830's and 1840's was the gradual but decisive reversal of this failure to live up to the widespread belief in public education. Led by men like Horace Mann, Henry Barnard, and Calvin Wiley, a movement for the improvement of the public schools spread across the country. By the time of the Civil War the movement succeeded in building in the North, at least, a school system which was free and open to all white children.

The essential elements of the educational structure and philosophy of today were worked out by 1860, though not, of course, practiced everywhere in the nation. Schools were to be supported by public funds and all members of the community were required to send their children to them or to some alternative school. To insure uniformity in the quality of instruction, the schools were to be placed under the supervision of a state authority. As a further safeguard for the quality of education, the state was to provide special, advanced schools—often called normal schools after the French institutions—for the training of teachers. Finally, in view of the diversity of religions and nationalities in America, instruction in the public schools would be secular and dedicated to the training of loyal citizens.

Free schools of some type always existed in all sections of the nation, not only in Puritan New England. In the nineteenth century, for example, there were a number of schools which, because of an endowment of one sort or another, were able to accept students without charge, or at least were in a position to offer instruction to children unable to pay. Rhode Island, New York, and some of the southern states for a while even supported free schools by lotteries. Some of the nation's large cities, like Boston and Charleston, boasted very good tax-supported schools. But in the days of Horace Mann, in the 1830's and 1840's, there were few systems of genuinely free public schools. The most common form of public education at that time was the so-called rate school. This was a school ostensibly supported by public funds—usually some kind of endowment—but these funds were heavily supplemented by the levy of rates or taxes upon the parents of the children who attended. Actually, of course, this was no more a free public system of education than the lottery-supported schools or the charity schools; it was neither free nor universal nor a system. "We want a COMMON and EQUAL education—also PUBLIC because it is of general concern," cried one Jacksonian radical newspaper in 1835. "It belongs to the public interest. As rational beings, it is in the INTEREST OF ALL, that ALL should be equally well educated." Because of the rate system's haphazard arrangement and support, reformers interested in a system of truly free schools worked vigorously to eliminate it.

It was not until the fifties, however, that the rate system began to be replaced by the free public school as we know it today—that is, open to all and supported by all. Massachusetts instituted its system as early as 1827, Vermont came along in 1850, Ohio followed two years later, Iowa in 1858, Rhode Island in 1868, Michigan and New Jersey in 1870, Indiana in 1871; the southern states achieved state-wide free schooling during Reconstruction.

The first step toward permanently secularizing the public schools was taken in New Jersey in 1844, when it was provided in the constitution that no school funds could be diverted to private educational institutions. This marked the beginning of the end of attempts to include religious instruction of any kind in public schools. Essentially, the movement to so secularize the schools stemmed from the recognition that Catholics would no more accept even the watered-down Protestantism that pervaded instruction in the public schools than Protestants would agree to the use of public funds to support Catholic education. By the end of the nineteenth century virtually all of the states included in their constitutions clauses that prohibited the expenditure of school funds on private religious education.

The common school was conceived as a device for welding a diversity of peoples into a single nation. Throughout most of American history it performed its task well, even when subjected to the strain of millions of newcomers during the heyday of immigration prior to the 1920's. The inculcation of patriotism and civic-mindedness in the young has been the function of the public school more than of any other social institution in the United States. Indeed, so successful has the common school been, that today Americans look to education for the ultimate, if not the immediate solution to their social problems. Individuals expect the schools to assure them of an improving livelihood, while society as a whole expects the schools to solve difficult and recalcitrant problems like segregation and racism. Indeed, the heated and sometimes violent conflicts over the nature and purpose of schools, which have punctuated the life of many American communities in the last few years, must be viewed as a measure of the exaggerated value Americans attach to education and the common school.

Once the basic structure of the elementary school was hammered out, the remainder of the modern educational system, in the course of time, followed as an extension of first principles. The first tax-supported high school, the English Classical School of Boston, was established in 1821; New York opened its first public high school in 1825. By 1860, some 320 high schools were in existence, of which 167, or over half, were located in the three states of New York, Massachusetts, and Ohio. Although the tuition academy dominated secondary education until well into the post-Civil War decades, the principle of free education for all would ultimately overtake secondary education as it had the grammar school. Moreover, in time, tuition-less college education, led by the City College of New York and the state universities, would place a crown upon the whole system. The Morrill Land Grant Act of 1862, which provided for federal land grants to each of the states for the founding or expansion of agricultural colleges, is one of the principal encouragements to popular higher education in the United States. Almost 70 colleges have been established under the provisions of the act.

For the world, as for America, the struggle for the truly public school in the Age of Jackson had important consequences. Though not all countries have necessarily accepted all our procedures, if they are democratic in philosophy they have accepted our assumptions. Most democratic nations have recognized, as Americans in the 1830's and 1840's made clear, that if the people are to take part in their own governance, then they must have access to the schools. And, for this to be true, the Americans of the early nineteenth century pointed out, the providing of schools must be recognized as a responsibility of society as a whole. It is in this sense that we can talk of the public school as a legacy from the Age of the Great Experiment.

Although the objects of reform were numerous in this era of ferment, there was one which swallowed up all the rest. Ever since the early 1830's the issue of slavery had figured with increasing prominence in the talk and politics of Americans. By the decade of the 1850's it lay like a weight on the minds and consciences of almost all Americans. As an issue it proved itself capable of rending churches, disrupting an ancient political party, turning the floor of Congress into a parody of deliberative debate, and igniting civil war on the plains of Kansas. Slavery, it is clear, was not just another object for reform. It was the greatest moral and social issue confronting Americans in the Age of the Great Experiment, for it divided the people as nothing else ever has. Its impact on American society then and for the future was at once devastating and enduring.

CHAPTER VI

The American Tragedy

WHEN Louis Kossuth, the Hungarian revolutionary, came to America in 1851, he was only one of many visiting Europeans who believed that America was "unequaled in general intelligence and in general prosperity," and "a glorious evidence of mankind's capacity to self-government. . . ." Some Europeans, however, could not fail to notice the fact of human slavery, which, as one English newspaper phrased it in 1845, "is a canker in the root of the seemingly fair and flourishing plant . . . and threatens to make the great republic of modern times a warning instead of an example to the world at large." The United States, John Stuart Mill tartly remarked, is a "country where institutions profess to be founded on equality, and which yet maintains the slavery of black men. . . ."

Simply because slavery was in truth a denial of American equalitarian pretensions, it increasingly dominated the affairs of the Republic. And even as it dominated the thinking of men, it was shaping Americans, both black and white, for a long time to come.

1. THE PECULIAR INSTITUTION

Slavery was an inheritance from the colonial period, and one common to all the states of the new Republic. In the course of the late eighteenth and early nineteenth centuries, however, several of the northern states found the institution at once repugnant to their conception of liberty and of little import in their economic life. Under such a combination of blights, slavery withered and died in a number of states before 1800; and in those states in the North where it did not, it was clearly on the road to extinction. Happily enough, farther south there was some promise of the same result if sufficient time

160

were allowed. Southern leaders of the Revolution like Washington, Madison, Jefferson, and Patrick Henry frankly looked forward to the day when slavery would be gone completely from the Republic, though they usually meant that they wanted the Negro to go, along with slavery.

The prospects for such a future were propitious in the latter part of the eighteenth century, inasmuch as tobacco, the staple of the slave-manned plantations of the South, was becoming an increasingly unprofitable crop. Should the economic and libertarian forces of the period pull in the same direction long enough, it was felt by many and hoped by even more, the anomaly of slavery among a people who believed that "all men are created equal" would soon cease to exist.

But toward the very end of the eighteenth century, two historical developments combined to infuse a new vigor into American slavery. The first and most important of these was the mechanization of English manufacturing, or the Industrial Revolution. Among the earliest industries to respond to mechanization was cotton textile manufacturing, with the immediate consequence of a precipitous increase in the demand for raw cotton, which in turn drove the price to very high levels. Prior to the Revolution no cotton of measurable quantities had been grown on the American mainland, though the West Indies had long exported the snowy "wool." The new rise in cotton prices, however, offered great incentive for the American production of the fiber. States like Georgia and South Carolina found that long-fiber cotton, which was readily separated from the seed, could be grown along their littorals and coastal islands. But efforts to expand cultivation of this sea-island cotton to the interior lands failed. The only cotton which would grow successfully on the uplands was a type in which the fiber tenaciously adhered to the seed, a fact which rendered its separation a tedious and expensive process even with slave labor.

With such economic incentive for ingenuity, it was inevitable that soon some device would be invented which would quickly and cheaply separate the short-fiber cotton from its seed. The inventor and the invention arrived in 1793 in the form of Eli Whitney and his gin. Immediately recognized as the answer to the ambitious planters' prayers, the gin and the unflagging English demand for cotton provided the necessary encouragement for the development of the Cotton Kingdom on the lands of western Georgia and South Carolina and in the new lands to the west. Intent upon reaping their profits as quickly as possible, the planters turned to the plantation and the Negro slave as the most expeditious means of production. Slavery was reborn, soon to flourish as never before.

By as early as the 1820's and the 1830's slavery was firmly established in the economy of the South. Even southern states like Kentucky, Virginia, North Carolina, and Missouri, which grew little or no cotton, gained a new economic interest in slavery from the fact that they found a ready market for their excess slaves in the rapidly expanding cotton states to the south. Moreover, these upper southern states continued to use Negro slave labor on their tobacco and hemp plantations.

At the same time in the North, however, slavery had either ceased to exist or was well on the way to legal extinction. This parting of the ways between the two sections of the country was freighted with ominous significance for the South and for the future of the Republic.

Though cotton cultivation certainly brought new life to the failing institution of slavery, this is not to say that the southern people thereby became a nation of slaveholders. In fact, despite the tons of paper and myriad hours of oratory expended on the slavery question in the ante-bellum years, the slaveholder was far from being the typical Southerner. The great majority of the southern white people held no slaves at all and therefore had no direct interest in or even connection with the institution. Out of a total of some 1.6 million white families in the South in 1860, only 384,000 owned the four million slaves. And even those who held slaves did not possess them in the number legendarily associated with the Old South of magnolias and white-pillared mansions. In 1860, 20 per cent of the slaveholders owned only a single Negro; fully two thirds of them possessed fewer than twenty slaves each. Over 99 per cent of the slaveowners held 100 or fewer slaves. The possession of 500 or more slaves, according to the Census of 1860, was indeed a rarity, since only fourteen "millionaires" enjoyed that distinction in all of the South.

Such census statistics should destroy any lingering illusion that the planter and his hundreds of slaves were typical or even commonplace figures in Dixie. Indeed, the Southerner with any slaves at all, let alone hundreds, was in the distinct minority, a curiosity amid the millions of plain people who owned no slaves at all and who, perhaps, rarely saw one. Statistically, the small yeoman farmer, working his land unassisted by the labor of black men, was the typical white Southerner in the ante-bellum era.

Furthermore, as the figures on slaveholding imply, the plantation itself was not typical either; small individually operated farms far exceeded plantations in number. In 1850, for example, the census reported 568,000 agricultural units in the South, of which only 101,-335, or 18 per cent of the total, could be classified as plantations—that is, a unit producing marketable quantities of one or more of the five basic staples of cotton, tobacco, sugar, rice, or hemp. If another definition of plantation is used, such as U. B. Phillips', of a farm with twenty or more slaves, then the proportion of plantations to farms shrinks still further, to less than one in ten.

But such figures on slaveholding and plantations, though often cited to demonstrate the relative unimportance of slavery in the ante-bellum South, are quite misleading if one seeks to measure the economic significance of slavery.[1] It was the function in the economy performed by Negro slave labor which gave slavery its crucial place in the life of the South. For though it is true that slaves made up a minority of the labor force, and their typical habitat, the plantation, comprised a very small proportion of the region's agricultural units, the slaves on the plantations produced the bulk of the section's marketable surplus, for, by definition, the plantation was a producer of surplus.

It was from the plantations that the exports came which paid for the South's imports from the shops, factories, and warehouses of Europe; the labor of slaves provided the wherewithal to maintain lawyers and actors, cotton factors and publishers, musicians in Charleston, Senators in Washington, and gamblers on the Mississippi River boats. In short, it was slavery which maintained, as the South realized, the culture and civilization of the region. Furthermore, the majority of the planters, agrarian and status-minded as they delighted in portraying themselves, were actually adventurously, and often ruthlessly, bent on profit and reinvestment. That is, they were agricultural entrepreneurs in a capitalist society; their central importance as a class resided not in their numbers, which was admittedly small, but in their ability to accumulate surplus for investment.

---

[1] As L. C. Gray has pointed out, the census figures can be expressed in such a way as to give quite a different picture of the incidence of slavery in the South. One out of every two persons in the southern population of 14 million was either a slave or a member of a slaveholding family.

Moreover, to focus attention, as some historians have done, on the large number of slaveowners who held only a few Negroes is to obscure the more significant fact that the majority of the slaves were held in units of a size well adapted to surplus-producing plantations. In 1860, according to the calculation of L. C. Gray, 53 per cent of the slaves in the South were held in parcels of twenty or more. If ten is taken as a good working unit for staple production, as it might well be, then three quarters of the slaves fell into this grouping. As a labor force, then, the slaves, though fewer than the working white farmers, were much more important in the economy because black labor, unlike white, was heavily concentrated in the surplus-producing sector. In substance, whether considered as capital or as labor, the slave regime was central to the southern economy.

Implicit in what has been said up to now about the importance of slavery in the economy has been the assumption that it was profitable. Because the profitability of the plantation regime has been frequently questioned, more extended comment is in order here.

Unfortunately, in discussing this question commentators and historians have not always been clear as to what they are proving. Though ostensibly showing the unprofitability of slavery, they often merely show that it is less efficient than a hypothetically free labor system. Charles Sydnor, for example, an astute modern historian who questioned the profitability of slavery, was actually doing nothing more than arguing that it was less efficient than free labor. Frederick Olmsted, the well-known northern traveler in the ante-bellum South, was guilty of the same error in his discussions of the profits derived from bound Negro labor.

In actuality, the question of the comparative costs of slave and free labor was and is an academic one, since the issue never really threatened the South's peculiar institution. Furthermore, a labor system is so tightly enmeshed in the web of custom and habit that it is rarely, if ever, overthrown by abstract comparison with another system's profits. Especially is this true when the labor system is actually producing profits.

There are several good general reasons for believing that, for the South as a whole, the slave regime was a profitable one during the decades immediately before the War.[2] According to the computations

---

[2] Specific examples of profit rates do not answer the question because we have too few of them to establish their representativeness, but they do illustrate

of Thomas Govan, for instance, the value of real and personal estate in the southern states between 1850 and 1860 jumped from $2.8 billion to $6.2 billion—an increment of over 100 per cent. It is difficult to believe that such economic growth could have taken place if slavery were unprofitable. Moreover, the ease with which the South, as compared with the other two sections, hurdled the Panic of 1857 suggests a sound and prosperous economy rather than one struggling to make ends meet.

The rising price curve for slaves—often erroneously cited as a reason why slavery would cease to show profits—is actually another proof that the South enjoyed an expanding rather than a stagnant or contracting economy. Under a slave system, as in a unionless free economy, a rising price for labor (wages in a free society) is an indication that enterprise is expanding at such a rate that the supply of labor is inadequate. The planter on old and wornout lands, it is true, may have found a rising price curve in slaves a brake upon his acquisitions of labor. But for the planter on new land, who, after all, was bidding up the price, the slave was well worth it; only with the Negro's labor could the planter reap the maximum advantage from the good cotton prices. Besides, even if the price of slaves climbed too high, demand would then fall off and the price would drop to accommodate itself to the shrunken demand.[3] In short, slavery would

the level of return on some plantations. James K. Polk's Mississippi plantation, according to John Bassett's examination, yielded annual profits ranging from 14 to 25 per cent. Elizafield, a Georgia rice plantation, produced enough wealth for its owner to add $10,000 in real estate value and $13,000 in personal property, including slaves, in the years between 1850 and 1860. Thomas Govan has carefully calculated, from records extending over periods of from four to eleven years during the 1840's and 1850's, that three plantations, two in Georgia and one in South Carolina, earned average annual profits of 3.7 per cent (after a managerial salary of $5,000 had been deducted), 6.6 per cent, and 12 per cent, respectively.

[3] It is often argued that slavery "froze" the South's capital in labor and thereby prevented the growth of manufacturing in that region. Whatever strictures may be laid against slavery as an economic situation, this is not one of them. The argument that putting capital into slaves rendered it unavailable for investment in manufacturing confuses the capital of the individual slaveholder with that of the section. It is true that by investing his profits in additional slaves, the planter had no excess for investment in manufacturing. But those who advance this argument forget that the southern slave trader, to whom the planter paid over his cash for the labor, was perfectly free to put the money into manufacturing, if he so desired. The failure of the ante-bellum South to develop manufacturing on a scale comparable with the contemporary

continue to produce profits for the economy as a whole. The fact that the prices for hiring slaves were also rising in the last decade of the ante-bellum period further supports the view that slavery was profitable. And since it was profitable, the contention that the Civil War was a needless war because slavery was on the way to extinction for lack of economic usefulness is more wishful thinking than hard fact.

But there was more to the South's defense of slavery than economics; there was also race. All the profits of all the plantations cannot explain the tenacity, the passion, with which the little people of the South—that majority of the people who held no slaves—rallied to the defense of the slave system, both before the war and in the armies of the Confederacy. Their stake in slavery is found in that institution's undoubted ability to prevent Negro domination and to provide psychological status where there was no other. For few Southerners hated the Negro so much as those whose economic position was almost indistinguishable from that of the slaves. Even non-slaveholders who happened to abhor the institution for moral or economic reasons were often silenced by slavery's undoubted ability to control the Negroes.

One such back-country farmer confessed his dilemma to Olmsted. "I wouldn't like to hev 'em free, if they gwine to hang around . . . because they is so monstrous lazy. . . . Now suppose they was free, you see they'd all think themselves just as good as we. . . ." Then came the fear of intermarriage: "How'd you like to hev a nigger steppin' up to your darter? Of course you wouldn't; and that's the reason I wouldn't like to hev 'em free; but I tell you, I don't think it's right to hev 'em slaves so; that's the fac—taant right to keep 'em as they is."

In 1860 Andrew Johnson, acknowledged spokesman for the South's little people against the pretensions of the slaveocracy, promised on the floor of Congress that in the defense of slavery all white men would be united. "When there was agitation in Tennessee, in 1856," he recalled, "I saw that the non-slaveholder was the readiest man to rise up and join the master in extirpating, if necessary, this race from existence, rather than see them liberated and turned loose upon the country."

North is therefore not traceable, in any direct sense, to the prevalence of slavery. Rather it would seem to be bound up with the general profitability of agriculture and the outlook of an agriculturally oriented people and society.

When all is said and done, then, profits and fear of the black man offer the most succinct explanation as to why the South, in the full glare of nineteenth-century humanitarianism, hugged to its bosom the moral and economic anachronism of slavery.

2. ALL SLAVES ARE BLACK

In the minds of many modern white Americans, the Negro is pictured as a man who was once a slave and one, moreover, who was essentially content in that status. This reading of the past has more than academic import, for, intended or not, it partly determined the subordinate status assigned the Negro in modern American culture. Other races, it is said, would not and could not have remained content in so degraded a status. But the Negro, the argument goes, is truly inferior simply because he has proved to be so adaptable to an inferior status.

There are a number of arguments which have been advanced to establish the essential contentment of the Negro in slavery, but perhaps the most persuasive is the fact that during the war, when the men were away from the plantations, there were very few slave revolts in the South. Indeed, all through the history of slavery, it can be added, the number of slave revolts was remarkably small. True, over two hundred revolts have been uncovered by diligent research, but even that number is insignificant when it is recalled that they spread out to something like two a year in an area the size of western Europe and among a servile population of two to four millions. Furthermore, many of these revolts were nothing more than temporary labor stoppages under a system which did not provide a means whereby dissatisfaction with immediate working conditions could be registered.

Furthermore, even the most celebrated instrument of protest, the Underground Railroad, heroic as its "conductors" and "passengers" were, tells us little about the attitude of the majority of the slaves. At most, according to the Road's sympathetic historian, an average of 2,000 slaves escaped annually between 1830 and 1860; compared with the millions held in bondage, these runaways are numerically and economically inconsequential.

In the same way, the sporadic suicides, self-mutilations by a sensitive slave, or the murder of a baby by a slave mother may illustrate the extremes to which some were driven by slavery, but they afford us little insight into the feelings of the many. Most unsatisfactory in shedding light on the Negro's conception of slavery are the reminiscences of the slaves themselves. Taken down long after freedom was attained, suffused with the romantic haze of years, or written by militant Negro abolitionists, they merely inform us of the variety of reactions to the system, but tell us little of the response of the slaves in general.

Actually, the arguments summarized above and rejected as inadequate reveal more about those who advanced them than about the attitude of the Negroes toward bondage. In looking for militant opposition to slavery, historians, northern and southern alike, have viewed slavery through their own stereotypes. Both used the same test for the Negroes' reaction to slavery—militant revolt. When the rebellions did not occur in the profusion expected, the liberal historian exaggerated those he did find; the Southerner, on the other hand, concluded that the Negro was content in slavery. But because the criterion of revolts was unrealistic from the outset, it revealed little about the Negro's attitude toward his status.

Widespread revolts were just not to be expected under the conditions of southern slavery. Psychological and physical obstacles to revolt were virtually insuperable. For example, the inevitable human element in slavery—the paternalistic, reciprocal relationship obtaining between many masters and their slaves—created bonds which greatly reduced the possibilities of successful or widespread revolt. E. F. Frazier, the Negro sociologist, for example, has observed that in many abortive conspiracies it was the faithful house slave who, to save his master, gave away the plot. Furthermore, the very rural, often frontier character of the South rendered any large-scale, organized revolt almost an impossibility, though individual, localized revolts could and did take place.

Those very areas, moreover, most susceptible to antislavery influences from the North—the border states—were also the localities where the treatment of the slave was traditionally most humane and consonant with the reciprocal loyalties of a big family. In such areas pressure for revolt was relatively weak, and distaste for violence against a good master was greatest. Moreover, it was in these same border states that the Underground Railroad was most active—a fact which meant, perforce, that the most aggressive and capable leaders were drawn off, leaving the least capable to cope with the formidable obstacles to organized revolt.

Finally, slavery must have seemed to many Negroes raised within its confines a part of the natural order, with which they might not be satisfied, but toward which they were incapable of militant and aggressive opposition because of their long acculturation.

But revolts are not the only criteria which can be used for the detection of dissatisfaction with slavery. Any standards which are used, though, must take into consideration the limitations which slavery imposed on the Negroes' ability and opportunities to express discontent. Once we cease to look for revolts as the major test of dissatisfaction under slavery, then we can find important evidence of widespread discontent.

The slave songs, for example, as the expression of a whole people, reveal much about the inner reactions of the Negroes to their lot. Rarely can a song of real exaltation be found; but the words of discouragement, dissatisfaction, and melancholy appear in profusion: "Nobody knows de trouble I've had"; "Why don't you give up de world?"; "My Father, how long?"; "We'll soon be free, de Lord will call us home." Sometimes the songs made direct reference to the burdens and anxieties of slavery, as in "O run, nigger, run, for the patrol will catch you"; "[Plantation] Bell da ring"; "Go in the wilderness"; then, finally, there are the many songs which bemoan the separation from loved ones—certainly a reflection of the realities of slavery.

Additional evidence that the Negroes were generally discontented with slavery is found in the fact that they escaped when a real opportunity to do so was presented to them. During the war, thousands of slaves deserted the plantations as the federal troops approached, seeking refuge and freedom within the Union lines. Moreover, over 185,-000 Negroes, most of whom were former slaves, voluntarily joined the Union Army to make war on the slave South.

Another indication of the widespread discontent under slavery is the superstitious reverence and awe in which the Negroes held the name of their emancipator. This sentiment was prevalent among former slaves even before Lincoln suffered his martyr's death and while they still had not tasted much of the sweets of freedom. It might also be added that southern slaveholders themselves testified to the Negro's desire for freedom when they acknowledged that manumission was the greatest boon a master could bestow upon a faithful Negro.

When these signs of pervasive discontent are taken together with the sporadic revolts, the conspiracies, the runaways, and the individual acts of defiance, a pattern of mass dissatisfaction with slavery is the inescapable conclusion. Contrary to the apologetics of southern slavery and modern myths, the Negro was no more a natural slave than other men.

In an earlier chapter we have already seen that the close association between the stigma of slavery and the Negro began early in the history of American society. The reinvigoration of slavery during the nineteenth century rendered that original attachment even more close. The most obvious measure of the stigma that had been fastened upon the Negro race by the middle of the nineteenth century was the legal status of the southern free Negro, of whom there were about 250,000 in 1860.[4]

The freedom of Negroes was entirely dependent upon their ability to maintain it; all men of black or brown skin in the South were presumed to be slaves unless their freedom papers or custom could prove the contrary. With zealous slave catchers not always careful to notice the limits of their authority, the tendency of the law was strongly in the direction of slavery. Indeed, sometimes the special criminal law for free Negroes created avenues for a return to bondage, as in Maryland, where punishment for first offenders included sale outside the state for a term of years—and some so punished apparently never returned to freedom.

But even if the blacks could prove their freedom, the quality of their liberty was strained. They could not travel in the same cars, live in the same hotels, or attend the same churches as whites; in some states, like North Carolina, they were excluded from the slaves' church meetings as well. Economically their job opportunities were limited by law and custom; and though political opportunities and privileges were denied them, they were taxed the same as whites, where additional taxes were not levied upon them.[5]

[4] There were also about a quarter of a million free Negroes in the North in 1860. There they were subjected to as severe social discrimination as in the South, but legal discrimination was much milder.

[5] Despite such restrictions on their economic opportunities, free Negroes in the South, particularly in cities like Charleston and New Orleans, owned considerable amounts of property. Estimates of the property run to several millions of dollars, including, in some cases, ownership of Negro slaves. The life of one free Negro, that of William Johnson of Natchez, has been documented by the publication of his diary in 1951, edited by W. R. Hogan and E. A. Davis. Johnson was born a slave in 1809, was emancipated in 1820, and soon became a respectable barber for whites. His business flourished in Natchez, where he employed several other free Negroes in his barber shop and earned

In a society justifying slavery as the proper status for the Negro race, there was little place for the free Negro; he was a pariah. As the defense of slavery in terms of race mounted through the 1850's, southern legislation increasingly reflected this view in a most literal fashion. In most states of Dixie, for instance, all newly manumitted Negroes were required to leave the state, an additional price thus being exacted from them for their liberty. Tennessee, Texas, Louisiana, and Maryland, in the last years of the slave era, enacted legislation designed to facilitate the enslavement of these anomalous persons. Arkansas actually passed legislation in 1859 to compel the emigration, on pain of enslavement, of all free Negroes in the state.

Unless he accepted the protection of slavery, the southern free person of color was visited with all the responsibilities of freedom and precious few of its privileges and immunities. Is it any wonder, then, that free Negro William Bass petitioned in 1859 for permission to submit to a master? His position as free Negro, he wrote, "is more degrading, and involves more suffering in this State, than that of a slave, who is under the care, protection and ownership of a kind and good master." As a free person of color, he continued, he "is preyed upon by every sharper," has little money, though able-bodied and capable of working. Moreover, he "is charged and punished for, every offense," whether guilty or not, "committed in the neighborhood."

For all his inferior position, however, the free Negro was feared in the South, for he always stood as a potential nucleus around which servile insurrection might organize. It was for this reason that the southern states in the 1840's and 1850's increased the obstacles to manumission, often to the point of prohibition. Some states, as we have seen, endeavored to hound them out of the community completely. South Carolina and five other southern states decreed, in their unassuageable anxiety, that free Negroes who came into port as ships' crew members had to spend the time of their sojourn in jail.

But the enduring impress of slavery was most deeply felt by the Negro who was a slave, and in 1860 over four million of the 4.3 million Negroes who lived in the South were held in bondage. To all

---

enough to lend money and invest in local enterprises. He often employed white men on his farm and even owned several Negro slaves. He was murdered in 1851 by a white man, who could not be convicted, though three trials were held, because the only witnesses to the slaying were Negroes—and they could not testify against a white man. At his death, Johnson was worth at least $25,000.

intents and purposes, therefore, the image in which the Negro beheld himself, and in which white men beheld him, was largely determined by his actual status under slavery.

Unlike the Indian who was enslaved, the Negro entered American slavery stripped of his native culture. Even anthropologists like Melville Herskovits, who maintain that some African cultural traits survived in America, cannot list more than a handful of minor customs of speech and dress to buttress their case. The culture of the Negroes was inevitably limited to that which slavery provided and which a slave status permitted them to absorb from the white men with whom they lived and worked.

The Negro's very demeanor and family pattern were conditioned by slavery. Under the duress of the whip he learned the need for deferential behavior; recognized that he must present a happy visage to his master, and that to appear too smart or too ready around white folks was dangerous. Married with a ceremony which pointedly omitted any perpetual vows, since all unions were dissolvable upon the sale of one of the partners, Negroes were conditioned to look upon marriage as a fiction which carried little meaning beyond the salving of the white man's conscience. One slave preacher, for instance, married couples "until death or *distance* do you part." Indeed, the slave family not only possessed very little spiritual or legal cohesion; it lacked even an economic bond. The master, after all, not the father, was responsible for the support of the wife and children. Under such circumstances it is remarkable that there was as much unity in the slave family as there was.

Habits of work, responsibility, and self-respect were geared to a low standard by slavery. Compelled to work, though deriving very little direct benefit from it, and exercising little responsibility in it, the slave easily became shiftless, careless, and irresponsible. Because many masters feared that if their slaves learned a skilled trade they would become "uppity" and hard to handle, the Negro was usually discouraged from improving himself. One Charlestonian, for example, spoke of the "baneful effects" of hiring out slaves because it produced in them an unwillingness "to return to the regular life and domestic control of the master." Laws in most of the southern states prohibited the teaching of reading and writing to slaves; and though some planters did not obey the law, there were many who did not need it to remind them that even a partly educated slave could be at least difficult and at most dangerous. In the clearer air of the eighteenth century, Southerner Thomas Jefferson recognized the moral crippling which slavery inflicted upon the Negro. "That disposition to theft," he wrote, with which they "have been branded must be ascribed to their situation, and not to any depravity of their moral sense."

Perhaps the most enduring monument to slavery and its effects upon the Negro was the elaboration of the doctrine of Negro inferiority. As we have seen, this belief began as early as the seventeenth century; but during the last decade of the ante-bellum period, the doctrine was dressed up in pseudoscientific garb and elevated to the position of a principal argument in justification of a labor system the world's morality had outgrown. "The Negro races stand at the lowest point in the scale of human beings, and we know no moral or physical agencies which can redeem them from their degradation," wrote Dr. J. C. Nott, the South's leading ethnologist in the 1850's. "It is clear," he concluded, "that they are incapable of self-government, and that any attempt to improve their condition is warring against an immutable law of nature." Slavery's boldest and learned apologist, publicist J. D. B. De Bow, contended that the physical differences between Negro and Caucasian rendered them morally and politically different. The "physical differences between the two races," he wrote, are so great "as to make what is wholesome and beneficial for the white man, as liberty, republican and free institutions, etc., not only unsuitable to the Negro race, but actually poisonous to its happiness."

The disabilities which slavery imposed on the Negro made proof of the black man's inferiority deceptively easy. As a slave the Negro was trained to be an inferior; then this very inferiority was used to support the argument that he was incapable of improvement. Only an occasional example of a successful free Negro could refute this circular reasoning, but such evidence was so limited that it could easily be dismissed as exceptional. In modern America, with its continuing discrimination against the Negro, a variety of this vicious circle persists, still confusing the thinking of white Americans on the nature and potentialities of the black man.

3. BUT ALL WHITE MEN ARE NOT FREE

Though unquestionably the Negroes felt the impress of slavery more profoundly than any other Southerners, the whites of the region were also touched by an institution which was central to their way of life. This was true despite the fact that the bulk of the white people had no immediate connection with the "peculiar institution."

By far the largest class of white men were yeoman farmers, of whom perhaps as many as 80 per cent, according to Frank Owsley, owned their own land—a happy situation not duplicated in the twentieth-century South. Generally prospering in the expanding southern economy of the fifties, the common man of that section was quite remote from the conventional poor white conjured up by the fertile imagination of the abolitionists of that day or dwelt upon by the southern "realists" of our own.

But with all due respect to these independent, hard-working, God-fearing farmers of the Old South, their numerical superiority does not overbalance the influence exerted by the slaveholding class. Through the possession of black labor, the small class of slaveowners actually dominated the economic, political, and intellectual institutions of the whole white South. And by virtue of this fact the South's civilization was increasingly shaped to fit the needs of the slave system.

In the fundamental matter of land distribution, for example, the owners of slaves tended to command the richest soil areas—a situation which was at once an explanation and a consequence of their prominent position in the Old South. It is true, as some southern historians have made clear, that the elbowing out of the yeoman by the slaveholder was not absolute, for these historians have shown that the two classes often held adjacent farms. But the contention that the slaveholders and nonslaveholders generally held lands of equal quality is hard to accept in the face of other evidence. It has been shown, for example, that on 300 selected holdings in Alabama and Mississippi, the cash value of the land per acre increased as the size of the holding. Thus in farms of one to fifty acres, the value per acre was $7.20; but in farms of 501 to 1,000 acres the value was $19.81 per acre, over twice as much. Furthermore, on a broader scale, as is well known, areas of the South having a high concentration of slaves coincided remarkably well with the richest land areas, e.g., along the Mississippi River Delta and in the so-called black belts stretching across central Georgia and Alabama.

The superior position of the slaveholder consisted of more than his having the best land; his class were more often landholders than were the nonslaveholders. In 1860 in the Georgia black belt, for instance, 92 per cent of the slaveowners were also owners of land, but only 58 per cent of the nonslaveholders were. Even in eastern Tennessee, generally thought to be the stronghold of the nonslaveholders, 92 per cent of the holders of slaves owned land, while only 55 per cent of the slaveless farmers were so fortunate. About the same proportions for the two classes obtained in the cotton-growing western part of the state. As a matter of fact, these proportions of land distribution among slaveholders and nonslaveholders held generally for all the states studied by Frank Owsley and his students at Vanderbilt University. It seems clear, therefore, that the great bulk of the landless folk in the South were nonslaveholders.

Such a distribution of the land further emphasizes what was obvious to the travelers and commentators of the period, namely, that to rise in southern ante-bellum society one needed slaves; the source and measure of wealth in this highly commercialized agriculture were not merely acres, but land worked by Negroes. In this situation lies the weakness of considering the plain folk the backbone of the antebellum South, as the historians of the Vanderbilt school are wont to do. Significance in a capitalistic economy, as we have observed before, is measured by wealth accumulation, not by numbers of persons.

Even southern white men remote from the plantation, like urban wage laborers, felt the effects of slavery. Negro bondage, for instance, must bear a good share of the responsibility for the fact that labor organization in the South lagged behind that in the North. In the South, "the courts were openly antagonistic to striking workers," Richard Morris has written, because many southern officials believed "that strike action, like anti-slavery agitation, was an attack on their 'peculiar' institution." And where official attitudes played no part, the success of a strike was always threatened by the omnipresent possibility that slaves could be hired to break it as happened at the Tredegar Iron Works at Richmond in 1847.

In still other ways, nonslaveholders were involved in the protection of slavery. It was the yeomen who held no slaves who were expected to make up the slave patrols which acted as the rural police of the slave society. Furthermore, the law prescribed severe penalties for any white Southerner who seemed to threaten the slave system. Heavy fines awaited the man who traded with slaves or taught them to read or write. In several states a white man was liable to capital punishment if he encouraged or aided a slave to escape. All the southern states declared it a felony to write or say anything which directly or indirectly might lead to rebellion or discontent among the Negroes. Even fraternization between a white man and another man's slave could catch the former in the tangles of the law.

Finally, it should not be forgotten that because the defense of slavery required Negroes to be incompetents in the law, justice sometimes miscarried. For example, when Professor George Whyte of William and Mary was poisoned by his nephew, the culprit could not be convicted because the principal witness against him was a Negro, legally incapable of testifying against a white man.

Since the law was so solicitous of the peculiar institution, it comes as no surprise that slaveholders dominated the political life of the South. This is not to say, it should be quickly added, that the South was ruled by a hereditary aristocracy or anything like it. That is no more than a hoary legend which ignores the many leaders of the region, like Alexander Stephens, Albert Gallatin Brown, Andrew Johnson, and Joseph Brown, who came from the very bottom of southern society. Indeed, the bulk of the Cotton Grandees of the late antebellum South were self-made men rather than sons of wealthy planters or aristocrats.

But regardless of their social and economic origins, the slaveholders dominated the political leadership of the South, especially on the national stage. Because slavery was wealth and because slavery was race, the peculiar institution lay at the core of southern politics, determining issues and influencing men in relation to itself, just as it ran like a dark thread through the fabric of the economy. Whereas in the 1830's and 1840's the South enjoyed two major political parties, by the middle of the fifties there was only one. The need to defend slavery at all costs destroyed the once powerful Whig party of the South. The great planters had long been more Whiggish than Democratic, but the tendency of northern Whigs to be antislavery by 1850 pushed more and more of the southern Whig planters into the once detested Democracy. At one time in the South—during the 1830's and 1840's—nonslaveholders and slaveholders had strongly disagreed over matters like the National Bank, the tariff, Andrew Jackson, and popular government, but the growing necessity to defend slavery finally overrode all these differences. In the name of racial solidarity, the issue of slavery covered over class antagonisms and gave a new, but false, unity to southern political thought. Ever since those days Southerners have been deprived of an adequate two-party system to express the diversity of their interests and political objectives.

Since the preservation of slavery was now the South's litmus test of acceptable politics, it was hardly to be expected that the frankly but mildly antislavery Republican party could receive a hearing in the Cotton Kingdom. And this despite the fact that the only anti-slavery principle of which the Republicans were guilty—opposition to the extension of slavery into the territories—was one in which most small southern farmers had no direct economic interest. So finely meshed was the political screening in the South in 1860 in behalf of slavery that Abraham Lincoln's name never appeared on a ballot in ten of the eleven states which were to make up the Confederacy. For millions of southern voters the compulsive defense of slavery and the fear of the Negro effectively restricted their choice of candidates as compared with that enjoyed by voters in the rest of the nation.

It should not be forgotten, however, that this political identification of the nonslaveholders with the interests of the slaveholders was freely undertaken, for it was carried out within the context of almost universal white manhood suffrage. To the majority of Southerners, the acquisition of slaves and the augmentation thereof were obviously a *summum bonum,* a recognized and desirable avenue of upward social movement. If the coin of economic and political advancement was slave ownership, few whites in the South thought the coinage base. But it was precisely this popular acceptance of slavery which made the institution the determinant of the contours of southern life.

If political freedom of choice was circumscribed by the demands of slavery, other fields of thought could not escape either. Already we have noticed that slavery saddled the southern people with a belief in the racial inferiority of Negroes which has persisted into our own time. Slavery also seemed to require the repudiation of one of the South's most precious gifts to America: the Jeffersonian, humanistic belief in the equality of all men.

In the waning years of the eighteenth century, the great Virginians had defended slavery only as an unwelcome inheritance from the past—necessary but evil. By the 1830's, the South was prepared to defend it as both necessary and good. "But let me not be understood as admitting," John C. Calhoun said in 1837, "even by implication, that the existing relations between the two races in the slaveholding States is an evil:—far otherwise: I hold it to be a good, as it has thus far proved itself to be to both and will continue to prove so if not disturbed by the fell spirit of abolition."

Caught in the contradiction between equality and slavery, the South chose slavery. Particularly was Jefferson's disquieting Declaration singled out for attack and scorn. "Is it not palpably nearer the truth to say," asked Chancellor Harper of South Carolina, "that no man was ever born free and that no two men were ever born equal, than to say that all men are born free and equal?" "It is as much in the order of nature," he further wrote, "that men should enslave each other, as that other animals should prey upon each other." For many Southerners the paradox of the Declaration of Independence and slavery was sufficiently embarrassing for them to want to forget it. After 1840, the Democratic party, out of deference to southern sensibilities, ceased to include the manifesto of its founder in its platform.

The suspicious profusion in which the defenses of inequality were advanced betrayed the moral conflict within the mind of the South. As early as the 1830's, Senator Pickens of South Carolina had conceded that "the truth is, the moral power of the world is against us. It is idle to disguise it." By mid-century the conflict of values had taken on excruciating sharpness. For by that time few nations of western European civilization still tolerated, much less defended, human slavery. It was true that semicivilized and reactionary Imperial Russia persisted in retaining serfdom, but that only further threw in embarrassing relief the anachronistic nature of American slavery.

During the forties and fifties, with the moral condemnation of slavery growing ever stronger outside the South, the demand for conformity and repression of dissent within the South became more frantic and insistent. Slowly the region was retreating into a pattern of life increasingly divergent from that of the rest of the nation. The South at one time had been the home of abolitionist societies, radical political clubs, and deistic thinkers, but now it was turning increasingly hostile to all thought which seemed to threaten the stability or survival of the slave system.

Reformers found an uncongenial atmosphere south of Mason and Dixon's line, because it was well known that reformers interested in temperance, women's rights, international peace, and so forth, frequently maintained close ties with abolitionists. Taking cognizance of these interconnections, one North Carolina editor boasted that the southern press "has uniformly rejected the isms which infest Europe and the Eastern and Western states of this country." Southern scientist Henry Ravenal urged the South to "shrink intuitively from all the novel and revolutionary notions which are infecting the masses of Europe and the free states of the North." Nor was it an accident that out of the 130 co-operative utopias established in the United States between 1800 and 1860, only two of them were in the South. The liberal fringes of religious life were snipped off too. By 1860 the Unitarian Church had all but disappeared from the South—a casualty, in large part, to the fact that most of its ministers were antislavery. "Scratch a reformer and you'll find an abolitionist" was the southern response to the intellectual and social ferment of the age of Emerson and Amelia Bloomer.

Where the ideas of the nineteenth century were congenial to southern ante-bellum values, they spread extravagantly. Though the novels of a romantic like Sir Walter Scott were popular in North and South alike, it was in the latter section that he became a literary idol. Upon his death Richmond newspapers were edged in black. Only in the South were knightly joustings held in full pseudo-mediaeval armor and regalia. It was from Scott's books that Southerners lifted the word "southron," which they self-consciously applied to themselves. The romantic picture of the organic, status society of the Middle Ages, which Scott dwelt on in several of his novels, seemed to shore up southern conservative ideas on society and slavery. Hence, south of the Ohio, Scott found a welcome place denied to contemporaries like Dickens and Shelley, who mixed their romanticism with urban, humanitarian, and irreligious beliefs largely foreign to the South.

Though in the main most Southerners supported slavery and were prepared to sacrifice their freedom of thought in its behalf, coercion and even bloodshed were still needed to provide that degree of uniformity which the peculiar institution seemed to require. Southern postmasters in the 1830's, for example, were given the power to remove abolitionist literature from the mails. Between 1830 and 1860, southern life was punctuated with numerous raids and mobbings of abolitionists and antislavery printers and speakers.

Northerners resident in the South were suspect merely on the ground of their nativity. For example, two northern teachers living in South Carolina were asked to leave town by a local committee, with the town's newspaper justifying such a manifestation of xenophobia in the following fashion: "Nothing definite is known of their abolition or insurrectionary sentiments," the paper conceded, "but being from the North and therefore necessarily imbued with doctrines hostile to our institutions their presence in this section has been obnoxious and at any rate suspicious." Even a proslavery, though Northern-born, educator, President Barnard of the University of Mississippi, was compelled to leave the South because of suspicion arising out of his nativity.

Nor were native Southerners exempt from coercive action. A college student who was discovered in Tennessee with abolitionist literature was given twenty lashes as a warning. An antislavery man in western Virginia in the 1850's was stripped, tied to a tree, and beaten until he agreed to sell his property and leave the state. Though violence of this kind could be duplicated in the North during the 1830's, by the last decade of the ante-bellum period denial of civil liberties to abolitionists in the free states was over. But in the South such restrictions increased and were actually extended to include anyone suspected of unorthodox sentiments, antislavery or otherwise.

Increasingly aware that southern ideas were different from those commonly accepted in the North, southern newspapers sought to insulate the section from outside ideas by calling for the purging of textbooks used in southern schools. They also urged the establishment of new colleges in the South in order to keep southern students out of the northern institutions, meanwhile suggesting that southern boys refrain from going North for their education. Southern xenophobes rejoiced when dozens of southern students left their northern schools in protest against the John Brown raid in 1859. A Professor Hedrick at the University of North Carolina was dismissed because he admitted that he intended to vote for Free-Soiler and Republican John C. Frémont in the election of 1856. The Raleigh *Standard* justified such tactics by writing "If there be Frémont men among us, let them be silenced or required to leave. The expression of Black Republican opinion in our midst is incompatible with our honor and safety as a people."

The South retreated within itself in the area of religion. In his book *Freedom of Thought in the Old South,* Clement Eaton attributes, in part, the growth of a narrow religious orthodoxy and the decline of Jeffersonian deism in the South of the 1830's and 1840's to the exigencies of the defense of slavery. "Only by a narrow and literal interpretation of the Scriptures," Eaton writes, "could slavery be given the high moral sanction of the Church." By the middle of the 1840's, southern and northern Baptists and Methodists could no longer remain in the same national organizations, so sectional churches were formed.

The significance of these efforts at conformity lies not in the force which may or may not have been employed. The important point is that on the whole the southern people during these years acquiesced in the suppression of free speech, free press, free assembly, and the free circulation of ideas in the name of slavery and the society which flourished upon it.

In this is to be seen the tremendous impact of Negro slavery upon the white South; the immediate victim was the liberalism of the eighteenth-century Virginians who had done so much to create a free Republic. The long-range consequence was a heritage of mob violence and extralegal sanctions in support of racial superiority—a heritage which has cast a pall over southern justice ever since. Truly history, in the form of slavery, laid a terrible curse upon the South, and by the middle years of the nineteenth century its exorcising was more difficult than ever before. But unhappily for the future of the region and the nation, the best the leaders of the South could do was to call the curse a blessing. This was the South's and the nation's tragedy.

The central place which slavery occupied in southern life has a direct bearing upon the coming of the Civil War—that culmination of the long history of slavery in America. If one is not concerned with the morality of owning slaves, then the fact that southern leaders were mainly slaveholders and defenders of slavery is no more worthy of comment than the fact that northern leaders usually possessed more land or money than their fellows and ardently defended property. But by the middle of the nineteenth century, for most people of the North and of western Europe, slaves were not property, but human beings. For slavery not only manifestly denied the American creed of equality; it was at variance with the prevailing values of western European civilization.

It is true that at one time Northerners and Europeans held slaves without moral qualms. For this reason, some writers have argued that Northerners and Europeans were hypocritical to belabor the South for its continued adherence to slavery. But this kind of argument misses the point that morals change over time; what was quite acceptable morally in the seventeenth or eighteenth centuries was no longer so in the nineteenth. To many people of the North, southern slavery was not an economic question, which the Southerners insisted it should be, but a moral issue transcending economic interests. The more the support of slavery was made the test of loyalty to the South, the more the region was estranged from the rest of the nation and the world of the nineteenth century.

Under such circumstances, it was not surprising that Southerners should begin to think of themselves as a separate people with their own culture and way of life. In an important sense, therefore, slavery and the agricultural setting in which it flourished constituted the primary "cause" for the Civil War.

Incidents like the Kansas-Nebraska Act, "Bleeding Kansas," the Osawatomie Massacre, the beating of Senator Sumner, the Dred Scott decision, the John Brown raid, all played their parts in the drama by providing occasions for the hardening of the differences between the sections. But underlying all of these circumstances and events was the broad and fundamental fact that a people who adhered to a slave system in the middle of the nineteenth century inevitably became a people different from those Americans who did not. As Calhoun said at the end of his life, it was "difficult to see how two people as different and hostile can exist together in one common Union." The various incidents of the 1850's fed the rising fires of southern nationalism, until in 1860–61 the South demanded self-determination. "When you deny to us the right to withdraw from a Government which . . . threatens to be destructive of our rights," Jefferson Davis told the Senate in 1861, "we but tread in the path of our fathers when we proclaim our independence, and take the hazard." The Civil War was actually the War for Southern Independence.

4. THE AMERICAN DILEMMA

Slavery furnished more than the basis for southern nationalism; it also aroused a powerful counterforce in the North. Though the abolition movement was a part of the general reform impulse of the 1840's and 1850's, the broader antislavery movement which culminated in the Republican party was almost as much a consequence of the South's interminable search for total security for its "peculiar institution" as it was the result of the reform movement.

Apart from the restrictions on freedom in the South, which were demanded in the name of slavery, southern leaders also insisted that the North co-operate in the preservation of slavery. The Fugitive Slave Act of 1850, which the South had won as a concession in the Compromise of that year, was an example of this. Under the new law the cards were heavily stacked in favor of the slave catcher. Jury trials for runaways were eliminated in the act because free-state juries were notoriously partial to escaped slaves. In a further effort to aid in the return of fugitives, the act prescribed that any commissioner who adjudged a Negro defendant a bona fide slave was to receive double the ordinary fee for his services.

Considering the proclivity of slave catchers for seizing any Negro and returning him or selling him into slavery, this law appeared to many in the North as an endeavor to extend the southern limitations on freedom into virgin fields. As a consequence, in many of the free states the act became a nullity. Then when the South, with the Kansas-Nebraska Act, further insisted upon northern support for the extension of slavery into areas where it had heretofore been prohibited, and to which it was obviously unsuited, a new political party sprang into being. This new Republican party was dedicated to halting the seemingly endless demands which the South advanced in behalf of slavery.

Prior to the advent of the Republican party in 1854–56, the opposition to slavery had come primarily from abolitionists, reformers who, out of deep moral conviction, hated slavery more than they loved the Constitution or the Union. William Lloyd Garrison, archpriest of abolition, said he would gladly permit the Constitution to be scrapped and the nation permanently divided if only Negro slavery could be ended in the United States. "No Union with Slaveholders" was the abolitionists' slogan. To such reformers slavery was a moral cancer consuming the essence of America, as it was also an insufferable injustice to the Negro; to achieve its extirpation no price was too costly, no pain too great.

Despite the fact that the abolitionists were amazingly active and provocatively articulate, they never won acceptance among most Americans either north or south of the Ohio. Northerners, it is true, ceased to mob abolitionist speakers by the late 1840's, but most of the people in the North would have little to do with such radicals. Part of this glacierlike hostility stemmed from the abolitionists' unabashed repudiation of the Constitution. Since slavery found sanction and legality in that document, abolitionists like Garrison called it "a covenant with death and an agreement with hell." After expressing such unconcealed contempt for the most venerated of American symbols, the abolitionists could not but fail in their attempt to galvanize the latent American belief in equality.

But if the abolitionists were unsuccessful in their efforts to arouse the North to a crusade against slavery, they did bequeath martyrs and heroes, like Owen Lovejoy, John Brown, Sojourner Truth, and many others, to the radical tradition of America. They also left an ideological Pandora's Box. For in their argument that there was a higher law than a Constitution which sanctioned slavery, they were preaching the dangerous doctrine that resistance to unjust laws is morally permissible.

The abolitionists were not the first nor the last Americans to justify breaking the law in the name of a higher morality. The speakeasy visitor during the prohibition era did it; so did the proslavery Southerner when he hurled abolitionists' printing presses into the river to silence them. More recent examples are white Southerners who refused to accept desegregation and students who resisted the draft because of the war in Vietnam. This slippery principle that laws may be broken if they flout moral opinion is obviously fraught with danger to a government of law, for there is no way to distinguish rationally among the reasons for disobeying the law. Yet, in the service of noble causes, the doctrine of the higher law has righted injustice, resisted tyranny, and protected the individual. It has also been nothing more than mob rule, denial of individual rights, and the end of government by law. In both forms, however, the idea of the higher law is historically and distinctly American.

Where the abolitionists failed, the Republican party was notably successful. Gunnar Myrdal, in his monumental study of the Negro in America, has described what he calls the American dilemma—the conflict between the traditional egalitarian creed and the actual treatment accorded the Negro. Already in the 1850's the moral conflict was dividing Americans against themselves. In the South the dilemma was resolved, or at least covered over, by the outright denial of the principle of equality; the Declaration of Independence was called, among other things, a tissue of "glittering generalities." But in the North, equality was increasingly accepted as a moral imperative. The newly formed Republican party now incorporated the disquieting Declaration of Independence in its appeal to Americans. Lincoln advised in 1858, "let us discard all this quibbling about this man and the other—this race and that race, and the other race being inferior. . . . Let us discard all these things, and unite as one people, throughout this land, until we shall once more stand up declaring that all men are created equal." At another time he said, "in relation to the principle that all men are created equal, let it be as nearly reached as we can."⁶

Though the Republicans seemed to subscribe to all kinds of divergent political and economic ideas, they were united in their opposition to the spread of slavery.⁷ This is not to say, however, that they were abolitionists. On at least two counts the average Republican differed from an abolitionist. For one thing, very few Republicans, though they opposed slavery, believed in social equality for Negroes. Lincoln spoke for many of his fellow Republicans when he said during the debates with Douglas in 1858 that he was not in favor of social equality for Negroes. The Negro, he said, "is not my equal in many respects—certainly not in color, perhaps not in moral or intellectual endowment. But in the right to eat the bread, without leave of anybody else, which his own hand earns," Lincoln added, "he is my equal and the equal of Judge Douglas, and the equal of every living man." In short, slavery was an evil because it denied the dominant American value of equality of opportunity. On this great issue, radical abolitionists and conservative Whigs, nativists and Jacksonian Democrats, could join hands in the formation of a new antislavery party.

⁶ The irony inherent in the transfer of Jefferson as a party idol from the Democrats to the Republicans was not lost upon Lincoln. When asked in 1859 to participate in a Republican celebration of Jefferson's birthday, he noted that the new party now claimed the Sage of Monticello, "while those claiming political descent from him have nearly ceased to breathe his name everywhere." It was in this letter that Lincoln made his famous remark that the Republicans, unlike the Democrats with their defense of slave property, "are for both the *man* and the *dollar;* but in cases of conflict, the man before the dollar."

⁷ The heterogeneity of the Republican party was not much different from that of most American political parties of importance. But in 1860, Howell Cobb, the Georgia statesman, pointed out that the heterogeneity also emphasized its essential antislavery bias. "The Black Republican party had its origin in the antislavery feeling of the North," he told his constituents. "The fact that it was composed of men of all previous parties, who then and still advocate principles directly antagonistic upon all other questions except slavery as it exists in the fifteen Southern States, was the basis of its organization and the bond of its union. Free-trade Democrats and protective-tariff Whigs, internal improvement and anti-internal improvement men, and indeed all shades of partisans, united in cordial fraternity upon the isolated issue of hostility to the South, though for years they had fought each other upon all other issues."

The second point on which the Republicans differed from the abolitionists was in the lengths to which they would go to oppose slavery. The abolitionists were willing to pull the Union down about their ears if it would end slavery. The Republicans, however, were conservatives who cherished the Union and fully endorsed the safeguards which the Constitution bestowed upon slavery in the South. They would not scrap the Constitution in a frantic effort to eliminate slavery, much as they might abominate the institution.

But, when, as Lincoln said, slavery seemed about to expand into areas heretofore prohibited to it, then a stand had to be taken against it. And, in such a setting, a stand could be made without repudiating the Constitution or the sanctuary which slavery enjoyed in the South. For it had always been held—at least before the Dred Scott decision —that Congress could constitutionally prohibit slavery in the territories.

Many modern historians and some contemporaries like Daniel Webster have called the opposition to the extension of slavery into the territories a trivial reason for bringing the nation to the brink of civil war inasmuch as the area was unsuited for plantation agriculture. But once the constitutionally conservative character of the Republican party and the American people is acknowledged, then the titanic struggle over slavery in the western territories takes on a deeper meaning. Everywhere else, slavery rested on the bedrock of the Constitution; only in this narrow, constitutional sphere could the great moral issue of slave versus free labor be fought out by a people convinced of the sanctity of their Constitution.

With the formation of the Republican party, the breakup of the Union became unavoidable. The new party's very reason for being stood athwart the South's drive for the expansion of slavery, and its almost immediate popularity in the more populous and growing North stood as a warning to the slave states that in time an antislavery government would gain power in Washington.

By the late 1850's the only alternatives to disruption of the Union, given the alignment of parties and the hardening sectional attitudes, were that the North should become a slaveholding area or that the South should cease to be one. The first possibility, despite some wild predictions by Southerners like George Fitzhugh and some politically inspired warnings by Northerners like Lincoln and Seward, was out of the question. The second was equally unlikely when weighed against the profits of slavery and the anodyne which the institution provided for southern racial fears.

Tightly wrapped in their own cultural assumptions, Northerners and Southerners were now incapable of compromise. All that was left was mounting recrimination. The North was here more often the aggressor because the force of European moral opinion was on its side; for the same reason the South could not help but be apprehensive. But because the South dominated the largest and oldest political party in the country, it was also defiant.

When in 1860 the South's political ascendancy seemed about to end, the region turned to secession as the final salvation for its peculiar institution and the civilization which was built around it. Secession, though, could serve as an answer to the South's problem only if the rest of the nation agreed. As it turned out, the new Republican party proved to be not only antislavery but strongly nationalistic.

Thus the immediate consequence of slavery was a terrible and costly war between the North and the South. At bottom, all the issues between the sections, whether of an incidental nature, like the John Brown raid, or of a broad character, like the conflicts over the tariff or the homestead bill, were in fact and in logic reducible to the question of slavery. To the men at the time and to an increasing number of modern historians, without the issue of slavery to divide the two sections, there would have been no Civil War.

Once the war came, however, it brought to an abrupt close one period of American history and opened the door to another of a much different order. The Civil War was not only a testing of the American people as a nation; it was a watershed in their history.

CHAPTER VII

Bringing Forth a New Nation

THE disruption of the American Union in 1861 has been explained in many ways, but, viewed against the perspective of European civilization as a whole, it was primarily the work of two of the most powerful forces then abroad in the world. One, as we have seen, was the rising tide of reform; the other was the elemental emotion of nationalism.

In the middle of the nineteenth century, nationalism was spreading like a fever through the ancient body of Europe; in America it seized the imaginations of the people, too, leading them into the most costly and bloody war of the century. For two decades the southern people had been growing in the conviction that their culture, entwined about the institution of Negro slavery, made them a separate nation. The election of 1860 precipitated this feeling into secession from the Union and an experiment in nationhood. But developing alongside this southern nationalism was another, one which insisted that the Union was eternal and indissoluble. Of this brand of nationalism, Abraham Lincoln was the Bismarck, as Jefferson Davis was the Kossuth of the South. It was Lincoln who with "blood and iron" sustained and cemented the loose confederation of the Fathers and created a new nation.

"Again and again it has been proved," wrote Heinrich Treitschke, the German nationalist, "that it is war which turns a people into a nation, and that only great deeds, wrought in common, can forge the indissoluble links which bind them together." Americans then and now would be loath to subscribe to this iron philosophy, but the driving force of the new nationalism which the War for the Union released suggests that it was an apt description of the making of the new America. "Before the War our patriotism was a fire-work, a salute, a serenade for holidays and summer evenings . . ." Ralph Waldo Emerson commented in 1864. "Now the deaths of thousands and the determination of millions of men and women show that it is real."

The War for the Union was a turning point in American history. After it Americans lived in a different nation, one in which freedom and equality now applied to all men, one in which the unity of the nation was beyond dispute, and one in which the power of the national government was supreme. The price of this change, however, was the ruthless denial of the southern white people's aspiration for nationhood.

1. A PEOPLE'S WAR

"We cannot escape history," Abraham Lincoln told his fellow Americans in 1862. "We of this Congress and this Administration will be remembered in spite of ourselves." Many other Americans of that generation were aware of the portentous times in which they lived. To George Ticknor of Boston it seemed in April of 1861 as if "the heather is on fire" throughout the North. After weeks of indecision and doubt, the commitment to war brought a sudden release of tension and a surge of patriotism. "I am proud of my country and my grand heroic brethren," exulted newspaperman Edmund Stedman in the fall of 1861. "The greatness of the crisis, the Homeric grandeur of the contest, surrounds and elevates us all." Within a matter of weeks, it seemed to a woman in New York, the whole nation had been transfigured by the guns which battered Fort Sumter. "How long it is since Sumter!" she wrote. "I suppose it is because so much intense emotion has been crowded into the last two or three weeks, that the 'time before Sumter' seems to belong to some dim antiquity. It seems as if we never were alive till now; never had a country till now."

Upon veterans the conflict left a never-to-be-forgotten imprint. "The war was . . . a very extraordinary war," recalled M. W. Tyler after half a century. "Nothing like it ever occurred before, and I doubt if anything like it will ever happen again." Twenty years after he left the Union Army, Oliver Wendell Holmes, Jr., said: "Through our great good fortune in our youth our hearts were touched with fire. It was given us to learn at the outset that life is a profound and passionate thing."

American emotional involvement in the great struggle has hardly abated in subsequent generations. During the years between 1862 and 1900, for example, over 480 short stories and novels were published about the war and its effects. One historian has counted 512 novels on the Civil War alone published between 1862 and 1948. Another literary measure of the war's impact over the years is the fact that the two best-selling novels in the whole history of American fiction are *Uncle Tom's Cabin* and *Gone With the Wind*—one concerned with the great issue which brought on the war, the other dealing with the consequences of the war. New serious and semipopular books on the war appear each year—over one hundred appeared in 1957—and clubs and societies devoted to exploring the history of the struggle are but further testimony to the unending fascination which that war still holds for Americans. What town or village in the states that fought in the war does not have its monument to the soldiers who fell in defense of the Union or the Lost Cause? Not even World War II, with its far-flung battle fronts and its intensity of moral purpose, has found a deeper place in the American heart and memory.

All wars pluck men from their families, but the War for the Union touched so many homes with the fear of death that it seemed a new kind of war. Edward Dicey, the English journalist traveling in the United States in 1862, met a woman who said she never knew anyone in the Army until a year earlier; but now, she said, she had sixty friends and relatives in the Union forces. Nor was this, Dicey added, an uncommon experience. The records of the war reveal that almost three million men served in the federal forces—about 15 per cent of the total population—and an even greater proportion stepped forward to defend the Confederacy. Lincoln's call for 500,000 volunteers in May of 1861 was answered by 700,000. Throughout the war the bulk of the Union Army was made up of volunteers, not draftees, since conscription procedures were neither efficient nor popular. "I very much doubt," commented Anthony Trollope in 1862, "whether any other nation ever made such an effort in so short a time. To a people who can do this it may be granted that they are in earnest. . . . The strong and unanimous impulse of a great people is seldom wrong."

The examples of supreme devotion to the cause were, as always, provided by the men in the armies. The soldiers of the Army of the Potomac knew very well that there were shirkers at home who were safe and often growing rich and fat; but they also believed the Union represented a cause worth dying for. "Well, if new men won't finish the job," wrote one of Grant's veterans in Virginia in 1864, "old men must, and as long as Uncle Sam wants a man, here is Ben Falls." Two months later Falls was dead at Spotsylvania Court House. The so-called Invalid Corps, made up of thousands of wounded veterans, bore testimony to the sense of involvement felt by many of the soldiers. Though entitled to a discharge, these men chose to serve their cause and country in noncombatant duties, such as guarding prisoners and communications. When the crucial election of 1864 arrived, the majority of the soldiers in the field did not vote for their old commander, McClellan, and his Peace Platform, but cast their ballots overwhelmingly for "old Abe" and a continuance of the war.

"The longer I lived in the country," Dicey decided in 1862, "the more I learned how deep the feeling of the North was; it was like all English feeling, and came slowly to the surface." The war's outcome seemed to be a responsibility weighing upon all, and each felt he had to meet it in his own way. When asked by his father why he insisted upon enlisting in 1862, sixteen-year-old Theodore Upson of Indiana replied simply, "Father, we must have more soldiers. This Union your ancestors and mine helped to make must be saved from destruction. I can go better than some others. I don't feel right to stay at home any longer." A much older man, Henry Hitchcock of St. Louis, told General Sherman that he joined in 1864 because "I could not stay at home and let other men do the fighting and run the risks while I was safely making money and enjoying the fruits of their toils. . . ." In Massachusetts an Irish immigrant begged for admission to Ben Perley Poore's battalion. "The prosperity of this country is my prosperity," he argued, "its life is in danger and I feel that I ought to en-list to save it."

The heroic activities of southern women in support of their cause are legendary, but equally prodigious were the exertions of northern women, notably in support of the Sanitary Commission. This forerunner of the Red Cross and the USO contributed in money and services at least $25 million to the Union troops. The wives and mothers of the soldiers as well as men too old to fight were outstanding in the organization and conduct of the Sanitary Fairs which were held in the large cities to raise extra funds for "the boys" at the front.

The war also affected the attitude of Americans toward revolution. Prior to the Civil War, as a people who had struck out for independence themselves, Americans wished well the struggles of other peoples for self-determination and freedom. So it was when the Greeks and Latin-Americans and Hungarians rose up in rebellion against their alien overlords during the first half of the century. But when the white South asserted that its strike for independence was in tune with the spirit of 1776, many Northerners could accept neither the analogy nor the justification implied. Suddenly the connection between justice and revolution that Americans had derived from their own history, was broken. At one time Thomas Jefferson had extolled revolution as not only the right of any people but as desirable in order to keep government responsive to the people's needs. After the southern revolt, however, revolution was no longer unambiguous. Now, even a revolution might be a bad thing. "The Civil War," Henry James wrote in 1879, "marks an era in the history of the American mind. It introduced into the national consciousness a certain sense of proportion and relation, of the world being a more complicated place than it had hitherto seemed, the future more treacherous, success more difficult. At the rate at which things are going, it is obvious that good Americans will be more numerous than ever; but the good American, in days to come, will be a more critical person than his complacent and confident grandfather. He has eaten of the tree of knowledge."

2. A BUSINESSMEN'S GOVERNMENT

When historians like Charles A. Beard and Louis Hacker, with a penchant for economic explanations, referred to the war as "the Second American Revolution," they had in mind the triumph of the northern business interest. They thought they could discern in the American struggle an analogy with the historic European bourgeois revolutions, such as took place in France in 1789. Neither the long previous history of the United States nor the years immediately prior to 1861 bear out this interpretation, however.

The impetus for war, as we have seen, came from the South, not from the North; the agrarians, not the bourgeoisie, risked war to gain their ends. Northern business had not been throttled by the admitted southern domination of the three branches of the federal government, and the census returns promised that even this domination would soon end. Moreover, business had received substantial aid from even the southern-dominated governments. Indeed, one of the justifications southern leaders advanced for secession was the alleged favoritism shown to northern shipping and manufacturing interests by the federal government. It is true that many northern manufacturers wanted a higher tariff, that some businessmen wanted a sounder monetary system, and that northern farmers wanted the public domain thrown open to free settlement, but the failure to obtain these wishes constituted neither a threat to northern prosperity nor a reason for a war against the South. Quite the contrary, as a number of recent studies have shown, northern businessmen were prominent among the leaders of the conservative forces in the North during the winter of 1860–61, working to compromise the conflicting demands of the sections and to heal the widening split in the Union.

The evidence for the contention that the war was a "revolution" is to be found in the events after 1861, not in those during the pre-secession years. To argue, as Beard and Hacker and others tend to do, from the results of the war back to the cause is to fall into the logical error of *post hoc, ergo propter hoc*.

But even if the Beard-Hacker analysis is weak as an explanation for the coming of the war, it does serve to remind us that along with the war came a new attitude toward business. With the South gone from the Congress, the business bias of the new Republican party was quickly translated into legislation. As John Sherman of Ohio put it, "those who elected Mr. Lincoln expect him . . . to secure to free labor its just right to the Territories of the United States; to protect . . . by wise revenue laws, the labor of our people; to secure the public lands to actual settlers . . . to develop the internal resources of the country by opening new means of communication between the Atlantic and the Pacific." In the course of the first Lincoln administration, all these economic demands and more were met.

For the first time since Jackson killed that "Monster," the Bank of the United States, the federal government essayed to bring some order into the currency chaos. For decades the circulating medium of the nation had been composed of good, solid gold and silver coins, issued by the federal government, on the one hand, and a host of paper "bills" issued by private banks on the other. This paper money was completely unregulated by the federal government and its backing varied from nothing except faith to virtually complete correspondence with gold. Receivers of such money could rarely be sure of the real value of such paper bills unless they were the issue of banks in a state like New York where the laws prescribed backing for note issue.

The National Bank Acts of 1863 and 1864 were designed to bring some stability into this situation. First, they authorized the establishment of National Banks which could issue paper money only against holdings of United States government bonds. (In a time of national deficit spending, this was also a clever device to sell bonds and simultaneously maintain their price.) Second, in order to eliminate the unreliable paper money of the private banks, and to provide a truly national currency, a prohibitive tax was placed upon the bills of banks not subscribing to the new act, a measure which compelled all note-issuing banks to become national. The result was a new uniformity in the nation's banking and currency structure and a valuable contribution to the industrial expansion of the postwar years.

The pre-eminence of an exclusively northern political party in the councils of government was also proclaimed by the passage of the first frankly protective tariff in twenty years. Furthermore, in the course of the war, the tariff was raised to its highest point yet. Its continued rise in subsequent years proved to be one of the chief gifts of the Republican party to the rapid industrialization of the nation's economy.

Another, if minor, fillip to the progress of industrialization was the passage, in 1864, of the Contract Labor Law, which facilitated the importation of foreign skilled labor into the expanding factories of the North. Although this law was repealed in 1868, the practice which it protected continued for another twenty years before organized labor was able to have it declared illegal.

Two other pieces of legislation further demonstrate the economic benefits which the North derived from the South's secession and reveal the close linkage between the new Republican government and the economic expansion of the subsequent decades. For almost ten years the country had been expecting the federal government to help in the construction of a transcontinental railroad, but sectional rivalries over the proper route had barred any action. In 1862, with the South gone, the matter was easily settled—the northern way—and the federal government committed itself to generous aid for the building of the road. With the Homestead Act of the same year, northern farmers were at last granted free land—up to 160 acres—a privilege for which their spokesmen had been contending for fifteen years. Though it is possible to exaggerate the amount of public lands awarded to actual settlers as compared with land speculators, there can be little question that the act, in its openhandedness with the national resources, constituted an encouragement to economic development by private enterprise.

It might well be said that in general the economic legislation of this first Lincoln administration set both the tone and the content of the Republican party program for the next forty years. And as a program it provided a climate in which the new entrepreneurs of the Gilded Age flourished mightily.

But if the war brought new support to the side of business and enterprise in the North, it visited just the reverse upon the South. As the battlefield of the war, the Confederacy bore the burden of the destruction which inevitably accompanies any war. But this was more than an ordinary war. It was a struggle by one people to destroy the other as a nation. As such, the mere defeat of armies could not be enough; the people of the South would have to be shown, by the most relentless of military attrition, that they as a people were incapable of resisting the power of the United States.

The truth of this was not clear to many Northerners at the beginning of the war, when the capture of Richmond was viewed as the main goal of the Union armies. To western generals like Grant and Sherman, however, it soon became apparent that only through a systematic destruction of the southern economy would the South's will to resist be broken once and for all. Grant first tested the immense military potentialities of "living off the country" at the time of Vicksburg in 1863; the value of the innovation was amply demonstrated by Wilson's raid into Alabama, by Sherman in his devastating march through Georgia and the Carolinas, and by Sheridan's destruction of supplies and communications in the Shenandoah Valley of Virginia. This was total war against the people and economy of the South, and, largely because of it and the increasing effectiveness of the blockade, the Confederacy was prostrate and helpless before the conqueror in less than two years after Vicksburg.

The price of such a military policy in suppressing a rebellion, however, is high; the South returned to the Union an impoverished section. The emancipation of the slaves alone wiped out perhaps $2 billion in capital, and the loss of property through deliberate destruction and war was no less. In 1860 the value of property in the South had been calculated at $4.4 billion; in 1870, even though five years of peace intervened, the figure had declined to $2.1 billion.

During these same ten years the wealth of the North had grown by 50 per cent.

When the war broke out, contrary to what some have argued, the ante-bellum South was no decadent civilization tottering to its ruin. Growing in wealth, proud of its culture, and flushed with confidence —too much so, as it turned out—the South was a flourishing region in 1860, brimming with promise for the future. The end came abruptly and terribly in the War for Southern Independence; rather than being a funeral pyre for a moribund culture, the war was a *Götterdämmerung*. And like an earlier Twilight of the Gods, the ante-bellum South lived on in legend as it had never lived in reality. But the destruction of the ante-bellum civilization did much more than create a legend; it introduced social and economic problems which have burdened the people of the region well into our own time.[1]

The emancipation of the slaves confronted the South, before all else, with an economic problem of great magnitude. The labor of the former slaves had to be brought to bear upon the land if the region was to recoup its losses—indeed, if it was to survive. The problem was complicated, though. Theoretically, the former slaves might have been turned into farmer-proprietors by giving them land. Thaddeus Stevens, the leader of northern Reconstruction, for example, was of this mind, for he advocated the division of the great plantations among the Negroes and the landless whites of the South.[2] Very few

---

[1] It is difficult to determine what role the destruction of property played in the slow recovery of the South. The very rapid recovery of West Germany after the enormous devastation wrought by World War II, for example, suggests that destruction *per se* is not always the determining factor. In ante-bellum days, stock raising was a significant part of the South's small-farmer economy, as it is once again today. The war, however, wrecked that ante-bellum diversification. It was not until 1900 that the number of livestock in the states of the former Confederacy reached the number for 1860. On the other hand, staple crops like tobacco and cotton reached 1860 levels of production by 1880. It appears that changes in farm labor and farm organization were more determining than the wide destruction.

[2] Though few of the Reconstruction leaders of the North gave much thought to the problem of the freedman's economic status, Thaddeus Stevens did. In March, 1867, for example, he pleaded with the Congress to grant each freedman forty acres of land and a small purse of money, the wherewithal to be obtained from the confiscation of the large estates of the South. "Homesteads to them [Negroes]," he said, "are far more valuable than the immediate right of suffrage, though both are their due." The only other political effort to give the Negro a stake and opportunity in the postwar South was that of South Carolina during the Radical ascendancy. The proposal was to buy up land

Northerners found this an acceptable solution, however, and for racial and social reasons, if nothing else, no Southerner endorsed it as even a possibility. Thus, at the very outset, it was in effect determined that the great majority of the Negroes would have to begin their life under freedom dependent upon others—their former masters, in fact—for the land which would permit them to make a living.

But even with the Negro as a dependent cultivator, the economic hurdles were not yet surmounted. The landowners, critically short of capital and cash, usually could not afford to hire gangs of freedmen as field workers. The makeshift solution which most readily suggested itself was what a later age would call sharecropping. By parceling out his otherwise useless land to the Negroes and taking a share of the crop, a planter could bring his acres to production without having to find sufficient cash to pay hired labor. The Negro, in turn, was given an opportunity to work land under his own supervision and perhaps to sell enough of his share of the crop to be able eventually to buy his own land.

On the surface, this system seemed to signal the breakup of the plantation economy. In all but appearance, however, it was the same old plantation, and even sometimes with the same owner, worked now, however, in small family plots instead of in gangs as under slavery.

But the real problem of the white farmer immediately after the war was not landlessness, but lack of capital. This dearth of ready cash occasioned the other innovation in southern agriculture born from the war's dislocations. In order to obtain seed, supplies, and equipment with which to work his land, the farmer gave a lien or legal claim on his crop to the local merchant who supplied him. Under this lien system, as it came to be called, the merchant with his indispensable credit moved to the center of the farmer's life. He was able to use his financial stake as a lever to compel the farmer to produce cash crops only, or, worse yet, a single crop like cotton, thus helping to saddle the region with one-crop agriculture and all its attendant evils. Furthermore, credit buying by the farmer encouraged extravagance on his part and fraudulent manipulation of the records on the part of the merchant. The net result was that the farmer often

---

for the former slaves, but the plan never got beyond the beginning stages. Some Negroes did own their own land, particularly in the Sea Islands off South Carolina, where they had seized it during the war, with the encouragement of the Union Army. But the vast majority of the freedmen were landless.

found it difficult to extricate himself from the mounting burden of debt fostered by his dependence upon the merchant. Once caught in a cycle of increasing debt, many small landowners of the South lost their land to their creditors and sank into tenancy.

The hope had been that sharecropping and crop lien would be only temporary crutches while the southern farmers recovered from the disastrous effects of the war. But things did not work out that way; neither system distinguished itself as a training ground for self-reliance, much less a ladder for upward social mobility. Instead, tenancy grew in the South; by 1900 over 45 per cent of the region's farmers, both black and white, were tenants—about double the ante-bellum proportion. In large part, of course, this increase was attribut-able to the inclusion of the freed Negro in the farming statistics, but it was still a realistic acknowledgment that the postwar South was economically much worse off than before the war.

Though the scars upon the land left by the war were gradually covered over and even the animosities engendered by the conflict softened through the years, sharecropping and crop lien did not pass away. Each census after the War for Southern Independence showed an increase in the number of tenants in the South, and not until the latter days of the New Deal was this trend reversed. Thus when President Franklin Roosevelt referred to the South as "the nation's economic problem No. 1" he was giving belated acknowledgment that the war was more than just a chapter in the history books.

3. A NATIONALIST'S DREAM

The destruction of the southern economy was only the most tangible result of the War for the Union. More importantly for the nation as a whole, victory for the Union signified the reintegration of the national state which almost half a century of bitter and relentless agitation over slavery had disrupted. "The war is over," young Theodore Upson wrote in his diary in June of 1865, "and the Union is saved!" The Union, however, was a quite different one from that which Upson fought to preserve. The day was now past when even a northern President like Franklin Pierce would refer to the United States as "the general agent," "the creature of the States." The doubts which assailed President James Buchanan as to the power of the federal government to suppress secession had been laid to rest with a finality only military victory can command. In 1869, the Supreme

Court, reading the war bulletins as well as the election returns, declared that the Union was "indestructible," the principle for which the North had gone to war. Never again would any state—even during the extreme segregation crisis of the 1950's—imagine that secession was a constitutional remedy for state grievances.

The repudiation of the doctrine of secession before the judgment seat of war, however, was only the first of the new and tightening bonds of Union. The armies which the North mobilized in the course of the war were like enormous forcing rooms for the quick flowering of nationalistic feeling. Men from different parts of the North, and even from areas of the South, mingled with one another in the common cause of the nation's survival. Natives and immigrants, especially Germans and Irishmen, were thrown together in a way which emphasized their common loyalty. Not since the Thirty Years' War in seventeenth-century Europe, Ella Lonn has written, had so cosmopolitan a group of Europeans been assembled in one army. "The heterogeneity of the northern Army was one of its most marked characteristics. . . . Not one of the three hundred regiments which marched out from New York was without one or more Teutons. Besides the companies of Germans from Cleveland, men of that nationality from the lake city served in twenty-two mixed Ohio regiments . . . as well as in regiments of Michigan, Missouri, Illinois, Indiana, and Pennsylvania, and in the American Fleet."

Often the service of the immigrant marked his transition from alien to citizen, and, more important, to acceptance as a fellow American. Bruce Catton in his superb history of the Army of the Potomac tells of Mike Scannell of Massachusetts, who, when called a "damned Yankee," was touchingly flattered. He replied to the astonished rebel: "Well, it is twenty years since I came to this country, and you are the first man who ever called me a Yankee." The hearty response of the Boston Irish to the call to the Union colors won them a place of new respect in the eyes of many old Bostonians; for years thereafter, anti-immigration agitation would find the going considerably tougher.

Though often having only a vague notion of the issues behind the conflict, the immigrant soldier nevertheless seemed to sense the implications which the war carried for the future of his adopted country. "We are having a war here in America," a young soldier wrote to his mother in Ireland. "The Southern states want to have a flag of their own and as many slaves as they can buy or steal. The North wants to keep the old flag and the country as Washington left it, and not to have slavery go any further; so they have gone to war about it, and I have enlisted and hope to fight for right and the country." One German, who arrived in New York City in 1860 and was dead in Virginia in 1864, wrote home about his decision to enlist. "I am a volunteer soldier in the Army of the United States to fight the rebels of South America for a sacred thing. All of America has to become free and united and the starry banner has to fly again over the new world."

Though it is true that the vast majority of the soldiers and sailors of the Union were volunteers, it should not be forgotten that the war introduced the first conscription act ever passed by the federal government. Never before had the central government stretched its hand so intimately into the very homes of the citizenry. This experience, which Southerners also knew under the Confederacy, was a precedent for the extensive and necessary use of the draft in the two great wars of the twentieth century.

The living monument to the profound nationalistic influence of the Army was the Grand Army of the Republic. In intent and in practice, this immense veterans' organization was the bridge which spanned the years between the emotions aroused by the War for the Union and the humdrum existence which stretched out afterward. The several hundred thousand veterans who joined this self-proclaimed incarnation of the cause of the Union were living testimony to the continuing significance of the war experience. Almost fanatical in its devotion to the welfare of the men who had served in the Union cause, the G.A.R., in subsequent years, proved itself to be a measure as well as a symbol of the deep well of national feeling which the war had uncovered.

4. THE TWILIGHT OF THE STATES

The sheer magnitude of the emergency which confronted the Lincoln administration in 1861 and after worked a permanent transformation upon the powers of the federal government. In part this was the inevitable consequence of the ever-increasing demands of a hard-fought war extending over far-flung battlefields and along some three thousand miles of seacoast. But it was also a result of the fact that the new Republicans and their President were bearers of a new nationalism which envisioned a central government of power and authority. Before the war was over, these two forces would completely overthrow the limited federal government which the Lincoln administration inherited in 1861. In its place would be a United States government truly supreme over states that once called themselves sovereign.

The sinews of war cost money, and in mere monetary terms the salvation of the Union was an expensive proposition—one which prompted changes in governmental financial policies. Federal expenditures skyrocketed from $66.5 million in 1861 to $474.8 million in 1862 and on up to the unprecedented level of $1,297 million in 1865—a peak not equaled until the entrance of the United States into the First World War. Under such conditions it was inevitable and imperative that the financial powers of the federal government would expand accordingly. For the first time in the history of the country, the government of the United States resorted to the printing press for money despite the fact that the Constitution specifically limited the federal government to the "coining" of money. Over $400 million in greenbacks were issued by the federal government to lubricate the economic machine. More than that, as we have seen, this new kind of federal government, this government with energy, went on to revamp the banking and currency structure of the nation, in the course of which it taxed out of existence the instrumentalities of the states. Never again would state bank notes be of any significance in the American economy. Currency affairs were now firmly in the hands of the national government, and the road from there to the Federal Reserve System and even to a managed currency was both clear and straight.

Unlike the Confederate Congress, which failed to lay adequate taxes, the United States in the very first year of the war greatly expanded the sources of internal revenue. Most important in this regard were the imposition of new and higher excise taxes and the laying of a tax on personal incomes for the first time in American history. The latter measure, untested in the Supreme Court before it was repealed in 1873, brought in almost 20 per cent of the total federal revenue in 1865.

Though some of the new fiscal instruments, such as the income tax and fiat money, were repealed after the war emergency, the American people had seen the federal government in its full panoply of power. The sight was not forgotten by Greenbackers, Populists, and other reformers in later years when they looked about for authority and weapons with which to attack the social and economic ills of the nation.

Nor did the swollen war expenditures shrink back to the trifling $66 million of the ante-bellum years. New obligations like veterans' pensions kept the federal budget and its bureaucracy far above the prewar level, and over the subsequent years they grew steadily.

Nor was the high protective tariff, which had come in with the war, repealed. Furthermore, contrary to the situation before 1860, there now were few states who doubted the constitutionality of protection; only expediency could be the objection. Thus another hotly disputed constitutional issue of the ante-bellum years—psychologically now so far in the distance—was rendered obsolete by the decisive verdict of the sword, which cut so many cords running into the past.

One of the most flagrant repudiations of state sovereignty by the central government was the acceptance of West Virginia into the Union. Though the Constitution clearly provides that no territory may be taken from a state without its consent, the western counties of Virginia were severed from the Old Dominion, never to be returned. The trick was turned by the creation of a rump government of Virginia Unionists who "agreed" to the secession of the western portion of the state. Lincoln had his doubts about the constitutionality of such a procedure, but, like Thomas Jefferson before him at the time of the Louisiana Purchase, he brushed them aside in the interest of the Union cause.

The most dramatic example of the way in which the war and the nationalist ideology of the Republican party continuously created the opportunities and necessity for enlarging the powers of the federal government at the expense of the states is provided by the handling of the delicate question of slavery. For decades the mark of a true friend of the Union was the refusal to question the legitimate existence of slavery in the southern states. All supporters of the Union, North and South alike, agreed that slavery was wrapped in the protecting folds of the Constitution itself and embedded in the compromises which the Founding Fathers had been compelled to make in 1787. Though, as Howell Cobb of Georgia shrewdly pointed out, the sole issue which united the Republican party was opposition to slavery, even this antislavery party conceded that there was no constitutional warrant for federal interference with the "peculiar institution" in the states of the South. The most the Republicans wanted to do was prohibit its spread to the territories. The secession of the South, however, removed the party's and the nation's scruples on the question of interference with slavery in the South.

This radical alteration in the nation's attitude toward slavery is all the more remarkable because it took place so rapidly.[3] Early in the war, in 1861, Union generals in the field, like Frémont and Butler, began to accept runaway slaves who entered their lines as either free men (Frémont's position—which was quickly countermanded by Lincoln) or as contraband of war (Butler's method), and therefore no longer the property of their masters. Seeking to formalize such penalizing of the slaveholders in rebellion, the Congress, in August, 1861, passed the Confiscation Act, declaring forfeit all claims to slaves actively engaged in aiding the rebellion. Almost a year later, Congress made it clear that the war was to be the occasion for striking at slavery more widely. The Act of July, 1862, provided that the slaves of all persons committing treason or supporting the rebellion were henceforth and forever free. The act also put an end to the Army's practice of returning fugitive slaves to their masters, unless the masters were adherents to the Union cause.

The growing movement to extend the federal power over the matter of slavery reached its crescendo in 1862. In April a goal was achieved for which the abolitionists had battled for twenty years: slavery was abolished in the District of Columbia. Then, in June, slave property was extinguished in the territories without compensation to the owners. Since the Supreme Court in the Dred Scott decision had denied Congress' power to end slavery in a territory, this latter action was palpably unconstitutional—but this was a new era and a new government. The final act which brought this mounting antislavery pressure before the conscience of the nation and the at-

---

[3] The antislavery attitude of the Republican party and administration was visible before the Emancipation Proclamation, but only occasionally. During the secession-crisis winter of 1860–61, for example, the President-elect and his party steadfastly refused to accept any compromise which countenanced slavery in the territories. "Let there be no compromise on the question of extending slavery," Lincoln instructed his followers in December, 1860. "If there be, all our labor is lost, and, ere long, must be done again. . . . Stand firm. The tug has to come, and better now than anytime hereafter." Another instance occurred in February of 1862, when the administration permitted N. P. Gordon, a slave trader, captured the year before, to be executed—the first slave trader to be executed in the forty-year history of American prohibition of the foreign slave trade.

tention of the world was the enunciation, in September, of the preliminary Emancipation Proclamation. And, significantly enough, it was under the guise of a war measure that this conclusion to a generation of agitation was achieved.

In his Proclamation, Lincoln reaffirmed his belief in the Declaration of Independence and the equality of all men, but he also extended the federal power, as the Congress had done earlier, over the most sacrosanct domestic institution in the United States. At one time men had come to blows regarding the power of Congress to control slavery in the territories, even though the territories were the creatures of the federal government. But now a nationalistic President and Congress did not scruple to end the hallowed institution in the allegedly sovereign states themselves.

Actually, at the time of its issuance, Lincoln's Proclamation did not free a single slave, since its terms applied only to those slaves held by masters in rebellion. Nevertheless, the edict marked a turning point in the history of bondage in America. It was not long thereafter that the Thirteenth Amendment, abolishing slavery throughout the Union, was started on its way to the states. Who could have predicted, three short years before, that such was to be the fate of the guarded and cherished institution of slavery? Riding on a tidal wave of nationalism, the antislavery crusade had ruthlessly swept away a $2 billion investment belonging to almost half a million Americans. As has been said, this was one of the greatest confiscations of private property in Anglo-Saxon history. That Union of "Liberty and Power" which old John Quincy Adams had worked to create and had yearned to see had finally come to pass.

The abolition of slavery did not, however, exhaust the flood of moral energy set free by the War for the Union; its tide did not ebb until freedom for the Negro and power for the federal government were firmly engrafted upon the Constitution itself. Whereas the Thirteenth Amendment to the Constitution put an end to the issue of slavery in American life,[4] the Fourteenth opened a broad new horizon of governmental power. This single amendment, with the possible exception of the commerce clause, has done more to bury states'

---

[4]In 1968 the Supreme Court ruled that the Thirteenth Amendment automatically prohibited any discrimination in housing on grounds of race on the principle that such discrimination was an attribute of slavery, which the amendment ended.

rights and to exalt the federal power than any other single amendment or clause in the Constitution.

Although obviously enacted to secure protection for the newly emancipated slave,[5] the power of the amendment has been felt in a dozen fields of American life. The courts have measured against it every conceivable variety of state law from slaughterhouse regulation to wages and hours legislation and on to segregated education. The use by the courts of the celebrated due-process clause of the amendment has been so protean and ingenious as almost to defy summary. This handful of words has been the basis for voiding dozens of state efforts at social reform as well as for justifying federal interference in the administration of justice within the states.

What is more, in the hands of the Supreme Court almost the whole Bill of Rights of the federal Constitution has been made an obligation of the states solely upon the authority of the due-process clause of this fecund amendment. In short, a host of domestic institutions and concerns, once strictly and admittedly within the domain of the states, have been slowly but inexorably transferred to the jurisdiction of the federal authority. Furthermore, the Fourteenth Amendment permanently made the civil rights of racial minorities a federal interest. This was accomplished not only by the due-process clause but also by the provision which threatened the state with loss of congressional representation if they counted Negroes in their population but did not grant them the vote. (Within three years, as we shall see in the next chapter, the Fifteenth Amendment was to make such enfranchisement mandatory throughout the nation.) This unprecedented interference with the suffrage, even indirectly, was yet another example of the subordination of the once-sovereign states to the burgeoning central leviathan. In the same amendment, in order to overturn completely and for all time the Dred Scott decision and its denial of citizenship to the Negro, citizenship was declared to be dependent upon place of birth. In this way it was placed beyond the discretion and authority of the states.

Although not directly connected with the forces of nationalism

[5] For years, under the influence of Charles A. Beard, historians have unfortunately confused the benefits business corporations derived from the amendment with the motivation for its origin. Jacobus tenBroek, *Antislavery Origins of the Fourteenth Amendment* (Ithaca, 1949), has put it back where it belongs: blood and flesh of the antislavery movement.

and freedom which the war fostered, the transformation of the office
of President during Lincoln's term is certainly attributable to the
war. As Woodrow Wilson observed, the Presidency is whatever the
incumbent can make of it, and Abraham Lincoln was personally a
strong leader and a committed nationalist. It seems indisputable,
nevertheless, that the trials of the war provided the necessary conditions for him to clothe the first magistracy of the Union in new
power.

In the course of the war the President stretched his war powers to
their outer limits. We have already seen how that power was used to
abolish slavery in the Confederacy, a usage of the power undreamed
of before 1860, except in the nationalist brain of John Quincy Adams.
Lincoln also suspended the writ of habeas corpus, suppressed free
speech and press, declared a blockade of the southern ports without
a declaration of war (despite the fact that four justices of the Supreme Court thought this action unconstitutional), spent money in the
early months of the war without congressional authorization, and
raised federal troops without an enabling act from Congress. As the
federal armies advanced, he undertook to reconstruct the rebellious
states and to provide for their return to the Union. "I conceive," he
explained to Senator Chandler in 1864, "that I may in an emergency
do things on military grounds which cannot be done constitutionally
by Congress."

Not even in the days of Andrew Jackson had there been a President so willing to act without waiting for congressional guidance or
approbation. Indeed, it might not be far wrong to see in much of the
truculence of the legislative branch during Reconstruction a natural
reaction to the four years of executive dominance which Lincoln exercised in the name of the War for the Union. In time of war, regardless of the cautious, circumspect men who were to occupy the
White House in later years, the Presidency would not be the same
after Lincoln had sounded the almost bottomless pool of its power.

5. A NEW WORLD POWER

That the Union emerged from the war more powerful and united
than before came as a surprise to many observers in London and
Paris. The end of the United States had been widely predicted. The
subtitle of Edward Freeman's study of federalism, published in 1863,
was suggestive of English upper-class prophecies: "From the Foun-

dation of the Achaian League to the Disruption of the United States."
And in the previous year, the British Chancellor of the Exchequer,
William Gladstone, declared that the southern leaders "have made a
nation. We may anticipate with certainty the success of the Southern
States as far as their separation from the North is concerned." The
French Emperor, Louis Napoleon, all through the early years of the
war toyed with the idea of recognizing the Confederacy, but the failure of the British to do so stayed his eager hand. He did not hesitate,
however, to take advantage of American internal preoccupations to
establish a French puppet regime in Mexico in defiance of the Monroe Doctrine.

All such anticipations of the downfall of the Union were reversed
by the military victories of 1864 and 1865. With the capitulation of
Lee, there could be no longer any doubt of the Union's survival, nor
of its awesome military might. Within a year of Lee's surrender, the
French agreed to withdraw their forces from Mexico. Europe was
beginning to feel the first stirrings of that military power, sprung
from a united people, which twice in the twentieth century would
come to redress the balance of the Old World.

"In the glare of our civil war, certain truths . . . have been
brought out with extraordinary sharpness of relief," wrote James R.
Lowell in 1865. One, particularly for Europe, "has been the amazing
strength and no less amazing steadiness of democratic institutions."
That steadiness was most obvious in the signal fact that in the midst
of a war which threatened the very existence of the Republic, an
election involving the fate of the administration itself was held on
schedule. There could be found no better example of democracy as
an orderly process of government carried out by leaders who believed in the wisdom of the people. At the beginning of the war,
Lincoln had said that it would show "that among free men there can
be no successful appeal from the ballot to the bullet." Northern victory had assured this. The years following would test whether any
nation "dedicated to the proposition that all men are created equal"
could make that principle work.

CHAPTER VIII

Dawn Without Noon

IN MAY of 1954, many Americans suddenly recognized, despite the fact that almost ninety years had passed since the War for the Union, that the sounds and clashes of that struggle were still echoing. The Supreme Court's decision that Negroes are entitled to equal status with whites in the public schools of the nation was but the latest of the efforts, beginning as far back as the time of Appomattox, to find for the Negro in America a place consistent with the national heritage of freedom and equality.

For a full two hundred years the character, the status, and the future of the great majority of black men in America were defined and molded by the institution of slavery. Then abruptly, within the course of four years of war, this customary and legal guide to race relations was completely swept away; white and black men alike had to set about establishing a new relationship. The determination of what that relationship should be has been slow, unsteady, and at times agonizing. Today, over a century after the enunciation of the Emancipation Proclamation, it has still not been finally determined; it is still capable of arousing deep-seated emotions among Americans.

1. EQUALITY BY FORCE

The first attempts to carve out a place for the black man in a white-dominated America were undertaken in the dozen years after 1865, which have since come to be called the Reconstruction period. That era, despite the cataclysmic character of the War for the Union, is best understood as a continuation of the history of the previous thirty years. The conflicts of the Reconstruction period are deeply rooted in the previous generation of sectional struggle over the issue of Negro slavery. The war, it is true, removed slavery from the congressional debates as effectively as it destroyed it in the South, but it failed to reconcile the opposite moral values which lay behind the two sections' conceptions of what slavery was and what the Negro was.

Many of the northern Radical Republicans, for example—men like Ben Wade, Charles Sumner, Thaddeus Stevens, William Fessenden, and John Bingham—had been in Congress during the antislavery struggle in the 1850's. They were still there when the Reconstruction of the former Confederacy was begun. For such men, the experiences of the years of antislavery and nationalistic agitation made it unthinkable that the South should be restored to the Union untouched by the fires in which they themselves had been tempered. And what was true of the leaders was true of thousands of ordinary men of the North whose lives were permanently altered by the moral fervor of the antislavery crusade and the emotionalism of the great War for the Union.

But the South, too, had a history by which its people had been molded. The Southerner's image of the Negro was shaped by the slave past, and its contours were shaken not at all by the rhetoric of the antislavery North or by the guns which finally destroyed the "peculiar institution." When the South came to legislate a status for the freedman, it would understandably draw upon the experience under slavery.

Under such circumstances, the cessation of hostilities between the sections brought not peace, but a political cold war, one which was more full of hate, bitterness, and misunderstanding than the hot war which preceded it. Since neither section had been able to transcend its historically derived conceptions about the nature of the Union, it was hardly to be expected that either would be able to rise above its history when dealing with the emotionally charged question of the freed Negro.

As the war overturned American thinking about slavery and the nature of the Union, so the Reconstruction re-educated the American people on the place the Negro should occupy in the United States. When the war ended, the position of the newly freed black man was ambiguous throughout the nation. In the North, though he was a citizen, society discriminated against him, and he was denied the ballot in all states except New York and five in New England. Moreover, as a measure of the North's attitude, within the previous five years the people of several northern states had over-whelmingly refused to extend the vote to Negroes. In the South, the Negro's ambiguous position was summed up in the fact that he was neither a slave nor a citizen.

But within half a decade, under the driving will of the Radical Republicans all this was reversed. The adoption of the Fourteenth and Fifteenth Amendments to the Constitution signified that the Negro was now to be a full citizen, equal in civil rights and voting privileges with white men. Insofar as modern Americans take pride from this inclusion of the Negro in the American dream of equality and opportunity, then it is to the Radicals that they are indebted. For it was solely because of the Radicals' control over the South that the requisite number of states were brought to ratify the two amendments. If not written into the Constitution then, when the conservative South was powerless to resist and the North was still imbued with its mission of reform, then the principle of Negro equality would probably never have been included in the national charter. This achievement of the Radicals is at least as much a part of the legacy of Reconstruction as the better-known corruption and the imposition of alien rule.

The accomplishment of the Radicals is especially noteworthy be-cause the obstacles were so formidable—not only in the South, but in the North as well. We have already seen that few states in the North in 1865 were prepared to grant Negroes the privilege of participating in the government. The North did, however, believe that the war had put a final end to Negro slavery. It was when that decision seemed to be challenged by the vanquished South that the equalitarian Radicals were presented with an opportunity to enlarge the area of the Negro's rights and privileges.

During the first year after Appomattox, there were a number of accounts from the defeated region to the effect that the former slaves were not being accorded their just rights. Even a reporter as friendly to the South as Benjamin Truman, President Johnson's personal observer, returned from his tour of the region with the impression that "even the greatest men of the South . . . believed that the Emancipation Proclamation was wicked and at least a mistake and a scourge to society."[1] Visitors less friendly to the

[1] Southern leaders were not loath to publicize their reluctance to see the end

South, like Republican Carl Schurz, found that "although the freed-man is no longer considered the property of the individual master, he is considered the slave of society and all independent state legislation will share the tendency to make him so. . . ." It was the so-called Black Codes passed by the newly elected legislatures of the southern states which seemed to offer the most accurate forecast of the future the South envisaged for the Negro.

Drawn up to take the place of the now defunct slave laws, the Black Codes were a compound of the old slavery statutes, northern apprenticeship and vagrancy laws, and British West Indian legislation dealing with emancipated slaves. Considering the history of slavery and the molding of the Negro under that institution, those parts of the Codes which fell short of equality before the law or of complete freedom are understandable, and on such grounds they have been defended. But seen in the light of northern experience and aspirations, the laws appeared to be a halfway station back to slavery.

It is true that the new laws expanded the rights of the freed Negro in permitting him to hold property, to sue and be sued, to make contracts, to marry, and so on. But it is equally true that the laws discriminated against black men. Negroes, for example, could testify in court only when their own race was involved, they could not carry firearms, and in several states restrictions were placed on their renting or owning land. Even more important, perhaps, was the fact that the laws required the freedman to work and forbade him to leave his job, thereby denying to him an important, if not indispensable, ingredient of freedom, namely, economic mobility.[2] When these pro-

---

of what they considered the most workable solution to the question of the Negro. The Governor of Mississippi told the legislature in 1865: "Under the pressure of Federal bayonets, urged on by the misdirected sympathies of the world . . . the people of Mississippi have abolished the institution of slavery. . . ."

[2] It has been argued that such provisions were necessary in order that economic production might be gotten under way again; that the Negro would not work unless compelled to. This argument falls to the ground, however, when it is recognized that the Codes were never put into any extensive practice (the United States military authorities and the Freedmen's Bureau suspended them and the later Radical state governments repealed them); yet the Negro certainly went to work and production increased. Such a defense of the Codes only serves to underscore the fact that the laws were actually devices to use the power of the state in the securing of a cheap, tractable, and convenient labor supply and not for the purpose of introducing the Negro to freedom.

visions are coupled with the knowledge that servitude without pay
was often the penalty for infraction of the Codes, it was only a short
step to believing, as did many Northerners, that the laws were in
effect re-establishing slavery. The people of the North were also
aware that the Codes left the Negroes at the mercy of their white
employers, since judges and juries were always white. Even under
the slave regime, the self-interest of the master, at least, had assured
a measure of justice for the black man in the white man's courtroom
or in the sheriff's office.

If the Black Codes reflected the influence of slavery on southern
thinking about the Negro, the northern reactions to the laws were
the result of the emotions left over from the long antislavery crusade.
For many Northerners the Codes seemed to demonstrate that the
South was trying to do by subterfuge what it was unable to do on the
battlefield—preserve slavery.

Those Northerners who could not be especially aroused against the
South by stories of atrocities against Negroes were often moved by
tales of outrages against southern white Unionists. Here, too, it
seemed as if the South was refusing to accept the verdict of the war.
"Hour after hour the democracy here are becoming more bold, more
insolent, more proscriptive," wrote one Virginian Unionist in 1866.
"Under democratic rule again," he warned, "hell would be a Garden
of Eden compared to the Southern States. . . ."

Under the skillful management of the Radical leadership, the unsettling reports of conditions in the South, the Black Codes, and the
pleas of southern Unionists appeared as insulting mockeries of the
North's wartime sacrifices and the long years of antislavery activity.
This was the first step in the Radicals' effort to convince the people
of the North that southern institutions needed federal renovation.

But before the Radicals could take advantage of the North's newly
aroused concern and act against the South, it was necessary that Lincoln's plan for the rapid restoration of the Union be set aside. The
President's plan, which his successor Andrew Johnson adopted, was
deliberately lenient to the defeated South in order that the Union as
it was in 1860 might be restored as speedily as possible. In pursuit
of this aim, the Presidential policy left the disposition of the status of
the Negro in the hands of the southern states.

By the end of 1865, all of the former Confederate states had completed the requirements under this plan and awaited only the re-

sumption of their seats in Congress to put the final seal upon their restoration to the Union. Since southern representation in Congress would have rendered impossible any further federal interference in the affairs of the South, the Radicals, who now controlled Congress, refused to seat the southern representatives.

By thus holding the southern states in a condition of constitutional suspended animation, the Radicals hoped to be able to work a social and political revolution upon the institutions of the region. Thaddeus Stevens, the leader of the Radicals in the House, made no secret of his aims. In January, 1866, he candidly told the House that he did not want the southern states returned to the Union until the Negro had been made a good citizen under the tutelage of northern missionaries. "I do not want them [the Southern states] to have the right of suffrage," he declared, "before this Congress has done the great work of regenerating the Constitution and the laws of this country according to the principles of the Declaration of Independence."

The goals of this revolution, as they unfolded in the next few years, included Negro equality, Negro suffrage, and a Negro-based Republican party in the South. Though only part of his ambitious program was apparent in 1865–66, there could be no doubt even then of the Radicals' desire to protect the Negro in his rights as a free man. In the spring of 1866, the Congress passed the Civil Rights and Freedmen's Bureau bills, both of which employed the federal power to insure the Negro's equality before the law and his equality of treatment in public places. The President's veto of these bills and the South's adamant opposition to them were answered by a new demand upon the defeated region. The Radicals now demanded as the price of readmission to the Union—in line with Stevens' statement in January—the ratification of the newly written Fourteenth Amendment to the federal Constitution.

Aside from its remarkably nationalistic tone, which we have already noticed, the Fourteenth Amendment proclaimed the equality of all Americans, black and white. Beginning by declaring that all persons born in the United States are citizens (thereby including Negroes), it went on to forbid any state to "make . . . any law which shall abridge the privileges or immunities of citizens of the United States," or to "deprive any person of life, liberty, or property, without due process of law," or to "deny to any person within its jurisdiction the equal protection of the laws." The amendment was submitted to the states, both northern and southern, in June, 1866, but its sweeping affirmation of equality was obviously directed first of all against those states which had been lately in rebellion.

The categorical and peremptory refusal of ten of the former Confederate states to ratify the amendment was a turning point in the history of Reconstruction. One cannot be sure, of course, what would have happened if the southern states had acted differently. We do know, though, that in the case of one state, Tennessee, whose ratification Congress accepted, readmission to the Union followed immediately, and Tennessee was not molested by congressional Reconstruction thereafter. If the other ten states had similarly been restored to the Union, then, presumably, there could have been no Radical Reconstruction as we know it simply because southern representation in Congress in concert with President Johnson could have stopped any such efforts. But even if the southern states were not restored to the Union, ratification of the amendment would have removed the primary justification for the later imposition of military rule. For it was in order to secure the necessary ratifying states that Congress later moved to the military subordination of the South. By refusing to ratify, the southern states gained little if anything, since it should have been obvious, given the temper of the country as revealed in the election triumph of the Radicals in 1866, that some effort to realize the equalitarian spirit of the times would succeed sooner or later.[3] By their intransigence, the southern states presented the Radicals with a lever with which to overturn the social structure of the Southland.

Viewed from the perspective of almost a century, the requirement that the southern states ratify the Fourteenth Amendment does not appear revengeful or vindictive,[4] but neither does it seem concil-

---

[3] It is interesting to note that the governors of Louisiana, Arkansas, and Virginia recommended ratification of the Fourteenth Amendment to their legislatures, but, of course, their advice was not heeded.

[4] Many historians, led by J. G. Randall, have come to refer to the Radicals as Vindictives. Such a simplistic view of the Radical motivation, however, obscures the remarkable lack of revenge displayed by the victors. Virtually no reprisals were taken against the South for the rebellion, despite the fact that the President of the United States was assassinated by a southern sympathizer. Probably never before in the history of any nation which had just suppressed a great rebellion could it be said, as was true of the United States, that not a single leader of the rebels was executed, or even tried for treason. Only one, Jefferson Davis, was imprisoned for any length of time, and he was released

iatory; few social revolutions, however, are easy to swallow. The amendment struck at the two most cherished canons of southern thought: states' rights and the inferiority of the Negro. The proud South was the prisoner of its history, and once again, as in the 1850's, it came up against the North's equally historical sense of mission and reform. And once again the North possessed the preponderance of power.

After the election of 1866 the North's support of the Radical program could be doubtful in no one's mind. The people of the North seemed prepared to go along with the social revolution which the Radicals were planning for the South. Moreover, they were apparently quite willing to have it apply to themselves, too, for the Fourteenth Amendment was ratified by over three-quarters of the northern states within the first year. The Radical election victory was overwhelming, even though President Johnson had embarked upon an unprecedented campaign against the Radicals and their program. New York returned a majority for the Republicans double what it had given Lincoln in 1864; New Jersey, traditionally Democratic, sent a majority of Republican congressmen; Pennsylvania elected eighteen Republicans and only six Democrats to the Congress; Michigan and Iowa returned solid Republican delegations. Only three border states, Delaware, Kentucky, and Maryland, went Democratic. All told, the Republicans secured 143 seats in a House of 192, enough to override any veto of the unfriendly President. The people of the North were solidly behind the Radicals' assertion that restoration of the Union must wait upon the South's acceptance of the equality of rights for Negroes.

"They have deliberated, they have acted," exclaimed Congressman James Garfield in February, 1867, when the ten southern states refused to ratify the Fourteenth Amendment. "The last of the sinful ten

---

after two years. None of the military leaders was held even momentarily, though a good number of them, like Lee, had left the federal service to join the Confederacy. The greatest economic blow levied against the South was the abolition of slave property without compensation, but this was not the work of the Radical Reconstruction. The evidence which is usually brought against the Radicals to show their vindictiveness does not support the charge so much as it demonstrates their interest in effecting a revolution in southern thinking and mores. Such enforced changes are admittedly painful, but hardly vindictive when viewed dispassionately. To persist in forcing through such changes is not any more vindictive than to redistribute Japanese land after World War II or to insist that anti-Semitism be prohibited in Germany.

has, with contempt and scorn, flung back into our teeth the magnanimous offer of a generous nation. It is now our turn to act." Armed with the victory at the polls, the Radicals now took their most extreme step. They placed the recalcitrant ten under military rule and, in addition to ratification of the Fourteenth Amendment, the southern states were required to extend the suffrage to the Negro and to revise their constitutions so as to grant equality to black men.

Since the northern states would soon be asked to grant suffrage to the Negro, it is instructive to set forth Thaddeus Stevens' justification for such a proposal. In placing his arguments before the Congress in January, 1867, Stevens candidly appealed to the three great principles for which the North had fought the war: the Negro, the Union, and the Republican party. "There are several good reasons for the passage of this bill," he began. "In the first place, it is just. . . . Have not loyal blacks quite as good a right to choose rulers and make laws as rebel whites? In the second place, it is a necessity in order to protect the loyal white men in the seceded States." With Negro suffrage, Stevens believed, pro-Union men in the southern states, both black and white, would constitute majorities, "control the States, and protect themselves." The final reason he offered was that "it would assure the ascendancy of the Union party. . . . I believe that on the continued ascendancy of that party depends the safety of this great nation."

To compel the South to accept Negro suffrage was to ask of that region more than the North at that time appeared willing to give.[5] But the North's opposition to Negro voting was deceptively weak, as the rapidity with which the Fifteenth Amendment was ratified demonstrated. In February, 1869, less than two years after Negro suffrage was imposed upon the South, the Fifteenth Amendment was on its way to the states. Ratification, with the assistance of the now Radicalized southern states, was achieved within thirteen months thereafter. By a combination of persuasion and emotion in the North, and ruthless suppression in the South, the Radicals had completed their revolution. In the eyes of the national Constitution the former slave was now a full citizen, equal before the law and in possession of the ballot.

[5] As late as 1868, only four states outside of New England and New York granted the suffrage to Negroes: Nebraska, Iowa, Minnesota, and Wisconsin. Colorado and Connecticut had rejected Negro suffrage in 1865; Ohio and Kansas did so in 1867; Missouri and Michigan in 1868.

2. HOW BLACK WAS BLACK RECONSTRUCTION?

But, it will be said, the price the South and the nation paid for this ideal of equality was outrageously high. And because the history of Reconstruction in the South has been so overlaid with myth and emotion, it is necessary at this point to digress somewhat in an attempt to put that unhappy decade into some perspective.

There is a myth of Reconstruction history to which most Americans, Northerners and Southerners alike, give credence. In brief outline it goes something like this. In 1867, a vengeful Congress placed the southern states under a military despotism which supported by its bayonets an alien regime in each of the states, composed of white adventurers—the carpetbaggers and scalawags—and their ignorant Negro allies. For a decade thereafter, the story continues, these regimes looted the treasuries of the southern states, impoverished the region with high taxes, denied the southern white people any say in their own governance, and spread terror throughout the Southland. Not until the withdrawal of federal troops in 1877, it is said, did this nightmare end and decency in government return to the South. As in most myths, there is some truth in this one; but a balanced picture of Reconstruction is quite different.

For one thing, though it is common to think of Reconstruction as lasting the ten years from 1867 to 1877, the actual duration of the military and Radical regimes varied considerably from state to state. Democratic or conservative governments came to power in Virginia and North Carolina as early as 1870 (in fact, Virginia never experienced a true Radical civilian government at all); in Georgia in 1871; in Texas, Arkansas, and Alabama in 1874; in Mississippi in 1876. Only South Carolina, Florida, and Louisiana depended upon the withdrawal of federal troops in 1877 for the overthrow of their Radical government. In brief, Radical Reconstruction, including the military phases as well as the civilian, lasted as short a time as three years in two states and as long as ten years in only three.

Because it is so often assumed that Radical Reconstruction was synonymous with military rule, the role of the Army in the South during this period must be precisely understood. Under the congressional plan of Reconstruction as set forth in the acts 'of 1867, the South was divided into five military districts, each under a major general. It was the responsibility of these generals to oversee the establishment of registration lists for voters for the constitutional conventions and the election of new governments in the states of their districts. Once this was accomplished, civil governments based on the new constitutions would assume power. Generally, the ending of military rule roughly coincided with the date at which Congress admitted the state to the Union. Thus military rule ended in 1868 in all of the southern states except Virginia, Texas, and Mississippi, and in those states it was over in 1869 or 1870. (Only in Georgia was military rule ever imposed again.) Often, it must be admitted, the Radical civil governments required or utilized the aid of militia and sometimes the federal troops to support their regimes, but this does not mean that an extraconstitutional government was in power. For the greater part of Radical Reconstruction, then, the southern states were under civil, not military, government, and, in most cases, these were governments which conservative white Southerners could influence with their votes. Indeed, it was by losing elections that many of the Radical governments fell into conservative hands before 1877.

But even when the southern states were under the military, it should not be assumed that the government was corrupt, oppressive, or unfair toward the whites. Contrary to the usual conception of the military occupation of the South, the number of troops actually stationed in the whole region was very small. No more than 20,000 men were involved in the whole "occupation," of whom fully 7,000 were concentrated in the two states of Louisiana and Texas. No garrison, except those in Richmond and New Orleans, which contained 1,000 each, numbered more than 500 men. The relative weakness of the military force, of course, is a measure of the southern acceptance of northern control.

Though weak in manpower, the military was supreme in law. In fact, the whole machinery of government and law was at the disposal of the Army; its authority was final. But the acquiescence in this on the part of the Southerners—for there was no organized opposition —is weighty testimony to the relative fairness of the administration. "It would be hard to deny that, so far as the ordinary civil administration was concerned," William A. Dunning, the authority on Reconstruction and no friend of the Radicals, has written, "the rule of the generals was as just and efficient as it was far-reaching. Criticism and denunciation of their acts were bitter and continuous; but no very profound research is necessary in order to discover that the animus of these attacks was chiefly political. . . ." There is good reason for believing, he continued, "that military government, pure and simple, unaccompanied by the measures for the institution of Negro suffrage, might have proved for a time a useful aid to social readjustment in the South, as preliminary to the final solution of political problems."

Even later, when the federal troops intervened in the South, it was with care and with a concern for fairness to the whites. President Grant in 1871, much disturbed by the attacks of the Ku Klux Klan upon Negroes, prevailed upon Congress to pass an act to aid in the suppression of the violence. Only once, however, did the President invoke the broad powers which Congress granted; this was in the famous incident of the nine counties of South Carolina in 1871. But even in this instance, Grant was careful enough to have the Attorney General investigate the situation in the area before he acted, and the President withdrew his order for one county when he found he was mistaken as to the disorders and conditions there.

In the prosecution of Southerners for infractions of the so-called enforcement acts, passed in 1870–71 to assist in the suppression of opposition to Negro suffrage, the federal courts tried hard to be fair. Out of the hundreds of cases against whites for infringements of these laws, there were relatively few convictions. One authority, William W. Davis, a Southerner, has estimated that only about 20 per cent of the cases under the acts resulted in conviction; and about 70 per cent of them were dismissed or nolle-prossed. "The Federal courts," Davis has written, "insisted on reasonable testimony, and the judges, with some notorious exceptions, were generally fair in their rulings." Moreover, he added, "White judges were inclined toward leniency in judging the white man prosecuted under the force acts on the testimony of black men." In summary, then, it would seem that justice was obtainable for the white man even during the grimmest days of so-called Black Reconstruction.[6]

Perhaps the explanation most commonly offered for the ascendancy of the Radicals and the Negroes in southern state governments

---

[6] Even a work as critical and penetrating as W. J. Cash, *The Mind of the South*, published as recently as 1941, contains exaggerated presentations of what happened during Reconstruction. "For ten years the courts of the South were in such hands that no loyal white man could hope to find justice in them as against any Negro or any white creature of the Yankee policy; for twenty years and longer they continued, in many quarters, to be in such hands that such justice was at least doubtful."

is that the conservative whites were disfranchised at the same time the Negroes were enfranchised. As a literal and nonquantitative statement, this is true, but as an explanation it will not hold water. At no time were sufficient whites deprived of the ballot to permit the Negroes and Northerners to take over the governments of the southern states by default.

Before the numbers involved can be discussed, the two different kinds or phases of disfranchisement must be understood. The first was during military rule, when Congress stipulated that those who had deserted federal office for the Confederacy or had voluntarily given aid to that cause were to be denied the suffrage and officeholding. Though it is impossible to obtain a completely accurate record of the number disfranchised under this rule (thousands of whites, for example, refused to register as a form of protest, but they are sometimes counted as disfranchised), the figure usually accepted is 150,000 for the whole South. This is to be compared with a total registration for whites in 1868 of about 630,000. Regardless of the size of the figure, under this disfranchisement only two elections were held, one for the choosing of the delegates to the state constitution conventions and the other for the selection of the officers of the new governments created under the constitutions. After that, the qualifications for voting would be those decided upon in the conventions and written into the new constitutions. And that was the second phase of disfranchisement.

Again, contrary to the usual opinion, the states, on the whole, in their Radical-dominated conventions were not as ruthless in disfranchisement as one might expect. And those which were, found that their disabling clauses were removed before ratification. In the end, only Louisiana, Alabama, and Arkansas actually enforced suffrage and officeholding restrictions against whites; the other seven states placed no legal obstacle in the way of white voting. Finally, it should be noted that the number of southern leaders upon whom the disabilities of the Fourteenth Amendment were visited was greatly reduced as early as 1872. At that date no more than 750 Southerners, those who had occupied high office under the United States in 1860–61 and had deserted to the southern cause, were still barred from officeholding. The disabilities against these men were not removed until the time of the Spanish-American War.

In view of the foregoing, it is illusory to look to white disfranchisement for an explanation of the electoral successes of the Radicals in the southern states. Rather it has to be sought in the fact that many whites did not vote, either in protest or because of indifference, while many Negroes did, either from understanding of the issues or from compulsion from their white and Negro leaders. It should not be forgotten, in this regard, that the proportion of Negroes in the southern states was uniformly greater at that time than it is now. Three states, for example—Louisiana, South Carolina, and Mississippi—contained a majority of Negroes, and one would expect, everything being equal, to encounter a Negro-Radical majority in those states. Moreover, a comparison of the number of Negroes registered in 1868 in each of the southern states with the number of Negro males over twenty-one as listed in the Census of 1870 discloses that only in Alabama was the actual number of Negro registrants out of line with the potential number as counted in the census. In all the other states the registration figures are plausible and not the result of obvious padding or fraud.

This is not to suggest that fraud did not occur in Reconstruction elections any more than it is meant to convey the impression that New York City elections at this time were innocent of fraud; undoubtedly there was much in both places and on both sides of the political fence. The purpose here, rather, is to show that there is solid justification for the strong showing which the Radicals made at the polls and that it is not to be casually attributed to the "counting out" of the whites. As a matter of fact, even under military-run registration in 1868, white voters outnumbered Negro voters in Georgia, Virginia, Texas, and North Carolina, a fact which rather effectively demolishes the argument that military reconstruction disfranchised the white majorities. Yet, of the two phases of disfranchisement, this was the stricter.

Looming over all discussions of Reconstruction, whether by Southerners or Northerners, is always the question of Negro domination. Surely, in the fear-ridden mind of the South, the unforgettable evil of Reconstruction was the participation of the Negro in government. Actually, though, aside from the exercise of the suffrage, which will be left until later, the Negro played a relatively minor political role in the Reconstruction of the southern states. Indeed, so limited were the number of offices available to Negroes that some of the Negro leaders, one southern authority has written, complained to their white mentors that their race was getting too few plums of office. Often northern whites who came to the South did not look with favor upon

Negroes in office, and Southerners who collaborated with the Radicals, retaining, at least in part, their southern-born attitudes on race, were chary of permitting too many Negroes to hold office.

Negroes, of course, did hold some offices under Reconstruction; in fact, outside of the position of Governor, which no Negro held in any state, black men filled each executive office at one time or another. In only one state, however, was a Negro a member of the Supreme Court; that was in South Carolina. The vast majority of Negro officeholders, however, were local officials like county superintendents of education and justices of the peace.

Contrary to the legend, Negroes did not dominate the legislatures of the southern states. The popularity of James S. Pike's sensational and partisan book, *The Prostrate State,* a contemporary description of the South Carolina legislature, has fostered the erroneous conclusion that such a body was typical of Radical regimes. In truth, Negroes were a majority in the legislatures of South Carolina and Louisiana only, and even there not for all the sessions of the period. Negroes were also a minority in all of the constitutional conventions called under the military, except, again, in the instance of South Carolina, and in Louisiana, where the whites and Negroes were equally divided. (South Carolina and Louisiana stand out in this regard because each contained a large and old city in which lived numbers of free Negroes who had some education and experience outside of slavery.)

Perhaps if there had been Negro domination, Reconstruction in the southern states would have been milder, for in both the conventions and the legislatures of the states the Negro members were the opposite of vindictive toward the whites. "I have no desire to take away any rights of the white man," said Tom Lee, delegate to the Alabama Constitutional Convention in 1867, "all I want is equal rights in the court house and equal rights when I go to vote." Even in the Negro-dominated legislature of South Carolina, there was no disfranchisement of whites beyond that prescribed for officeholding in the Fourteenth Amendment. Whenever the question of amnesty for Confederates came up in the United States Congress, where several Negroes sat during Reconstruction, the Negroes were usually found on the side of leniency toward the white man.

The South Carolina convention was extreme and unrepresentative of its sister conventions when it sought to ban terms of opprobrium like "Nigger" and "Yankee." South Carolina was also out of line with the other states when it provided for racially integrated schools; only two other states followed that example. For the overwhelming majority of Southerners, Reconstruction did not involve the mixing of races in the public schools. Nor did it mean the legalization of intermarriage between the races; the ante-bellum statutes prohibiting such unions were retained by the Radical regimes. The Negroes, in the main, wanted equality, not dominance.

Among the advantages which Radical Reconstruction brought to the southern states were the new constitutions which the Negroes and Radical whites wrote in each of the states. These organic laws stand up well upon comparison with earlier and subsequent ones in the South. As E. M. Coulter of the University of Georgia, and no friend of Reconstruction Radicals, has written, "The Constitutions finally turned out were much better than the Southerners had ever hoped for: in fact, some of them were kept for many years after the whites again got control of the governments." Generally they were "more democratic than the documents they supplanted, made so by increasing the electorate through Negro suffrage, requiring the total population as the basis for representation, reducing the terms of office, and by adding such principles as homestead exemptions and non-imprisonment for debt." The constitutions also provided for "free education for all and favored the economic development of the South," Coulter concludes.

Unquestionably, the evil most often charged against Reconstruction was the extension of the suffrage to a people the overwhelming majority of whom had only recently emerged from the dependent status of slavery. It is true that Negro suffrage in the South, aside from the intense fears it stirred up in the whites, was conducive to fraud, deception, and, at the very least, thoughtless voting. But viewed through the glasses of hindsight and with the recognition that universal suffrage is fundamental to a democratic society, the enfranchisement of the Negro appears considerably less "radical" today. The insouciant manner in which the suffrage was proffered to former slaves and the universality of the extension are certainly open to question, but the elementary justice of some form of Negro suffrage cannot be denied by any sincere advocate of democratic government.[7]

---

[7] It should not be thought that illiteracy was one of the legitimate arguments against Negro suffrage. Thousands of southern whites enjoyed the fran-

Unfortunately, on the matter of the suffrage, neither white Southerners nor northern Radicals were prepared to adjust their conception of the Negro to reality. Though some free Negroes were obviously capable of voting intelligently in 1865, as Lincoln, for example, recognized, and most Negroes would be after the mentally crippling effects of slavery had had a chance to be outgrown, few Southerners could shed their blanket view of the Negro as an incompetent. "The fact is patent to all," a South Carolina convention of whites asserted in 1867, "that the Negro is utterly unfitted to exercise the highest functions of the citizen." The South would not change. "Left to itself," southern historian Francis Simkins has concluded, "the region would not have accorded the Negro the vote or other manifestations of equality. . . ."

On the other hand, the northern Radicals, fearful that the South, once back in the Union, would deny the vote to all Negroes, and especially desirous of creating a large number of new Republicans, went to the other extreme and decreed universal Negro suffrage. This solution, however, overlooked the obvious disabilities which slavery had temporarily stamped upon a majority of the Negroes and seriously underestimated the tenacity of the historically ingrained racial feeling of the whites. Today the only comfort which can be drawn from the thoughtless and opportunistic policy of the Radicals is that it did provide a means for the inclusion of the Negro in the electorate, even if the means almost smothered the ideal with disrepute.

Radical Reconstruction in the South left a more permanent monument than the Negro's transient experience in public office and a nobler one than the southern white's nightmares of racial amalgamation. This was the laying of the foundation of southern free public education. Almost all of the Reconstruction conventions and legislatures erected or revived systems of free public education —a not insignificant manifestation, it might be noted parentheti-

chise even though they could neither read nor write. In 1880, for example, white illiterates averaged over a quarter of the population in Georgia, Alabama, and North Carolina. J. T. Trowbridge, the journalist, who made a tour of the South in 1865–66, concluded that the Negroes should be granted the suffrage. "They are," he wrote, "by all moral and intellectual qualifications, as well prepared for it as the mass of poor whites in the South." In a good number of states of the Union at this time, even immigrants were granted the vote prior to their acquisition of citizenship. The only valid argument against universal Negro suffrage, it would seem, was the lack of independent experience which was inherent in the Negro's former slave status.

cally, of the Radical propensity for making over Dixie in the image of the North. In most of the southern states, these Reconstruction efforts in behalf of public education remained after 1877 to become the bases upon which post-Radical governments built their school systems. Though the South had always had some free schools and even some local public-school systems, free education as it was known in the North by the 1850's began in the South only after the War for Southern Independence.

The other educational achievement of Radical Reconstruction in the South was the conversion of the whites to the view that Negro education was not only desirable but a necessity. This was largely the work of the Freedmen's Bureau. Prior to Radical Reconstruction in Georgia, for example, as Mildred Thompson has pointed out, the postwar government provided public education only for whites. Education for the Negroes was viewed as a waste of effort and perhaps even dangerous. All over the South in 1865–67, northern whites who attempted to instruct Negroes were subject to attack and violence. The blazing Negro schoolhouse of this period was the predecessor of the later burning cross.

Despite such opposition, the Freedmen's Bureau succeeded in establishing Negro schools before 1867. At its height, the Bureau operated over 4,000 primary schools, 74 normal schools, and 61 industrial schools for Negroes. George Bentley, a recent historian of the Bureau, concludes that by 1867 Negro and white alike in the South had come to accept the necessity for public education of the former slave. "Certainly in this respect," Bentley observes, "the Bureau had performed a commendable service for the Negroes, for the South and for the nation."

By the time the reader has gotten this far in the "other side" of Reconstruction, he is probably somewhat annoyed at the absence of references to the well-known corruption and fraud so much a part of the conventional picture of the period. He is convinced that this noisome aspect will be conveniently forgotten. There is no denying the disreputable character of all too many of the Radical state governments. Certainly the histories of Louisiana, South Carolina, Florida, and Alabama during this period provide rather painful examples of what corruption can be and what government should not be.

But again it is necessary to emphasize that the total picture is not all dark. Mississippi, for example, under Radical Republican rule enjoyed a government as administratively honest as most Democratic ones, and in some ways decidedly more honest. "The only large case of embezzlement among the state officers during the post-bellum period," writes James Garner, the historian of Mississippi Reconstruction, "was that of the Democratic state Treasurer in 1866." Mildred Thompson, writing about her native state, says that in comparison with states like Alabama and South Carolina, Georgia under Radical Reconstruction "shows a marked moderation in her government, a lesser degree of reconstruction evils, less wanton corruption and extravagance in public office, less social disorder and upheaval. In Georgia," she concludes, "Negroes and carpet-baggers were not so conspicuous, and conservative white citizens were better represented."

Though Virginia escaped entirely the period of Radical Reconstruction which other southern states endured after the cessation of military rule, she did not escape extravagance. In 1869, the first and last election under military rule brought the defeat of the Radicals in a free polling. But under the conservatives who then took office, Virginia contracted as staggering a public debt as those run up in the Radical-dominated states. Even the usual stories of the high taxes imposed by the Radical governments in the various states are susceptible of a different interpretation when put into some perspective. In 1870, for instance, when the average tax rate for the southern states was 15 mills, that of Illinois was 45.

The fraudulent dealings of the Radical regimes appear less exceptional and noteworthy if they are placed within the context of the times. For instance, it is instructive to realize that after the end of Reconstruction, each of the conservative Democratic governments in Georgia, Alabama, Virginia, Mississippi, Louisiana, and Tennessee had treasurers or other officials who absconded with or embezzled state funds, the individual defalcations often running to half a million dollars. Then, of course, the years of Reconstruction also included the Tweed swindles in New York City, in which perhaps over $100 million was robbed from the public treasury. And on the national level, the frauds and stealings carried out under the unseeing eye of President Grant serve to round out the picture.

Though not at all excusing the Radical frauds, the corrupt climate of the times does make it clear that the Radical pilferings were little more than particular instances of a general postwar phenomenon. And once this fact is grasped, it becomes apparent that it is not corruption which has fastened disrepute upon these short-lived regimes, but the fact that Negroes participated in them. "Corruption and extravagance increased the intolerance with which the Negro regimes were regarded," southern historian Francis Simkins has written, "yet even if these regimes had shown exemplary statesmanship they would have been unacceptable to white Southerners as long as Negroes comprising any part of them were regarded as political equals."

3. CASTE WILL OUT

The tragedy of Reconstruction is that it failed. Rather than liberating the South from its fear of the Negro, Reconstruction exacerbated it; instead of re-establishing a two-party political system, it further fastened a benumbing single party upon a region which once had led the nation in political creativity. Yet neither that section nor the North was alone responsible for the failure; both have to bear the national burden—the South for its intransigent conservatism, the North for its bungling idealism.

As is apparent today, it was imperative in those first years after Appomattox that a way be found whereby the nation and the Negro might confidently look forward to the former slave's full and equal participation in American life. But the unique opportunity of those first years was squandered. Neither Southerners nor Northerners were capable of disenthralling themselves, as Lincoln had counseled; both continued to act within their historically determined attitudinal patterns. Lincoln himself, for that matter, failed to grasp the crucial nature of the postwar era, so far as the Negro was concerned. His plan for the rapid restoration of the southern states indicated that he was quite prepared to throw away the single opportunity for realizing the equalitarian precepts of the Declaration of Independence to which he so often referred. And though the Radicals succeeded in enshrining in the Constitution their vision of equality for all, thereby illuminating the path the nation was ultimately to follow, they were woefully unequal to the complicated and delicate task of implementing their vision. Having failed to meet the problem of the black man at its inception, white Americans have been compelled to grapple with it in each succeeding generation down to our own day.

The inability of the Radicals to translate their equalitarian ideals into reality through the use of force[8] brought an end to the first phase of the search for a place for the Negro in America. During the years

[8] At the risk of seeming to condone the often cynical methods employed by the Radicals in the South, the principle behind Reconstruction deserves some

which followed, the South was left free to work out for itself what it considered the Negro's proper niche. Contrary to popular conceptions of Reconstruction and its aftermath, the South was neither united nor decided on what that position should be. The evolution of the region's place for the Negro would take another generation.

The southern leaders and people in 1867 had been extremely doubtful about the wisdom of Negro suffrage; but when Reconstruction came to a close, they did not move to eliminate the Negro from southern politics. Instead there was a substantial period during which the South freely experimented with Negro voting. In states like Mississippi and South Carolina, where the Negroes were a majority, a policy of bringing them into the Democratic party was tried. During the 1880's in South Carolina, for instance, several Negro Democrats sat in the legislature. A Negro was nominated by the Mississippi State Democratic Convention of 1877 for the office of secretary of state, and it was not unusual in that state for fusion tickets to be set up in black counties with Negro candidates. Such moves, however, were scattered instances, rather than general conditions; most Negroes remained in the Republican party.

As Republicans the Negroes in the South after 1877 continued to vote and to hold office, though when they threatened the supremacy of the whites, fraud, violence, and intimidation were used to right the balance. Negroes served in the South Carolina legislature right down to 1900, usually elected, of course, from predominantly Negro districts; during the 1880's and 1890's black representatives sat in the legislatures of North Carolina, Mississippi, and Tennessee. Negroes also represented the South in Washington after Reconstruction. Be-

---

attempt at a defense. It is a common argument that force cannot change ideas or dissolve prejudices, and that, therefore, from the outset Reconstruction flew in the face of experience. It is true that ideas are best changed by sincere, inner conversion, but this is not always possible; and weak as enforced conversion may be as a foundation on which to build sympathy and understanding, it is sometimes the only alternative. In both Japan and Germany after 1945, the western powers, notably the United States, undertook to impose certain concepts and forms of democratic life upon the defeated peoples. The only essential difference between these efforts to change people's minds by compulsion and that of Reconstruction was in method; the modern effort was, all things considered, intelligently and efficiently handled. The principle, however, was precisely the same as that which animated Radical Reconstruction in the South. It would seem that only those who oppose the principle of forcible democratization of Germany and Japan can consistently condemn the leaders of Radical Reconstruction for trying to solve by force, albeit ineptly, the problem of the black man in a white America.

tween 1877 and 1900, Negro representatives and senators from the South appeared in every Congress of the United States except the Fiftieth (1887–89). The Fifty-first Congress (1889–91), for example, counted three Negroes, one each from North Carolina, South Carolina, and Virginia.[9] All this came to an end, however, at the turn of the century, a pivotal date in the nation's search for a place for the Negro.

The first permanent law for segregating Negroes from whites in railroad cars was passed as early as 1881 in Tennessee, but it is erroneous to assume, as many have done, that the so-called Jim Crow laws went onto the statute books contemporaneously with the withdrawal of federal troops. Aside from bans on intermarriage and the initiation of legal segregation on trains, the large body of discriminatory legislation that characterized race relations in the South until very recently was unknown before 1898.

Before that date the mingling of whites and Negroes in public places was often quite unrestricted. In 1878, Thomas Wentworth Higginson, scion of a prominent Boston family, abolitionist, and former officer in a Negro regiment in the war, toured South Carolina to see the results of the resurgence of white conservative rule. He found the Negroes traveling on first-class cars, serving on the police force, and generally mingling with the whites in public places. Almost twenty years later in 1897, when a move was afoot to enforce segregation on railroad cars, a Charleston editor, by implication, indicated how little segregation there was in South Carolina. "Our opinion is that we have no more need for a Jim Crow system this year than we had last year, and a great deal less than we had twenty and thirty years ago." Such a system, he said, "would be a needless affront to our respectable and well behaved colored people." One anonymous Northerner, writing in the *Atlantic Monthly* in 1882, was told by the head of a racially mixed school in the South that "mixed schools" would come to the South. The author himself became convinced "that there will soon be mixed schools, for white and colored children, in many parts of the South. There are already a few such schools." Southern leaders acknowledged this possibility, he went on, and "they are not disturbed by the prospect."

---

[9] All during these same years, the North sent no Negro representatives at all, though it is only fair to add that the number of Negroes in that section was then very small. Not until 1929 did the first northern Negro sit in the Congress of the United States.

Writing in *Harper's Monthly* three years later, Charles Dudley Warner, on a visit to the South, noted that "In New Orleans the street cars are free to all colors; at the Exposition white and colored people mingled freely. . . ." A Negro clergyman, he reported, assisted at the services of the major white Episcopal church in that city. He was told by one Negro woman that in Mobile the Negroes had their votes courted by white politicians, and served in minor municipal offices and on the police force. Even the whites' Opera House, this woman told him, was turned over to the Negroes for an exhibition which the whites also attended.

To many visitors from the North, the South in the mid-eighties seemed to be making great strides in the direction of relaxation of racial discrimination. Part of this impression was merely a reflection of increasing northern sympathy for the southern point of view now that the emotion-packed years before 1865 were receding. But a substantial part was obviously a mirroring of the true situation. The end of the Reconstruction and the restoration of white rule had not resulted in the erection of a wall between Negroes and whites in the South.

But those who thought they detected a trend toward equality were destined for disappointment. Instead of expanding the realms of equality for the Negro, the South ultimately developed a pattern of race relations which clearly marked the Negro as a second-class citizen. The 1880's was a period when the legal racial pattern was still in flux, but already there were several signs pointing in the direction the South would go. For example, though there were very few laws requiring segregation, discrimination certainly existed, particularly in hotels, theaters, and on trains. And already in the 1880's, the ugly practice of lynching was spreading ominously. Between 1882 and 1903, almost 2,000 Negroes were lynched in the southern states, as against 567 white persons.

It was the Farmers' Revolt, coming to a head in the early 1890's, which finally brought the balance down on the side of increased restrictions on the Negro. The first form this took was the legal elimination of the Negro from southern politics. Aside from the small farmer's ever-present fear and hatred of the Negro, the aroused agrarian movement had new and compelling reasons for wanting to see the Negro deprived of the vote once and for all. The farmers believed, and sometimes rightly so, that the Negro vote was often mobilized against them, corruptly or otherwise, by the conservatives and the business interests against which they were fighting. Nor were these conservative leaders reluctant, if it served their purpose, to accuse the newly formed farmers' party of splitting the white vote and thereby endangering white supremacy. The complete removal of the Negro from politics, the farmers reasoned, would permit the whites to fight out their differences untroubled by the explosive and confusing issue of white supremacy. A further impetus to the elimination of the Negro from politics was given by politicians like "Pitchfork Ben" Tillman of South Carolina and James Vardaman of Mississippi, who were eager to use the poor man's Negrophobia as a handy vehicle to power.

The movement to eliminate the Negro voter permanently and constitutionally was led by the Mississippi Constitutional Convention of 1890, and the pattern arrived at there became the model for the rest of the southern states. During the nineties and the opening years of the new century, a veritable parade of southern constitutional conventions literally wrote an end to Negro participation in southern politics. To circumvent the prohibitions of the Fifteenth Amendment and yet eliminate effectively the bulk of the Negro voters, the conventions resorted to ingenious subterfuges. Poll taxes, complicated balloting procedures, and literacy tests were among the devices employed to strike Negroes from the registers.

Because the mass of poor white farmers had always harbored deep fears of the black man, these new constitutional provisions were only a translation into law of their own emotions and attitudes. But such legal narcissism exacted a price. The procedures adopted to exclude the Negro from the suffrage also operated to disfranchise thousands of poor, untutored white men who could not surmount any of the hurdles. White registration under the new Louisiana constitution, for instance, dropped 39,000 from what it had been only three years before under the old constitution; Negro registration fell over 125,000. But even this contraction in the white electorate—the reversal of a century of uninterrupted suffrage expansion—seemed worth the candle if it meant the elimination of a threat to white supremacy.

Under the momentum of these political changes, the southern states at the turn of the century began to issue a flood of legislation narrowing the Negro's sphere of activity and carefully defining his place in southern life. Segregation of the races was decreed on streetcars (only Georgia had such a law in the nineteenth century), in waiting rooms, in hospitals, in cemeteries, in housing, in prisons, at drinking fountains, and even in telephone booths (Oklahoma, 1915). Actually, the races were already segregated in practice in many of these areas without laws as sanctions, but in some instances the new laws, in logically extending the principle of separation of the races pressed the application even into minor aspects of life, such as drinking fountains and telephone booths. Certainly no such rigid and petty segregation of the races had existed in the South before; to that extent, at least, the law was creating "custom" rather than only reflecting it.

The segregation proposals of the late 1890's came as a shock to some white Southerners. One editor in Charleston, S.C., for example, where segregation was probably the least advanced in the South, voiced his opposition to legally enforced segregation on trains. He attempted to ridicule into oblivion the principle by carrying it out to what he thought was an obvious absurdity. "If there must be Jim Crow cars on the railroads, there should be Jim Crow cars on the street railways," he wrote. "Also on passenger boats . . . if there are to be Jim Crow cars, morever, there should be Jim Crow waiting saloons at all stations, and Jim Crow eating houses. . . . There should be Jim Crow sections of the jury box, and a separate Jim Crow dock and witness stand in every court—and a Jim Crow Bible for colored witnesses to kiss. It would be advisable also to have a Jim Crow section in county auditors' and treasurers' offices for the accommodation of colored taxpayers." But, as C. Vann Woodward has dryly observed, "What he intended as a *reductio ad absurdum* and obviously regarded as an absurdity became in a very short time a reality. . . . All the improbable applications of the principle suggested by the editor in derision had been put into practice—down to and including the Jim Crow Bible."

The southern solution to the problem of the races was to be a caste system for the black man in a society "dedicated to the proposition that all men are created equal."

4. THE SOUTH KNOWS THE NEGRO BEST

The gradual solidification of the Southern Way for the Negro did not take place in a vacuum. The South's erection of a system of caste for its black people was largely possible because of the encouraging attitude of the North. As the fervor of reform died down during the last two decades of the century and more materialistic considerations captured the nation's interest, the North came to accept the South at its own evaluation as the section which best knew the Negro and his capabilities.

How far the North traveled toward the acceptance of a caste position for the Negro is seen in two interpretations of the Fourteenth Amendment by the Supreme Court in 1883 and 1896. At the time of both decisions, it should be emphasized, the Court was composed almost entirely of northern Republicans. For example, when the Court handed down its decision in the Civil Rights Cases in 1883, only one Democrat—from California—and only two Southerners, both of whom were Republicans, were on the bench. In 1896, when the Court decided *Plessy* v. *Ferguson* on separate but equal railroad facilities, there still were only two Southerners. And, ironically enough, one of them, Justice Harlan of Kentucky, was the sole dissenter, as he had been in the earlier Civil Rights Cases.

The Court made it clear in its 1883 decision that the South would have a free hand in determining the civil rights of Negroes, the provisions of the Fourteenth Amendment notwithstanding. The Civil Rights Act of 1875—the statute at issue before the Court—provided that innkeepers, theater owners, hotel managers, and the like must accord equal treatment to members of all races. The Court held the act unconstitutional on the ground that the Fourteenth Amendment, upon which authority the statute rested, was only a limitation upon state-enforced discrimination and did not empower the federal government to prohibit discrimination on the part of individuals.[10] Though Harlan's biting dissent exposed the narrowly legalistic reasoning of the Court, his voice was a lone one in a nation longing for surcease from moral crusading.

At the end of the century, in the Plessy decision, the Court demonstrated its further willingness to move in step with the South on the question of segregation. The Court ruled that a Louisiana law which required separate railroad cars for the races was no contra-

---

[10] Justice Bradley, in writing the opinion of the Court, gave utterance to the growing northern disillusionment and weariness with the problems of the Negro. After a man has been released from slavery, Bradley said, "there must be a stage in the progress of his elevation when he takes the rank of mere citizen, and ceases to be the special favorite of the laws, and when his rights as a citizen or a man, are to be protected in the ordinary modes by which other men's rights are protected." As Harlan pointed out in his dissent, this argument missed the whole point; it was not that the Negro was asking for more than other men; he was pleading to be treated in the same way as other men, which was all the law presumed to do.

vention of the protections of the Fourteenth Amendment so long as the facilities for Negroes were equal to those for the whites. Yet the Court had promised, upon the occasion of the Civil Rights Cases thirteen years before, that any state action looking toward discrimination would fall under the ban of the amendment.

With the 1896 decision, the Court opened the way for the deluge of segregation statutes which soon separated the races in many areas of southern life. As a further indication of the close approximation of northern and southern conceptions of the Negro's place, it should be noted that both of the Court's decisions were viewed in the North as national, as against sectional, approaches to the rights of Negroes.

Only a southern Justice of the Court and a former slaveowner— John Marshall Harlan—saw the betrayal inherent in the decisions. In a ringing affirmation of the constitutional meaning of American freedom and citizenship, he appealed to the spirit as well as the letter of the Fourteenth Amendment. "The white race deems itself to be the dominant race in this country," he observed. "And so it is, in prestige, in achievements, in education, in wealth and in power. . . . But in view of the Constitution, in the eye of the law, there is in this country no superior, ruling class of citizens. There is no caste here. Our Constitution is color blind, and neither knows nor tolerates classes among citizens. . . . The law regards man as man, and takes no account of his surroundings or of his color when his civil rights as guaranteed by the supreme law of the land are involved." He then went on to warn his brethren: "In my opinion, the judgment this day rendered will, in time, prove to be quite as pernicious as the decision made by this tribunal in the Dred Scott case."[11]

By the end of the nineteenth century, molders of public opinion in the North had begun to look at the Negro through southern eyes. "I do not see," commented E. L. Godkin, editor of the liberal weekly, *The Nation,* "how the Negro is ever to be worked into a system of government for which you and I would have much respect." The history of the Negro race "leads to the belief," concluded Professor Albert B. Hart, himself the son of abolitionists, "that he will remain inferior in race stamina and race achievement." President Eliot of

[11] The one major example of northern dissent from the increasingly restrictive view of the Negro's place was the enactment of civil rights statutes in some fifteen northern states during the 1880's and 1890's. This was after the Supreme Court declared the federal Civil Rights Act unconstitutional. These state laws, of course, had no effect in the South, and even in the North they were only rarely invoked and supported.

Harvard said in 1907 that if the number of whites and blacks in Boston was nearly equal, "we might feel like segregating the one from the other in our own schools. It may be," he added, "that as large and generous a work can be done for the Negro in this way as in mixed schools. . . ."

In 1890, Henry W. Grady, publicist and spokesman for the business-minded New South, journeyed to Boston to deliver his last great oration. His speech, "The Race Problem in the South," was a spirited defense of the Southern Way, of the need for the South to be free to work out its own solution to the Negro question. "Hardly had he finished," reported the Boston *Herald* in describing the reaction of the predominantly Republican gathering, "when the audience rose en masse and joined in one great cheer." Boston, the very cradle and nursery of militant abolitionism, had capitulated to the South at last.

Even Negroes could find some merit in the southern position. Certainly it would be false to argue that Booker T. Washington and the masses of his people who followed his leadership agreed with the southern conception of the black man's proper place in American life. But it is equally certain that Washington's view of the black man's place was a limited one, summed up in his celebrated analogy of the fingers of the hand. "In all that is purely social we" (meaning whites and Negroes) "can be as separate as the fingers, yet one as the hand in all things essential to mutual progress." Moreover, the unprecedented praise which white Southerners heaped upon his Atlanta Exposition Address of 1895, in which he set forth his conception of the Negro's place, betrays how closely his position coincided with that of the white South. His whole philosophy of race relations was a retreat from the militant cry for equality and opportunity which had been the outlook of the earlier leader of the race, Frederick Douglass.

It has often been argued that Washington was being only realistic when he set forth a limited role for the Negro at that time. Be that as it may, the fact remains that, though he did not explicitly condone caste, Washington was, by agreeing to work within it, putting the ultimate stamp of approval upon the southern image of the Negro.

By the time of the First World War, it appeared that the American solution to the question of the races was strikingly parallel, if not similar, to that of South Africa. One South African, Maurice Evans, coming from his homeland to look at the American South, could only exclaim, "How often the very conditions I had left were reproduced before my eyes, thousands of miles melted away and Africa was before me." It seemed only natural that America, with a similar racial composition and therefore many of the same problems, would travel along the road with South Africa and move ever closer to total separation of the races. But, as we of the mid-twentieth century know, this did not happen; today, as South Africa seems to be hurtling toward racial catastrophe, America continues to press toward equality and integration, even though the path is rocky and progress maddeningly slow.

Not until late in the twentieth century—in the 1930's—was there a noticeable reversal of the progressive solidification of a caste place for the Negro. But the reversal did come because many Americans, Northerners and Southerners, white and black, never lost sight of the American dream of justice and equality, which the Radicals of Reconstruction had securely fixed in the Constitution itself. Like ceaseless waves beating at a seemingly immutable cliff, these amendments have eaten slowly—sometimes almost imperceptibly—into the structure of social and political inequality that had been built around black men in America. Indeed, thanks to these amendments and the decisions of the United States Supreme Court, the legal basis of discrimination has been completely dismantled since the path-breaking decision on school desegregation in 1954. Even the long-standing legal prohibitions against interracial marriage were overthrown by the Court in 1967. Moreover, Congress in the Civil Rights acts of 1964, 1965, and 1967 has thrown the weight of the law behind the drive for equality for the Negro in jobs, voting, and housing. But if the struggle to remove the legal bases for discrimination has been largely won, the fight for equality still continues, for discrimination against the black man in jobs and housing, in particular, clearly still remains, denying to Negroes that equal opportunity which the Radical program of 1867 promised but did not provide.

The advent of the Negro as a free man was only a part of the new shape the postwar America was assuming. Material forces of great potency were already at work during the war, and in subsequent years industrialization emerged as one of the molders of a new society. The sources of this new force demand some explanation.

CHAPTER IX

Machines, Men, and Socialism

SOMETIMES men living through an epoch of great change are so intent upon the immediate problems of their time as to be oblivious to the momentous tides swirling about them. David A. Wells, American economist and publicist, however, was not of this breed. Writing in 1889, he fully recognized that man's control "over the forces of Nature" had progressed so far that man "has been able to do far more work in a given time, produce far more product" per worker, and "reduced the effort necessary to insure a comfortable subsistence in a far greater measure than it was possible for him" to do twenty or thirty years before. Wells, in short, had put his finger on the quintessence of the industrial revolution which followed the Civil War. The years between 1865 and 1914 witnessed one of the great industrial expansions of all time; America emerged from that period the arsenal of two world wars and the prime industrial power of the planet.[1]

In the course of such a movement, however, the United States perforce underwent profound social change. The first to feel the new forces were the people who worked in the factories. The labor unions which they organized grew in importance and power along with industry, and the form they assumed was in many respects a reflection of the American environment in which they developed.

---

[1] The rate of American industrialization was not especially high; the annual rate, for example, was lower than that of either the U.S.S.R. or Canada. But the absolute increase in American production up to 1929 far exceeded that of any of the major industrial powers of the world. Most important of all, of course, is the further fact that the volume of United States production exceeded that of any other country by the opening of the twentieth century.

1. REVOLUTIONARY CHALLENGE

Between 1860 and 1914, the population of the United States tripled, while the number of workers in manufacturing increased five and one half times; the value created by manufacturing rose almost twelve times; and the capital invested in industry multiplied twenty-two times. In 1890, for the first time the value of manufactured goods surpassed that of agricultural commodities, although farm production was then at an all-time high and rising every year. By the turn of the century, the United States was already an industrial nation.

As industry expanded, railroad lines were flung across the nation at a prodigious rate. In the first thirty years of railroad construction, roughly between 1830 and 1860, some 30,000 miles of track had been laid. Within eight years after the surrender of Lee at Appomattox, the trackage was twice what it had been in 1860. By the end of the century, the United States railroad net was greater than that of all Europe: almost 200,000 miles of steel rails binding a continental empire, a people, and a market. Here, too, David Wells spelled out the implications of the new order, observing in 1885 that it cost less than seven tenths of one cent to transport a ton one mile on the average American railroad. "To grasp fully the meaning and significance of these figures," he pointed out, one has merely to realize that a ton of goods "can now be carried on the best managed railways for a distance of a mile, for a sum so small that outside of China it would be difficult to find a coin of equivalent value to give a boy as a reward for carrying an ounce package across a street. . . ."

Fundamental to the revolution in production was geography. Too often the largess of nature within the confines of the territory of the United States is overlooked in accounting for American success as an industrial power. For even the most advanced techniques cannot make up for fuel deficiencies and scarcity of resources. The French lack of good coal resources and the consequent limitation placed upon industrialization is a case in point.

The resources of the United States can only be described in Gargantuan terms: tremendous quantities of all the major minerals needed for industrialization—coal, iron ore, copper, minor metals like zinc and gold and silver, and huge quantities of the newly discovered black gold of oil; agricultural lands of virginal richness, extending across a continent; an invigorating climate of sufficient diversity to permit long growing seasons for fiber crops like hemp and cotton and food crops like sugar; forests providing ample lumber for a booming industry.

Superimposed on this geographic foundation of plenty was a framework of political unity which permitted goods to circulate freely. Once Americans mastered the techniques of rapid transportation and the integration of raw materials with finishing processes, the diversity of the sprawling territory and its resources would provide new markets and sources of supply unhindered by the political or linguistic barriers which, for example, hindered a France in the eighteenth century and a Germany as late as the middle of the nineteenth century.

But fundamental as geography and resources may have been, in and of themselves they offer no dynamic explanation for the rapid industrialization of the postwar years. The resources had lain unused for centuries and the climate was unchanged for millennia, while a people of a nonindustrial culture—the Indians—occupied the territory. Americans themselves, for that matter, had lived in parts of the country for upward of two centuries before they brought to life the bounty of nature buried beneath the soil. The explanation for the new quickening of industrial activity is not to be found in the raw materials; it must be looked for in the history of the people.

Even before the War for the Union, the bases of economic growth had been laid. The transportation network of canals, steamboat lines, and railroads, which we have already looked at, provided an indispensable foundation for growth. So did the manufacturing that for two decades had been developing in the burgeoning cities of New England and the Middle Atlantic states. Most economic historians would argue, in short, that the United States was already well on the road to industrialization prior to the Civil War; indeed, some would go so far as to contend that the war actually came as an interruption to growth. Thomas Cochran, for example, has pointed out that the *rates* of growth for railroad construction, pig iron, and cotton textile production, among others, actually declined during the war years and then shot upward in the postwar years. From his figures he concludes that the war as such may well have had a retarding effect on economic growth. Since Cochran's evidence is entirely quantitative by design and therefore he must leave out determinants of growth that cannot be measured or counted, his conclusions are not entirely convincing. His figures, however, do warn us that the war was not as unalloyed a push toward industrialization as some historians heretofore have assumed.

Among the possible factors that Cochran does not take into consideration, because the consequences cannot be measured, are government actions. Yet we know that federal expenditures increased from about $65 million annually before the war to a high of $1,296.8 million in 1865; by 1870 the figure stabilized at around $300 million, considerably above the prewar figure. Such expenditures by the federal government alone certainly provided a fresh impetus to the economy. Nor does Cochran take into account the possible effects of that legislation already referred to as favorable to northern business and which was enacted during the war—measures like banking and currency stabilization, the protective tariff, and the Homestead Act. His method also ignores activities begun during the war, which would be measured in statistics of production only years later, such as the construction of railroads. Although it was clearly the war, with the secession of the South, as we have seen, which permitted the enactment of the Pacific Railway Act of 1862, the road was not actually completed until years after the war was over. Thus, that railroad construction would not have appeared in Cochran's figures as a warborn impetus to growth, though in fact it was.

Government aid to railroad construction, incidentally, is a good example of the way in which one encouragement to growth, begun during the war, continued to be employed long after the war was over. Though government contributions to internal improvements were certainly not novel in America, never before had they been made on such a lavish scale as after 1860.

The federal and state governments, not to mention the municipalities scattered throughout the country, all seemed to feel, if one can judge from their actions, that to aid in the construction of railroads was to participate in the destiny of America. The government contributions were enormous for a nation where good government had often been equated with frugality. Cash loans totaling over $150 million were made to railroads by the federal, state, and local governments. In addition, a number of states and cities granted tax exemptions to railroad companies as an encouragement to construction —a concession, incidentally, which brought savings of at least $12.6 million to the railroads. State and local governments purchased at par almost $149 million worth of railroad securities, which, it has been conservatively estimated, returned the railroads about $50 million more than they could have realized from the sale of the securities to private purchasers. Foremost among the aids of government were the 134 million acres of public lands granted to some seventy railroads by the federal government and the 48.9 million acres granted by nine states. These gifts of land, if brought together, would comprise an area larger than the United Kingdom, Spain, and Belgium combined. Depending on how one estimates the value of these lands, the railroads received between $130 million and $500 million as an outright gift.

Beyond a doubt, the aid from the community in the construction of the railroads was substantial, but one can overemphasize its effect on total railroad building. For instance, the trackage of the roads receiving the federal grants of land comprised only about 8 per cent of the total in the country. Furthermore, after 1871 the policy of land grants, begun as far back as 1850, was discontinued. Even a transcontinental railroad like the Great Northern was constructed without any federal land grants, and many another, though less ambitious, railroad in the later years of the century could say as much.

Nor should it be casually supposed that land grants and other aids from government were necessarily fraudulently acquired or even socially undesirable. For one thing, there was a *quid pro quo:* the railroads furnished the government with transportation at reduced rates. Furthermore, the loans which the government made were almost completely repaid, with interest, although, it must be added, not until the federal government went to court. From a social standpoint there was a sound basis for the assistance. A substantial part of the lands granted to the railroads acquired worth only because the railroads built through to them; by rendering the lands accessible to settlers, the railroads largely created their value.[2] Though this point can be exaggerated, it carries especial weight in regard to those trans-Mississippi states and territories where transportation of bulk items was almost wholly dependent upon the railroad.

A recognition of such facts, however, should not obscure the important point that the aids of government were indispensable to the construction of many, if not most, of the western roads. It is inconceivable that canny private investors, particularly in the first decades of the railroad age, would have put their money into rails running

---

[2] In actuality, of course, the government "gave" nothing when it made land grants. It was the homesteader who bought land from the railroads who made the contribution to railroad construction. Generally, he paid a higher price when he bought from a railroad than he would have had the land been purchased from the federal government.

through dry and empty plains, obviously bare of both freights and markets. But such prudent men would take a different attitude if their investments were guaranteed, as they often were, by state or local governments or supported by federal land grants and loans.

In the end, though, the part which government played in the powerful thrust of industrialization after 1860 cannot be accurately measured or accounted for in dollars, acres of land, or legislative enactments. There was also something much more subtle. It was the warm, reassuring attitude of sympathy in which government in America bathed business enterprise. Such a friendly atmosphere was eminently conducive to investment and entrepreneurship, and was probably worth as much as all the gifts and laws put together. The degree of government beneficence displayed toward business is measured by the outright hostility and suspicion displayed toward labor. Recall, for example, the massive federal intervention in the great railroad strike of 1877, and in the labor troubles at Coeur d'Alene and Pullman and Chicago later in the century. Remember too the notorious use made by the federal courts of the Sherman Antitrust Act to hamstring labor organization—what John Peter Altgeld was to call "government by injunction."[3] Economic historian Joseph Schumpeter has argued that capitalistic enterprising is a delicate flower, easily discouraged and impeded by governmental threats and interference. If this be so, then the late nineteenth century in America was a veritable hothouse for such flora.

This rapid and successful expansion of the industrial machine was also encouraged by the great influx of immigrants in the postwar era. Before the war, the annual immigration was measured in thousands; in the years after, it was often counted in millions. In the decade of the eighties, for example, over five million newcomers entered the United States, becoming eager workers and avid customers of American business. In any balance sheet of the nation's industrial assets, the manpower of these strangers to America must be included.

[3] At the time of the coal strike of 1902, President Theodore Roosevelt learned how dependent the business leaders had become upon governmental defense of their interests. In a letter to a friend, T. R. told how the coal operators with whom he had been mediating refused to deal with the union and even "in at least two cases assumed an attitude toward me which was one of insolence. . . . One of them demanded outright and several of them hinted that they were going to demand that I use the United States Army in their interests. . . . They kept referring to Cleveland's course in the Debs' riots as offering a parallel, which was of course either ridiculous or dishonest on their part. . . ."

But this second wave of industrial expansion in American history was a product of things as well as of people. The hundreds of inventions of the period were, in some cases, of fundamental importance to the expansion of industry: the Bessemer process in steel, for instance, which made this versatile metal usable on a wide scale for the first time; the Siemens-Martin process, which permitted even poor ores to be converted into steel; refrigeration, which laid the foundation for a nationwide meat-packing industry; the telephone, the electric lamp, the internal combustion engine, and so on. A catalogue of major inventions of the period would almost be a list of the great industries which sprang up in the new age. And along with such spectacular inventions went numerous improvements, adaptations, minor gadgets, like the typewriter, which, by being widely adopted, allowed the machine to sink deep into the everyday life of Americans.

The machine has always been welcome in America;[4] indeed it is almost a symbol of American industry. Europeans frequently poke fun at the American's preoccupation with gadgets, contraptions, and machines; they even imply it reveals our lack of human concern. But there is historical reason behind the American's machinemindedness. As a country chronically short of labor, America has generally welcomed machines because it has needed them; where labor costs are high, employers readily turn to machines in order to save on their wage bills. This willingness to use machines is, in turn, closely related to the high standard of living in America. Machines spelled high productivity of labor, and the key to any rising standard of living is increased production per worker. The wider the acceptance of the machine, the greater the possibility of a rising wage for the individual worker.

The American addiction to the machine was apparent to foreign observers fifty years ago. In the fall of 1902, Alfred Mosely, an enterprising English businessman, succeeded in bringing the secretaries of twenty-three major British trade unions to the United States for the purpose of studying the "secret" of American productivity. The reports of these delegates from the trade unions are suffused with admiration for the advantages machines afforded the American as

---

[4] In 1789 the rector of the Swedish Churches in Pennsylvania told the American Philosophical Society: "Machines for abridging human labour are especially desired in America as there can be no competition between them and the arms of industrious labour, while these have full employ on her extensive land; which must be the case for ages."

compared with the British worker. "The number of labour-saving appliances in use for almost everything is perfectly astounding," said G. D. Kelley of the Lithographers. "American employers believe that machines rather than men or women ought to be driven," concluded T. A. Flynn of the Tailors, "and the clever workman who, by invention or suggestion, enables his employer to carry out this ideal is encouraged in a manner delightfully real and sincere."

The close connection between this interest in machinery and an improving status for the worker was clearly seen by W. C. Steadman. "The American workers do not work any harder than their English brethren," he observed, "the tendency being to use improved machinery of the latest type, and should a new machine be put in today and a better one come out tomorrow that will turn out more work it will be put on one side for the latest and the best, no matter what the cost." This is in contrast with the situation in England, he noted, where we "use machinery to decrease wages, in America it means more wages and shorter hours, and workmen are encouraged by their employers" to make suggestions and improvements. Another delegate, after contrasting American employers' readiness to adopt new machinery with the English employers' continued use of obsolete machines, went on to say: "I don't pretend to think that the American employer loves his workmen more than does the British employer, but he recognizes" that up-to-date machinery "pays, while the other does not."

Though Americans were interested in using machines, they did not always have to invent them; many basic inventions, like the Bessemer and Siemens-Martin steel processes and the internal combustion engine, were of European origin. This fact serves to remind us that American industrialization, coming late in the century, enjoyed the signal advantage of being able to tap the accumulated industrial and technological experience of the European nations, particularly England's.

European assistance to American industrialization amounted to more than technology. An underdeveloped country at that time, the United States had access to the accumulated capital of the whole western world, and the movement of European capital into America was substantial. By the conclusion of the nineteenth century, $3.4 billion of European capital was tucked away in American enterprises. When the First World War broke out, American industry had absorbed over $7 billion of the Old World's capital. Thanks to the international tranquillity of the nineteenth century and the marvelous interchangeability afforded by the gold standard, American industry experienced a minimum of difficulty in borrowing the savings of the hard-working Victorian bourgeoisie. At any other time in history (for that golden age of peace and free exchange was of relatively brief duration), the process of American industrialization would have been more like the strenuous capital accumulation of the Russians and the Indians in the twentieth century. The advantages which accrued from the ability to tap other people's savings are graphically demonstrated in a comparison of national savings. It has been estimated that Americans saved between 11 and 14 per cent of their national income as against probably well over 20 per cent saved by the British during their rise to eminence. It is believed that Soviet Russia has been compelled to set aside more than 20 per cent of the national income in order to finance her industrialization. Americans, it would appear, had it considerably easier than other countries.

When one has set down all the possible factors which might account for this surge of industrialization, there still seem to be some missing ingredients. One of importance is the very spirit of the people themselves. What made them work; what made them strive for wealth, status, improvement? For certainly these qualities are as necessary as mineral wealth or salubrious climate. Was it the Puritan past, the remarkable mobility of American society, which offered incentive to all, the unexampled opportunities for the industrious, the speculative streak which ran through all Americans ever since Columbus took a chance? It would be hard to say, but certainly they all aided in sparking that drive for work and activity which then, as now, is the trade mark of the American. Also among the people were the entrepreneurs—not merely the capitalists who supplied the money, but those men who possessed a genius for industrial production and who, by throwing together the resources of a nation, the labor of millions, and the capital of the western world, built American industry.

Who were these entrepreneurs; what made them tick; how was it that they so dominated the American economy during those years? This is neither the place nor yet the time to answer such important questions, since historians have only just begun to explore the question of the crucial role of the entrepreneur in economic growth. We

can do little more than set forth some of the less controversial or
obvious features of the entrepreneurs who dominated late-nineteenth-
century America.

Some time ago, in an investigation of major industrial leaders like
Rockefeller, Vanderbilt, Guggenheim, Armour, Carnegie, and others,
Charles A. Beard attempted to generalize about the social origins of
the entrepreneurs. As a class he found them coming from the lower
strata of society, sons of farmers, generally rather poorly educated,
and often foreign-born, as in the case of Carnegie. As a group, he
thought the giants were representative of a new class of men come to
economic power in America.

More recent investigations, however, using a broader sampling,
have arrived at a much different picture. Whether one looks at a
sample of fifty-one railroad presidents, as Thomas Cochran did, or
at the successful businessmen who appear in the *Dictionary of American Biography,* as C. Wright Mills did, the conclusion is inescapable that these industrial leaders were not men who came up from
the bottom. The level of education, for example, which they attained
was far above that of most people of their day. Over 50 per cent of
those born between 1820 and 1879 attended college in an age when
high school was still the exception for most Americans.

In another study William Miller found that 70 per cent of those
born between 1850 and 1879 came from upper- or upper-middle-class
families. Moreover, as against Beard's findings, almost 48 per cent
of them had fathers who had been businessmen, and only 21.5 per
cent came from farm families. Something like 90 per cent of these
men were native-born. The conclusions of a study of three hundred
executives of important firms in the 1870's can serve as a summation
of all these investigations. The authors found that the typical entrepreneur was "American by birth, of a New England father, English in national origin, Congregational, Presbyterian or Episcopalian
in religion, urban in early environment," and "born and bred in an
atmosphere in which business and a relatively high social standing
were intimately associated with his family life. Only at eighteen did
he take his first regular job, prepared to rise from it, moreover, not
by rigorous apprenticeship begun when he was virtually a child, but
by an academic education well above average for the times." In short,
the men who were getting to the top, even in the 1870's—that alleged
era of self-made men—had not been poor farm boys or uneducated
immigrant lads starting at the bottom, but instead men who had been

given rather exceptional opportunities to make the race to the top.[5]

When, however, we turn from the social origins of these men to their personality traits, generalization is much less easy, even if one confines himself to the best-known leaders. Vanderbilt may have been ruthless and gruff, uneducated and uncultured, but Carnegie was subtle and articulate; Rockefeller was taciturn but commanding, quiet but implacable. The common factor eludes us.

One characteristic which does stand out as almost universal is their passion for their work. In a study of forty-three careers of well-known captains of business, Chester Destler discovered that only two of them actually retired in order to rest; the others either never retired or had to be compelled to for one reason or another. Numerous stories of their application to their job come to mind; some are almost noble, many are close to being sordid, but all demonstrate that the job was the thing. Rockefeller's attention to detail was legendary; at one point he indignantly inquired of a subordinate where a few hundred missing bungs from the oil barrels were, for he had detected a discrepancy in the routine accounts. At another time he painstakingly revised the number of drops of solder used in sealing oil cans in order to save the expenditure of a single extra drop. More human perhaps is the picture of J. J. Hill, the railroad magnate of the Great Northern, getting down from his train one bitter Minnesota winter's night to help his men shovel snow from the tracks.

The strike for the main chance is common among the life histories of the giants; often it appears early in their careers. William A. Clark, for example, later of the copper trust, plunged into the wilds of Montana with a load of tobacco, confident that he could sell the weed at monopoly prices to the miners there. Collis P. Huntington, subsequently of Central Pacific fame, built up his San Francisco grocery business by beating his competitors out into the Bay to meet the supply ships from the East.

---

[5] The social origins of the top business leaders of the mid-twentieth century seem to be about the same, according to Mabel Newcomer, *The Big Business Executive, the Factors That Made Him, 1900–1950* (New York, 1955), p. 149. "The typical executive of 1950," Miss Newcomer concludes, "is a native American, the son of a small, independent business man. His family's income was moderate. . . . His parents managed to put him through college, with such contributions as he himself made to his own expenses through part-time employment, mostly in summer." She notes that a college education is, in some ways, a better way to the top than inherited wealth. And because college education is so accessible, the opportunities for a poor boy's reaching the upper levels of business leadership seem to be greater now than fifty years ago.

Though lust for wealth was a part of the thinking and most likely the mainspring of all great entrepreneurs, one would be settling for half a man if he thought that this was all there was to them. To work so hard and so unflaggingly as they did for an additional million or two after the million mark had long been passed is not explicable in terms of simple greed. Instead, Rockefeller's urge to bring order out of chaos in the oil industry, Harriman's dream to encircle the world with his rail and steamship lines, or Ford's ambition to produce a cheaper and better automobile than anyone else suggests that a mechanism more human than profit was driving them. These men were looking for adventure, for challenge; they were men playing "the Great Game," as Allan Nevins has called it. Perhaps for the latter portion of the nineteenth century this was the equivalent of war for which William James was seeking. Though it was hardly "moral," as James hoped it would be, it was still peaceful, invigorating, and undeniably productive.

Diverse as these men may have been in personality, there can be little question as to the means which they employed. Of forty-three noted leaders of business whom Chester Destler studied, thirty-six used monopoly or near monopoly to gain their ends. Thirteen used political corruption, sixteen of them mulcted their own companies for their personal advantage, and twenty-three charged exorbitant rates if the traffic would bear it. There is no way of knowing to what extent this example was followed by lesser-known entrepreneurs, but there seems no reason to believe they were significantly more scrupulous about methods.

It is one thing to note how the entrepreneurs built their empires; it is another to make an ethical judgment on their practices. Recently, the so-called Robber Barons have come in for more spirited defense than at any time since the days of William Graham Sumner.[6] But to defend the methods of these leaders on the ground that the job was done, as some historians have, is to be guilty of justifying the means by the ends. But to go even further, as Allan Nevins has, to justify them and their methods on the ground that the industrial power they built enabled the United States to win two world wars is to commit the more grievous crime of excusing men in the name of

[6] *The Saturday Review,* February 6, 1954, carried a lively debate on the subject of the Robber Barons between the man who popularized the term— Matthew Josephson—and Allan Nevins, who has been foremost in defense of the gentlemen in question.

consequences they never intended. Such a procedure drains the whole matter of any moral content. Furthermore, to plead the extenuation of the climate of business ethics of the time, as still others have done, is to lose sight of the fact that there were, after all, many men who, objecting to the ruthless claw-and-fang tactics of the titans, were quick to point out the undesirable aspects of it. Besides, were not the workers who objected to the low wages and antiunion tactics of the great combines a part of the climate of opinion? All of which suggests that perhaps the question cannot be answered in purely moral terms.

The most we can say is that the industrial machine was built and that the social and human cost was high. But then perhaps we must also ask ourselves whether any nation has transformed its way of life at any time in history without exacting a frightful human toll. Compared with the social costs in the England of the nineteenth century and the Russia of the 1920's and 1930's, the American industrial revolution was cheaply done.

2. THE INDUSTRIAL LEVIATHAN

To many Americans who lived through the era of the trusts, it seemed as if industrialization was synonymous with what Louis Brandeis stigmatized as "Bigness." For at the same time that industrialists pushed for a free, highly competitive economy in conformity with the most theoretical postulates of capitalist economics, in their daily work they were busily engaged in building ever larger, oligopolistic industrial empires. This consolidation of small units of production into larger ones, this concentration of control in business, has manifested itself wherever the factory has taken root: in newly emergent Japan with the Zaibatsu, in Imperial Germany with the cartels, in rising America with the "trusts," and in the older industrial nations like France and Britain. The forms of such concentration have varied widely, from actual mergers to mere loose agreements to divide the market, as in pools and cartels. But the purpose behind them has always been the same—the control of the market and the elimination of competition. Here was the paradox, for only with competition was industrial capitalism able to function as it was expected to—as both a producer of the maximum amount of goods and a system of fair distribution. When industrial capitalism forsook competition, it soon failed to fulfill its promise as a system of production and distribution. When that happened, political attacks upon the system were not far away.

One of the great consolidation movements of American industry took place in the 1890's and the early years of the twentieth century —the era of the Sugar Trust, the Beef Trust, the Steel Trust, the Oil Trust, and the Money Trust. Symbolic of the era is the United States Steel Corporation, organized in 1901 as the first billion-dollar corporation in history. At the moment of its creation, this fusion of some 200 companies in the steel and iron business controlled 60 per cent of the production in the whole industry. So effective was its control that the price of steel rails in the country was stabilized for over a decade at $28 a ton.

During the latter half of the nineteenth century, a number of other industries provided examples of consolidation. In the cotton goods industry, for example, between 1850 and 1905 the number of factories remained substantially the same, but the value of the production per establishment rose over 600 per cent. The agricultural machinery industry underwent an even more dramatic concentration; over half of the companies disappeared from independent production at the same time that the value of output of each of the remaining establishments increased almost 3,300 per cent! Examples not quite as eye-catching, but equally as indicative of the spread of concentration, could be named for other major industries of the country. Even a relatively new industry like electrical machinery manufacturing showed a 400 per cent increase in production per establishment in the course of the twenty-five years before 1905.

The same tendency was observable in railroading. In 1910, 67 per cent of the total trackage in the United States was owned by only fifty-four giant companies, each of which had over 1,000 miles of track. The prime individual example of railroad consolidation was that afforded by Edward Harriman. Obsessed with the idea of dominating the railroads of the country, he succeeded, by the time of his death in 1909, in building an empire of rails which extended from the west to the east coasts, from the North to the South; only death deprived him of Manchurian lines that he hoped to link with his American roads through Pacific steamboat routes which he also owned. His best-known effort at cornering the railroads of the country was made in conjunction with J. J. Hill, when they created the Northern Securities Company, a holding company controlling almost all the railroads west of the Mississippi. This affront to competition, however, was dissolved by order of the Supreme Court in 1904.

Consolidation of enterprises was only one sign of the maturing character of the American economy; the growth of investment banking was another, and, like consolidation, it tended to attenuate competition. As Werner Sombart has pointed out in regard to European capitalism, the advent of the investment banker signalizes the last stage of a maturing capitalism. Only after a long period of capital accumulation, and at a time when the size of individual firms has grown beyond the resources of self-financing, does the financier assume a crucial importance in the economy.

By the 1880's and 1890's the investment banker, with pools of capital at his disposal, was in ever-mounting demand from railroads requiring financial reorganization and from firms buying up competitors or marketing large security issues. It was then that the House of Morgan began to acquire its world-wide renown, attaining an almost mythical eminence as a symbol of financial power. Morgan successfully managed the reorganization of several important railroads, notably the Southern, in the late nineties, as well as gathering the necessary capital for the creation of the mammoth U.S. Steel Corporation in 1901. During the depression of 1893, J. P. Morgan enjoyed the unexampled prestige of being appealed to by the President of the United States for assistance in protecting the financial standing of the government itself.

The central position of the banker in the economy was officially recognized in 1912 with the appointment of the Pujo Committee of the United States House of Representatives for the investigation of what was popularly known as the Money Trust. The committee found that a small group of financiers, numbering Morgan of New York and London, and Kidder, Peabody of Boston, among them, "have . . . been more destructive of competition than anything accomplished by the trusts. . . ." By controlling the credit and capital supply in the nation, these bankers, the committee report went on, "strike at the very vitals of potential competition in every industry that is under their protection," and if they are permitted to continue, they "will render impossible all attempts to restore normal competitive conditions in the industrial world. . . ."

The Pujo Committee reported that the House of Morgan and its affiliated banks—the First National and the National City—held

341 directorships in 112 corporations having aggregate resources of over $22 billion. Such concentration of control and power, though neither complete nor absolute, was, nevertheless, highly suggestive of the distance the American economy had moved from the economist's ideal of perfect competition. Certainly, only halfhearted competition could be expected among firms each having members of the same banking house sitting on the boards of directors. In this and other ways it was clear that the penetration of finance into industry was muting competition in America.[7]

Industrial concentration, no matter whether it took the subtle forms of finance or the ruthless form of driving a competitor to the wall, presented a challenge to society; such aggregations of wealth and economic power in relatively few hands could be dangerous as well as beneficent. Just as the essence of the art of politics is balancing freedom with authority, so in an advanced capitalist state the essential economic problem is balancing efficiency and maximum production against protection for the consumer. Once competition is forsaken in pursuit of the economic advantages of great combinations, the built-in protections of theoretical capitalism cease to be operative. It is therefore necessary to work out institutions of control which will protect society but at the same time not shackle the enormous productive power and efficiency which seem to be inherent in concentration. The social need for some control over the concentration of economic power became so glaring and insistent by the end of the 1880's that all the major political parties in the country included antitrust planks of one sort or another in their platforms. For as Henry Demarest Lloyd summed it up in 1884: "If the tendency to combination is irresistible, control of it is imperative."

The American people in the years before 1914 arrived at two different solutions to the question of industrial concentration, both of which are still operative today. The first one is symbolized by the Interstate Commerce Commission, created in 1887 as an answer to the economic power of the railroads. In the railroad-building era after the Civil War, towns and shippers had vied to attract the revolutionary iron horse to their locality only to find that it was a genie which could destroy them. Often in a monopoly position, the rail-

---

[7] Nor has the problem ended in our own time. In 1951–53 the federal government presented a five-million-word case against the leading investment houses of the country, charging a conspiracy among them to restrain competition. The case was dismissed, however, in September, 1953, as unproved.

roads did not hesitate to use their power. Higher rates for a short haul than for a long one were common; under-the-counter refunds for one shipper and not for another were frequently used as devices to reward the big shipper. Setting rates as high as the traffic would bear was virtually standard procedure for any railroad worth its salt.

Though protests against such cavalier treatment of the consumer and shippers had been heard as early as the 1870's, no satisfactory answer to the problem was worked out until the Interstate Commerce Act of 1887, an act which signaled a significant departure from the laissez-faire ideals of the day. Ordinarily, in accordance with the textbooks on classical economics, Americans had relied upon competition as the regulator of prices and the restraint on monopoly. The railroad, however, was not easily or generally amenable to such control. It was not feasible, for example, to build competing roads when the traffic was limited. Besides, the initial cost of a railroad was so great as to be a major obstacle to the free entry of competitors into the industry.

In view of such theoretical considerations and the more practical one of actual injustice to the consumers, the federal government revived an old mercantilistic practice—that is, a regulatory body which would undertake continuous supervision of the industry. This was the Interstate Commerce Commission. It is true that for two decades after its creation the Commission was almost totally ineffective in regulating rates or anything else about railroading, but the new principle had been set forth; in time the powers were forthcoming in profusion. The Interstate Commerce Act of 1887, therefore, marks the beginning of the federal government's interference in the operation of the capitalist economy through the agency of the now familiar regulatory commission.

The second device which Americans brought to bear upon the irresponsible power of industrial concentration was not only novel but unique when compared with the experience of other industrial countries.[8] The philosophy behind the Sherman Antitrust Act of

[8] *The New York Times,* July 5, 1957, reported that the lower house of the Parliament of West Germany approved, on July 4, a new anticartel law, which, in effect, became the first antitrust law in Germany. The Common Market countries in the 1960's also adopted anticartel legislation, which in some respects was stiffer than that obtaining in the United States under the antitrust acts. But as an article in *The New York Times,* January 7, 1962 (Financial Section, p. 1), pointed out, the American approach to trusts was quite different still from the European. Europeans do not fear the merger—

1890 was that the federal government should act to re-establish and preserve competition throughout the economy. This was to be done by the issuance of dissolution orders and, after the passage of the Clayton Act in 1914, through punitive and criminal penalties.[9] To this day—as the daily newspaper with its accounts of antitrust suits reveals—the primary means for controlling industrial concentration and monopoly in America resides in the antitrust statutes. Such an approach is uniquely American, since no other industrial country has put prohibitions against interference with competition into statutory law. "The Sherman and Clayton Acts," Franklin Roosevelt observed in 1944, "have become as much a part of the American way of life as the due process clause of the Constitution."

3. THE RECONSTRUCTION THAT TOOK

Although the industrialization of the United States after 1865 is usually taken to be a northern phenomenon, in reality it was nationwide, affecting even the agrarian South. In ante-bellum days, the intellectual and economic leaders of the South had repeatedly called for a union of mill and cotton on the soil of Dixie. But it was only when the old plantation-slave system lay shattered that the South turned to manufacturing with anything more than the most preoccupied interest. The industrial movement received the blessing of the rising leaders of the New South—men like Henry Grady of Georgia, "Marse Henry" Watterson of Kentucky, General Bullock of Georgia, and Daniel Tompkins of North Carolina who saw the future of the South intimately linked with the triumphant business interests of the North. Why shouldn't the South, they reasoned, have industries protected by tariffs and railroads built by government subsidies; why shouldn't the South overcome its agrarian weakness by girding itself in the iron power of industry as the North had done? Eagerly the ordinary folk of the South followed their new leaders. Many a small back-country cotton mill in the 1880's acquired its initial capital from numerous small contributions of the plain people desirous of

---

that is, large-scale enterprises—only cartels or market agreements. "By and large," the *Times* article says, "the European approach is to control the abuses of monopoly power rather than to prevent or eliminate monopoly."

[9] Not until the passage of the Federal Trade Commission Act in 1914 was the principle of the regulatory commission—first applied to railroads in 1887 —made applicable to industrial combines. And then it was done only in a tangential manner, as in restraints on advertising.

setting up a new industry in their depleted farming region. Moreover, poor hill farmers and their wives and children were only too ready to supply the muscle necessary to man the machines of the new dispensation.

In the early years of the twentieth century, the cotton manufacturers of the North could not fail to see the handwriting on the wall; the South was the coming center of cotton milling. New England may have won the war, but it lost the economic struggle. In 1915, fully 60 per cent of cotton manufacturing in the United States was carried on in the South. By that time many a northern mill was moving south, drawn by the region's special advantages: proximity to the raw material, cheap, unorganized labor (primarily white because Negroes were employed in the mills only as menials), ample coal for power, and a mild climate which saved on fuel bills.

But the South was compelled to pay a price for this ascendancy in cotton manufacture. The southern mill town, set down in a rural locale, was really a miniature manorial estate, in which the workers were not only beholden to the company for their jobs, but for the roof over their heads, the food on the table, the recreation of their off hours. Unlike in the North, where towns and cities were usually the mill sites, the southern mills created the towns, leaving no area of independence for the individualistic farmers who became the new factory hands.

Often the whole family became enmeshed in the system: where father's earnings were not sufficient, mother would enter the factory along with the children. It was not unusual for half the working force in mills before 1900 to be made up of women, and in some mills children comprised a quarter of the employees. Working and sanitary conditions in the southern mills were as bad as they have been traditionally everywhere at the beginning of an industrial revolution. The sweatshops of the North, so abominated in southern literature and propaganda before the war, had now come to the land of Dixie.

Though cotton milling was the most dramatic example of the increasing tempo of industrialization in the South, it was not the only one. Steel and iron manufacture and coal mining became major industries in the middle and lower South during the years before the First World War. The opening up of the tremendous oil reserves of Texas at the turn of the century signaled the beginning of the industrialization which has transformed the state in recent years. Sulphur and other chemical production expanded in Louisiana, and lumbering flourished in virtually all of the forested southern states. Though always centered in the South, tobacco manufacturing shot forward after 1865, especially as the cigarette became increasingly popular.

By the time the First World War broke out in Europe, the American South had been "northernized" to a degree only hoped for by the most ambitious of Reconstructionists. Moreover, this was permanent change, for the northern industrial way had been voluntarily accepted by the South. As Tom Sawyer knew, such an internally motivated conversion is the most efficacious kind.

Actually, of course, this was no more than a beginning. The introduction of the factory barely penetrated the surface of southern life; for the great majority of the people, both black and white, the land and the seasons were still the center of their lives as they had been for their fathers. But for the future, the industrializing of the South was a portent; it signified the beginning of the integration of the South into the nation. The decisive break with the agrarian tradition had been made; the re-creation of the South in the image of the North was begun. With the factory came the city, both of them slowly remolding the rural South as they have been remaking American civilization in general. Today, for the first time since the South began to drift apart from the rest of the nation, these new social forces are pulling that region once again into the main current of American life.[10]

4 . DOLLARS MEAN SUCCESS

The spread of the factory throughout the land lent further credence to the old belief that in America opportunities were almost unlimited and that material success was a sign of virtue. Indeed, for someone like Horatio Alger, Jr., the virtues of money-making were already assumed, and he exulted in the wide opportunity for success. "In this country, fortunately," he wrote, "there are few places where an industrious man cannot get a living, if he is willing to accept such work as falls his way. This willingness often turns the scale and converts

[10] As recently as 1880, only 12.7 per cent of the cities in the nation were located in the South; in 1950, over 28 per cent of urban communities were to be found there. The impact of urbanization on a controversial problem like desegregation, for instance, can hardly be exaggerated. Indeed, it can be said that it is mainly in the urban South, where the progress in desegregation, whether of schools, accommodations, or jobs, is really taking place. The rural South has hardly begun to change in this respect.

threatening ruin into prosperity and success." Andrew Carnegie, of course, was one of the most articulate preachers of the cult of success of the period, as well as its most widely known exemplar. It was John D. Rockefeller's opinion that no matter how poor some persons might be, they possessed "infinite possibilities. They have but to master the knack of economy, thrift, and perseverance and success is theirs."

Though Americans since at least the days of Benjamin Franklin had talked of how to get ahead in a world organized around money-making, it was not until the industrial age that the teaching of the secrets of material success became a thriving business itself. The publication of handbooks in the art of success became very popular; of the success books printed before 1900, four fifths of them appeared after 1865, and 80 per cent of them were published in the northeastern section of the country, where industry and commerce—and the opportunities for success—were centered.[11]

The popularizing of the "bitch-goddess success," as William James caustically phrased it, was the job of others besides publicists and businessmen. Clergymen, particularly Protestants, were prominent in prescribing the proper avenues for the attainment of earthly rewards. Their recipes usually included a heavy dose of conventional morality and "right" living. Russell Conwell, of "Acres of Diamonds" fame, was a Baptist minister; Lyman Abbott, who followed Henry Ward Beecher in the pulpit of Brooklyn's Plymouth Church, published *How to Succeed* in 1882. The founder of the Christian Endeavor Society, Francis E. Clark, was a Congregational minister and the author of two self-help books, one published in 1884 and another in 1885. The ultimate in what one writer has called "the partnership between God and Mammon" must have been reached when Episcopal Bishop William Lawrence concluded, "Godliness is in league with riches."

In hard fact, the road to success in industrial America was not an easy one—as the social origins of entrepreneurs rather convincingly inform us. But limited as the opportunities were, they were there. A

---

[11] As was to be expected, a variety of the Horatio Alger myth—work-hard-and-you-will-be-successful—ultimately filtered into juvenile literature, too. The effort in 1955–56 to unearth the true author of the famous story *The Little Engine That Could,* as reported in *The New York Times Book Review,* April 8, 1956, turned up the fact that the tale was an oral tradition of the 1880's and 1890's before it actually appeared in print. This would place it in the center of the success-story era. The fable teaches the moral that if one tries hard enough, success in any endeavor is thereby assured.

study of social mobility in the industrial town of Newburyport, Massachusetts, between 1850 and 1880 offers some hard evidence on both the breadth of opportunity and the limits on upward movement in industrial America. Most unskilled workers it was found did not move very far upward on the social scale; in twenty years only 5 per cent had moved into non-manual jobs; most had moved only "one step" up to semiskilled worker. Only 10 per cent of sons of unskilled workers moved into the top bracket of non-manual worker, but that was double the rate of their fathers. Most important, though, in this study by Stephan Thernstrom, was the finding that the great majority of workers, regardless of their level of skill, were able to accumulate property, whether in real estate or in savings. Thernstrom found that after twenty years at least two-thirds of the workers owned property, with the median amount being $600 or at least a year's wages. It was this "property mobility" that Thernstrom concludes really sustained the belief in the promise of America.

Certainly Europeans were impressed by the opportunities for advancement available to the average citizen and worker in America. All but one of the twenty-three British workers who came to the United States in 1902 with the Mosely Industrial Commission felt that the opportunities to rise in Britain were inferior to those in this country. As Mr. Cox of the Steel Workers Union put it, "If I were just starting life . . . with my present knowledge, I would go to America." "The road to comparative wealth" in America, added Mr. Flynn of the Tailors, "is more easy to find, and the possibilities it leads to are boundless." The American social escalator was not infallible, but it was apparently working well enough for the world to believe in it.

This worship of success, this striving for wealth and position, so typical of the period, left its mark upon Americans. Insofar as it taught that all men could succeed, it served to enhance the American belief in social equality and actually assisted in maintaining the open society. By extolling hard work, the Alger myth made all labor honorable and undermined any lingering aristocratic snobbery about the degrading character of honest labor. But on the other hand, such worship of success reinforced the sometimes crude materialism which has been a part of the American character since colonial times.

In yet another way the cult of success affected subsequent American history. One of the ingredients of the cult has been the image of the businessman as an enemy of privilege and a friend of the common man.[12] The high degree of acceptance which this idea received from Americans in general is to be measured in the failure of the anti-business protest movements of the era, like Greenbackism, Populism, and Socialism, to name only the most prominent ones. The interests of the business community have been so closely identified with the cult of success that popular disenchantment with the singular virtue of the businessman has usually been of short duration. Brief periods of popular distrust of business leadership, such as during the Progressive and the New Deal eras, have been preceded and followed by long periods of adulation.

Indeed, in our time, it is clear that that part of the American Dream which promises success to every poor, hard-working, frugal American boy still lives. Each year, for the last twenty or so, the Horatio Alger Award has been solemnly presented to business leaders who have made the long stride from rags to riches, and paperback reprints of Horatio Alger's stories may once again be purchased by the upward-looking masses.

5. THE WORKERS' RESPONSE

To say that the labor movement was affected by the industrialization of the postwar years is an understatement; the fact is, industrial capitalism created the labor movement. Not deliberately, to be sure, but in the same way that a blister is the consequence of a rubbing shoe. Unions were labor's protection against the forces of industrialization as the blister is the body's against the irritation of the shoe. The factory and all it implied confronted the workingman with a challenge to his existence as a man, and the worker's response was the labor union.

There were labor unions in America before 1865, but, as industry was only emerging in those years, so the organizations of workers were correspondingly weak. In the course of the years after Appomattox, however, when industry began to hit a new and giant stride, the tempo of unionization also stepped up. It was in these decades,

---

[12] The popular image of the businessman, as reflected in folklore, however, has never been a favorable one. But then, in middle-class America, the makers of folklore are not the dominant class. Kenneth Porter, in an article "The Business Man in American Folklore," asks, "Whoever heard of the really *good* business man in American folklore, other than in Jim Fisk's Robin-Hood role?"

after many years of false starts and utopian ambitions, that the American labor movement assumed its modern shape.

Perhaps the outstanding and enduring characteristic of organized labor in the United States has been its elemental conservatism, the fantasies of some employers to the contrary notwithstanding. Indeed, it might be said that all labor unions, at bottom, are conservative by virtue of their being essentially reactions against a developing capitalism. Though an established capitalist society views itself as anything but subversive, in the days of its becoming and seen against the perspective of the previous age, capitalism as an ideology is radically subversive, undermining and destroying many of the cherished institutions of the functioning society. This dissolving process of capitalism is seen more clearly in Europe than in America because there the time span is greater. But, as will appear later, organized labor in the United States was as much a conservative response to the challenge of capitalism as was the European trade union movement.

Viewed very broadly, the history of modern capitalism might be summarized as the freeing of the three factors of production—land, labor, and capital—from the web of tradition in which medieval society held them. If capitalism was to function, it was necessary that this liberating process take place. Only when these basic factors are free to be bought and sold according to the dictates of the profit motive can the immense production which capitalism promises be realized. An employer, for example, had to be free to dismiss labor when the balance sheet required it, without being compelled to retain workers because society or custom demanded it. Serfdom, with its requirement that the peasant could not be taken from the land, was an anachronistic institution if capitalism was to become the economic ideology of society. Conversely, an employer needed to be unrestricted in his freedom to hire labor or else production could not expand in accordance with the market. Guild restrictions which limited apprenticeships were therefore obstacles to the achievement of a free capitalism.

The alienability of the three factors of production was achieved slowly and unevenly after the close of the Middle Ages. By the nineteenth century in most nations of the West, land had become absolutely alienable—it could be bought and sold at will. With the growth of banking, the development of trustworthy monetary standards, and finally the gold standard in the nineteenth century, money or capital also became freely exchangeable. Gradually, over the span of some two centuries, the innovating demands of capitalism stripped from labor the social controls in which medieval and mercantilistic government had clothed it. Serfdom as an obstacle to the free movement of labor was gradually done away with; statutes of laborers and apprenticeships which fixed wages, hours, and terms of employment also fell into disuse or suffered outright repeal. To avoid government interference in the setting of wage rates, the English Poor Law of 1834 made it clear that the dole to the unemployed was always to be lower than the going rate for unskilled labor. Thus supply and demand would be the determinant of wage levels. Both the common law and the Combination Acts in the early nineteenth century in England sought to ensure the operation of a free market in labor by declaring trade unions to be restraints on trade.

Like land and capital, then, labor was being reduced to a commodity, freely accessible, freely alienable, free to flow where demand was high. The classical economists of the nineteenth century analyzed this long historical process, neatly put it together, and called it the natural laws of economics.

To a large extent, this historical development constituted an improvement in the worker's status, since medieval and mercantilist controls over labor had been more onerous than protective. Nevertheless, something was lost by the dissolution of the ancient social ties which fitted the worker into a larger social matrix. Under the old relationship, the worker belonged in society; he enjoyed a definite if not a high status; he had a place. Now he was an individual, alone; his status was up to him to establish; his urge for community with society at large had no definite avenue of expression. Society and labor alike had been atomized in pursuit of an individualistic economy. Herein lay the radical character of the capitalist ideology.

That the workingman sensed the radical change and objected to it is evident from what some American labor leaders said about their unions. Without rejecting the new freedom which labor enjoyed, John Mitchell, of the Mine Workers, pointed out that the union "stands for fraternity, complete and absolute." Samuel Gompers' eulogy of the social microcosm which was the trade union has the same ring. "A hundred times we have said it," he wrote, "and we say it again, that trade unionism contains within itself the potentialities of working class regeneration." The union is a training ground for democracy and provides "daily object lessons in ideal justice; it breathes into the working classes the spirit of unity"; but above all, it affords that needed sense of community. The labor union "provides a field for noble comradeship, for deeds of loyalty, for self-sacrifice beneficial to one's fellow-workers." In the trade union, in short, the workers could obtain another variety of that sense of community, of comradeship, as Gompers put it, which the acid of individualistic capitalism had dissolved.

And there was another objection to the transformation of labor into an exchangeable commodity. The theoretical justification for the conversion of the factors of production into commodities is that the maximum amount of goods can be produced under such a regime. The increased production is deemed desirable because it would insure greater amounts of goods for human consumption and therefore a better life for all. Unfortunately for the theory, however, labor cannot be separated from the men who provide it. To make labor a commodity is to make the men who provide labor commodities also. Thus one is left with the absurdity of turning men into commodities in order to give men a better life!

"Labor is a commodity of a peculiar sort," John Mitchell pointed out. "It is a part of the very being of the man who sells it. The commodity sold is a human creature, whose welfare in the eyes of the law should be of more importance than any mere accumulation of wealth on the part of the community." For the very same reason, Samuel Gompers bestowed the label "Labor's Magna Carta" upon Section 14 of the Clayton Act, which specifically denied that labor was a commodity.

Seen in this light, the trade union movement stands out as a truly conservative force. Almost instinctively, the workers joined labor unions in order to preserve their humanity and social character against the excessively individualistic doctrines of industrial capitalism.[13] Eventually, the workers' organizations succeeded in halting

[13] V. I. Lenin, that archetypical radical, was well aware of the basically conservative origins and character of the trade union movement. In his *What Is to Be Done?* (1902), he contrasted trade unionism with revolutionary socialism. "The history of all countries shows," he wrote, "that the working class, exclusively by its own efforts, is able to develop only trade-union consciousness," that is, combining into unions, etc. Socialism, however, is the product of the intellectuals.

the drive to the atomized society which capitalism demanded, and in doing so, far from destroying the system, compelled it to be humane as well as productive.

The essential conservatism of the labor movement is to be seen in particular as well as in general. The organizations of American labor that triumphed or at least survived in the course of industrialization were conspicuous for their acceptance of the private property, profit-oriented society. They evinced little of the radical, anticapitalist ideology and rhetoric so common among European trade unions. Part of the reason for this was the simple fact that all Americans—including workers—were incipient capitalists waiting for "the break." But at bottom it would seem that the conservatism of American labor in this sense is the result of the same forces which inhibited the growth of socialism and other radical anticapitalist ideologies. This question will be dealt with at some length at the end of this chapter.

"The overshadowing problem of the American labor movement," an eminent labor historian has written, "has always been the problem of staying organized. No other labor movement has ever had to contend with the fragility so characteristic of American labor organizations." So true has this been that even today the United States ranks below Italy and Austria in percentage of workers organized (about 30 per cent as compared, for instance, with Sweden's 90 per cent). In such an atmosphere, the history of organized labor in America has been both painful and conservative. Of the two major national organizations of workers which developed in the latter half of the nineteenth century, only the cautious, restrictive, pragmatic American Federation of Labor lived into the twentieth century. The other, the Knights of Labor, once the more powerful and promising, as well as the less accommodating in goals and aspirations, succumbed to Selig Perlman's disease of fragility.

Founded in 1869, the Noble Order of the Knights of Labor recorded its greatest successes in the 1880's, when its membership rolls carried 700,000 names. As the A.F. of L. was later to define the term for Americans, the Knights did not seem to constitute a legitimate trade union at all. Anyone who worked, except liquor dealers, bankers, lawyers, and physicians, could join, and some thousands of women workers and Negroes were members in good standing of this brotherhood of toilers. But the crucial deviation of the Knights from the more orthodox approach to labor organization was its belief in worker-owned producers' co-operatives, which were intended to make each worker his own employer. In this way, the order felt, the degrading dependence of the worker upon the employer would be eliminated. "There is no good reason," Terence V. Powderly, Grand Master Workman of the order, told his followers, "why labor cannot, through co-operation, own and operate mines, factories and railroads."

In this respect the order repudiated the direction in which the America of its time was moving. It expressed the small-shopkeeper mentality which dominated the thinking of many American workers, despite the obvious trend in the economy toward the big and the impersonal. As the General Assembly of 1884 put it, "our Order contemplates a radical change, while Trades' Unions . . . accept the industrial system as it is, and endeavor to adapt themselves to it. The attitude of our Order to the existing industrial system is necessarily one of war." Though the order called this attitude "radical," a more accurate term, in view of the times, would have been "conservative" or "reactionary."

In practice, however, the Knights presented no more of a threat to capitalism than any other trade union. Indeed, their avowed opposition to the strike meant that labor's most potent weapon was only reluctantly drawn from the scabbard. The Constitution of 1884 said, "Strikes at best afford only temporary relief"; members should learn to depend on education, co-operation, and political action to attain "the abolition of the wage system."

Though the order officially joined in political activity and Grand Master Workman Powderly was at one time mayor of Scranton, its forays into politics accomplished little. The experience was not lost on shrewd Samuel Gompers, whose American Federation of Labor studiously eschewed any alignments with political parties, practicing instead the more neutral course of "rewarding friends and punishing enemies."

In a farewell letter in 1893, Powderly realistically diagnosed the ills of his moribund order, but offered no cure: "Teacher of important and much-needed reforms, she has been obliged to practice differently from her teachings. Advocating arbitration and conciliation as first steps in labor disputes she has been forced to take upon her shoulders the responsibilities of the aggressor first and, when hope of arbitrating and conciliation failed, to beg of the opposing side to do what we should have applied for in the first instance. Advising against strikes we have been in the midst of them. While not a political party we have been forced into the attitude of taking political action."

For all its fumblings, ineptitude, and excessive idealism, the Knights did organize more workers on a national scale than had ever been done before. At once premature and reactionary, it nonetheless planted the seeds of industrial unionism which, while temporarily overshadowed by the successful craft organization of the A.F. of L., ultimately bore fruit in the C.I.O. Moreover, its idealism, symbolized in its admission of Negroes and women, and more in tune with the mid-twentieth century than the late nineteenth, signified its commitment to the ideals of the democratic tradition. For these reasons the Knights were a transitional type of unionism, somewhere between the utopianism of the 1830's and the pragmatism of the A.F. of L. It seemed to take time for labor institutions to fit the American temper.

In the course of his long leadership of the American Federation of Labor, Samuel Gompers welcomed many opportunities to define the purposes of his beloved organization. But probably none tried his soul so much as that day in 1914 when Morris Hillquit of the Socialist party questioned him before the United States Commission on Industrial Relations. In the course of the colloquy, the sharp contrast between the highly philosophical and theoretical aims of the Socialists and the stubbornly unphilosophical, practical spirit of the Federation's eminent leader was spread upon the record for all to see.

After sparring for a while, Hillquit asked "whether the American Federation of Labor and its authorized spokesman have a general social philosophy or work blindly from day to day?" Obviously nettled, Gompers refused to answer on the ground that the question was an insult. Finally, when Hillquit withdrew the words "blindly from day to day," the trade union leader launched into a recital of the A.F. of L.'s aims, carefully avoiding any theoretical formulations. It sought, he said, to "accomplish the best results in improving the conditions of the working people, men and women and children, today and tomorrow and tomorrow—and tomorrow's tomorrow; and each day making it a better day than the one that had gone before."

Pressed by Hillquit for some measure of what "better" meant, Gompers irascibly replied that anyone knew, without benefit of philosophy, that a wage of $3 a day was better than one of $2.50 and an eight-hour day superior to one of twelve. To Hillquit's leading suggestion that $4 and seven hours were even better, the union chief readily agreed, saying, "the best possible conditions obtainable for the workers is the aim." But Hillquit's effort to expose the philosophical poverty of the union's aims and Gompers' stubborn defense of cautious, practical unionism can best be appreciated the way it happened:

> Mr. Hillquit: Yes, and when these conditions are obtained—
> Mr. Gompers: (interrupting) Why, then we want better.
> Mr. Hillquit: (continuing) You will strive for better?
> Mr. Gompers: Yes.
> Mr. Hillquit: Now my question is, Will this effort on the part of organized labor ever stop until it has the full reward for its labor?
> Mr. Gompers: It won't stop at all.

Hillquit, working hard to convince Gompers that labor and socialism had common aims, pushed his questioning still further. The old cigarmaker, however, knew what he was doing.

> Mr. Hillquit: Then, the object of the labor union is to obtain complete social justice for themselves and for their wives and for their children?
> Mr. Gompers: It is the effort to obtain a better life every day.
> Mr. Hillquit: Every day and always—
> Mr. Gompers: Every day. That does not limit it.
> Mr. Hillquit: Until such time—
> Mr. Gompers: Not until any time.
> Mr. Hillquit: In other words—
> Mr. Gompers: (interrupting) In other words we go further than you. (Laughter and applause in the audience.) You have an end; we have not.

In the final words of Gompers, "You have an end; we have not," are summed up the great gulf which separated successful trade unionism in America from socialism. Dedicated as Gompers obviously was to organized labor and more specifically to the A.F. of L., he did not permit utopian idealism to influence his clear-eyed view of the American scene. The almost mystical identification with all workers which both the Knights and the Socialists exhibited had no analogue in the American Federation of Labor, which confined itself to the welfare of craft workers and the preservation of that group's position as the elite of the working class. Any other course, the Federation felt, would bring disintegration to the labor movement. This was business unionism, neither idealistic brotherhood nor belief in the unity of the proletariat.

"The trade unions are the business organizations of the wage-earners," Gompers explained in 1906, "to attend to the business of the wage-earners." Later he expressed it more tersely: "The trade union is not a Sunday school. It is an organization of wage-earners, dealing with economic, social, political and moral questions." As Gompers' crossing of swords with Hillquit demonstrated, there was no need or place for theories. "I saw," the labor leader wrote years later, in looking back on his early life in the labor movement, "the danger of entangling alliances with intellectuals who did not understand that to experiment with the labor movement was to experiment with human life. . . . I saw that the betterment of workingmen must come primarily through workingmen."

In an age of big business, Samuel Gompers made trade unionism a business, and his reward was the survival of his Federation. In a country with a heterogeneous population of unskilled immigrants, reviled and feared Negroes, and native workers, he cautiously confined his fragile organization to the more skilled workers and the more acceptable elements in the population. The result was a narrow but lasting structure.

Though never ceasing to ask for "more," the A.F. of L. presented no threat to capitalism. "Labor Unions are *for* the workingman, but against no one," John Mitchell of the United Mine Workers pointed out. "They are not hostile to employers, not inimical to the interests of the general public. . . . There is no necessary hostility between labor and capital," he concluded. Remorselessly pressed by Morris Hillquit as Gompers was, he still refused to admit that the labor movement was, as Hillquit put it, "conducted against the interests of the employing people." Rather, Gompers insisted, "It is conducted for the interests of the employing people." And the rapid expansion of the American economy bore witness to the fact that the Federation was a friend and not an enemy of industrial capitalism. Its very adaptability to the American scene—its conservative ideology, if it was an ideology at all—as Selig Perlman has observed, contained the key to its success. "The unionism of the American Federation of Labor 'fitted' . . . because it recognized the virtually inalterable conservatism of the American community as regards private property and private initiative in economic life."

This narrow conception of the proper character of trade unionism
—job consciousness, craft unionism, lack of interest in organizing
the unskilled, the eschewing of political activity—which Gompers
and his Federation worked out for the American worker continued
to dominate organized labor until the earthquake of the depression
cracked the mold and the Committee for Industrial Organization
issued forth.

6. NOBODY HERE BUT US CAPITALISTS

"By any simple interpretation of the Marxist formula," commented
Socialist Norman Thomas in 1950, "the United States, by all odds the
greatest industrial nation and that in which capitalism is most advanced, should have had long ere this a very strong socialist movement if not a socialist revolution. Actually," he correctly observed,
"in no advanced western nation is organized socialism so weak."
Nor was this the first time Socialists had wondered about this. Over
fifty years ago, in the high noon of European socialism, Marxist
theoretician Werner Sombart impatiently put a similar question:
"Warum gibt es in den Vereinigten Staaten keinen Sozialismus?"

The failure of the American working class to become seriously
interested in socialism in this period or later is one of the prominent
signs of the political and economic conservatism of American labor
and, by extension, of the American people as a whole. This failure
is especially noteworthy when one recalls that in industrialized countries the world over—Japan, Italy, Germany, Belgium, to mention
only a few—a Socialist movement has been a "normal" concomitant
of industrialization. Even newly opened countries like Australia and
New Zealand have Labour parties. Rather than ask, as Americans
are wont to do, why these countries have nurtured such frank repudi-
ators of traditional capitalism, it is the American deviation from the
general pattern which demands explanation.

In large part, the explanation lies in the relative weakness of class
consciousness among Americans. Historically, socialism is the gospel
of the *class-conscious* working class, of the workingmen who feel
themselves bound to their status for life and their children after
them. It is not accidental, therefore, that the major successes of
modern socialism are in Europe, where class lines have been clearly
and tightly drawn since time immemorial, and where the possibility
of upward social movement has been severely restricted in practice

if not in law. Americans may from time to time have exhibited class consciousness and even class hatred, but such attitudes have not persisted, nor have they been typical. As Matthew Arnold observed in 1888, "it is indubitable that rich men are regarded" in America "with less envy and hatred than rich men in Europe." A labor leader like Terence Powderly was convinced that America was without classes. "No matter how much we may say about classes and class distinction, there are no classes in the United States. . . . I have always refused to admit that we have classes in our country just as I have refused to admit that the labor of a man's hand or brain is a commodity." And there was a long line of commentators on American society, running back at least to Crèvecoeur, to illustrate the prevalence of Powderly's belief.

The weakness of American class consciousness is doubtless to be attributed, at least in part, to the fluidity of the social structure. Matthew Arnold, for example, accounted for the relative absence of class hatred on such grounds, as did such very different foreign observers as Werner Sombart and Lord Bryce. The British union officials of the Mosely Commission, it will be recalled, were convinced of the superior opportunities for success enjoyed by American workers. Stephan Thernstrom in his study of Newburyport gave some measure of the opportunities for economic improvement among the working class when he reported that all but 5 per cent of those unskilled workers who persisted from 1850 to 1900 ended the period with either property or an improvement in occupational status.

Men who are hoping to move upward on the social scale, and for whom there is some chance that they can do so, do not identify themselves with their present class.[14] "In worn-out, king-ridden Europe, men stay where they are born," immigrant Charles O'Conor, who became an ornament of the New York bar, contended in 1869.

---

[14] Twenty-five years ago, when *Fortune* magazine asked a sampling of Americans what class they belonged to, some 47 per cent said, "middle class" and only 15 per cent answered, "lower or working class." That these striking results can be misinterpreted if they are taken to mean that Americans do not recognize classes was shown by Richard Centers, *Psychology of Social Classes* (Princeton, 1949). Centers presented his sample with a choice of classes, including "working class," instead of leaving the question open-ended, as was done in the *Fortune* poll. Under these conditions 51 per cent of his sample selected "working class." Repetitions with two other samples yielded substantially the same results. Centers' data indicated that Americans, when pressed, *do* recognize classes in their society. But the *Fortune* data showed that Americans instinctively hold to the ideal of a society with a great middle class.

"But in America a man is accounted a failure, and certainly ought to be, who has not risen above his father's station in life." So long as Horatio Alger means anything to Americans, Karl Marx will be just another German philosopher.

The political history of the United States also contributed to the failure of socialism. In Europe, because the franchise came slowly and late to the worker, he often found himself first an industrial worker and only later a voter. It was perfectly natural, in such a context, for him to vote according to his economic interests and to join a political party avowedly dedicated to those class interests. The situation was quite different in America, however, for political democracy came to America prior to the Industrial Revolution. By the time the industrial transformation was getting under way after 1865, all adult males could vote and, for the most part, they had already chosen their political affiliations without reference to their economic class; they were Republicans or Democrats first and workers only second—a separation between politics and economics which has become traditional in America. "In the main," wrote Lord Bryce about the United States of the 1880's, "political questions proper have held the first place in a voter's mind and questions affecting his class second."[15] Thus, when it came to voting, workers registered their convictions as citizens, not as workingmen. (In our own day, there have been several notable failures of labor leaders to swing the labor vote, such as John L. Lewis' attempt in 1940 and the C.I.O.'s in 1950 against Senator Taft and the inability of union leaders to be sure they could hold their members to support Hubert Humphrey in the Presidential election of 1968.) To most workers, the Socialist party appeared as merely a third party in a country where such parties are political last resorts.

Nor did socialism in America gain much support from the great influx of immigration. It is true that many Germans came to this country as convinced Socialists and thus swelled the party's numbers, but they also served to pin the stigma of "alien" upon the movement. Even more important was the fact that the very heterogeneity of the

---

[15] It is interesting to note that this generalization, though apparently true as applied to labor, does not fit the farmer, who, historically, was a farmer before he was a voter. Is it for this reason that his economic interest has sometimes taken precedence over his political allegiance, as in the Populist movement, and in the farm block of the twentieth century?

labor force, as a result of immigration, often made animosities between ethnic groups more important to the worker than class antagonism. It must have seemed to many workers that socialism, with its central concern for class and its denial of ethnic antagonism, was not dealing with the realities of economic life.

In the final reckoning, however, the failure of socialism in America is to be attributed to the success of capitalism. The expanding economy provided opportunities for all, no matter how meager they might appear or actually be at times. Though the rich certainly seemed to get richer at a prodigious rate, the poor, at least, did not get poorer —and often got richer. Studies of real wages between 1865 and 1900 bear this out. Though prices rose, wages generally rose faster, so that there was a net gain in average income for workers during the last decades of the century. The increase in real wages in the first fifteen years of the twentieth century was negligible—but, significantly, there was no decline. The high wages and relatively good standard of living of the American worker were patent as far as the twenty-three British labor leaders of the Mosely Commission were concerned. The American is a "better educated, better housed, better clothed and more energetic man than his British brother," concluded the sponsor, Alfred Mosely, a businessman himself.

But America challenged socialism on other grounds than mere material things. Some years ago an obscure Socialist, Leon Samson, undertook to account for the failure of socialism to win the allegiance of the American working class; his psychological explanation merits attention because it illuminates the influence exercised by the American Dream. Americanism, Samson observes, is not so much a tradition as it is a doctrine; it is "what socialism is to a socialist." Americanism to the American is a body of ideas like "democracy, liberty, opportunity, to all of which the American adheres rationalistically much as a socialist adheres to his socialism—because it does him good, because it gives him work, because, so he thinks, it guarantees him happiness. America has thus served as a substitute for socialism."

Socialism has been unable to make headway with Americans, Samson goes on, because "every concept in socialism has its substitutive counterconcept in Americanism." As Marxism holds out the prospect of a classless society, so does Americanism. The opportunities for talent and the better material life which socialism promised for the future were already available in America and constituted the image in which America was beheld throughout the world.[16] The freedom and equality which the oppressed proletariat of Europe craved were a reality in America—or at least sufficiently so to blunt the cutting edge of the Socialist appeal. Even the sense of mission, of being in step with the processes of history, which unquestionably was one of the appeals of socialism, was also a part of the American Dream. Have not all Americans cherished their country as a model for the world? Was not this the "last, best hope of earth"? Was not God on the side of America, as history, according to Marx, was on the side of socialism and the proletariat?

Over a century ago, Alexis de Tocqueville predicted a mighty struggle for the minds of men between the two giants of Russia and the United States. In the ideologies of socialism and the American Dream, his forecast has been unexpectedly fulfilled.

Industrialization was a new and potent force in American life; even when only emergent, it was reshaping the face of America. The factory, in league with the city, would eventually transform the America of Jefferson and Jackson. But these were not the only forces at work in the years after 1865—the wave after wave of immigrants which washed over America also left their impress on the American.

---

[16] In *Toward a United Front* (New York, 1933), pp. 49–51, Samson has an amusing and provocative page or two on the similarities between utterances of American statesmen and the slogans of socialism. One concerns President Hoover's avowal that America would abolish poverty. "Who has ever heard a responsible spokesman of European capitalism announce that it is the aim of, let us say, the French or the English 'system' to 'abolish poverty'?" asks Samson. "Normally, phrases such as this are uttered by spokesmen of the working class. Socialism is, normally, the philosophy of the working class."

CHAPTER X

Out of Many, One

THOUGH historians have long celebrated the ancient *Völkerwander-ung* of the German tribes in the last centuries of the Roman Empire, during the nineteenth and early twentieth centuries the outpouring of peoples from the land mass of Europe and Asia dwarfed all previous mass immigrations. In little more than a century, between 1820 and 1930, over 62 million people uprooted themselves from their native lands to seek a better life in the newer lands around the globe.

Almost two thirds of these enterprising souls came to the United States. No other country even approached America as a goal, the next most popular, Canada, receiving only a little more than 10 per cent of the world's migrants. If this meant that America was the promised land for the majority of the emigrants, it also meant, as George Santayana has pointed out, that in the process the United States was set apart psychologically from Europe. "The discovery of the new world exercised a sort of selection among the inhabitants of Europe," he wrote. "The fortunate, the deeply rooted, and the lazy remained at home; the wilder instincts or dissatisfactions of others tempted them beyond the horizon. The American is accordingly the most adventurous, or the descendant of the most adventurous, of Europeans."

In yet another way immigration helped to make the United States different from Europe and, for that matter, from any other new country. Other new countries like Australia and Argentina, it is true, are as much the product of immigration as the United States, but all such countries were peopled by a very narrow range of nationalities. For example, over 80 per cent of the immigration to Australia has been from the British Isles (not including Ireland); 74 per cent of people migrating to Canada came from the United States and Great

Britain; almost four fifths of Argentina's immigrant population derived from Italy and Spain. Only in America were many nationalities mixed together. Though no one of the peoples involved in the building of America contributed more than one seventh of the total alien population, five (Germans, British, Irish, Austro-Hungarian, and Italian) have each contributed more than a tenth of the immigrants; two others, the Russians and the Scandinavians, have made up 8.5 and 6.2 per cent respectively. In short, the diversity of peoples has been much more than a mere sprinkling; it has involved great blocs of nationalities.

1. THE WIDENING STREAM

From its inception, America has been the frontier of Europe and the goal of those who were bold enough to take a second chance. All through the seventeenth, eighteenth, and nineteenth centuries, people flowed to the New World—direct responses to the economic, military, or religious troubles convulsing the Old World. During the seventeenth century, for example, the religious and economic discontent in England drove people to New England and the Chesapeake colonies; in the early eighteenth century, economic discontent in Ireland and Germany introduced the leaven of Scots-Irish and Germans into the English stock of America. But between 1820 and 1920, by far the greatest and presumably the last of the great waves of Europeans flooded to America; in that single century, 38 million came to the United States.

If one charted the annual arrivals of this last wave of immigrants, the graph would assume a pattern of peaks and valleys—but until 1914, the trend would always be upward. Along this over-all upward trend, however, two major peaks would stand out: one in the 1850's and another in the five years between 1905 and 1910.

The dates of these two peaks can serve as convenient markers for differentiating between the so-called old and new immigration. Unfortunately, these terms are somewhat misleading, since they apply to the European geographic origins of the immigrants rather than to time of arrival. But their widespread use makes them convenient nonetheless. The first peak is associated with the old immigrants—that is, those who came primarily from northern and western Europe: England, France, the Low Countries, Germany, and Scandinavia; the second with the new immigrants, the great peasant peoples of eastern and southern Europe: Italians, Greeks, Poles, Russians (including Jews), and Slavs in general. The usage "old" and "new" has some justification in that before 1880 the peoples of southern and eastern Europe were almost unknown on the immigrant ships which put in at Castle Garden in New York. As late as the decade 1881–91, in fact, these peoples constituted only a little over 18 per cent of the immigrants from Europe. But in the 1890's the immigrants from northern and western Europe, though they continued to come in substantial numbers, were almost lost in the masses of people who now spilled out of the lands east of the Elbe River and south of the Alps.

The actual numbers of immigrants coming into the United States in the early years of the twentieth century were almost unbelievable. In the years before 1880, the annual arrivals had never reached half a million, and only once before the end of the century did their numbers exceed three quarters of a million. After 1896, however, when the numbers of immigrants from eastern and southern Europe for the first time surpassed those from the north and the west, annual immigration frequently topped the million mark. In each of six different years before 1915, over a million new Americans arrived; in fact, between 1902 and 1914, more than half a million immigrants poured into the country every single year, and in most of the years the figure was above three quarters of a million. In the space of those twelve years, the total number of immigrants far exceeded all the new arrivals between 1820 and 1880—the peak period for the old immigration.

It is not within the scope of this book to inquire into the forces which impelled this movement of peoples to America; that subject is more properly European than American. But the image in which the simple European peasant beheld the United States was largely the product of the millions of immigrants who came and saw the mountains, the plains, the cities, the farms, and, above all, the people of America. And the pull which brought still more immigrants was compounded from what these newcomers saw and heard in the new land.

Thousands of letters from America, written by the recently arrived to their home folk, or more often to the local newspaper in the old country, gradually filled out an image of America in which opportunity, equality, and hope for the future were writ large. "This is a free country and nobody has a great deal of authority over another," wrote one Swede from Illinois in 1850. "There is no pride and nobody needs to hold his hat in his hand for anyone else. This is not Sweden, where the higher classes and employers have the law on their side so that they can treat subordinates as though they were not human beings." To Johann Schmitz forty years later, as he eagerly told his brother about America, the hat was still a symbol of what the new country stood for. "And what is nicer yet is the fact that this is a free land. No one can give orders to anybody here, one is as good as another, no one takes off his hat to another as you have to do in Germany." To a Norwegian in Minnesota in 1866, it seemed that the lack of occupational distinctions was the great attraction of America. "The principle of equality has been universally accepted and adopted," he wrote extravagantly, after the manner of the newly arrived. "The artisan, the farmer, and the laborer enjoy the same degree of respect as the merchant and the official."

The material satisfactions which the immigrant often experienced in America were sometimes exaggerated when he wrote back to those who had feared to take the risk of emigration. (And did not such an accent on material possessions contribute to the European's notion of America's commitment to materialism and worship of quantity?) "Generally our animals are larger here than they were in our home parish in Norway," boasted one immigrant from Minnesota in 1859. "Our cows milk very well, and the milk and cream are richer here than they were in Norway. . . . No bolts are used in our irons; we heat them by putting them on a stove lid, and they are much better for ironing than those we had in Norway."[1]

Some emigrants to America returned home, for one reason or another, giving Europeans an opportunity to see and hear with their own senses what America was like, for not infrequently the returned ones showed traces of their sojourn in America. One Italian landlord, for example, complained that "the men who come back from America walk through the streets as if they were our equals. . . ."

---

[1] Not all letters home were in praise of the new Canaan. J. N. Bjorndalen in Wisconsin wrote to his parents in 1844 to warn them against the tendency of his fellow migrants to play up the beauties of the new world: ". . . almost all reports and letters received in Norway from America are good," he observed drily. "But this is very wrong; only about a third part of these letters is true. People only write down accounts of the good, although they themselves have had no experience of it. . . . I do not advise any of my relatives to come to America. If you could see the conditions of the Norwegians in America at present, you would certainly be frightened; illness and misery are so prevalent that many have died. . . ."

Theodore Saloutus, in writing about the repatriated Greeks who had lived in America, remarked that these former Americans upon their return were frequently in the vanguard of progress in the old country. They brought practicality, industry, and orderliness to the Greek villages to which they returned. Often they inspired their fellow Greeks to be up and doing; they unconsciously stirred up in their neighbors a discontent with present conditions. "They bring back a more democratic spirit," one Greek labor leader told Saloutus. "They know more about machines. . . . They often encourage sports. . . . The returned Greek-Americans are staunch defenders of America."

Edward Steiner, that romantic chronicler of the immigrant, wrote that landlords and manufacturers in Europe told him the Americans "have trained" the returning emigrants in the habits of industry and "that we have quickened their wits. . . ." Even those Americans who by the twentieth century were becoming apprehensive as to where the new tide of immigration was leading could not escape being aware of the changes in the returning European after a sojourn in the United States. One haughty Bostonian remarked to Steiner that the returning aliens "carried themselves so differently from those who came over. . . ." One Slavic woman, on a visit from America, added her mite to the building up of a realistic picture of life in the United States when she said that, contrary to European impressions, American women worked hard. But, she added, they were not required to submit to beatings by husbands.

"America has been a blessing to us," a Hungarian statesman was reputed to have admitted. "Had Columbus not discovered it, Europe would still be in servitude and had it not been rediscovered by our peasants, they would not have had a chance to get their necks from under the yoke." This image of America as the hope of the oppressed, as the home of the common man, as the opportunity for the industrious, was implanted and nurtured in the European heart and mind by the immigrants who came to America and stayed—and even by those who elected to return. Like most mirrors, this one held by the immigrants contained flaws and distortions, but it was sufficiently accurate to satisfy most of those who acted upon the reflection of America it cast.

A vast reservoir of good will, of hope, of aspiration, was thus created in the worn-out, hard-bitten soul of Europe. America was rich, America was good, America was hope, America was the future. In a democratic age when the feelings and votes of the common people are taken into account, this warm feeling toward America possesses hard value as well as soft sentiment. Makers of American foreign policy have had this good will as something upon which they could depend and build—and, unhappily enough, squander. It was the gift of the immigrant and of the America which he found here.

2. HEWERS OF WOOD AND DRAWERS OF WATER

Ever since the first trying years at Jamestown, America has been wheedling people from Europe in order to put their magical labor to work upon the natural richness of the new country. This seemingly unquenchable thirst for men's labor has lain at the root of the broad welcome which America has accorded the workers of the world. For, despite their excursions into nativism, Americans in the nineteenth century were as grateful for the new hands and muscles as John Smith had been two hundred and fifty years before.

An indication of this appreciation is evident in the various efforts to calculate the value which the immigrants added to the nation's wealth. Just after the Civil War, the United States Treasury solemnly and prudently declared each immigrant to be worth $800 in the ledger of the national economy. The estimate was raised appreciably by Representative Levi Morton of Indiana in 1880. Scorning a recent government calculation of the immigrant's contribution, Morton asserted that the true value was beyond computation. "Mr. Chairman, what estimate can we place upon the value to the country of the millions of Irish and Germans to whom we largely owe the existence of the great arteries of commerce extending from the Atlantic to the Pacific and the results of that industry and skill which has so largely contributed to the wealth and prosperity of the country?" As late as 1892, by which date many Americans were having sober second thoughts about the westering human stream which never stopped, a writer in the *North American Review* was still blessing the alien's gift of labor. "By reason of this incoming, our almost limitless resources have been partially developed, forests leveled, railroads built, and canals dug . . . and the wilderness has been made to blossom. . . ."

As a class, the immigrants were "hewers of wood and drawers of water" in America; moreover, in proportion to their numbers they performed more of the nation's work than did the native-born. As one friend of the immigrant pointed out in 1893, though the foreign-born population in 1870 comprised "one-seventh of the entire population," it performed "something more than one-fifth of all the work." In 1880, this same writer went on, foreign-born workers constituted almost a third of the labor force, even though immigrants made up only 13.3 per cent of the total population.

Such disproportion is not the consequence of exploitation so much as it is the result of the peculiar age distribution of the immigrant population. The great majority of the immigrants came to the United States in the prime of life—in the working years between fourteen and forty-five. For example, four-fifths of the immigrants in 1900 fell within this age range, though less than three fifths of the native population did. Nor were Americans blind to the economic value of this age grouping. "Thus, immigration brings to us a population of working ages unhampered by unproductive mouths to feed," commented economist John R. Commons in 1906. "Their home countries have borne the expense of rearing them up to the industrial period of their lives," he thriftily pointed out, "and then America, without that heavy expense, reaps whatever profits there are on the investment." Europe was a kind of labor "farm" where workers were conveniently and cheaply raised to full size before they entered American industry.

For an America ever reaching out for more and more labor, the ratio of the sexes in the immigration which came after the 1880's was better than could have been expected. The older immigrant nationalities had often come in families, a mode of migration which tended to distribute the sexes more or less evenly. The new peoples, however, emigrated more often as single men, or married men who had left their families behind. For instance, in the decade of 1901–10, almost 70 per cent of the newcomers were men; whereas in the decade 1850–60, less than 60 per cent were. But it is significant that in both periods there was an excess of men, which, when taken together with the favorable age distribution, meant that immigration provided much more productive labor than was to be expected from any normal increase in population.

Though it is true that the labor of the typical immigrant, especially after 1880, was not skilled, this should not cause us to overlook the skills which the immigrant added to the wealth of America. Emigrants from industrialized and commercial northern and western Europe were noteworthy in this regard, particularly the Germans who came in the 1840's and 1850's. This nationality dominated cabinetmaking and pianomaking in New York City, for example. Even entrepreneurs in the latter industry, like Steinway, were immigrants. Germans were also prominent as skilled bakers, tailors, and shoemakers in New York. Englishmen, coming from a technically advanced society, often came, both before and after the war, as skilled workers, such as machinists, mechanics, and shipbuilding workers. In the years after 1865, the backbone of the American glass industry was made up of skilled Belgian workers.

The skills which these workers brought, however, comprised only a part of the immigrant's contribution to American industrial development; common, unskilled labor was the more important addition. But if important, such labor was also lowly. As an unskilled worker, the immigrant, severely limited in his choice of occupation, most often found himself in jobs at the bottom of the ladder, sometimes in occupations which no native, except perhaps a despised Negro, would accept. Before 1860, the Irish were especially conspicuous as unskilled workers. In the Boston of the 1850's, for example, they bore virtually the same relation to the culture of that city as the Negro slaves did to the contemporary South: both constituted the broad base on which rested an elegant civilization. Of all the employed Irish in Boston in 1850, 62 per cent were working as laborers or as domestic servants; in 1855, the state census revealed that 98 per cent of New York City's 20,000 common laborers were immigrants. After the war, the story of the unskilled is essentially the tale of the immigrant in general, so we shall save that until later.

But before 1860, the economic importance of the immigrants was not confined to industry. Many of the newcomers helped to level the forests and plow up the black earth of the western prairies. By 1860, immigrants in a new state like Minnesota constituted at least one fifth of the inhabitants of forty-nine of the sixty-four counties; in brand-new, sparsely settled counties, the immigrants sometimes made up a majority. Even in an older state like Illinois, by then two generations in the Union, immigrants, especially Germans, comprised 20 per cent or more of the population in something like one fifth of the counties. Germans were also numerically prominent in portions of Iowa, where in eight or nine rural counties in 1860, every fifth person was an immigrant.

Wisconsin before 1860 was the most indebted to the immigrant for its agricultural growth. Immigrants comprised almost a quarter of the state's one million inhabitants at the outbreak of the war, with the Germans surpassing the total for the English, Canadian, Norwegian, and Irish. In twenty-two of the state's fifty-eight counties immigrants constituted a third or more of the population, and in some of those counties they were a clear majority.

Although at the end of the nineteenth century most of the immigrants were becoming industrial workers upon arrival in America, many thousands continued to push out to the new lands of the Far West and the Great Plains. Immigrants of older ethnic groups, like Germans and Scandinavians, for example, continued to be drawn to the traditional settlements of their nationalities,[2] but now some of the "new" nationalities were beginning to become prominent in agriculture. Italians, for instance, in 1910 were the most conspicuous immigrant people in thirteen of the sixteen California counties which reported 20 per cent or more immigrant population. The foreign-born made up 21 per cent of the population of the State of Washington in 1910; almost another quarter were second generation immigrants. Eastern Europeans like Finns and Russians were prominent in several of the rural counties, while in others "old immigrants" like Norwegians, Germans, and Swedes were important.

On the Great Plains of Middle America in the twentieth century, the immigrant still occupied a conspicuous place in agriculture. Though Nebraska is rarely thought of as the goal of immigrants, in 1910 six counties in that state reported that the foreign-born made up one fifth or more of their population. Two agricultural counties, Colfax and Cuming, in the center of the state, counted almost three quarters of their populations as first- and second-generation immigrants, mostly from Germany and Austria.

Though by the twentieth century the immigrant played only a small part in the drama of settlement and agriculture, in some Midwestern states, like the Dakotas, he was the star. The foreign-born in South Dakota, for example, comprised 20 per cent of the 1910 population in no less than seventeen counties; indeed, in three of these, one out of every three persons was an immigrant. Two thirds of the inhabitants of all but three of these seventeen counties were first- and second-generation immigrants. Even more significant insofar as in-

---

[2] For example, as late as 1910 both Wisconsin and Illinois still counted one fifth of their populations as foreign-born, with Germans and Scandinavians predominating over all other ethnic groups. In at least nine Wisconsin counties Germans made up over a majority of the immigrants, and in each of these counties the foreign-born were more than 20 per cent of the total population.

fluence went was the fact that individual nationalities tended to cluster together. For example, three quarters of the foreign-born in three counties were Russians (actually Germans who had emigrated from Russia). In three other counties, Norwegians made up more than half the immigrant population.

If Wisconsin in the first half of the nineteenth century was largely the creation of the European peasant, the rich state of North Dakota was the product of the immigrant at the very end of the century. In 1910 the foreign-born comprised 27 per cent of the people of the state, and another 43 per cent were children of immigrants. There was not a single county in which the foreign-born comprised less than 15 per cent of the population, and there were twenty-eight counties in which they constituted more than a quarter. The 40,000 first-generation Norwegians were the largest ethnic group, with Russians (actually German-speaking people) running second with 32,000. The latter, in conformity with their traditional cultural exclusiveness even in Russia, were highly concentrated in five or six counties, where they often made up more than two thirds of the foreign-born population.

Important as the immigrant was in agriculture, the fact remains that the typical immigrant in the years after 1890 was a worker in a factory or mine. In 1910, only 14 per cent of the foreign-born were in agriculture and forestry, but 43.5 per cent were engaged in manufacturing. When the Congressional Immigration Commission of 1907 investigated the economic impact of immigration, it discovered that the labor supply in industry after industry was dominated by the foreign-born. In basic industries like iron and steel making, coal mining, construction work, copper mining and smelting, and oil refining, the foreign-born, on the average, comprised over 60 per cent of the labor force. Labor in cotton-goods manufacturing, once the province of native-born farm girls, as at Lowell in the beginning of the nineteenth century, was now almost 70 per cent foreign-born. By 1910, the clothing industry, even though always sprinkled with foreign workers, was drawing almost three quarters of its operatives from immigrant groups.[3] In terms of quantity of labor, it is evident from such figures that American industry would have expanded at

[3] Certain industries, it should be noted, were conspicuous for their small percentages of foreign-born: boots and shoes counted only 27.3; collars, cuffs, and shirts, 13.3; cigars and tobacco, 32.6; and glass, 39.3.

a much slower pace if the muscle and brain of the immigrant had not been available.

All through American history, opponents of the immigrant have pointed to the working foreigner as the thief of the native worker's job. Undoubtedly the immigrant replaced a native-born worker, but it usually was a displacement which benefited the latter. "When the foreigner came in," observed one writer in the *North American Review* in 1892, "the native engineered the jobs, the former did the shoveling. The American in every walk and condition of life . . . has been the 'boss' ever since. The foreigner plows and sows, the native reaps . . . one digs the canals, the other manages the boats; the one burrows in the mines, the other sells the product, and so on through all the various occupations."

Though the effect of the immigrant upon the native's occupational status is often described as a wedge or upward thrust, it is more accurately visualized as the filling of an economic vacuum. Before the native worker could move up the occupational ladder of the national economy, his place had to be taken by new workers coming in at the bottom—and these new workers were the immigrants. Rather than being a wedge pushing the native into a better job, the immigrant was himself sucked into the industrial system by the vacuum created by the upward movement of the natives. But regardless of the analogy employed, it is clear that the native's rise would have been much slower if there had not been an inflow of unskilled immigrant labor at the bottom.

The Immigration Commission found conspicuous examples of this occupational effect in the bituminous and anthracite coal industries and in iron and steel manufacture. In bituminous coal, for example, all white-collar jobs, the Commission's report stated, "are occupied by native American or older immigrants and their children, while the southern and eastern Europeans are confined to pick mining and to unskilled common labor." The same phenomenon was observed in six different communities in which glass manufacturing was the major industry. Sometimes, as in the case of the glass industry, the very survival of the industry was dependent on the new immigrants. Native and "old" immigrant workers were attracted to other industries, and unless cheap "new" immigrant labor had been available, an industry like glassmaking would have been hard put to secure sufficient labor.

This tendency for the older nationalities as well as the natives to move up on the occupational scale was also apparent in other spheres. Indeed, it was the usual thing for older nationalities in America to move up a notch socially as newer groups came in at the bottom. The process was discernible not only in industry but, as we shall see, in politics as well. Thus the flow of immigrants into this country has acted as a reinforcement of the social fluidity of the society. And mobility, it should not be forgotten, is broader than vertical motion through the social structure; it also includes horizontal movement across the face of the land. Both forms of movement have been highly characteristic of Americans, and immigration has been a stimulus to both.

When the peasants and farmers of eastern Europe took places in American factories and mines, they exerted an economic influence beyond the supplying of labor. Largely unskilled in even the elementary crafts of America's industries, these peasants provided an incentive for manufacturers to increase the mechanization of their processes. Because they were unable to obtain sufficient skilled labor, many employers were willing to mechanize so that they might utilize the cheap unskilled labor which was pouring into the country. "A large number of illustrations of this tendency might be cited," two authorities in the field of immigration have stated. "Probably three of the best, however, are the automatic loom and ring spindles in the cotton-goods manufacturing industry, the bottle-blowing and casting machines in bottle and other glass factories, and the machines for mining coal." The Immigration Commission made the same observation regarding the introduction of technological improvements in glass manufacturing.

The whole process was an interacting one. As an employer hired unskilled peasants to fill out his labor requirements, he was encouraged, if not compelled, by this addition to utilize machinery in tasks these people were not trained to do. Once the machines were installed, the employer acquired a vested interest in continued use of such unskilled labor, and so expanded his use of machinery until the whole cycle spiraled up to maximum mechanization. This practice of employing machinery in tandem, as it were, with the vast supply of unskilled labor became so common that one prominent economist was prompted in 1906 to complain that America was sacrificing skills to profits. "Were it not for immigration," John R. Commons argued, "American industries would ere now have been compelled to give more attention to apprenticeship and the training of competent mechanics."[4] Though America did not actually become as devoid of mechanics as Commons feared, certainly the stimulus of the new immigration contributed to that widespread use of machinery which so impressed visitors like the labor leaders of the Mosely Commission in 1902.

To bring together in this way the evidence for the importance of the immigrant in the industrial expansion of America is to run the danger of making the tail wag the dog. For, contributory as immigration was, it neither created the jobs nor provided the initial stimulus for the enormous expansion of industry which America experienced during the latter years of the nineteenth century. Immigration was a consequence, not a cause, and the proof of this is readily observable in the relation between immigration and the business cycle.

As one would expect, the rise and fall of immigration closely correlated with the ups and downs of the business cycle, but the important detail in this relationship was that the decline in the business cycle always preceded a drop in immigration. Within six months after a downturn in business, Harry Jerome has shown, the influx of foreigners fell off. From this it is apparent that the causal factor was business conditions, not the flow of foreign labor. It was the discouraging news from America in a recession and the consequent fall-off in remittances to the old country[5] which stanched the flow of people from abroad. Similarly, it would be the encouraging letters and fat money orders which would broaden the stream at a brighter time. The

[4] Sometimes, because of the immigrant, the geographical distribution of industries was given a special and unpredictable twist. Industries like the manufacture of cigars and tobacco, silk, and men's and women's clothing were located, the Immigration Commission pointed out, in close proximity to iron and steel and anthracite coal centers. The explanation of this development was that the consumer industries were following the cheap woman and child labor available in the homes of the immigrant men employed in the basic industries.

[5] A measure of the "pull" which America exerted upon immigrants is found in the fact that well over three quarters of the immigrants landing in the years 1908–10 gave "joining relatives" as their reason for coming. Authorities on immigration also emphasize the importance of remittances in financing and encouraging emigration to America. Even such a small ethnic group as the Greeks, according to Theodore Saloutus, sent back $4.6 million in 1910 and $8.2 million in 1914. Italians in the single year of 1907, it has been estimated by one authority, sent back $85 million. Not infrequently, a single money order from an immigrant might contain more hard cash than the peasants in an eastern European village could hope to see in a lifetime.

economic opportunities of America were created here; the flood of
peasants was primarily a response to that attraction.

3. IMMIGRANTS HAVE VOTES

For many Americans today the impress of the immigrant on American civilization is summed up in the political boss and the big city
machines. Though the political influence of the immigrant undoubtedly can be exaggerated, it was certainly powerful; and during the
nineteenth century, as the immigrant ships set ashore their cargoes, it
was increasingly noticed. "One of the functions of the Irish race in
America," one observer wrote in all seriousness in 1894, "is to administer the affairs of American cities." Cities as far apart in miles
and character, he went on, as New York, Omaha, New Orleans, San
Francisco, Pittsburgh, and St. Louis, not to mention eleven others,
were "among the cities led captive by Irishmen and their sons" in
the arena of politics. Indeed, as early as the 1880's, Irish mayors
were being elected in New York and Boston and other cities where
the Celts had thickly settled. Nor were the Irish alone in their new-
found opportunities for political activity and careers. Perhaps the
best known of the early Germans in politics were Carl Schurz of
Missouri and Gustav Schleicher of Texas, both of them refugees from
the abortive 1848 uprising in Germany. Later in the century, in 1893,
John Peter Altgeld became Governor of Illinois, the first naturalized
citizen to do so, and then went on to become a power in the national
Democratic party, kept, however, from the Presidential nomination
in 1896 by his foreign birth.

Not until after the First World War were representatives of the
second great wave of immigration, the "new immigrants," prominent
in politics. Then Italians like Pastore of Rhode Island, DiSalle of
Toledo, La Guardia and Marcantonio of New York, and a Czech
like Anton Cermak of Chicago made the headlines. In 1949, Joseph
Mruc became the first Pole to be mayor of Buffalo. It is only since
the Great Depression that any significant federal recognition by way
of choice appointment has been granted these newer immigrant
groups. The first Italo-American was appointed to the federal bench
in 1936, but the first Polish-American did not receive that recognition until Truman's administration. For the Presidential campaign of
1968, both major parties selected Vice-Presidential candidates who
were second generation immigrants from eastern and southern Eu-

rope: Edmund Muskie, of Polish descent, and Spiro Agnew, of Greek origin.

In politics, as in industry, the bottom slowly rose to the top as the immigrant learned the ways of America and mastered the levers of political power. For basically, an immigrant group's achievement of prominent political office was a function of its numbers and its political organization. Immigrant leaders attained high elective office through the bloc voting of their nationality, such as occurred with the Irish and Germans; prominent appointive office was achieved when a nationality was recognized as a potent political force, as has recently been the case with Italians and Poles in the federal judgeships. In time, and for the same reasons, even disadvantaged and almost politically friendless groups like the Puerto Ricans and Mexicans, it can be predicted, will receive similar appointments.

It would be a mistake, however, to assume that the influence of the foreign-born at the polls has been confined to the election of ethnic brethren. Even before 1865, for example, national issues were occasionally decided by the votes of immigrants, for in some states the franchise preceded citizenship; even where it did not, fraud or at most a five-year wait bestowed the ballot upon the newcomer. That the foreign vote may well account for the election of Abraham Lincoln in 1860 was suggested some years ago by William A. Dodd. The election, Dodd showed, was won in the Northwest, but only narrowly, and "by the votes of the foreigners whom the railroads poured in great numbers into the contested region." As Dodd wrote, "The election of Lincoln, and, as it turned out, the fate of the Union were thus determined not by native Americans but by voters who knew least of American history and institutions." Subsequent elections like those of 1884 (the year of "Rum, Romanism, and Rebellion") and 1916, when Woodrow Wilson did not carry a single state in which Catholics were important because of dissatisfaction with his Irish and Mexican policies, demonstrate the tendency of immigrant groups to vote in accordance with their national origins.

Even in our own time, as Samuel Lubell has shown in his book *The Future of American Politics,* the clan voting of the immigrant is often determinate. Looking into the districts and the precincts, Lubell found time and again that the ethnic nerve of the voters was much more sensitive than the economic or political. For example, though the lower-income levels of the population tended to support Roosevelt in both 1936 and 1940, sometimes economic self-interest foundered on the rock of nationality. "Roosevelt's heaviest losses" in 1940 "came in German-American and Italo-American wards," writes Lubell, for by that election the President's hostility toward Hitler and Mussolini had become overt. On the other hand, Lubell shows, high-income Jews—not likely to support F.D.R. on economic grounds—registered strong support for Roosevelt in 1940 under the sting of Hitler's anti-Semitism. When ethnic background and low income pulled in the same direction, as it did for Buffalo's Polish-Americans in 1940, "the vote for Roosevelt was prodigious." Polish wards went Democratic nine to one, with some precincts reaching twenty to one, to give the President "his heaviest pluralities in the whole country."[6]

According to Jack Redding's account in his behind-the-scenes book, *Inside the Democratic Party,* Truman in 1948 was greatly indebted for his victory to the votes thousands of immigrants gave him in return for foreign policies like the Marshall Plan, the Truman Doctrine, and the Berlin airlift. Truman even carried German-American wards that had gone Republican under F.D.R.

Mr. Lubell, together with Ray Billington, has done American political history a distinct service by showing, as Lubell has phrased it, that "the hard core of isolationism in the United States has been ethnic and emotional and not geographical." Too often it has been assumed that the isolationist politics of the Middle West are a function of that section's distance from ocean-borne menaces. Now it has been shown by Lubell and others that it is the German background of many of the citizenry of the region which largely accounts for the reluctance to accept an internationalist foreign policy in the twentieth century. The truth of this proposition is suggested also by the relative absence of isolationist sentiment in the Middle West when the State Department directs its barbs at countries other than Germany.

Lubell is careful to point out, nonetheless, that emotional attachment to the homeland is not the sole cause of the isolationism of the Germans and other nationalities. Just as often, perhaps, it is the fruit of the cultural isolation in which the immigrants often live. What this

[6] Lubell also shows the immigrant effect on a broader scale. In 1940, F.D.R.'s majority dropped 7 per cent from 1936. There were twenty counties in the country where his loss exceeded 35 per cent; of these counties, nineteen were predominantly German-speaking in background. Another thirty-five counties showed a drop of 25–35 per cent in the Roosevelt majority; in all but four of these, Germans were "first or second strongest nationality of origin."

often meant in fact is illustrated by an incident told by Joseph Dorfman in his biography of Thorstein Veblen. The economist's mother
was so insistent upon maintaining the Norwegian language and culture that none of her children was even aware that she knew English
until they were almost adults. Though the case of Veblen's mother
was undoubtedly extreme, many immigrants were so culturally isolated—Lubell cites the excellent example of the German-speaking
Russians of isolationist North Dakota—as to be effectively walled off
from just those influences which were making other Americans more
international in outlook. As a result, the immigrants often remained
at least as isolationist as most Americans had been in the nineteenth
century. But whether it was emotional attachment to the homeland
or cultural insulation which fostered the opposition to international-
ism, it arose out of the immigrant background.

The isolationism of many immigrants is one side of the foreigners'
influence upon the foreign policy of the United States; the other is
almost the opposite, since it involves the attempt to prescribe action
for American policy. For even when cut off from American culture,
the immigrant still retained, quite naturally, an interest in the country of his birth. Since immigrants also vote in America, this sentimental connection with the homeland can, and often does, influence
the determination of American foreign policy. The appeals made to
the Italians and the Irish by the opponents of the Versailles Treaty
in 1919, to the Germans in 1939–41 by the isolationists, or to the
Poles by the Republicans after Yalta in the late 1940's are all cases
in point. Harold Ickes in his recently published diary reveals that
Roosevelt in early 1938 told him that the embargo on arms to Loyalist Spain could not be lifted because to do so "would mean the
loss of every Catholic vote next fall. . . ." Certainly, large numbers
of Jewish voters make it necessary for our government officials to
think twice in working out a policy toward Israel or the Arab world.
Because no other country contains as large or as diverse a population, the United States in its conduct of foreign affairs is confronted
with difficulties which are unique and more complicated than elsewhere.

4. MELTING POT OR SALAD BOWL?

As immigration reshaped the economy and politics of America, it
also remolded other aspects of society. For instance, the immigrant

was intimately involved in the growth of the city, that social development which loomed over all others in the late nineteenth century. Increasingly, as the century approached its end, the city became the destination of the immigrant just as it was the goal of a growing number of native farm boys seeking to exchange the plow for the lathe.

Most contemporaries were well aware that the typical new immigrant was a city dweller. But he was more than that: he was a dweller in a big city. At the turn of the century, one half of all the foreign-born lived in the 160 cities of 25,000 population or more. For some nationalities the proportions were even higher: three quarters of the Russians—mainly Jews—and almost two thirds of the Irish and Italians lived in cities of such size. Though less than one fifth of the American people as a whole lived in the big cities (100,000 or more population), almost two fifths of the immigrants did. The clustering of foreigners in the great city is even more striking when it is recognized that one third of the second-generation stock also lived in the thirty-eight cities of over 100,000 population, though only one tenth of the old native population lived in those cities.

This conjunction of the city and the foreigner aroused sinister thoughts in the minds of Americans still wedded to the farm—and most natives in the early years of the twentieth century still lived in a rural environment. Always suspicious of the city anyway, the rural man became more so as he saw tenement piles and ramshackle company towns crowded with people whose customs, religions, and looks differed from his own. Moreover, the immigrants, as city dwellers, with all that that word connoted to the rural mind, absorbed from the rest of America more than the share of suspicion and distrust which their foreign origin alone could be expected to evoke. In short, by being urban as well as foreign, the large numbers of immigrants tended to enhance social tensions, thus further impeding the quick acceptance which every immigrant hoped to find in his new homeland. The most obvious manifestation of these tensions, as we shall see later, was nativism.

For the history of American urbanization, the nationality ghettos of the big cities were certainly the immigrants' most obvious contribution. But these conglomerates of the foreign-born, large and obtrusive as they often were, should not completely overshadow the contribution which the immigrant made to the building of new cities. Such new towns were quite different from those which in the earlier days of the Republic were hacked out of the forest or founded at the juncture of trade and travel routes. The immigrant cities were a direct product of America's expanding industry and large numbers of newcomers, brought into being by the clustering of immigrant workers around a new ore mine or a new steel mill.

These towns were the frontier of the new industrial expansion. The hard and soft coal areas of Pennsylvania, West Virginia, Alabama, Ohio, and Illinois all gave birth to a number of such towns, as did the iron ore ranges of Minnesota and the copper mining sites of Michigan. The Immigration Report of 1910 told of one steel town, West Seneca, New York, located just outside Buffalo; only ten years old, it already had a population of 20,000, of whom four fifths were immigrants. Another such newly founded town was Hungary Hollow, Illinois, in which 15,000 Bulgarians were employed in the steel mills in 1910. Charleroi and Kensington, Pennsylvania, and Ford City, Ohio, were examples of new immigrant cities springing up around the glass factories located there.

Whether one looks at the old cities which were being swelled by the new additions from abroad or at the new ones which were being created by the newcomers, the irony still remains: the spectacular urbanization of America at this period was in large part the product of European peasants.

When the people of one culture move into another, they often have to shed layer after layer of old habits and ways of thought, much as one peels an onion. To some extent this was true of the Europeans who came to America, and especially so of those peasants who exchanged their rural life for an American city. But the danger inherent in the peeling of an onion—that so many layers will be removed that nothing is left—was no threat to the immigrants; most of them retained a number of their traditional habits.

Few of the immigrants, for instance, divested themselves of their religion or church,[7] and because they did not, they enriched the unique religious heritage of America. The churches which the immigrants brought with them have increased the diversity of sects in America so that in the 1950's, with something like 235 distinct reli-

[7] Part of this, as Will Herberg has pointed out, is inherent in the nature of American culture. Though demanding much of the newcomer, it has not demanded uniformity of religion. "The newcomer is expected to change many things about him as he becomes American—nationality, language, culture," Herberg observes. "One thing, however, he is *not* expected to change—and that is his religion." *Protestant-Catholic-Jew* (New York, 1955), p. 35.

gious bodies in this country, at least sixty are the direct result of immigrants.

The heterogeneity of nationalities carved new sects out of old denominations, as well as creating entirely new churches. The Lutherans, for example, split into a dozen national churches; the Mennonites have thirteen varieties; the Eastern Orthodox Church is divided into nine national sects. A host of minor sects have been spawned by the diversity of immigrant nationalities—churches like the Armenian Orthodox Church in America, the Assyrian Jacobite Apostolic Church, the Free Magyar Reform Church of America, and three varieties of German Dunkers. "The tendency toward conformity with the new civilization is, strangely enough, responsible for much of the denominationalism of America," explains H. Richard Niebuhr. "It separates various generations of immigrants from each other so effectively that new schisms result." Recent immigrants, finding "themselves ill at ease among their partly Americanized kindred . . . feel compelled to organize new denominations which will be truer to the Old World customs."

Though the variety of sects is uniquely American, it is not as sociologically significant as the fact that all religion in the United States is divided into three great segments. As Will Herberg has pointed out, "By and large, to be an American today means to be either a Protestant, a Catholic, or a Jew. . . . Unless one is either . . . one is a 'nothing'; to be a 'something,' to have a name, one must identify oneself to oneself, and to be identified by others, as belonging to one or another of the three great religious communities in which the American people are divided."

Of these three "great communities," two are the creation of the immigrants. Without the immense nineteenth-century emigration to the United States from Ireland, Italy, Poland, and other Catholic countries, the Roman Catholic Church in America would still be merely a missionary church among the heretics as it was in the eighteenth century. The same is true of Judaism, the third of the religious divisions of Americans. It has been raised to its present importance solely by the large numbers of German and Russian Jews who swelled the tiny Spanish and Portuguese colonies of the seventeenth and eighteenth centuries.

Immigrants have not only fleshed out the substance of the Roman Catholic Church, but one nationality—the Irish—has long dominated the leadership—a consequence, in large part, of the Celts having gotten here "fustest with the mostest." Even today, the hierarchy is topheavy with Irish names.

But the immigrant influence upon the Church extends beyond leadership. It would seem that the Irish domination has been largely responsible for the prudishness or puritanism which, until recently, has been so strikingly characteristic of the American branch of the Roman Catholic Church. In America, as in Eire, the Church has taken an excessively prudish attitude on matters concerning nudity, sex, and marriage.[8] It is true, of course, that Catholic doctrine on birth control and sexual behavior is universal rather than national, but this fact does not prevent a national tinge from showing. Thomas Sugrue, the well-known American Catholic layman, speaks of "The intensely sentimental Catholicism of Spain; the fiercely Puritanical Catholicism of Ireland; the relaxed and affectionate Catholicism of Italy. . . ." It is difficult, for instance, to imagine an American church dominated by a French or Italian hierarchy indulging in the present American Church's ban on motion pictures and books which too realistically depict the natural, if sometimes lascivious, relations between men and women.

It would be misleading, however, to leave the impression that the Catholic Church was alone among the immigrant churches in exhibiting a puritanical streak. Protestant immigrant sects also displayed such attitudes, and none of them, let it be said at once, traced their descent from the original Puritans. A number of the immigrant churches, particularly branches of the Lutheran Church, attempted to regulate courtship habits, marital duties, and social pastimes like dancing, drinking, and card playing—usually in the direction of min-

[8] An example of the great concern for modesty is afforded in a handbook for Catholic parents, *Parents, Children and the Facts of Life,* by Henry V. Sattler, bearing the imprimatur of the Bishop of Paterson. "Teach children a routine in dressing and undressing which will expose them as little and as briefly as is reasonably possible. Teach them also to avoid too much curiosity about their own sex." Seán O'Faoláin, in an essay in J. A. O'Brien, *The Vanishing Irish* (New York, 1953), p. 121, tells of his experience in the Irish Church: "Since my boyhood I have heard my elders fulminating about keeping company, night courting, dancing at the crossroads, V necks, silk stockings, late dances, drinking at dances, girls who take part in immodest sports (such as jumping and hurdling), English and American books and magazines, short frocks, Bikinis, cycling shorts, and even waltzing which I have heard elegantly described as 'belly-to-belly dancing.' Perhaps the most extreme example of this kind of thing was to hear woman described from a pulpit to a mixed congregation as the 'unclean vessel.'" Mary Laverty, in the same collection, also tells of the excessive prudery of the Irish clergy.

imizing pleasure. Marcus Hansen tells the story of a group of Scandinavians in Wisconsin in the 1850's who, after a Sunday of picnicking, drinking, and dancing, were vehemently attacked the next day
in the native American press for their un-American and un-Christian
behavior. Though stunned by the unexpected assault, the immigrants
were even more taken aback when their ministers defended the criticism. The clergymen explained that though such revels were permissible in Norway and were not sinful, in the new country they only
drew reproaches and hostility from Americans; therefore the Church
must disapprove. Such spontaneous puritanism, as Hansen called it,
was not uncommon in the churches of the immigrants as the leaders
and members sought to make their peace with disapproving neighbors.

"The process of Puritanization can be followed by anyone who
studies the records of a congregation or the minutes of a synod,"
Hansen tells us. "Discipline became more and more strict. One after
another, social pleasures that were brought from the Old World fell
under the ban. Temperance and Sunday observance were early enforced; then card playing and dancing were prohibited. Simplicity in
dress and manner of living became prime virtues."

There was another reason for the puritanism of the immigrant
churches. Rather than see the community lose its identity in the
American environment, the Church instinctively threw up protective
barriers. Activities like dancing, card playing, and drinking, which
could serve as vehicles for American encroachment, were banned or
discouraged by the churches. Originally intended to preserve the old
ways, the strict moral code remained even after its *raison d'être* had
passed away. Thus, in a roundabout fashion, these aliens—so divergent from their neighbors at the outset—ended by accepting and
further advancing that brand of morality called puritanism, which so
often has been considered typically American.

To many ethnic groups, the silent terror of being in a new land,
thousands of miles from native roots, strengthened rather than weakened the loyalty to and dependence upon the old religion. They could
not help but contrast their firm religious beliefs with the indifference
they found among the natives. "I think," one disgusted Norwegian
preacher wrote from Wisconsin, "that the largest faction here in the
West consists of veritable heathens who neither have been baptized
nor have learned to know Christianity." Certainly, for the Irish, the
ancient Church proved to be confessor, teacher, counselor, social

director, almsgiver, and even political leader for a people ignored by the institutions and scorned by the citizens of the new land. The Lutheran Church of the Germans and Scandinavians of the Middle West performed a similar if less pervasive function.

From such bonds of intimacy, born of the immigrants' needs, sprang an attachment between the people and their Church which no American tradition of secularism or indifference could disrupt or seriously impair. It may not be far wrong to attribute the greater church attendance and religiosity of Americans in the twentieth century, as compared with the eighteenth, to the great immigration of the intervening century.

If the immigrant reinforced the Puritan strain in the American tradition, he also enhanced the conservative streak which runs all through American culture. In politics, religion, and economics, as we have seen, the weight of the immigrant has been thrown into the scales in favor of the traditional, the tried, the accepted. Even where he was not innately conservative, his cultural isolation has meant loss of contact with the stream of ideas which were changing America, and he has appeared as a conserver of old ways. At other times, the immigrants deliberately eschewed the new, as when they shunned Populism in politics and secularism in religion, and sought their security in conformity with the dominant patterns of American life. For even when the immigrant was prepared to mingle with the native Americans, he wanted nothing more than to be like them, to take the *status quo* as a bench mark by which he could maintain his bearings in novel surroundings.

In 1908, at the height of the last great surge of immigration, a naïve and sentimental play about American immigrants, written by an English Jew, captured the imaginations of American theatergoers. Played before numerous audiences throughout the country, *The Melting Pot* of Israel Zangwill also ran through many editions in book form. Its title has been immortalized as the classic description of the immigrant's reception and future in America. "There she lies, the great Melting Pot," exclaimed the hero, David Quexano. "East and West, and North and South, the palm and the pine, the pole and the equator, the crescent and the cross—how the great Alchemist melts and fuses them with his purging flames!"

But, one is tempted to ask, is this really what happens to the immigrant in America? Do the various national traits "melt and fuse" to form a new American culture when it is clear that many of them remain untouched and persistent? Some traits, to be sure, do disappear after a while. After one or two generations most of the sharply deviant contours are worn down to the common pattern, the brassy earrings, the large mustachios, the garlicked breath, and the atrociously accented English being replaced by appropriate American substitutes. But true as that may be, it does not make a melting pot, for the dropping of old habits for new is not fusion or melting.

As we have already seen, some habits from the old country were not discarded; in those instances the children of immigrants even into the third and fourth generations retained their differences. In view of such failure to melt and fuse, the metaphor of the melting pot is unfortunate and misleading. A more accurate analogy would be a salad bowl, for, though the salad is an entity, the lettuce can still be distinguished from the chicory, the tomatoes from the cabbage.

Contrary to the conception implied by the figure of the melting pot, American civilization has not been homogeneous and uniform; even today it is diverse and pluralistic. The evidence is all around us: in the varieties of languages, of foods and restaurants, of religions and festivals, of newspapers and books, of costumes and dances, of literatures and theaters. Though some immigrant habits and mores are undoubtedly lost in America, others are not; and they remain, not fusing into a new cultural synthesis but persisting as living remnants of many cultures, spicing and enlivening the broader stream of American life. As a result of these resistant, undigested bits of foreign ways within the United States, American culture has been more colorful, more cosmopolitan, more diverse than any other people's since the days of Trajan and Hadrian and down until the creation of modern Israel. But as foreign language newspapers die off one by one, as they have been doing, and the great tide of immigration lies increasingly farther in the past, the cultural diversity that has been one of the hallmarks of American civilization also begins to slide into homogeneity.

5. WHO ARE AMERICANS?

With strange and different foreigners spreading throughout the country, congregating in the cities, voting with political machines, pushing their way into farms and factories, it was to be expected that there would be a reaction on the part of the native population.

Nor is it surprising that the two great outbursts of antiforeign sentiment—1830–60 and 1890–1914—should coincide with the two peaks of immigration. Always it was the numbers of these newcomers which worried the older Americans.

The earlier of the two anti-immigrant movements, that of the nativists, or Know-Nothings as they came to be called in the 1850's, was directed primarily against the growing influence of the immigrant in politics and the sudden upsurge of the Roman Catholic Church, for which immigration was largely responsible. Despite the ugly turn which the anti-immigration movement in the 1830's took when it resorted to mob violence against Catholics and immigrants, the principal purpose animating the nativist movement of the 1850's was the elimination of the foreigner as a political force. For this reason the key planks of the Know-Nothing party were the extension of the waiting period for naturalization from five to twenty-one years and the exclusion of the foreign-born from public office. At no time, in contrast with later movements, did the Know-Nothings seek a restriction upon the flow of immigrants into the country. There were compelling economic reasons why this was so—the need for labor being among the most important—but the fact remains that Know-Nothingism, no matter what else it stood for, was not a restrictionist movement.

Indeed, the nature of the Know-Nothing movement is far from simple. Americans are often tempted, if by nothing more than their reverence for their alien ancestors, to look upon the nativist or Know-Nothing response to immigration as a tale of simple bigotry. But a critical examination of the movement, only a sketch of which can be given here, suggests that something more was involved than just the corroding influence of intolerance.

The history of nativism in Massachusetts offers a good example of the complex character of the nativist reaction to the immigrant. The nativists of Massachusetts in the 1850's were really a coalition of two quite dissimilar groups—old-line Whigs, who were concerned over the growing numbers of Irish in the state, and liberal Whigs and Democrats interested in counteracting the conservative policies of the dominant Democratic party. Since the Irish were almost invariably Democrats, and conservative, it was possible for the conservative Whigs and liberal Whigs and Democrats to join in a common front against the conservative Democrats and Irish, albeit for different reasons. To the social reformers and liberals, many of whom disliked the bigotry of the out-and-out nativists, joining the Know-Nothing or American party was justifiable in the interests of reform as the only practical means for welding together the divided opponents of the conservative Democratic party. The stratagem worked and the American party was swept into office in 1855.

That this was more a victory for reform than for bigotry is shown by the events which followed the election. The Know-Nothing legislature did not enact any nativist legislation, but it did pass a series of reform laws: protection for runaway slaves and free Negroes, improvements in the educational and jury systems, and expansion of the rights of women. Viewed against such a background, it does not seem so strange that a dedicated antislavery and reform leader like Massachusetts' Senator Henry Wilson was willing to be associated with the Massachusetts Know-Nothings.

Not all nativists, of course, can be properly fitted into this pattern,[9] but those who do, demonstrate that the native reaction to the immigrant was more than a simple fear of the new and the different; sometimes it was recognition that the foreigner was innately conservative and an obstacle to reform.

Underneath the political manifestations of native anxiety regarding these outlanders was the undeniable fact that the immigrants were different. Their dress was queer, their language was either unknown or wrongly accented, their religion was sometimes saturated with bloody memories of the religious strife of the sixteenth century, and, perhaps most disturbing of all to the natives, their pleasures, like lager beer gardens and St. Patrick's Day revelries, seemed to be at wide variance with what was considered moral in America. One German church worker traveling in America, for example, was told by immigrants that "we can't work with Americans; they are too good for us. They regard us as the greatest sinners if we drink a glass of beer or have a fete on Sunday afternoon."

Regardless of the distaste which these strangers seemed to arouse in Americans, Know-Nothingism failed to attain any of its goals,

---

[9] In the South, for instance, Know-Nothingism was genuinely conservative, using as its appeal the Southerner's fear that the immigrant endangered the institution of Negro slavery. It is ironic that in Massachusetts the typical immigrant was an Irish Catholic; from this it was generalized that the immigrant was politically conservative. In the South, however, the immigrants heard from most were the handful of antislavery Germans in Texas and those in the North; consequently, the typical immigrant in the minds of Southerners seemed to be an enemy of the "peculiar institution."

the movement declining even more rapidly than it rose. Moreover, the immigrants' enthusiastic support of the Union cause in 1861 smothered the last traces of public nativism for a generation. Not until the new wave of immigrants began to dash upon American shores in the last decade of the century was there any significant revival of anti-Catholic and antiforeign sentiment comparable to that of the 1830's and 1850's.

The counterpart of the Know-Nothings at the end of the nine-teenth century was the American Protective Association. This or-ganization was more anti-Catholic than anti-immigrant, but, since the two were so closely connected in the public mind, no real distinc-tion was made between them. The A.P.A. was notorious for its half-truths and lies about the evil and subversive propensities of the Roman Catholic Church. Such blatant bigotry, however, was more a throwback to the worst in nativism than a new approach to the immigrant's influence in America.

A broader, though much less organized, movement than the A.P.A., and one which was destined to achieve its goal, also de-veloped in the early years of the "new" immigration. This was a movement to restrict both the numbers and the kinds of people who could enter the United States—an approach to the immigrant which was new to American thought. The first concrete step in this direction was taken in 1882, when Congress, responding to the fears of Cali-fornians and others, prohibited the future immigration of Chinese.

During the remaining years of the century, a number of broadly based groups and organizations displayed mounting concern over the possible changes and dangers the rising flood of immigrants would inflict upon American society. Businessmen, for instance, though torn between their economic self-interest in cheap immigrant labor and their worry over social disturbances sparked by foreigners, began to speak out in favor of some kind of restriction on immigration. Labor leaders were similarly of two minds on the subject, but by the late nineties organized labor was taking a stand in favor of cutting down on immigration. T. V. Powderly, of the Knights of Labor, did so in 1892, and he was followed by the A.F. of L. in 1897.

The whole movement was given intellectual underpinning by men like Professors John W. Burgess of Columbia and N. S. Shaler of Harvard, President F. A. Walker of M.I.T., and Senator Henry Cabot Lodge of Massachusetts. For years these learned gentlemen and others like them preached the gospel of the Anglo-Saxon heritage of Americans, warning in elegant tones against the degradation which awaited the country if the immigrant tide—particularly that part of it originating in eastern and southern Europe—was left unchecked.

Anglo-Saxonism, moreover, was popular as well as academic. It was apparently accepted, for example, by the nativist Junior Order of United Mechanics, which boasted 224,000 members in 1914. The order's chaplain told a House committee that he wanted to see that type of immigrant "to come from which we came . . . I glory in my kinship," he remarked. "My father on one side, was a German, my father upon the other was an Englishman. . . . That is the kind we can absorb. . . . They belonged to that independent race . . . who . . . came with the idea already imbedded in their hearts and minds of the beauties of self-government."

To achieve the dual purpose of limiting numbers and at the same time discriminating between desirable and undesirable peoples, the advocates of restriction hit upon the literacy test. Thanks to the popular educational systems of the nations of northern and western Europe, immigrants from those countries would be able to pass such a test, but those people from the more backward countries of eastern Europe would not. The literacy test provided just the right mesh to satisfy the ethnic bias of the restrictionists.

Three times measures providing for a literacy test were driven through Congress by public concern over the ability of America to absorb so many different kinds of people. And each time they were vetoed. Woodrow Wilson spoke for his predecessors when he told the Congress in his veto of 1915 that the literacy tests represented a "radical change in the policy of the Nation." Heretofore, he pointed out, we have kept only incompetents, the sick, and the anarchistic from our shores. "In this bill it is proposed to turn away from tests of character and of quality and impose tests which exclude and restrict; for the laws here embodied are not tests of quality or of character or of personal fitness, but tests of opportunity. Those who come seeking an opportunity," he told the Congress, "are not to be admitted unless they have already had one of the chief of the opportunities they seek, the opportunity of education. The object of such provisions," he correctly observed, "is restriction, not selection." But the vetoes were only temporary holding actions; the literacy test became law in 1917 over Wilson's second veto.

The arguments in support of restriction did not stop with educational tests. Some leaders, like Madison Grant, New York patrician and president of the Museum of Natural History, injected the dangerous doctrine of race into the question of the immigrant. "Mental, spiritual and moral traits," Grant asserted in 1916, "are closely associated with the physical distinctions among the different European races. The Alpine race [i.e., eastern Europeans] is always and everywhere a race of peasants. . . . The Nordics are, all over the world, a race of soldiers, sailors, adventurers, and explorers, but above all, of rulers, organizers and aristocrats in sharp contrast to the essentially peasant character of the Alpines."

Racist views like Grant's were not confined to the study or select company; variants of them were a part of acceptable discourse at the seat of government. "Our capacity to maintain our cherished institutions stands diluted by a stream of alien blood, with all its inherited misconceptions respecting the relationship of the governing power to the governed," contended Congressman Albert Johnson, chairman of the House Committee on Immigration in 1927. Heretofore the Negro had been the primary target of racist thought, but under the impact of the new immigration such thinking was applied to the newcomers as well. In substance, racism, once confined to whites' attitudes toward black men, now spread to include certain kinds of immigrants as well.

The principal step in the restriction of immigration was taken in the twenties. After a generation of discussion about racial characteristics and the ability of American society to assimilate certain nationalities, it was to be anticipated that restriction would not limit itself to a mere reduction in numbers. To be sure, a severe reduction of numbers was provided for in the 1924 law; no more than 150,000 could enter the country within a single year, though as recently as 1921 over 800,000 had come in. But more significant than the large cut in numbers was the law's effort to deal with the question of western versus southern European immigration, always the central concern of restrictionists and racists. The law provided that each of the world's nationalities should be granted an annual quota of immigrants, the number of which should bear the same relation to the total of 150,000 which each nationality within the United States bore to the total population.

Superficially at least, a theory of American culture was evident here. It assumed that the people of the United States had attained the proper ethnic mixture and no further change was desirable; immigrants were to come into the country in proportion to the numbers

already here. If examined a little more closely, the measure also revealed a decided ethnic bias against the eastern and southern Europeans. This was clear from the original version of the act, which used
1890 as the base year for the calculation of the proportions—a date,
it will be remembered, when the number of "new" immigrants was
very small. But even the final provisions, which dispensed with base
years, displayed favoritism toward the Teutons and Celts, for the
method of calculation tended to discriminate against the Slavic and
Mediterranean peoples. For purposes of setting quotas, the total population of the United States was to be broken down into countries
of origin, regardless of how far back the first generation came over.
This was a procedure which obviously favored the northern and
western Europeans, since they had been the earliest immigrants and
by 1920 would count the most descendants.

Despite opposition from some liberal-minded Americans and from
the nationalities discriminated against, the national origins approach
to immigration remained American policy for over forty years. Then
in 1965, largely as a result of pressure from Presidents John F. Kennedy and Lyndon B. Johnson, Congress abandoned the policy entirely, supplanting it with one that opened America's gates to immigrants from any country who had relatives already here or who
might bring needed skills. Under the new law all countries enjoyed
equal quotas, up to a maximum of 20,000 a year; moreover, the
old prohibition against Asian immigrants was dropped entirely. The
American people, in short, had returned to their historic policy of
offering a broad welcome to all strangers from "the palm and the
pine, the pole and the equator, the crescent and the cross."

Even during its years of restrictive policies, it ought to be added,
the United States followed practices considerably broader than those
of some other countries. New countries of the British Commonwealth,
like Canada, Australia, and New Zealand, for example, have from
the beginning tended toward national exclusiveness in accepting immigrants. More recently, frankly restrictive legislation has reinforced
this tendency. Canada, in its basic immigration statute of 1910, for
example, placed northern Europeans and Americans on a "preferred"
basis, and permitted southern and eastern Europeans to enter only as
servants and farmers, or for special occupational reasons. Both Australia and New Zealand have been most assiduous in banning Asians
from their soil, and both countries have also raised bars against non-
Britishers as well. In fact, the Undesirable Immigrants Exclusion Act

of 1919 of New Zealand prohibits the landing of any person not of British birth and parentage, unless in possession of a special permit.

The Latin American countries have not been notably restrictive on grounds of ethnic origin, but they have sought to exclude certain occupational groupings, such as commercial and industrial workers. The emphasis in their policies, if one can generalize about several disparate countries at once, is on encouraging agricultural workers, and sometimes actually prohibiting, as in Mexico, the immigration of persons intending to enter commerce.

When compared with other nations, then, and for all their concern over the deleterious consequences of cultural mixture, Americans have accepted the new meaning which the immigrant has given to the national motto. "E Pluribus Unum" once referred to thirteen separate political states; today it might well stand for the peoples who came to America and here achieved unity through their cultural diversity.

The immigrant flood was only one of the three powerful social forces which were transforming America in the years after Appomattox. The other two were the factory and the city, industrialization and urbanization. The former we have already canvassed; it now remains to turn to the city.

CHAPTER XI

Alabaster Cities and
Amber Waves of Grain

SEEN in the broad perspective of man's history, at least as archeologist V. Gordon Childe contemplates it, the "Urban Revolution" dates from the sixth millennium before Christ. But, as that phrase has meaning for modern men, the Age of the City in the life of western man was the nineteenth century of the Christian era. In the course of that century, throughout the world of European civilization, millions of farmers and peasants forsook their land to stream into the strange man-made world of the city. As a result, in the middle of the twentieth century, for the first time in human history, the typical heir of European culture is a dweller in the city. Today countries as diverse in history and geography as England and Australia are highly urbanized. Seventy per cent of the population of England and Wales live in cities of 20,000 or more; over half of the people of Australia live in cities of 100,000 or more.

Though situated on the geographical periphery of European civilization, the United States also passed through the urban revolution of the latter half of the nineteenth century. Cities, to be sure, were not unknown in America before that time; almost from the first settling there had been a few like Boston, New Amsterdam, Charleston, Philadelphia, and Newport. But for almost two centuries they were little more than good-sized towns comprising no more than a small proportion of the population. As late as 1850, for example, less than 13 per cent of Americans lived in cities, of which only nine contained more than 50,000 people.

After 1865, however, the pace of urbanization noticeably quickened; by 1920, the census could report that over half the American people, for the first time in their history, lived in cities. At that time W. B. Munro, a lifelong student of urban institutions in the United States, wrote, "The City of today is responsible for most of what is good, and for most of what is bad, in our national life and ideals." Since then, the spread of the city has been reinforced rather than checked; for in 1950, 60 per cent of Americans lived in cities. "Cities like sex," commented one authority in 1945, "are here to stay."

1. THE LURE OF THE CITY

The causes for the expansion of cities are complex, but they are all firmly rooted in man's ceaseless effort to wrest more than mere subsistence from nature. For in a quite literal sense, the birth of cities has always been dependent upon the soil; urban life is not possible until the return from agriculture is sufficient to permit some men to be freed from the eternal search and labor for food. This elementary step in human social evolution was first taken some 8,000 years ago in the New Stone Age, when agricultural technique was first systematically used. What was necessary thousands of years ago has continued to be essential at every subsequent stage in the rise of urban civilization; always the migration of men from the land to the city has been bound by the iron hoops of agricultural productivity.

Because of this fundamental relation between the barren city and the life-supporting soil, an urbanized society, as we use the term today, was not technically possible before the nineteenth century. For it was not until that century that agricultural technology and technique were sufficiently productive to permit the majority of men to be released from the interminable tilling of the soil. As recently as 1787 in the United States, it required nine farm families to feed one urban family. The impressive advances in agricultural productivity since then are graphically summed up in the fact that in 1945 eight urban families were being handsomely supported by a single farm family.

The force which drew countrymen from their farms to the city was economic opportunity. Sometimes this amounted to no more than a little better life than a farmer was able to eke out of a worn-out tenant's plot; sometimes it was a wide-open door to fame and fortune for a man whose talents were lost in a rural environment.

That the growth of cities in the nineteenth century is primarily associated with industrial expansion is shown in a general way by the following table, showing percentage increase of urban population each decade.

1860–1870	59.3	1910–1920	29.0
1870–1880	42.7	1920–1930	27.3
1880–1890	56.7	1930–1940	7.9
1890–1900	36.4	1940–1950	18.2
1900–1910	39.3		

From even a cursory inspection of the table, it is obvious that the rate of urbanization in the United States has been slowly falling off. But a closer look reveals that this decline has not been smooth; instead, it has been punctuated by interruptions or dips in the line of fall. Three such dips stand out: 1870–80, 1890–1900, and 1930–40. Each of these decades was characterized by a severe depression. Since after each of these decades urbanization increased—as, for example, in the 1940–50 decade, where it doubled the rate of the 1930's—it is apparent that the fall-off is due to the lack of economic opportunity in the city.

Though basically the growth of cities is the result of people moving in from the farms, that does not tell the whole story. The eternal problem of the city is the inability to supply the population with food and the factories with raw materials. Even when agricultural productivity has risen greatly, the growth of the city is still held in leading strings to the efficiency of transport. Until the steam locomotive came upon the scene in the nineteenth century, it was difficult to imagine a society in which most of the people did not live on the land; the mere transportation of the quantity of food and goods necessary to sustain them was beyond the capacity of the horse and the boat. As the way of life of a whole society, urbanism in the nineteenth century was new in man's experience, and the railroad was not the least of the several social and technological changes which made it possible. Indeed, it is possible to visualize urbanism as a new constellation of social forces—increasing agricultural production, surplus rural population, and the mechanized factory—held together by the loadstone of the railroad.

But when one has set down the economic and technological forces which undoubtedly account in large part for the growth of urbanism in America, one causal factor remains unmentioned—what A. M. Schlesinger has aptly called "the lure of the city." Always and paradoxically, the city to rural folk was repellent because of its "sinfulness" and strangeness; yet at the same time, its lights, its noises, its gaiety, its variety, its mystery were irresistible. Hamlin Garland relates in the story of his youth that he never forgot, while performing the dreary chores of the farm, the wonder of the town drugstore and its soda fountain, and above all the bustle of people and activity. For many who knew the city, its gregariousness was worth more than anything the isolated farm could promise or provide. This was illustrated in a story common in the 1890's when Americans were beginning to inquire into the "lure" which the city exercised. An Irish woman, starving in the city, was given work and a home out in the country. But in a matter of weeks she was back in her old haunts and miserable circumstances. When asked why she left her job to starve in the city again, she replied, "Paples is more coompany than sthumps."

Both the economic pull and the lure of the city were evident in the novels of the time depicting the farm boy's trek to the bright lights. "Generally speaking," concluded G. A. Dunlap, after studying over a hundred novels concerned with the newcomer to the city, "he came to find there more favorable surroundings or enlarged opportunities."

2. THE SEEDTIME OF THE CITY

In our table of urban increase after 1865, the decade of the eighties stands out as having the largest increment of population. The reasons for this are not hard to discover, for the decade was one in which city-building forces seemed to converge. The economy in general and industry in particular, after finally pulling itself out of the long depression of the seventies, was now hitting its stride. At the same time, mounting rural discontent over falling farm prices and ever-increasing waves of immigration provided hundreds of thousands of people for the building of cities.

The urban expansion in that decade is impressive. The census, for example, reported that 101 cities of 8,000 or more population doubled their size during the eighties. Examples of the growth of individual cities were sometimes not far short of spectacular. Birmingham, Alabama, for example, skyrocketed from 3,000 in 1880 to over 26,000 ten years later; El Paso multiplied itself thirteen times. Kansas City, Kansas, increased its population by 1,000 per cent, and even a large city like its namesake in Missouri jumped from 60,000 to over 132,000. Minneapolis achieved perhaps the most incredible expansion of any large city, rising from 47,000 to over 164,000. Omaha was not far behind, for it reached 140,000 in 1890, though in 1880 its population was only 30,500. In a somewhat smaller class, but remarkable for its rate of growth, was Duluth, which leaped from 3,300 to 33,100 in the course of these ten years. Two other Middle American cities deserve mention for their rapidity of growth: Sioux City, Iowa, which climbed over 500 per cent to reach almost 38,000, and Wichita, Kansas, which jumped from less than 5,000 to 23,000 ten years later.

Though the Middle West was the center of urbanization in this decade, the Far West also made tremendous strides in city building. Spokane, Washington, for example, grew from a mere 350 to 20,-000, Tacoma jumped from 1,100 to 36,000, and Seattle recorded a growth of 1,100 per cent. Fresno, California, rolled up an eightfold increase and Denver, though a good-sized city of 35,000 in 1880, more than tripled itself by 1890.

The same census which reported the expansion of the city also documented the depopulation of the rural communities. Almost 40 per cent of the 25,746 townships of the nation in 1880 reported a drop in population in 1890. The Midwest, as the center of urban growth, was also the region of striking examples of rural decimation. Almost 50 per cent of Indiana's townships, for instance, showed a decline in population for the 1880's, though the state as a whole grew in numbers. Fifty-four per cent of Illinois' and 58 per cent of Ohio's townships lost people in a decade when the states as a whole were increasing in population. In Michigan, the Census of 1890 reported almost 7,500 fewer farmers than in the previous return, though the population of the state had climbed almost half a million.

In New York and New England, the historic springs of Middle Western settlers, two thirds and more of the townships of New England and New York reported fewer people in 1890 than in 1880. It was said that in a single county in New York, 400 empty farmhouses were to be seen. Over 1,440 abandoned or vacant farms were counted in New Hampshire by the state commissioner of agriculture.

By 1910, the urban population fell only a little short of comprising half of the nation: 46 per cent. One has only to look beneath such a broad statistic to recognize that a good part of the nation was much more urbanized than even that figure suggests. Almost 85 per cent of the people of New England and over 70 per cent of the inhabitants of the Middle Atlantic states made their homes in towns and cities.

In the tier of states which stretched from Pennsylvania to the Mississippi, north of the Ohio River—the area which was becoming the heart of industrial America—over 50 per cent of the people were classified as urban folk. Fifty-five per cent of the people living in the three states which faced the Pacific Ocean were living in cities. Indeed, the decade between 1900 and 1910 saw the Pacific coastal states set the pace of urbanization for the rest of the nation, as the Midwestern states had done in the 1880's. Whereas the country as a whole increased its urban population by only 35 per cent, the three Pacific states more than doubled their city dwellers in the first ten years of the twentieth century.

The most dramatic manifestation of urbanization is the great city —urban centers which counted 100,000 or more in population. By 1910, almost 45 per cent of the people of the Middle Atlantic states lived in a relatively few great cities, and a third of the population of the Pacific coastal states did. It was also in 1910 that the census recognized twenty-five so-called Metropolitan Districts, which, in reality, were twenty-five large cities surrounded by contributory and contiguous smaller cities and towns. In effect, the Metropolitan District was an acknowledgment that many small cities which were contiguous were actually providing an environment very close to that of a great city. It also provided a new measure of the extent to which America had become urbanized; in 1910, over 22 million people, out of a total of 92 million, lived in these twenty-five Metropolitan Districts.[1]

As the great city and the metropolis developed, the urban satellite soon followed. "Dormitory cities" out from the industrial city began to appear as early as the 1880's; in that decade Brookline, Massachusetts, was already being termed the "bedroom" of Boston. In 1884, when a branch line of the Pennsylvania Railroad was run out, Chestnut Hill assumed the same relationship to Philadelphia and, about the same time, Lake Forest became Chicago's "dormitory." More recently, whole counties have taken on this function for the great metropolis of New York: Essex in New Jersey, Nassau on Long Island, Fairfield in Connecticut, and Westchester in New York.

There were other kinds of satellites, too. Small industrial towns surrounding a great city and drawing on its labor pool were increas-

---

[1] The movement into the urban conglomerate continues. In 1951, almost a quarter of the people of the nation were living in *eight* of the largest of these great urban centers; in 1910, the same percentage of the population was spread among twenty-five such districts.

ingly evident. Pittsburgh, for example, was rimmed with little steel towns in the years after 1880: Homestead, Duquesne, McKeesport, Aliquippa, and Ambridge. Graniteware manufacturing towns like Granite City, Alton, and East St. Louis, all in Illinois, grew up across the Mississippi from Missouri's great city of St. Louis. A somewhat different type of industrial satellite was the town established by the company to house its workers and to enable it to exert a greater control over the employees. Pullman, Illinois, and Gary, Indiana, just outside Chicago, were examples of these.

The rapidity with which the city spread across America, engulfing more and more of the people, was only the exterior of the Urban Revolution. Its deeper significance was to be sought in the kind of environment the city provided.

3. MEN MAKE CITIES

Eager as many a countryman appeared to be to get to the city, the physical aspects of the object of his trek must have often been disillusioning upon arrival. The Census of 1880 contains a wealth of data on the unsavory countenance of the American city, and almost any random selection from it calls up pictures of primitive conditions. Take, for example, the report on sanitation in the old and established city of Philadelphia. "The custom almost universally practised of turning sink-and-slop water on the ground," the report said, "allowing it to flow across the sidewalks, and stagnate in the street-gutters, has such a pernicious influence upon the atmosphere that one feels an indescribable sense of relief in going to the park or moving out of town, where the air is not laden and polluted with the fetid vapors and foul odors everywhere prevailing in Philadelphia." It was further said that across the river in New Jersey, Camden emptied the night soil from its privies upon the "gathering grounds of the public water supply." Manufacturing wastes were run into the Delaware River without check from the Camden side, and on the other bank Philadelphia emptied its sewers into the same waters. This was the very same river, it should be added, from which Philadelphia drew a good part of its drinking water.

Such lack of concern over sanitation was more typical than exceptional in American municipalities in 1880. Indianapolis, with a population of over 75,000, did not have more than 10 per cent of its homes equipped with water closets; the night soil removed from the city's thousands of privies was emptied into the White River. In Baltimore, with a population of over 330,000, there were "no sewers to speak of . . . all chamber slops," the census reported, being "deposited in cess-pools or privy-vaults." As might have been anticipated, the city's 80,000 cesspools, thanks to the porous soil, constituted a menace to the wells of drinking water. A sampling of thirty-five wells and springs showed that twenty-three were "filthy" in the official opinion, and all the rest in bad or suspicious condition, except for a single one, which was classed as "good."

Paved streets were so rare, even in the large cities, that they might be classified as municipal luxuries. Though Minneapolis, for example, contained almost 47,000 people and 200 miles of streets, none of the streets was paved and the sidewalks were nothing but pine planking. "One of the serious drawbacks" of a great city like New Orleans, the census recognized, was the fact that less than one fifth of its 500 miles of streets were paved, though its population exceeded 200,000. Heavy rains turned the streets into "almost impassable mire" and during a drought the same streets were "extremely dusty." Although Atlanta, Georgia, was approaching a population of 40,000, only three of its 100 miles of streets were paved; the rest were only dirt roads.

Gradually, during the remainder of the century, brick paving crept over the streets of American cities, but it was not until the twentieth century that asphalt, the paving of the great cities of Europe for half a century, could rival brick. It was largely the advent of the bicycle and then the automobile which provided the stimulus for laying a smoother and quieter pavement in the cities of America.

Americans have never distinguished themselves, except perhaps for the TVA, by their social planning; for the most part, social institutions have been left to develop freely and under the stimulus of individual interest. Only later, if at all, do Americans get around to shaping them to the various needs of the people. This attitude was particularly evident as the cities of the nineteenth century began to mushroom across the nation. Occasionally a city, like New York in 1810, actually worked out a plan for its future growth, but usually the cities grew as they would, without plan and without guidance.

Very few of the municipal governments made any provision for recreation in the growing cities, even though it should have been obvious that the new urban environment was almost devoid of the old rural facilities for play. New York, it is true, set an admirable example in the 1850's with its great Central Park, which became the wonder of American municipal life. But few other cities were so thoughtful or farsighted. Several big cities like Newark and Jersey City in New Jersey, Allegheny and Pittsburgh in Pennsylvania, Brooklyn in New York, and Cleveland in Ohio actually devoted more of their areas to cemeteries than they did to recreational parks. Whereas New York led the list with 19.8 per cent of its land given over to parks, Newark could spare less than 1 per cent, though 1.7 per cent was taken up with cemeteries. Only four of the cities of 100,000 population in 1880 devoted more than 5 per cent of their acreage to recreation.

One of the distinguishing features of urban living was the high density of population, a fact which must have been painfully apparent to anyone who walked along the crowded streets and saw the closely packed tenements bulging with humanity. In 1890, the average number of persons per dwelling in the United States was 5.45, but for New York City the average was 18.52. For Cincinnati it was 8.87; for Boston, 8.52; for Chicago, 8.60; for Hartford, 8.12. In Montana, the ratio was 4.9.

The tenement, which was largely responsible for the city's higher density, came to New York as early as the 1830's, attaining the distinction of a problem in the 1850's.[2] By the 1890's, land-use maps for New York afforded ample testimony of the almost incredible coverage of the land by the dumbbell style of tenement. This type of housing, first introduced in 1879 as a "sanitary" improvement, received its name from the shape of the floor plan, the slim indentations on the side forming a narrow air shaft between the otherwise closely set buildings. The design was eagerly taken up by landowners anxious to squeeze the maximum of rent from their city footage, and soon, as one writer has said, the tenement "spread over Manhattan Island like a scab." For acre after acre the poor of the city were crammed into these airless, unsanitary, unattractive firetraps. Other cities, like Boston, followed the example of New York and introduced the

[2] The apartment house for the middle and upper classes did not arrive until the 1870's and 1880's, even though the tenement for the poor was long in evidence and the "flat" had been accepted in Paris for a hundred years. To New Yorkers and Bostonians of the upper classes, the apartment had a flavor of French immorality about it. "It was no easy matter for the French-trained [Richard Morris] Hunt . . . to persuade respectable New Yorkers to take advantage of the apartment house," two recent historians of American building have written. "They were as provincial as the rest of the country at the time and were convinced that the 'French flat' would lead to a breakdown of the American family."

dumbbell; some cities, like Philadelphia, did not, but other types of multiple dwellings in row after monotonous row served much the same purpose of utilizing every precious foot in an overcrowded city.

The result of such lack of planning and unconcern for beauty and attractiveness was a dull and uninteresting urban face. Lord Bryce, for example, when traveling in the United States in the 1880's, thought that only eight or nine cities in the whole country displayed any distinction or charm. The rest, he wrote, "differ from one another only herein, that some of them are built more with brick than with wood, and others more with wood than brick. In all else they are alike, both great and small." And then he went on to describe the result of the miserable amount of imagination expended on city planning. "In all the same wide streets, crossing at right angles, ill-paved, but planted along the sidewalks with maple trees. . . . In all the same shops, arranged on the same plan, the same Chinese laundries with Li Kow visible through the window, the same ice cream stores, the same large hotels . . . the same street cars passing to and fro with passengers clinging to the door-step, the same locomotives ringing their great bells as they clank slowly down the middle of the street."

For most of the nineteenth century, the size of the city was rather rigidly limited by the slow-moving horse-drawn trolley or omnibus. It was not until the 1870's that American cities were freed from this leash on their growth through the introduction of new means of rapid transit. New York tried the elevated steam train, which had the distinct drawback of spraying oil and live ashes on passers-by below, and of being economically feasible in only the very largest of cities. Nevertheless, Kansas City, Brooklyn, Chicago, and Boston, in their desperate search for rapid urban transportation, followed the New York example. At the same time, several cities, like Philadelphia and Chicago, were experimenting with the cable car, a device first used in San Francisco on its steep hills.

The real break-through in the transportation bottleneck, however, came toward the end of the 1880's when Richmond, Virginia, successfully introduced the electric trolley. This vehicle initiated a minor revolution in urban transportation, for it was practical in both large and small cities and it was relatively swift without being dangerous. In short order the trolley became the typical mode of urban transit; by 1895, there were over 10,000 miles of trolley tracks in the cities of the nation. Though even the greatest metropolises used the trolley, they also employed the electrically driven subway and elevated rail-way, Boston beginning its subway in 1895 and New York in 1905. But it was the noisy but efficient trolley that dominated the main streets of America's cities and towns right up until the Second World War. By then, because the multiplicity of automobiles rendered the trolley's lack of maneuverability a traffic obstruction, it was con-demned to extinction.

Transportation was only one of the problems which were unknown on the farm but assumed weighty proportions in the city. Garbage and waste disposal, for instance—a relatively simple matter on the farm—posed formidable tests of man's ingenuity and knowledge of chemistry once the city concentrated the refuse of thousands of peo-ple. It would be decades before garbage and sewage disposal was no longer a pressing problem of the city. Though in the humid sections of the nation the location of potable water was only a minor chore of settlement, in the city it became a desperate search, and aqueducts of the cities were pushed farther and farther into the back country, as they still are today, in a ceaseless quest for sufficient and pure water. Similarly, danger from fire, theft, and bodily harm increased many times as men exchanged the comparative isolation of the farms for the swarming dangers of the city.

4. BUT CITIES ALSO MAKE MEN

Though it was not until 1920 that most Americans lived in cities, urban values had long set the tone and defined the aspirations of American culture. Indeed, the history of the latter part of the nine-teenth century, as we shall have occasion to see a little later, can be written in terms of the gradual spread of urban life until it pervaded the uttermost crannies of society. But for the moment it would be well to pause and try to point up those differences which have tra-ditionally drawn a line between life in the city and life on the farm. The rural man has instinctively recognized this line, and when he has crossed it he has known himself to be in a different world. Sociologi-cally and psychologically, what does it mean when one goes from the country to the city?

One can exaggerate the differences between urban and rural life, to be sure. It is true that the "city" is not a single type of environ-ment, but actually a *range* of environments. A city of 3,000 people, for example, is obviously quite a different social milieu from one of three million, as any New Yorker will be quick to point out to the booster from Zenith.

Despite this, however, there are sound reasons for treating all cities as essentially a single environment. The primary reason is that all cities have more in common with one another than any of them do with the countryside. This is best illustrated by the differences in the occupations in cities as against those which are found in the country. All occupations, except farming, flourish in the city; only one, farming, exists in the country. In 1930, for example, 99.5 per cent of the agriculturally employed population lived in communities of less than 2,500 people—i.e., in areas which did not meet the census definition of a city. It does not take much imagination to recognize that, from this fact alone, the city and the country must be considerably different. Think of the complexity of life, of habits, of work which results from an environment in which a great variety of occupations is to be found, as compared with the simplicity which inevitably follows where there is mainly only one. Furthermore, all cities, even the tiniest, are knit together by their aspirations. They want to be like big cities, not like the countryside. This ambition, which is sometimes exhibited as boosterism, inevitably sets the city psychologically apart from the country. As Oswald Spengler pointed out, the city "is a place from which the countryside is henceforth regarded, felt, and experienced as 'environs,' as something different and subordinate."

Finally, it can be pointed out that the number of small cities—say, below 10,000 population—which because of their size might be thought to blur the clean line between city and country make up only a small proportion of the population. In 1910, for instance, people in towns of 10,000 or less made up only 9 per cent of the population, when the total urban ratio was something like 45 per cent. In short, though a sharp line such as the census draws with its minimum of 2,500 may be difficult to accept, there can be little question that, as between the city and the country in general, the social gulf is much wider than that between any given city and another.

"The man of the land and the man of the city are different essences," Spengler wrote. "First of all they feel the difference, then they are dominated by it, and at last they cease to understand each other at all." Whether there are "essences" may be debatable, but there can be little doubt that the city transforms the countryfolk who come to make their homes there. Harriet Arnow, in her novel *The Dollmaker,* has brilliantly described some of these changes, as in this passage: "Slowly her hand dropped from the doorknob, and she turned back to Clovis. It wasn't the way it had used to be back home when she had done her share, maybe more than her share of feeding and fending for the family. Then, with egg money, chicken money, a calf sold here, a pig sold there, she'd bought almost every bite of food they didn't raise. Here everything, even to the kindling wood, came from Clovis."

As the novel makes quite clear, much more than a loss of wifely independence was involved in the move from the Kentucky hills to industrial Detroit. Privacy was lost through the thin walls of the city apartment; the impersonality of the city permitted cheating at the store, both by the customer who did not know the merchant and by the storekeeper because he was not known by the purchaser. The social pressure to "adjust" to the new ways, the rift between parents and children because their rates of accommodation differed and because the children were now subjected to novel influences like the movies, the Girl Scouts, and the soap operas, are all oddly reminiscent of the immigrant's struggle to adjust to and understand his new world. Actually, of course, the similarities are not so odd; to go from the farm to the city was as much a movement out of one culture into another as to come from Europe. The Kentucky farm folk of *The Dollmaker* were no more prepared than European immigrants for the frightening kitchen gadgets, the chlorinated water, the work hours unrelated to the sun, and the absence of greenery, which were among the constituents of urban life.[3]

As the city and the country differed in their material aspects, so they differed in, what was perhaps more important, the habits of mind of the people who lived there. As Robert MacIver has pointed out, the fact that there are no farmers in the city serves to produce a quite different outlook on life among city people as compared with rural. For the latter, he writes, "there is no sense of a common and

[3] A story by the nineteenth-century Spanish writer Leopoldo Alas suggests that the city has had the same effect on rural people wherever it might be. In Alas' story Dona Berta, the heroine, came for the first time to Madrid after a long life in a remote rural area. "Contemplating Madrid when it was deserted reconciled her somewhat to it. The streets seemed less hostile, more like the small, narrow lanes she knew; the trees more like the 'real trees.' . . . She was afraid of the multitude . . . but most of all, she was afraid of being run down, trampled, crushed by horses, by wheels. . . . The trolley looked like a cautious monster, an insidious serpent to her. She imagined that the guillotine was something like those hidden wheels that slid like a knife along the two iron lines." *Great Spanish Stories* (New York, 1956), p. 193.

vital dependence on the aspects of the seasons and the vagaries of the weather. There is no sense of a common earth, a common fortune and a common fate. . . . There are no impressive signs to call out at the same moment those universal comments and reflections which make man feel kin to man—the devastation of the storm, the flow of the sap, the fall of the leaf." Unlike rural men, the urban dwellers are diverse in origins, in interests, in occupations, in their whole lives. Where the rural family is relatively isolated, the urban family is closely involved with many other people; yet the breadwinner is outside the home site for most of the daylight hours. Even recreation in the city is conditioned by the environment; sports are for spectators, not participants.

Relieved in large part from the pressure of competition by the fact of his isolation, the rural man lives a relatively simple, outdoor life in contrast with the competitive, indoor, anxious search for prestige and position which the highly mobile and social environment forces upon the city dweller. Rural life, to be sure, like nature itself, changes through time, but in contrast city life races; people are constantly moving in and out; businesses are succeeding and failing; the very face of the city itself, man-constructed as it is, is also man-destroyed.

This very fluidity of urban existence induces a change in the character of the countryfolk who come under its influence. "The city calls more for alertness, the quick mind that responds to the changing occasion" than does the farm, McIver has concluded. "What is seen superficially in manners is revealed more profoundly in morals. 'Urbanity' belongs to the city." It is the rural community which holds fast to the old morality, to the traditional ways; it is the city which is so used to change that it accepts it with equanimity. But the city pays a price for this, too. The corollary of the urban man's repudiation of the social anchor of tradition is an increased burden of anxiety. Insofar as the environment of the city loosens the hold of religion, the family, and traditional morality, to that extent it undermines the social forces which sometimes are all that keep men steady in times of stress.

Essentially the city is movement—vertically and horizontally. The ladders of social mobility, like the means of horizontal transportation and hustle and bustle, are concentrated within the city: the Church, the government, education, the law, the courts, the army, the arts, journalism, and so forth. The very hierarchy of occupations in the city, of which there is no counterpart in the country, encourages and too often compels a struggle for movement in which many rise and many fall. And if, as sociologist Louis Wirth has observed, "mobility is an index of metabolism," then the city is almost consuming itself in its own activity.

It would seem to follow, then, that as the nation becomes progressively urbanized, the competitiveness of the city will add its considerable weight to that historic American drive to excel, to keep up with the Joneses, to rise in the social scale.

But if the city has encouraged the drive to excel, it at least has provided the opportunity. Toward the end of the Dark Ages, as cities began to reappear upon the map of Europe, the hallmark of the emergent city was freedom; *"Stadtluft macht frei"* was the urban slogan of the twelfth century. In the twentieth century, one urban planner still finds the essence of the city to be its air of freedom. "In our industrial society, the city represents a particularly precious form of freedom—freedom of choice of work," Charles Ascher wrote in 1945. "If one skill becomes obsolete, there are facilities to learn another and the chance to practice it. Father can work in a mill, son in a filling station, daughter in an office."

The site of all past civilizations, as the word itself implies, has been the city, and so it is today. Uniformly, literacy has been higher in cities than in country districts, just as it has been greater in urbanized New England than in the rural South. At one time in the 1890's it was calculated that American cities produced twice as many names in *Who's Who* as the proportion of urban people warranted. One student investigated the origins of 6,000 French men of letters for the five centuries prior to 1895 and found that cities produced thirteen times as many prominent figures in proportion to the population as did the country districts. Then, as now, it is obvious that the city, wherever it is found, is the center of art, the theater, the newspaper, publishing—indeed, the center of all endeavors concerned with the printed and written word or the transmission of ideas.

Cities are also paradoxes. "Their rapid growth and large size testify to their superiority as a technique for the exploitation of the earth," two sociologists have written, "yet by their very success and consequent large size, they often provide a poor local environment for man." And that "poor local environment" is something else besides inadequate housing, noise, filth, crime, and crowded conditions, though they are bad enough. It also includes psychological factors like competitiveness, anxiety, insecurity, and loneliness.

"In the city there is little or no sense of neighborhood," wrote Josiah Strong, a crusading clergyman of the 1890's. "You may be separated from your next neighbor by only a few inches, and yet for years never see his face or learn his name. Mere proximity does not imply social touch." This phenomenon, which all who have lived in the city immediately recognize as typical, is perhaps the most paradoxical aspect of the city. It seems, almost, as if there is a social law that decrees that the more people there are in a city, the slighter the contact among them. To young men just arriving from the country, Strong remarked, "the first thing that is impressed on them is their own utter loneliness, which often seems unendurable." In such loneliness a sociologist like Sorokin has located the cause for the consistently higher suicide rate of the city—a rate, incidentally, which has steadily increased in the United States as urbanization has proceeded. In 1860, the suicide rate per 100,000 was 3.18; in 1922, it was 11.9.

But it is not only in regard to suicides that the city is a greater threat to human life than the country. For the most part, a person born in the city could not anticipate living as long as he might, had he been born on a farm. For example, the parents of a baby boy born in a city in 1901 could expect him to attain the age of forty-four, but farm parents of a male child would be able to look forward to slightly more than ten additional years of life for their offspring. Since the turn of the century, the spread between rural and urban life expectancies has narrowed, but it is still there.

It is only fair to add that the city as distinguished from industrialization may not be responsible for the short life expectancy of city dwellers; there is evidence, for example, that it is industrialization which is the true cause. But since it is almost impossble to separate industry from its natural habitat, and since no cities are without some industry, we are justified in concluding that between the twin forces of the factory and the city, men are robbed of several years of life.

A similar difficulty in separating the influence of the factory from that of the city is met with when we deal with rural-urban differences in birth rates and family sizes. It is well known that the birth rate is lower and the family size smaller in cities as compared with rural communities.[4] But it is also well recognized that family size and birth rate decline as income increases, and since it is equally acknowledged that wealth is more highly concentrated in cities than in rural areas, we cannot know whether the downward changes in these indices are the result of rising incomes or of the environment of the city. It is logical to assume, nonetheless, that the urban milieu plays some part, if only because the children in the city constitute an economic loss rather than an asset as they do on the farm. Moreover, contraceptive knowledge and equipment have usually been more available in the city than in the country.

The precise causal factors, however, are not so important as far as American civilization is concerned. More significant is the fact that these population and mortality trends are closely associated with urban life. If the United States continues to fall under the influence of the city—as everything seems to suggest it will—then these urban characteristics will become increasingly descriptive of American life as a whole.

It is not necessary, however, to speculate about the future effects of urbanization and industrialization; the past impact is spread upon the record for all to see. One of the first areas to feel the alchemy of industrial and urban change was agriculture.

5. THE HAND THAT FEEDS IS BITTEN

The broad foundation on which both industrial and urban expansion rested in the nineteenth century was the great improvement in farming—an event which agricultural historian Carl Taylor has called "as significant in its effects as the Industrial Revolution" in England a century before. Between 1865 and 1900, a mountain of foodstuffs and raw materials poured from the farms of America. Wheat production climbed from 152 million bushels in 1866 to 500 million in 1880 and then soared up to 675 million in 1898. The output of corn exceeded even these levels: 730 million bushels in 1866, 1,500 million in 1880, and 2,330 million in 1898. Though the Civil War had

---

[4] Urban fecundity has been so low that for most of the last fifty years cities in the United States have failed to reproduce themselves. Only the influx of immigrants and countryfolk has kept cities growing. In 1930, for example, the net reproduction rate for cities was 88.0, where 100 represents bare replacement of the population. The rate at that time for rural-farm population was far above replacement: 159. Only since World War II has the urban reproduction rate gone above 100. Before 1900, the birth rate of cities was lower than that of rural areas, but the net reproduction rate was above 100.

all but extinguished cotton production in the United States, the snowy fiber made a spectacular comeback; in 1898, something over 11 million bales or 4 billion pounds were grown in the American South.

The torrent of production was of such proportions that even the rapidly expanding population of the United States could not absorb it; it gushed out to engulf the world. Whereas in the 1850's the United States exported about 19 million bushels of wheat and 33 million pounds of beef products, by the late 1870's the annual exportation of these agricultural commodities increased sevenfold. Yet this was only the beginning of the flood of food and fiber which surged across the face of the world from the American cornucopia, the crest not being reached until the opening years of the twentieth century. In 1901, the wheat surplus of the country was 234 million bushels; in 1906, the exports of beef products exceeded 731 million pounds; and it was not until 1910 that the exportation of pork products fell below an annual rate of one billion pounds. It almost seemed as if the grim prognostications of old Thomas Malthus were being smothered in foodstuffs.

Such production, however, was only possible because the American farmer, in the years between 1870 and 1900, transformed raw nature at an unprecedented pace. It was as if the cover of half a continent was ripped off in those thirty years. Between 1870 and 1900, 225 million acres of improved land were added to American farms, or 37 million acres *more* than had been put to the plow in all of the two and a half centuries since Jamestown was settled.

The beginnings of this incredibly rapid opening of the lands of the country go back to the years of the War for the Union. The passage of the Homestead Act in 1862, for example, permitted the rapid transfer of enormous quantities of public lands into private hands, both directly to settlers and otherwise through fraud. Similarly the land grants to railroads immediately after the war resulted in millions of acres of government lands being thrown on the market for private exploitation.

The great spurt in agricultural expansion is only partly explained by the increase in the amount of land opened up to cultivation; of equal importance was the coming of the machine to the farm. Like the opening of the land, the mechanization of agriculture was pushed by the war. With perhaps a million farmers in the Union armies at a time when the nation's demand for food was increasing, those left behind on the farms were compelled to turn to machinery. The success of machines, particularly reapers and threshers, in producing a greater wheat crop than during peacetime assured the future use of such labor-saving instruments.

Through the remaining four decades of the century, man power was generally replaced by horse power as the thresher, grain drill, hay mower, corn and fodder cutters, and other machines came into wider and wider use. Furthermore, as other machines were invented and introduced, they too brought the superior power of the horse to the service of the farmer. By as early as 1880, four fifths of the wheat grown in the nation was cut by machine; in the 1880's and 1890's, a mechanical corn harvester also came into use, to be followed soon by a corn binder.

Some of the machines were enormous savers of time and labor. One government witness before the Industrial Commission of 1901 testified that in the mid-nineties a bushel of corn could be shelled by a steam sheller in one and a half minutes; by hand it used to take 100 minutes. When farmers reaped, bound, and threshed by hand, the witness reported, it took 160 minutes for each bushel of wheat; with a combine, the same tasks were completed with only four minutes of human labor. In the 1880's and 1890's, great steam tractors were rumbling over the flat, open prairies of the Dakotas and the bonanza farms of California as men tried to harness steam power to the needs of agriculture. Though the cotton belt enjoyed no significant harvesting improvements, the productivity of the southern farmer was nevertheless increased by the growing use of mechanical planters, stalk cutters, and fertilizer distributors.

After 1860, the recourse to machinery in agriculture steadily advanced. The Census of 1850 reported that $6.8 million was invested in farm implements and machinery; in 1880, the figure had risen ten times; and by 1900, it was $101.2 million. Furthermore, such figures, rather than overestimating the increase in the use of farm machinery, actually tended to minimize it, since prices of farm implements fell during the years after 1865. As in industry, the key to the expansion of agricultural production was improved technology and the intensification of capital.

Unquestionably the greatest stimulus to production in the latter half of the nineteenth century was the ever-widening market. Within the nation, the railroad net, with its progressively finer mesh, provided improved marketing facilities for farm goods, while fresh arrivals of immigrants meant new stomachs to be filled and bodies to be clothed by the produce of the farms. But the growth of American agricultural production outran even the rapidly expanding national market. As early as the 1880's, American wheat was flowing like water into the remote crevices and valleys of western and central Europe. "Austrians and Hungarians stood aghast," William Trimble has written, "to see it sold even in the markets of Trieste and Fiume, the long-time places of exportation." In 1900, 34 per cent of American wheat, 10 per cent of the corn, and 66 per cent of the cotton crop was exported. A witness before the Industrial Commission of 1901 estimated that "about one-fourth of the total agricultural production of the country is exported."

The immediate effect of the entrance of American farmers into the world agricultural market was near catastrophe for many European countries. Despair settled over the farms of Europe as prices and land values plummeted. Between 1871 and 1891, for instance, the price of wheat fell 27 per cent in Germany and about 30 per cent in Sweden. In the face of such a decline in farm income, many European farmers were ruined and pressed down into the status of agricultural laborers; many sought relief by flight to El Dorado itself, the source of their misery. Landlords also felt the pressure from American fecundity. Rents on the large estates of Prussia fell 20 to 30 per cent; land values in the United Kingdom tumbled almost 50 per cent between 1874 and 1894. Under such conditions, it is not surprising that Dr. Alexander Peez, the Austrian statesman, spoke of the enormous American grain exports as "the greatest economic event of modern times," comparable in significance with the influx of American gold in the sixteenth century, which produced the Price Revolution.

This second Price Revolution to emanate from America was only possible because another revolution, one in communications, was under way. Thanks to the telegraph, the improved marine steam engine, the submarine cable, and the steady decline in rail and shipping rates, the separate national economies of the North Atlantic basin were being integrated into a single intercontinental market. Thanks to the rapid and tightly knit system of international communications and transport, the expanding industrial economy of Europe was able to look to America as the breadbasket of its industrial and urban population. To America, the creation of an international market for its agricultural output meant that the United States would be able to balance the payments on its own imports. Between 1873 and 1900, the United States enjoyed a favorable balance of trade every year save two. That it was agriculture which made this possible is shown by the fact that in all those years farm commodities made up three quarters or more of total American exports. This was the farmer's contribution to the acceleration of American industrialization.

But if the commercialization of agriculture ensured favorable trade balances for the economy as a whole, for the farmer it meant loss of control over his market. The price of wheat, for example, was now determined by forces outside America, since the almost instantaneous communications and the cheap, efficient transportation made world supply and demand the determinant of prices. A poor harvest in America, which in earlier days might at least have had the mitigating consequence of higher prices, now might mean nothing of the sort; a bumper crop in faraway Russia or in distant India could just as easily drive the price down.

Indeed, American farmers soon found that the expansion of the world's agricultural production, of which America's was but a part, brought a steady fall in farm prices all through the 1880's and 1890's. Entrance into a world market, as far as the farmer was concerned, meant that there was no longer any possibility that he or his government could exercise any significant control over farm prices at all. Unfortunately, this fact was never clear to the American farmer, if one is to judge from the protest literature he issued; he always held the trusts, the grain elevators, the railroads, and Wall Street chiefly responsible for his falling income. It was only after the farmers had wrestled with these local devils that they turned, in the twentieth century, to the fundamental source of their woes: the impersonal, almost mysterious interaction of world supply and demand over which no trust and no monetary policy ruled. But before we deal with the farmers' efforts to ameliorate the impact of the market, it is worth while to indicate the nature of that impact.

6. THE FARMER COMES OF AGE

Despite the idyllic image of the independent subsistence farmer conjured up by agrarian philosophers like Thomas Jefferson and John Taylor of Caroline, the commercialization of agriculture was as inevitable as time. As early as 1776, Adam Smith had shown that economic efficiency and material abundance followed specialization and the division of labor. Once this principle was learned in industry, it was foreordained that farming would pick it up, too. For after all, idealize him as one might, the fiercely independent frontiersman who, in addition to raising his own food, also built his home and made his own furniture and tools, while his wife made the family's clothes, candles and soap, and whatnot, lived a hard life of never-ending toil. And even when his years of work were done, his home was still crude, his furniture makeshift, his clothes coarse, and his diet monotonous. Under such conditions, the farmer and his wife, when new markets became available, were only too happy to see their home industries transferred to the factory, the products of which could now be purchased with the cash obtained from the sale of a commercial crop.

For a number of years before the Civil War, this transfer of home industries to the factory had been in process. By the end of the century, the vast majority of the farmers had given up the home manufacturing of their ancestors and concentrated their labor and talents on the raising of one or two cash crops. In substance, the farmer had become a businessman, producing and selling a commodity in an intricately interconnected market of exchangeable commodities.

The effect was to change the farmer's way of doing business. "The old rule that a farmer should produce all that he required and that the surplus represented his gains, is part of the past," observed the Chicago *Prairie Farmer* in 1868. "Agriculture, like all other business, is better for its subdivisions, each one growing that which is best suited to his soil, skill, climate, and market, and with its proceeds purchase his other needs." Later, in 1904, the *Cornell Countryman* frankly declared the Jeffersonian Arcadia outmoded. "Now the object of farming is not primarily to make a living, but it is to make money. To this end it is to be conducted on the same business basis as any other producing industry."

On a wider scale, commercialization changed the patterns of agricultural production. For example, with the creation of a national railroad net, eastern farmers were brought into competition with the virgin and richer farm lands of the West. For New England this often resulted in the wholesale abandonment of farms; in other areas, such as New York and Pennsylvania, the only recourse was a shift to perishable crops like dairy products and vegetables, which were out of the reach of western competition. Thus, for some, the wider markets meant increased opportunities; for others, it meant economic death or drastic shifts in old habits. In all cases, the impersonal but powerful forces of the market were narrowing the freedom of choice available to the heretofore free-wheeling, individualistic farmer.

Attention to the problems and changes which commercialization bestowed upon the American farmer must not obscure the fact that most of the material advantages he sought were actually forthcoming. "This is a new age to the farmer," George Holmes, a statistician for the Department of Agriculture, told the Industrial Commission in 1901. "He is now, more than ever before, a citizen of the world. Cheap and excellent books and periodical publications load the shelf and the table in his sitting room and parlor. He travels more than he ever did before, and he travels longer distances. His children are receiving a better education than he received himself, and they dress better than he did when he was a child. They are more frequently in contact with town and city life than he was."

Yet this was apparently not enough. Eight years after Holmes testified, and still during a period of farm prosperity, President Theodore Roosevelt told the Congress, "It would be idle to assert that life on the farm occupies as good a position of dignity, desirability and business results as farmers might easily give it if they chose. One of the chief difficulties," the President said, "is the failure of country life, as it exists at the present, to satisfy the higher social and intellectual aspirations of country people."

Contradictory as these two summaries of the farmers' life are, they actually symbolize the consequences of commercialization. On the one hand, the farmers enjoyed the variety and cheapness of goods which the market and expanding industry placed at their disposal; but on the other, they were discontented and insecure because, as mere cogs in the great machine of the market, they were exposed to every shock which the system sustained. Though involvement in the market brought sweets, it also demanded hostages to fortune.[5]

Moreover, it was a fact that the more the farmer savored the de-

---

[5] Even mechanization, lamented the president of the Grange when he appeared before the Industrial Commission, seemed to bring too few advantages to the individual farmer. Asked whether it was not true that mechanization reduced production costs, he replied, "It has reduced the cost of production to some extent, but what is strange to say, in those cradling days [that is, before the mechanical reaper] it appeared to be as easy for the farmer to pay his lawful debts then as it is now, and if you put that question to 100 farmers, I venture to say that 99 of them would say, 'much easier.'" Moreover, he regretfully observed, with all the mechanical aids, the farmer seemed to work as long as ever.

lights of the larger world, the more meager farm life appeared to him. One manifestation of this was the steady depopulation of the countryside in the later decades of the century; another was President Theodore Roosevelt's call in 1908 for a Country Life Commission. It was the President himself who asked, "How can the life of the farm family be made less solitary, fuller of opportunity, freer from drudgery, more comfortable, happier, and more attractive?" Such a question was itself a severe indictment of what life on the farm was. And when the Commission had completed its inquiry, it reported in the same vein as the President's charge: "Agriculture is not commercially as profitable as it is entitled to be for the labor and energy that the farmer expends and the risks that he assumes" (no one seemed willing to admit that the farmer was now a producer in a market in which the supply was far outrunning the demand) "and . . . the social conditions in the open country are far short of their possibilities." One of the striking evils of farm life, named again and again in the hearings, was heavy drinking. The commissioners concluded in their report that "Intemperance is largely the result of the barrenness of farm life, particularly the lot of the hired man." In brief, farming was hardly the wholesome, satisfying existence Americans had thought it was; the problem of "How you gonna keep 'em down on the farm" long antedated any visit to Paree.

If a taste of the fleshpots of Egypt had rendered the farmers discontented with the agrarian life Jefferson and others had taught them to prize, it had not always been so. It is true that the apotheosis of the independent, hard-working, simple but honest farmer had always been an ideal rather than an actuality, but once there had been more truth than distortion in it. Richard Hofstadter is perfectly right when he argues that American agriculture has always been tainted with the search for the main chance; has always been highly enterprising, even speculative, rather than static and traditional. But when he further declares that the "United States failed to develop . . . a distinctively *rural* culture," he is using European agricultural mores as the norm. To do that is quite misleading, for the agrarian ideal of America, the truth of which Hofstadter seems to deny, took the independent, forward-looking, free *American* farmer as its typical figure, not the tradition-directed European peasant. The putative father of the myth, Thomas Jefferson, certainly thought of his idealized yeoman as struck from a far different mold from that which shaped the downtrodden European peasant. None of the agrarian philosophers were singing the praises of European peasants; they were celebrating the progressive American farmer as they knew him in the fields of America.

It is true, as Rudolph Heberle pointed out in 1929, that "The agricultural population in the United States . . . is mobile to a high degree if compared with the country population of Europe. The facility with which the American farmer changes from one farm to another has always astonished the European observer." But if the occupational mobility of the city and the country in America is compared, then the relative stability of farm life is quite apparent. Only 22.5 per cent of the businessmen of Minneapolis, for example, followed their fathers' occupation, but 63.7 per cent of the sons and daughters of Minnesota farmers did so. In short, compared with the European, the American farmer was mobile; but compared with the city dweller, he was traditional, secure, conservative, and steady.

According to agricultural historian Paul Johnstone, so it was in the years before 1860. The farm home, he says, was a "Gibraltar of security," and because "no one was far from hardship and none had excess of ease," poverty did not bring loss of self-respect. Moreover, "when opportunity was not at hand, it could be found just over the horizon." At one time, then, there had been hard substance to the dream of Arcadia, and though farmers, like most Americans in the nineteenth century, contended for a foothold on the ladder of social advancement, this does not deny the independence and security which farming brought to its practitioners in the years before 1870.

But in subsequent years the pervasiveness of the commercial spirit gradually reduced the truth of the ideal to microscopic proportions. The rhetoric has remained, however, for even in the middle of the twentieth century the virtues of farm living are said to be almost miraculously regenerative. "The big farm produces crops," asserted Roger M. Kyes, businessman and later Deputy Secretary of Defense in the Eisenhower Administration, "the small farm produces men." Compare this with the statement from W. H. Harvey, *A Tale of Two Nations,* a popular Populist novel of 1894: "As the country makes the body better than that developed in the city, so also, even in a greater degree it does the mind and soul. It is man-making." The Country Life Commission Report of 1909 contains many such examples of a continuing belief in the special powers of agricultural life. An assistant secretary of agriculture, who appeared before the Industrial Commission, offered the opinion that "the undesirable class [of immigrants] does not usually go out on the farms; they can not stay on the farm without becoming pretty good people."

At the same time that the farmer-businessman was aspiring to be a part of the glittering civilization of the urban world, that civilization was stretching out to encompass him. Even in such a minor aspect of life as reading matter, the farmer found himself accepting the urban view of things. Before 1860, the fiction printed in farm journals almost invariably concerned the vicissitudes of rural life and the villain was usually a city slicker. By the turn of the century, however, the great national farm magazines—and they were the main ones—carried fiction of the same type and locale as the urban periodicals. Rural folk, like the people of the city, were now reading stories based on urban assumptions and depicting the life of the city. In the twentieth century, the telephone, the mass newspaper, the mail-order catalogue, the automobile, improved highways and roads, rural free delivery, the radio, the movies, and, most recently, television have advanced still further the farmer's emulation of urban ways. And where the farmer himself might be slow to respond to such stimuli, his more worldly-wise and adaptable children added to the pressure.

As early as 1896 one sociologist noted, with obvious regret, the insidious influence of the city upon the sheltered life of the farm. "The isolated farmer and his family have begun to be affected by the strain of modern life in a deplorable way," complained Frank Giddings in his textbook in sociology. "They are no longer ignorant of the luxuries of the towns and the simple manner of life no longer satisfies them. The house must be remodeled and refurnished; the table must be varied; clothing must be 'in style,' and the horses, carriages and harnesses must be more costly." By the early decades of the twentieth century, urban values had penetrated the countryside to such an extent that it was no longer possible to talk of a sharp division beween urban and rural life; there were now only varying degrees of urbanism.

7. THE FARMER AS POLITICIAN

Though few farmers objected to the material benefits which the commercialization of agriculture bestowed upon them, a great many of them protested the steady fall in farm prices which accompanied it. All during the last decades of the nineteenth century farm prices fell at a faster rate than prices in general—a fact which persuaded many farmers that they were victims of a conspiracy as well as an economic squeeze.

In an endeavor to stay the steady deterioration of the farmers' economic position, a number of farm organizations sprang into existence in the 1870's and 1880's. Some, like the Patrons of Husbandry, began as farmers' fraternal and social clubs, but soon shifted to being pressure groups advocating the regulation and control of railroads and grain elevators. Others, like the Agricultural Wheel and the various Farmers' Alliances of the 1880's, were, from the outset, deliberate attempts at meeting the challenge of declining farm prices in an economy which was increasingly dominated by big business. These latter organizations also attacked the railroads for their high rates and the trusts for their exorbitant prices, but no purely economic pressure group seemed capable of improving the farmers' worsening position.

As a result, in 1892 the aroused farmers turned to politics as a way out; the People's party was born. In its first election that year, the Populist party, as it was also called, made surprising gains at the expense of the two major parties. James Weaver, the Presidential candidate, captured over a million votes, and in local contests Populists were elected to five U.S. Senate seats, ten congressional seats, and three gubernatorial chairs—a substantial achievement for the first important third party since the rise of the Republicans in the mid-1850's.

The platform of the People's party throws considerable light on the changes through which American agriculture was passing. As an industry develops, James Malin has pointed out, it first concerns itself with the problems of production and only secondarily and at a later time with the problems of distribution. By the last decade of the nineteenth century, at about the time of the Populist protest, the industry of agriculture had more than surmounted the problems of production; more goods were being put out by American farms than the world could absorb. It was now the distribution of these surpluses which constituted the major problem confronting the agricultural industry.

In a dim way, the Populist revolt recognized this fact. Its major farm planks, for example, dealt with matters of distribution like prices (inflation through paper money or free silver), transportation (railroad rate regulation and so forth), and credit (the subtreasury plan, whereby a farmer could borrow government funds at a low interest rate against his stored crop). But these same planks, especially those regarding prices and credit, also greatly encouraged production, a fact which in itself revealed the confusion in the economic thinking of the Populists. The weakness or error in Populist economics was not its heretical and inflationary demands, but rather the failure to acknowledge the fundamental problem of overproduction. For the most part, Populist remedies for the farm situation were directed at the symptoms and not at the disease.

That this was not because of general ignorance on the subject is apparent from the writings of contemporaries. C. Wood Davis, for example, writing in *Forum* in 1890, put his finger directly upon the real cause. Between 1870 and 1890, he showed, the population in the United States rose 30 per cent; but during the same period, the number of farms went up 51 per cent, the number of bales of cotton increased 90 per cent, and the acres of land devoted to corn and wheat jumped 50 per cent. "The logical conclusion," Davis pointed out, "is that the troubles of the farmers are due to the fact that there are altogether too many farmers" and too great production of farm commodities.[6]

But that kind of analysis was not for the Populists. *Coin's Financial School,* the leading Populist tract, and a veritable Bible of free-silver agitation, only ridiculed the overproduction diagnosis. Coin (the fictitious teacher of free-silver principles in the pamphlet) said "that overproduction could not be claimed so long as tens of thousands were going hungry; and that the only overproduction admitted by all, was millionaires." To which can only be added E. L. Godkin's remark that "Of the world outside," the farmer "knows and cares nothing."

Though the Populists were blind to the role the surplus played in the making of their problems, an investigation of the focal points of

[6] Davis proved to be a remarkable prophet in an area where the future has often confounded the seer. In a subsequent article in *Forum* that year, entitled "When the Farmer Will Be Prosperous," he predicted a turn for the better by the end of the nineties—almost the precise years in which it did come. His major point was that it was dependence upon the foreign market which made agricultural prices and income so unstable, and that when American consumption caught up with production there would then be an equilibrium between supply and demand which would assure the farmer a decent living. In its essentials, this prediction was about what happened after 1900 and before 1914, when the balance was shattered by the abnormal demands of the European war.

Populist strength further supports the argument that overproduction was the mainspring of much of the farmers' unaccustomed radicalism. For example, wheat-producing Kansas, Nebraska, and North and South Dakota gave a third or more of their votes to the Populist ticket in 1892; but equally agricultural Iowa, Illinois, and Wisconsin cast less than 5 per cent of their votes for the People's party candidates. The difference may be explained by the differences in the diversification of crops in the two groups of states. In the latter group, the development of dairying and corn-hog production had done much to stabilize farm income, since the farmers there were less dependent upon the foreign market. As a result, there was less economic pressure to drive them to radical political measures.

Though cotton might be expected to play the same role in the South as wheat in the Midwest, the election results do not clearly bear out this assumption, probably because the race question complicated, where it did not stifle, the growth of a third party in that section. Nevertheless, cotton states like Texas, Alabama, Georgia, and Mississippi were conspicuously more Populist in their voting than more diversified and noncotton states like Kentucky, Virginia, Tennessee, and North Carolina.

It is surely no accident that the withering away of the farmer's militancy at the opening of the twentieth century was accompanied by a decline in the agricultural surplus. Whereas in 1897–1901 the United Kingdom purchased 72 million bushels of wheat and 74 million bushels of corn each year from the United States, in 1910–14 that country's average annual importations of these crops were only 27 million and 10 million respectively. Germany's annual importation of American corn fell more than 80 per cent, and bacon imports dropped over 95 per cent between 1900 and 1910. Despite this decline in foreign purchases, however, American farm prices in general rose almost 90 per cent between 1899 and 1910. It would seem that in those years before the outbreak of World War I, industry and agriculture in the United States had finally reached an equilibrium in which the farmer and those he fed and clothed were relatively satisfied.

The happy future promised by this equilibrium, however, was shattered by the intrusion of the First World War. Agricultural acreage and production were pushed far out of line with the domestic market, and the way was paved for the prolonged farm depression of

the 1920's and 1930's and the seemingly interminable surplus problem that has for so long perplexed the nation. The world population
explosion, however, promises that the farm surplus will soon cease
to be a problem. Already, in 1966, the Secretary of Agriculture
raised the quotas on agricultural production because the great surpluses that plagued the country in the 1940's and 1950's had been
depleted.

8. STANDING JEFFERSON ON HIS HEAD

As a political movement, the farmers' revolt was full of meaning
for the future of American politics. Unfortunately, much sentimentality has been expended in depicting the Populist-Democratic defeat
of 1896 as the farmers' last stand against the overpowering and ruthless forces of industrialism and the money power. Though this view
has a measure of truth in it, Populism is more accurately viewed as a
manifestation of a transitional phase in the history of American agriculture. Populism was at once the last gasp of the agrarian myth and
the coming of age of the farmer as businessman.

As befits a leader who stood at the juncture of two eras in the
history of the American farmer, William Jennings Bryan in his famous "Cross of Gold" speech in 1896 appealed to both the old and
the new farmer. Proudly he called the farmer "as much a business
man as the man who goes upon the Board of Trade," only to fall
back upon the tried and true agrarian creed that if the farms are destroyed, "the grass will grow in the streets of every city in the country." This confusion as to the commercial farmer's actual role in the
economy was also apparent in Populism's overtures to urban labor.

The farmer as a son of toil had always been celebrated by the
agrarian tradition; after all, did not the farmer labor with his hands,
was not his bread earned in the sweat of his brow?[7] And true to the
tradition, the platforms of the angry farmers proclaimed the unity
of all labor. "The interests of rural and urban labor are the same,

---

[7] Though the farmer was becoming more and more involved in the market
during the 1890's, his socioeconomic role could be confusing even to a Columbia University professor. C. E. Emerick, writing in the *Political Science
Quarterly* in 1897, wrestled with the question in this manner: "The farmer, it
is true, is to some extent a capitalist—and to some extent, also, by coordinat-
ing capital and labor, he acts as entrepreneur. But the farmer is by distinction
a laboring man. . . ."

their enemies are identical," asserted the St. Louis platform of 1892. The Omaha platform of the same year endorsed several labor demands like the eight-hour day and opposition to Pinkerton police, as well as declaring a secondary boycott of the Rochester clothing manufacturers, against whom the Knights of Labor were then striking.

But all this was thinking with rhetoric rather than with realities; it was appealing merely to the common American heritage of Jeffersonian and Jacksonian symbolism and not to the hard facts of economic life. Clear-eyed Samuel Gompers of the American Federation of Labor saw the emptiness behind the words and, though touched by the idealistic sentiments, he could not overlook the economic gulf which separated the farmers and the urban workers. The People's party, he wrote in the *North American Review* in 1892, is not a labor party, and "in the nature of its makeup" it cannot ever be a party "in which the wage-earners will find their haven. Composed, as the People's Party is, mainly of *employing* farmers without any regard to the interests of the *employed* farmers of the country districts or the mechanics and laborers of the industrial centres, there must of necessity be a divergence of purposes, methods, and interests." The union of such forces, he concluded, is "impossible, because it is unnatural."

The validity of Gompers' analysis was reflected in discussions of the "farm labor problem" which were already a feature of the farm journals in the 1880's. The farmers were employers for the most part, and the deeper the commercial spirit invaded agriculture, the more profoundly the farmer accepted the assumptions of a businessman and alienated himself from the working man who worked for wages, whether he was on the farm or in the factory.

After the debacle of 1896, the business side of the schizoid farmer's movement was dominant; thereafter we hear little of the Jeffersonian rhetoric but much of parity, export debentures, equity fees, and crop allotments. Rather than being the last stand of the farmers, 1896 was the first step in their road to success. In business-minded America, the farmer as an entrepreneur and salesman has been much more successful in gaining the ear of the government and the nation than he ever was as a latter-day agrarian philosopher.

Naïve and unrealistic as Populism's appeal to urban labor may have been, the new and radical demands in the new party's platforms constituted a turning point in the history of modern American political reform. Populism brought to a national audience a bushel of new solutions to American problems; some were bizarre, but most were long overdue and of interest to all Americans, not just farmers. In addition to obviously agrarian proposals like the subtreasury plan and free silver, and labor planks like the eight-hour day, the platform also went on record in favor of the graduated income tax; the public ownership of railroads, telephones, and telegraphs; the direct election of senators; and the initiative and referendum, to name only the best-known.

The important point is that underlying several of these reforms was the clear assumption that government was charged with responsibility to regulate the economy. As an idea, of course, this was not new, but before the Populists it had never been linked so effectively with popular aspirations and problems, and never before had it been actively championed by so many Americans.

The Populist views of the responsibilities of government in the economy were doubly important because, in 1896, the Democratic party was inoculated with the virus. Though dedicated Populists like Henry D. Lloyd and Tom Watson fulminated against the alliance with the Democrats in that year, the alliance was the beginning of the triumph of Populism's philosophy of government. It was also the signal for a decisive shift in the ideology of the Democratic party and ultimately of the nation itself.

For a century the party of Jefferson and Jackson had carried high upon its banners the legend "That government is best which governs least." In the years before 1860, the party had pushed its states' rights –laissez-faire philosophy to such an extreme that when the War for the Union was won, the new nationalism of the people denied the Presidency to the Democracy for nearly a generation. And then, when a Democrat did assume the Presidential power, he turned out to be a firm believer in the old tradition. When Grover Cleveland was presented with a bill appropriating a small amount of money for the relief of drought-stricken farmers in Texas, he needed only to consult traditional Democratic doctrine to decide to veto it. In his veto message Cleveland appealed to the "limited mission" of government and the necessity "that the lesson should constantly be enforced that though the people support the Government the Government should not support the people." Stanchly adhering to his party's ancient faith, even in the face of the Green Uprising of the 1890's, Cleveland earned the deep-seated disgust of dirt farmers and urban intellectuals everywhere, but especially in his own party.[8]

During the last years of Cleveland's second administration, the deep dissatisfaction with the laissez-faire heritage of the party impelled many Democrats to look toward a union with the Populists. There had always been important points of contact between the two parties. The Populists, for example, also revered Jefferson and Jackson, although for somewhat different reasons. For many Democrats the virtues of these heroes were largely associated with their championing of local government and limitations on the federal power. The Populists, on the other hand, conveniently overlooked that part of their heroes' thinking and loved them for their espousal of the agrarians and for their opposition to monopoly. But such a convenient historical memory was nothing new for Americans when they employed their history for contemporary purposes. It was ironical, though, that the author of the Kentucky Resolutions and the author of the Maysville veto should be stood on their heads and made into symbols of national power. And it approached humor when hard-money Andy Jackson was expected to buttress free silver and cheap money.

Despite the Populists' advocacy of an interventionist national government, the Democratic party, at its convention in 1896, took on the leadership of the farmers' revolt and the issue of cheap money. In doing so, the party underwent a historic change of course. For though it is true that the Democratic platform of that year said little about most of the other Populist demands, the party's obvious willingness to use the power of the national government to manipulate the currency supply and its denunciations of the National Banks amply demonstrated that a new philosophy animated its members. Moreover, during the campaign the Democratic standard bearer,

---

[8] To see how far Cleveland lagged behind Populist sentiment, one has only to compare his statement with one uttered by the Populist Governor of Kansas in 1893. "The Government must make it possible for the citizen to live by his own labor. . . . If the Government fails in these things, it fails in its mission. . . . What is the State to him who toils if labor is denied him and his children cry for bread? . . . The people are greater than the law or the statutes, and when a nation sets its heart on doing a great and good thing, it can find a legal way to do it." The close similarity of this statement with many utterances in and out of government during the early days of the New Deal is striking and at least partly explained by the fact that depression stalked the land in 1893 and 1933.

William Jennings Bryan, by strongly supporting labor unions and denouncing court injunctions against labor, further revealed the party's departure from the ancient tenets of economic liberalism. In fact, the overwhelming defeat of the Cleveland forces at the convention could be interpreted in no other way than as a sharp slap at the ancient laissez-faire tradition of the party. Like a snake sloughing off its old skin, the Democratic party was shaking itself free of its fear of the national government—a fear it had inherited from Jefferson and the ante-bellum leaders of the South who had dominated the party for so long. The process was to be pushed still further by Woodrow Wilson in the next century and brought to completion by Franklin Roosevelt and Harry Truman.

It would be misleading, however, to leave the impression that the Democratic party was the sole vehicle of this sea change in the American conception of the federal government. Both the Republican party and the nation at large took up the new view. The Populist agitation, for all its focus on the farmers' problems, had galvanized the reform spirit throughout the country.

The proof of this is to be read in the series of Populist measures, once denounced as either subversive or outlandish, which, by other hands, were translated into law in the years between 1900 and 1914. The power of the I.C.C. to regulate railroads was greatly strengthened in 1906 and 1910; postal savings banks were established in 1911; the income tax and the direct election of senators came in 1913. Also in 1913 the Populist demand for a flexible currency and the end of the National Banking System was achieved with the establishment of the Federal Reserve System. Even the Populist's favorite measure, the subtreasury plan, can be said to have been put into law with the passage of the Warehousing Act of 1916. In an important sense, therefore, the farmers' revolt was the forerunner of the much more successful Progressive movement which followed. Populism not only provided the stimulus but, as enacted legislation testifies, it sometimes set the goals.

The transformation of the American farmer into a businessman was only the most obvious result of the industrialization and urbanization of the nation. Ancient and established institutions like the Church and the home were also being transformed by the forces of the new era.

CHAPTER XII

New World A-Comin'

"THE generation which was beginning to take shape and character when I came of age," President W. J. Tucker of Dartmouth wrote concerning the years after 1865, "was to have the peculiar fortune, whether to its disadvantage or to its distinction, of finding its own way into what we now call the 'modern world.' " In the years between 1880 and 1915, industrialization and urbanization, like two gigantic hands touching the spinning clay on a potter's wheel, refashioned the contours of American society; institutions with long lineage and stability like the Church and the home were shaken and altered. To an American who was alive in 1870, the world of forty years later lost many of its familiar bench marks. This was so for more profound reasons than the fact that the automobile was beginning to appear in the streets or because two brothers had kept some pieces of wood and iron in the air for a few minutes.

More than this, the new world of the city and the factory confronted the American Dream with a spiritual challenge which almost overwhelmed it. But when the challenge had been met, the America which emerged, despite its industrial and urban character, remained in spirit remarkably like the old, still loyal to the old tradition of equality, humanitarianism, individualism, and social justice. For, like the political Revolution of 1776, the Progressive movement of the early twentieth century was distinguished almost as much by what it conserved as by what it introduced.

1. JESUS VERSUS RICARDO

To the rural mind the city was tantalizing; it was both attractive and repulsive, good as well as evil. "Every city has been a Babylon, and every city has been a New Jerusalem," Plymouth Church's Reverend Lyman Abbott said, "and it has always been a question whether the Babylon would extirpate the New Jerusalem or the New Jerusalem would extirpate the Babylon." To many in the 1880's and 1890's it seemed that Babylon had won out.

Looking about him in 1887, the Reverend Josiah Strong saw "great perils threatening our Christian civilization, such as wealth, its worship and its congestion, anarchism and lawlessness, intemperance and the liquor power, immigration and a superstitious Christianity," and all of them, he noticed, "are . . . massed in the city. And not only so, but in the city every one of these perils is enhanced." And so it seemed to others more worldly. A friendly foreign visitor like Lord Bryce was appalled at the corruption in municipal government which gnawed away at the self-respect of Americans and threatened the continuance of democracy itself. Continue as you are, he told some Americans, and "you will set us liberals back in Europe five hundred years."

The churches could not long escape what Strong later aptly called "the Challenge of the City." From the beginning the roots of religion had penetrated deep into the consciousness of Americans; since the Revolution several great revivals had broadened the popular base of Protestantism. But in the year which followed the Civil War, there was an almost palpable recession of religious interest under way among a broad class of Americans. "Everybody knows," a churchman told the students of Andover Theological Seminary in the mid-1880's, "that the Protestant Churches, as a rule, have no following among the workingmen." Attending church in Chicago, dressed as a workingman, Princeton Professor Walter Wyckoff noticed that "I was conspicuously lonely as a representative of the poor." His fellow workers admitted to him that in their rural homes they had been regular in church attendance, but that "the habit had dropped completely from them upon coming to live in town." One worker said, "The rich folks build their churches for themselves, and they keep them for themselves, and I ain't never going to interfere with that arrangement." And the richly decorated urban churches, with their high-priced pews and sedate air, bore him out. A survey made in Pittsburgh in 1888 revealed that though business and professional men made up only 10 per cent of the population, they constituted 60 per cent of the membership of the Protestant churches.

Many churches stood empty and unused amid the congested working-class districts of the great cities. Between 1868 and 1888, for example, although nearly 200,000 people moved into the part of New York City below 14th Street, seventeen Protestant churches moved out, their places being taken by only two Roman Catholic churches and a single synagogue. One minister complained that "to the mass of workingmen Sunday . . . is a day for labor meetings, for excursions, for saloons, beer-gardens, baseball games and carousals," rather than a time to attend church. It was notorious that the urban citizenry were increasingly breaking the Sunday laws which rural-dominated state legislatures imposed upon them. It came as no surprise, therefore, that in the 1880's three markedly urban states, New York, Massachusetts, and California, relaxed or abandoned their Sunday laws. Among the cities of the nation a retreat from the old-time religion was in full swing.

Contrary to the opinions of some shortsighted churchmen, the estrangement of the urban working class from Protestantism was something more than a shift in interest or an increase in human depravity. At bottom it stemmed from the failure of the churches to adapt themselves to the altered face of American society. Because, historically, Protestantism in America, like the nation at large, was rural, the Church was bewildered by the city; nothing in its history prepared it for the problems now thrown up by urbanization. Long accustomed to class relations remarkably free of conflict, the Protestant churches, suffused with the Calvinist ethic of individual achievement and responsibility, could not easily understand an era characterized by class warfare, ruthless monopolies, and the squalor of tenement-filled cities. Moreover, many of the urban workingmen were immigrants and Catholics and therefore beyond the appeal of the Protestant churches.

The churches were suspicious of, when they were not openly hostile to, the new urban proletariat, who bore slight resemblance to the steady, conservative farmers of an earlier America. "You can count on the ends of your fingers all the clergymen who take any interest in the labor problem," Terence Powderly of the Knights of Labor complained in 1892. The workers, Samuel Gompers of the A.F. of L. said a little later, "have come to look upon the Church and the ministry as apologists and defenders of the wrongs committed against the interests of the people simply because the perpetrators are the possessors of great wealth." The Reverend Washington Gladden was told by one worker in the 1880's that the reason he and his fellows did not attend church was that it seemed to be a place for employers only. "Of course," he admitted, "the manufacturers can and should dress better than the laborer; but when we see them so full of religion on Sunday, and then grinding the faces of the poor on the other six days, we are apt to think they are insincere." Nor was Henry Ward Beecher's remark that any workingman worth his salt could support a family on a dollar a day, providing he did not drink or smoke, conducive to the increase of workingmen in the Protestant churches.

All men of the cloth, however, were not Beechers either in moral obtuseness or income. (Beecher was reputed to have an income in excess of $20,000 a year when he uttered his dictum.) The implications of the great railroad strike of 1877, in which thousands of workers ran amuck destroying trains, roundhouses, and yards in angry protest against a wage cut, were not lost on a minister and philanthropist like Charles Loring Brace of New York. "There is something always impressive," he wrote at that time, "in these blind, passionate movements of the laboring classes for the larger share of the goods of life. . . . The great problem of the future is the equal distribution of the wealth. . . . I believe myself that, in general, the laboring classes do not receive their fair share. Strikes are one of their means of getting more. . . ." In later life, the well-known exponent of the social gospel, Washington Gladden, recalled that it was in the late 1870's and early 1880's that his attention was first drawn to the impending social conflict between capital and labor. Hard-fought strikes of the 1880's, he remembered, "brought very strongly before my mind the critical character of the relations between the men who are doing the work of the world and the men who are organizing and directing it." Because the growing hostility between capital and labor was tearing Protestantism apart as it was rending the nation, churchmen were soon compelled to seek out explanations and remedies in places which were far removed from theology or their usual social circles.

Instinctively almost, leading churchmen appealed to the universal character of Christianity as an antidote to the social cleavage. "Christianity, from the nature of it," Samuel Loomis told the students at Andover Seminary in 1886, "cannot remain the religion of classes; it must be the religion of the whole people or none." The churches will never re-establish contact with the urban masses, Washington Gladden cautioned in the same year, until they recognize that these " 'masses' are composed to a large extent, of . . . wage earners," and the churches must "adjust their theories and their methods" to that fact if they wished "to see daylight shine through this dark problem of church neglect." The new social setting was "most disturbing" to the popular "influence of the church," W. J. Tucker recalled in reviewing the period. "The study of the enlarged and more complicated economy was thus necessary if the church was to maintain or recover its influence." Unless the Church is successful in its appeal to the working class, Samuel Loomis warned, the workers, "perishing in their blindness, will involve all Christendom in common ruin."

As tension between workers and employers was successively built up, discharged, and built up again in bitter strikes such as those of 1877, 1886, 1892, and 1894, an increasing number of Protestant clergymen found it difficult to reconcile the doctrines of Jesus with the impersonal and ruthless functioning of a laissez-faire economy. "Jesus Christ knew a great deal more about organizing society," Washington Gladden wryly commented, "than David Ricardo ever dreamed of knowing, and the application of his law to industrial society will be found to work surprisingly well." The historic alliance between religion and business which began with the Calvinists was coming under searching scrutiny. Many churchmen, Gladden noted, were recognizing that the doctrine of laissez faire not only meant "let well enough alone . . ." but also "let ill enough alone!"

But the clergymen of the new view were well aware that mere exhortation and appeal to Christian principles could not be expected to undermine this sacrosanct shibboleth. Inasmuch as capital has combined, Gladden told a labor audience in 1886, then let the workers "combine, and let the people say Amen." In 1893, Josiah Strong insisted that even though real wages may have been rising in the last decade or so, the more basic question was whether the laborer was "receiving his just dues." And he concluded that the rampant poverty and destitution in the cities made it clear that the worker "has not had his due share, and ought not to be satisfied until justice is done him." During the Homestead strike of 1892, several religious journals recognized, almost for the first time, the claims of labor to a fair hearing. The *Christian Union* called the disturbance a part of "the transition from an aristocratic to a democratic industrial organization."[1]

---

[1] But the conversion of large numbers of clergymen, it should be noted, was

In 1887, a number of Episcopalians in New York City organized the Church Association for the Advancement of the Interests of Labor, which gradually spread to other cities of the nation. Five years later, the Baptists, led by Walter Rauschenbusch, established the Brotherhood of the Kingdom, pledging themselves to—among other things—"obedience to the ethics of Jesus." Significantly, the purpose was the re-establishment of the true meaning of the Kingdom of God and "to assist in its practical realization in the world."

The most obvious and earliest sign that the churches were acting to establish contact with the urban masses was the so-called institutional church—that is, one which performed social services for its members. "Too long has Rome been allowed a practical monopoly of the humanitarian agencies of religion," declared the Cincinnati Conference of the Methodist Church in 1889. One Congregational church in Connecticut took up the new humanitarian and social work with such zeal that fashionable people called it "the church for ex-drunkards." Despite the appellation, membership grew. A wealthy urban church like St. Bartholomew's in New York assumed the burdens of the new duty, building an elaborate parish house in 1891 at a cost of $400,000, most of the sum being donated, ironically enough, by the Vanderbilts. St. Bartholomew's was only one of a large number of Episcopal churches that built parish houses for the new activities among the urban masses. Among the Baptists, Russell Conwell's Temple in Philadelphia, built in 1890 at a cost of a quarter of a million dollars, offered a wide variety of athletic, literary, and benevolent activities.

The institutional church pushed its activities out into the city itself. Volunteer women went out into the streets and into the tenements to seek out the deserving poor; co-operative ventures among several churches were initiated in order to provide church services to those working people who had no nearby churches. It was in these years that youth organizations like Christian Endeavor (Congregational), Epworth League (Methodist), and the Brotherhood of St. Andrew

---

a slow process. As late as 1892, a survey revealed that the overwhelming majority of Congregational ministers in Massachusetts believed that the discontent among the working population bore "little or no effect upon the attitude of the workingmen toward the churches." And in 1886, at the time of the Haymarket bombing, the *Congregationalist* belligerently advised, "when anarchy gathers its deluded disciples into a mob, as at Chicago, a Gatling gun or two swiftly brought into position and well served, offers, on the whole, the most merciful as well as effectual remedy."

(Episcopal) were started. In short order these organizations undertook projects among the working class.

While the laboring class's lack of interest compelled some Protestant churches to replant their roots in the cities, the urban challenge
brought forth a new church, conceived in the city itself. Imported
into the United States from England in the 1870's, the Salvation
Army by the 1880's was by far the largest Protestant denomination
active in the slums and streets of the cities of America. Deliberately
shaped to help lighten the soul-crushing burdens of discouragement,
intemperance, and poverty, the Army performed a host of services
ranging from cheap ice in summer to warm lodgings in winter. The
Army's work with the poor was essentially humanitarian and only
secondarily theological; before it exhorted, it fed the hungry and
clothed the naked. Without ever forgetting the spiritual message they
carried, the "slum angels" and other workers of the Army brought
genuine compassion into the lives of the poor. Such realism and sympathy were repaid with success.

Much as the urban friars of the thirteenth century had stirred up
the ire of indolent and uninterested priests of the medieval Church,
the Army in the early years aroused the enmity of the staid and established churches. A popular story summed up the success the
Army enjoyed and the ecclesiastical hostility it provoked. When
asked by his vicar whether he liked the Salvation Army, a bishop replied, "Well, I cannot say that I do, but to be honest I must confess
I believe God does." As the leaders of the Army well knew, the sen-
sationalism of the drum and the soup kitchens, when coupled with
unremitting and practical humanitarianism, constituted the Army's
most compelling appeal to the working class. "The Salvation Army
in no sense desires to become respectable," declared Ballington
Booth, the son of the founder and the head of the American branch
in 1893. "We are not going to give up the ungloved hand for the kid
glove; the drum for the church bell; the cornet for the piano or
organ."

By the opening of the twentieth century, the Army, once hounded
and even despised by the older churches, had won a place as an institutional church born to the manner, ideally suited for the work of
adapting Christianity to the new conditions of the city. "I have long
recognized the Salvation Army as one of the most potent, if not the
most potent, force for the betterment of mankind now at work for

the safety of mankind," concluded Governor Albert Cummins of Iowa in 1904.

Once the churches embarked upon the path of attempting to square social practices with the ethics of Jesus, the institutional church and the Salvation Army proved to be merely halfway stations along the way; much more thoroughgoing renovations of religious thought were to follow. Some of the impetus came from outside the churches. Economist Richard Ely of Johns Hopkins, with his influential *Social Aspects of Christianity,* directed attention to the religious implications of the contemporary social situation at the same time that he revealed the underlying religious thought animating much of the growing literature of discontent. The same could be said about *Social Reform and the Church,* a book by another economist, John R. Commons, in which, among other things, it was said that "the object of sociology is to teach us to love our neighbors." Pressed by empty churches on the one hand and appalled by the gulf between Christian ethics and social practice on the other, many Protestant clergymen began to listen to academicians like Commons and Ely and ministers like Gladden. As churchmen studied economics, talked with workers, and visited slums, a theological and philosophical basis for a new mission of the Church gradually emerged. The social gospel, as a later generation would call it, was being hammered out on the anvil of social realism.

Although in the past the theological seminaries had been rather unresponsive to the play of social forces, in the last decade of the nineteenth century they took the lead in propagating the new ideas. In his autobiography, William Jewett Tucker confessed that as a lecturer at Andover Seminary in the 1880's he had deliberately taken on a "Lectureship on Pastoral Theology" which no one else wanted in order that he might widen its content. "It became," he recalled, "an open door through which I had free access to those special problems which were confronting the Church. It became entirely logical, under the construction put upon this lectureship, to emphasize the new and enlarged functions of the church in modern society." Moreover, his *Outlines on Social Economics,* distributed in the late 1880's, inspired many a pastor already in his pulpit. "I am growing more and more interested in the sociological problem," one minister in Topeka, Kansas, wrote Tucker in 1889, "I am coming to believe that the second service of the Church should be directed to this line of work, and I have a church here that is ready to follow in this departure from the old traditional conception of what constitutes proper church work." Washington Gladden lectured at Yale in 1886 on "The Relation of the Church and Ministry to Socialism." In 1892, seven seminaries initiated professorships or lectureships in social ethics; two years later, such courses were added in three more theological centers. And in the same year a professor of sociology was added to the staff of the Episcopal Theological School in Cambridge. During the summer of 1895, Oberlin sponsored a conference for clergymen at which the theme was "The Causes and Proposed Remedies for Poverty." Not only was the conference directed by an economist, John R. Commons, but it featured Socialists and labor leaders among its speakers.

The doctrine of the social gospel achieved its most eloquent expression in the personality and numerous writings of Walter Rauschenbusch of Rochester Theological Seminary. Over and over again his books appealed for a recognition of the social mission of Christianity. "The chief purpose of the Christian Church in the past has been the salvation of individuals," he wrote in *Christianizing the Social Order* in 1912. "But the most pressing task of the present is not individualistic. Our business is to make over an antiquated and immoral economic system; to get rid of laws, customs, maxims, and philosophies inherited from an evil and despotic past; to create just and brotherly relations between groups and classes of society" and thereby make it possible that men might "live and work in a fashion that will not outrage all the better elements in them. Our inherited Christian faith dealt with individuals; our present task deals with society."

Constantly striving to show the social implications of the Christian message, Rauschenbusch declared, "The purpose of all that Jesus said and did and hoped to do was always the social redemption of the entire life of the human race on earth." Under this interpretation, the obligation of the Christian ministry was clear and inescapable. "The ministry must apply the teaching functions of the pulpit to the pressing questions of public morality," he wrote in 1907. In practice this meant to Rauschenbusch that "Every step taken in industrial life to give the employees some proprietary rights in the business, and anything placing owners and employees on a footing of human equality, would deserve commendation and help."

The Church, in short, in the estimation of Rauschenbusch, should range itself on the side of the working class.

Though many rural churches of Protestantism escaped the fire of the new doctrine, and even whole denominations like the Presbyterians were slow to react, the year 1914 found the social gospel permeating the major denominations of Protestantism. The Methodist "Social Creed," setting forth in 1908 a variety of goals for the amelioration of labor conditions, was one of the outstanding fruits of the movement. Included in the Creed were such purposes as "a living wage in every industry," "abolition of child labor," "the highest wage that each industry can afford," and "the recognition of the Golden Rule . . . as the supreme law of society and the sure remedy for all social ills." That same year the Federal Council of Churches of Christ in America was formed by thirty-three Protestant denominations. Since the Council drew its statement of social principles almost verbatim from the Methodist Social Creed, it stood as tangible evidence that the Protestant churches were now willing to commit themselves to the realization of the principal demands of the working people.

The new social outlook of the churches was evident in the report which the Federal Council of Churches issued in 1920 upon completing its investigation into the national steel strike of 1919. The report, for all its endeavor to achieve objectivity, was animated with sympathy for the strikers, as it was heavy with indignation at the callousness of the employers. Protestantism had come a long way since the days of Henry Ward Beecher, half a century before.

The acceptance of the social gospel spelled the transformation of American Protestantism. At one time thoroughly saturated with the individualism of the frontier and the Calvinist ethic, the Protestant Church became, in the words of W. J. Tucker, "as conspicuously the agency of 'social service' as it had been the 'means of grace' in the work of individual salvation." Heretofore a prime support of the doctrine of laissez faire, the churchmen were now included among its sharpest critics—as many clergymen still are in modern America.

With the triumph of the social gospel, Protestantism not only profoundly altered its social outlook but regained much of its lost prestige among the people. There was a period, John Mitchell, president of the United Mine Workers, commented in 1913, "when it was taken for granted that clergymen . . . were unable to comprehend trade unionism." But today, he continued, "many of the denominations as such, and the prevailing opinion among clergymen as individuals, have pronounced for unions. . . ." Under such circumstances, he went on, "it may be regarded as an accepted fact that the church is today emphatically on the side of union labor." Another group, social workers, once critical of the churches' aloofness from the social issues of the day, had returned to the fold. In 1905, it was reported that three quarters of the social workers in the American Institute of Social Service were "faithful church members."

So completely and pervasively was the social gospel accepted that it has become, in the words of a European religious historian, "the distinguishing characteristic of American Christianity." It is true that since the late 1930's the primacy of interest which the social gospel previously enjoyed has been somewhat reduced by the rise of neoorthodoxy. But the core of the social doctrine is still a powerful force in American theology. To illustrate this, one has only to recall that Reinhold Niebuhr, though the best-known neo-orthodox theologian, is also a member of the executive committee of the Americans for Democratic Action. Even those who do not consider themselves exponents of the social interpretation of Christianity now recognize, as F. E. Johnson put it in 1940, that "there is no necessary incongruity between what has been called the Social Gospel and the basic concerns of traditional Christianity; that, on the contrary, a vigorous social ethic is vital to orthodoxy, while our liberal social Christianity needs to discover its roots in the historical Christian faith."

In conquering the churches, the social gospel extended its influence through society at large. By helping to heal the widening breach between the working class and the rest of society, by demanding a fair share of American abundance for the worker, the social gospel was instrumental in halting the dangerous drift toward class division so imminent in the 1880's and 1890's. Rather than being an "opiate of the people," as Karl Marx had described religion, the churches in industrial America consciously ranged themselves on the side of the poor and the downtrodden, striving to achieve social justice for all. In doing so they threw a formidable obstacle in the path of socialism in the United States.

On the other hand, a Protestantism shot through with the social gospel is a veritable hothouse of reform movements and social protest; it can no longer be an automatic defender of the *status quo*. Indeed, considering the transcendent standard by which society is judged under the social gospel, those who apply such a yardstick can never be satisfied. After the advent of the social gospel, it was possible to advocate social reform in the language of religion. It is not accidental that reform leaders like Woodrow Wilson and Franklin Roosevelt used religious phrases to clothe their pleas for reform. Religious allusions, for example, frequently occurred in the speeches of Franklin Roosevelt. The New Deal, he said in 1934, "is as old as Christian ethics, for basically its ethics are the same. . . . It recognizes that man is indeed his brother's keeper, insists that the laborer is worthy of his hire, demands that justice shall rule the mighty as well as the weak." By broadening the definition of Christianity to include justice for all members of society, the ministers of the social gospel made it possible to harness the long religious heritage of the people in behalf of the realization of the American Dream of justice, equality, and opportunity.

Whereas the urban effect upon Protestantism was at first shattering and only later beneficial, upon Roman Catholicism at first it was not apparent at all. This was true if only because the Catholic Church in America, flourishing largely among the poor immigrants of the cities, required little instruction in the degradation of poverty and the squalor of tenement living. Those Protestant clergymen who were beginning to be concerned over their own churches' alienation from the people were frankly envious of Rome's appeal. "The Catholic Church," remarked Samuel Loomis in 1887, "is emphatically the workingman's church. She rears her edifices in the midst of the densest populations, provides them with many seats and has the seats well filled." Richard Ely, the economist, complained in the middle eighties that Protestant ministers had difficulty being fair to labor, though this was not true of Catholic priests. "It is not a difference of good will," Ely emphasized, "so much as a difference of knowledge. The Catholic revealed an acquaintance with the movements of the masses—the Protestant ignorance." When President Theodore Roosevelt discussed his proposed arbitration commission with union leader John Mitchell during the coal strike of 1902, Mitchell asked, as Roosevelt reported it, that "a Roman Catholic prelate" be put on the body "as the great mass of miners were Roman Catholics." Obviously these Catholic workers trusted their churchmen.

But, for all its centuries of diverse historical experience in social adjustment, the Roman Church was only less unprepared for the new era than Protestantism; it too had to adapt as industrialization transformed society. Because the seat of Catholic authority was in Rome, it was not until 1891, with Leo XIII's encyclical *Rerum Novarum,* that the American Church could speak with authority in the idiom of the industrial age. In that justly famous document, the Church, in the words of the Pope, now came out in favor of the "dignity of labor," "the equality of rich and poor," the undesirability of child labor, the need for protections of the worker in industry, and "the employers' moral obligation to pay fair wages."

Even with such an invitation to social reform through religion, the Catholic Church in America, with notable and rare exceptions like Father Edward McGlynn and Archbishop Ireland, was slow to respond. One historian, writing of Boston in the urban age, observed that "the Archdiocese of Boston failed to send a single priest into the army of social reform, which recruited so many Protestant ministers during the period 1880–1900."

By the time of the First World War, however, adjustments in Catholic official attitudes were beginning to appear. In 1917, Father John A. Ryan was granted permission to establish the *Catholic Charities Review,* a request which had been denied him only a few years earlier. Immediately after the war, the four bishops composing the leadership of the National Catholic War Council issued a "Program of Social Reconstruction," in which the meaning of Leo's great encyclical on labor was spelled out for postwar America. In short order there followed the formation of the National Catholic Welfare Council and its Department of Social Action which issued, in 1920, a collection of church social documents, significantly entitled *Church and Labor.* Thus Catholicism, even within the relatively rigid limits imposed by the international character of its authority, endeavored, like Protestantism, to shape itself to deal with the challenge of the new era.

As has been implied, social Christianity constituted much more of a psychological wrench for Protestantism than for Catholicism. The latter, after all, having attained intellectual maturity within the social and historical context of the predominantly agrarian economy of the High Middle Ages, was never very friendly toward rationalistic capitalism. Unlike Calvinistic Protestantism, Catholicism did not especially prize thrift, frugality, hard work, sobriety, and wealth accumulation, which were so helpful in the growth of capitalism. As American Protestantism and Catholicism drew together in social ideology in the course of the early twentieth century, they moved farther away from the ethic of work and saving which had nurtured the expansion of capitalism and contributed to its enormous productive capacity. As modern American economist Kenneth Boulding has pointed out, "the 'lost gospel'—the old gospel of individualism, of self-help—is in many respects a sound one. Indeed, the middle-class nature of Protestantism is testimony to its long-run success." It was Protestantism which taught the middle class the virtues of "hard work, thrift, family limitation, productivity and frugality. . . . There is hardly any better overall recipe for economic development, whether for the individual or for a society." But, Boulding observes, "the old doctrines are discredited in the churches today." And, it should be added, it was the old gospel which supplied the energy to run the great engine of American production. One wonders what effect a reversal of that historic religious economic ethic will have upon capitalism's great achievement of production. And if it does interfere with productivity, what effect will that have on the American promise of abundance for all?

2. BE IT EVER SO SMALL

If the forces of the new era widened the domain of religion, they had the opposite effect upon the family and the home. In both a literal and figurative sense, the home shrank, working a significant alteration in the position of women and children in American society.

The initial force, of course, was industrialization. Wherever that process has taken place, whether in Europe, Asia, or the United States, it has demanded the labor of women and children. Even before 1860, tens of thousands of women stood before machines in the factories of New England and the Middle Atlantic states. Indeed, in that year women held, proportionately, more jobs in manufacturing than they did in 1900—a fact which illumines their important role in the beginnings of industrialization. But our concern here is not with the significance of women in the process of economic growth, but with the effect of industry upon the status of women. In this regard, the noteworthy fact is that as industry spread across the face of the nation in the 1880's and after, the number of women in the labor force grew steadily. Whereas in 1870 only 14.8 per cent of the women over sixteen years of age were gainfully employed, in 1900 the figure was up to 20.6 per cent; by 1910 it was 24.3. It should be noted that the flow of women into the labor force between 1860 and 1914 far exceeded the increase in the number of women in the country. Thus during the 1880's, though the feminine population grew about 28 per cent, the number of women workers jumped over 50 per cent.

Though the factory provided many of the occupational opportunities for women in this period, it was by no means the only one. In service industries like domestic service, telephone and telegraph, nursing, and teaching, women far outnumbered men. In business offices, that holy of holies of the American male, the woman worker became increasingly in evidence as the new invention, the typewriter, was widely introduced. It is true that the number of women in the professions was quite small, but Lord Bryce in the 1880's noticed that American women "have made their way into more of the professions more largely than in Europe." In fact, he wrote, "it is easier for women to find a career, to obtain remunerative work of an intellectual as of a commercial or mechanical kind, than in any part of Europe."

Undoubtedly, what opportunities there were in the professions for women are to be attributed to the opening of higher education to the sex. By the end of the century the battle for women's education had been won, largely by the establishment of women's colleges with curricular and educational standards deliberately raised to the level of the best men's institutions. Unlike the older men's colleges, which were founded by churches, a number of the women's colleges, like Vassar (1861), Smith (1870), Wellesley (1870), and Bryn Mawr (1885), were founded upon fortunes derived from industry and commerce. For this reason it might be said that the woman's college was doubly symbolic of the decisive role industrialization played in changing women's place in American society.

By providing opportunities for work outside the home, industrialization served to weaken the dependence of women in the family upon the breadwinning father. It was now possible for women to begin to experience the wider world. In 1903, Mrs. Bessie Van Vorst, a matron of society who wished to sample the life of a working girl, took a job in a Pittsburgh pickle factory. After only a day or two of the deadening drudgery of the factory, Mrs. Van Vorst could continue no longer and was compelled to stay away from work for two days. At the end of that time, however, she began to want to go back to work—exhausting as she knew it was. "Two days of leisure without resources or amusement make clear to me," she explained afterward, "how the sociability of factory life, and freedom from personal demands, and escape from self can prove a distraction to those who have no mental occupation, no money to spend on diversion. It is easier to submit to factory government . . . than to undergo the arbitrary discipline of parental authority." This was one form of independence which industrialization offered to women.

The other kind, which was more material than spiritual, was equally important in accounting for women's leaving the home. As a girl worker in a woolen shirt mill in Perry, New York, put it, "My father gives me all the money I need, but not all the money I *want*. I like to be independent and spend my money as I please." Though as a matter of hard fact few women workers were in such a fortunate economic situation at home, it is nevertheless true that financial independence for women was a significant by-product of industrial expansion. Certainly in many a home the father's pre-eminence was shaken when it was possible for the daughters and even the wife to support themselves against his actual or potential tyranny. And over the years the number of married women in the labor force has steadily increased. In 1890, only 13.9 per cent of working women were married; fifty years later, the figure was 36.4. As early as 1898, the day nursery, indispensable for the working mother, assumed significant proportions, for in that year the National Federation of Day Nurseries met for the first time.

In an even more obvious fashion, urbanization was cutting the home to smaller dimensions. The private house, so common in the rural and small-town environment, was given up in the great city where land was measured by the square foot instead of the acre. In New York City, for instance, the number of private houses annually constructed dropped from 1,300 in 1886 to a mere 40 in 1904. The multifamily dwelling, the tenement or the apartment house, had become the typical home of the urbanite. And as the physical dimension of the home shrank, so did the family size, despite the fact that public morality frowned upon contraception and federal and state laws prohibited the circulation of information about techniques. In the single decade 1890–1900, the average number of persons in families declined in over three quarters of the cities of 25,000 population or more.

This falling off of the urge to procreate was particularly noticeable among upper-class educated women—that is, among those most affected by the new forces. One New York City woman physician in 1904 asserted that "having a family is not an American ideal. Among my patients I find that the majority do not want any children; certainly not more than one." Urban resistance to childbearing received national attention in 1903, when President Theodore Roosevelt publicly denounced "the man or woman who deliberately avoids marriage, and has a heart so cold as to know no passion and a brain so shallow as to dislike having children." Such a person, the President declared, "is in effect a criminal against the race, and should be an object of contemptuous abhorrence by all healthy people."

The exhortation of even a President, however, was not strong enough to overcome contrary forces. Only 53 per cent of the members of the Vassar College classes of 1867 to 1897 were married, it was reported in 1915. And an investigation of 17,000 alumnae of eight women's colleges and coeducational Cornell turned up the fact that by 1918 less than 40 per cent of them had married. Educational and occupational opportunities newly available to women were making them independent in their choice of husbands, and many apparently had doubts as to the desirability of matrimony at all.

The questioning of the hallowed institution of matrimony extended even to those who were married. Foreign observers of American society have generally been impressed with the close internal bond of the family in the United States, yet, paradoxically, marriages in this country have usually been less durable than those in Europe. As industrialization and urbanization grew apace after 1870, the divorce rate in America was not only higher than Europe's, but it rose higher each decade. For instance, between 1870 and 1880, the population as a whole increased some 30 per cent, but divorces rose almost 80 per cent. In the following decade, the number of divorces increased three times as fast as the population. At the end of the century, the American states were granting seventy-three divorces for each 100,-000 of the population as compared with ten awarded in Australia, two in England, thirty-two in Switzerland (the highest in Europe), and twenty-three in France. At that time, as now, divorce more frequently occurred among urban than rural families and, as the United States has become increasingly urban, marriages have more frequently ended in divorce. The divorce rate in 1966 was more than two and one half times what it was in 1900.

Though a high divorce rate obviously betokens great marital instability throughout the society, it nevertheless can be interpreted more favorably. A long duration for marriage is by no means a conclusive measure of marital happiness; on the contrary, a long-lived marriage may merely conceal unrelieved misery. The ready availability of divorce makes it reasonably certain that long marriages are also happy marriages. Since it is the institution of marriage which has provided the principal agency for the limiting of women's place in society, liberalization of divorce laws has been a demand of the woman's movement, and its attainment has been an important step in the achievement of freedom for women. The truth of this is borne out by the fact that in the late nineteenth century almost two thirds of the divorces were granted to wives; in the twentieth century the proportion is even greater.

On the farm, children were a source of labor and an integral part of the working unit of the family. This situation was altered, however, in the city. Inasmuch as there were few household and no farm tasks which the children could perform, nor any meadows and woods in which they could amuse themselves, the position of children in the urban family changed. Furthermore, because industry could make good use of child labor, society was confronted with the urgent necessity for protecting youngsters against economic exploitation. As early as 1880, the census reported that one million children between the ages of ten and fifteen years were gainfully employed; within ten years, the number increased 75 per cent.

"Responsible citizens often say that they do not believe in play," H. S. Curtis, an authority on the adaptation of children to urban life, wrote in 1917, "and that the child ought to work, but these people fail to realize, apparently, that the work of children has disappeared, and the choice is not between work and play, but between play and idleness." Though hard to believe today, before 1885 there were no public playing places for children in any city of the country. At that date, a women's philanthropic society, seizing on an example witnessed in Germany, dumped heaps of sand at two places in the streets of Boston. The children's response to this rather belated recognition of their instinct for play was sufficiently encouraging for three piles to be put out the following year; from such beginnings the practice spread to other localities and cities.

But it was a long way from piles of sand to organized playgrounds. At the end of the century, the actual number of cities which had progressed to supervised play facilities added up to no more than a baker's dozen. The movement, however, gained impetus in 1899 when the New York Board of Education set up thirty-one playgrounds attached to the public schools. The providing of supervised play areas for city children was adopted by other cities. In 1906, the Playground and Recreational Association of America was founded and by 1915 over 430 cities maintained playgrounds for their children.

But playgrounds in the city are far removed from country meadows; the play habits of children were compelled to change to fit the limits of the city. "Most of the traditional games of the world have grown up under conditions of plenty of space and plenty of time," James Gulick has pointed out. "Relatively few games can be found that are useful where 500 children are turned out for a ten-minute recess into a yard where 50 can play comfortably." A game like "monkey-chase," developed in a Connecticut orchard and requiring a grassy running space, "could not bear transplanting to the city." On the other hand, a gambling game like "craps . . . is a typical city game, invented by the children of the city. . . . Craps is the almost inevitable outgrowth of modern city conditions; it bids fair to become the national game of the tenements." As Gulick noted, it can easily be played in a limited space, it is quiet, and it is well suited to limited time; "it can be played in five minutes or five hours. It adapts itself to any number of players, five, ten, or any indefinite number."

The belief in play as an important part of the life of the child has paralleled the growth of the city. In 1917, H. S. Curtis observed that the playground was only the most primitive contribution of the Play Movement. The next stage was one which was only beginning in the United States, he wrote, but had already captured much attention in Europe. "It is built on the assumption that play is essential to development of children and that it must be furnished to every child every day." On this philosophy are founded the kindergarten, the nursery school, and the progressive approach to education, all typically urban devices which first assumed significant proportions during the first years of the twentieth century.

3. THE NEW WOMAN

In offering new opportunities to women outside the home, industrialization constituted one of the silent but potent forces behind the so-called feminist movement. It is true that the forging of the intellectual weapons for women's emancipation long antedated the factory, for the celebrated declaration of feminine "independence" was announced at Seneca Falls, New York, in 1848. But from a social standpoint, it was only with the increase in economic opportunities resulting from the spread of the factory that the movement of women out of the traditional home assumed noticeable proportions.

The term "emancipation," however, when applied to the women's movement is somewhat misleading. Although it is perfectly true that women have been subordinate to men during most of history, it is equally true that they have shared in the rewards and perquisites of power, prestige, and wealth as no other "oppressed" group ever has. Women as wives and mistresses, rulers and leaders, as intellectuals and salonières, have always been a "force in history," to use Mary Beard's phrase. In contrast to minorities like Negroes, Jews, and Indians, women have been included in the innermost circles of the ruling males, enjoying advantages, protection, and succor usually ruthlessly denied a subject class. Thus, as Mrs. Beard has observed, when a bill was introduced in the New York legislature in 1848 to grant married women greater property rights, it "was drawn by a member of the legislature who was eager to safeguard the rights of his wife, and it was vigorously pressed by another member equally eager to protect the interests of his daughter." In substance, just because women are a sex, they have been vouchsafed a measure of equality customarily withheld from an inferior class—namely, marriage with the master class. In fact, to render the paradox of women as subordinates even more involved, what for the normal minority group represents the achievement of complete equality, that is, marriage with the dominant class, for the feminine "minority" has been the avenue whereby women's most complete subjection has been effected.

In other ways, however, the social position of women was analogous to that of Negroes. Thus, women were denied the vote, kept from holding office, from filling certain jobs, and from participation in certain kinds of activities, all on the grounds that they were incapable of performing these roles. For example, during a good part of the nineteenth century higher education was said to be beyond the capacity of women, just as it was said to be too demanding for black men. Women, too, again like Negroes, learned to accommodate themselves to those with power—that is men—so that they cajoled rather than demanded, just as Negroes would play "dumb" or shuffle foolishly because that kind of deferential behavior was what white men wanted and responded positively to. Finally, women, like Negroes, are highly visible socially so that prejudice against them is

immediately triggered and cannot be assuaged or eliminated by covert
association and familiarity, as might occur with a Jew or a Catholic.
Thus for women, as for Negroes, discrimination has been more tenacious and pervasive than for other minorities.

Simply because women were at once like other minorities and yet
not like them, the women's movement of the nineteenth century and
after is best seen as an extension of the opportunities open to women.
This widening of the social base of women's activities was accomplished in two ways. One we have already noticed: the expansion of
women's work through the growth of industry and urbanization. The
other was less obvious but no less important. Because the home in
the city was smaller and managed with relative ease, the woman
who did not work in the factory or at the office was almost compelled to seek diversion outside the narrow confines of the family. In
One Woman's Life, Robert Herrick described the changes which
came over the home life of a married woman in the city. Milly, the
heroine of the novel, lived an easy life in a small apartment, with one
child and a servant or two who did most of the work. Hers was,
writes Herrick, "much like the lives of many thousands of young
married women in our transition period." She just did not have
"enough to do to occupy her abundant energy and interest in life.
. . . And modern life had also so skillfully contrived the plebeian
machinery of living that there was little or nothing left for the woman
to do, if she were above the necessity of cooking and washing for
her man." Such generalizations, of course, apply almost exclusively
to women of the middle class. But that does not weaken their importance, since the movement for women's rights was almost entirely
the work of middle-class women.

The smallness of the home was only one factor which gave more
time to women of the city; many of the time-honored chores of the
housekeeper were being lightened or eliminated. Gradually more and
more household tasks, once considered *de rigueur* for the homemaker, left the home to be performed commercially. Cheap ready-
made clothing was commonplace in the city by the middle of the
nineteenth century, and in the years after the Civil War what sewing
had to be done could be facilitated by the mechanical home sewing
machine. In 1853, six companies produced 23,000 such machines,
but twenty years later their combined production exceeded half a
million. The indispensable duty of daily cooking, which was more

often a heavy chore than a wifely delight, was made somewhat pleasanter and easier by the commercial sale of gas for fuel and illumination. During the 1880's, the commercial laundry began to assume a prominent place in the lives of many middle-class women, thereby relieving them of a great part of the drudgery of housekeeping.

As far as the art of cooking was concerned, food preparation was simplified by packaged cereals like Quaker Oats and Wheatena, which supplanted the rural cornmeal mush. Home-baked bread, though always tasteful and a fond memory of former rural residents, was time-consuming in a household burdened with a bewildering variety of tasks. Women eagerly supported the expansion of the baking factory in the 1880's and 1890's, thereby hastening the removal of one more ancient chore from the urban home. At about the same time, canned vegetables were taking a prominent place on urban tables. "Housekeeping is getting to be ready made, as well as clothing," commented one woman, with a measure of exaggeration, in *Good Housekeeping* in 1887. Commercially produced ice, first widespread in the seventies, removed dependence on changes in the weather and systematized the most satisfactory means for the preservation of food.

The well-organized transportation system of an urban-industrial society made it possible for the first time for menus to have variety and style. The frontier and rural character of this country, if in no other way, was always impressed upon foreign visitors by the deadly monotony of the popular American diet. Farm cookery, nostalgia to the contrary notwithstanding, always leaned heavily upon the frying pan, and in winter fresh fruits and vegetables were unknown on the farm table. The variety of foods available in the city a large part of the year encouraged diversification in menus and titillated palates in a manner either unthought of or impossible in the country regions. A gauge of this new and, one might add, gratifying interest in food was the establishment of cooking schools in the mid-1870's. Within three years after it opened in 1874, the New York Cook School counted 1,200 students. During the 1880's, cookbooks began to appear in profusion for the first time, with perhaps the acme being reached in 1896 by Fanny Farmer of the Boston Cooking School, whose book was destined to assume in short order the proportions of a classic.

Many thousands of middle-class American women soon discov-

ered, as did Milly Rindge in Herrick's novel, that the restricted urban
home afforded married women new leisure for outside activities.
Women's organizations grew as the cities grew. Though some of
these groups were made up of workingwomen, many were composed
of middle-class women released from the drudgery of the home and
searching for avenues of social expression. Though organizations like
the Daughters of the American Revolution, United Daughters of the
Confederacy, Colonial Dames of America, and United States Daughters of 1812—all founded in the 1890's—are obvious reflections of
a resurgence of nationalism, they are also indicative of this growing
surplus of female social energy. What one might call economic organizations of women were also formed during these years. The
American Association of University Women, organized in 1881,
and the National Association of Deans of Women, founded in 1891,
mirrored the increasing participation of middle-class women in higher
education. The great range of women's organizations is suggested by
three which differed widely in purpose and membership: the National Consumers' League (1899), The Junior League (1901), and
the National Woman's Trade Union League of America (1903).

The number of such societies of women were the wonder of foreign
visitors. When Lord Bryce tried to explain why American women
have "an average of literary taste and influence higher than that of
women in any European country," he gave as one of his reasons
"the leisure which they possess as compared with men."

These organizations, however, should not be thought of as so
many sponges sopping up excess womanly energy and time, but serving no social purpose. On the contrary, their impact on society was
scarcely short of astounding. For though the mention of a woman's
club brought a smile to most masculine faces in the early twentieth
century, as it does in our own post-Hokinson era, the clubs were
actually enormously effective in the 1890's and later. Many a town
or city owed its library, children's playgrounds, or a charming park
to the efforts of the local woman's club. Frequently, there were no
other civic organizations in the town.

The club movement achieved such power and prestige that in 1901
an act of Congress awarded the General Federation of Women's
Clubs a national charter. Then in 1904, the president of the Federation, Mrs. Sarah Decker, pushed the clubs into high gear as social
improvement agencies with her famous remark: "Ladies . . . Dante
is dead . . . and I think it is time that we dropped the study of

his inferno and turned our attention to our own."[2] The General Federation as one measure of women's exodus from the home is impressive; by 1914, over a million women were members.

The Women's Christian Temperance Union was another major woman's organization which was obviously a direct response to changes in the home and in the social milieu. Under the leadership of Frances Willard, the W.C.T.U., with a quarter of a million members, became a school on a national scale for the education of women in social affairs and the need for social reform. Despite its title, the W.C.T.U., after the middle 1880's, was active in a number of reforms unconnected with the evil of drink. The power of the W.C.T.U. was put behind movements for the protection of workingwomen, for laws raising the age of consent, for kindergartens, for the training of girls for domestic service, and for the realization of international peace through arbitration. Frances Willard herself was a member of the Knights of Labor and an important figure in the early history of the Populist party, as well as an experimenter with vegetarianism, phrenology, and theosophy.

The work of the W.C.T.U., like the organization itself, is symbolic of the radiating effects of the emergence of women from what feminist Charlotte Perkins Gilman called the "smallest, oldest, lowest" work of the world—that of the home. Just as the espousal of the temperance cause by women ultimately helped to bring prohibition to America, so the women's attacks on the peculiarly urban evil of prostitution stimulated legislation in an aspect of social life which had heretofore been virtuously skirted. The Mann Act of 1910, sometimes called the White Slave Act, was one such measure on the federal level. Though Americans could never bring themselves to consider regulated prostitution, the agitation stirred up over the "social evil" resulted in a massing of information on the subject which, in turn, permitted the eradication of the grosser evils of the trade,

[2] Since it is commonly held that the woman's movement was essentially a suffrage lobby, it is relevant here to point out that the General Federation of Women's Clubs did not officially discuss the suffrage issue until 1910 and that even the W.C.T.U. was brought to accept the suffrage plank only after a bitter campaign by Frances Willard. The suffrage aspect of the women's movement has been omitted in the text because it is so well known and because it has unfortunately obscured the larger and fundamentally more important aspects of the popularization of women's opportunities. Many women in the 1890's and after who were interested in a wider sphere for women felt, like Ernestine Geyer in Herrick's *One Woman's Life,* "Things aren't done in this world by voting about 'em."

such as recruitment through the seduction of innocent girls, and forcible submission. Moreover, for the first time, the causal connection between sweatshop working conditions and recruitment into commercial vice was so plain that none could blink it away.

The manner in which industrialization added a new depth to the literature of the woman's movement is illustrated in the voluminous writings of Charlotte Perkins Gilman. Her first major work, *Women and Economics,* published in 1899 and widely circulated in the United States and abroad in subsequent years, was a powerful and reasoned case for the economic independence of women if they were to achieve true freedom on a broad scale. Ever mindful of the needs of society, Gilman stressed the loss which society sustained when the peculiar creative talents of women were denied expression.

The significance and nature of these talents were apparent in the diversity of work undertaken by a growing number of women in the nineties and the early years of the twentieth century. In a field like social work and industrial relations, women like Florence Kelley of Chicago, Mary Simkhovitch of New York, and Vida Scudder of Boston not only distinguished themselves, but incidentally offered a striking example of the interacting effects of the new social forces. Once the social conditions of an urban, industrial society permitted women to participate fully in the work of the world, their energies and abilities, in turn, could be utilized for making the raw, new society a better place for human habitation.

4. NEW POLITICIANS WITH OLD PRINCIPLES

That hurricane of reform called Progressivism, which blew through all levels of American political and social life in the years between 1900 and 1917, was many things, but above all it was a response to the challenge of the city and the factory, an attempt to bring to heel the untamed forces which had almost reduced the American Dream to a mockery.

For three decades the voices of protest—the labor unions, the churches, the Populists, the publicists, the utopian novelists—had been increasing in number and growing in volume, but the orgy of corruption and chicane, the piling up of corporate and individual wealth, continued while the squalor of the cities spread and the poverty of the farms deepened. The decade of the nineties, which experienced the deepest depression up to that time, brought fresh examples of class cleavage and class hate: the bloody struggle between workers and Pinkerton police at Homestead in 1892; the deliberate starving of the Pullman employees in 1894; the clashes between federal troops and striking railway workers in Chicago; the pitiful march of Coxey's Army of unemployed, dramatizing the workers' desperate need for work. While thousands of workers struggled to keep their jobs or to eke out an existence on a reduced wage, the New York *Tribune* reported in 1892 that there were "only 4,047 millionaires" in the country. It truly seemed as if American society had been riven into the many poor and the few rich; that the ideal of an America of equality of opportunity for all, of social justice, of decency in government, had become a nightmare in which the ideals had been inverted as in some kind of social Black Mass.

Progressivism changed all this; its advent was like a bright spring day after the bleak, depressing, soul-crushing days of February. Hope and spiritual uplift seemed to flood back into the hearts of Americans, even if the country was not actually transformed into a paradise. It seemed worth living in America again now that, even in the age of the city and the factory, men and women were trying to breathe life into the American Dream.

In 1907, in the midst of the Progressive ferment, sociologist E. A. Ross published *Sin and Society,* a book which, in its brief compass, set forth the underlying philosophy of the new reform movement and illumined the way in which the forces released by industrialism had transformed the old question of good and evil. Under the heading "New Varieties of Sin," Ross dramatically directed attention to the necessity of re-evaluating moral responsibility in an age when no man was an island unto himself. "Modern sin," he wrote, "takes its character from the mutualism of our time. . . . Nowadays the water main is my well, the trolley car is my carriage, the banker's safe my old stocking, the policeman's billy my fist. My own eyes and nose and judgment defer to the inspector of food, or drugs, or gas, or factories, or tenements, or insurance companies. I rely upon others to look after my drains, invest my savings, nurse my sick, and teach my children." Unfortunately, he continued, when all men are so interdependent and the web of connection is at once tight and far-flung, the moral focus becomes blurred, and no one assumes responsibility for the evil he commits. "The modern high-power dealer of woe wears immaculate linen, carries a silk hat and a lighted cigar, sins with a calm countenance and a serene soul, leagues and months from

the evil he causes. . . . Modern sins are impersonal. . . . The hurt
passes into that vague mass, the 'public' and is there lost to view."
In a less complex society one could know and trust those upon whom
one depended, but in this new order, though the dependence was infinitely enhanced, personal knowledge of people was in inverse ratio.

The reformers of the early twentieth century to a greater or less
degree appreciated the new morality imposed by social change. Sometimes, as we shall see, their awareness was translated into legislation
designed to meet the problem; sometimes the problem was beyond
legislation. But in any case, an increasing army of reformers and writers in the first decade of the twentieth century threw a flood of light
upon the social results of the factory and the city—results which were
threatening to overwhelm, if not destroy, the old America.

Foremost among such publicists were the so-called muckrakers,
who for a decade and in dozens of books and magazines unmercifully
pricked the American conscience. Lincoln Steffens, for example, disgusted by the corrupt political machines in the cities and states of the
nation, probed and questioned until he was able to reveal in his
Shame of the Cities and *Shame of the States* the unholy alliance between business wealth and corrupt politics. The complacency of the
nation was shattered by David Graham Phillips' sensational report
on "The Treason of the Senate," in which some of the biggest names
in "the greatest deliberative body in the world" were charged with
and convicted of history's most heinous crime.

Before, during and after the exposures of corruption, movements
were afoot to bring some decency and reform to a number of cities
and states. Reformers like Samuel Jones of Toledo and Tom Johnson of Cleveland showed that cities could be run honestly if they
were divorced from the extraneous and often corrupting influence of
state and national politics and if knowledgeable men could be encouraged to run for office. New forms of local government were created to deal with the special problems of the cities. The commission
form of municipal government and the city-manager plan date from
these years between the late 1890's and 1910. Both were attempts to
fit government to the novel and complex requirements of urban life.
By our own time, several hundred American communities have
adopted some form of the commission-manager system in order to
bring businesslike operation into the running of their urban machinery.

Out of the determination to break the grip of machine politicians and corporate wealth upon government, the Progressives took up the fight for new devices of popular government. Because corrupt or reactionary legislatures often impeded efforts at reform, the new leaders turned to the initiative, recall, and referendum as the means whereby the people might "initiate" legislation themselves, remove from office those who had betrayed their trust, and pass on controversial legislation which seemed too vital to entrust to the judgment of indifferent legislatures. The adoption of the Australian or secret ballot (it was provided by the government instead of by the political parties, as had heretofore been the case) threw one more obstacle in the path of corruption at the polls. None of these devices, nor all of them together, it must be admitted, made saints out of politicians or eliminated the political machine, but politics was a more honorable profession when the Progressives were finished than it had been for two generations.

The squalor and congestion of the city also came in for sensational exposure at the hands of Progressives like Jacob Riis, Jane Addams, Florence Kelley, and Mary Simkhovitch. Addams' Hull House in Chicago and Lillian Wald's house on Henry Street in New York became bywords among the many poor who received warm shelter and sympathy there and at other settlement houses. Under the insistent prodding of Riis' exposures, the legislature passed new tenement laws providing for decent living conditions among the poor. At long last "the scab" of the dumbbell tenement began to recede from New York City.

The poverty, sickness, and degradation which woman and child labor brought in their train also came under vigorous attack. Robert Hunter's *Poverty* and John Spargo's *The Bitter Cry of the Children* trenchantly brought home to even the most hardened reader the painful details of what persistent poverty, inadequate housing, and urban living were doing to the mothers and the future of the nation. The workers' acclaim and the nation's headlines were captured by Louis D. Brandeis when he convinced the Supreme Court, that fountainhead of conservatism, in his monumental sociological brief in the case of *Muller* v. *Oregon* in 1908, that the regulation of hours and conditions of work for women was not a denial of the liberties guaranteed in the Fourteenth Amendment. State after state in the course of the Progressive era enacted legislation to protect women and children in their working conditions. Toward the end of the period, the federal government stepped in to prohibit child labor completely, but the act was struck down by the Supreme Court.

It was the great corporations, however, which undoubtedly drew most of the Progressives' fire, for from that direction seemed to arise the greatest threat to a democratic society. Grown to enormous proportions, ramifying throughout the economy, these industrial combines appeared to have made themselves masters of all America. "Some of the biggest men in the United States . . . are afraid of somebody, are afraid of something," Woodrow Wilson said. "They know that there is a power somewhere so organized, so subtle, so watchful, so interlocked, so complete, so pervasive, that they had better not speak above their breath when they speak in condemnation of it." This concern of the Progressives was translated into a wave of state and national legislation which endeavored to throw up protections against concentration of economic power. Many of the states, for example, set up within their boundaries regulatory commissions and stringent rules for corporations. The so-called Seven Sisters Acts, pushed through the New Jersey legislature by Governor Woodrow Wilson, transformed that state from the haven of corporations to one of the Union's strictest monitors of industrial behavior.

On the national level, laws in 1903, 1906, and 1910 supplied the Interstate Commerce Commission with weapons which for the first time enabled it to tame the railroads' power to do evil. The Clayton Antitrust Act of 1914 set forth a long array of objectionable, monopolistic procedures by corporations with criminal and civil penalties attached to them. In substance, it sought to plug up the holes in the old Sherman Act of 1890. As a further safeguard, the Federal Trade Commission was created in 1914 to serve as a kind of watchdog over the practices of the business world, empowered to publicize corporate activities contrary to the public interest and to take the delinquents to court.

As an agency which carried on a continuous policing of the amoral world of business in the interest of the consumer and free enterprise, the F.T.C. was helping to create a new morality for the corporation. Indeed, the whole corpus of regulatory legislation of the Progressives looked in that direction. Insofar as business morals have improved since the days of the nineteenth-century Buccaneers of Business, this is the result of the new police and the new climate of opinion encouraged by the Progressive movement.

And as Richard Hofstadter has observed, there was certainly an improvement in business responsibility during the Progressive years. At the opening of the twentieth century, he writes, "thoughtful American businessmen, pressed by the threat of union organization, condemned by muckrakers, and smarting under the comparisons with the most efficient managers of Europe, began to address themselves to poor working conditions and employee morale, and to the reformation of their haphazard shop methods. Between 1900 and 1910, 240 volumes on business management were published. . . . The emerging business schools, nonexistent in the country before 1898, provided numerous new agencies for discussion, education, and research in the field of management. Employers began to study personnel problems, consider devices for cutting fatigue and improving work conditions, and launched in some cases upon their own welfare and pension programs and profit-sharing schemes."

The passage of legislation for inspection and certification of the purity of food and drugs by government was a similar realistic avowal that in a modern industrial-urban society it was no longer safe to depend upon personal reputations or personal knowledge as a guarantee of the wholesomeness of food or the therapeutic value of drugs. The laissez-faire precept, *caveat emptor,* was too callous and too dangerous now.

Long convinced that the great corporations were dependent for their power as well as for their excessive profits on the protective tariff, the Progressives undertook to knock out that prop of monopoly. Unsuccessful in their first assault in 1909, they did better in 1913, when the Wilson administration succeeded in substantially cutting the tariff for the first time since it had begun to rise in 1861.

In the Tariff Act of 1913, the Progressives included a tax on corporate and personal incomes. This tax was a symbol of the new attitude. In taxing incomes according to the ability to pay, the Progressives were taking notice of the highly interdependent nature of their society. At a time when a man's income was a direct consequence of his individual labors, a graduated tax might have appeared unjust. But for a society wherein the amassing of wealth was totally dependent upon the co-operation of many men and institutions, this was not the case. No matter how sycophantic one might be, it was difficult to argue that the "great American fortunes" were the result of individual exertions. They were truly social products, taxable by society. The income tax symbolizes, as nothing else does, the new industrial age. Rooted in the realities of the society, it was at the same time the principal equalizer of the great disparities of wealth which seemed to be at once an evil and an integral part of industrialism.

But Progressivism was more than merely a random response to the insistent problems of the new social order. Implicit in the disgust which the Progressives felt for the corruption and power lust of the Gilded Age and fundamental to the reforms which they advocated was a vague vision of what America should be. It was against this vision that the Gilded Age was measured and found wanting; it was for the achievement of this dream that the reforms were pushed.

The vision was not new, however; it was not a product of the emergent new society. Though the Progressives were overwhelmingly city men and dealing with urban problems, they espoused ideals developed in an earlier and rural period of the nation's history. For seen in terms of goals rather than means, the Progressives embraced the same large purposes for which the Jeffersonians and the Jacksonians fought: equality of opportunity, opposition to monopoly, humanitarianism, and belief in democracy. Like so much else in the American experience, the Progressives were more a conservative than an innovating force. Though it is true that to one who had lived through the Gilded Age, Progressivism seemed radical and novel, to one who sees it against the backdrop of an earlier era in American thought, it was but a latter-day Jeffersonianism.

But it was a Jeffersonianism shaped to fit the demands of a new society. In this lay the Progressives' strength, their weakness, and their lasting contribution to modern America. A philosophy well rooted in the American past strengthened them because it drew upon the common heritage; it weakened them because it circumscribed their reform efforts within the limits of a philosophy derived from a vastly different social context. But the philosophy bequeathed to modern Americans an outlook which spoke up strongly for freedom, equality of opportunity, and individualism despite all the social and economic forces which pulled in the opposite direction. That these ideals are still relevant to America is largely the result of the Progressives. They poured hard substance into ideals which at the time seemed outmoded in a world of factories and cities.

If Populism was the instinctive and ill-considered reaction of troubled farmers to the onrush of urbanism and industrialism, Progressivism was the urban middle class's recognition that the misgovernment, poverty, and class hatred of the new society must be eliminated. But whereas the farmers' response grew out of the elemental impulse of self-preservation, the Progressives were goaded to reform by no such force. Indeed, as city people, they were a rising, not a declining, class in the new society. Certainly it was not economic discontent which drove the Progressives to undertake their reforms. The first decade of the twentieth century was noteworthy for its prosperity; indeed, the single recession of the period, the Bankers' Panic of 1907, affected most people as little as its title suggests. In short, one looks in vain for an economic spur to such a perversive age of reform.

The springs of the reforming spirit are rather to be found in the sudden feeling that the vital juices of America were being drained away in the sewer of the Gilded Age. The ground had long been prepared for this spiritual rebirth, but for some reason it was not until 1900 that the slow accretion of protest, the gradual heightening of social sensitivity, coalesced into a swell of reform.[3]

The pith of Progressivism then, and its importance for Americans today, are to be found in the same fact. As a philosophy Progressivism was a revitalization, a restatement of traditional American ideals; in substance it was the application of Christian morality and Jeffersonian principles to the twentieth century—an effort to shape society to the dimensions of an ideal. In short, it was moral. Indeed, unless one accepts the moral nature of Progressivism, one misses the heart which vivified the body of the movement. It was a supreme effort to bring back into American public life decency and old-fashioned concern for morality and humanitarianism. In a sense, it was an attempt to make Americans worthy of their history. "We stand in the presence of a revolution—not a bloody revolution," Woodrow Wilson

---

[3] Not all recent historians would place as much emphasis upon the business-controlling role of the Progressive movement as I have done here. Robert Wiebe, *Businessmen and Reform* (Cambridge, 1962), for example, has shown that businessmen were active in at least the early Progressive movement, principally in behalf of government regulation of business, largely because in that way some needed order would be brought into economic affairs. Gabriel Kolko, *The Triumph of Conservatism: A Reinterpretation of American History, 1900–1916* (New York, 1963), goes much further. He argues that businessmen who participated in the so-called Progressive movement for the regulation of business were really conservatives who used governmental power to serve the interests of business. This contention is at once too semantic and too one-sided to be helpful, but the evidence presented by Wiebe and Kolko (as distinct from Kolko's interpretation) makes it clear that just as railroad regulation in the 1880's sprang from more than the demands of farmers, so some Progressive economic reforms were pushed or supported by some businessmen, though not all businessmen liked the measures.

said in 1912, "but a silent revolution, whereby America will insist upon recovering in practice those ideals which she has always professed, upon securing a government devoted to the general interest and not to special interest."

Pervasive as moral concern was among the vast majority of Americans who espoused Progressivism, in some it amounted almost to a confession of guilt for having delayed too long in redeeming the Promise of America. Only a repressed feeling of guilt can account for much of the utter sentimentality with which some of the muckrakers and social workers portrayed the conditions of the poor. The sense of guilt was laid bare in a poem "Tortured Millions," published in the celebrated muckraking magazine *McClure's*. After reciting the personal gains which the poet enjoyed at the cost of the workers' degradation, the poem closes with these lines:

> O thou Eternal Law, I wish this was not to be.
> Nay, raise them from the dust and punish me.

It was for just such attitudes, though admittedly less explicitly expressed, that Lloyd Morris aptly described Jane Addams, the social worker, and Emma Goldman, the radical, as "sentimentalists with swollen consciences," an epithet which is applicable to other Progressives as well.

Such feelings of guilt are closely related to the Protestantism which was the religion of most Progressives. By virtue of the absence of recognized expiatory channels like confession and penance, self-accusatory guilt is peculiarly Protestant. But the Protestant source of Progressivism runs deeper; it is to be found in the soul-searing experience through which the Protestant churches had been passing for nearly a decade and a half. Richard Hofstadter calls Progressivism "a phase in the history of the Protestant conscience, a latter-day Protestant revival. . . ." In a real sense, Progressivism was the social gospel in practice.

Though not all historians would subscribe to the accent on the religious sources of early twentieth-century reform implied here, the religious understratum to the social protests of the 1880's and 1890's is too pervasive to be ignored. Recall, for example, the deep religious conviction and phraseology in such influential and supposedly secular works as Henry George's *Progress and Poverty* and Edward Bellamy's *Looking Backward*. Or, as an even more striking example, the American Economic Association's rejection, at its founding in 1885, of the "doctrine of laissez-faire" because it is "unsafe in politics and unsound in morals. . . ." At about the same time Richard Ely, the secretary of the Association, was telling the members that what "we wish to accomplish . . . lies in the direction of practical Christianity. . . ." The existence of a Christian Socialist movement in the 1890's similarly testified to the religious element which underlay the incipient reform movement. That the mass of people also felt the contradictions between Christian ethics and their society is apparent from the fabulous success of a third-rate novel like Charles Sheldon's *In His Steps; What Would Jesus Do?* Published in 1897, the novel quickly became one of the greatest best sellers of all time, well over two million copies being sold in America alone.

Sheldon's book, coming late in the nineties, was a bridge between the new religious upsurge of that era and the Progressive movement which followed. The novel concerns a minister and his church who decide to carry on their daily lives according to their understanding of the precepts of Jesus. All decisions were to be weighed in the scale of "What Would Jesus Do?" In the course of the book, those who follow this principle sound and act like the Progressives of a later day. They show concern for the plight of the workers; they display a recognition of the role of the environment in shaping people's actions and thoughts. Those who are well-to-do exhibit a sense of guilt for their money; respectable people are encouraged to participate in politics as their duty to society; railroad regulation is demanded; settlement houses are established; and several of the characters display the isolationism of the later Progressives by preferring missionary work at home rather than in foreign lands.

The Progressives, for their part, often gave voice to a religious sentiment. In his autobiography, Frederick Howe, the prominent Cleveland Progressive, wrote that, though he discarded his strict religious upbringing early in life, it constituted only an outward divestment. "From that religion my reason was never emancipated," he recalled, ". . . early assumptions as to virtue and vice, goodness and evil remained in my mind long after I had tried to discard them." Such a persistence of religious values, he concluded significantly, "is, I think, the most characteristic influence of my generation." Among the national political leaders of Progressivism, the religious element in their language and thought has often been noticed. "If I did not believe that the moral judgment would be the last and final judgment in the minds of men as well as at the tribunal of God," Woodrow Wilson said, "I could not believe in popular government." And who needs to be reminded of William Jennings Bryan's intense religious nature? Or that when Theodore Roosevelt shouted at the Progressive convention, "We stand at Armageddon and we battle for the Lord," the nearly hysterical delegates burst into perfervid singing of "Onward, Christian Soldiers"?

The intimate connection between political Progressivism and the social gospel can be traced down to even finer links. Both Theodore Roosevelt and Woodrow Wilson as Presidents consulted on their social programs with Walter Rauschenbusch, the nationally known exponent of the social gospel. And Robert La Follette, the other great national Progressive leader, was powerfully influenced both in his youth and later by his friendship with John Bascom, another prominent clerical advocate of social Christianity.

Though Americans of a later and more cynical age frequently look upon Samuel ("Golden Rule") Jones with bemused tolerance, his firm conviction that Christianity was practical is of central importance to an understanding of the moral impulse of Progressivism. A well-to-do manufacturer in Toledo in the 1890's, Jones quickly earned the soubriquet "Golden Rule" because of his saintlike and consistent application of that ethical rule of thumb. In his factory, for example, the sole regulation he insisted upon was that single precept of Jesus. As tangible witnesses to his conviction, he built for the entertainment and enlightenment of his employees Golden Rule Park and Playground and Golden Rule Hall. First elected mayor of Toledo in 1897 on the Golden Rule Platform, he was still in office at his death in 1904.

Jones enjoyed the support of all classes of society even though his radical approach to government earned him powerful and relentless enemies. (The day he died, it is said, the Toledo street car companies' stocks jumped twenty-four points!) Moreover, naïve and innocent as his thought sometimes appears, Jones attracted to himself both as friend and leader some of the most sophisticated men of the time, notably Brand Whitlock, who became Jones's mayoral successor, Frederick Howe, and Tom Johnson of Cleveland. What humble folk and men of affairs alike responded to in Jones were his idealism and his faith in the goodness of men and the teachings of Jesus. Jones, like many another Progressive, exemplified Santayana's definition of an American—"an idealist working on matter."

Years later, Brand Whitlock wrote that most men never realized what Golden Rule Jones taught, "namely that, above all the laws men make with political machines . . . there is a higher law, and that the Golden Rule is a rule of conduct deduced from that law. . . ." For most Progressives it was always clear that their fight was a moral one, a struggle of good against evil.

It should also be said that the moralistic outlook of the Progressives was a long-term weakness, if a short-term strength. Tending to see the world in black and white, the average Progressive battled against monsters he could not really lick, or else he contented himself with only the illusion of victory. Thus many of the reform measures of the era, like the Federal Trade Commission, the antitrust laws, and the initiative and referendum, soon proved themselves inadequate to deal with the complexities of economic and political life. Though, as we shall see later, there were Progressives of an increasingly relativistic strain of thought, most of them displayed a highly moralistic approach to the world, such as religion in America has exhibited ever since the Puritans. Being highly moral, Progressivism was often also absolute. In this regard, it was a throwback to an earlier and simpler America, for by the opening years of the twentieth century a relative morality was the coming thing.

The social ethics of Protestantism were but one of the sources of the new reformers' moral purpose; the other was derived from the political idealism of the early Republic. Jefferson's vision of America was just as much the ideal of the twentieth-century reformer as it had been of Democrat Andrew Jackson, Republican Abraham Lincoln, and Populist Tom Watson. "I hear men talk about following in the footsteps of Jefferson," Progressive John Peter Altgeld said in 1902. "Why, Jefferson was the great radical of his day! He referred everything back to the people; he wanted everything left in the hands of the people. . . . Were Jefferson alive today, his voice would be heard from ocean to ocean demanding that the people themselves must own the monopolies." Rather than discard the presumably outdated Jeffersonian image of America, the Progressives proceeded to update it, thereby salvaging for the twentieth century the Jeffersonian vision of a free and open society in the New World.

The shibboleths and touchstones of the Jeffersonian-Jacksonian tradition ran all through the electrifying campaign speeches of Woodrow Wilson in 1912. As he himself said, "The New Freedom is only the old revived and clothed in the unconquerable strength of modern America." His New Freedom was little more than the equality of opportunity which permeated Jacksonian Democracy. The purpose of government, Wilson said, was "to set business free," in order that it might "follow its own right laws." "I stand," he declared, "as the party behind me stands, for regulated competition of a sort that will put the weak upon an equality with the strong."

Competition and individualism, so close to the heart of the earlier agrarian creed, still were meaningful slogans to the leaders of Progressivism. "The supreme task of the American people," Progressive Senator Albert Cummins of Iowa told the Senate in 1908, "is stimulating, fostering and protecting the competitive factor in American business." To Charles McCarthy of Wisconsin, the righthand man of Senator Robert A. La Follette, Progressivism meant the "beginnings of a new individualism." In the forefront of the radical wing of Progressivism was John Peter Altgeld of Illinois, the pardoner of the Haymarket anarchists. Yet in the 1890's, he told a group of students: "This is an age of individual achievement. . . . If you are sent out to bring something, bring it, and not an explanation. If you agree to do something, do it; don't come back with an explanation. Explanations as to how you came to fail are not worth two cents a ton. Nobody wants them or cares for them."

Long before the Progressive era, Jefferson, in a plea for unity in American society, had said, "We are all Republicans, we are all Federalists." But for all their admiration of Jefferson, the Populists had ignored his counsel of harmony, boasting instead of their class allegiance. The Progressives, on the other hand, placed themselves above and outside of classes, presuming to speak for Americans without reference to economic interest. In this respect Progressivism was a vehement denial of the cleavage into classes which the economic strife of the preceding Gilded Age had seemed to portend for the American future. In part this lack of class consciousness resulted from the movement's drawing its members from almost all classes. If small businessmen were the special darlings of the Progressive program, farmers, laborers, and consumers were nonetheless members of the family. Even the rich were not excluded, for, as George Mowry has noted, "few reform movements in American history have had the support of more wealthy men."

But there was more to it than that. Lack of class consciousness sprang from a long American tradition in favor of social unity and in opposition to class divisions. "It was essential," Theodore Roosevelt wrote at the time of the coal strike of 1902, "that organized capital and organized labor should thoroughly understand that the third party, the great public, had vital interests, and overshadowing rights in such a crisis. . . ." "I should be ashamed of myself if I excited class feeling of any kind," Woodrow Wilson told an audience in 1912. "The government of our country cannot be lodged in any special class. . . ." When Robert La Follette was attacked for setting class against class, one of his newspaper supporters in Wisconsin rushed to his defense. "We challenge . . . his enemies to cite one line in which Bob La Follette has ever arrayed class against class, one speech in which he has not been as concerned for the civic-minded rich man as for the poor. . . ." In speaking for the people as a whole, the Progressives were refurbishing a sense of social unity inherited from an earlier America and one which the corrosive acid of capital and labor strife had almost obliterated.

On the surface it might appear that Progressivism and socialism would have much in common. Both were direct responses to the challenge of industrialization and urbanization. But their conceptions of the good society were as far apart as the continents which spawned them. Where socialism sought to exacerbate class division, Progressivism tried to heal it; where socialism denied the validity of private property, Progressivism attempted to strengthen it; where socialism looked forward to the co-operative society, Progressivism sang the praises of the individual.

Yet simply because both movements grew from the same soil, the triumph of Progressivism marked the end of a significant Socialist movement in the United States. It would not be far wrong to see in the reform movement of the early twentieth century one of the most formidable obstacles to the growth of socialism in America. Nor is it accidental that the high point of socialism's popularity in this country was reached in 1912, the same year Progressivism captured the national government. Never again would any Socialist or Communist candidate receive as large a percentage of the votes as Eugene Debs did in 1912.

Like a safety valve on a steam engine, the reforms of the Progressive era seemed to draw off the popular pressure for drastic social change which had been building up during the many years of untrammeled industrialism. With that release of pressure, socialism lost its only chance for power. "The accomplishments of the Interstate

Commerce Commission are the greatest triumphs of modern times in scientific government," moderate Progressive Samuel Untermyer concluded in 1911. "It saved us from government ownership of the Railroads, as the like regulation of Industrial Corporations will save us from Socialism." Especially conscious of this role of Progressivism was Theodore Roosevelt. Irritated by the attacks made upon him by the coal operators during the strike of 1902, he asked testily, "Do they not realize they are putting a very heavy burden on us who stand against socialism; against anarchic disorder?"

No better summation of that blending of the old ideals with the new social forces can be provided than a statement of Fred Howe in 1907. He began by reiterating the old Jeffersonian goals of American reform. "The great problem now before the American people is, how can opportunity be kept open; how can industry be saved from privilege; how can our politics be left to the unimpeded action of talent and ability?" But then he acknowledged that these old goals must be achieved through new means. "This is the problem which the city has to solve, even more than the state or the nation. For in the city the life of the future is to be found." Snipping here, pasting there, the Progressives fitted the old American Creed to the new conditions of an industrial and urban society in a more than tolerable fashion. Despite their name, the Progressives stand forth as true exemplars of American conservatism.

It would be misleading, however, in pointing out the dominant conservative aspects of Progressivism, to lose sight of those elements in the movement which were novel. From what has been said about the reforms of the Progressives, it is apparent that the Jeffersonian principle of the limited state found no analogue in Progressive thought. The seeds of the welfare state which were beginning to sprout in Populism grew under the forcing frame of Progressivism, to reach full flower in the hothouse of the New Deal. Populism buried the limited state, once and for all; no Progressive endeavored to resurrect it.

There was yet another new element which Progressivism introduced into American thought. Although most Progressives were naïvely but strongly absolutistic in their morality, there were also a number of intellectuals in the movement who were discarding that outlook. Though small in number, these Progressives developed a view of the ancient problem of evil which was conspicuously relativistic and social. For "we now see, or begin to see, if vaguely," Brand Whitlock remarked, "that, except in metaphysics, there is no such thing in our complex life as an absolute good or an absolute bad, and to the problem of evil we begin to apply the conception of economic influences, social influences, pathological influences . . . most of us know little or nothing about." From Golden Rule Jones, Whitlock had learned that criminals "were all people, just folks, and that they had so much more good than bad in them, that if some way could be devised whereby they might have a little better opportunity to develop the good, there was hope for all of them." Corruption, the apathy of the citizenry, and "poverty, vice, crime and disease," Frederick Howe concluded, "are due to causes economic and industrial. They are traceable to our institutions, rather than to the depravity of human nature." Herbert Croly, the high priest of Progressive ideology, observed, "Jefferson believed theoretically in human goodness, but in actual practice his faith in human nature was exceedingly restricted." The Progressives went far beyond Jefferson in seeing men as essentially good and merely corrupted by environment.

The origins of this moral relativism can be traced to the new environment of the city. In a rural society, the milieu is provided by nature; it is given, like an axiom in a geometry book—something one assumes. Under such conditions, it made sense for men to believe that each individual was the master of his future; that his destiny was a more or less direct consequence of his own moral choices. The advance of the city and the onslaught of industrialism, however, destroyed that uncomplicated and illusory sociology. In the industrial city, the framework in which men worked out their morality was socially created, put together by the hands of man, not the hands of God. The evil which flourished in this environment was easily conceived of as the creation of men's collective action; from this it would follow that no one man was responsible for the evil which he personally committed. Hence someone like Golden Rule Jones refused to believe that the criminals and prostitutes with whom his office brought him into contact were truly responsible for their transgressions. Nothing was any longer absolute, not even evil.

If moral relativism now became increasingly commonplace in the upper intellectual reaches of society, men farther down on the scale would soon recognize that "we are all in the same boat together."

Under the pressures of the Great Depression, this acknowledgment that man possessed only limited moral and economic independence would come completely out into the open as economic debacle dragged down good and evil men into common ruin.

CHAPTER XIII

The Third American Revolution

TWICE since the founding of the Republic, cataclysmic events have sliced through the fabric of American life, snapping many of the threads which ordinarily bind the past to the future. The War for the Union was one such event, the Great Depression of the 1930's the other. And, as the Civil War was precipitated from the political and moral tensions of the preceding era, so the Great Depression was a culmination of the social and economic forces of industrialization and urbanization which had been transforming America since 1865. A depression of such pervasiveness as that of the thirties could happen only to a people already tightly interlaced by the multitudinous cords of a machine civilization and embedded in the matrix of an urban society.

In all our history no other economic collapse brought so many Americans to near starvation, endured so long, or came so close to overturning the basic institutions of American life. It is understandable, therefore, that from that experience should issue a new conception of the good society.

1. "HUNGER IS NOT DEBATABLE"

The economic dimensions of the Great Depression are quickly sketched—too quickly perhaps to permit a full appreciation of the abyss into which the economy slid between 1929 and 1933. The value of stocks on the New York Exchange, for example, slumped from a high of $87 billion in 1929 to a mere $19 billion in 1933. Wholesale prices dropped 38 per cent by 1933 and farm prices seemed almost to have ceased to exist: they were 60 per cent below the low level of 1929. Within less than three years, realized national income plummeted to almost half of what it had been in the last boom year; and the same was true of industrial production. The human cost of this catastrophic breakdown in the complicated industrial machine, *Fortune* magazine estimated in September, 1932, was 10 million totally unemployed or 25 million people without any source of income.

To worsen matters, the industrial stagnation was accompanied by a spreading fever of bank failures. First here and there, then all over the country, the banks began to close their doors in the faces of their depositors. By the beginning of 1933, the financial self-confidence of the nation reached a dangerously low level, requiring the new administration of Franklin Roosevelt, as its first official act, to order the closing of all banks. In all, more than 10,000 deposit banks failed in the five years after 1929. If the banks, the custodians of the measure of value, proved to be unsound, men might well wonder what was left to cling to as the winds of disaster gained in fury.

Unnerving as the failure of the banks undoubtedly was, for most people the Great Depression became starkly real only when unemployment struck. No one knew whom it would hit next; the jobless were everywhere—in the cities, in the towns, on the farms. Their helplessness, their bewilderment, were often written in their faces, reflected in their discouraged gaits, and mirrored in their run-down dwellings. John Dos Passos reported seeing the unemployed of Detroit in 1932 living in caves scooped out of giant abandoned sand piles. Though it was said that no one would be allowed to starve, *Fortune,* in September, 1932, suggested that some had already. The magazine counted the millions of the unemployed and told of families subsisting on a single loaf of bread for over a week or of going without food for two or three days on end. Discarded and spoiled vegetables or wild dandelions were the substance of meals for some families. Other reports in 1933 told of at least twenty-nine persons who died of starvation in New York City. Moreover, thousands must have died from diseases which gained an easy foothold in weakened and underfed bodies; but these unfortunates were never counted. Food, casually consumed in good times, suddenly became the focus of existence for thousands. In their desperation some urban folk actually tried to wring their food from the barren soil of the city. In Gary, Indiana, for example, 20,000 families were raising food on lots lent by the city; Robert and Helen Lynd reported that in Middletown in 1933, 2,500 of the town's 48,000 people eked out their food budgets with relief gardens.

The spreading unemployment generated new and deep-seated fears. When the unkempt veterans of the First World War camped in Washington in 1932, demanding a bonus to tide them over their joblessness, a fearful and unsure President had them dispersed by troops armed with tear gas. And when Congress in that same year voted a 10 per cent cut in government salaries, President Hoover sent a secret message urging that the enlisted men of the Army and the Navy be excluded from such decreases so that in case of domestic troubles the federal government would not be compelled to rely upon disgruntled troops.

Nor was it only the federal government that felt uneasy in the presence of the specter which was stalking the land. Malcolm Cowley, in an eyewitness account, described how the trucks bearing the disillusioned veterans out of Washington were quickly sped through town after town, the local authorities fearing that some of the unemployed veterans would jump off and become burdens on already overtaxed communities. Cowley tells of one citizen in Washington, not a marcher at all, who was hurriedly bundled into a truck by mistake and could not get off until he reached Indianapolis!

Driven by their desperation, some Americans began to talk of violence. Mutterings of revolution and threats to return with rifles were heard among the bonus marchers as they left Washington. Out on the farms, the dissatisfaction of the veterans was matched by sullen farmers who closed the courts and disrupted mortgage auctions to save their homes. The ugly turn which the discontent could take was revealed by the arrest of a man in Wisconsin in 1932 on suspicion of having removed a spike from the railroad track over which President Hoover's train was to pass. In that bleak year it was not uncommon for the President of the United States to be booed and hooted as he doggedly pursued his ill-starred campaign for re-election. To Theodore Dreiser, as the cold night of the depression settled over the land, it seemed that Karl Marx's prediction "that Capitalism would eventually evolve into failure . . . has come true."

Even for the Lords of Creation, as Frederick Lewis Allen was to call them, the Great Depression was an unsettling and confusing experience. "I'm afraid, every man is afraid," confessed Charles M. Schwab of United States Steel. "I don't know, we don't know, whether the values we have are going to be real next month or not." And in the very early months of the Roosevelt administration, Harold Ickes, attending a dinner of the Chamber of Commerce of the United States, could sense the pitiable impotence to which the nation's industrial leaders had sunk. "The great and the mighty in the business world were there in force," he rather gleefully noted in his diary, "and I couldn't help thinking how so many of these great and mighty were crawling to Washington on their hands and knees these days to beg the Government to run their businesses for them."

But it was the unspectacular, the everyday dreariness of unemployment that must have cut the deepest and endured the longest as far as the ordinary American was concerned. The simplest things of life, once taken for granted, now became points of irritation. "I forget how to cook good since I have nothing to cook with," remarked one housewife. Children lost their appetites upon seeing the milk and mush "that they have seen so often." Even the rare treat of fresh meat could not awaken an appetite long accustomed to disappointment and pallid food.

The routine entertainments of the poor were casualties to unemployment. "Suppose you go to a friend's house and she gives you a cup of tea and something," the wife of an unemployed worker told a social worker. "You feel ashamed. You think, now I got to do the same when she comes to my house. You know you can't so you stay home." Shifts in entertainment patterns among the unemployed were revealed in a study made of some 200 families in New Haven. Before the breadwinner lost his job, some 55 per cent went to the movies; once unemployment hit, however, only 16 per cent did. In the days when work was to be had, only 13 per cent found recreation in "sitting around the house," but now 25 per cent did so. With the loss of their jobs, 12 per cent of the men admitted they "chatted and gossiped" for recreation, although none of them did when they had work.

Unemployment's effect upon the family was often more profound and far-reaching. In recounting the case history of the Raparka family, one sociologist wrote that when Mr. Raparka "lost his job in the fall of 1933, he dominated the family. Two years later it was Mrs. Raparka who was the center of authority." Again and again social workers chronicled the alteration in the father's position in the family during a period of unemployment. Humiliation settled over many a father no longer able to fulfill his accustomed role in the family. "I would rather turn on the gas and put an end to the whole family than let my wife support me," was the way one unemployed father put it. One investigator found that one fifth of her sample of fifty-nine families exhibited a breakdown in the father's authority, particularly in the eyes of the wife. For example, one wife said, "When your husband cannot provide for the family and makes you worry so, you lose your love for him."

Fathers discovered that without the usual financial power to buy bikes or bestow nickels, their control and authority over children were seriously weakened and sometimes completely undermined. In one family where the father was unemployed for a long time, his role was almost completely taken over by the eldest son. The father himself admitted: "The son of twenty-two is just like a father around the house. He tries to settle any little brother-and-sister fights and even encourages me and my wife." In the same family, a younger son who was working summed up his relationship to his parents in a few words. "I remind them," he said, "who makes the money. They don't say much. They just take it, that's all. *I'm* not the one on relief." In such circumstances, it is no exaggeration to say that the massive weight of the depression was grinding away at the bedrock of American institutions.

The ties of a home struck by unemployment were weak and the opportunities for fruitful and satisfying work were almost totally absent in 1932–33. *Fortune* reported in February, 1933, that something like 200,000 young men and boys were traveling around the country on railroad trains for lack of anything better to do. Tolerated by the railroads because of their obvious poverty and lack of jobs, the boys were often suffering from disease and malnutrition. The authorities in Los Angeles asserted, for example, that 25 per cent of those coming into the city needed clinical attention and 5 per cent required hospitalization. During a single season, one railroad announced, fifty such footloose boys were killed and one hundred injured. From Kansas City it was reported that girl wanderers, dressed in boy's clothing, were on the increase. To many such young people, now grown, the Great Depression must still seem the most purposeless, the most enervating period of their lives.

What Robert and Helen Lynd concluded for their study of Middletown in 1935 can be applied to America as a whole: ". . . the great knife of the depression had cut down impartially through the entire population cleaving open lives and hopes of rich as well as poor. The experience has been more nearly universal than any prolonged recent emotional experience in the city's history; it has approached in its elemental shock the primary experiences of birth and death."

2. THE END OF LAISSEZ FAIRE

Perhaps the most striking alteration in American thought which the depression fostered concerned the role of the government in the economy. Buffeted and bewildered by the economic debacle, the American people in the course of the 1930's abandoned, once and for all, the doctrine of laissez faire. This beau ideal of the nineteenth-century economists had become, ever since the days of Jackson, an increasingly cherished shibboleth of Americans. But now it was almost casually discarded. It is true, of course, that the rejection of laissez faire had a long history; certainly the Populists worked to undermine it. But with the depression the nation at large accepted the government as a permanent influence in the economy.[1]

Almost every one of the best-known measures of the federal government during the depression era made inroads into the hitherto private preserves of business and the individual. Furthermore, most of these new measures survived the period, taking their places as fundamental elements in the structure of American life. For modern Americans living under a federal government of transcendent influence and control in the economy, this is the historic meaning of the great depression.

Much of what is taken for granted today as the legitimate function of government and the social responsibility of business began only with the legislation of these turbulent years. Out of the investigation of banking and bankers in 1933, for example, issued legislation which separated commercial banking from the stock and bond markets, and insured the bank deposits of ordinary citizens. The stock market, like the banks, was placed under new controls and a higher sense of responsibility to the public imposed upon it by the

[1] A complementary and highly suggestive way of viewing this trend away from laissez faire, of which the events of the 1930's are a culmination, is that taken in K. William Kapp, *The Social Costs of Private Enterprise* (Cambridge, Mass., 1950). Kapp observes that for a long time private enterprise had shifted the social costs of production—like industrially polluted water, industrial injuries, smoke nuisances and hazards, unemployment, and the like —onto society. The decline of laissez faire has, in this view, actually been a movement to compel industry to pay for those social costs of production which it has hitherto shirked.

new Securities and Exchange Commission. The lesson of Black Tuesday in 1929 had not been forgotten; the classic free market itself—the Exchange—was hereafter to be under continuous governmental scrutiny.

The three Agricultural Adjustment Acts of 1933, 1936, and 1938, while somewhat diverse in detail, laid down the basic lines of what is still today the American approach to the agricultural problem. Ever since the collapse of the boom after the First World War, American agriculture had suffered from the low prices born of the tremendous surpluses. Unable to devise a method for expanding markets to absorb the excess, the government turned to restriction of output as the only feasible alternative. But because restriction of output meant curtailment of income for the farmer, it became necessary, if farm income was to be sustained, that farmers be compensated for their cut in production. Thus was inaugurated the singular phenomenon, which is still a part of the American answer to the agricultural surplus, of paying farmers for *not* growing crops. The other device introduced for raising farm prices, and still the mainstay of our farm policy, came with the 1938 act, which provided that the government would purchase and store excess farm goods, thus supporting the price level by withdrawing the surplus from the competitive market. Both methods constitute a subsidy for the farmer from society at large.[2]

Though the Eisenhower administration in the 1950's called for a return to a free market in farm products, at least in part—that is, the removal of government supports from prices—Congress refused to go along. Under Kennedy and Johnson government subsidy for agriculture has been continued as it undoubtedly will be under the Nixon administration. A free market in agriculture was in operation during the twenties, but it succeeded only in making farmers the economic stepchildren of an otherwise prosperous decade. Moreover, today the farm bloc is too powerful politically to be treated so cavalierly. Furthermore, the depression has taught most Ameri-

---

[2] On the day that the first AAA was declared unconstitutional, a Gallup poll revealed that, although the nation as a whole did not like the AAA, the farmers of the South and Midwest did. As a result, invalidation of the act by the Court did not mean the end of such a policy, but only the beginning of a search to find a new way of accomplishing the same end. Hence there were successive AAA's, whereas, when NRA was declared unconstitutional in 1935, it was dropped, primarily because neither business nor labor, for whose interests it had been organized, found much merit in its approach to their problems.

cans—and western Europeans as well—that a free market is not only a rarity in the modern world, but that it is sometimes inimical to a stable and lasting prosperity. All of the countries of western Europe also provide government subsidies to agriculture.

Perhaps the most imaginative and fruitful innovation arising out of the depression was the Tennessee Valley Authority, which transformed the heart of the South. "It was and is literally a down to earth experiment," native Tennesseean Broadus Mitchell has written, "with all that we know from test tube and logarithm tables called on to help. It was a union of heart and mind to restore what had been wasted. It was a social resurrection." For the TVA was much more than flood and erosion control or even hydroelectric power—though its gleaming white dams are perhaps its most striking and best-known monuments. It was social planning of the most humane sort, where even the dead were carefully removed from cemeteries before the waters backed up behind the dams. It brought new ideas, new wealth, new skills, new hope into a wasted, tired, and discouraged region.

At the time of the inception of the TVA, it was scarcely believable that the "backward" South would ever utilize all the power the great dams would create. But in its report of 1956, the Authority declared that the Valley's consumption of electricity far exceeded that produced from water sites: almost three quarters of TVA's power is now generated from steam power, not from waterfall. In large part it was the TVA which taught the Valley how to use more power to expand its industries and to lighten the people's burdens. Back in 1935, Drew and Leon Pearson saw this creation of consumer demand in action. "Uncle Sam is a drummer with a commercial line to sell," they wrote in *Harper's Magazine*. "He sold liberty bonds before, but never refrigerators."

Measured against textbook definitions, the TVA is unquestionably socialism. The government owns the means of production and, moreover, it competes with private producers of electricity.[3] But prag-

[3] The extent of the intellectual change which the depression measures introduced can be appreciated by a quotation from President Hoover's veto in 1931 of a bill to develop a public power project in what was later to be the TVA area. "I am firmly opposed to the Government entering into any business the major purpose of which is competition with our citizens." Emergency measures of such a character might be tolerated, he said. "But for the Federal government deliberately to go out to build up and expand such an occasion to the major purpose of a power and manufacturing business is to break down the initiative and enterprise of the American people; it is destruction of equal-

matic Americans—and particularly those living in the Valley—have had few sleepless nights as a consequence of this fact. The TVA does its appointed job, and apparently it is here to stay. For when the Eisenhower administration sought to establish an alternative to the expansion of the TVA power facilities by awarding a contract for a steam plant to a private firm—Dixon-Yates—friends of the TVA in and out of Congress forced the cancellation of the contract. And despite Eisenhower's unfortunate reference to it as "creeping socialism," the TVA has been absorbed into that new American Way fashioned by the experimentalism of the American people out of the wreckage of the Great Depression.

Undoubtedly social security deserves the appellation "revolutionary" quite as much as the TVA; it brought government into the lives of people as nothing had since the draft and the income tax. Social security legislation actually comprises two systems: insurance against old age and insurance in the event of loss of work. The first system was completely organized and operated by the federal government; the second was shared with the states—but the national government set the standards; both were clear acknowledgment of the changes which had taken place in the family and in the business of making a living in America. No longer in urban America could the old folks, whose proportion in the society was steadily increasing, count on being taken in by their offspring as had been customary in a more agrarian world. Besides, such a makeshift arrangement was scarcely satisfying to the self-respect of the oldsters. With the transformation of the economy by industrialization, most Americans had become helpless before the vagaries of the business cycle. As a consequence of the social forces which were steadily augmenting social insecurity, only collective action by the government could arrest the drift.

To have the government concerned about the security of the individual was a new thing. Keenly aware of the novelty of this aim in individualistic America,[4] Roosevelt was careful to deny any serious departure from traditional paths. "These three great objectives—the

---

ity of opportunity amongst our people; it is the negation of the ideals upon which our civilization has been based."

[4] Characteristically enough, as his memoirs show, President Hoover had long been interested in both old-age and unemployment insurance, but always such schemes were to be worked out through private insurance companies, or at best with the states—never under the auspices of the federal government. "It required a great depression," he has written somewhat ruefully, "to awaken interest in the idea" of unemployment insurance.

security of the home, the security of livelihood, and the security of social insurance," he said in 1934, constitute "a minimum of the promise that we can offer to the American people." But this, he quickly added, "does not indicate a change in values."

Whether the American people thought their values had changed is not nearly as important as the fact that they accepted social security. And the proof that they did is shown in the steady increase in the proportion of the population covered by the old-age benefit program since 1935; today farm workers as well as the great preponderance of nonfarm workers are included in the system. Apart from being a minimum protection for the individual and society against the dry rot of industrial idleness, unemployment insurance is now recognized as one of the major devices for warding off another depression.

It is true, as proponents of the agrarian life have been quick to point out, that an industrialized people, stripped as they are of their economic self-reliance, have felt the need for social insurance more than people in other types of society. But it is perhaps just as important to recognize that it is only in such a highly productive society that people can even dare to dream of social security. Men in other ages have felt the biting pains of economic crisis, but few preindustrial people have ever enjoyed that surfeit of goods which permits the fat years to fill out the lean ones. But like so much else concerning industrialism, it is not always easy to calculate whether the boons it offers exceed in value the burdens which it imposes.

For the average man, the scourge of unemployment was the essence of the depression. Widespread unemployment, permeating all ranks and stations in society, drove the American people and their government into some of their most determined and deliberate departures from the hallowed policy of "hands off." But despite the determination, as late as 1938 the workless still numbered almost ten million—two thirds as great as in 1932 under President Hoover. The governmental policies of the 1930's never appreciably diminished the horde of unemployed—only the war prosperity of 1940 and after did that—but the providing of jobs by the federal government was a reflection of the people's new conviction that the government had a responsibility to alleviate economic disaster. Such bold action on the part of government, after the ineffective, if earnest approach of the Hoover administration, was a tonic for the dragging spirits of the people.[5]

[5] It was the misfortune of Herbert Hoover to have been President at a time

A whole range of agencies, from the Civil Works Administration (CWA) to the Works Progress Administration (WPA), were created to carry the attack against unemployment. It is true that the vast program of relief which was organized was not "permanent" in the sense that it is still in being, but for two reasons it deserves to be discussed here. First, since these agencies constituted America's principal weapon against unemployment, some form of them will surely be utilized if a depression should occur again. Second, the various relief agencies of the period afford the best examples of the new welfare outlook, which was then in the process of formation.

Though in the beginning relief programs were premised on little more than Harry Hopkins' celebrated dictum, "Hunger is not debatable," much more complex solutions to unemployment were soon worked out. The relief program of the WPA, which after 1935 was the major relief agency, was a case in point. In 1937, *Fortune* magazine commented on "the evolution of unemployment relief from tool to institution"—a recognition of the importance and duration of relief in America. "In 1936, the federal government was so deeply involved in the relief of the unemployed," *Fortune* contended, "that it was not only keeping them alive, but it was also giving them an opportunity to work; and not only giving them an opportunity to work but giving them an opportunity to work at jobs for which they were peculiarly fitted; and not only giving them an opportunity to work at jobs for which they were peculiarly fitted, but creating for them jobs of an interest and usefulness which they could not have expected to find in private employment." The statement somewhat

---

when his considerable administrative and intellectual gifts were hamstrung by his basic political philosophy, which, instead of being a guide to action, served as an obstacle. Much more of an old-fashioned liberal than a reactionary, and deeply attached to the Jeffersonian dogma of the limited powers of the federal government, Hoover was psychologically and philosophically unable to use the immense powers and resources of his office in attacking unemployment. Back in 1860–61, another President—James Buchanan—had been paralyzed in the midst of a national crisis by his limited conception of the federal power, but in that instance his inaction was palliated by the fact that his successor was to take office within less than three months. Hoover, however, wrestled with the depression for three years. During that trying period he did a number of things to combat the depression, but he always stoutly held to his rigid intellectual position that federally supplied and administered relief would destroy the foundations of the nation. Never has an American President, including the two Adamses, defied overwhelming popular opinion for so long for the sake of his own ideals as Herbert Hoover did then; and never has a President since Buchanan fallen so quickly into obscurity as Hoover did after March 4, 1933.

distorts the work of the WPA, but it sums up the main outlines of the evolution of the relief program.

The various artistic and cultural employment programs of the WPA are excellent examples of how relief provided more than employment, though any of the youth agencies like the Civilian Conservation Corps or the National Youth Administration (it subsidized student work) would serve equally well. At its peak, the Federal Writers' Project employed some 6,000 journalists, poets, novelists, and Ph.D.'s of one sort or another; unknowns worked on the same payroll, if not side by side, with John Steinbeck, Vardis Fisher, and Conrad Aiken. The $46 million expended on art—that is, painting and sculpture—by the WPA in 1936–37 exceeded the artistic budget of any country outside the totalitarian orbit—and there art was frankly propagandistic. *Fortune,* in May, 1937, found the American government's sponsorship of art singularly free of censorship or propaganda. The magazine concluded that "by and large the Arts Projects have been given a freedom no one would have thought possible in a government run undertaking. And by and large that freedom has not been abused." During the first fifteen months of the Federal Music Project, some fifty million people heard live concerts; in the first year of the WPA Theater, sixty million people in thirty states saw performances, with weekly attendance running to half a million. T. S. Eliot's *Murder in the Cathedral,* too risky for a commercial producer, was presented in New York by the Federal Theater to 40,000 people at a top price of 55 cents.

"What the government's experiments in music, painting, and the theater actually did," concluded *Fortune* in May, 1937, "even in their first year, was to work a sort of cultural revolution in America." For the first time the American audience and the American artist were brought face to face for their mutual benefit. "Art in America is being given its chance," said the British writer Ford Madox Ford, "and there has been nothing like it since before the Reformation. . . ."

Instead of being ignored on the superficially plausible grounds of the exigencies of the depression, the precious skills of thousands of painters, writers, and musicians were utilized. By this timely rescue of skills, tastes, and talents from the deadening hand of unemployment, the American people, through their government, showed their humanity and social imagination. Important for the future was the foresight displayed in the conserving of artistic talents and creations for the enrichment of generations to come.

The entrance of the federal government into a vast program of relief work was an abrupt departure from all previous practice, but it proved enduring. "When President Roosevelt laid it down that government had a social responsibility to care for the victims of the business cycle," *Fortune* remarked prophetically in 1937, "he set in motion an irreversible process." The burden of unemployment relief was too heavy to be carried by local government or private charities in an industrialized society; from now on, the national government would be expected to shoulder the responsibility. "Those who are on relief and in close contact otherwise with public matters realize that what has happened to the country is a bloodless revolution," wrote an anonymous relief recipient in *Harper's* in 1936. The government, he said, has assumed a new role in depressions, and only the rich might still be oblivious to it. But they too "will know it by 1940. And in time," they will "come to approve the idea of everyone having enough to eat."[6] Few people escaped the wide net of the depression: "Anybody sinks after a while," the anonymous reliefer pointed out. "Even you would have if God hadn't preserved, without apparent rhyme or reason, your job and your income." That the depression was a threat to all was perhaps the first lesson gained from the 1930's.

The second was that only through collective defense could such a threat be met. By virtue of the vigorous attack made upon the economic problems of the thirties by the government, the age-old conviction that dips in the business cycle were either the will of God or the consequence of unalterable economic laws was effectively demolished. As recently as 1931, President Hoover had told an audience that some people "have indomitable confidence that by some legerdemain we can legislate ourselves out of a world-wide depression. Such views are as accurate as the belief that we can exorcise a Caribbean hurricane." From the experience of the depression era, the American people learned that something could and ought to be done when economic disaster strikes. No party and no politician with a future will ever again dare to take the fatalistic course of Herbert Hoover in 1929–33.

---

[6] The providing of work relief instead of the dole did more than fill hungry stomachs; it re-established faith in America and in one's fellow man. "I'm proud of our United States," said one relief recipient. "There ain't no other nation in the world that would have sense enough to think of WPA and all the other A's." The wife of one WPA worker was quoted as saying, "We aren't on relief any more—my man is working for the government."

As the enactment of the Employment Act of 1946 showed, the prevention of depression now occupies top listing among the social anxieties of the American people. The act created a permanent Council of Economic Advisers to the President, to keep him continuously informed on the state of the economy and to advise him on the measures necessary to avoid an economic decline. And the Joint Committee on the Economic Report does the same for Congress.

Today political figures who indignantly repudiate any "left-wing" philosophy of any sort readily accept this inheritance from the depression. "Never again shall we allow a depression in the United States," vowed Republican candidate Eisenhower in 1952. As soon as we "foresee the signs of any recession and depression," he promised, ". . . the full power of private industry, of municipal government, of state government, of the Federal Government will be mobilized to see that that does not happen." Ignoring the fact that as a prospective federal official he had promised more than he could deliver, he innocently and accurately added, "I cannot pledge you more than that." Sensing the tremendous importance of the matter to the American people, Eisenhower made substantially the same statement three other times—at Yonkers, Peoria, and Pittsburgh. At Yonkers he said that he had "repeated this particular pledge over and over again in the United States" and that he and his associates were "dedicated to this proposition. . . ."

In the White House, Eisenhower continued to reflect this underlying and persistent fear that a depression would once again stride through the land. According to the account in Robert Donovan's semiofficial *Eisenhower: The Inside Story,* at session after session of the Cabinet during the recession of 1953–54, it was the President who stressed the urgency of the economic situation. It was he who constantly prodded Arthur F. Burns of the Council of Economic Advisers to prepare plans with which to forestall a serious drop in the economic indicators. Indeed as late as June, 1954, just after Burns had delivered an optimistic report on the condition and future of the economy, as Donovan tells it, "The President . . . was still concerned about whether the administration was doing enough. Even though it jarred the logic of some members of the Cabinet, he insisted, everything possible must be done to restore vigor to the economy. It was important, the President said, to produce results and to err on the side of doing too much rather than too little."

In the midst of the recession of 1957–58, Vice-President Richard Nixon, speaking on April 24, 1958, specifically repudiated the traditional approach of expecting the economy to right itself without government intervention. "Let us recognize once and for all," he told his audience, "that the time is past in the United States when the Federal Government can stand by and allow a recession to be prolonged or to deepen into depression without decisive Government action." Though Eisenhower was obviously worried that hasty measures might bring on further inflation, on May 20, in a public address, he agreed with the Vice-President that the government had "a continuing responsibility . . . to help counteract recession." In the same speech the President enumerated concrete measures already taken, such as extension of unemployment benefits, speeding up of defense and civilian procurement, acceleration of government construction projects, and the easing of credit by the Federal Reserve.

The evident acceptance of the new obligations of government in the economy on the part of the first Republican administration since the New Deal is strikingly suggestive of the shock which the depression dealt conventional economic thought in America.

3. REVOLUTION IN POLITICS

In passing through the dark valley of the depression, Americans discarded more than conventional economics; they also revised their political preferences. Like downswings in other times, the depression of the thirties spawned a number of ephemeral political aberrations like the Share the Wealth of Huey Long, the oldsters' rebellion led by Dr. Francis E. Townsend, and the soured Populism of Father Coughlin's crusade for Social Justice. But the most portentous shift in popular political thought was the Roosevelt Revolution—the raising of the Democratic party to the predominant position in American political life. As the War for the Union became the stock in trade of the Republicans after 1865, so the Great Depression became the Democrats' primary justification; they have made as steady use of the tattered shirt as the Republicans did of the bloody shirt. And the tactic has worked; during the fifties and sixties, as the national elections show, there have been many more Democrats than Republicans in the country. Although Republican Eisenhower was elected by large majorities in 1952 and 1956, only in his first election was he able to carry a Republican Congress into office with him. Not since 1848 has a winning President failed to bring a House of Representatives of his own party into power. Eisenhower's failure to do so in 1956, despite his immense personal popularity, and Nixon's inability to do so in 1968 suggest that most American voters are still loyal to the Democratic party, despite their willingness to support an occasional Republican Presidential candidate. The grip of the depression on the American psyche has barely loosened a full generation after 1940.

The massive shift in popular opinion from the Republican to the Democratic party was a direct result of the wide range of social groups to which the Democratic administration offered succor and recognition. Midwestern farmers, for example, had always been deemed safe within the Republican fold, but after the AAA program they eagerly joined the Roosevelt coalition. And as late as 1948, at least, it was evident that many were still there, for the farmers held the key to Harry Truman's unexpected victory that year. Numerous relief payments to workers, labor legislation, and the benevolent interest of the President himself succeeded in tying the working classes of the city more firmly and in greater numbers than ever before to the wheels of the Democratic chariot. In the election of 1956, under the impact of the Eisenhower charisma, some urban groups deserted the Democrats, but they were back in the fold in 1960 to help elect John F. Kennedy and most of them were still there in 1968 to offer their support to Hubert Humphrey. And even when some of the big cities voted for Eisenhower in 1956, they continued to support Democratic candidates for Congress, suggesting that it was Eisenhower's personal, not his Republican, appeal that won them.

Perhaps the most unexpected result of the revolution was the transfer of the Negro vote from the Republicans, where it had lain for three generations, to the Democrats. Like so much else in the twentieth century, this change in the Negro's voting habits is closely linked to the growth of industrialization. For almost half a century after the end of slavery, about 90 per cent of the Negro population of the country lived in the South; in 1910, for example, the figure was 89 per cent. But with the expansion of northern industry during the First World War, there was an increasing demand for skilled and unskilled labor. For the first time in American history, large numbers of Negroes, attracted by the new opportunities in northern industry, left the South. In the seven years after 1916, it has been estimated, as many as a million Negroes migrated northward. Northern industrial centers experienced enormous increases in their Negro populations between the censuses of 1910 and 1920. In Akron, Ohio, for example, the increase was over 780 per cent; in Cleveland, 307 per cent; and in Detroit, the automobile industry attracted enough new workers to swell the Negro population by over 620 per cent. This emigration from the South continued through the twenties. Whereas in the Census of 1920 15 per cent of the Negro population lived outside the South, in 1930 20 per cent of the Negroes made their homes in the North and the West. In the course of the single decade of the twenties, the Negro population in the North jumped over 64 per cent, while it grew in the South by only 5 per cent. So massive was this new migration, much of which came out of the Deep South,[7] that in 1920, for the first time in the history of the nation, the statistical center of the Negro population reversed its historic southwestern course and shifted north and east.

In moving out of the South the black man divested himself of two distinguishing social and political characteristics. In the South the Negro was typically rural and usually disfranchised, despite the Fifteenth Amendment. Once in the North, the Negro became primarily a city dweller, and he was permitted to exercise the vote. The new urban setting of the Negro, of course, was dictated by the industry which drew him northward. In 1930, over 88 per cent of the northern Negroes and 82 percent of Negroes in the West lived in cities; by contrast, 68 per cent of the Negroes in the South lived on the land. The concentration of Negroes in northern cities was even greater than these figures suggest; one third of them lived in only four northern cities. The conjuncture of the ballot and urban concentration created a formidable Negro voting power for the first time in the North. It is not surprising, therefore, that the election of the first Negro congressman outside of the South—that of De Priest in 1929—occurred in Chicago only a decade after the massive migration to the North. Not much before that date were

---

[7] Heretofore most Negro migration, which rarely exceeded 10,000 annually, had come from the states of the upper South. The new migration, however, was significant in that it was drawn from the lower South. Between 1900 and 1910, for example, a mere 2,000 Negroes left South Carolina for Pennsylvania; in the following decade, 16,196 did. Only 781 Negroes left Alabama for Ohio in the ten years before 1910; in the subsequent decade, 17,500 made the trip —and so it went in state after state in the Deep South. This movement of Negroes out of the area of their greatest concentration, of course, has had a profound effect not only on the future of the Negro in the South but has also exposed white hostility in the North.

there enough northern Negroes to compel politicians and parties to take them into account.

What party allegiance they would assume, however, was determined by other considerations. As Mark Hanna, the powerful Republican boss at the turn of the century, said, "I carry the Negro vote around in my vest pocket." He did; and other Republican bosses before and after him could say the same. To tell the truth, where could the Negro find sympathy but in the Republican party, the party of the Emancipator? As the Negro leader Frederick Douglass is supposed to have warned his followers: "The Republican party is the ship; all else is the sea." Was it to be expected that the black man could look for support from the Democrats, the party of the Southern white man? Well, at least not until Republican promises on behalf of the black man had worn thin enough to force his looking elsewhere.

During the optimism of the Progressive period, a few middle-class Negroes and intellectuals did talk of playing off the Democrats against the inertia-ridden Republicans. Some Negro leaders, for example, urged support of Woodrow Wilson in 1912 on the ground that he was untainted with the "lily-white" practices of which both Taft and Theodore Roosevelt were plainly guilty. Disillusionment for those Negro leaders, however, was fast in coming. True to his southern training and the southern bias of his party, Wilson in office quickly introduced segregation into the federal service in Washington. Thus it turned out that Progressivism, in both its Democratic and Republican forms, failed to include the Negro in its vision of a better America. The incipient movement for a two-party system for Negroes was halted for another two decades.

In the depths of the depression, even though there was some dissatisfaction with Hoover among Negro leaders, it is clear that the rank-and-file black voter clung to his Republican faith. The name Franklin Roosevelt carried no magic for Negroes in 1932. In the black wards of Chicago that year, Roosevelt picked up only 23 per cent of the vote—a ratio smaller than Al Smith's in the prosperous year of 1928. It was the same among the Negroes in Cleveland; Detroit Negroes awarded F.D.R. only a little more than a third of their votes.

By 1936, however, the somersault had been executed. At that election Chicago's Black Belt gave Roosevelt 49 per cent of its votes; the Negroes of Cleveland went all out for the President—62 per cent—even though in 1932 they had awarded Hoover 72 per cent of their ballots. Roosevelt garnered almost two thirds of the Negro vote in Detroit, and the four Negro wards in Philadelphia each gave him a majority of 5,000. The swing to the Democrats had been forecast in 1934, when the first Democratic Negro congressman in American history was elected from Chicago. Between 1936 and 1940, exactly half of the eighteen Negroes elected to state legislatures were Democrats. Though a tendency has been developing among some Negro leaders since the Second World War to be more critical of their new Democratic allies, Samuel Lubell reported that in the election of 1950 there was "less of a break among Negroes than among any other major group in the Roosevelt Coalition." Despite the fact that civil rights had become a supercharged issue in the country at the time of the 1956 elections, Negroes, particularly in the North, continued to adhere to their recent Democratic conversion.[8]

What brought about this dramatic reversal? Part of the answer, of course, lies in the demographic facts of migration, but, as the Negro voting in 1932 demonstrates, the really operative force was the Roosevelt administration's recognition of the Negro. It is noteworthy that very little of the Democratic appeal to the Negro before 1940 can be illustrated in pronouncements or even in particular pieces of legislation. Only rarely does one find in the literature of Franklin Roosevelt and his New Deal such self-conscious appeals to the Negro as, say, in Harry Truman's Fair Deal or in Lyndon Johnson's famous address at Howard University in 1964.

There are several reasons for this. Primary, of course, is the fact that Truman's Fair Deal developed after the Roosevelt regime had already given the Negro a bigger and higher platform from which to articulate his demands. Moreover, because F.D.R., as a working politician, was always conscious of his party's southern wing, he would rarely antagonize the Southerners on the race issue alone. Fur-

[8] In a postelection survey of the Negro vote, *The New York Times,* November 11, 1956, p. 60, reported that "the party of Lincoln still has a long way to go to regain the politico-racial domination that it held so firmly from post-Civil War days until Franklin D. Roosevelt smashed it twenty years ago." And since the Democratic party under Kennedy and Johnson has made common cause with the Negro, the allegiance of black voters to that party has been almost unanimous. In the election of 1964 some Negro districts voted over 90 per cent for Lyndon Johnson. Even in 1968 Hubert Humphrey won the great majority of Negro votes, North and South.

thermore, Roosevelt as a leader was only tangentially aware of the Negro as a special case, as a minority to be singled out for exceptional treatment or concern. It was Eleanor Roosevelt, not Franklin, who went out of her way to be racially democratic and to concern herself with minority problems.

Nonetheless, the Roosevelt administration in its relatively undramatic fashion did much for the Negro, and this too stemmed from both the character of Franklin Roosevelt and the underlying philosophy of his administration. Just as the federal government found a place for the artist, so its humane outlook could not exclude the Negro. Thus if white men were to be given relief work, so must Negroes; and if so, then why not on an equal basis? "We are going to make a country in which no one is left out," the President said in another connection. And there was nothing to suggest that he had any mental reservations about race when he said it. Besides, although F.D.R. would do little publicly to antagonize his southern allies on the race question, his political perspicacity told him that in the North his power was heavily dependent upon city machines, many of which could or did benefit from Negro votes.

From the very outset the Democratic regime in Washington accepted the black man. Negroes were sprinkled through almost all its agencies either as advisers or as employees in a lesser capacity. The administration consulted and bestowed office upon nonpolitical Negroes (the Republicans had generally used Negroes as political appointees) like William H. Hastie, later to be the first Negro federal judge; Robert C. Weaver, the economist who later, under Lyndon Johnson, became the first Negro to sit in the Cabinet; and Mrs. Mary Bethune, the educator. When low-cost housing went up, Negroes got their share; Negro youths were welcome in the CCC and the NYA just as the whites were, though in the former the races were segregated. Recreational centers, hospitals, and schools were built for Negroes with federal money. Evenhandedly distributed federal relief funds were a gift from heaven to the black man, who was traditionally "hired last and fired first." As one Negro newspaperman told Samuel Lubell, "The really important thing about WPA is that it is a guarantee of a living wage. It means Negroes don't have to work for anything people want to give them." In the votings conducted by the AAA among farmers and those supervised by the National Labor Relations Board among workers, Negroes were treated the same as white men, even though in the South these same black men were excluded from political elections. In short, the Roosevelt administration took a number of concrete steps toward accepting the Negro as a full citizen—a simple innovation of portentous consequences. It would be difficult hereafter for any party in power to do less.

All the credit for converting the Negro from his Republicanism, however, should not go to positive acts of the Democratic administration; the objective economic and social environment also deserves some. Negroes, for example, began to secure jobs in a greater variety of occupations than ever before; under the impact of the depression, some employers were willing to hire Negroes for the first time, if only because the black worker accepted lower wages. Moreover, the C.I.O. unions now began to organize Negro workers on an equal basis with whites. To accomplish this end, Negro organizers were sent among the steel, maritime, and auto workers, and, when the permanent Congress of Industrial Organizations was formed in 1938, a clause in the constitution prohibited any constituent union from discriminating on grounds of race. The startling improvement in the Negro's position in the thirties could not help but redound to the benefit of the party in power.

By 1940, the capturing of the Negro vote by the Democrats was an accomplished fact, and the party platform of that year, using the word "Negro" for the first time, boasted of its friendship for the black man. "Our Negro citizens," the platform proclaimed, "have participated actively in the economic and social advances launched by this Administration." It would not have been an exaggeration, for once in the history of political platforms, if it had been noted that this was about the first time since the 1870's that any party could truthfully say half as much.

4. REVOLUTION IN LABOR

The change wrought in the political affiliations of Negroes by the depression was as nothing compared with the catalytic and subversive effect it worked upon the labor movement. And, analogous to the change in the preference of the Negro voter, the alteration in the position and power of labor was indebted to the action of the Roosevelt administration, the Democratic Congress, and the new social atmosphere of the depression era.

During the prosperity of the twenties the labor movement had gone into a decline rare in the history of unionization. The usual tendency had been for membership to rise in prosperous times and to decline in bad. But whereas in 1920 organized labor could claim its largest membership to date—some five million workers—by 1929 barely three million could be counted. Thus labor entered the depression under the handicap of declining membership. But instead of killing off many unions, as depressions had done earlier, the depression of the thirties seemed to stimulate a new and aggressive organizing spirit among the workers. In the light of the later tremendous expansion of union membership, it might be said that the depression created a class consciousness among American workingmen for the first time sufficient to permit large-scale unionization.

Despite the fact that the vast majority of unionized workers were then in the American Federation of Labor, that body was not destined to be the instrument of the new unionization. The Federation was too cautious, too saturated with Samuel Gompers' commitment to craft forms of organization and his fear of governmental interference, to be able to capitalize on the unrest among the workers. It is true that some Federation leaders like John L. Lewis of the Miners and Hillman of the Clothing Workers were pressing hard for new organizing drives among the workers of the still unorganized great industries of the country like textiles, steel, rubber, automobiles, and aircraft. But such men were a small minority in the Federation.

The deepening of the economic slump, however, did open crevices in the Federation's high wall of tradition. At the 1932 convention in Cincinnati, John L. Lewis convinced the convention to go on record in favor of state unemployment systems. To the old-timers in the Federation this was a serious and dangerous departure from Gompers' inflexible principle of "voluntarism"—that is, no government interference on either side in the match between capital and labor. Lewis also cajoled the delegates—apparently bewildered and shaken by the enormity of the economic crisis—into accepting the principle of a legislatively limited working day—a further repudiation of Gompers' principles.

Then came the opening notes of the Rooseveltian performance, foremost among which was the National Industrial Recovery Act. This measure contained a labor clause—the well-known 7a—which guaranteed to workers the right of free choice of union and committed the employers to dealing with such unions. Spurred by this government encouragement, both spontaneous organization and A.F. of L.-affiliated unionization surged forward. More than 1,100 federal and local unions in the mass production industries of automobiles, aluminum, and rubber were brought into being by 1935; union membership for these industries shot up from less than 11,000 in 1933 to over ten times that figure in 1935. President Green of the A.F. of L. announced that between 60,000 and 70,000 workers had been added to the Federation in Akron alone in 1933, most of them in the rubber industry. Capitalizing on Roosevelt's acceptance of section 7a, John L. Lewis told the miners, "The President wants you to join a union." The United Mine Workers, though wasting away all through the twenties, attracted 300,000 members to its rolls in the spring and early summer of 1933. The Ladies Garment Workers Union added 100,000; the Amalgamated Clothing Workers gathered in another 50,000 during the middle months of NRA's first year. At the A.F. of L. convention of 1934, the Executive Council reported "a virtual uprising of workers for union membership. Workers," the Council said with amazement, "held mass meetings and sent word they wanted to be organized."

The emphasis on craft organization and the cautious philosophy of the American Federation of Labor, however, were not equal to the task of organizing and canalizing this upsurge among the workers in the mass production industries. The craft form, where unionization proceeded along the lines of the job, rather than the factory, made no sense whatsoever in any of the great industries where the mass of workers were semiskilled or unskilled rather than skilled. Moreover, to divide the workers in a plant according to occupations resulted in endless jurisdictional disputes among the unions. Ultimately the mishandling of the organizational problem reflected itself in loss of membership. For example, though in 1934 the A.F. of L. had over 150,000 members in its 100 locals in the automobile industry, by 1936 the membership had dwindled away to 19,000. A willingness to try new forms and to include the unskilled and semiskilled, who bulked so large in the mass production industries, was urgently needed if organized labor was to benefit from the workers' new interest in unions.

The obvious failure of the A.F. of L.'s approach to the mass industries came to a head in the heated Atlantic City convention of October, 1935. Beetle-browed, leonine John L. Lewis of the industrially organized Miners raised his stentorian voice in behalf of the unorganized. "Heed this cry from Macedonia that comes from the hearts of men," he cried to the impassive leaders of labor's elite.

"Organize the unorganized and in doing this make the A.F. of L. the greatest instrument that has ever been forged to befriend the cause of humanity and champion human rights." Defeated at every turn on the floor of the convention (except perhaps in his famous right hook to the nose of arch-conservative William Hutcheson of the Carpenters), Lewis and his fellow rebels, the day after the convention closed, organized the Committee for Industrial Organization. Composed of ten of the more aggressive and spirited of the A.F. of L. unions, this committee sparked the mighty organizing effort which transformed American industrial and labor relations in the next handful of years. Within a year after the formation of the C.I.O., the A.F. of L. expelled the constituent unions. The split in the labor movement, destined to remain unhealed for twenty years, was a fact.

In view of the consequences, however, that split was the most promising thing that ever happened to Samuel Gompers' beloved American Federation of Labor in particular and to the American workingman in general. The C.I.O.—formed into the permanent Congress of Industrial Organizations in 1938—undertook a massive and energetic invasion of unorganized mass industries like steel, automobiles, textiles, rubber, aircraft, and lumber—all industries which had implacably resisted the union organizer for over a generation. One by one, with varying degrees of violence and resistance, they fell to the determination, the guts, and the persistence of the new unionism. In time the A.F. of L. also joined in, and by 1940 total union membership in the country had risen to 8.5 million from 3.7 million only five years earlier. Under the impact of the depression, the American labor movement had come of age.

Aside from the new and vital spirit which the C.I.O. breathed into the labor movement, its great innovation was its effective use of the industrial-union form. So successfully was this form adapted to the economic structure that the industrial union soon captured a prominent place in the once craft-dominated A.F. of L. By 1940 about a quarter of the A.F. of L.'s four million members were in industrial unions and a quarter of the C.I.O.'s workers were in craft unions. Furthermore, by organizing recent immigrants, the unskilled, Negroes, and women on a scale and with a determination never attempted by the A.F. of L., the C.I.O. revived a broad approach to unionism which had been sidetracked in America ever since the A.F. of L. had beaten out the old Knights of Labor.

The enormous expansion of unionization in the last years of the depression was not solely attributable to the novel spirit among the unions and the workers. Much of the impetus came from the new attitude of the government. We have already seen the catalytic effect the NRA had on the rush toward unionization, and it would be difficult to exaggerate that effect. When that act was declared unconstitutional in 1935, its place was taken by the National Labor Relations Act (the Wagner Act), in itself perhaps the most revolutionary single measure in American labor history.

The Wagner Act started from the same premise as section 7a of the NRA—that is, that workers should be free to choose their own unions and employers must abstain from interfering in this choice. It also required that employers accept duly constituted unions as legitimate representatives of their employees and bargain with them. The act also set up a board—the National Labor Relations Board— whose duty it was to supervise elections for the certification of unions as representatives of a majority of the workers in a plant, and to hear complaints against employers for having interfered with union organizing. The Board was also empowered to hear complaints against employers for refusing to bargain with a certified union.

In two different ways, the act threw the enormous prestige and power of the government behind the drive for organizing workers. In the first place, it flatly declared unionization to be a desirable thing for the national economy, forbidding employers to interfere in the process of organization. Five so-called unfair labor practices were listed, all of them acts which only an employer could commit; the act listed no "unfair" practices of labor. (Actually, the courts had built up such a large body of common-law interpretations of unfair labor practices by unions that it was hardly necessary to add to them in the act.) Moreover, as an additional indication of its belief in the labor movement, the law virtually outlawed the company union— that is, the labor organization sponsored by the employer. In the second place, once a union was formed, and it had been certified by the Board as speaking for a majority of the workers, the employer, under the act, had no alternative but to recognize it as the representative of his employees. Though it is true that many employers refused to accept the constitutionality of the law—usually on the advice of their lawyers—until after the Supreme Court decision of 1937 in the Jones and Laughlin Steel case, this placing of the government on the side of unionization was of central importance in the success of many an organizational drive of the C.I.O., notably those against Ford and Little Steel.[9]

The passage of this controversial act marked, insofar as labor was concerned, an acceptance of governmental assistance which would have made old Sam Gompers apoplectic. All during his leadership of the A.F. of L., labor had consistently refused to accept (except for the war emergency) government intervention at the bargaining table of labor and business. But by accepting governmental assistance, the American labor movement not only departed from its own traditions, but from those of European labor as well. Although well aware of the benefits to be derived from such government support as the American movement received, labor in England and on the Continent has not abandoned its historic independence of the state. European labor unions have preferred to remain untouched by the quasi-governmental status in which the American labor movement has permitted itself to be clothed. Labor's bête noire, the Taft-Hartley Act, is an obvious confirmation of the truism that dependence on government is a knife which cuts both ways.

Another, though less important, difference between American and European labor practices is the attitude toward the union and closed shops. Largely because of the historic fragility of American labor organizations, unions in the United States have found it desirable, if not imperative, to insist that all workers in a given shop or plant join the union to which a majority of workers belong. The Wagner Act reinforced this practice by making it an unfair labor practice for an employer to refuse to sign an agreement requiring all of his employees to join the union.

European employers have rarely signed such agreements, and the Swiss, French, German, English, and Swedish labor unions have gone on record as opposing such closed or union shop agreements. Indeed, in the basic Matignon agreement between French capital and labor in 1936, the unions voluntarily agreed to management's right to hire and fire regardless of union membership. Generally speaking,

[9] Even before the Wagner Act had won the support of the Supreme Court, Presidential "pressure" and prestige helped the C.I.O. attain some of its most telling victories, like that over General Motors in February of 1937. The sensational exposure of union-busting tactics of employers by Senator Robert La Follette's investigating committee, beginning in 1936, was still another form of governmental assistance to the cause of labor.

labor and the courts alike in Europe have looked upon the closed shop as an infringement of a worker's right to join or not join any association he pleases. Unionism, however, is considerably stronger there than here, and the workers can be confident that the open shop is not an excuse for refusing to deal with unions at all, as it has proved to be in the United States.

The Wagner Act broke new ground in labor law, going even beyond the epoch-making Norris-La Guardia Act of 1932. This latter act, passed after years of agitation and half a dozen tries on the part of labor and liberal congressmen and senators, severely restricted the use of antiunion injunctions issuing from federal courts in the course of labor disputes. So expertly was the act drawn that it overthrew in one stroke a mountain of legal obstacles to labor organization and activity which ingenious judges and lawyers had quarried out of the common law. In substance, though, the main achievement of the act could be summed up in the phrase "laissez faire in labor relations." Labor would now be free to use its full economic power, without judicial hamstringing, just as employers had always been free to use theirs. In no way, it should be emphasized, did the Norris-La Guardia Act compel, or even advise, employers to accept unions or to bargain with them.

That innovation came only with the Wagner Act. As a federal court of appeals said in 1948, "prior to the National Labor Relations Act no federal law prevented *employers* from discharging employees for exercising their rights or from refusing to recognize or bargain with labor organizations. The NLRA created rights *against employers* which did not exist before then." In this lay the revolution in governmental attitudes toward organized labor.

So lusty and powerful did organized labor grow under the new dispensation that by the time the Second World War was over, a strong movement was afoot to amend the Wagner Act in order to protect the interests of the employer and to secure the national welfare against certain powerful national unions. The result was the Taft-Hartley Act of 1947, actually an amendment to the original 1935 act. Without entering into the details, suffice it to say that this amendment now added certain unfair labor practices of which unions might be guilty, such as the secondary boycott, and bestowed special powers upon the federal government for effectively handling paralyzing nationwide strikes. But the central core of the National Labor Relations Act was left unimpaired, as it remains today. The American people under Republican as well as Democratic regimes have re-affirmed more than once the principle that it is the obligation of the federal government to protect a worker in the free exercise of the right to join a union and that all employers must bargain collectively with a certified union.

Enormous as was the assistance which labor received from government in the form of the NLRA, there was still another piece of legislation which offered a boost to labor. This was the Wages and Hours Act of 1938, which set minimum wages and maximum hours for workers in industries engaged in interstate commerce. Since its example has been followed by several industrial states like New York, the principle of a legislative floor under wages and a ceiling on hours has been extended beyond the constitutional limits of the federal government's power. Because the minimum set by law was well below the going industrial wage, the act did not affect most workers, but it helped considerably to pull up wages in certain unorganized industries. Furthermore, it helped to narrow the wage differences between northern and southern industries. During the first two years of the act, nearly a million workers received increased wages under its provisions and over three million had their hours shortened. Subsequent to that time, the minimum wage has been progressively increased from the original 40 cents an hour to the present (1968) $1.60, thereby putting a rising floor under the nation's industrial wage scale. Furthermore, in abolishing child labor in all industries involved in interstate commerce, the act achieved a long-sought goal of the labor and liberal movements in the United States. And once again, it is worth noticing, it was accomplished through the powerful intervention of an active federal government.

Seen against a broader canvas, the depression, together with government support, profoundly altered the position of labor in American society. Girded with its new-found power and protections, Big Labor now took its place beside Big Business and Big Government to complete a triumvirate of economic power. And when it is recognized that through the so-called farm bloc in Congress agriculture also has attained a sort of veto power on the operations of the economic system, it is not difficult to appreciate the aptness of John Galbraith's description of modern American capitalism as a system of "countervailing power." Instead of competition being the regulator of the economic system, Professor Galbraith persuasively argues, we now have a system of economic checks and balances—Big Labor,

Big Business, Big Agriculture, and so forth—no one of which is big enough or powerful enough to control the total economy. Though Galbraith's argument is not totally convincing, his conception of the American economy is much closer to reality than is the old competitive model. And insofar as Professor Galbraith's analysis is correct, it is clear that this system of countervailing power came into being during the depression, with the rise of Big Government, Organized Agriculture, and Big Labor.

5. WAS IT A NEW OR OLD DEAL?

One of the most enduring monuments to the Great Depression was that congeries of contradictions, naïveté, humanitarianism, realistic politics, and economic horse sense called the New Deal of Franklin D. Roosevelt. As the governmental agent which recast American thinking on the responsibilities of government, the New Deal was clearly the offspring of the depression. As we have seen, it was also more than that: it was a revitalization of the Democratic party; it was the political manifestation of that new spirit of reform which was stirring among the ranks of labor and the Negro people.

In their own time and since, the New Deal and Franklin Roosevelt have had a polarizing effect upon Americans. Probably at no time before Roosevelt has the leader of a great democratic nation come to symbolize as he did the hopes and the fears of so many people.[10] Not even Jackson, in whom Roosevelt himself recognized a President of his own popularity- and hatred-producing caliber, could rival him. Two decades after Roosevelt's death, the mention of his name can still evoke emotions, betrayed by the wistful look in the eye or in the hard set of the jaw.

For the Democratic party, Roosevelt was like a lightning rod, drawing to himself all the venom and hatred of the opposition, only to discharge it harmlessly; nothing, it seemed, could weaken his per-

[10] According to Harold Ickes, Roosevelt was profoundly struck by the adoration which was bestowed upon him by his admirers. During the 1936 campaign, the President told Ickes "that there was something terrible about the crowds that lined the streets along which he passed. He went on to explain what he meant, which was exclamations from individuals in the crowd, such as 'He saved my home,' 'He gave me a job,' 'God bless you, Mr. President,' etc." In May, 1936, Marquis Childs published an article in *Harper's,* entitled "They Hate Roosevelt," in which he described and tried to account for the unreasoning hatred for the President on the part of what Childs called the upper 2 per cent of the population.

sonal hold on the affections of the majority of Americans. That something more was involved than sheer popularity is shown by the example of Dwight Eisenhower. Though held in even greater popular esteem, Eisenhower was unable to invest his party with his own vote-getting power; Republicans lost while Eisenhower won. The difference between F.D.R. and Ike is that one stood for a program, a hope, and a future, while the other stood for himself as a good, well-intentioned man whom all instinctively trusted and perhaps even admired. The one was a leader of a nation, the other a popular hero. Roosevelt is already a member of that tiny pantheon of great leaders of Americans in which Washington, Jackson, Lincoln, and Wilson are included; it is difficult to believe that Eisenhower will be included. His monument is more likely to be inscribed: "The best-liked man ever to be President."

In the thirties, as now, the place of the New Deal in the broad stream of American development has been a matter of controversy. Historians and commentators on the American scene have not yet reached a firm agreement—if they ever will—as to whether the New Deal was conservative or radical in character. Certainly if one searches the writings and utterances of Franklin Roosevelt, his own consciousness of conservative aims is quickly apparent. "The New Deal is an old deal—as old as the earliest aspirations of humanity for liberty and justice and the good life," he declared in 1934. "It was this administration," he told a Chicago audience in 1936, "which saved the system of private profit and free enterprise after it had been dragged to the brink of ruin. . . ."

But men making a revolution among a profoundly conservative people do not advertise their activity, and above all Franklin Roosevelt understood the temper of his people.[11] Nor should such a statement be interpreted as an insinuation of high conspiracy—far from it. Roosevelt was at heart a conservative, as his lifelong interest in history, among other things, suggests. But he was without dogma in his conservatism, which was heavily interlaced with genuine concern for people.[12] He did not shy away from new means and new ap-

---

[11] It is significant that only once during the 1932 campaign, according to Ernest K. Lindley, did Roosevelt call for "a revolution"; and then he promptly qualified it to "the right kind, the only kind of revolution this nation can stand for—a revolution at the ballot box."

[12] When an economist suggested to F.D.R. that the depression be permitted to run its course and that then the economic system would soon right

proaches to problems when circumstances demanded it. His willingness to experiment, to listen to his university-bred Brains Trust, to accept a measure like the TVA, reveal the flexibility in his thought. Both his lack of theoretical presuppositions and his flexibility are to be seen in the way he came to support novel measures like social security and the Wagner Act. Response to popular demand was the major reason. "The Congress can't stand the pressure of the Townsend Plan unless we have a real old-age insurance system," he complained to Frances Perkins, "nor can I face the country without having . . . a solid plan which will give some assurance to old people of systematic assistance upon retirement." In like manner, the revolutionary NLRA was adopted as a part of his otherwise sketchy and rule-of-thumb philosophy of society. Though ultimately Roosevelt championed the Wagner bill in the House, it was a belated conversion dictated by the foreshadowed success of the measure and the recent invalidation of the NRA. In his pragmatic and common-sense reactions to the exigencies of the depression, Roosevelt, the easygoing conservative, ironically enough became the embodiment of a new era and a new social philosophy for the American people.

"This election," Herbert Hoover presciently said in 1932, "is not a mere shift from the ins to the outs. It means deciding the direction our nation will take over a century to come." The election of Franklin Roosevelt, he predicted, would result in "a radical departure from the foundations of 150 years which have made this the greatest nation in the world." Though Hoover may be charged with nothing more than campaign flourishing, it is nevertheless a fact that his speech was made just after Roosevelt's revealing Commonwealth Club address of September. Only in this single utterance, it should be remembered, did Roosevelt disclose in clear outline the philosophy and program which was later to be the New Deal. "Every man has a right to life," he had said, "and this means that he has also a right to make a comfortable living. . . . Our government, formal and informal, political and economic," he went on, "owes to everyone an avenue to possess himself of a portion of that plenty [from our industrial society] sufficient for his needs, through his own work." Here were the intimations of those new goals which the New Deal set for America.

---

itself—as Frances Perkins tells the story—the President's face took on a "gray look of horror" as he told the economist: "People aren't cattle you know!"

Accent as heavily as one wishes the continuity between the reforms of the Progressive era and the New Deal, yet the wide difference between the goals of the two periods still remains. The Progressive impulse was narrowly reformist: it limited business, it assisted
agriculture, it freed labor from some of the shackles imposed by the
courts, but it continued to conceive of the state as policeman or judge
and nothing more. The New Deal, on the other hand, was more than
a regulator—though it was that too, as shown by the SEC and the
reinvigoration of the antitrust division of the Justice Department.
To the old goals for America set forth and fought for by the Jeffersonians and the Progressives the New Deal appended new ones. Its
primary and general innovation was the guaranteeing of a minimum
standard of welfare for the people of the nation. WPA and the whole
series of relief agencies which were a part of it, wages and hours
legislation, AAA, bank deposit insurance, and social security,[13] each
illustrates this new conception of the federal government. A resolution offered by New Deal Senator Walsh in 1935 clearly enunciated
the new obligations of government. The resolution took notice of the
disastrous effects of the depression "upon the lives of young men and
women . . ." and then went on to say that "it is the duty of the
Federal Government to use every possible means of opening up opportunities" for the youth of the nation "so that they may be rehabil-
itated and restored to *a decent standard of living* and ensured proper
development of their talents. . . ."

But the guarantor state as it developed under the New Deal was
more active and positive than this. It was a vigorous and dynamic
force in the society, energizing and, if necessary, supplanting private
enterprise when the general welfare required it. With the Wagner
Act, for example, the government served notice that it would actively
participate in securing the unionization of the American worker; the
state was no longer to be an impartial policeman merely keeping
order; it now declared for the side of labor. When social and economic problems like the rehabilitation of the Valley of the Tennessee
were ignored or shirked by private enterprise, then the federal gov-

[13] Social security is an excellent example of how, under the New Deal, reform measures, when they conflicted with recovery, were given priority. In
siphoning millions of dollars of social security taxes from the purchasing
power of the workers, social security was a deflationary measure, which must
have seriously threatened the precariously based new economic recovery. For
this reason and others, Abraham Epstein, the foremost authority in America
on social security, denounced the act as a "sharing of poverty."

ernment undertook to do the job. Did private enterprise fail to provide adequate and sufficient housing for a minimum standard of welfare for the people, then the government would build houses. As a result, boasted Nathan Straus, head of the U.S. Housing Authority, "for the first time in a hundred years the slums of America ceased growing and began to shrink."

Few areas of American life were beyond the touch of the experimenting fingers of the New Deal; even the once sacrosanct domain of prices and the valuation of money felt the tinkering. The devaluation of the dollar, the gold-purchase program, the departure from the gold standard—in short, the whole monetary policy undertaken by F. D. R. as a means to stimulate recovery through a price rise—constituted an unprecedented repudiation of orthodox public finance. To achieve that minimum standard of well-being which the depression had taught the American people to expect of their government, nothing was out of bounds.[14]

[14] The proposition that the New Deal marked a sharp change in attitudes and practices has not been accepted by all historians, to say the least. Although the literature on the subject is canvassed in the bibliographical essay at the end of this book, the two principal schools of criticism are worth setting forth here. On this subject orthodox and New Left historians seem to be in substantial agreement. Arthur Link in his *American Epoch* (New York, 1967), p. 433, sums up the orthodox argument: "The chief significance of the reform legislation of the 1930's was its essentially conservative character and the fact that it stemmed from half a century or more of discussion and practical experience and from ideas proposed by Republicans as well as by Democrats."

The New Left criticism is vigorously set forth in Barton Bernstein, "The New Deal: The Conservative Achievements of Liberal Reform," in his collection of essays, *Towards a New Past: Dissenting Essays in American History* (New York, 1968), pp. 264–65: "The New Deal failed to solve the problem of depression, it failed to raise the impoverished, it failed to redistribute income, it failed to extend equality and generally countenanced racial discrimination and segregation. It failed generally to make business more responsible to the social welfare or to threaten business's pre-eminent political power. In this sense, the New Deal, despite the shifts in tone and spirit from the earlier decade, was profoundly conservative and continuous with the 1920's."

My reasons for disagreeing with the orthodox view have already been set down above. My disagreement with the New Left historians is a little different. They have set forth a measure of radical change that *no* movement in United States history can fulfill. Such a "consensus" approach to American history may be useful in comparing the United States with other societies, but it ignores the important and noticeable shifts in outlook and practice within the United States that the historian must recognize if he is to avoid making the American past nothing more than a stately, homogenized progression from the seventeenth century to the present. It is in that sense that I speak of the New Deal as a revolution. Certainly the men of the 1930's and

But it is not the variety of change which stamps the New Deal as the creator of a new America; its significance lies in the permanence of its program. For, novel as the New Deal program was, it has, significantly, not been repudiated by the Eisenhower administration, the first Republican government since the reforms were instituted. Verbally, it is true, the Republican administration has had to minimize its actual commitments to the New Deal philosophy, and it tended to trust private business more than the New Dealers did— witness, for example, its elimination of the minor governmental manufacturing enterprises which competed with private firms. But despite this, the administration's firm commitment to the guaranteeing of prosperity and averting depression at all costs is an accurate reflection of the American people's agreement with the New Deal's diagnosis of the depression. Nor has the Republican party dared to repeal or even emasculate the legislation which made up the vitals of the New Deal: TVA, banking and currency, SEC, social security, the Wagner Act, and fair treatment of the Negro. The New Deal Revolution has become so much a part of the American Way that no political party which aspires to high office dares now to repudiate it.

It may or may not be significant in this regard (for apothegms are more slippery than precise) but it is nonetheless interesting that Roosevelt and Eisenhower have both been impressed with the same single sentence from Lincoln regarding the role of government. "The legitimate object of Government," wrote Lincoln, "is to do for a community of people whatever they need to have done but cannot do at all or cannot do so well for themselves in their separate or individual capacities." Twice, in 1934 and again in 1936, F. D. R. in public addresses used this expression to epitomize his own New Deal, and Robert Donovan in his officially inspired book on the Eisenhower administration writes that this same "fragment of Lincoln's writing . . . Eisenhower uses time and again in describing his own philosophy of government." Between Lincoln and Eisenhower there was no Republican President, except perhaps Theodore Roosevelt, who would have been willing to subscribe to such a freewheeling description of the federal power; in this can be measured the impact of the New Deal and the depression.

1940's thought an important change in outlook and approach of government toward society was taking place. The historian cannot rely only upon his own criteria for measuring change; he must be sensitive to what contemporaries thought was happening as well.

The conclusion seems inescapable that, traditional as the words may have been in which the New Deal expressed itself, in actuality it was truly a revolution in ideas, institutions and practices, when one compares it with the political and social world that preceded it. In its long history, America has passed through two revolutions since the first one in 1776, but only the last two, the Civil War and the depression, were of such force as to change the direction of the relatively smooth flow of its progress. The Civil War rendered a final and irrevocable decision in the long debate over the nature of the Union and the position of the Negro in American society. From that revolutionary experience, America emerged a strong national state and dedicated by the words of its most hallowed document to the inclusion of the black man in a democratic culture. The searing ordeal of the Great Depression purged the American people of their belief in the limited powers of the federal government and convinced them of the necessity of the guarantor state. And as the Civil War constituted a watershed in American thought, so the depression and its New Deal marked the crossing of a divide from which, it would seem, there could be no turning back.

The decade of the 1930's witnessed another turning point from which there was no turning back. The menace of Hitler and Japan during the late 1930's initiated a revolution in American foreign policy that still continues. It is to the background and nature of that revolution in America's relations with the world that we must now turn.

CHAPTER XIV

The Making of a World Power

IN THE course of transforming itself from an agrarian republic into a great industrial state, the United States also changed from a minor participant in the affairs of the world to one of the chief powers of the globe. For most of its history, down to the end of the nineteenth century, Americans had found it possible as well as desirable to remain aloof from the political affairs of Europe and the rest of the world. But by the twentieth century the rapid growth of American economic strength and therefore American military and political power decreed that the United States could no longer remain outside the mainstream of world diplomacy.

The transition from isolation to involvement was unsteady and sometimes painful. After backing into empire, Americans soon had second thoughts and abandoned their brief role as imperial master, only to turn to other departures from tradition, with equally ambiguous results. Thus the first crusade to Europe ended in disillusion and withdrawal. Yet the United States of the twentieth century could not really recapture its nineteenth-century isolation, try as it might. Therefore the second crusade to Europe marked a true turning point, for from that experience there was no turning back. But the road ahead was filled with surprises. And though it would seem after 1945 that nothing remained untouched by change, the fact was that from the beginning to the present, in foreign affairs as in other matters, there was an American approach that was at once distinctive and persistent.

1. A NEW DIPLOMACY FOR A NEW ERA

As we have seen in an earlier chapter, to most Americans the Revolution was the culmination of a long history of their growing self-awareness as a distinct and fortunate people. The birth of the republic signalized in the minds of Americans a "new order in the world," as the Great Seal of the United States phrased it. It should come as no surprise, then, that in their dealings with other nations, the United States, from its birth, sought to perpetuate that sense of difference. Indeed, the most distinctive element in American foreign policy for most of United States history—isolation—arose out of the special experience of Americans during the colonial and early years of independence.

It is not merely coincidental, for example, that the most influential pamphlet advocating independence argued for American isolation from the affairs of Europe. "As Europe is our market for trade," wrote Tom Paine in *Common Sense,* "we ought to form no partial connection with any part of it. It is the true interest of America to steer clear of European contentions, which she never can do while, by her dependence on Britain, she is made the make-weight in the scale of British politics." Paine's assertion of difference between Americans and Europeans was not new. Certainly at least since the French and Indian War, Americans had been giving vent to expressions of their identity as a people, for they were convinced that they were not only different from Europeans but better. Even sophisticates like Benjamin Franklin were sure before the Revolution that the moral level of America was higher than that of England or Europe. Thus when the struggle for independence compelled Americans to deal with Europe diplomatically, they did not hide their sense of difference and superiority. At the French court, Franklin deliberately dressed simply, even untidily, in tacit criticism of the niceties of European protocol and pretension. When crusty John Adams was advised by French Foreign Minister Vergennes to make the necessary adjustments to European diplomatic conventions, he haughtily and self-righteously replied that "the dignity of North America does not consist in diplomatic ceremonials or any of the subtleties of etiquette; it consists solely in reason, justice, truth, the rights of mankind, and the interests of the nations of Europe."

More lay behind Adams' statement than simple revolutionary fervor or diplomatic inexperience. Significantly absent from his catalog of diplomatic purposes were phrases like "balance of power" or "reasons of state," which were then, as now, the common coin of diplomatic intercourse. The omissions, like the inclusions, were not accidental. The American leaders aimed to fashion a fresh diplomacy that would be worthy of their new republic and of the enlightened age in which it was born. As might be expected, it was the American *philosophe,* Thomas Jefferson, who made the clearest connection between the age of the Enlightenment and the foreign policy of new America. Power and force in foreign affairs, Jefferson wrote to Madison in 1789, "were legitimate principles in the dark ages which intervened between antient [*sic*] and modern civilization, but exploded and held in just horror in the eighteenth century. I know of but one code of morality for man whether acting singly or collectively." Such a single standard meant abhorrence of war and rejection of force and of political alliance that enmeshed nations in the balance of power. Indeed, in 1804 Jefferson wrote that he considered the balance of power as "the pest of the peace of the world, as the workshop in which nearly all the wars of Europe are manufactured."

As Jefferson's remarks suggest, the new diplomacy meant the separation of American from European interests. At the beginning of American diplomatic affairs, this separation was uppermost in the minds of the nation's leaders. When Congress in 1776 drew up a model treaty for the instruction of its agents seeking aid from France, the only diplomatic connection it was prepared to agree to was commercial. Congress would not even hold out to France the bait of possessions in the New World, which might be captured from the British in joint operations. The only concessions that the wary Americans were prepared to make, at least in the beginning, was the promise that they would not conclude a separate peace if French aid precipitated war between England and France. In the end, of course, the alliance with France that was signed in 1778 did obligate the United States to help France protect its colonies in the New World, and the ties were political as well as commercial. But this change was dictated by the realities of survival; the French would not provide the required aid on less favorable conditions. Later, in 1783, John Adams recalled clearly the pristine and narrow aims of the United States in its dealings with foreign countries in 1776. His first principle, he said, had been that "we should calculate all our measures and foreign negotiations in such a manner, as to avoid a too great dependence upon any one power of Europe—to avoid all obligations and temptations to take part in future European wars; that the business of America with Europe was commerce, not politics or war." The accuracy of Adams' summation of the American attitude is shown by events once the war for independence was won.

Freed from the need for a political alliance, such as has been entered into with the French, Congress quickly reverted to the policy of separate interests and purely commercial connections with foreign states. Thus when the group of Armed Neutrals in Europe invited the new United States to join them, Congress in June, 1783, turned down the invitation, despite its admitted agreement with the goals of the group. "The true interest of these states," Congress resolved, "requires that they should be as little as possible entangled in the politics and controversies of European nations."

This was the idea of the two hemispheres, which received its classic expression in Washington's Farewell Address in 1796. In that document, too, the distinction was drawn between commercial and political ties. "The great rule of conduct" for the United States in foreign relations, the retiring President wrote, was that "in extending our commercial relations" to foreign nations the United States ought "to have with them as little *political* connections as possible." Washington's statement of the distinction points up the fact that the isolation recommended by the Founding Fathers was never a Chinese or Japanese policy of cutting the nation off from contacts with other peoples or civilizations. In fact in some respects the aim of the vigorous, even aggressive new Republic was just the opposite. Rather than withdrawing within itself, it sought markets and trade around the globe, wherever a profit beckoned or an opportunity opened.

Commercial relations, in substance, were to be encouraged. The underlying basis for the doctrine of the two hemispheres, as Washington made evident, was that "Europe has a set of primary interests which to us have none or very remote relations. Hence she must be engaged in frequent controversies, the causes of which are essentially foreign to our concerns. Hence, therefore, it must be unwise in us to implicate ourselves by artificial ties in the ordinary vicissitudes of her politics or the ordinary combinatons and collisions of her friendships or enmities."

Washington's advice that Americans not "entangle our peace and prosperity in the toils of European ambition, rivalship, interest, humor, or caprice," neatly summed up what many Americans had concluded from their history as a people separated from Europe yet often embroiled in Europe's quarrels. In a sense, therefore, Washington's advice was accepted before he offered it, and its realism accounts for its being readily followed in the years that followed.

Implicit in the doctrine of the two hemispheres was the idea that as long as Europe had interests in the New World, the United States would not be free of embroilment in the affairs of Europe. As the diplomatic history of the United States for the first quarter of the nineteenth century was to show, Washington's advice was capable of being followed only as European interests in the New World were reduced. The primary step was the purchase of Louisiana in 1803; with it isolation became a realistic policy for the first time and for the foreseeable future. If France had occupied Louisiana, as Napoleon intended, and had developed it as a colony, the relations of the United States with Europe would have been much different. Even Francophile Jefferson was prepared to contemplate a political alliance to counteract the French, for, as he wrote in 1802, "The day that France takes possession of New Orleans, we must marry ourselves to the British fleet and nation." For with Napoleonic France on its flank, the fledgling United States would have had to look to Britain as a counterweight. In such a situation a policy of no European alliances would have been impossible because it would have been unrealistic.

The acquisition of Louisiana, however, did not prevent the United States from continuing to be involved in Europe's war. As an important neutral, dependent upon trade with Europe, the United States could not escape the consequences of the efforts of England and Napoleonic France to deny the ocean-borne trade to each other. The War of 1812 was the result. But if the war denied the American desire for isolation and peace, the ideological line linking the Farewell Address and the Monroe Doctrine is straight and clear. Indeed, it was the Latin American wars for independence that finished what the Louisiana Purchase began—the removal of almost all of Europe's interests from the New World. Both the Farewell Address and the Monroe Doctrine originated as protests against European intervention in American affairs. Washington's advice grew out of his concern over the effect of the French alliance upon domestic politics as well as foreign policy. The immediate causes for Monroe's dictum were Tsarist Russia's movement to extend its dominion southward from Alaska and the threat of the monarchical powers of continental Europe to suppress the recent colonial revolutions in Spanish America.

Important and influential as the Monroe Doctrine was destined to become in the foreign policy of the United States, its significance and meaning at the time can certainly be exaggerated and misunderstood. In 1823, when the doctrine was enunciated, the United States had no intention of going to war to prevent European intervention in the affairs of the newly independent republics to the south. In fact, as is now well known, the United States counted upon the commercial and political interest of Great Britain to provide the muscle behind Monroe's doctrine. The catalyst for Monroe's famous statement was the suggestion of George Canning, foreign secretary of Great Britain, in the summer of 1823, that his country and the United States issue a joint statement warning the continental monarchies against intervention in Latin America. But shrewd nationalist John Quincy Adams, Monroe's Secretary of State, pointed out that the United States did not need public support from Britain. All the necessary support would be forthcoming, Adams pointed out, because it was the desire to carry on trade with the newly independent states of Latin America that was the real source of British opposition to the re-establishment of European rule. Besides, Adams pointed out, "it would be more candid, as well as more dignified, to avow our principles explicitly to Russia and France, than to come in as a cock-boat in the wake of the British man-of-war."

It is worth recognizing, moreover, that for many years after Monroe set it forth in his annual message of December, 1823, the principle received neither recognition in Europe nor acknowledgment in the United States. Not until the 1850's were the principles of the doctrine connected with Monroe's name in the public press, and not until the 1860's can the historian be sure that it is a cardinal principle of American foreign policy. In 1864, at the time that France was supporting Maximilian of Austria as Emperor of Mexico, the House of Representatives clearly enunciated the doctrine of nonintervention. It resolved that "it does not accord with the policy of the United States to acknowledge any monarchical government erected on the ruins of any republican government in America under the auspices of any European power." Here were set forth the essential elements of Monroe's doctrine. Monarchy—as in Brazil—was acceptable so long as it was native and not imposed—but no new colonies would be countenanced. As John Quincy Adams bluntly told the British minister in 1821: "Keep what is yours, but leave the rest of the continent to us." Monroe in his enunciation of principles did not mention the transference of a European colony to another European power, but as early as 1811 the principle of no-transfer had been enunciated by both Congress and the President in regard to Florida. By 1870, no-transfer was regarded as a part of the Monroe

Doctrine itself. In the end, however, it must be said that like Washington's Farewell Address, the Monroe Doctrine said little that was new; it codified the central principles that the United States had worked out or acted upon in previous years. And it is for that reason that it was so readily accepted then and later.

While the doctrine of the two hemispheres contained in the Monroe Doctrine is well known, less well recognized is the ideological justification for the split between the hemispheres. The usual interpretation has been that Monroe's dictum was a defense of American security in view of the proximity of the former Spanish colonies to the United States. Certainly security played a role in the enunciation of the doctrine, but the words of Monroe reveal an additional, ideological concern, which is worth emphasizing in the light of later ideological concerns in American foreign policy. "The political system of the allied powers," Monroe pointed out, referring to the states of the Triple Alliance, "is essentially different . . . from that of America. . . . We owe it, therefore, to candor and to the amicable relations existing between the United States and those powers to declare that we should consider any attempt on their part to extend their system to any portion of this hemisphere as dangerous to our peace and safety." The repeated use of the word "system"—not power or influence—is conspicuous and significant. The ideological or moral element in Monroe's statement is also present in John Quincy Adams' remarks in 1823, as he sought to differentiate the premises of foreign policy of the United States from that of European states. "The policy of all the European nations toward South America," Adams wrote, "has been founded upon selfish principles of interest, incongruously combined with erroneous principles of government. Since the restoration of the Bourbons, the European alliance of emperors and kings has assumed as the foundation of human society the doctrine of unalienable *allegiance*. Our doctrine is founded upon the principle of unalienable *right*. The European allies, therefore, have viewed the *cause* of the South Americans as rebellion against their lawful sovereign. We have considered it as the assertion of natural right." Adams' contention that the foreign policy of the United States rested upon different principles from that of the European states had been put in even stronger moral terms by a committee of Congress twenty years before. "The Government of the United States is differently organized from any other in the world. Its object is the happiness of man; its policy and its interest, to pursue right by right means. War is the great scourge of the human race, and should never be resorted to but in case of the most imperious necessity. A wise government will avoid it, when its views can be attained by peaceful measures. Princes fight for glory, and the blood and the treasure of their subjects is [*sic*] the price they pay. In all nations the people bear the burden of war, and in the United States the people rule."

This clear assertion of a connection between the people, domestic institutions, and foreign policy has been characteristic of American pronouncements. It has not only given them a self-righteous cast, as in the one just quoted, but it has also made American foreign policy highly moralistic in its goals. Americans have rarely accepted the characteristically European dicta of Clausewitz that war is "nothing more than the continuation of politics by other means" and of Clemenceau that peace is "the continuation of war by other means." From the outset, war has been bad and peace has been good, to be desired by all except madmen.

It was just this attitude that George Kennan, in a famous series of lectures in 1951, roundly condemned as "the legalistic-moralistic approach to international problems. This approach runs like a red skein through our foreign policy of the last fifty years," he said. "It is the belief that it should be possible to suppress the chaotic and dangerous aspirations of governments in the international field by the acceptance of some system of legal rules and restraints." Kennan based his strictures upon the experience of the United States in foreign affairs since 1898, but it is evident that the attitude which he denounced began long before the Spanish-American War. As we have seen, the idea that Americans as a new and enlightened people were morally superior to Old Europe suffused American thought in general and foreign policy in particular. To this was added the conviction of men like Jefferson and Madison that there was a universal right or natural law that was above and beyond the standards of the existing diplomatic system. Jefferson, it will be recalled, had even gone so far as to say that states and individuals were to be governed by a single standard of behavior. As Paul Varg has written, "Americans prided themselves on being the model Republican society that the rest of the world would emulate. Others were held in bondage by privileged classes, but America was the land of opportunity, where demonstrated individual worth rather than birth was the test of a man. This concept, prominent during the Revolution, continued to flourish and made it easy to look upon every issue that arose with foreign nations as a moral question."

This moral or idealistic outlook, Kennan recognized, has become even more conspicuous in the twentieth century. "There have been other nations as rich as we," Woodrow Wilson pointed out, "there have been other nations as powerful, there have been other nations as spirited; but I hope we shall never forget that we created this Nation, not to serve ourselves, but to serve mankind." A later Secretary of State, who always admired Wilson, offered similar testimony to the continuing American belief that United States policy was different from that of Europe. In his memoirs Cordell Hull remarked, "During the First World War I had made an intensive study of the system of spheres of influence and balance of power and I was grounded to the taproots in their iniquitous consequences. The conclusions I then formed in total opposition to this system stayed with me." Franklin Roosevelt's Four Freedoms, which he first announced at the Atlantic Charter meeting with Churchill in 1941, are highly charged with idealism and moralism. Each of Roosevelt's Freedoms, for example, was expected to be achieved "everywhere in the world."[1] Even a diplomat as supposedly tough-minded as Dean Acheson could give voice to a moralistic basis for American foreign policy that has a real Wilsonian ring to it. "And the basic objective of American foreign policy," Acheson said in 1951, "is to make possible a world in which all people . . . can work, in their own way, toward a better life. . . . We are children of freedom. We cannot be safe except in an environment of freedom."

Contrary to the traditional interpretations, Wilson's contribution to the development of an American approach to foreign affairs was not the introduction of idealism or moralism. Idealism had been a feature of the American approach to foreign affairs from the beginning. Wilson's innovation was to use American power to advance and sustain idealism. The Founding Fathers, like Wilson, believed in an ordered, peaceful world community, but no American leader before Wilson had contemplated using American power to achieve it. Since Wilson, of course, the idealistic strain in American policy has

[1] Robert Sherwood expressed some doubt that Roosevelt really believed the Four Freedoms. But F.D.R.'s close friend Harry Hopkins assured Sherwood: "He believes them." Sherwood reported, however, that to the British government the Four Freedoms were "no more than a publicity handout."

been pronounced. All the Presidents since Franklin Roosevelt have used American power to support and advance the American belief in an ordered, peaceful, politically stable world in which the exchange of goods and the flow of capital may be as unimpeded as possible.

Indeed, such a use of power suggests that idealism has been by no means the only ingredient of American policy. From the earliest days a tough realism or sense of self-interest has also informed American foreign relations. Perhaps the classic expression was that of Secretary of State John Quincy Adams in 1821 when he was being importuned to throw the support of the United States behind the Greeks' war for independence from the Turks. "Wherever the standard of freedom and independence has been or shall be unfurled," he made clear, there will America's "heart, her benedictions and her prayers be. But she goes not abroad in search of monsters to destroy. She is the well-wisher of the freedom and independence of all. She is the champion and vindicator only of her own." Otherwise, Adams warned his eager compatriots, "she would involve herself beyond the power of extrication in all the wars of interest and intrigue, of individual avarice, envy and ambition, which assume the colors and usurp the standard of freedom." Over a generation later, when once again revolution was threatening the old European order, other Americans echoed Adams' words. The revolutions of 1848 throughout Europe struck a responsive chord in American hearts and minds, for at stake was the principle of self-determination on which the United States itself had been founded. Not surprisingly, therefore, when Louis Kossuth, one of the leaders of the unsuccessful Hungarian uprising against the Austrians, came to the United States, he found wide popular interest in his cause. At the same time, however, he encountered little desire to involve the nation directly in the cause of revolution in Europe. As Henry Clay told Kossuth in 1852, it was best for the cause of freedom that the United States stay out of "the distant wars of Europe" and "keep our lamp burning brightly on this western shore, as a light to all nations." As in the days of the Puritans and the Revolution, America would be as a city upon the hill—an example and model for all, but not a searcher after "monsters to destroy." Felix Gilbert has summed up the dual character of American foreign policy succinctly. "Settled by men who looked for gain and by men who sought freedom, born into independence in a century of enlightened thinking and of power politics, America has wavered in her foreign policy between Idealism and Realism."

Indeed, the consistent adherence to the policy of the two hemispheres or isolation is to be explained by reference to both idealism and realism. Such a policy suited well the limited power and the local interests of nineteenth-century America. Separated from Europe by a broad ocean and immersed in its business of settling a continent, the United States had little reason or occasion for a new adventure or foreign expansion. It could afford to be idealistic because such an approach to foreign policy was realistic.

By the end of the nineteenth century, however, Americans began to question the tradition of staying in the western hemisphere. The occasion for the momentous shift was Spain's difficulties with its last colony in the New World, but the operative forces were more domestic than foreign. As we have already noted in earlier chapters, during the last half of the nineteenth century, industrialization was the great shaping force in American society. It is not accidental that in the decade of the 1890's, just as industrialization was triumphing, Americans were seized by an unprecedented interest in overseas empire.

2. LOOKING OUTWARD

In one sense, the move toward empire by the United States was not new at all. From the beginning of its history, the United States had been an empire, both in size and in its tendency to enlarge itself. Nor was the expansion of the United States across the continent always a peaceful operation. There were constant wars against the Indians as well as a major war against neighboring Mexico. By any reckoning except that of Americans themselves, who liked to think they carried out the will of Providence, those wars and territorial acquisitions were imperialistic. But most modern Americans—and historians, too, for that matter—have generally accepted the view of contemporaries that the continental expansion of the American people was "natural" and a part of Manifest Destiny. To reach from ocean to ocean and from Great Lakes to Gulf seemed too geographically neat not to be a part of the Divine intention. What has seemed less natural and therefore in need of explanation (and justification) was the movement of the United States beyond its continental borders. It is this movement that receives the name imperialism. Whether it is called that or, more neutrally, overseas expansionism, it has seemed to fly in the face of the traditional patterns of American behavior on the international scene. Hence diplomatic historian Samuel Flagg Bemis has called the acquisition of the Philippines "The Great Aberration."

The explanation of the outward turning of the American people at the end of the nineteenth century is a complex one. It begins long before the 1890's. In one sense it begins in the early nineteenth century, when Americans first conceived of the idea that movement to the Pacific Ocean was a part of their "manifest destiny." For it was with feet firmly planted on the Pacific coast that Americans first began to look across the ocean to new lands and markets. In fact, as Norman Graebner has shown, the decision to occupy the Pacific coast and to incorporate Oregon and California into the Union was tied up with the Asian trade almost from the beginning. The acquisition of Texas at about the same time and the annexation of West Florida at an earlier time were clearly consequences of the westward movement. Americans migrated into Spanish territory and then became sufficiently numerous either to revolt or to ask the United States to take them over. But that process of agrarian imperialism cannot account for the acquisition of the lands along the Pacific coast. When California and the Oregon territory were acquired in the late 1840's the number of Americans in either place was negligible. There were a good number of Americans in Oregon's Willamette Valley, to be sure, but United States claims to that part of the Oregon territory were neither new nor contested. The Pacific coastal areas came to the attention of American leaders and the public as a consequence of maritime activities across the Pacific and from the expectation that they would provide jumping-off places for Americans seeking to tap the markets and trade of Asia. The object of the Polk administration's diplomatic conflict with the British was the great harbor of Puget Sound, where there were no American settlers, and which the British confidently claimed. Secretary of State William Seward's acquisition of Alaska and the Midway Islands in 1867 was also dictated by a belief, as he said, that "the Pacific Ocean, its shores, its islands, and the vast regions beyond will become the chief theater of events in the world's hereafter."

Neither the acquisition of a Pacific frontage nor Alaska, however, moved the United States of the immediate post-Civil War years into extra-continental expansion. Indeed, even Seward's acquisition of Alaska was ridiculed as the purchase of a useless icebox. Grant's interest in extending American suzerainty over Santo Domingo in

1870 was killed off by a resolute Senate and public, which firmly rejected expansion outside of the established continental boundaries. In short, neither the prophecies of a Secretary of State nor the activism of an imperial-minded President could move Americans to colonial acquisition. But what officials could not achieve in 1870, other less personal forces would do in the 1890's.

Not since the 1790's was the influence of domestic affairs on foreign policy more evident than during the last decade of the nineteenth century. The immediate cause for the acquisition of a colonial empire during those years was the Spanish-American War, for it was from that brief struggle that the imperialist acquisitions flowed. But the causes for that war, like the causes for the acquisition of new overseas territories, are themselves rooted in domestic as well as foreign affairs. The principal question is "Why did a sincerely reluctant administration go along with the undeniably popular demand for war in 1898?" For as one Bostonian wrote in early 1898, he had not met a man of the upper class "who considers that we have any justifiable cause for war. Below that crust," however, he went on, "the wish for war is *almost* universal."

The popular interest in the cause of Cuba, even at the cost of war with Spain, stemmed from a number of sources. Certainly the rising recognition at home and abroad of the United States as a great industrial power caused many Americans to think about a new role for their country in the world. It was during the 1890's, for example, that Europeans began to complain about the "American invasion," by which they meant the mounting competition in their own home markets from United States manufactures. They had long been used to the United States as a formidable competitor in agricultural commodities, but now America was also the world's foremost producer of manufactured goods. Americans took pride in their economic power and easily translated it into nationalism. It is not surprising, for example, that during the 1890's a large number of patriotic societies, like the Sons of the American Revolution and the Daughters of the American Revolution, were founded. That was also the decade in which the cult of the national flag began; for the first time the flag salute and the flag itself were introduced into the public schoolroom. Speakers at public functions seemed to vie with one another in praising the power and the virtue of the United States. "The place of this nation is at the end of the column of civilization," intoned one speaker at a veterans' convention in 1896. "Not that we would put other nations down. . . . Our idea has always been and is now to point to other nations the way to come up higher."

More prominent and influential voices advanced similarly nationalistic sentiments. The intellectual if not the actual leader of these public figures was Admiral Alfred T. Mahan, a writer on naval affairs. His book *The Influence of Sea Power Upon History* (1890) was only the first of his works to urge the United States to a course that would put it in a class with the other great naval and imperialist powers of the time. Navies, colonies, and markets all went together to make a nation powerful, Mahan pointed out. America's destiny was clear. "Whether they will or no," he prophesied in 1893, "Americans must now begin to look outward." His views were echoed by important political figures like Theodore Roosevelt and Senator Henry Cabot Lodge as well as by influential editors like Walter Hines Page and Albert Shaw.

Not all the popular interest in looking outward derived from pride or the search for national power and prestige. It also seemed to arise from uncertainty and fear. For before there was expansion in the nineties there were social unrest, hard times, and farm discontent. The depression of 1893 triggered off huge strikes, alarming marches of industrial workers upon Washington, and the rise of widespread political discontent that in time would transfigure the Democratic party. Some conservatives understandably looked to war and international involvement as a means of silencing or at least muting that unrest and discontent. "While it might be putting it too strong to say that war is needed in this country now," wrote one Kansas newspaper, "yet who is there who does not believe, and in fact know, that such a thing would clear the atmosphere and stamp out the growth of socialism and anarchy, discontent and sectional prejudices that are gaining a foothold in this nation." One member of President Cleveland's cabinet in 1896 thought that the excessive nationalism of the time was "unaccountable except on account of the unrest of our people, and the willingness to turn from domestic to foreign affairs." Moreover, to many humanitarian-minded, Christian Americans, intervention in Cuba was necessary to stop the cruel war against the Cuban people and to free them from Spanish rule. Thus radical Democrats like William Jennings Bryan could become as aroused over Cuba as bellicose Republicans like Theodore Roosevelt.

But there were also more mundane reasons why many of America's leaders in the middle nineties were turning outward in their in-

terests. One was the growing capacity of American industry to produce goods at an enormous rate. One measure of the heightened capacity is that in 1897 for the first time in United States history the
value of manufactured exports exceeded imports. That same year also
saw the largest margin of difference between exports and imports in
United States history, suggesting the growing dependence of the
American economy on foreign markets. Indeed, so great was American economic capacity in the 1890's that responsible statesmen and
businessmen wondered whether the nation could absorb the surpluses.
As early as 1890 Secretary of State James G. Blaine had called attention to the need for new foreign markets if United States factories
were not to be stifled by their own excess production. Some Republican leaders tried to meet the problem by expanding American trade
abroad through reciprocity agreements. Thus the McKinley tariff of
1890 contained a reciprocity clause and the Republican platform of
1896 included a strong plank in favor of reciprocity. Nor were Republicans alone in their recognition of the problem. Democratic Secretary of State Walter Q. Gresham in 1894 thought there was a danger of social upheaval since "our mills and factories can supply the
home demand by running six or seven months in the year." The
onset of the depression of 1893 made the search for new markets
even more urgent. Democrats like Secretary of the Treasury William
L. Wilson defended a low tariff on the ground that it would open up
new markets and thereby improve the position of labor, for as things
stand, Wilson pointed out, "There is not one of our leading industries
that can find free and healthful play within the limits of our home
markets." Cleveland and his Secretary of the Treasury John Carlisle
thought that new markets would help to stanch the outflow of gold
that plagued the administration in the early months of the depression. During the depression of 1893 the National Association of
Manufacturers was founded to help open up new markets in Latin
America. It is not without significance that Richard Olney, Cleveland's Secretary of State, who took a strong stand against Britain in
the Venezuelan crisis, in later years looked back upon the year
1895 as the time when it became clear that United States foreign
relations took a new turn. Writing in 1898, he said there was a "crying need of . . . more markets and larger markets for the consumption of the products of the industry and inventive genius of the
American people." Home markets were simply not enough.

Into this complex of attitudes and needs the Cuban insurrection of

1895 came as a fortuitous, but highly consequential event. For three years Americans watched with mounting involvement as Spain sought to suppress the Cuban rebels and thereby forestall United States intervention in Cuba. But when it became evident that Spain could not crush the rebellion and yet would not grant independence to the Cubans, the United States entered into war in behalf of the Cubans. With the declaration of war the American urge to empire gained a new and propitious field of endeavor. Cuba itself was not available for annexation, because the so-called Teller Amendment to the declaration of war promised independence to the island. But nothing had been said about the Pacific possessions of Spain and it was among them that American imperialism found its expression.

The first concrete manifestation of the new imperialism was a reawakening of interest in the annexation of the Hawaiian Islands. In 1893 the Harrison administration had negotiated an annexation treaty only to have the new anticolonialist President Grover Cleveland withdraw the treaty from the Senate's consideration. In early July, 1898, however, less than three months after the war with Spain had begun, Hawaii was annexed by joint resolution of Congress, which required only a simple majority. Significantly, at about the same time, the United States took possession of Spanish-held Guam Island and unoccupied Wake Island in the Pacific. With Hawaii, Midway, Wake, and Guam the United States now possessed a series of coaling stations or "stepping stones" that stretched three-quarters of the way from California to China. The next natural "step" was the Philippines.

Some historians, in accounting for the United States naval attack upon Manila, even before American troops had landed in Cuba, have placed much emphasis upon the activities of Theodore Roosevelt as Assistant Secretary of the Navy. It is true that before war with Spain broke out, Roosevelt, while temporarily in charge of the department, ordered Admiral George Dewey, stationed in Asian waters, to be prepared to attack the Philippines in the event of war with Spain. It is equally true that Roosevelt was an imperialist as well as a believer in the social therapy of war. But it seems evident now that the McKinley administration's interest in the Philippines was not thrust upon it. It is significant, for example, that when the Secretary of the Navy returned to his post he did not countermand Roosevelt's order to Dewey. Moreover, there was nothing sinister or even unusual in Roosevelt's order to advance upon a possession

of Spain in the event of war with that country; it was the prudent
and the expected thing to do. As a result of that attack, however, before the war was over in Cuba, the Philippines were in American
hands, with President McKinley faced with the decision of what to
do with them.

McKinley's decision to keep the Philippines was undoubtedly compounded from a variety of motives. Certainly there was a strong feeling around the country that the United States ought to have an empire, or so McKinley seemed to feel after he had made a speaking
tour sounding out public opinion. Within the administration there was
also fear that if the United States did not take the islands, Japan or
Germany might, and such an eventuality was felt to be neither good
for the Filipinos nor for continuing American influence in the western Pacific. Then there was also the question of the economic interest of the United States in Asia.

Considering the activities of the McKinley administration in the
weeks prior to the decision, the interest in the China trade looms
large among the explanations as to why the Philippines were kept. It
is true that prior to the outbreak of war with Spain over Cuba, most
United States businessmen were not pushing for war, believing that
hostilities would disrupt trade rather than advance it. But talk about
the vast market of China had been a staple of public and private
discussion for years. And in the face of the burgeoning production
of American factories, the opening of new markets was high on the
agenda of the administration. The permanent acquisition of the Philippines, just off the coast of China and at the Asian end of the newly
acquired stepping stones of Hawaii, Wake, and Guam, would give
the United States a special and advantageous avenue to the great
Asian market. As Mark Hanna, President McKinley's close adviser
and a businessman himself, said, possession of the Philippines would
permit the United States to "take a large slice of the commerce of
Asia. That is what we want. We are bound to share in the commerce
of the Far East and it is better to strike for it while the iron is hot."
Even in July, 1898, when the annexation of Hawaii was before the
Senate, Senator George F. Hoar was telling President McKinley that
supporters of annexation were asserting that Hawaii was essential
"in order to help us get our share of China."

American imperialism, then, differed from the classic European
form in that it did not seek administrative control over markets and
peoples, but principally access to markets. Political control could

be left in local hands. As one midwestern Congressman pointed out in regard to the annexation of Hawaii: "I can distinguish between the policy that would scatter colonies all over the islands of the sea and the land of the earth and that policy which would secure to us simply those facilities of commerce that the new commercial methods make absolutely essential." (The island stepping stones would provide the necessary coaling stations for naval and merchant vessels as well as stations for undersea cables.)

It was this distinction between colonial and commercial imperialism on which the McKinley administration acted when it acquired the Philippines. Perhaps the neatest if highly partisan summary of the American urge to acquire Pacific real estate was given by the well-known Republican orator Chauncey M. Depew at the Convention of his party in 1900. "The American people now produce $2 billion worth more than they can consume, and we have met the emergency, and by the providence of God, by the statesmanship of William McKinley, and by the valor of Roosevelt and his associates, we have our market in Cuba . . . in Puerto Rico . . . in Hawaii . . . in the Philippines, and we stand in the presence of 800 million of people, with the Pacific as an American lake, and the American artisans producing better and cheaper goods than any country in the world. . . . Let production go on . . . let the factories do their best, let labor be employed at the highest wages, because the world is ours, and we have conquered it by Republican principles."[2]

Two subsequent developments in United States foreign affairs add substance to the interpretation that American interest in the Philippines was dictated more by concern for trade than for territory and subject peoples. The first is that within a matter of two years—i.e., by 1901 at the latest—the apparent urge of Americans for territorial expansion subsided, apparently for good. No more territory has since been acquired, except for shreds for special purposes like the Panama Canal Zone or the Virgin Islands. Furthermore, almost all of the territory gained during the Great Aberration has been either relinquished entirely—as in the case of the Philippines—or incorpo-

---

[2] An even more self-interested assertion, if that is possible, was Henry Cabot Lodge's at the same convention: "We make no hypocritical pretense of being interested in the Philippines solely on account of others. While we regard the welfare of these people as a sacred trust, we regard the welfare of the American people first." For anyone familiar with Woodrow Wilson's approach to foreign policy, this statement by Lodge goes a long way to explain why neither man trusted or respected the other.

rated into the United States proper, as in the instances of Hawaii
and Alaska. Indeed, the revulsion against territorial acquisition set
in so quickly that as early as 1907, erstwhile fervent imperialist Theodore Roosevelt was calling the Philippines the "Achilles' Heel" of
the United States defenses in the Pacific. In 1916, the Jones Act
promised eventual independence to the Philippines, which was
granted exactly thirty years later.

The second series of events to suggest that United States expansion
in 1898 was dictated by commercial rather than colonial concerns
is the enunciation of the Open Door policy by Secretary of State John
Hay in 1899.[3] As Hay saw the great powers on the verge of carving
up China into closed spheres of economic activity, he attempted to
forestall the possibility that the United States, as a latecomer into
Asia, would be "frozen out" of the supposedly great China market.
Hence in September, 1899, he sent to each of the European powers
active in China identical notes, asking that they give "formal recognition" that all would "enjoy perfect equality for their commerce and
navigation within" the spheres of interest of the others. Because the
response of the big powers was evasive and vague and Hay's standard of acceptance extremely loose, historians have often cited the
Open Door notes as an especially egregious example of American
ineptitude and self-deception in foreign affairs.

It is quite true, as Hays admitted in 1901 in response to a Japanese inquiry, that the United States was not prepared "to attempt
singly or in concert with other powers, to enforce these views in the
east by any demonstration which could present a character of hostility to any other power." And it is also true that in the twentieth
century the United States itself sought exclusive privileges in China,
in violation of its own principle of the Open Door. But whatever
the defects in the Open Door policy—and there were a number—the
fact remains that the purpose of the policy was to keep the opportunities of the allegedly vast China market open to American busi-

[3] A. Whitney Griswold, *The Far Eastern Policy of the United States* (New
York, 1938), makes much of the alleged British inspiration behind Hay's
Open Door policy. The fact is that Hay had long been thinking in such terms,
and by the time he sent his notes, British interest in the idea had dissipated.
See Foster R. Dulles, *America's Rise to World Power, 1898–1954* (New York,
1955), p. 64n. Unfortunately, an influential commentator on American foreign policy, George Frost Kennan, in his *American Diplomacy, 1900–1950*
(Chicago, 1951), perpetuates the Griswold error, using it as another example
of United States naïveté in foreign policy matters.

ness. To that extent, the Open Door continued the policy that brought the United States across the Pacific on its island stepping stones— access to the potential trade of China.[4]

The Open Door is important, too, because it was an extension of two cardinal principles of early American policy: freedom of trade and self-determination. For in the course of the twentieth century the Open Door came to include the idea that the territorial integrity of China must be maintained. These two ideas became the cornerstones of United States policy in Asia. Ironically, at one time the United States expected Japan to be a partner in holding the door open in Asia, for Japan, like the United States, was a latecomer to the trade and markets of China. But even before the First World War it was evident that Japan, with its own growing interests in China, was going to be the most hostile opponent of the idea. For that reason one is tempted to see the Open Door notes of 1899 as the first steps on the road to Pearl Harbor.

If the Spanish-American War and the acquisition of a new overseas empire marked the abandonment of the traditional policy of the United States, in a less obvious sense the events of the late nineties constituted no real departure at all. The country, to be sure, was now involved in areas once only peripheral to its concerns. Asia thereafter would be a continuing and growing interest for the United States, so that in 1966 President Lyndon Johnson could speak of the United States as a Pacific power. In that sense, the Spanish-American War was a significant turning point in the history of American relations with the world. But if one defines isolation as George Washington did, as meaning no entangling alliances with Europe, then one must look elsewhere for the first real break with tradition. For even with the acquisition of the Philippines the United States was still free to act as it saw fit; its unilateral freedom had

---

[4] Diplomatic historian Richard W. Leopold, in *The Growth of American Foreign Policy* (New York, 1962), Chapter 10, lists four general reasons for the imperialism of the 1890's: 1. The strategic root—bases, etc. 2. Economic root—markets, etc. 3. Religious root—missionaries. 4. Emotional root—adventure, tensions within society, racism, national pride. Of the four he finds the last the "most significant. Indeed, it may be argued that the American people quickly turned away from overseas dependence because once their emotional needs were satisfied, the other pressures were too weak to uphold a policy that did not accord with their traditional ideals or the principles upon which their institutions rested." It could be said, however, that if the China market was the goal, imperialism fell off because by 1900 that market was in reach and turned out to be rather unimportant.

not been circumscribed by any multilateral commitments. Most Americans after 1898 still thought of themselves as isolated from the affairs of the world. In 1943, for example, Walter Lippmann, who in 1915 became one of the editors of the *New Republic,* recalled, "I cannot remember taking any interest whatsoever in foreign affairs until after the outbreak of the First World War. . . . I remained quite innocent of the revolutionary consequences of the Spanish-American War."

3. THE MOST FATEFUL STEP

Nothing more clearly illustrates the American sense of isolation from the affairs of Europe than the domestic reaction to the outbreak of the European war in August, 1914. President Wilson not only proclaimed American neutrality, but he felt he could also ask Americans to be neutral in thought as well as in deed. One Boston newspaper quipped at about the same time, "The worst has befallen in this cruel war. The price of beans has risen." The significance of the country's gradual but steady movement toward war is not that a declaration of war resulted, but that for two and a half years most Americans, from the President on down, believed that the United States could remain out of the war. That it was not able to stay out has been a subject of consuming interest ever since, to both historian and citizen alike. During the 1920's and 1930's in particular, writers like C. Hartley Grattan and Walter Millis, as well as professional historians like C. C. Tansill, pressed hard upon the public the idea that American involvement in war in 1917 was the result of economic and other causes that did not reflect the true national interest. More recent historians, however, have tended to find the economic causes inadequate. It is true that the initial friendliness toward the Allied cause was strengthened by a burgeoning trade in goods and munitions, the sales of which helped to bring the United States out of a mild depression in 1914. And it is also true that Secretary of State William Jennings Bryan resigned over the issue of loans to belligerents because he feared the effect of the growing economic connections between the United States and the Allies upon the United States policy of neutrality. Today, however, most historians reject a purely or even largely economic explanation for the decision for war in 1917. Certainly one reason for rejecting that explanation is that by 1916 the economy of the country was at such a high level that even if Allied trade had been cut off, prosperity probably would not have been seriously endangered. But the principal reason for considering economic influence minor is that, as far as the decision makers were concerned, such influences, so far as they can be traced, were weak or nonexistent. Uppermost in Wilson's mind was neutral rights. And it is around his handling of this concern that modern historians' analyses revolve.

Wilson's emphasis upon the protection of United States rights as a trading neutral was quite in keeping with the American diplomatic tradition. The doctrine that "free goods make free ships" was one of the cardinal principles set forth by the Continental Congress in the Model Treaty of 1776. Madison and Jefferson had both emphasized the advantages to be' gained by the United States as a neutral engaged in trade during a war. "The new world will fatten on the follies of the old," was Jefferson's cynical way of putting it. As diplomatic historian Richard Leopold has written, "Second only to isolationism as a polestar of American diplomacy in the formative years was the principle of neutrality."

Wilson's conception of neutral rights—which followed established international law—asserted that the United States was free to trade in noncontraband goods with any belligerent it pleased and that its nationals were free to travel unmolested on belligerent ships. This view of neutral rights, it is worth emphasizing, clashed as vigorously with British practices as it did with German. In fact, the clash was more resounding since Great Britain was a major sea power and thereby was in a position to interfere with American trade with blockaded Germany. Indeed, for a while in 1915–16, when difficulties with the Germans were in a period of quiet, Anglo-American relations were near the breaking point over the right of Americans to trade with Germany without interference. The issue that set Britain's anti-neutral behavior apart from Germany's was the submarine.

Inasmuch as Great Britain was the primary sea power of the time, it was able to blockade Germany with surface ships and thus did not need to resort to the new naval weapon of the submarine. Germany, on the other hand, as a land power with a navy inferior to Britain's, was impelled to make maximum use of a weapon that promised to overcome that inferiority. The submarine enabled Germany to carry out a blockade of the British Isles—an achievement that would have been impossible with surface ships, given the superiority of the British Navy. But in order to use the submarine effectively as a blockad-

ing weapon, Germany had to break two of the principal rules of traditional international warfare—namely, that, in sinking merchant
ships, warning was to be given and the lives of crews and passengers
safeguarded. The latter requirement meant that they were to be
picked up or taken to safety. This rule originated before the invention of the submarine and for a blockading surface vessel the requirement presented no difficulties. For a submarine, however, the
rule was impractical—there was no room for any extra personnel in
the narrow confines of a U-boat—and essentially self-destructive.
The only security the thinly armored and weakly armed submarine
possessed against surface warships or even armed merchantmen was
its ability to approach undetected under water. To give warning or
to pick up survivors was to deprive the submarine of its single advantage as a weapon and to invite destruction.

The Germans were well aware that the submarine did not fit into
the traditional canons of international law, but, given their inferior
surface navy, they could not forego the advantages that would accrue
from its use. Under insistent pressure from Wilson in 1915 and 1916
they grudgingly agreed, first, to sink no passenger liners and then,
in the Sussex pledge of May, 1916, to sink no unarmed merchant
ship of either neutral or belligerent registry. Wilson was not able to
secure promises from the Allies, however, that they, in turn, would
refrain from arming their merchant ships. Given the continued Allied
use of armed merchant ships, it was inevitable that the Germans
would break the Sussex pledge and thereby force Wilson to take the
United States into war against Germany. Wilson always believed that
his policy of firmness toward the Germans without war was what the
American people wanted. When William Jennings Bryan resigned
in 1915, for example, Wilson conceded to him that it was not clear
that there was a sure way of realizing "the double wish of our people,
to maintain a firm front in respect of what we demand of Germany,
and yet do nothing that might by any possibility involve us in war."
Unlike Bryan, Wilson was prepared to take the risk. Unfortunately
for Wilson's desire to satisfy the "double wish" of the American
people, the German Army and Navy were convinced that only
through all-out submarine warfare could the Allies be defeated. Over
the long term, fear of United States involvement did not deter them.
The submarine was their most potent weapon against Britain, and
American support of the Allies was considered so great already that
full participation in the war was not deemed too high a price to pay

for full and unrestrained use of a powerful and probably indispensable weapon. Thus when the Germans announced on January 31, 1917, the resumption of unrestricted submarine warfare, Wilson had little alternative, given his assertion of United States' rights and honor in the past, particularly at the time of the Sussex pledge in May, 1916.[5] He waited two months as German submarines piled up irrefutable evidence of Germany's intention to carry out an all-out war against shipping in the North Atlantic, even at the cost of American lives and ships. Having only humiliation as an alternative, Wilson chose war.

Ever since the First World War, two large questions about that conflict have troubled both the American people and the historians. One, which has been running like a red thread through this discussion of American entrance into the war, is: Could the United States have stayed out of that war? The other question is: If it had been possible to stay out, should the United States have stayed out? Put another way, was entrance into the First World War a mistake? The answer given to all of these questions by many Americans during the 1920's and 1930's was a resounding "Yes."[6] Let us look at the two questions separately.

On a purely practical level it is highly probable that the United States could have avoided getting into war in 1917, if it had been willing to abandon its conception of international law and its rights as a neutral. It was very unlikely that Germany would have attacked the United States without provocation; without trade between the United States and the Allies there would have been no occasion for conflict or incidents between the United States and Germany. But whether the American people, much less their conscientious President, in the context of 1917, would have accepted a voluntary abandonment of traditional rights is another question. In 1812, when the United States was much less formidable, it went to war over neutral rights; in 1917 a similar cause could hardly help but evoke a similar

[5] Apparently Wilson was well aware of the dilemma the Sussex pledge placed him in. He told his Secretary of the Navy in late 1916 that he did not like the slogan of the Democratic Presidential campaign of that year: "He kept us out of war." "I can't keep the country out of war," he told Daniels. "They talk of me as though I were a god. Any little German lieutenant can put us into the war at any time by some calculated outrage."

[6] In 1937, according to a public opinion poll, 71 per cent of the American people thought that entrance of the United States into World War I had been a mistake.

response from a much stronger United States. Wilson, it is true, upheld a higher standard than some other leaders in the government. Secretary of State Bryan, for example, was prepared to go a long way in abandoning neutral rights in behalf of peace. And in 1916 some Senators recommended that Americans be prohibited from traveling on belligerent ships since it was the killing of Americans that made German infractions of neutral rights seem so much more intolerable than British interference with American trade. Wilson, however, would have none of it. "For my part," he wrote in 1916 to one Senator supporting the McLemore resolution, which would have prohibited Americans' traveling on belligerent ships in the war zone, "I cannot consent to any abridgment of the rights of American citizens in any respect. The honor and self-respect of the nation is involved. We covet peace and shall preserve it at any cost but the loss of honor. To forbid our people to exercise their rights for fear we might be called upon to vindicate them would be a deep humiliation indeed. . . . It would be a deliberate abdication of our hitherto proud position as spokesman . . . for the law and right. . . . Once accept a single abatement of right, and many other humiliations would certainly follow, and the whole fine fabric of international law might crumble under our hands piece by piece."

Later, in the 1930's, the revulsion against Wilson's adamant defense of neutral rights and international law was so severe that the whole structure he defended was abandoned. The so-called Neutrality Laws of 1935–37 forbade Americans to travel on belligerent ships in time of war, to lend money to belligerents, or to sell munitions to warring nations. Americans in the 1930's applied what they considered the lessons of the First World War to the problem of war in their own time. Probably never before had history been used so deliberately and mechanically in the formulation of foreign policy.

The great assumption behind the neutrality legislation of the 1930's was that if the United States could have stayed out of war in 1917, it ought to have done just that. Since the Second World War, however, this assumption has been increasingly questioned. (As so often happens in historical interpretation, subsequent developments quite rightly change the historical meaning of an event. Hitler's attempt to dominate Europe made men see German power in 1917 in a different, though not necessarily more accurate light.) Walter Lippmann and others have argued that the real reason the United States went to war in 1917 was not because of neutral rights, though they provided the occasion. The true reason was in order to preserve the balance of power in Europe, to prevent Germany from dominating the continent, a development that very likely would have occurred if the Allies had been defeated. And that defeat might well have occurred if American troops had not been sent to France. Some idea of what that defeat would have meant is suggested by the Treaty of Brest-Litovsk, which a victorious Germany imposed upon Bolshevik Russia in 1918. In that settlement Germany received control over the Russian Baltic provinces, domination over Poland, and a protectorate over the Ukraine, which was to be separated from Russia. It seems reasonable that a similarly Carthaginian peace would have been imposed on France, Belgium, and Italy if Germany had won in the West as it did in the East. Such a peace would have left Germany master of the continent and a threat to Britain, the rest of Europe and even the United States.

But however sound may be the argument that the United States ought to have entered World War I, the contention that in 1917 such considerations shaped the decision for war is not borne out by the evidence. As Robert Osgood has shown, not even bellicose Theodore Roosevelt argued that the security of the United States depended upon the defeat of Germany. His insistent appeals for more action against Germany by President Wilson were usually couched in terms of a struggle against an enemy of civilization rather than a threat to the United States in any specific sense. Similarly, Ambassador Walter Hines Page and Secretary of State Robert Lansing, two of Wilson's closest official advisers who favored war against Germany, rarely spoke of the need to preserve the balance of power in Europe, even in their private letters. Wilson himself, his closest friend Colonel Edward House reported, took the view in the fall of 1914 that "even if Germany won, she would not be in a condition seriously to menace our country for many years to come. . . . He did not believe there was the slightest danger to this country from foreign invasion, even if the Germans were successful." And as Ernest May has pointed out, "Wilson had not retracted" that statement at the time he made the decision for war. Arthur Link, Wilson's biographer, would like to think that considerations about the balance of power in Europe played a role in Wilson's decision. But even he has to admit that there is no direct evidence to sustain that view.

Certainly Wilson's public defense of American entrance into war was devoid of any appeal to self-interest or a threat to American security in the foreseeable future. In fact, Wilson's principal argument before and after the decision for war was that America acted in behalf of principle, not self-interest. In his war message, for example, he called the submarine not a threat to United States security, but "a war against all nations. . . . The challenge is to all mankind." Two days before he sailed for Paris, after the war, to attend the meetings with the heads of state drafting the peace treaty with Germany, Wilson told an audience, "We are about to give order and organization to this peace not only for ourselves, but for the other peoples of the world as well. . . . It is international justice we seek, not domestic safety merely." Later, in defending the treaty, he said, "My friends, we did not go to France to fight for anything special for America. We did not send men 3,000 miles away to defend our territory. We did not take up the gage that Germany had thrown down to us because America was being especially injured. America was not being specially injured. We sent those men over there because free people everywhere were in danger and we had always been, and will always be, the champion of right and of liberty."[7]

4. THE FLIGHT FROM COMMITMENT

When Wilson led Americans into war he promised that a new international order would emerge from the struggle. Even though the treaty drawn up at Versailles was not the peace without victory for which Wilson had called, the President was confident that his League of Nations would in time right the inequities imposed by the peace treaty. The failure of the United States to join the League was therefore a major defeat and disappointment to him. As Wilson knew, the League was quite in line with the American tradition of a world legal order that would ensure peace. No previous President, it is true, had pressed such an institution, but its underlying assumptions were close to those of Jefferson and Madison when they spoke of natural law and a new order in international affairs.

The fact of the matter is that the defeat of the League did not stem from any deep hostility on the part of Americans. Neither in

---

[7] What a contrast there is between Wilson's conception of why the United States went to war and that of Senator William Borah, the well-known isolationist! In 1917 Borah said he voted for war on one basis only: "I join no crusade; I seek or accept no alliance; I obligate this government to no other power. I make war alone for my countrymen and their rights, for my country and its **honor.**"

the Senate nor in the country at large was there ever a majority solidly opposed to an international organization. Even in the Senate, as Arthur Link has pointed out, the fight over the League was between strong and mild internationalists. The so-called hard-line isolationists, like Henry Cabot Lodge, William Borah, and Hiram Johnson, whose opposition is well known, were always in a decided minority in the Senate and the country. In November, 1919, for example, 85 per cent of the Senators were prepared to accept a league of some kind. At all times during the Senate discussions, there was a majority willing to accept the League on Wilson's terms, though a two-thirds majority was required for acceptance of a treaty. Even that two-thirds vote could have been obtained if Wilson had been willing to accept some reservations from the more internationalist-minded Republicans. As far as the country as a whole was concerned, the *Literary Digest* reported in April, 1919, that 718 newspapers favored the League, 181 opposed it, and 478 were conditional on the issue. In no section of the country was there a majority of newspapers in opposition to the treaty. Indeed, Senator Henry Cabot Lodge, who was hostile to the League from the outset, was so apprehensive about public opinion and the reaction of the Senate to the treaty that, as chairman of the Senate Foreign Relations Committee, he deliberately delayed for weeks before bringing it before the committee. In substance, there never was a large-scale opposition to Wilson's League. On the other hand, it is equally clear that neither the Senate nor the country at large felt the same passion for the League that Wilson did. Because of his leadership and the American tradition in foreign affairs, the country and the Senate seemed ready to go along with him, at least to the extent of accepting American membership in some kind of international organization. Wilson's refusal to compromise or to accept changes in the Covenant and his physical breakdown prevented the translation of general support for *a* league into hard Senatorial agreement on membership in *the* League of Nations.

The failure of the United States to join the League has been seen by many Americans, then and later, as a welcome return to the old isolation and freedom from entanglement with Europe. It was certainly the latter, but whether it was also the former is another question. Many citizens and statesmen alike may have wished for a return to the old days, but as the postwar decade was soon to show, that road was no longer open. The very position of the United States in the world was now altered, making a return to the nineteenth-century practices in foreign policy impossible as well as anachronistic. The United States was simply too powerful militarily and economically to be able to slip back into its old relationship with the world.

One sign that new circumstances dictated new policies even to a Republican and anti-Wilsonian administration was the series of international agreements negotiated at Washington in 1921–22. These agreements on naval disarmament (Five Power Treaty), on the territorial integrity of China (Nine Power Treaty), and on the political organization of the western Pacific (Four Power Treaty) were all part of the effort to bring some order into the relationships among the powers in the Pacific. In that sense the treaties were a part of the larger international order that European statesmen had begun to construct, immediately after the war, with the Versailles Treaty.

The Washington treaties clearly signaled the new importance and power of the United States in world affairs. In the Five Power Treaty on naval disarmament, for example, the United States was accorded parity in battleships with Great Britain, the traditional mistress of the seas. In the Nine Power Treaty the American policies of the Open Door and the territorial integrity of China were now formally accepted by the principal powers interested in Asia. Later events would show that Japan's acceptance was more verbal than substantive, but the shift in the relations among the powers in the Pacific area that the treaties as a whole exemplified was clearly more than verbal. Great Britain, which had been allied with Japan since 1902, now abandoned that alliance in favor of friendship with the United States, which it obviously viewed as the dominant power in the Pacific.

There were no comparable agreements regarding Europe, but during the 1920's the United States became increasingly active economically in Europe. Again, the fundamental cause was the new and dominant position achieved by the United States economically and financially. For one of the several consequences of the war was that the United States changed from a debtor nation (borrowing money from other nations) to a creditor nation (lending capital to others). American capital now became an important ingredient in the postwar economy of western and central Europe. Indeed, the steady flow of United States capital into Germany made it possible for that country to meet its reparations payments to the Allies. For a while during the 1920's, the State Department tried to channel this economic power in behalf of its own foreign policies, a practice that Herbert Feis has called "The Diplomacy of the Dollar." By permitting

American firms and banks to invest or lend money only to those countries whose policies fitted the preconceptions of American statesmen, the superior economic position of the United States became an arm of foreign policy. At one point, for example, the State Department turned down a loan to a brewery in Czechoslovakia because to support an alcohol-producing enterprise violated the American domestic policy of prohibition. On the other hand, the State Department did not prevent loans to steel manufacturers in Germany. These were also the years during which Herbert Hoover's Department of Commerce was active in foreign economic affairs. Hoover sought to use the power of the United States to prevent producers of raw materials like rubber and coffee from raising or maintaining prices through international agreements and other devices.

A further instance of United States involvement in the world during the so-called isolationist 1920's was the Kellogg-Briand Pact of 1928. The lack of realism in a multilateral agreement to renounce war as an instrument of national policy is certainly patent. The whole idea, in the 1920's as later, has been easily ridiculed. But the Kellogg-Briand Pact was an international agreement with a number of countries and to that extent revealed the United States' continuing and ineluctable involvement in the affairs of the world in general and in Europe in particular.

Yet, if these ventures into agreements with European and Asian states in the 1920's seemed departures from past practices, in another sense they exemplified a continuity with the past. And in linking the postwar years with the preceding decades, these agreements served to connect the policies of the past with those of the 1930's. That linkage was the insistence, on the part of the United States, that in no way was its traditional freedom of action to be curtailed by any agreement into which it entered. This had been American policy ever since 1800, when the French alliance was finally terminated; it had been reflected in Wilson's careful insistence that the United States was an Associated, not an Allied power when it entered war in 1917. The Senate displayed a much more exaggerated form of the same fear of "entanglement" during the debates on the Washington treaties. Anxious Senators ransacked dictionaries and treatises on international law to be sure that none of the agreements could be even remotely considered an alliance. In the end, the Senatorial anxiety was assuaged only by appending formal reservations that no alliance or commitment to force had been created by the treaties. Similarly, in

the Nine Power Treaty the United States supported the concept of
the territorial integrity of China, but it did not commit itself to do
anything to insure or protect that principle, either alone or in concert with other signatories. Also, in the Kellogg-Briand Pact, the
United States vowed not to use war as an instrument of national
policy, but this pious agreement did not obligate the United States
to go to any country's defense. Totally absent from all of the formal
international agreements of the 1920's was the obligation to work
with other powers as the Covenant of the League required. Similarly, men like Secretary of Commerce Herbert Hoover, who wanted
the United States to use its enormous economic power to help shape
the world as Americans liked it, still kept intact the freedom of action they cherished for their country.

The isolationism of the 1920's, in short, did not preclude agreements with other powers about matters of importance to the United
States. Nor did it preclude the use of American economic or even
military power, as in Central America, just so long as the United
States retained its freedom of action on the international scene. The
new isolationism was, in brief, nationalistic, activist, and not untouched by idealism. The last attribute was best expressed by Senator
Borah—an irreconcilable opponent of the League in 1919, an advocate of the Kellogg Pact in the 1920's, and an isolationist in the
1930's. During the Senate debate in July, 1919, Borah said, "If I
have had a conviction throughout my life with which it has been
possible for me to be consistent at all times, it has been the conviction that we should stay out of European and Asiatic affairs. I do
not think we can have here a great, powerful, independent, self-governing Republic and do anything else; I do not think it possible for
us to continue to be the leading intellectual and moral power in the
world and do anything else. I do not think we can achieve the task
now confronting us, that of establishing here an industrial democracy, as we have achieved a political democracy, and do anything
else."

If the isolationist past was the principal intellectual force shaping
the foreign policies of the 1920's and 1930's, the impact of the First
World War was a close rival. All through the two decades men referred to the horrors of war in a way that had not been evident after
the Spanish-American War or even after the Civil War. The desire
to reduce the dangers of a new war, for example, provided a large
part of the impetus for the Washington Conference of 1921–22. For

one thing, Senator Borah initiated the whole idea with a demand for a disarmament conference. For another, it was Secretary of State Charles Evans Hughes' dramatic recommendation, at the opening of the conference, that sixty-six battleships be scrapped that captured the most interest then and since. The Kellogg-Briand Pact similarly issued from the body of the peace movement. Leaders for peace, like Nicholas Murray Butler and James T. Shotwell sparked the popular drive to outlaw war, and others interested in world peace, like Jane Addams and Senator Borah, carried the idea to fulfillment, even over the amused objections of more realistic members of the public and the Senate.

A similar dread of a new war runs all through the arguments of the isolationists during the 1930's. "Our civilization is at stake," said one Senator. "We went through the valley of the shadow of death seventeen years ago. In God's name let us not go through another." Representative Louis Ludlow, who introduced an amendment to the Constitution to require that a popular referendum be held to declare war, spelled out the fears of many Americans, especially isolationists. "The next war will be a war in which machinery will overshadow manpower," he wrote in a book in 1937, "with airplanes raining poison and peoples fighting each other with weapons of wholesale massacre. No longer will active participation in wars be limited to the combatant armies on the field of battle. Henceforth whole populations will be involved." Witnesses before the Senate Munitions Investigating Committee, he went on, "predicted that the next war will destroy civilization." Other isolationists emphasized the repression that war would bring. "War means the setting up of a complete dictatorship here," warned Congressman George H. Tinkham in July, 1941. "It means the abolition of free economics, the imposition of censorship and espionage, in short, the establishment of totalitarian government." Because many isolationists believed that reform and democracy would be threatened by war, many of Franklin Roosevelt's Republican supporters on the domestic front—like Senators William Borah, Gerald P. Nye, Robert La Follette, and Representative William Frazier—were his opponents on foreign policy. Some progressive-minded isolationists like Norman Thomas, the Socialist leader, and Charles A. Beard, the historian, were so convinced that war would destroy democracy and impede social progress that they remained opposed to Roosevelt's foreign policy right down to Pearl Harbor and beyond.

The isolationists of the 1930's also feared compromising the nation's freedom of action in foreign affairs, which had seemed so important to the opponents of the League. Isolationist Charles A. Lindbergh, for example, in a radio address in the fall of 1940 specifically entered "a plea for American independence." Why, he asked, with 130 million people, "are we being told that we must give up our independent position, that our frontiers lie in Europe and that our destinies will be decided by armies fighting on European soil?" Three months later in January, 1941, a less prominent isolationist admitted that he would like to see Great Britain win. "But I would not like to see her win at the expense of diverting ourselves from our plain duty as I see it to be—neutral." This concern about maintaining freedom of action also helps to explain why an outspoken isolationist like Senator Robert A. Taft could say, "It is not nearly so dangerous to become involved in a war in the Pacific as in the European war . . ." In the Far East there was no danger of multilateral restrictions on United States international behavior as there was in Europe. Intervention in Europe would mean allies; intervention in the Pacific meant only hostility toward Japan, which was only half as bad in the eyes of unilateralists. It might bring war, but it would not entail alien restrictions on American actions.[8]

Americans may have seemed wedded during the 1930's to a continuing policy of aloofness from European affairs, but they could no more stay out of the European war that began in the fall of 1939 than they had been able to stay out of the First World War. The

[8] Simply because isolationists in the 1930's were concerned with preserving the United States' freedom of action, they tended to be more interested in building up United States' defenses than some of their later opponents would concede. Insofar as isolationists were unilateralists, they were nationalists—which meant that often they wanted American military power increased. Hence many isolationist Congressmen willingly supported military appropriations during the 1930's. The same Congresses that enacted the neutrality legislation of 1935 and 1937, for example, passed $17 billion in military and Navy appropriations. Until 1940 both the American Legion and the Veterans of Foreign Wars, two highly nationalistic organizations of veterans, supported an isolationist position on foreign policy.

This willingness of isolationists to support preparedness measures, it ought to be said, changed in 1940, when the international scene had altered and Roosevelt's policy became clearly pro-Ally. At that point military preparations seemed to isolationists to be a way of enmeshing the nation in the European war. Hence the dwindling number of isolationists strongly opposed preparedness measures. The high-water mark of isolationist power to limit military preparedness was the near defeat of the extension of the draft in the fall of 1941. The measure came within one vote of being defeated in the House.

significant difference between the two lay in the events that followed. After 1941 Americans abandoned their traditional allegiance to unilateralism.

That shift in outlook, however, was neither sudden nor easy. Even Franklin Roosevelt, in October, 1935, after the outbreak of war between Italy and Ethiopia that summer, voiced the traditional view. "Despite what happens in continents overseas," he told the country, "the United States of America shall and must remain, as long ago the Father of Our Country prayed that it might remain—unentangled and free." With such an outlook he could sign the neutrality legislation of the middle thirties despite some misgivings. Actually, the so-called Neutrality Laws abandoned, as we have seen, the principles of neutrality for which the nation had stood from its founding.

The rise of Hitler, his successes in Europe in 1938 and after, and the growing power of Japan in China and the Pacific, however, posed a threat to the balance of power in the world. As a result, many Americans, including Franklin Roosevelt, began to rethink their traditional view of America's role in the world. Indeed, as Robert Osgood has pointed out, the significant fact about the isolationists of the 1930's was not their number, but the number of their opponents, especially after 1939. For the first time since the 1790's there was a large and growing number of Americans who were advocating that the United States take sides in a European conflict. After the fall of France in the early summer of 1940, the country was unmistakably on the side of the British and the French, though still reluctant to go to war. As late as January, 1939, a majority of Americans had not believed that the United States ought to defend countries like Mexico, Brazil, or the Philippines if they were attacked. By August, 1940, well over a majority thought all of these places should be defended by the United States. In short, Americans felt a threat to their security in 1940 that had been absent in 1917; consequently they had a new and realistic view of the world—perhaps for the first time in the twentieth century. When the battle of Britain in the fall of 1940 revealed the pressing need of England for massive support from the United States, the American people were prepared to go along with Roosevelt's suggestion for "Lend-Lease," which gave the British, in effect, a blank check to draw upon American production in order to resist the Nazis. To confirmed isolationists the passage of Lend-Lease in March, 1941, marked a major turning point. "We have torn up 150 years of traditional foreign policy," Senator Arthur Vandenberg wrote in his diary at the time. "We have tossed Washington's Farewell Address into the discard. We have thrown ourselves squarely into the power politics and power wars of Europe, Asia, and Africa. We have taken the first step upon a course from which we can never hereafter retreat."

Vandenberg's prophecy was more accurate than he could have anticipated. The reason he was right lay in the changing attitude of Americans in the face of rising German and Japanese power. That Americans were increasingly fearful of the Germans and Japanese is shown by their willingness to accept the Roosevelt administration's bold support of Britain. Neither public opinion nor Congress prevented the President from doing what he thought was demanded by Britain's plight, even when it involved using the Navy to patrol the North Atlantic in league with the British Navy, or placing soldiers on Greenland and Iceland to prevent those Danish possessions from falling into the hands of the Germans after the Nazi occupation of Denmark. Roosevelt's meeting in August, 1941, with Churchill at Argentia Bay, Newfoundland, to write the Atlantic Charter and to agree on postwar aims was undoubtedly the most unneutral act ever committed by a professed neutral. Yet the Atlantic meeting aroused surprisingly little hostile sentiment except among a small group of die-hard isolationists. The country, in short, was accepting the idea of support of Britain short of war; it was apparently also supporting Roosevelt's policy of countering the Japanese conquest of China and the Japanese threats against the French, Dutch, and British colonies in southeast Asia.

Despite his bold action and acute sense of the need for support of the British, F.D.R. did not believe the American people would sustain him if the exigencies of the situation demanded full-scale war against Germany or Japan. Indeed, to this day, no one knows whether he wanted war, if that should be necessary to stop Hitler. Some historians, drawing upon public opinion polls, have argued that Roosevelt may well have overestimated the influence of the isolationist minority. Public opinion, for example, was several months ahead of Congress on such measures as the lifting of the arms embargo and the establishing of compulsory military training. (In September, 1940, for example, 53 per cent of Americans thought the defeat of Hitler was more important than staying out of war. In January, 1941, some 68 per cent of Americans favored all-out aid to Britain, even at the risk of war.)

If Roosevelt was in a dilemma over his fear of isolationist sentiment on the one hand and his concern that Britain might go down before the Nazis, on the other, his problem was resolved by the Japanese attack on Pearl Harbor. At the moment of attack, though, it almost seemed that the event may have precipitated the United States into the wrong war at the wrong time. To Roosevelt and his advisers the principal threat rightly came from Germany, not Japan. But the Japanese assault meant that priority would have to be given to an Asian, not a European war; the American people would have stood for nothing less. Yet, considering the greater power of the German armies, mere left-handed American help to the Allies in Europe, while concentrating on Japan, might not have been sufficient to keep Britain and Russia afloat. Whether Roosevelt ultimately was prepared to ask for war against Hitler as well as Japan is unknown, though when Secretary of War Stimson advised him to do just that on December 8, he declined. Four days after the attack on Pearl Harbor, Hitler came to Roosevelt's rescue and the aid of the Japanese by himself declaring war on the United States. Roosevelt was free to give Europe first priority.

The entrance of the United States into the Second World War, as we now can see, was a watershed in history. The First World War, it is true, had linked the destinies of the United States and Europe, but that association had been at once brief and widely regretted among Americans. By 1941, however, the events of the preceding years, particularly since 1938, had worked their effects upon the minds of Americans. One measure of that change was the reevaluation of the historical meaning of American entrance into the First World War. In November, 1939, the proportion of Americans who thought Wilson's policies regarding World War I were wrong was double that of those who thought he had been right. By April, 1941, however, the proportions were almost reversed: only 39 per cent of Americans thought Wilson had been mistaken in 1917. In the interim it had become clear that the world order created and sustained by the Versailles Treaty, the Washington agreements, and the Kellogg-Briand Pact was in a shambles. And in place of that order, the Germans and the Japanese were forging a world that would be unfriendly to and perhaps even dangerous for the United States and the nations of western Europe. Some new international order, in which the United States would be an active participant instead of an aloof observer, was obviously called for by the American people.

A further sign of the abandonment of the old unilateralism or isolationism, was the widespread interest, even enthusiasm, during the war for the creation of a new international organization to be set up after the defeat of Germany and Japan. In 1943 both houses of Congress passed resolutions favoring United States participation in an international body, and, at the Teheran conference in December and at Yalta in February, 1945, Roosevelt, Stalin, and Churchill discussed plans for a postwar international peace-keeping body. Thus, before the war was over in Europe, the United States had virtually committed itself to participation in an international organization that contemplated the use of force to keep the peace.[9] Nevertheless, Roosevelt was careful to associate Republicans and Senators with the planning of the postwar organization, if only to avoid the difficulties that his Democratic predecessor Woodrow Wilson had run into in 1919. (As Robert Sherwood later testified about Roosevelt, "The tragedy of Wilson was always somewhere within the rim of his consciousness.") The precautions were probably unnecessary. By 1945 there simply was no significant sentiment opposed to United States participation in the United Nations organization. When the Charter came before the Senate for "advice and consent," only two votes were cast against membership. Like a voice from the past came word that ailing, but still sturdily isolationist Senator Hiram Johnson of California would have voted nay if he had been able to attend.

5. CHALLENGE AND RESPONSE

The events that led up to war in 1941 and the war itself undoubtedly account for the willingness of Americans to join a new international organization in 1945. But those events do not account for what is clearly the most striking shift in American policy since the founding of the Republic—the extension of American military power

[9] The final United Nations Charter called for an international army to carry out the will of the Security Council, but the Soviet Union and the United States have not yet been able to agree upon its composition, and so none has been created. Herbert Hoover, an old supporter of Woodrow Wilson, though not on the question of the League, and a Quaker, was one of the few opponents of the idea of using force to preserve the peace. "After all," he wrote in 1942, "the preservation and advancement of civilization cannot be based on force." Roosevelt's view, which he often summed up in the analogy of a constable preserving order in a small town, was echoed by his Secretary of State Cordell Hull. "During my study of the prewar economic situation in Europe," he wrote in his memoirs, "I had formed the firm conclusion that balance of power had to be replaced by an association of nations."

around the globe. Surely that had been neither the intention nor the expectation in 1945. Franklin Roosevelt may have been anxious to see the United States as an active member of the new United Nations organization, but he was realistic enough to recognize that at the end of the war American troops would be quickly returned home. At Yalta he told Churchill and Stalin, as the British Prime Minister recalled it, that "he felt he could obtain support in Congress and throughout the country for any reasonable measures designed to safeguard the future peace," but he "did not believe that American troops would stay in Europe much more than two years." And so intense were the demands of the public and of servicemen alike for a rapid demobilization, that within a year after the victory over Germany the U.S. armed forces of 15 million had been cut in half.

Ironically enough, it was the very completeness of the victory over Nazi Germany that helped to bring American military power to Europe for the first time during peace. The defeat of Germany meant that Russian power flowed easily into its place—that is, into the very heart of Europe. Indeed, even as the war was coming to an end, some American officials began to be apprehensive about this massive westward extension of Russian military force. And at the Potsdam Conference, in the summer of 1945, U.S. Ambassador to the Soviet Union Averell Harriman told Secretary of the Navy James Forrestal that he "was very gloomy about the influx of Russia into Europe." When Secretary of War Henry Stimson saw the repressive character of Soviet government in Berlin during his attendance at the Potsdam Conference, he wrote a strong memorandum to President Truman expressing doubt that peace with such a nation was possible. At any rate, he counseled the President that the United States ought not to share its atomic secrets with Russia until greater personal freedom was granted in the Soviet sphere. Whether Truman's abrupt termination of Lend-Lease shipments to the Soviet Union on May 8 was a part of this newly aroused fear of Russia is doubtful. The administration said it was merely complying with the law, but the Russians took the action as an unfriendly gesture and protested. The shipments were resumed a month later after a conciliatory visit to Stalin by Harry Hopkins, but Russian suspicions were not entirely allayed. Nor were American fears quieted, for Stalin continued to consolidate his position in eastern Europe, especially in Poland.

Truman's abrupt manner in dealing with the Russians has often been contrasted with Roosevelt's. Expressive of Roosevelt's attitude and approach toward the Russians is a note that Harry Hopkins passed to Roosevelt during the Yalta Conference regarding reparations. "The Russians have given in so much at this conference that I don't think we should let them down. Let the British disagree if they want to," he wrote. And that is the way the record reads. Truman, on the other hand, at his first meeting with Foreign Secretary Vyacheslav Molotov, according to Truman's own account, gave Molotov such a dressing-down for alleged Soviet misbehavior in Poland that the Russian said he had "never been talked to like that in my life." It is just that contrast between Truman's and Roosevelt's approaches to the Russians that has spawned the widely held feeling that if F.D.R. had lived, there would have been no Cold War. Obviously there is no sure way of knowing. But a brief exploration of the question can serve as an introduction to a consideration of the roots of the Cold War.

It is true, as those who say Roosevelt would not have allowed the Cold War to begin, that Franklin Roosevelt's approach to the postwar world rested on the assumption that world peace would depend upon good relations between the Soviet Union and the United States. At the several wartime conferences with Stalin, Roosevelt made clear his belief that the Russian dictator could be cajoled, argued, and charmed into abandoning the Russian and Communist suspicion of the West in general and of capitalists in particular. As Churchill's memoirs inform us, the British Prime Minister was not infrequently annoyed at Roosevelt's deliberate effort to score points with Stalin at Churchill's expense. Indeed, as early as March, 1942, Roosevelt rather brutally told Churchill: "I think I can personally handle Stalin better than either your Foreign Office or my State Department. Stalin hates the guts of all your top people. He thinks he likes me better and I hope he will continue to do so." Roosevelt's willingness finally to accede to Stalin's demand for three votes in the UN Assembly was but one concrete manifestation of his conciliatory approach toward the Russian dictator. And as Herbert Feis has pointed out, as late as March, 1945, when Churchill called F.D.R.'s attention to what he considered Russian violations of the Yalta agreement concerning eastern Europe, Roosevelt would not rise to the bait. He still saw himself as mediator between Churchill and Stalin.

Unlike Churchill, Roosevelt viewed the postwar world as one in which the interests of the big powers were reconcilable, even if they were not identical. Unlike Churchill, too, Roosevelt did not think in terms of power blocs or rivalries between the great powers. Like his former boss Woodrow Wilson, Roosevelt looked toward a new world polity in which spheres of influence, balance of power, and the other apparatus of European—as opposed to American—diplomatic intercourse would be eliminated.

It is inaccurate, however, to label Roosevelt as simply an idealist. Insofar as F.D.R. recognized that the peace of the postwar world rested on the relations between the two great powers he was certainly being realistic. For it was indisputable then, and even more so since, that in the hands of the Russian and American leaders lay the prospects for peace. Roosevelt was also realistic in a more mundane way. He was willing to make concessions to Stalin in the interests of peace, but he was never willing to concede what he considered basic principles, such as the independence of eastern Europe, which he felt had been agreed upon at Yalta. Thus, ten days before his death, on April 1, he wrote Stalin that the Yalta agreements on Poland would have to be honored. Soon thereafter he also told Churchill that the western Allies must hold the line against any Russian pressures that might change that understanding. It is these last statements that give substance to the assertion that if F.D.R. had lived American relations with Russia after the war would not have been much different from what they were in fact under Truman. Actually, as the foregoing makes clear, the evidence is pretty thin and conjectural. A more important reason for believing that the Cold War was likely, regardless of the man in the White House, is that the interests of the two powers in the years after 1945 were sharply divergent. It was these divergent interests, themselves the outgrowth of the different histories of the United States and Russia, that made impossible the kind of consensus between the two nations on which Roosevelt's approach to the postwar world depended.

What was to be Russia's place in postwar Europe? That question lays bare the first divergence of interest between the Soviet Union and the United States. For when the war against Hitler ended, Russian military and political power stood on the Elbe River, in the center of Europe, far from its traditional place on the periphery. To the east of the Elbe lay Poland, Bulgaria, Hungary, Roumania, Czechoslovakia, and Yugoslavia—all except the last occupied by Soviet troops. As the events of 1945 showed, and those of subsequent years would reinforce, the occupation of the eastern European nations was not simply for the purpose of safeguarding Russian communications to Germany. At Yalta and at every subsequent meeting, the Russians made clear that the states bordering the Soviet Union must have governments friendly to Russia, which usually meant they must be Communist, whether immediately or in the near future.[10] To be sure, the Russian occupation of eastern Europe was dictated by other than ideological considerations. Certainly the memory of past invasions of the motherland from Europe figured in the thoughts of the Russian leaders. Since the seventeenth century, Russia had been invaded by the Swedes, the Poles, the French, and twice by the Germans. In the eyes of the West, however, the subordination of the nations of eastern Europe to Soviet power and ideology threatened the balance of power on that continent. Neither Napoleon nor Hitler had been permitted to dominate as much of Europe without provoking hostility and eventually war. It was this threat and those memories that aroused the fears of Harriman, Stimson, and Forrestal in the spring and summer of 1945, and prompted Churchill's famous Iron Curtain speech at Fulton, Missouri, in March, 1946.

Moscow's domination of eastern Europe also flew in the face of long-held and deeply felt American principles of self-determination and economic and political freedom.[11] Some recent historian-critics of American diplomatic policy have emphasized the economic goals behind American insistence on self-determination in eastern Europe, arguing that it is nothing more than the old Open Door policy of obtaining markets for American business. Undoubtedly, as these historians have shown, a desire for markets and raw materials was a part of the American opposition to Soviet control over eastern Europe. But a less narrow and less doctrinaire conception of men's motives would also suggest that American policy makers had long been equally concerned with political freedom of choice for itself and

---

[10] Of Russia's European neighbors, only Finland and Norway escaped the pressure for a Communist regime; even so, in Finland, the government has been careful in its policies not to give offense to the Russian colossus.

[11] In December, 1792, Secretary of State Thomas Jefferson laid down the following principle to the United States minister at London: "We certainly cannot deny to other nations that principle whereon our government is founded, that every nation has a right to govern itself internally under whatever forms it pleases, and to change these forms at its own will; and externally to transact business with other nations through whatever organ it chooses, whether that be a King, Committee, Assembly, Convention, President, or whatever it be. The only thing essential is the will of the people." A similar statement was written to the American minister in Paris on the same day.

for other nations. At the very least, the Open Door policy, in origin and in subsequent practice, had a political as well as an economic dimension. That is but another way of saying it symbolized that combination of idealism and realism that has been characteristic of American foreign policy from the beginning.

East and West also diverged regarding their respective conceptions of the future of Germany. Once Germany was defeated the unspoken differences between United States and Russian interests regained their voices. To the West, a defeated and devastated Germany, now that the Nazis were gone, was a burden that had to be supported. But to the Russians, and to a certain extent to the French, too, Germany was a potential menace as well as a source of reparations for damages inflicted by the Nazis during the war. In both instances, German economic self-sufficiency and political independence would be ruled out. Thus at Yalta and after, Stalin insisted upon enormous reparations from Germany. At one point he asked that 80 per cent of all German industry be made available for reparations, which would have made Germany incapable of supporting itself. After much discussion with the West, Stalin settled for a considerably reduced figure. But even after Russia ceased to exploit German wealth, it feared German military revival. That the Russian insistence upon strict control over Germany and the restricting of its economic power was not only a Communist but also a national concern is shown by France's attitude during the first two years. Like the Russians, the French opposed the principle of ultimate unification and at one point went so far as to oppose the issuance of common postage stamps for all of Germany.

Finally, there was the ideological difference between the Russians and the West. Fear of the ideological expansion of Communism ran back a quarter of a century in the mind of Churchill, who always regretted, as he once put it, that he had not been able to strangle Bolshevism in its cradle. Nor was a similar fear absent from the minds of other Europeans and Americans,[12] especially when they witnessed the willing subservience of Communists and Communist par-

[12] Arno Mayer, *The Political Origins of the New Diplomacy, 1917–1918* (New Haven, 1959), and N. Gordon Levin, Jr., *Woodrow Wilson and World Politics. America's Response to War and Revolution* (New York, 1968), present provocative and persuasive arguments for seeing the ideological origins of the Cold War in 1918–19 in the form of Wilsonian liberalism and Leninist Bolshevism. But ideology, it is worth adding, is only one cause for the post-1945 conflict between the United States and the U.S.S.R.

ties outside the Soviet Union to the policies and interests of the Russian government. For their part, the Russians were convinced that capitalism predisposed a nation to war and the world to instability. Stalin himself said as much in a speech in February, 1946, which received widespread publicity in the West, where it was viewed as a signal that the Russians would never make an accommodation with the capitalist world. Supreme Court Justice William O. Douglas, a well-known liberal, went so far as to call Stalin's speech the "declaration of World War III." The response to Stalin's speech came unofficially a month later when Winston Churchill in the conspicuous presence of President Truman delivered his so-called Iron Curtain speech at Fulton, Missouri. Summing up both the national and ideological threat of the Soviet Union, he said, "Nobody knows what Soviet Russia and its Communist International organization intends to do in the immediate future, or what are the limits, if any, to their expansive and proselytizing tendencies." For the next five years, these Communist "tendencies" would beset western Europe with espionage, political strikes, and fear of military attack.

On top of these fundamental differences between the United States and the Soviets came a series of incidents that deepened differences, aroused suspicions, and made the Cold War a reality by early 1947. In March, 1946, the Soviet's refusal to evacuate Iran, as promised at the beginning of the wartime joint British-Soviet occupation, precipitated a United States and Iranian appeal to the Security Council of the United Nations. The sharp American reaction and an aroused public opinion compelled the Soviet Union to remove its troops in May. Then in rapid succession Stalin took a series of actions that made clear that he wanted to have nothing to do with the world being arranged by the West under the leadership of the United States. Russia refused to join the World Bank and the International Monetary Fund, and rejected the terms of a billion-dollar loan from the United States, even though only a year earlier Molotov had been pressing for American help in restoring his devastated country. About the same time, also, Russian troops evacuated Manchuria, carefully leaving behind in the hands of the Chinese Communists large quantities of captured Japanese arms and equipment that would be useful in the civil war against Chiang Kai-shek's Nationalist government. As if to suggest that a decision had been made to stay indefinitely in Germany, Stalin halted the dismantling of industrial equipment in the Russian zone of Germany. Hereafter East Germany would manufacture goods for Russia rather than be simply a source of loot. That summer, also, the U.S.S.R. abruptly rejected the United States' plan for the international control of nuclear energy. Two months later Stalin insisted that the Turks share their control of the straits of the Dardanelles with Russia.

Although from the standpoint of the Russians some of these actions and demands could be justified, in the eyes of the ordinary American citizen Russian behavior in 1946 smacked of intransigence, truculence, and ingratitude. To the Russians the Baruch plan for the international control of nuclear weapons constituted a restriction on their opportunities to develop a bomb of their own, on which we now know they were feverishly working. But to Americans, the rejection of the Baruch plan, like the spurning of the United States loan, was nothing but an ungrateful response by a suspicious Stalin to a generous gesture by the United States.

The official American reaction to Russia's series of actions was made clear in September, 1946, when Secretary of State James E. Byrnes, who had never been overly optimistic about getting along with the Russians anyway, announced that the United States would no longer wait for Soviet agreement on the unification of Germany. The United States and Britain proceeded to merge their two zones and the Germans were encouraged to develop their own, independent economy. The French, almost as skeptical of the consequences of German unification as the Soviets, refused to accept the American invitation until September, 1949. With the division of Germany, the Cold War became a reality; it would be the frame of reference of American foreign policy for the next quarter of a century. As Dean Acheson prophesied in June, 1946, "We have got to understand that all our lives the danger, the uncertainty, the need for alertness, for effort, for discipline will be upon us. This is new for us. It will be hard for us." For Americans, perhaps, the most difficult part was the abandonment of the traditional goal of complete victory over an enemy. Their history had not prepared them for protracted struggle during which power was to be measured and restrained rather than simply applied in pursuit of "victory."

The policy that was worked out to meet the exigencies of the Cold War was indeed revolutionary in the fundamental meaning of that word; it overturned established ways in the conduct of American foreign policy. The revolution began when Britain, weakened by war and postwar economic disorder, warned the United States in

February, 1947, that it could no longer sustain Greece in its civil war against Communist guerillas supported by Yugoslavia. Upon learning that Britain would have to abandon its traditional post as the stabilizing power in the eastern Mediterranean, President Truman took the momentous step of committing the United States to giving economic and military aid to Greece and to Turkey, then threatened by the Soviet Union. No United States troops were sent then or later to Greece. But Truman's message to Congress in explanation of his policy began a novel, and what subsequent events would show to be, a far-reaching commitment. "I believe," he told Congress, "that it must be the policy of the United States to support free peoples who are resisting attempted subjugation by armed minorities or by outside pressures." For the first time in its history during peace, the United States was undertaking an obligation to interfere in events in Europe. It was the beginning of what came to be called the policy of containment of Soviet Communism, which would be the central theme of the United States foreign policy for the next generation.

From the outset, there were two prongs to the containment policy.[13] One was simply military—that is, to oppose by force Communist or Soviet military force, whether local or foreign. (The immediate instance was the Greek government which was fighting against Communist guerillas, who were being aided by Yugoslavia, then a loyal Communist ally of the Soviet Union.) The other was to make the conditions of life in the country threatened by a Communist takeover sufficiently rewarding to the inhabitants that they would have little incentive to support Communist parties or doctrine. The most successful example of the latter approach was the Marshall Plan, by which the United States undertook in 1948 to rehabilitate western Europe and thereby prevent Communism from taking over, either by force or by the ballot. Moreover, this imaginative use of American industrial and agricultural techniques, wealth, and economic efficiency did more than help restore the devastated and de-

[13] Generally the intellectual origins of the containment policy are said to be George F. Kennan's article "The Sources of Soviet Conduct," in *Foreign Affairs,* July, 1947, which had circulated earlier within the government. Most readers interpreted that article as counseling military as well as political and economic containment of Soviet power, but in his recent *Memoirs, 1925–1950* (Boston, 1967), pp. 358–60, Kennan asserts that he never intended or counseled that military power be used, even indirectly, as in Greece. How the policy was otherwise to be implemented is not clear.

moralized economy of western Europe. By bringing the states of western Europe into a common endeavor, the Marshall Plan set the stage for the even more successful and path-breaking Common Market, which came into being in the late 1950's.

Within the context of the Cold War, the success of the Marshall Plan was measured by the Soviet Union's hostility toward it and what it stood for. Thus when Secretary of State George Marshall offered to include in his program the states of eastern Europe and the Soviet Union itself, Stalin refused, not only for himself, but for Poland and Czechoslovakia as well, despite their clear interest in the proposal. Then just before the European Recovery Program was enacted by Congress, Communist worker's groups, undoubtedly with Soviet encouragement, took over the Czechoslovak government, putting it behind the Iron Curtain. As the Marshall Plan was being put into effect in the summer of 1948, the Russians further demonstrated their hostility to the new economic plans of the West by beginning a blockade of West Berlin, which was located 100 miles inside the Soviet zone of Germany.

These Soviet pressures on the West caused several of the countries of western Europe to seek a more reliable defense than that provided by the United Nations or their own individual efforts. Out of their concern emerged the North Atlantic Treaty Organization, which the United States and Canada as well as twelve European countries formally organized in 1949. The heart of the treaty was that each of the signatories agreed that an attack upon one was an attack upon all. The Treaty of Washington that formalized NATO was the first long-term military alliance into which the United States had entered since the alliance with France in 1778.[14] The NATO alliance also marked a retreat from the traditional principle of United States foreign policy that force was not to be used to affect the behavior of foreign states, except in self-defense. In these striking departures from traditional practices are measured the revolution in American foreign policy from 1945 to 1949. The revolution is evident in another way. The necessary financial support for the Truman Doctrine

[14] This statement is not strictly true since, in the Treaty of Rio de Janeiro made with the nations of Latin America in 1947, the United States and each of the signatories covenanted to look upon an attack on one as an attack on all. But under the Monroe Doctrine the United States had long viewed an attack on any nation of the western hemisphere as an attack upon itself, so that the 1947 treaty was not the revolutionary act the Treaty of Washington clearly was.

and the European Recovery Program was voted overwhelmingly by
a Congress with a majority of Republicans in the House of Representatives. The revolution, in short, took place among the American
people and the Republican party as well as among the planners of
the State Department.

Although President Truman had enunciated the principle of resisting Communist power in regard to Greece and Turkey, the words
he used placed no limits on the American commitment. In 1947 it
was probably not considered noteworthy that he had left the limits
unspecified, but events in 1950 soon made it clear that in the minds
of Truman and his advisers there was indeed a global commitment.
The precipitating event was the invasion of South Korea by Communist North Korea in June, 1950.

In the climate of opinion and state of knowledge of 1950, the invasion of South Korea was only too easily seen as a deliberate effort
on the part of the Communist leaders to expand in Asia now that
their opportunities for expansion in Europe had been closed off by
the Marshall Plan and the North Atlantic Alliance. Today, however,
that assumption of the 1950's does not seem to be the full explanation, though there seems little reason to doubt that the Russians supported and even approved of the attack. For one thing, the absence
of the Soviet representative from the United Nations Security Council, when he might have vetoed support for the South Koreans, still
awaits explanation. Even when invited to return by the Secretary
General, he refused. As a result of his absence, the United States
decision to aid the South Koreans received the moral sanction of
the United Nations and the material support of a number of its
members. For another thing, despite Truman's assumption at the
time, the decision to invade the South may not have been a deliberate
testing of the United States. Almost a year earlier General Douglas
MacArthur, the American commander in occupied Japan, in a speech,
had omitted Korea from the list of countries in the western Pacific
region that he said constituted the defense perimeter of the United
States. Only six months before the invasion, Secretary of State Dean
Acheson also left out Korea in drawing a similar line. Finally, since
the division of Korea into North and South was singularly artificial
and merely a consequence of the postwar impasse between the United
States and the Soviet Union, the invasion may have been as much the
product of local Korean ambitions as broader Communist goals,
whether Russian or Chinese. Certainly the protégé of the United

States in the South, Syngman Rhee, was so anxious to invade the North and reunite his country by force that the American authorities there denied him any heavy military equipment for fear that he would do just that and thereby precipitate a war. The Russians, however, apparently had no such scruples, so that when they evacuated Korea they left behind ample offensive military equipment for a powerful attack on the South.

The Korean War is significant in world history as well as in United States foreign policy. On the world level the Korean War was the first example in history of collective security practiced by a formally constituted international organization. The system had worked just as the internationalists of the 1930's had said it ought to. Aggression had been stopped by the combined efforts of the nations of the world. Looked at more closely, however, it was evident that the will and power of one nation—that of the United States—were decisive in making collective security work. Viewed even more closely, it was equally clear that American will was energized principally because Russia, the enemy in Europe, was thought to be behind the Korean invasion. In short, the intervention in Korea was an act of "selective security" rather than proof of the validity of collective security as men had defined that term in the 1930's. For, without the background of the Cold War and the newly created NATO alliance, it is not at all clear that the United States would have intervened simply because a North Korean army invaded the southern part of Korea. Yet, as the leading historian of the struggle has written, "Rarely in history has a great power sacrificed so much for so little material gain. . . . For the Korean decision was primarily a political decision in the Jeffersonian tradition of American idealism." Like containment itself, David Rees continues, it was "a fusion of idealism, economic aid, diplomacy, and force."

For the United States the Korean War proved to be as formative in the development of policy and action in Asia as the collapse of Britain in 1947 had been for the working out of European policy. From the decision to intervene in Korea, as from the earlier decision to assume the burdens dropped by the British, flowed not only the primary decision to resist aggression but a number of others as well. As a result of the Korean invasion, the policy of containment, worked out in and for Europe, and successfully applied there, now came to Asia. When, in the course of 1945 and early 1946, American policy makers decided that resistance to Communism as an ideological and military force was necessary, they faced a formidable task. Communism threatened to expand not only in Europe, but in Asia as well. For with the withdrawal of the Japanese from China in 1945, the Communists and Chiang Kai-shek's Nationalists entered upon a bitter civil war for the control of China. The United States offered some support to Chiang—as did the Russians in 1945—but that support proved to be misplaced, since the Nationalists were unable to withstand the steady advance of Mao Tse-tung's Communists. After a futile effort in 1946–47 to mediate the dispute between the two Chinese factions, the United States washed its hands of Chiang to concentrate on keeping western Europe free of Communist control. In 1949, almost totally defeated, Chiang fled the mainland for the island of Formosa, with the Communists in close pursuit. The United States did nothing. Since Formosa had been promised to China at the Cairo Conference, American officials merely waited for the Communists to mount an invasion of the island, and thus liquidate the civil war. Significantly, in the same speech in which he omitted Korea from the defense perimeter of the United States, Secretary of State Dean Acheson omitted Formosa as well.

This hands-off policy of the United States in regard to the Chinese civil war, however, came to an abrupt end with the invasion of South Korea in the summer of 1950. For at the same time that President Truman ordered military support to be sent to the South Koreans, he also ordered the U.S. Seventh Fleet to station itself between Formosa and the mainland. The ostensible purpose was to prevent both sides in the Chinese civil war from attacking one another, but the true aim was to prevent the Chinese Communists from attacking Formosa and thereby outflanking the American position in Korea. And before the latter conflict was over, the United States would be engaged in a full-scale, if unofficial, war with China itself in the hills of North Korea. The war could not be won in the usual way and so it ceased by mutual agreement rather than victory for either side.

That the war should end in that manner constitutes another important consequence of the Korean War for Americans. For most of their history, Americans have been in the unusual and fortunate position of being able to debate what *ought* to be done in foreign policy, rather than being confined, as most nations are, to a discussion only of what is possible. This is the principal reason, one suspects, that American foreign policy has often been discussed in moral, rather than power terms. How was it possible for Americans to enjoy this luxury? One reason is that from their beginning as a people Americans have been free from powerful enemies close at hand. Neither Spain nor Mexico was strong, and England, which was an enemy for a while, was far away. Had the situation been otherwise, it seems clear that Americans would have learned early the realities and the normal limits in foreign affairs. Another reason is that until well into the twentieth century Americans have set rather limited and even local goals for their foreign policies, such as acquiring territory from weak neighbors or controlling the Caribbean. Hence their power was never put to a demanding test. More recently, as the goals of Americans have become more ambitious, as during the Second World War, when the United States fought on two widely separated continents, American military and economic power has kept pace. Thus, for a long time the truism that no nation is omnipotent, which is known to all other peoples from experience, had been hidden from Americans. During the Korean War, however, Americans learned that there were limits to their power, for an all-out war with China would have brought with it not only enormous expenditures of lives and wealth but perhaps nuclear war as well. To those still unconvinced by the experience of Korea, the longer and even more frustrating war in Vietnam forcefully demonstrated that even for Americans the goals of foreign policy, like power itself, can no longer be unlimited.

Not the least of the consequences of the Korean War was the United States involvement in Vietnam. Today the split between Communist China and the Soviet Union is evident to all. But in 1950 and for years thereafter today's commonplace was still unsuspected. In fact, at that time it was an axiom of official as well as popular thought that Communists were all alike and that they cooperated and worked together in international affairs as smoothly and effectively as they did within their own countries. As a consequence, the invasion of Korea was interpreted as a rerun of the 1930's, when the West had been too divided and selfishly nationalistic to make a common front against Hitler and Mussolini. As Harry Truman later wrote about the attack on South Korea, "If this was allowed to go unchallenged, it would mean a third world war, just as similar incidents had brought on the Second World War." The President was undoubtedly thinking also of more recent events in Europe where timely cooperation between the United States and the countries of western Europe had reduced substantially the threat of Communism and Soviet power.

Thus the policy that had worked so well in Europe was applied to Asia. The first step was to repel the invasion of South Korea, the second was to protect Formosa from the Chinese Communists, and the third was to support the French in Indo-China.

When the French returned to take over their colony of Indo-China from the defeated Japanese in 1945, the United States was not eager to help them achieve that objective. By and large the United States stood aloof from the French effort to fight the rising nationalism of Asia that was fast bringing the old colonialism to an end. The triumph of the Communists in China and the outbreak of the Korean War, however, completely changed the American outlook. Convinced that a single hand directed the activities of the Communist empire that stretched from the Elbe to the Mekong, the United States in 1950 took measures to shore up the threatened frontiers of the non-Communist world. At the same time that Truman ordered the Seventh Fleet to interpose itself between Formosa and the mainland, he sent military advisers to help the French in their colonial war against the Vietminh, the Communist-led opponents of the French. Ultimately, American aid to the French in their war against Ho Chi Minh reached 78 per cent of the total cost of the war. When the French in 1954 proved unable or unwilling to continue manning the bastions of anti-Communism in Asia, Secretary of State John F. Dulles organized the Southeast Asia Treaty Organization in emulation of the successful NATO in Europe. SEATO, however, unlike NATO, had little substantial power outside of the United States contribution, since the two largest non-Communist Asian countries, Indonesia and India, were not included. Its formation, though, once again testified to the powerful and continuing influence of the European example in the development of a policy in Asia. But that which had worked so well in industrial and politically advanced Europe, found little success in agricultural and politically underdeveloped Asia. The isolationists of the 1930's had sought to avoid war in their day by blindly applying the "lessons" of 1917, only to find they did not help. So the men of the 1950's and 1960's by mechanically drawing "lessons" from the events of the 1940's ended with a protracted and costly war in Asia and a divided country at home.

Yet, despite the dissatisfaction with the war in Vietnam, there has been continuity between the foreign policy of Lyndon Johnson and the American past. President Johnson himself was fond of pointing out that three American Presidents before him had sanctioned his policy in Vietnam. But he might have gone further than that. The ideological justification for the United States military activity in Vietnam was that the United States was seeking the rule of law in international relations by punishing aggressors. That is the same goal that Franklin Roosevelt advocated in the 1940's when he wrote the Atlantic Charter and pressed for United States' participation in the United Nations. It is the same goal for which Wilson fought at Versailles and across the country in 1919. It is the goal which the Founding Fathers pursued when they envisioned the United States as propounding a new kind of foreign policy for itself and the world. It was to be a foreign policy based not upon the balance of power or spheres of influence but upon justice, self-determination, and international cooperation. The Founding Fathers, like Secretary of State Dean Rusk himself, saw behind the affairs of nations a natural law that was worthy of being followed. What was new was the idea that the United States had a responsibility to police that law. To the Founding Fathers, as to men of the nineteenth century, only public opinion and moral force were expected to be exercised to keep the peace; military power was reserved for the defense of clear-cut national interests. It was first Wilson, then Franklin Roosevelt, and most recently Lyndon Johnson, who have sought to put the power of the United States behind the law. In that sense American attitudes toward foreign policy were at once unchanging and revolutionized in the course of the twentieth century.

Critical Bibliographical Essay

THE works cited herein make no pretense of exhausting the literature; they do not actually include all the books I have read, but they do constitute the principal materials from which I have drawn information and ideas. For this revised edition I have added works published since the first edition when I thought the new works were significant or when they caused me to change my mind about some subject covered in the text. Some titles have been dropped, usually on the ground that they have been superseded or in order simply to keep this essay from becoming unmanageable. Books cited or discussed in the body of the book are generally not included here; nor have I listed the more obvious collections of printed sources used.

I. THE BEGINNINGS

For the colonial period as a whole, I have relied heavily on Herbert L. Osgood, *The American Colonies in the Seventeenth Century* (3 vols., New York, 1904–7), and Charles M. Andrews, *The Colonial Period of American History* (4 vols., New Haven, 1935–38). The early chapters of Ralph H. Brown, *Historical Geography of the United States* (New York, 1948), have been the source of my generalizations about the nature of the land.

Louis Hacker's provocative *Triumph of American Capitalism* (New York, 1940) has sparked much of my thinking, though my conclusions are much different from his. The essay on the businessman in France by John Sawyer in William Miller, ed., *Men in Business* (Cambridge, 1952), is the basis for my remarks contrasting the American and French businessman. The significance of the absence of a feudal past in America is set forth with verve by Louis Hartz in *The Liberal Tradition in America* (New York, 1955). Richard Morris, *Studies in the History of American Law* (New York, 1930), Chapters I and II, discusses the departures from European property law. For the efforts to establish quasi-feudal regimes in the colonies, I have drawn on John Johnson, *Old Maryland Manors*

(Baltimore, 1883); Clarence Rife, "Land Tenure in New Netherlands," in *Essays in Colonial History Presented to Charles McLean Andrews by His Students* (New Haven, 1931); and Samuel G. Nissenson, *The Patroon's Domain* (New York, 1937).

Though John Winthrop's *History of New England from 1630–1649,* edited by J. Savage (Boston, 1853), is a partisan account by a leader of the oligarchy, it is a mine of information on the early history and mores of the Puritan settlement. At the other end of the seventeenth century, Cotton Mather's *Magnalia Christi Americana* (Hartford, 1820) performs the same function and the additional one of including many sources for Puritan thought and action in the course of the century. An excellent collection of Puritan writing is Perry Miller, *The American Puritans* (New York, 1956), in paperback edition.

The writings about the Puritans bid fair to exceed even the great output of the notoriously prolific Puritans themselves. The dean of such commentators was undoubtedly Perry Miller. As anyone familiar with his work must recognize, my interpretation of the Puritans is heavily indebted to his books: *Orthodoxy in Massachusetts, 1630–50* (Cambridge, Mass., 1933); *The New England Mind: Seventeenth Century* (Cambridge, Mass., 1953); and its sequel, *From Colony to Province* (Cambridge, Mass., 1953). Two of the number of works belaboring the Puritans deserve to be mentioned here if only because they have done so much to produce an opposite reaction in me: James Truslow Adams, *The Founding of New England* (Boston, 1926), and the first part of Vernon L. Parrington's *Main Currents in American Thought* (New York, 1930). Both these books represent the high-water mark of the effort to give scholarly clothing to the popular impression that the Puritans were a narrow-minded, repressed, antidemocratic people.

A less partisan approach to the Puritans was already begun in the 1920's with Kenneth Murdock's *Increase Mather* (Cambridge, Mass., 1926), which did much to rescue that divine from, among other things, Parrington's imputations of ignorance. The 1930's saw a number of historians step forward to take a second and fresher look at the Puritans: Herbert Schneider, *The Puritan Mind* (New York, 1930); Samuel Eliot Morison, *Puritan Pronaos* (New York, 1936), and his *Harvard College in the Seventeenth Century* (Cambridge, Mass., 1936). Though I have not always followed Professor Morison's almost total defense of the Puritans, his influence on my handling of them has been great. Clifford K. Shipton, "A Plea for Puritanism," *American Historical Review,* XL (April, 1935), 460–67, is a direct answer to James Truslow Adams. Ralph Barton Perry's *Puritanism and Democracy* (New York, 1944) is broader in scope and more temperate than Morison's work, and seeks to relate the Puritans to the democratic ideal in America. Not all recent treatments of the Puritans, however, have been favorable, as both the title and content of Thomas J. Wertenbaker's *Puritan Oligarchy* (New York, 1947) demonstrate. Perry Miller, *Roger Williams* (Indianapolis, 1953), and Mauro Calamandrei, "Neglected Aspects of Roger Williams' Thought," *Church History,* XXI (September, 1952), 239–58, have thrown much new and important light on this controversial Puritan. See also Edmund Morgan, *Roger Williams* (New York, 1967).

The nature of the Puritan's outlook on life has been singled out by a number of writers for special treatment. Henry Bamford Parkes, "Morals and Law Enforcement in Colonial New England," *New England Quarterly,* V (July, 1932), 431–52, was an attempt to test the implications of Charles Francis Adams' famous essay, "Some Phases of Sexual Morality and Church Discipline in Colonial New England," *Proceedings* of the Massachusetts Historical Society, 2nd Ser., VI (1891), 477–516. Parkes found the Puritans purer than Adams implied. Edmund Morgan in "The Puritans and Sex," *New England Quarterly,* XV (December, 1942), 591–607, and in *The Puritan Family* (Boston, 1944) carried the investigation further and on a broader front. His short biography of John Winthrop, *Puritan Dilemma* (Boston, 1958), is an excellent introduction to Puritan thought and practice. His *Visible Saints* (New York, 1963), emphasizes the importance of Church membership in Puritan thought. Since the death of Perry Miller, Morgan is the leading historian on Puritanism. Percy Scholes, an English musicologist of note, in *The Puritans and Music in England and New England* (London, 1934) has made a firm case in their favor which, in my opinion, Cyclone Covey, "Puritanism and Music in Colonial America," *William and Mary Quarterly,* 3rd Ser., VIII (July, 1951), 378–88, has not been able to shake, though he deliberately attempts to. Though Emil Oberholzer, *Delinquent Saints* (New York, 1956), is no apologist for the Puritans, his thorough monograph offers ammunition to both sides in the controversy regarding Puritan morals.

The seminal essays on the relation between Puritanism and capitalism are Max Weber, *The Protestant Ethic and the Spirit of Capitalism* (New York, 1930), and R. H. Tawney, *Religion and the Rise of Capitalism* (New York, 1937). Much water has passed under the historiographical bridge since these studies, but no writer on Puritanism has yet succeeded in ignoring the connection they descried between Puritan morality and economic growth. Bernard Bailyn, *The New England Merchants in the Seventeenth Century* (Cambridge, Mass., 1955), is noteworthy for its clear demonstration of the acceptance by the merchants of Puritan doctrine as well as the undermining which economic activity worked upon the Zion in the wilderness. I am much indebted to Frederick B. Tolles, *Meeting House and Counting House* (Chapel Hill, N.C., 1948), for the incisive pointing up of the similarity in Quaker and Puritan ethics as they bear on wealthmaking. Edward B. O. Beatty, *William Penn as Social Phi-*

losopher (New York, 1939), and the essay on Penn in Joseph Dorfman, *Economic Mind in American Civilization* (2 vols., New York, 1946), present a jaundiced view of Penn with which I do not completely agree, but they are important. Sydney V. James, *A People Among Peoples* (Cambridge, Mass., 1963), is one of the notable works on colonial Quakers published in the last fifteen years. Lois K. Mathews, *The Expansion of New England* (Boston, 1909), is the standard study on the outward movement of the Puritans.

Three studies on the relations between Puritanism and democracy, aside from Ralph Barton Perry's, mentioned earlier, need to be cited here, for from them I have drawn many of my data on the subject: Herbert Osgood, "The Political Idea of the Puritans," *Political Science Quarterly*, VI (March, 1891), 1–28; (June, 1891), 201–231; H. Richard Niebuhr, "The Idea of Covenant and American Democracy," *Church History*, XXIII (June, 1954), 126–35; B. Katherine Brown, "Freemanship in Puritan Massachusetts," *American Historical Review*, LIX (July, 1954), 865–83. A revealing study of a Puritan community is Sumner C. Powell, *Puritan Village* (Middletown, Conn., 1963). On the provincial level, of prime importance is George Lee Haskins, *Law and Authority in Early Massachusetts* (New York, 1960).

All who write on the history of seventeenth-century Virginia are indebted, as I am, to the various studies of P. A. Bruce: *Economic History of Virginia in the Seventeenth Century* (2 vols., New York, 1896), *Institutional History of Virginia in the Seventeenth Century* (New York, 1910), and *Social Life of Virginia in the Seventeenth Century* (2nd ed., Lynchburg, Va., 1927). The last book, however, has been superseded by Thomas J. Wertenbaker, *Planters of Colonial Virginia* (Princeton, 1922), and Louis B. Wright, *First Gentlemen of Virginia* (San Marino, Calif., 1940). The best modern and fullest study of the colonial South is Wesley Frank Craven, *The Southern Colonies in the Seventeenth Century, 1607–1689* (Baton Rouge, La., 1949). An excellent short interpretation of Virginia society is Bernard Bailyn, "Politics and Social Structure in Virginia," in James M. Smith, ed., *Seventeenth Century America* (Chapel Hill, N.C., 1959).

The literature on the history of slavery is enormous and still growing. Oscar and Mary Handlin, "The Origins of the Southern Labor System," *William and Mary Quarterly*, 3rd Ser., VII (April, 1950), 199–222, was the starting point for my thinking about the origins of racism, though my conclusions are now quite opposed to theirs. The monumental study of racial attitudes in the colonial years, Winthrop D. Jordan, *White Over Black* (Chapel Hill, N.C., 1969), takes a position on the question of origins close to mine. See also the highly erudite study of attitudes toward slavery in these same years in the whole western world by David Brion Davis, *The Problem of Slavery in Western Culture* (Ithaca, N.Y.,

1966), especially Part II. I have found much important material in James C. Ballagh, *A History of Slavery in Virginia* (Baltimore, 1902); J. R. Brackett, *Negro in Maryland* (Baltimore, 1889); Susie Ames, *Studies of the Virginia Eastern Shore in the Seventeenth Century* (Richmond, 1940); John Russell, *Free Negro in Virginia, 1619–1865* (Baltimore, 1913); Lorenzo Greene, *Negro in Colonial New England, 1620–1776* (New York, 1942); and B. C. Steiner, *History of Slavery in Connecticut* (Baltimore, 1893).

II. The Awakening of American Nationality

In varying degrees I have drawn upon a number of works dealing with the eighteenth-century colonies. Lawrence Gipson, *The British Empire Before the American Revolution* (Caldwell, Ida., 1936), presents in the first three volumes a masterly survey of the colonies around 1750. Max Savelle, *Seeds of Liberty* (New York, 1948), is an excellent survey of the colonial mind. The long, meaty introductory chapters on the economic, social, and political character of the colonies in Clinton Rossiter, *Seedtime of the Republic* (New York, 1953), have been both stimulating and informative. James Truslow Adams, *Provincial Society, 1690–1763* (New York, 1927), a volume in the History of American Life Series, provided me with much detailed information, as did Evarts B. Greene, *Revolutionary Generation, 1763–1790* (New York, 1943), the next volume in the series. Greene's earlier book, *Foundations of American Nationality* (New York, 1922), was the springboard for a good part of this chapter. The quotation pointing up the contemporaneous growth of capitalism and the American colonies is from G. O. Virtue, "Capitalistic Aspects of the Colonial Economy," in *Explorations in Economics* (New York, 1936). The sources for my generalizations about colonial architecture are Fiske Kimball's highly respected *Domestic Architecture of the American Colonies and of the Early Republic* (New York, 1922) and the more recent and most readable Hugh S. Morrison, *American Architecture from the First Colonial Settlements to the National Period* (New York, 1952). The only book dealing in any comprehensive way with colonial scientific interests is the recent Brooks Hindle, *The Pursuit of Science in Revolutionary America, 1735–1789* (Chapel Hill, N.C., 1956).

The standard history of the family in America is the old, but still useful, Arthur Calhoun, *A Social History of the American Family* (3 vols., Cleveland, 1917–19). There is a great need for a synthetic study of the family in America before 1900. Herbert Moller, "Sex Composition and Correlated Culture Patterns of Colonial America," *William and Mary Quarterly,* 3rd Ser., II (April, 1945), 113–53, is somewhat prolix, but its data are valuable. A good survey of the literature on the colonial family as seen through the new demographic studies is Philip J. Greven, Jr., "Historical Demography and Colonial America," *William and Mary Quarterly,* 3rd Ser., XXIV (July, 1967), 438–54. A number of studies on the position of women in the colonial period are available. I have drawn upon Elizabeth Dexter, *Colonial Women of Affairs* (Boston, 1924); Mary Benson, *Women in Eighteenth Century America* (New York, 1935); and Julia C. Spruill, *Women's Life and Work in the Southern Colonies* (Chapel Hill, N.C., 1938). Richard B. Morris has a most valuable discussion of women's legal rights in his *Studies in the History of American Law,* already mentioned. Edmund Morgan, in his *Virginians at Home* (Williamsburg, Va., 1952), tried to do for the southern colony what he did for New England, but with less success.

My sources for the distribution of immigrants have been the standard Albert B. Faust, *The German Element in the United States* (2 vols. in one, New York, 1927), and Charles A. Hanna, *The Scotch-Irish* (2 vols., New York, 1902). Ian C. C. Graham, *Colonists from Scotland: Emigration to North America 1707–1783* (Ithaca, N.Y., 1956), is especially noteworthy for its rescuing of the important Scottish immigration from being lost in the mass of Scots-Irish. My understanding of the Great Awakening has been enhanced by reading Leonard J. Trinterud, *The Forming of an American Tradition. A Reexamination of Colonial Presbyterianism* (Philadelphia, 1949), and Perry Miller, *Jonathan Edwards* (New York, 1949), which, like everything Professor Miller touched, throws new light and meaning on our religious history. An important study emphasizing the religious character of the colonial revivals is Edwin Scott Gaustad, *The Great Awakening in New England* (New York, 1957). Less successful, but highly erudite in its survey of sermons is Alan Heimert, *Religion and the American Mind* (Cambridge, 1966). For statistics on church membership I am indebted to Edwin S. Gaustad, *Historical Atlas of Religion in America* (New York, 1962).

The best general treatment of the political connections between England and the colonies is still Leonard Labaree, *Royal Government in America* (New Haven, Conn., 1930). I have relied upon Charles Grove Haines, *The American Doctrine of Judicial Supremacy* (New York, 1914) and Joseph Henry Smith, *Appeals to the Privy Council from the American Plantations* (New York, 1950), for my discussion of the judicial relations of the colonies with Britain. Richard B. Morris's chapter on the Zenger trial in *Fair Trial* (New York, 1952) has been the chief source for my handling of that incident. It needs to be supplemented, however, by Leonard Levy, *Legacy of Suppression* (Cambridge, Mass., 1960), a study of the idea of a free press in the colonial years. Robert E. Brown, *Middle Class Democracy and the Revolution in Massachusetts, 1691–1780* (Ithaca, N.Y., 1955), emphasizes convincingly the democratic practices in colonial Massachusetts; Robert E. and B. Katherine Brown,

Virginia, 1705–1786: Democracy or Aristocracy? (East Lansing, Mich., 1964), makes the same point for Virginia. Chilton Williamson, *American Suffrage from Property to Democracy, 1776–1860* (Princeton, N.J., 1960), also argues that suffrage was wide even before the Revolution. Michael G. Kammen, ed., *Politics and Society in Colonial America* (New York, 1967), contains a number of important articles on the suffrage in the colonial period, among which is Milton Klein, "Democracy and Politics in Colonial New York," *New York History,* XL (July, 1959), 221–246, which I have drawn upon. An important critique of those who would make too much of the breadth of the colonial suffrage as a measure of democracy is J. R. Pole, "Historians and the Problem of Early American Democracy," *American Historical Review,* LXVII (April, 1962), 626–646.

Except for the valuable and unique Jackson Turner Main, *The Social Structure of Revolutionary America* (Princeton, N.J., 1965), the sources for social attitudes and structure in the pre-Revolutionary era are primarily the writings of travelers and colonials. The *Works* of that indefatigable American Benjamin Franklin are filled with comments on the society of the new country. The *Letters of Cadwallader Colden* in *Collections* of the New-York Historical Society, Vols. 52–56, 67–68, are valuable for the opposite reason: Colden was most unsympathetic with the American aspirations of his day. *Gottlieb Mittelberger's Journey to Pennsylvania in the Year 1750 and Return to Germany in the Year 1754 . . .* (Philadelphia, 1898) contains much interesting information because the German is so unfriendly to America. The same can be said about Comptroller Weare, "Observations on the British Colonies on the Continent of America," in *Collections* of the Massachusetts Historical Society for the year 1792, 1st Ser., Vol. I. Michel Guillaume St. Jean de Crèvecoeur, *Sketches of Eighteenth Century America,* is a mine of information, but not always to be taken without qualification. His *Letters of an American Farmer* is, of course, a classic, but subject to the same limitation. Like Franklin, *Letters of Benjamin Rush,* edited by L. H. Butterfield (2 vols., Princeton, 1951), offer material from an enthusiastic American. *American Husbandry* (New York, 1939), a famous agricultural treatise of the period, written anonymously and edited by Harry J. Carman, has information on social conditions as well as agriculture. *The Carolina Backcountry on the Eve of the Revolution,* edited by Richard J. Hooker (Chapel Hill, N.C., 1953), contains interesting material on religious activities in the journal and other writings of Charles Woodmason, an Anglican itinerant preacher. I have also used *The Journal and Letters of Philip Vickers Fithian, 1773–1774,* edited by H. D. Farish (Williamsburg, Va., 1943), and Per Kalm, *The America of 1750,* edited by Adolph B. Benson (2 vols., New York, 1937). *Gentleman's Progress; the Itinerarium of Dr. Alexander Hamilton, 1744,* edited by Carl Bridenbaugh (Chapel Hill, N.C., 1948), offers much material on the state and attitudes of the colonies north of Maryland.

More and more, historians have been turning to an investigation of the growth of American nationality in the years before 1776. One of the most provocative, and one which I have followed closely, is Albert J. Harkness, Jr., "Americanism and Jenkins' Ear," *Mississippi Valley Historical Review*, XXXVII (June, 1950), 61–90. Much material, incidentally, in this connection is to be found in William Sachse, *The Colonial American in Britain* (Madison, Wis., 1956). Two books of Michael Kraus have pioneered in showing the growth of an American consciousness in the midst of an Atlantic civilization: *Intercolonial Aspects of Colonial Culture on the Eve of the Revolution* (New York, 1928) and *The Atlantic Civilization: Eighteenth Century Origins* (Ithaca, N.Y., 1949). Richard L. Merritt, *Symbols of American Community, 1735–1775* (New Haven, Conn., 1966), through an examination of newspapers, offers a novel measure of increasing national awareness as the revolution approached. Using more conventional means, John W. Blassingame, "American Nationalism and Other Loyalties in the Southern Colonies, 1763–1775," *Journal of Southern History*, XXXIV (February, 1968), 50–75, reaches a similar conclusion on American identity prior to 1776. Carl Bridenbaugh's *Cities in Revolt* (New York, 1955), a continuation of his earlier *Cities in the Wilderness* (New York, 1938), argues convincingly for the point that an American feeling was growing fast in the cities of the mid-eighteenth century. Many of my conclusions on this subject are indebted to his work. Bridenbaugh's study of the *Colonial Craftsman* (New York, 1950) also contains information on the nature of society. Though Leonard Labaree's *Conservatism in Early American History* (New York, 1948) does not go along with the newer views on the mobility within colonial society, his book cannot be overlooked, for it is a corrective to those who would ignore the rigidities in the social stratification. My paragraph on linguistic changes in American English was derived from H. L. Mencken's *The American Language* (4th ed., New York, 1936). See also Albert H. Marckwardt, *American English* (New York, 1958).

III. A NEW KIND OF REVOLUTION

For the periods before and after the Revolution, the writings of the important participants are a mine of information on attitudes. I have explored with profit the standard published works of John Adams, Benjamin Franklin, Fisher Ames, Alexander Hamilton, Thomas Jefferson, George Washington, and Benjamin Rush. *The Correspondence of General Thomas Gage* (2 vols., New Haven, 1933) highlights the irresolution of the British Ministry and dispels the colonial illusion that military power was being exerted against them before 1774.

The debate about the causes for the Revolution has spawned a tre-mendous literature; only representative samples can be mentioned here. To Charles H. Lincoln, *Revolutionary Movement in Pennsylvania, 1760–1776* (Philadelpia, 1901), perhaps belongs the honor of first presenting in scholarly fashion the thesis that the Revolution was an internal strug-gle between classes as well as a revolt against British control. Carl L. Becker, *History of Political Parties in the Province of New York, 1760–1776* . . . (Madison, Wis., 1909), pushed the same argument. In addi-tion to showing the class divisions over revolution, A. M. Schlesinger, *The Colonial Merchants in the American Revolution, 1763–1776* (New York, 1918), also bore down hard on the economic causes for the com-ing of the break with England. Louis Hacker set forth the most blatant economic explanation for the Revolution in "The American Revolution: Economic Aspects," *Marxist Quarterly,* I (January–March, 1937), 46–67, and in Chapters 10–12 of his later *Triumph of American Capitalism.* Earlier Charles M. Andrews in his *Colonial Background of the American Revolution* (New Haven, 1924) argued that the Revolution was an out-growth of the colonial experience and not a consequence of English eco-nomic restrictions. In his later work, *The Colonial Period of American History,* IV, 425–28, Andrews set forth a blistering denunciation of the Hacker school of thought regarding the influence of British mercantilism. I have followed the Andrews point of view. John C. Miller, *Origins of the American Revolution* (Boston, 1943), comes closer to Andrews' view, but does not repudiate the economic. Most recently, Lawrence Gipson, *The Coming of the Revolution, 1763–1776* (New York, 1954), argues for the long-term causes, but because of the chronological limits of his book he does not go into the matter. Relatively unique among modern explanations for the coming of the Revolution is Robert E. Brown, *Middle Class Democracy in Massachusetts and the Revolution* (Ithaca, N.Y., 1955), wherein it is contended that the Revolution was an effort to preserve democracy against British tyranny. Merrill Jensen, "Democ-racy and the American Revolution," *Huntington Library Quarterly,* XX (August, 1957), 321–41, in its repudiation of Brown's thesis sums up my own objections. I do not, however, go along with Jensen in subscrib-ing to a democratic versus aristocratic struggle after the Revolution.

My disbelief in any fundamental economic explanation for the coming of the Revolution stems from a number of works; foremost is Lawrence Harper, "The Effect of the Navigation Acts on the Thirteen Colonies," in R. B. Morris, ed., *Era of the American Revolution* (New York, 1939), a superb piece of quantitative historical investigation. Douglass C. North, *Growth and Welfare in the American Past* (Englewood Cliffs, N.J., 1966), using the methods of the "new economic history," finds the burden smaller than Harper did. I have accepted A. C. Bining's con-clusions in *British Regulation of the Colonial Iron Industry* (Philadelphia,

1933). The *coup de grâce* was dealt one aspect of the economic explanation for the coming of the revolution by O. M. Dickerson, *Navigation Acts and the American Revolution* (Philadelphia, 1951). Thomas Abernethy, *Western Lands and the American Revolution* (New York, 1937), shows that British limitations on westward expansion had no appreciable effect on Revolutionary sentiment.

For my interpretation of the coming of the Revolution I have also used Edmund and Helen Morgan, *Stamp Act Crisis* (Chapel Hill, N.C., 1953); Charles R. Ritcheson, *British Politics and the American Revolution* (Norman, Okla., 1954); Vincent Todd Harlow, *The Founding of the Second British Empire, 1763–1793* (London, 1952), to name only the most recent studies. An excellent examination of a neglected cause of the Revolution is Carl Ubbelohde, *The Vice-Admiralty Courts and the American Revolution* (Chapel Hill, N.C., 1960). Highly favorable to the imperial point of view on the West is Jack M. Sosin, *Whitehall and the Wilderness* (Lincoln, Neb., 1961). Much detailed information was obtained from the old but full William E. H. Lecky, *A History of England in the Eighteenth Century* (8 vols., London, 1878–90). For the political and constitutional ideas of the era I have used Randolph G. Adams, *Political Ideas of the Revolution* (Durham, N.C., 1922), Charles H. McIlwaine, *The American Revolution: a Constitutional Interpretation* (New York, 1923), and Robert L. Schuyler, *Parliament and the British Empire* (New York, 1929). The extent to which historians have accepted the constitutional and political character of the Revolution is clearly measured in H. Trevor Colbourn's, *The Lamp of Experience: Whig History and the Intellectual Origins of the American Revolution* (Chapel Hill, N.C., 1965); Bernard Bailyn, *Ideological Origins of the American Revolution* (Cambridge, Mass., 1967), which draws its conclusions from an examination of the pamphlet literature spawned by the Revolution; and the suggestive article by Gordon S. Wood, "Rhetoric and Reality in the American Revolution," *William and Mary Quarterly*, 3rd Series, XXIII (January, 1966), 3–32.

Though in interpreting the period after the Revolution historians have been taking sides for some time, the factual, detailed investigations upon which judgments may be based are few. Charles A. Beard's *An Economic Interpretation of the Constitution* (New York, 1935), originally published in 1913, can be said to have opened the debate by arguing that the period between 1776 and 1789 was characterized by a struggle between economic classes for control of the central government. His *Economic Origins of Jeffersonian Democracy* (New York, 1915) continued this line of argument into the Federalist-Jeffersonian era. Merrill Jensen's *The Articles of Confederation* (Madison, Wis., 1940), and *The New Nation: A History of the United States During the Confederation, 1781–1789* (New York, 1950), have attempted, unsuccessfully to my mind, to support the Beardian case. The evidence and methodology in Beard's first book have been criticized and superseded by a wealth of new evidence in Forrest MacDonald, *We the People: The Economic Origins of the Constitution* (Chicago, 1958). My understanding of the Jeffersonian Democratic-Republicans has benefited from reading E. Wilder Spaulding, *New York in the Critical Period* (New York, 1932); Eugene Link, *Democratic-Republican Societies, 1790–1800* . . . (New York, 1942); and Elisha Douglass, *Rebels and Democrats* (Chapel Hill, N.C., 1955), though I do not agree with their general acceptance of fundamental divergence of philosophy between the Jeffersonians and Federalists. First-rate on the 1790's is William N. Chambers, *Political Parties in a New Nation* (New York, 1963). *The Journal of William Maclay* (New York, 1927); William Manning, *Key to Liberty* (Billerica, Mass., 1922); and Charles Warren, *Jacobin and Junto* (Cambridge, Mass., 1931), are writings of Republicans which I have used with profit. *The Records of the Federal Convention of 1787* (4 vols., New Haven, Conn., 1911–37), edited by Max Farrand, are a prime source for the conservative view in this period. I have followed J. P. Warren, "The Confederation and Shays' Rebellion," *American Historical Review*, XI (October, 1905), 42–67, in emphasizing the conservatives' concern over lack of central power in the Articles of Confederation. An important addition to the literature on the Confederation years is E. James Ferguson, *The Power of the Purse: A History of American Public Finance, 1776–1790* (Chapel Hill, N.C., 1961).

The starting point for all subsequent studies of the social implications of the American Revolution is J. Franklin Jameson, *The American Revolution Considered as a Social Movement* (Princeton, 1926). Criticism of Jameson's thesis has been piecemeal rather than total, though Frederick B. Tolles attempted a comprehensive review in "The American Revolution Considered as a Social Movement: a Re-Evaluation," *American Historical Review*, LX (October, 1954), 1–12, but without doing justice, it seems to me, to the large amount of evidence against Jameson's position. C. S. Crary, "Forfeited Loyalist Lands in the Western District of New York—Albany and Tyron Counties," *New York History*, XXV (July, 1954), 239–258, and Harry Yoshpe, *Disposition of Loyalist Estates in the Southern District of the State of New York* (New York, 1939), emphasize the absence of any significant redistribution of land through revolutionary seizures. A critical reading of Robert O. DeMond, *Loyalists in North Carolina During the Revolution* (Durham, N.C., 1940), leads to much the same conclusion. A gem of an essay on the nature of the Loyalists is William H. Nelson, *The American Tory* (New York, 1961). Lee M. Newcomer, *The Embattled Farmers* (New York, 1953); Robert J. Taylor, *Western Massachusetts in the Revolution* (Providence, 1954); and Allan Nevins, *The American States During and After the Revolution*

1775–1789 (New York, 1924), all supplied information and insights which have contributed to my conception of the so-called Critical Period. The principal study on the Anti-Federalists is now Jackson Turner Main, *The Anti-Federalists* (Chapel Hill, N.C., 1961).

Three authorities have been the main source for my generalizations regarding constitutional changes after the Revolution: Walter F. Dodd, *Revision and Amendment of State Constitutions* (Baltimore, 1910); Fletcher Green, *Constitutional Development in the South Atlantic States, 1776–1860* (Chapel Hill, N.C., 1930); and, most detailed of all, W. C. Webster, "Comparative Study of the State Constitutions of the American Revolution," *Annals* of the American Academy of Political and Social Science, IX (1897), 380–420. I also used the authoritative source collection, F. N. Thorpe, ed., *The Federal and State Constitutions* (7 vols., Washington, 1909).

The old but still valuable Philip Schaff, "Church and State in the United States," in *Papers* of the American Historical Association, II (1888), 391–543, has been most influential in my thinking about the American doctrine of separation of Church and State. Evarts B. Greene, *Religion and the State* (New York, 1941), was of great value, as was A. P. Stokes's monumental *Church and State in the United States* (3 vols., New York, 1950). Leo Pfeffer, *Church, State and Freedom* (Boston, 1953), is argumentative, but important.

Of social commentary, the most valuable for my interests was Johann Schoepf, *Travels in the Confederation,* translated and edited by Alfred J. Morrison (2 vols., Philadelphia, 1911). J. P. Brissot de Warville, *New Travels in the United States* (2 vols., London, 1794), and *Moreau de St. Méry's American Journey, 1793–1798,* Kenneth and Anna M. Roberts, editors (Garden City, N.Y., 1947), also supplied some data.

My conclusion that the American Revolution was a conservative one was prompted by reading the last chapter of Clinton Rossiter's *Seedtime of the Republic* (New York, 1953) and Daniel Boorstin's provocative *The Genius of American Politics* (Chicago, 1953). The same idea was advanced in Friedrich Gentz's essay, first published in 1800, *The French and the American Revolutions Compared,* translated by John Quincy Adams (Chicago, 1955). For a strong case on the other side, which does not quite convince me, see the superb Robert R. Palmer, *The Age of the Democratic Revolution,* I (Princeton, N.J., 1959).

IV. To Make a More Perfect Union

The history of the westward movement and the diplomacy of Expansion have been well dealt with in general volumes upon which I have drawn liberally: Ray Billington, *Westward Expansion* (New York, 1949); Thomas A. Bailey, *A Diplomatic History of the American People* (3rd ed., New York, 1947); Albert Weinberg, *Manifest Destiny* (Baltimore, 1935), which is a superb study of the ideas Americans have used to justify their expansion; Roy F. Robbins, *Our Landed Heritage* (Princeton, 1942), a comprehensive account of the evolution of land policy; and Helene Zahler, *Eastern Workingmen and National Land Policy, 1829–1862* (New York, 1941).

There are a number of surveys of the economic history of the United States; I have found Edward Kirkland, *A History of American Economic Life* (3rd ed., New York, 1951), the most stimulating. More detailed for this period and covering much more than its title suggests is George Rogers Taylor, *Transportation Revolution, 1815–1860* (New York, 1951). Louis Hunter, *Steamboats on the Western Rivers* (Cambridge, Mass., 1949), is indispensable. I have followed Henry Clyde Hubbard, *The Older Middle West 1840–1880* (New York, 1936), in the discussion of the importance of the railroads linking the West and the East.

The genuine and deep concern of government with economic development during the pre-Civil War years is now well recognized among historians. Oscar and Mary Handlin, *Commonwealth, A Study of the Role of Government in the American Economy: Massachusetts, 1774–1861* (New York, 1947), and Louis Hartz, *Economic Policy and Democratic Thought: Pennsylvania, 1776–1860* (Cambridge, Mass., 1948) were among the first to emphasize the point, though both studies sometimes make more of their evidence than is warranted. More convincing, though narrower in conception since it deals only with aid to internal improvements, is Carter Goodrich, *American Promotion of American Canals and Railroads, 1800–1890* (New York, 1960). The whole literature on the subject of government support of economic development has been admirably summed up and critically appraised in Robert A. Lively, "The American System: A Review Article," *Business History Review,* XXIX (March, 1955), 81–96.

The standard treatments on the labor movement of the pre-Civil War years are John R. Commons *et al., History of Labour in the United States,* Vols. I and II (New York, 1918), and Norman Ware, *Industrial Worker, 1840–1860* (New York, 1924). I have also used Caroline F. Ware, *Early New England Cotton Manufacture* (New York, 1931), and Hannah Josephson, *Golden Threads* (New York, 1949), for the Lowell girls. For my treatment of Eli Whitney I have relied upon Jeannette Mirsky and Allan Nevins, *The World of Eli Whitney* (New York, 1952), which is a remarkable job of integrating original sources into a smoothly flowing text.

All discussions of Turner's theories must begin with the collection of his essays, *The Frontier in American History* (New York, 1921). The literature about Turner and his theories is simply too large even to list here; it is categorized and annotated in Ray Billington, *America's Fron-*

tier Heritage (New York, 1966). The book is also a defense of the Turner thesis by a knowing historian. Benjamin F. Wright, "Political Institutions and the Frontier," in Dixon R. Fox, ed., *Sources of Culture in the Middle West* (New York, 1934), is one of the earliest criticisms of Turner's thesis as it relates to democracy in the West. The best and most penetrating over-all critique of Turner's ideas is contained in two articles of George W. Pierson, "The Frontier and Frontiersmen of Turner's Essays," *Pennsylvania Magazine of History and Biography,* LXIV (October, 1940), 449–78, and "The Frontier and Our Institutions," *New England Quarterly,* XV (June, 1942), 224–55. The long quotation from Tocqueville's letter on his observations in Michigan is from Pierson's magnificent *Tocqueville and Beaumont in America* (New York, 1938). Richard Hofstadter, "Turner and the Frontier Myth," *American Scholar,* XVIII (Autumn, 1949), 433–43, sums up the anti-Turner literature. The most important support for Turner's ideas on democracy and the frontier comes from Stanley Elkins and Eric McKitrick, "A Meaning for Turner's Frontier," *Political Science Quarterly,* LXIX (September, 1954), 321–53; (December, 1954), 565–602.

The safety-valve thesis has come in for very extended empirical investigation. Foremost in this regard is Carter Goodrich and Sol Davison, "The Wage Earner in the Western Movement," *Political Science Quarterly,* L (June, 1935), 161–85, and LI (March, 1936), 61–116. The weakness of the factual data for believing that a safety valve was working is demonstrated unintentionally in Joseph Schafer, "Was the West a Safety Valve for Labor?" *Mississippi Valley Historical Review,* XXIV (December, 1937), 299–314, which was intended as an answer to Goodrich and Davison. Studies which also offer evidence for disbelieving in the safety valve include Rufus S. Tucker, "The Frontier as an Outlet for Surplus Labor," *Southern Economic Journal,* VII (October, 1940), 158–86; Clarence Danhof, "Farm-making Costs and the 'Safety-Valve': 1850–1860," *Journal of Political Economy,* XLIX (June, 1941), 317–59; Carl N. Degler, "The West as a Solution to Urban Unemployment," *New York History,* XXXVI (January, 1955), 63–84; and Fred A. Shannon, "A Post-Mortem on the Labor-Safety-Valve Theory," *Agricultural History,* XIX (January, 1945), 31–37. The best answer to Shannon is Ellen von Nardoff, "The American Frontier as Safety-Valve: The Life, Death, Reincarnation, and Justification of a Theory," *Agricultural History,* XXXVI (July, 1962), 123–42. H. J. Habakkuk, *American and British Technology in the Nineteenth Century* (Cambridge, Eng., 1962), makes much of empty land as an inducement to use machines.

My thinking about the implications of the frontier for the making of American character has been stimulated by Fred A. Shannon's *An Appraisal of Walter Prescott Webb's The Great Plains* (New York, 1940), though I do not agree with all of Professor Shannon's strictures against

Webb. Needless to say, I have read Webb's *The Great Plains* (Boston, 1931) with great profit. For my summary of comparative frontiers I have used James G. Leyburn, *Frontier Folkways* (New Haven, 1935); section 4, Chapter VII, of the *Cambridge Economic History of Europe*, Vol. I (Cambridge, 1941); James Westfall Thompson, *Feudal Germany* (Chicago, 1928); Richard Shryock, "British versus German Traditions in Colonial Agriculture," *Mississippi Valley Historical Review*, XXVI (June, 1939), 39–54. W. D. Wyman and E. B. Kroeber, *The Frontier in Perspective* (Madison, Wis., 1957), contains several essays on the frontier influence in lands outside the United States.

V. THE GREAT EXPERIMENT

As at perhaps no other time in our history, the United States in the three decades before 1860 was scrutinized by foreigners; their impressions are contained in literally dozens of books, many of which I have perused in writing this chapter. Beyond all others, that of Alexis de Tocqueville, *Democracy in America* (2 vols., New York, 1948), is the most critically perceptive. Harriet Martineau, *Society in America* (2 vols., New York, 1837), and Achille Murat, *A Moral and Political Sketch of the United States of North America* (London, 1833), are among the most friendly, while Frances Trollope, *Domestic Manners of the Americans,* edited by Donald Smalley (New York, 1949), is probably the most acid. The writings of two Americans should also be mentioned here: James Fenimore Cooper, *The American Democrat* (New York, 1956), which was an American's answer to the strictures of European conservatives upon the western democracy, and Philip Hone's *Diary,* edited by B. Tuckerman (2 vols., New York, 1889), which offers the views of a home-grown conservative in Jacksonian America. Douglas T. Miller, *Jacksonian Aristocracy. Class and Democracy in New York, 1830–1860* (New York, 1967), emphasizes the conservative streak in Jacksonian America.

Leonard White's long-needed and readable study of administrative history of the period, *The Jacksonians* (New York, 1954), has been my chief authority for the treatment of the changing character of government. I have supplemented it with Clinton Rossiter, *The American Presidency* (New York, 1956), and Fletcher Green, *Constitutional Development in the South Atlantic States, 1776–1860* (Chapel Hill, N.C., 1930). The nature of parties and popular participation in politics has been persuasively reinterpreted in the work of Richard P. McCormick, notably in two articles: "Suffrage Classes and Party Alignments: a Study in Voter Behavior," *Mississippi Valley Historical Review*, XLVI (December, 1959), 397–410 and "New Perspectives on Jacksonian Politics," *American Historical Review*, LXV (January, 1960), 288–301, and in a recent book: *The Second Party System: Party Formation in the Jacksonian Era* (Chapel Hill, N.C., 1966).

The most stimulating and comprehensive treatment of the Jacksonian era remains Arthur M. Schlesinger, Jr., *Age of Jackson* (Boston, 1945), for it has spawned a whole shelffull of studies on the era. My interpretation of Jacksonian economic thought, however, is closer to that expressed in Richard Hofstadter, *The American Political Tradition* (New York, 1951), Chapter III. John William Ward, *Andrew Jackson, Symbol for an Age* (New York, 1955), is a stimulating analysis of the image of Jackson in popular literature: its method and conclusions are in line with those advanced in Marvin Meyers, *Jacksonian Persuasion* (Stanford, Cal., 1957). Lee Benson in *The Concept of Jacksonian Democracy* (Princeton, N.J., 1961) concludes among other things, without persuading me, that the name of the period ought to be changed. His assertion that the parties of the era were not divided by class is vigorously and convincingly rejected in Frank Otto Gatell, "Money and Party in Jacksonian America: A Quantitative Look at New York City's Men of Quality," *Political Science Quarterly,* LXXXII (June, 1967), 235–52.

I have derived much insight into Jacksonian ideas from the handy collection of sources edited by Joseph Blau, *Social Theories of Jacksonian Democracy* (New York, 1954). William Leggett and the radical Loco-Focos are analyzed and put into historical perspective in Richard Hofstadter, "William Leggett, Spokesman of Jacksonian Democracy," *Political Science Quarterly,* XLVIII (December, 1943), 581–94; and Carl N. Degler, "The Locofocos: Urban 'Agrarians,'" *Journal of Economic History,* XVI (September, 1956), 322–33. Theodore Sedgwick, Jr., a supporter and friend of Leggett, has edited *A Collection of the Political Writings of William Leggett* (2 vols., New York, 1840). The economic implications of Jacksonian ideas are admirably dissected by one who is unconvinced of their soundness on finances in Bray Hammond, "Free Banks and Corporations: the New York Free Banking Act of 1838," *Journal of Political Economy,* XLIV (April, 1936), 184–209, and "Banking in the Early West: Monopoly, Prohibition and Laissez-Faire," *Journal of Economic History,* VIII (May, 1948), 1–25. Obviously, I have followed Hammond in this regard. The long-needed biography of the great Jacksonian spokesman, Thomas Hart Benton, by William Chambers, *Old Bullion Benton* (Boston, 1956), is somewhat weakened by a rather uncritical acceptance of the Schlesinger view of the war against the Bank. I have used with great profit Carl B. Swisher's *Roger B. Taney* (New York, 1935) and Benjamin F. Wright, *The Contract Clause of the Constitution* (Cambridge, Mass., 1938), in dealing with the Charles River Bridge case.

My generalizations and quotations on the reform movement as a whole have been drawn primarily from Alice Felt Tyler, *Freedom's Ferment*

(Minneapolis, 1944), a survey of the movement; Merle Curti, *Growth of American Thought* (New York, 1943), Chapters XII, XIV, XV; Arthur Ekirch, *The Idea of Progress in America, 1815–1860* (New York, 1951); George D. Lillibridge, *Beacon of Freedom; the Impact of American Democracy upon Great Britain, 1830–1870* (Philadelphia, 1955); and the source collection of Irving Mark and Eugene L. Schwaab, *Faith of Our Fathers* (New York, 1952).

There is a crying need for a broad, interpretive study of the ideas and forces behind the educational revival of the 1830's and 1840's. In lieu of that I have rested my conclusions on the standard works now available: Ellwood P. Cubberley, *Public Education in the United States* (Boston, 1919); Paul Monroe, *Founding of the American Public School System* (New York, 1940); Sidney Jackson, *America's Struggle for Free Schools* (Washington, 1941), which really deals only with a few states; and B. A. Hinsdale, *Horace Mann and the Common School Revival in the United States* (New York, 1900).

VI. THE AMERICAN TRAGEDY

The best over-all treatment of the ante-bellum South in one volume is Clement Eaton, *The Growth of Southern Civilization 1790–1860* (New York, 1961); it is written by a Southerner with a national outlook. Vol. V in the ten-volume History of the South, Charles S. Sydnor, *The Development of Southern Sectionalism, 1819–1848* (Baton Rouge, 1949), is a model study and is in striking contrast with the subsequent volume in the series, Avery Craven, *Growth of Southern Nationalism, 1848–1861* (Baton Rouge, 1953), which is largely focused on the national scene and deals hardly at all with developments in the South. The much older and more popular book of William A. Dodd, *Expansion and Conflict* (New York, 1915), also by a Southerner, I have found suggestive and informative. Though my assumptions regarding slavery and the Negro are quite different from those of U. B. Phillips, in substance my conception of the "Central Theme of Southern History" is his. His essay of that name can be found in the collection, *The Course of the South to Secession*, edited by E. M. Coulter (New York, 1939). From a somewhat different angle, Jesse T. Carpenter's *The South as a Conscious Minority, 1789–1861* (New York, 1930) has been influential with me. Robert R. Russel, *Economic Aspects of Southern Sectionalism, 1840–1861* (Urbana, Ill., 1922), endeavors to explain the growth of southern self-consciousness in terms of economic interest, but I think it unconvincing.

The subject of southern Negro slavery seems to be perennially interesting if one is to judge from the number of words devoted then and now to its discussion. The unquestionably basic work on the subject of southern economics and one upon which I have relied is Lewis C. Gray, *History of Agriculture in Southern United States to 1860* (2 vols., Washington, 1933). The best-known worker in the vineyard of slavery history is U. B. Phillips; the fruits of his scholarship are *American Negro Slavery* (New York, 1933, though first published in 1918) and *Life and Labor in the Old South* (Boston, 1929). Phillips has come in for increasingly severe criticism for his very mild strictures against slavery as a system and his southern-born callousness to the moral crippling to which slavery subjected the Negro, but the facts and details of his books still repay study. A modern scholar, northern in birth and orientation, has essayed to write a general institutional history of slavery within a more modern framework of anthropological and sociological knowledge. Kenneth Stampp, *The Peculiar Institution* (New York, 1956), is now the best treatment of slavery, but it sometimes romanticizes the Negro and tends to see harshness and guilt in the slaveowner. Stampp and Phillips are compared in Stanley Elkins' stimulating but misleading book *Slavery* (Chicago, 1959). Persuasive in the main, and congenial to my own view of the slave South is Eugene Genovese, *The Political Economy of Slavery* (New York, 1965). The classic sources on the ante-bellum South are the journalistic accounts of the acute northern observer Frederick Law Olmsted: *Journey in the Seaboard Slave States* (2 vols., New York, 1904), and *Journey in the Back Country* (New York, 1861). I have also used the reissue of his *Cotton Kingdom*, edited by Arthur M. Schlesinger (New York, 1953). The collection of sources *Plantation and Frontier* (2 vols., Cleveland, 1909), edited by U. B. Phillips, is indispensable. That great southern nationalist of the 1850's, J. D. B. De Bow, edited a broad-ranging compendium of sources on the South of that decade which I have used: *Industrial Resources of the Southern and Western States* (3 vols., New Orleans, 1852–3).

Specialized studies in aspects of southern slavery and economics in the ante-bellum period abound, and I have relied upon a number of them. Though Phillips and a good number of other scholars have argued that slavery was unprofitable, the balance is now shifting; Thomas P. Govan, "Was Plantation Slavery Profitable?" *Journal of Southern History*, VIII (November, 1942), 513–35, though tentative in conclusion, convinced me in the affirmative. Stampp in his recent book and Robert W. Smith, "Was Slavery Unprofitable in the Ante-bellum South?" *Agricultural History*, XX (January, 1946), 62–64, also conclude that slavery was profitable. Especially persuasive in showing how profitable slavery was and richly documented is A. H. Conrad and J. R. Meyer, "The Economics of Slavery in the Ante-Bellum South," *Journal of Political Economy*, LXVI (April, 1958), 95–130. Robert R. Russel, "Economic History of Negro Slavery," *Agricultural History*, XI (October, 1937), 308–21, and "The General Effects of Slavery Upon Southern Economic Progress," *Journal of Southern History,* IV (February, 1938), 34–54, have been important in delineating the importance of slavery in the economy. I have also drawn data from, though not always agreeing with, the conclusions in Alfred H. Stone, "Free Contract Labor in the Ante-Bellum South," and Walter F. Fleming, "Slave Labor System in the Ante-Bellum South," both of which are in Vol. V of *The South in the Building of the Nation* (10 vols., Richmond, 1909–13). The literature on the profitability of slavery is well summarized and assessed in Harold D. Woodman, "The Profitability of Slavery: a Historical Perennial," *Journal of Southern History,* XXIX (August, 1963), 303–25.

The most important new interpretation of the character of southern society is the work of the so-called Vanderbilt school, led by Frank Owsley. Though L. C. Gray a long time ago recognized the importance of the nonslaveholder in the southern economy, only since Owsley has any systematic study been made of that class. The pioneer study was Frank and Harriet Owsley, "The Economic Basis of Society in the Late Ante-Bellum South," *Journal of Southern History,* VI (February, 1940), 24–25; a broader study, drawing upon the work of his students, is Frank Owsley, *Plain Folk of the Old South* (Baton Rouge, 1949). I have also used James C. Bonner, "Profile of a Late Ante-Bellum Community," *American Historical Review,* XLIX (July, 1944), 663–80; and Herbert Weaver, *Mississippi Farmers, 1850–1860* (Nashville, 1945). Though I have not followed the Owsley group in assigning a central role in the southern economy to the yeoman, I have found its picture of general prosperity a convincing one. My criticisms of the Owsley school have been sparked by the involved but penetrating work of Fabian Linden, "Economic Democracy in the Slave South," *Journal of Negro History,* XXXI (April, 1946), 140–89. Other studies on plantation life and economy I have used with profit include Weymouth T. Jordan, *Hugh Davis and His Alabama Plantation* (University, Ala., 1948); John Spencer Bassett, *Southern Plantation Overseer as Revealed in His Letters* (Northampton, Mass., 1925); Frederick Bancroft, *Slave-Trading in the Old South* (Baltimore, 1931); and Charles S. Sydnor, *Slavery in Mississippi* (New York, 1933).

The most extreme case for the rebelliousness of the Negro in bondage is made in Herbert Aptheker, *American Negro Slave Revolts* (New York, 1943); the evidence in R. A. and A. H. Bauer, "Day to Day Resistance to Slavery," *Journal of Negro History,* XVII (October, 1942), 388–419, suffers like that in Aptheker's book from lack of representativeness. The best study on the underground railroad, emphasizing the role of the Negro slave, is Larry Gara, *Liberty Line* (Lexington, Ky., 1961). B. A. Botkin has edited a collection of slave reminiscences: *Lay My Burden Down* (Chicago, 1945). Two Negro scholars have written remarkably objective studies of their own people which I have used: E. Franklin Frazier, *The Negro in the United States* (New York, 1949) and John Hope Franklin, *From Slavery to Freedom* (New York, 1947), a history of the Negro in America. There are many studies of the free Negro under slavery, as there are many individual state studies of slavery. I have used John Hope Franklin, *Free Negro in North Carolina, 1790–1860* (Chapel Hill, N.C., 1943); J. M. England, "The Free Negro in Ante-Bellum Tennessee," *Journal of Southern History*, IX (February, 1943), 37–58; and L. P. Jackson, *Free Negro Labor and Property Holding in Virginia, 1830–1860* (New York, 1942). Richard C. Wade, *Slavery in the Cities* (New York, 1964), is an important addition to the understanding of slavery and the origins of segregation.

Three studies, though largely unconcerned with slavery historically, throw much light on the impact of slavery on the Negro: Abram Kardiner, *The Mark of Oppression* (New York, 1951), which discusses the long-range psychological effects of slavery; Gunnar Myrdal *et al.*, *The American Dilemma* (2 vols., New York, 1944), a wide-ranging study of the Negro in America; and Melville Herskovits, *The Myth of the Negro Past* (New York, 1941), which shows, unintentionally, how weak is the case for persistence of African culture in America. Miles Mark Fisher, *Negro Slave Songs in the United States* (Ithaca, N.Y., 1953), though it tries to show, by analyzing the slave songs, that the Negro longed for Africa, proves just the opposite by the paucity of evidence. For my discussion of slave songs I have used the compendium of William F. Allen, *Slave Songs of the United States* (New York, 1929, first published in 1867). For the reaction of Negroes during the war, I have followed Bell I. Wiley, *Southern Negroes, 1861–65* (New Haven, 1938).

That the South was not ruled by an oligarchy is demonstrated in Fletcher Green, "Democracy in the Old South," *Journal of Southern History*, XII (February, 1946), 3–23, but the pre-eminence of the issue of slavery is admitted. The effects of slavery upon the urban white worker are delineated in Richard B. Morris, "The Measure of Bondage in the Slave States," *Mississippi Valley Historical Review*, XLI (September, 1954), 219–40. I am greatly indebted to Clement Eaton's superb volume *Freedom of Thought in the Old South* (Durham, N.C., 1940) for much of my description of the constrictive intellectual effects of slavery; other studies leading in the same direction are his "Mob Violence in the Old South," *Mississippi Valley Historical Review*, XXIX (December, 1942), 351–70; and Charles S. Sydnor, "The Southerner and the Laws," *Journal of Southern History*, XI (February, 1940), 3–23, which, while denying the Southerner is any more prone to lawlessness than other Americans, admits that slavery encouraged extralegal action. Rollin Osterweis broke new and important ground when he showed the intellectual connection between slavery, romanticism, and nationalism in *Romanticism and Nationalism in the Old South* (New Haven, 1949); I have learned much from this work.

Southern defenses of slavery have been set forth in detail, though without much critical analysis, in William S. Jenkins, *Pro-Slavery Thought in the Old South* (Chapel Hill, N.C., 1935). Winifred Carsel, "The Slaveholders' Indictment of Northern Wage Slavery," *Journal of Southern History*, VI (November, 1940), 504–20, and Harvey Wish, *George Fitzhugh, Propagandist of the Old South* (Baton Rouge, 1934), set forth the counterthrust of the South. I have also used collections of the proslavery writings of Southerners: *Pro-Slavery Argument* (Philadelphia, 1853), and E. N. Elliott, ed., *Cotton Is King and Pro-Slavery Arguments* (Augusta, Ga., 1860).

The distinction I make between antislavery and abolition is derived from a reading of a number of studies of the period. Outstanding in this regard is Dwight Dumond, *Antislavery Origins of the Civil War in the United States* (Ann Arbor, Mich., 1939), and Russel B. Nye, *Fettered Freedom: Civil Liberties and the Slavery Controversy* (East Lansing, Mich., 1949). Theodore C. Smith, *Liberty and Free Soil Parties in the Northwest* (New York, 1897), and Julian P. Bretz, "The Economic Background of the Liberty Party," *American Historical Review*, XXXIV (January, 1929), 250–64, offer much material on the growth of northern opposition to slavery on grounds other than morality. Until the last decade, much of the writing on abolition and antislavery was almost hostile, especially toward leaders like William Lloyd Garrison. Representative of this attitude was Gilbert H. Barnes, *Antislavery Impulse, 1830–44* (New York, 1933). Views much more favorably disposed toward even the extreme abolitionists are to be found in recent works like Louis Filler, *The Crusade Against Slavery, 1830–1860* (New York, 1960), James M. McPherson, *The Struggle for Equality* (Princeton, N.J., 1964), and Martin Duberman, ed., *The Antislavery Vanguard* (Princeton, N.J., 1965).

The view that slavery could not expand after 1860 has been most vigorously stated in Charles W. Ramsdell, "Natural Limits of Slavery Expansion," *Mississippi Valley Historical Review*, XVI (September, 1929), 151–71. The question of which of the sections was more aggressive is canvassed in C. S. Boucher, "In Re: That Aggressive Slaveocracy," *Mississippi Valley Historical Review*, VIII (June, 1921), 8–79, in which the South is said to have been more divided than aggressive; and in Russel B. Nye, "The Slave Power Conspiracy: 1830–1860," *Science and Society*, X (Summer, 1946), 262–74, in which the South's defense of slavery is seen as a threat to liberty and therefore aggressive, though not as a deliberate conspiracy. My own view is closer to Nye's than Boucher's. Southern historian Thomas Govan, in "Was the Old South Different?"

Journal of Southern History, XXI (November, 1955), 447–55 is one of the recent writers who sees slavery as the determining cause of the antebellum South's culture and the ensuing war. That is the central point also of Genovese, *The Political Economy of Slavery,* already mentioned.

The literature on the coming of the Civil War is so voluminous and controversial that it has to be discussed in detail or not discussed at all. Since space does not permit the former course, the latter will have to be taken. Two surveys of the literature, however, can be noted: Howard K. Beale, "What Historians Have Said about the Causes of the Civil War," in Social Science Research Council, *Theory and Practice in Historical Study: A Report of the Committee on Historiography* (New York, ca. 1946), which deals with a host of writers and neatly categorizes them; and Thomas J. Pressley, *Americans Interpret Their Civil War* (Princeton, 1954), in which the works of several major historians are critically dissected in detail.

VII. Bringing Forth a New Nation

The standard survey on the Civil War, now even more valuable because of its revision by David Donald, is J. G. Randall and David Donald, *The Civil War and Reconstruction* (2nd ed., Boston, 1961). The bibliography is unsurpassed. In *Roots of American Loyalty* (New York, 1946), Merle Curti has several good chapters on the making of a new nation. The popular literature resulting from the war is listed in R. W. Smith, "Catalogue of the Chief Novels and Short Stories by American Authors dealing with the Civil War and Its Effects, 1861–1899," *Bulletin of Bibliography,* XVI (September–December, 1939), 193–94; XVII (January–April, 1940), 10–12 (May–August, 1940), 33–35 (September–December, 1940), 53–55 (January–April, 1941), 72–75, and delightfully discussed and analyzed in Robert Lively, *Fiction Fights the Civil War* (Chapel Hill, N.C., 1957).

Reminiscences and reporting on the war are voluminous. A handy compendium which I have used is *The Blue and the Gray,* edited by Henry Steel Commager (2 vols., Indianapolis, 1950). I have also quoted from Theodore Upson, *With Sherman to the Sea* (University Station, La., 1943); Mason W. Tyler, *Recollections of the Civil War* (New York, 1912); William T. Lusk, *War Letters* (New York, 1911); *Letters of a Family During the War for the Union* (2 vols., New Haven, 1899); *Touched with Fire; Civil War Letters and Diary of Oliver Wendell Holmes, Jr., 1861–4,* edited by Mark DeWolfe Howe (Cambridge, Mass., 1946); Henry Hitchcock, *Marching with Sherman* (New Haven, 1927); John Beatty, *Memoirs of a Volunteer, 1861–3,* edited by H. S. Ford (New York, 1946). Anthony Trollope's *North America* (New York, 1862) is interesting in the light of his mother's earlier criticisms of the North.

Another Englishman, Edward Dicey, also portrayed the North sympathetically in *Six Months in the Federal States* (London, 1863). Bruce Catton's *A Stillness at Appomattox* (Garden City, N.Y., 1954) is already a minor classic in its genre of portraying the impact of the war upon the soldiers who fought it.

My thinking about the military aspects of the war has been greatly influenced by reading General J. F. C. Fuller's lively and controversial *Grant and Lee* (London, 1933) and *The Generalship of Ulysses S. Grant* (New York, 1929). Ella Lonn's *Foreigners in the Union Army and Navy* (Baton Rouge, 1952) is the basis for my statements on the importance of the immigrants; Mary Dearing, *Veterans in Politics, the Story of the GAR* (Baton Rouge, 1952), and Wallace Evan Davies, *Patriotism on Parade* (Cambridge, Mass., 1955), supplied information for my description of the G.A.R. Frank Owsley's disenchanted treatment of *King Cotton Diplomacy* (Chicago, 1931) is the standard authority on the diplomacy of the Confederacy.

The immediate economic consequences for the South are set forth in James L. Sellers, "Economic Incidence of the Civil War in the South," *Mississippi Valley Historical Review*, XIV (September, 1927), 179–91. Ralph Andreano, ed., *The Economic Impact of the American Civil War* (Cambridge, Mass., 1962), contains a selection of important articles on the effects of the war. The adjustments in southern agriculture are handled admirably in Fred Shannon's *The Farmer's Last Frontier* (New York, 1945) and in more detail in the first four chapters of Robert Preston Brooks, *Agrarian Revolution in Georgia, 1865–1912* (Madison, Wis., 1914). I have also used Oscar Zeichner, "The Transition from Slave to Free Agricultural Labor in the Southern States," *Agricultural History*, XIII (January, 1939), 22–32, and Marjorie Mendenhall, "The Rise of Southern Tenancy," *Yale Review*, XXVII (Autumn, 1937), 110–29.

The standard study on *The Social and Industrial Conditions in the North During the Civil War* is by Emerson D. Fite (New York, 1930), but it is little more than a hodgepodge of facts. My conception of the Lincoln administration's economic policies was aided by reading Reinhard Luthin, *The First Lincoln Campaign* (Cambridge, Mass., 1944), which stresses the economic elements in Lincoln's appeal more than I do. J. G. Randall, *Lincoln, the Liberal Statesman* (New York, 1947), in which the title essay is the last, tries to make Lincoln into a Manchesterian liberal, but without complete success. The lack of northern business interest in war is clearly set forth in Philip Foner, *Business and Slavery* (Chapel Hill, N.C., 1941), and in Ollinger Crenshaw, "Rural and Urban Voting in the Election of 1860," in Eric F. Goldman, ed., *Historiography and Urbanization* (Baltimore, 1941). The relative lack of interest in the tariff is demonstrated in Richard Hofstadter, "The Tariff Issue on the Eve of the Civil War," *American Historical Review*, XLIV (October,

1938), 50–55. Paul W. Gates, "The Homestead Law in an Incongruous Land System," *American Historical Review,* XLI (July, 1936), 652–81, and Fred Shannon, "The Homestead Act and the Labor Surplus," *American Historical Review,* XLI (July, 1936), 637–51, show that free land went more to speculators and the corporations than to bona fide settlers. The history and significance of the Contract Labor Law has been carefully analyzed by Charlotte Ericksen in *American Industry and the European Immigrant, 1860–1885* (Cambridge, Mass., 1957). My thinking about the nationalistic character of the Republican party has been much stimulated by William A. Dunning, "The Second Birth of the Republican Party," *American Historical Review,* XVI (October, 1910), 500–518. My conception of the intellectual impact of the war has been strongly influenced by George M. Frederickson, *Inner Civil War* (New York, 1965). I am greatly indebted to J. G. Randall, *Constitutional Problems Under Lincoln* (New York, 1926), for my understanding of this aspect of administration policy.

VIII. Dawn Without Noon

The basic collection of sources on Reconstruction is Walter F. Fleming, ed., *Documentary History of Reconstruction* (2 vols., Cleveland, 1906–7), upon which I have drawn often. Herbert Aptheker, ed., *Documentary History of the Negro People in the United States* (New York, 1951), contains a section on the Reconstruction period in which the selections are designed to show the Negro's positive contributions. The view of a moderate Northerner in the years immediately after the war is J. T. Trowbridge, *The South: A Tour of Its Battlefields and Ruined Cities* (Hartford, 1866). The two contradictory reports of the South's reaction to defeat are Carl Schurz's, to be found in his *Speeches, Correspondence and Political Papers,* edited by Frederic Bancroft (6 vols., New York, 1913), and Benjamin Truman's *Report* in Senate Executive Documents, 39th Congress, 1st Session, No. 2. The history of Reconstruction in Mississippi is told by a Negro Republican in John Lynch, *Facts of Reconstruction* (New York, 1913). It is highly suggestive in regard to the possibilities of Negro-white collaboration before the debacle of the Grant regime aborted them. For a long time the standard account of an "eyewitness" of South Carolina Reconstruction was James S. Pike's *Prostrate State* (New York, 1874), but Robert F. Durden, *James Shepard Pike* (Durham, N.C., 1957), has shown it to be superficially prepared and animated by a desire to embarrass the Grant regime. One carpetbagger of unquestioned liberal views has revealed his efforts in the South in Louis F. Post, "A Carpetbagger in South Carolina," *Journal of Negro History,* X (January, 1925), 10–79. I have found John William de Forest, *Union Officer in the Reconstruction* (New Haven, 1948), invaluable for visualizing the day-to-day problems of a conscientious Northerner dealing with ignorant ex-slaves in a society trying to live under a new dispensation. Though reports of Georges Clemenceau, later Premier of France and then a Washington correspondent, in *American Reconstruction, 1865– 1870* (New York, 1928), deal with events at the capital, they offer a European view of the Radicals' efforts to remold the South.

Though the writing on Reconstruction has been enormous and, since 1900, largely favorable to the southern point of view, Claude Bowers, *The Tragic Era* (Cambridge, Mass., 1929), has probably done more than any other book to delineate the view now so commonly accepted regarding the enormities of Reconstruction. William A. Dunning's *Reconstruction, Political and Economic 1865–1877* (New York, 1907) and *Essays on the Civil War and Reconstruction* (New York, 1898) are still important, but they are marred by the then prevalent attitude of seeing the Negro as incapable of taking a place as a full citizen. I am indebted to several of the works on Reconstruction which Dunning's students completed: C. Mildred Thompson, *Reconstruction in Georgia* (New York, 1915); James Garner, *Reconstruction in Mississippi* (New York, 1901); J. G. de R. Hamilton, "Southern Legislation in Respect to Freedmen, 1865–1866," and W. W. Davis, "Federal Enforcement Acts," both in *Studies in Southern History and Politics* (New York, 1914).

Soon after the students of Dunning completed their investigations of individual states, re-evaluations of some of them began to appear; a pioneer in looking at Reconstruction from a positive point of view was Francis Simkins and Robert H. Woody, *South Carolina During Reconstruction* (Chapel Hill, N.C., 1932). R. W. Shugg, *Origins of Class Struggle in Louisiana* (University, La., 1939), covers the 1850's as well as the Reconstruction and sees the latter period as much more than a conflict between southern whites on the one hand and northern carpetbaggers and Negroes on the other. Vernon L. Wharton, *The Negro in Mississippi, 1865–1890* (Chapel Hill, N.C., 1947), stresses the achievements of Negroes in that state and plays down the so-called atrocities of the era. James S. Allen, *Reconstruction: The Battle for Democracy* (New York, 1937), though the work of a dedicated Marxist with an ax to grind, is important for its canvassing of the Negro's attempt to get land for himself after slavery. The fullest, as well as the most readable discussion of the effort to grant land to the freedman in South Carolina is Willie Lee Rose, *Rehearsal for Reconstruction* (Indianapolis, Ind., 1964). The role of the Negro school in early Reconstruction is carefully and fairly treated in Henry Swint, *Northern Teacher in the South, 1862–1870* (Nashville, Tenn., 1941). E. M. Coulter, *The South During Reconstruction, 1865– 1877* (Baton Rouge, La., 1947), fails to build upon the new turn taken in Reconstruction studies and so continues the essentially biased attitude toward the Negro so common in earlier works. More in tune with the revisionist views are John Hope Franklin, *Reconstruction: After the Civil War* (Chicago, 1961), and Rembert Patrick, *The Reconstruction of the Nation* (New York, 1967). I have relied for much of my information regarding disfranchisement on two articles by William A. Russ, "Negro and White Disfranchisement During Radical Reconstruction," *Journal of Negro History,* XIX (April, 1934), 171–92, and "Registration and Disfranchisement under Radical Reconstruction," *Mississippi Valley Historical Review,* XXI (September, 1934), 163–80. Early Reconstruction and the role of Andrew Johnson have been significantly reinterpreted in three important works: Eric McKitrick, *Andrew Johnson and Reconstruction* (Chicago, 1960); LaWanda and John Cox, *Politics, Principle, and Prejudice, 1865–1866* (New York, 1963); and W. R. Brock, *An American Crisis: Congress and Reconstruction, 1865–1867* (New York, 1963). All are critical of Johnson.

Understandably, the reinterpretation of Reconstruction has been led by Negro scholars, notably W. E. B. Du Bois. His "Reconstruction and its Benefits," *American Historical Review,* XV (July, 1910), 781–99, was followed by Alrutheus A. Taylor's pedestrian but informative volumes *Negro in South Carolina During Reconstruction* (Washington, 1924), and *Negro in the Reconstruction of Virginia* (Washington, 1926). By the time Du Bois wrote his general study of the period, *Black Reconstruction* (New York, 1935), derived largely from his winnowing of the Dunning and other studies, he had become a Marxist, hence this pathbreaking book is seriously marred by his attempt to fit Reconstruction history into the mold of the class struggle. Kenneth Stampp, *The Era of Reconstruction, 1865–1877* (New York, 1966), though not a work of original research, is now the best introduction to new viewpoints on the period, the literature of which has grown so rapidly that it threatens to rival that on the Civil War. The full, critical bibliography in Stampp will have to take the place of any extensive discussion here of that burgeoning literature. My interpretation of the Freedmen's Bureau has been drawn from Paul Peirce, *The Freedmen's Bureau* (Iowa City, 1904), George Bentley, *A History of the Freedmen's Bureau* (Philadelphia, 1955), and John and LaWanda Cox, "General O. O. Howard and the Misrepresented Bureau," *Journal of Southern History,* XIX (November, 1953), 427–56. The respectable nature of some so-called scalawags has been convincingly argued in David Donald, "The Scalawags in Mississippi Reconstruction," *Journal of Southern History,* X (November, 1944), 447–60.

The period after Reconstruction has been substantially reinterpreted in the work of C. Vann Woodward. His major work, *Origins of the New South, 1877–1913* (Baton Rouge, La., 1951), should be supplemented with his *Tom Watson, Agrarian Rebel* (New York, 1938) and the *Strange Career of Jim Crow* (New York, 2nd rev. ed., 1966). I am deeply indebted to these books. Articles in the periodical press of the time attest to the ambiguity of southern white attitudes toward the Negro in the 1880's, about which Woodward writes: A South Carolinian, "The Result in South Carolina," *Atlantic Monthly*, XLI (January, 1878), 1–12; T. W. Higginson, "Some War Scenes Revisited," *Atlantic Monthly*, XLII (July, 1878), 1–9; "Ought the Negro to Be Disenfranchised? Ought He to Have Been Enfranchised?" *North American Review*, CXXVIII (March, 1879), 225–83; Anonymous, "Studies in the South," *Atlantic Monthly*, L (September, 1882), 349–61, and by the same author, "The South Revisited," *Harper's Monthly*, LXXIV (March, 1887), 634–40. More systematic, scholarly studies to test Woodward's thesis, however, have not been persuasive. Although Charles E. Wynes, *Race Relations in Virginia, 1870–1902* (Charlottesville, Va., 1961), and Frenise A. Logan, *The Negro in North Carolina, 1876–1894* (Chapel Hill, N.C., 1964), conclude that Woodward's thesis of ambiguity in the Negro's status is accurate, their evidence does not seem to support their conclusions. In short compass, the problem is examined well in Joel Williamson, ed., *The Origins of Segregation* (Boston, 1968). Paul Lewinson, *Race, Class and Party* (London, 1932), is an early attempt to trace the gradual disfranchisement of the Negro. Francis Simkins, *Tillman Movement in South Carolina* (Durham, N.C., 1926), tells the story for one state; Albert K. Kirwan, *Revolt of the Rednecks* (Lexington, Ky., 1951), does it for Mississippi. I have also drawn upon Raymond R. Nixon, *Henry Grady* (New York, 1943), a biography of a leader of the New South.

The North's lack of interest in the black man, as well as the declining position of the Negro are well set forth, though not without some bitterness, in Rayford Logan, *The Betrayal of the Negro* (New York, 1965); George B. Tindall, *South Carolina Negroes, 1877–1900* (Columbia, S.C., 1952), reveals the progress and disabilities of the Negro in a key state during this period. Vernon Lane Wharton, *The Negro in Mississippi, 1865–1890* (Chapel Hill, N.C., 1947) was a path-breaking monograph on its subject. The legal discrimination against the Negro in both North and South is chronicled in Gilbert T. Stephenson, *Race Discriminations in American Law* (New York, 1910). More sympathetic to the Negro is Ray Stannard Baker, *Following the Color Line* (New York, 1908). Somewhat carpingly, Samuel D. Smith tells the story of *The Negro in Congress, 1870–1901* (Chapel Hill, N.C., 1940). I have drawn my data on lynching from *Thirty Years of Lynching in the United States, 1889–1918* (New York, 1919) and J. E. Cutler, *Lynch Law* (New York, 1905), Chapters 5 and 6. The most recent biography of the great leader of the Negroes in this period is Samuel R. Spencer, Jr., *Booker T. Washington and the Negro's Place in American Life* (Boston, 1955), in which an effort is made to justify the pragmatic position Washington assumed. Until Louis Harlan's biography appears, the best short treatment of Washington can be found in August Meier, *Negro Thought in America, 1880–1915* (Ann Arbor, Mich., 1963). Paul Buck, *Road to Reunion, 1865–1900* (Boston, 1937), tells without criticism the North's growing acceptance of the inferiority of the Negro. Two contemporary accounts of conditions in the South upon which I have drawn are Maurice Evans, *Black and White in the Southern States* (London, 1915); and Albert B. Hart, *The Southern South* (New York, 1910), the latter by a Harvard professor more puzzled than indignant at what he sees.

IX. MACHINES, MEN, AND SOCIALISM

For the expansion of American industry I have relied upon a number of standard surveys of economic development: Allan Nevins, *Emergence of Modern America, 1865–1878* (New York, 1927); Ida Tarbell, *Nationalizing of Business, 1878–1898* (New York, 1936); H. U. Faulkner, *The Decline of Laissez-Faire, 1897–1917* (New York, 1951). Edward Kirkland, *Industry Comes of Age* (New York, 1961), is disappointing because of its emphasis upon opinion, but it is the most recent and broadest survey of the industrialization of the United States. Most suggestive of all has been the contemporary *Recent Economic Changes* (New York, 1895) of David A. Wells. Charles R. Van Hise, *Concentration and Control* (New York, 1912), provided many examples of corporate concentration. I profited much from Hans B. Thorelli, *Federal Antitrust Policy* (Baltimore, 1955). The standard and unsuperseded authority on early southern industrialization is Broadus Mitchell, *Rise of the Cotton Mills in the South* (Baltimore, 1921). The statements of English workingmen on the wide use of machinery in America have been taken from A. Mosely, *Reports of the Delegates, Mosely Industrial Commission to the United States, October–December, 1902* (London, 1903). Thomas Cochran seriously questions the easy assumption that the Civil War encouraged economic development in his "Did the Civil War Retard Industrialization?" *Mississippi Valley Historical Review*, XLVIII (September, 1961), 197–210. But see a qualified rebuttal, by Harry N. Scheiber, "Economic Changes in the Civil War Era: An Analysis of Recent Studies," *Civil War History*, XI (December, 1965), 396–411.

Aside from the general accounts, I have also used for the railroads Robert R. Riegel's interesting *Story of the Western Railroads* (New York, 1926); the classic Charles F. Adams, Jr., and Henry Adams, *Chapters of Erie* (Boston, 1871); and, for financial consolidation, E. G. Campbell, *Reorganization of the American Railroad System, 1893–1900* (New York, 1938). The role of the land grant in railroad construction has received much attention; the pioneer article is Robert S. Henry, "The Railroad Land Grant Legend in American History Texts," *Mississippi Valley Historical Review*, XXXII (September, 1945), 171–94; see also the replies and criticisms in XXXII (March, 1946), 557–76. I have followed, in the main, Henry's position. T. C. Cochran, "Land Grants and Railroad Entrepreneurs," *Journal of Economic History,* X (Supplement, 1950), 53–67, calls attention to the importance of the grants in financing the roads. That the government received no financial gain from the grants is shown in Paul W. Gates, "The Railroad Land-Grant Legend," *Journal of Economic History,* XIV (Spring, 1954), 143–46. The basic work for calculating the governmental support to the roads is *Public Aids to Transportation* (4 vols. in 2, Washington, 1938–40), a governmental publication.

For my treatment of financial consolidation I have relied upon Louis Brandeis, *Other People's Money* (New York, 1914), a contemporary analysis of the findings of the Pujo Committee; George W. Edwards, *The Evolution of Finance Capitalism* (London, 1938); and the somewhat sensational Lewis Corey, *House of Morgan* (New York, 1930).

The literature on individual entrepreneurs and businesses is voluminous and of very uneven quality. The classic indictment of the great business leaders of the period is Gustavus Myers' indignant *History of the Great American Fortunes* (New York, 1936), first published in 1910. In the same vein is the famous Matthew Josephson, *Robber Barons* (New York, 1934). An attempt at rehabilitating one of the most notorious leaders is Allan Nevins, *John D. Rockefeller* (2 vols., New York, 1940). Keith Sward's *Legend of Henry Ford* (New York, 1948) is caustic in the older tradition. Much more sympathetic is Roger Burlingame, *Henry Ford* (New York, 1955). A number of leaders are popularly dealt with in Stewart Holbrook, *Age of the Moguls* (Garden City, N.Y., 1953). With humor and irony Oscar Lewis describes the activities of Crocker, Stanford, Huntington, and Hopkins in *The Big Four* (New York, 1946). Another railroad giant receives sympathetic treatment in Stewart Holbrook, *James J. Hill* (New York, 1955). Some of the giants have left expressions of their aims; I have used John D. Rockefeller, *Random Reminiscences of Men and Events* (New York, 1916); Henry Ford, *My Life and Work* (New York, 1926); and Andrew Carnegie, *Autobiography* (Boston, 1920).

My generalizations about the social origins of the entrepreneurs of the period depend upon a number of studies: C. Wright Mills, "The American Business Elite: A Collective Portrait," *Journal of Economic History,* V (December, 1945), 20–44; William Miller, "American Historians and the Business Elite," *Journal of Economic History,* IX (November, 1949), 184–208; F. W. Gregory and I. D. Neu, "Industrial Elite in the 1870's," in William Miller, ed., *Men in Business* (Cambridge, Mass., 1952); and Thomas C. Cochran, *Railroad Leaders, 1845–1890* (Cambridge, Mass., 1953). The kinds of business practices engaged in by the giants are categorized in Chester McA. Destler, "Entrepreneurial Leadership Among

the 'Robber Barons'; A Trial Balance," *Journal of Economic History,* VI
(Supplement, 1946), 28–49. The social impact of the age of the entrepreneurs is set forth in Irvin Wyllie, *Self-Made Man in America* (New
Brunswick, N.J., 1954). I learned about other aspects of the same subject from R. Richard Wohl, "The 'Rags to Riches Story': An Episode of
Secular Idealism," in Richard Bendix and Seymour M. Lipset, eds., *Class,
Status and Power* (Glencoe, Ill., 1953); and Sigmund Diamond, *Reputation of the American Businessman* (Cambridge, Mass., 1953), in which
it is shown that by the end of the century the businessman had become
in popular thought an ordinary man instead of a genius beyond the emulation of the common herd. See also K. W. Porter, "The Business Man
in American Folklore," *Bulletin of the Business Historical Society,* XVIII
(November, 1944), 113–30.

For the labor movement as a whole, I have used in varying degrees
Norman Ware, *The Labor Movement in the United States, 1860–1895*
(New York, 1929), which despite its title is a history of the Knights of
Labor only; Foster Rhea Dulles, *Labor in America* (New York, 1949);
Philip Foner, *History of the Labor Movement in the United States* (2
vols., New York, 1947–55). Valuable for delineating the ideological dif-
ference between the Knights and the A.F. of L. is the study of the
Knights by Gerald N. Grob, *Workers and Utopia* (Evanston, Ill., 1961).
The two books which have sparked my thinking on the conservative na-
ture of the labor movement are Karl Polanyi, *The Great Transformation*
(New York, 1944), and Frank Tannenbaum, *A Philosophy of Labor*
(New York, 1951). Selig Perlman, *A Theory of the Labor Movement*
(New York, 1928), uses conservative in the conventional sense of
"friendly to property."

The writings of some of the labor leaders are invaluable for understanding the assumptions of the movement: Terence Powderly, *The Path
I Trod,* edited by H. J. Carman, H. David, and P. N. Guthrie (New
York, 1940); Samuel Gompers, *Seventy Years of Life and Labor* (2
vols., New York, 1925), and *Labor and the Common Welfare* (New
York, 1919); John Mitchell, *Organized Labor* (Philadelphia, 1903), and
The Wage Earner and His Problems (Washington, 1913). The quotation
from Gompers before the U.S. Commission on Industrial Relations is
from Vol. II of the *Final Report and Testimony* (11 vols., Washington,
1916). Louis S. Reed, *Labor Philosophy of Samuel Gompers* (New York,
1930), was also helpful.

In considering the failure of socialism, several works on the move-
ment proved enlightening. The foremost study of the leader Eugene V.
Debs is Ray Ginger, *Bending Cross* (New Brunswick, N.J., 1949).
Howard Quint, *Forging of American Socialism* (Columbia, S.C., 1953),
which deals only with the early years, and David A. Shannon, *Socialist
Party of America* (New York, 1955), both discuss the limited appeal of

the movement and I am indebted to both of them. Norman Thomas' thought on the subject is contained in *Socialist's Faith* (New York, 1951). The failure of other radical movements like anarchism and the Industrial Workers of the World to attract large segments of the American working class is canvassed or illuminated in Paul F. Brissenden, *The I.W.W.* (New York, 1919), and John S. Gambs, *The Decline of the I.W.W.* (New York, 1932); Chester McArthur Destler discusses anarchism in *American Radicalism, 1865–1901* (New London, Conn., 1946). The limited nature of the demonstrative behavior of labor is clearly set forth in Donald L. MacMurry's *Coxey's Army* (Boston, 1929). Sidney Hook essays an answer to the question "Why Has Socialism Not Been More Successful in the United States," in Donald D. Egbert and Stow Persons, eds., *Socialism and American Life* (2 vols., Princeton, 1952). The answer of Leon Samson is contained in his *Toward a United Front* (New York, 1933). David Shannon's essay on the same subject, in C. V. Woodward, ed., *The Comparative Approach to American History* (New York, 1968), is excellent. The classic study on social movement is Pitirim Sorokin, *Social Mobility* (New York, 1927), which I have used with profit. A first-class empirical study of social mobility is now available in Stephan Thernstrom, *Poverty and Progress* (Cambridge, Mass., 1964), which I have relied upon. The differences between the American and the European worker are recognized in Robert W. Smuts, *European Impressions of the American Worker* (New York, 1953), and in the observations of contemporaries like James Bryce, *The American Commonwealth* (3rd ed., 2 vols., New York, 1901); H. G. Wells, *The Future in America* (New York, 1906); and Matthew Arnold, *Civilization in the United States* (Boston, 1900).

X. OUT OF MANY, ONE

The great source for the distribution of immigrants is the census reports after 1850. Even in a relatively early census like that of 1860, it is possible to carry investigation of immigrant population to the county level. For the twentieth century I have used the very complete and detailed Census of 1910. For the early years of the twentieth century, the *Report* of the United States Immigration Commission (41 vols., Washington, 1911–13) contains a wealth of data, though rather unorganized. I have used extensively the more convenient *Abstracts of Reports of the Immigration Commission* (2 vols., Washington, 1911). Though valid criticisms of bias have been brought against the conclusions of this report, its data are still unsurpassed for the period. Isaac Hourwich, *Immigration and Labor* (New York, 1912), is an early attack on the conclusions of the Commission; Chapter V of Oscar Handlin, *Race and Nationality in American Life* (Boston, 1957), is the most recent. I am much indebted to William S. Bernard *et al.*, eds., *American Immigration Policy: A Reappraisal* (New York, 1950), for comparisons of American immigration policy with that of other countries.

In recent years a number of collections of immigrant sources have been published. One of the oldest in the broad field of immigration policy, and still valuable, is Edith Abbott, *Historical Aspects of the Immigration Problem* (Chicago, 1926). I have drawn much from Theodore C. Blegen, ed., *Land of Their Choice; the Immigrants Write Home* (Minneapolis, 1955). George M. Stephenson published some letters of immigrants in "When America was the Land of Canaan," *Minnesota History*, X (September, 1929), 237–60, and the same was done in Henry S. Lucas, ed., *Dutch Immigrant Memoirs and Related Writings* (2 vols., Assen, Netherlands, 1955). The impact of America on returned immigrants is illuminated in Theodore Saloutus, *They Remember America: The Story of the Repatriated Greek-Americans* (Berkeley, Calif., 1956), and Merle Curti and Kendall Birr, "The Immigrant and the American Image in Europe, 1860–1914," *Mississippi Valley Historical Review*, XXXVII (September, 1950), 203–30. The rather romanticized approach toward immigration in Edward Steiner's volumes appeared at the height of the last great wave of immigration: *The Immigrant Tide* (New York, 1907) and *On the Trail of the Immigrant* (New York, 1906), and I have drawn on them.

The standard authority on immigration before 1860 is Marcus Hansen, *Atlantic Migration, 1607–1860* (Cambridge, Mass., 1940). No comparable study has been made for the new immigration, though Oscar Handlin, *The Uprooted* (Boston, 1951), does cover the period. Handlin's interest, however, is primarily in the immigrants' adjustment here, rather than the process of migration itself. More detailed and a model of its kind is his earlier work, *Boston's Immigrants, 1790–1865* (Cambridge, Mass., 1941). The New York immigrant scene is canvassed as closely, though not as strikingly, in Robert Ernst, *Immigrant Life in New York City, 1825–1863* (New York, 1949). The best general study on immigration is Maldwyn Jones, *American Immigration* (Chicago, 1960).

Aside from the immigration *Report* and special studies mentioned already, on the role of the immigrant in the economy I have used Isaac Hourwich, *Immigration and Labor* (New York, 1912), which is essentially a defense of the immigrants; while John R. Commons, *Races and Immigrants in America* (New York, 1907), like the Immigration Commission, raises questions as to their influence, but not their economic value. The same can be said of Jeremiah Jenks and W. Jett Lauch, *The Immigration Problem* (New York, 1912). Harry Jerome, *Migration and Business Cycles* (New York, 1926), is the basic work on the subject, from which I have learned much. The important role of the immigrant in the leadership of labor unions is demonstrated in P. A. Sorokin, "Leaders of Labor and Radical Movements in the United States and Foreign Countries," *American Journal of Sociology,* XXXIII (November, 1927), 382–411. The periodical literature of the day is filled with comment on the contribution of the immigrant.

For my discussion of the political role of the immigrant, I am especially indebted to Samuel Lubell's illuminating researches in *The Future of American Politics* (2nd edition, Garden City, N.Y., 1956); the same view of the connection between isolationism and immigrant background was advanced in Ray Allen Billington, "The Origins of Middle Western Isolationism," *Political Science Quarterly,* LX (March, 1945), 44–64. Oscar Handlin, "The Immigrant and Politics," in David F. Bowers, ed., *Foreign Influences in American Life* (Princeton, 1944), puts great emphasis on the conservative politics of immigrants, though ignoring the Germans in the Socialist movement. The importance of the immigrant in the election of 1860 is demonstrated in William E. Dodd, "Fight for the Northwest," *American Historical Review,* XVI (July, 1911), 774–88, but somewhat modified in Andreas Dorpalen, "The German Element and the Issues of the Civil War," *Mississippi Valley Historical Review,* XXIX (June, 1942), 55–76.

My thinking on the connection between religion in America and immigration has been greatly stimulated by Will Herberg, *Protestant-Catholic-Jew* (New York, 1955). Of a somewhat different nature, but certainly complementary, is H. Richard Niebuhr, *Social Sources of Denominationalism* (New York, 1929). My discussion on immigrant Puritanism is indebted to Marcus Hansen, "Immigration and Puritanism," in his book *Immigrant in American History* (Cambridge, Mass., 1940). On the nature of Catholicism in America, Thomas Sugrue, *A Catholic Speaks His Mind on America's Religious Conflict* (New York, 1952), is important for calling attention to the variety within the Church. Carl Wittke, "The Immigrant Theme on the American Stage," *Mississippi Valley Historical Review,* XXXIX (September, 1952), 211–32, points up another manifestation of immigrant influence and stereotype.

For the nativist movement, Ray Billington, *Protestant Crusade, 1800–1860* (New York, 1938), has long been the standard treatment, but it suffers from the failure to recognize that anti-Catholicism had a variety of roots, not all of them in the soil of bigotry. Handlin in his *Boston's Immigrants* offers a most suggestive corrective and it is substantially that which I have followed. A similar approach is taken in Harry J. Carman and Reinhard H. Luthin, "Some Aspects of the Know-Nothing Movement Reconsidered," *South Atlantic Quarterly,* XXXIX (April, 1940), 213–34; William G. Bean, "An Aspect of Know-Nothingism—The Immigrant and Slavery," *South Atlantic Quarterly,* XXIII (October, 1924), 319–34, and "Puritan versus Celt, 1850–1860," *New England Quarterly,*

VII (March, 1934), 70–89. The differences between northern and southern nativism appear, by implication, in W. Darrell Overdyke, *Know-Nothing Party in the South* (Baton Rouge, 1950).

The movement for restriction of immigration is well described and analyzed in John Higham, *Strangers in the Land* (New Brunswick, N.J., 1955); the New England movement for restriction, with the focus on Boston, is treated in Barbara Miller Solomon, *Ancestors and Immigrants* (Cambridge, Mass., 1956). Much of my discussion has been taken from Higham's searching examination. Confirmation of Higham's view that business as well as labor desired limitation on immigration by the end of the nineteenth century is forthcoming in Morrell Heald, "Business Attitudes Toward European Immigration, 1880–1900," *Journal of Economic History,* XIII (Summer, 1953), 291–304. Madison Grant's racist view of the new immigrant is contained in his *Passing of the Great Race* (New York, 1916). The standard treatment of restriction is Roy L. Garis, *Immigration Restriction* (New York, 1927). It needs to be supplemented by Robert A. Divine, *American Immigration Policy 1924–1952* (New Haven, Conn., 1957).

XI. ALABASTER CITIES AND AMBER WAVES OF GRAIN

There is a wealth of material on the growth of cities in the censuses of the United States beginning in 1880, when *Social Statistics of Cities* was issued in two volumes. Thereafter the Bureau of the Census included increasing detail on cities; especially useful for comparative purposes is the *Statistical Atlas of the Twelfth Census* (Washington, 1903), in which a summary of historical changes for individual cities is to be found. The stimulating work of Lewis Mumford, *Culture of Cities* (New York, 1938), has been the beginning of my thinking on the subject of urban life. The classic statistical work is the path-breaking Adna Weber, *The Growth of Cities in the Nineteenth Century* (New York, 1899). Two books of Josiah Strong, *New Era* (New York, 1893) and *Challenge of the City* (New York, 1907), contain statistical data and stimulating suggestions by a perspicacious contemporary. For a long time the standard historical authority has been Arthur M. Schlesinger, *The Rise of the City, 1878–1898* (New York, 1933), of which only a part, unfortunately, is devoted to the subject of the title. See also his "The City in American History," *Mississippi Valley Historical Review,* XXVII (June, 1940), 43–66. There is still no satisfactory history of the city in the United States, but Blake McKelvey, *The Urbanization of America* (New Brunswick, N.J., 1963), is a start. Briefer and more general is Constance McL. Greene, *The Rise of Urban America* (New York, 1965). Helpful also is Charles N. Glaab, ed., *The American City, A Documentary History* (Homewood, Ill., 1963). The difficulties and pitfalls of interpreting history in terms of cities are well set forth in William Diamond, "On the Dangers of an Urban Interpretation of History," in Eric Goldman, ed., *Historiography and Urbanization* (Baltimore, 1941), primarily a critique of Schlesinger. I have learned much from Christopher Tunnard and Henry Hope Reed, *American Skyline* (Mentor ed., New York, 1956), which is a history of urban building in the United States.

The impact of the city on society has been primarily the province of sociology, and I have drawn freely upon a number of texts and studies in this field. A pioneer study in this area is J. G. Thomas, *Urbanization: Its Effects on Government and Society* (New York, 1927), which is suggestive but too exuberant in its pretensions to be uncritically used. More temperate is Louis Wirth, "Urbanism as a Way of Life," *American Journal of Sociology*, XLIV (July, 1938), 1–24; and Charles S. Ascher, "What Are Cities For," and Chauncey D. Harris and Edward L. Ullman, "The Nature of Cities," in *Annals* of the American Academy of Political and Social Science, Vol. 242 (November, 1945). I have also used the very readable Robert MacIver, *Society* (New York, 1949); Wilbur C. Hallenbeck, *American Urban Communities* (New York, 1951); Svend Riemer, *The Modern City* (New York, 1952); and S. A. Queen and D. B. Carpenter, *The American City* (New York, 1953). Pitirim Sorokin, *Society, Culture and Personality* (New York, 1947), has some data on the growth of cities. Eric E. Lampard, "American Historians and the Study of Urbanization," *American Historical Review*, LXVII (October, 1961), 49–61, is very critical, but also narrow in its conception of urbanization. The city in literature is dealt with rather unimaginatively in G. A. Dunlap, *The City in the American Novel, 1789–1900* (Philadelphia, 1934). Pitirim A. Sorokin and Carle C. Zimmerman, *Principles of Rural-Urban Sociology* (New York, 1929), did much to point up for me the difference in the city and country environments.

The standard and best treatment of the history of agriculture after the Civil War is Fred A. Shannon, *Farmer's Last Frontier* (New York, 1945), which I have relied upon. The problem of the surplus is admirably dealt with in William Trimble, "Historical Aspects of the Surplus Food Production of the United States," American Historical Association, *Annual Report, 1918*, I, 221–40. I have also used Edwin G. Nourse, *American Agriculture and the European Market* (New York, 1924), a searching economic analysis of the problem. The mechanization of agriculture is told in detail in Leo Rogin, *The Introduction of Farm Machinery . . . During the Nineteenth Century* (Berkeley, Calif., 1931), and in the famous essay by E. E. Edwards, "American Agriculture—The First 300 Years," in *Yearbook of Agriculture, 1940* (Washington, n.d.), pp. 171–276. Some material is also to be found in Vols. 10 and 11 of the *Report of the Industrial Commission* (18 vols., Washington, 1901). See also L. B. Schmidt, "The Agricultural Revolution in the United States,"

Science, LXXII (December 12, 1930), 585–94. The whole question of the relation between industrialization and mechanization of agriculture is discussed and attempts made at measurement in Pei-kang Chang, *Agriculture and Industrialization* (Cambridge, Mass., 1949). The subject is well canvassed for America in Theodore Saloutus, "The Agricultural Problem and Nineteenth-Century Industrialism," *Agricultural History,* XXII (July, 1948), 156–74. The failure of tenancy as a ladder to land ownership is dealt with convincingly by LaWanda F. Cox, "Tenancy in the United States, 1865–1900," *Agricultural History,* XVIII (July, 1944), 97–105.

For my conception of the farmer under the impact of industrialism, I have leaned heavily upon Paul H. Johnstone, "Old Ideals versus New Ideas in Farm-Life," in *Yearbook of Agriculture, 1940,* pp. 111–170. The differences between the American farmer and the European peasant are brought out in Joseph Schafer, *Social History of American Agriculture* (New York, 1936). *A Systematic Sourcebook in Rural Sociology,* edited by Pitirim Sorokin *et al.* (3 vols., Minneapolis, 1930–32), provided convenient source material on the subject, as did the *Report of the United States Country Life Commission* (Washington, 1909). See also Horace Plunkett, *The Rural Life Problem in the United States* (New York, 1910), the work of an Englishman, and the two books on New York State agricultural mores by James M. Williams, *Our Rural Heritage* (New York, 1925) and *The Expansion of Rural Life* (New York, 1931). The persistence of the myth of the idyllic life of the farmer is demonstrated in Elmer T. Peterson, ed., *Cities Are Abnormal* (Norman, Okla., 1946), and in two excellent scholarly studies of the historic connection between the democratic ethos and farming: A. Whitney Griswold, *Farming and Democracy* (New York, 1948), and Henry Nash Smith, *Virgin Land* (Cambridge, Mass., 1950).

All studies of the Populist movement begin with John D. Hicks, *Populist Revolt* (Minneapolis, 1931) which is still very useful but rather uncritical about the validity of the farmer's complaints. Carl C. Taylor, *Farmer's Movement, 1620–1920* (New York, 1953), is broader in scope but no more critical of the farmer's diagnosis of his ills. Completely untouched by romantic illusions about the farmer is Richard Hofstadter, *Age of Reform* (New York, 1956), and I am much indebted to it. It needs to be corrected in places, however, by Walter T. K. Nugent, *The Tolerant Populists* (Chicago, 1963), an excellent study of Kansas Populism, and C. Vann Woodward, "The Populist Heritage and the Intellectual," *American Scholar,* XXIX (Winter, 1959–60), 55–72. I have followed the stimulating suggestions of B. H. Wilcox, "An Historical Definition of Northwestern Radicalism," *Mississippi Valley Historical Review,* XXVI (December, 1939), 377–94. I have profited greatly from the illuminating suggestions of James C. Malin, "Notes on the Literature of

Populism," *Kansas Historical Quarterly,* I (February, 1932), 160–64, and "The Background of the First Bills to Establish a Bureau of Markets, 1911–12," *Agricultural History,* VI (July, 1932), 107–29. For the twentieth century I have also used Frederic L. Paxson, "The Agricultural Surplus: A Problem in History," *Agricultural History,* VI (April, 1932), 51–68, and Theodore Saloutus and John D. Hicks, *Agricultural Discontent in the Middle West, 1900–1939* (Madison, Wis., 1951). The fumbling attempt to unite labor and the Populists is traced in Chester McArthur Destler, *American Radicalism, 1865–1901* (New London, Conn., 1946), Chapters 8, 9, and 11.

XII. NEW WORLD A-COMIN'

A number of the religious and philanthropic leaders put their thoughts into print during and after the period. The autobiography of William Jewett Tucker, *My Generation* (Boston, 1919), contains much information; so does Samuel Lane Loomis, *Modern Cities and Their Religious Problems* (New York, 1887). The most vocal of the early spokesmen for a new approach to religion was Washington Gladden; I have used his *Applied Christianity* (Boston and New York, 1886), *Social Salvation* (Boston and New York, 1902), and his memoirs, *Recollections* (Boston and New York, 1909). Josiah Strong, *Challenge of the City* (New York, 1907) and *New Era* (New York, 1893), are also important expressions of concern for religion in the midst of the city. *The Life of Charles Loring Brace* (London, 1894), edited by his daughter Emma, contains many letters of this influential New York philanthropist and minister. The two works of Walter Rauschenbusch I have used extensively are *Christianizing the Social Order* (New York, 1919, though originally published in 1912) and *Christianity and the Social Crisis* (New York, 1907). Some material is also to be found in Walter Wycoff's account of his experience as a disguised itinerant worker: *The Workers* (2 vols., New York, 1897–98).

An important article on the urban impact on religion is A. M. Schlesinger, "Critical Period in American Religion, 1875–1900," in *Proceedings of the Massachusetts Historical Society,* LXIV (June, 1932), 523–47. Timothy L. Smith, *Revivalism and Social Reform* (New York, 1957), argues for interest in social matters by the churches in the years before 1860. A path-breaking article on the role of religion in labor reform in the late nineteenth century is Herbert G. Gutman, "Protestantism and the American Labor Movement; The Christian Spirit in the Gilded Age," *American Historical Review,* LXXII (October, 1966), 74–101. Three books are standard in the field now and I am greatly beholden to all of them: Aaron I. Abell, *Urban Impact upon American Protestantism, 1865–1900* (Cambridge, Mass., 1943); Charles H. Hopkins, *Rise of the*

Social Gospel in American Protestantism, 1865–1915 (New Haven, 1940); and, perhaps the best of all and certainly the broadest in scope, Henry F. May, *Protestant Churches and Industrial America* (New York, 1949). May also makes a good case for the connection between the social gospel and Progressivism. Charles A. Barker's full biography of *Henry George* (New York, 1955) also emphasizes the close ties between religious idealism and the reform movement of the 1880's and 1890's. For a less popular reform movement, James Dombrowski does the same in his *Early Days of Christian Socialism in America* (New York, 1936). For the Salvation Army I have drawn upon Frederick Booth-Tucker, *Social Relief Work of the Salvation Army in the United States* (Albany, 1900), and Herbert A. Wisbey, Jr., *Soldiers Without Swords* (New York, 1955). The effect of the new movement upon Catholicism is apparent in John A. Ryan and Joseph Husslein, eds., *The Church and Labor* (New York, 1924), a collection of sources and essays. Robert D. Cross, *The Emergence of Liberal Catholicism in America* (Cambridge, Mass., 1958), nicely distinguishes between conservatives and liberals within Catholicism. Some discussion is also contained in Arthur Mann, *Yankee Reformers in the Urban Age* (Cambridge, Mass., 1954). *The Trends in Protestant Social Idealism* are traced by Neal Hughley (New York, 1948). The quotations from Kenneth E. Boulding are in "Religious Foundations of Economic Progress," *Harvard Business Review*, XXX (May–June, 1952), 33–40.

A broad yet full study of the women's rights movement, based upon extensive research, is Eleanor Flexner, *Century of Struggle* (Cambridge, Mass., 1959). Less thorough or full, but stimulating in approach, is Andrew Sinclair, *The Better Half* (New York, 1965). Mabel Newcomer, *A Century of Higher Education for American Women* (New York, 1959), is in a class by itself. Not to be missed for what it shows about the changing ideas of women regarding equal rights is Aileen Kraditor, *The Ideas of the Women Suffrage Movement, 1890–1920* (New York, 1965). Much factual information on the changing place of women is to be found in the two volumes in the History of American Life Series: A. M. Schlesinger, *Rise of the City*, and H. U. Faulkner, *Quest for Social Justice* (New York, 1931). More contemporary than historical, but with much information on the early twentieth century, is Ernest R. Groves, *The American Woman* (New York, 1937). The same can be said of Willystine Goodsell, *A History of Marriage and the Family* (rev. ed., New York, 1934). Ideas concerning *Marriage, Morals and Sex in America* (New York, 1953) are traced by Sidney Ditzion, but with a little too much attention paid to the bizarre. Some interesting comments on the American woman at the turn of the century are to be found in Hugo Münsterberg, *American Traits from the Point of View of a German* (Boston and New York, 1902). A book which I used, but which the feminists of the period berated, was Mrs. John Van Vorst and Marie Van Vorst, *The Woman Who Toils* (New York, 1903). Arthur Mann, *Yankee Reformers in the Urban Age* (Cambridge, Mass., 1954), makes some important comments on the nature of the new woman as exemplified especially in Vida Scudder of Wellesley College. Mary I. Wood, *History of the General Federation of Women's Clubs* (New York, 1912), is an official and dull recital of activities. Economic data on women are contained in S. P. Breckinridge, *Women in the Twentieth Century* (New York, 1933), and Helen Sumner's *History of Women in Industry in the United States* (Washington, 1910), Vol. IX in *Report on the Condition of Woman and Child Wage Earners in the United States* and Vol. X, *History of Women in Trade Unions* (Washington, 1911), by John B. Andrews and W. D. P. Bliss.

I have also used a number of studies of individual women leaders; especially noteworthy is Mary Earhart, *Frances Willard* (Chicago, 1944); see also Josephine Goldmark, *Florence Kelley's Life Story* (Urbana, Ill., 1953); Rheta Dorr, *What Eight Million Women Want* (Boston, 1910); and Katherine Anthony, *Susan B. Anthony* (Garden City, N.Y., 1954). There is no biography of Charlotte P. Gilman except her autobiography, *The Living of Charlotte Perkins Gilman* (New York, 1935), though one is certainly justified. Her ideas are summarized and criticized in Carl N. Degler, "Charlotte Perkins Gilman on the Theory and Practice of Feminism," *American Quarterly,* VIII (Spring, 1956), 21–39. The modernity of Gilman's views is demonstrated, inadvertently, in Betty Friedan, *The Feminine Mystique* (New York, 1963).

My presentation of the movement for children's play is indebted to C. E. Rainwater, *Play Movement in the United States* (Chicago, 1921); Henry S. Curtis, *The Play Movement and Its Significance* (New York, 1917); and Luther Halsey Gulick, *A Philosophy of Play* (New York, 1920).

Several of the intellectuals of the Progressive movement have left statements of their aims and philosophy; they were indispensable for the writing of this section: Frederick Howe, *Confessions of a Reformer* (New York, 1925), and his earlier book, *The City, the Hope of Democracy* (New York, 1906); Brand Whitlock, *Forty Years of It* (New York, 1914), and *Letters and Journal of Brand Whitlock,* edited by Allan Nevins (New York, 1936); Robert M. La Follette's *Autobiography* (Madison, Wis., 1913); the major "theoretical" work of the movement was Herbert Croly, *Promise of American Life* (New York, 1911). A bridge between contemporary and later appraisals of the movement is Lincoln Steffens' *Autobiography* (New York, 1931), in which he is much less sanguine about reform than he had been at the time. Harry Barnard, *"Eagle Forgotten"; the Life of John Peter Altgeld* (Indianapolis, 1938), clearly points up the aspiring middle-class roots of the Progressive mind of even the most radical variety; Alfred D. Chandler, Jr., "The Origins of Progressive Leadership," in *Letters of Theodore Roosevelt,* edited by E. E. Morison (Cambridge, Mass., 1951–54), Vol. VIII, Appendix III, does the same for all the leaders of the political movement. The letters of Roosevelt open a broad window into the mind of the most famous Progressive. *The New Freedom* (New York, 1913), a collection of Woodrow Wilson campaign speeches in 1912, is indispensable for understanding the Democratic variety of Progressivism. Charles McCarthy, *The Wisconsin Idea* (New York, 1912), is an exposition of the third facet of Progressivism, that of the La Follette followers.

The literature on the Progressive movement is constantly increasing. The first major critique of the movement was John Chamberlain, *Farewell to Reform* (New York, 1932), which is shot through with the bitter defeatism of the liberal in the midst of the Great Depression. More optimistic and much less interpretive is C. C. Regier, *Era of the Muckrakers* (Chapel Hill, N.C., 1932). Still true to the spirit of the Progressive era is Louis Filler, *Crusaders for American Liberalism* (New York, 1940), but in the same year the acid pen of Matthew Josephson touched Progressivism in *The President-Makers* (New York, 1940). Highly critical of the movement, but brilliant in its fusion of political and literary events and in its style, is Part I of Alfred Kazin, *On Native Grounds* (Anchor ed., New York, 1956). Impressions of the era, especially as drawn from literature, are to be found in Lloyd Morris, *Postscript to Yesterday* (New York, 1947). A detailed but important study of the Progressive mind is George E. Mowry, "The California Progressive and His Rationale: A Study in Middle Class Politics," *Mississippi Valley Historical Review,* XXXVI (September, 1949), 239–50. Russel Nye sees the Middle Western Progressive as more individualistic and more Jeffersonian in philosophy than the eastern in his *Middle-Western Progressive Politics* (East Lansing, Mich., 1951). The first half of Eric Goldman's *Rendezvous with Destiny* (New York, 1953) is a searching and provocative analysis of the changing ideas before and during the Progressive era; he makes much of the relativistic approach to society and politics taken by some of the Progressive intellectuals. Though not primarily concerned with the Progressive movement, Morton White, *Social Thought in America* (New York, 1949), throws much light on the growing relativism in the thought of the early twentieth century. David W. Noble, *The Paradox of Progressive Thought* (Minneapolis, 1958), is prolix, but useful. The best discussion of the transition from the old to the new "liberalism" is that contained in Charles Forcey, *The Crossroads of Liberalism* (New York, 1961). Richard Hofstadter, *Age of Reform* (New York, 1955), has influenced my thinking considerably, but its assertion of a "status revolution" during the Progressive years is unproved.

Recently the literature on the Progressive period has stressed the role of businessmen in the reform movement. Earliest and most balanced is Robert Wiebe, *Businessmen and Reform* (Cambridge, Mass., 1962); Gabriel Kolko in two books has carried Wiebe's line of attack to the point of seeing business and government in league, rather than at odds, as the traditional view of the Progressive era has often depicted the situation. See his *The Triumph of Conservatism: A Reinterpretation of American History, 1900–1916* (New York, 1963), and *Railroads and Regulation, 1877–1916* (Princeton, N.J., 1965). Samuel P. Hays, *Conservation and the Gospel of Efficiency* (Cambridge, Mass., 1959), shows, too, that the conservation movement of the time was not hostile to business goals. The Progressives' emphasis upon efficiency is shown in another area in Samuel Haber, *Efficiency and Uplift* (Chicago, 1964).

XIII. THE THIRD AMERICAN REVOLUTION

The impact of the depression on American life has hardly begun to be assessed, but some general treatments were already being drawn up during the era. Most detailed, but confined to a single town, is the critical and painstaking dissection of Muncie, Indiana, by Robert and Helen Lynd, *Middletown in Transition* (New York, 1937). Frederick Lewis Allen made a superficial survey of the thirties in *Since Yesterday* (New York, 1940), which makes no pretense of being analytical. More scholarly, but more pedestrianly written, is Clarence J. Engler, *Some Social Aspects of the Depression, 1930–1935* (Washington, 1939), in which the social costs of the debacle are assessed. The *Journal of Sociology,* XLVII (May, 1942), devoted its entire issue to "Recent Social Changes" in the period 1932–42. It emphasizes the changes in the family and in the role of government. Dixon Wecter made a survey of the era in *The Age of the Great Depression* (New York, 1952), upon which I have relied for many facts. Popular and broad in scope and very readable is Caroline Bird, *The Invisible Scar* (New York, 1966). A rather superficial, but lively, survey of the literary aspects of the decade is Leo Gurko, *Angry Decade* (New York, 1947).

My presentation of the immediate impact of unemployment has been drawn from several studies by sociologists and from surveys in the periodical press: R. C. Angell, *The Family Encounters the Depression* (New York, 1936); Mira D. Komarovsky, *The Unemployed Man and His Family* (New York, 1940); and E. W. Bakke, *Citizens Without Work* (New Haven, 1940). See also "No One Has Starved," *Fortune,* VI (September, 1932), 19–29 ff., for an ironic examination of the extent of misery in the depths of the depression; the story of the wandering youths is in *Fortune,* VII (February, 1933), 46. The eyewitness accounts of the

Bonus Army and the unemployed in Detroit are reprinted in *The New Republic Anthology, 1915–1935* (New York, 1936), pp. 424–34. An anonymous article, "I'm On Relief," *Harper's Magazine*, Vol. 172 (January, 1936), 200–209, gives voice to the new attitude toward governmental responsibilities. *Fortune* surveyed the general unemployment situation almost yearly; a detailed investigation of one family is to be found in Vol. XIII (February, 1936), 63–68 ff.; the survey of the arts programs is "Unemployed Arts," *Fortune*, XV (May, 1937), 109–17 ff. David Shannon, ed., *The Great Depression* (New York, 1960), is a superb collection of contemporary sources. Jane de Hart Mathews, *The Federal Theater, 1935–1939* (Princeton, N.J., 1967), is a fine study of an important New Deal innovation; equally good as to the insights it provides into the New Deal as innovator is Paul K. Conkin, *Tomorrow a New World: The New Deal Community Program* (Ithaca, N.Y., 1959).

The literature on the new legislation of the period is very great, though most of the New Deal agencies have not been subjected to scholarly or monographic analysis. One still depends on contemporary accounts. On control of banks I used Ferdinand Pecora, *Wall Street Under Oath* (New York, 1939), by the counsel for the congressional investigation; and a critical article, Bernard Flexner, "The Fight on the Securities Act," *Atlantic Monthly*, CLIII (February, 1934), 232–50. The history of social security proposals which I used for background is Isaac M. Rubinow, *The Quest for Security* (New York, 1934); the leading authority on social security at the time, Abraham Epstein, opposed the program in "Our Social Insecurity Act," *Harper's Magazine*, Vol. 172 (December, 1935), 55–66. For an expression of the new approach to government's role, see G. R. Leighton and Richard Hellman, "Half Slave, Half Free: Unemployment, the Depression, and the American People," *Harper's Magazine*, Vol. 171 (August, 1935), 342–53. The standard authority on the TVA is C. H. Pritchett, *The Tennessee Valley Authority* (Chapel Hill, N.C., 1943), and I have also used the relevant portions of Broadus Mitchell, *Depression Decade* (New York, 1947), here and elsewhere in this chapter. Odette Keun, *A Foreigner Looks at the TVA* (New York, 1937), is very sympathetic, as is the contemporary Drew and Leon Pearson, "The Tennessee Valley Experiment," *Harper's Magazine*, Vol. 170 (May, 1935), 699–707. Donald Davidson presents a jaundiced but not unfair picture of TVA in the second volume of his *The Tennessee* (2 vols., New York, 1948).

The altered position of the Negro is dealt with in detail in E. L. Tatum, *Changed Political Thought of the Negro, 1915–1940* (New York, 1951); Henry Lee Moon, *Balance of Power: The Negro Vote* (Garden City, N.Y., 1948); E. D. Waldron, "The Negro Exodus From the South,"

Current History, XVIII (September, 1923), 942–44; and in Gunnar Myrdal's *American Dilemma* and Samuel Lubell's *The Future of American Politics.*

For the new labor movement I have relied on Edwin W. Witte, *The Government in Labor Disputes* (New York and London, 1932), for the period of the twenties; R. R. Brooks, *When Labor Organizes* (New Haven, 1937); Edward Levinson's dramatic and very sympathetic *Labor on the March* (New York, 1938); and Leo Huberman's sensational but factual *Labor Spy Racket* (New York, 1937) for the great organizing drives. The most recent broad study of organized labor in the 1930's is Walter Galenson, *The CIO Challenge to the AF of L* (Cambridge, Mass., 1960). It contains valuable data and conclusions. Excellent on labor in general in the early depression is Irving Bernstein, *The Lean Years* (Boston, 1960). On the implications of the new labor laws I am indebted to Charles O. Gregory, *Labor and the Law* (New York, 1946); Harry A. Millis and Emily C. Brown, *From the Wagner Act to Taft-Hartley* (Chicago, 1950); and Kurt Braun, *The Right to Organize and Its Limits* (Washington, 1950).

The volume of writings about Franklin D. Roosevelt and his New Deal by both contemporaries and scholars is so huge that it cannot begin to be surveyed here. Only some pertinent items and particularly those that actually went into the writing of my chapter will be mentioned. There has been a growing literature on the question of continuity and change. Arthur Link, *American Epoch* (3rd ed., New York, 1967), Chapter 19, still argues for continuity from the Progressive years; from somewhat different angles Andrew Scott, "The Progressive Era in Perspective," *Journal of Politics,* XXI (November, 1959), 685–701, and Richard S. Kirkendall, "The Great Depression: Another Watershed in American History?" in John Braeman, *Change and Continuity in Twentieth-Century America* (New York, 1966), press the same point, though less effectively. My own position is reflected in Richard Hofstadter, *The Age of Reform,* Chapter VII, and in the biographical approach taken in Otis Graham, Jr., *An Encore for Reform* (New York, 1967). Most recently the New Deal has come into criticism for its failure to grapple fundamentally with the problems of American society, and, in that sense, these New Left critics agree with those who see in the New Deal more continuity than alteration from earlier reform movements. Notable in this group is the penetrating Paul K. Conkin, *The New Deal* (New York, 1967), the introductory essay by Howard Zinn in his collection of sources, *New Deal Thought* (Indianapolis, Ind., 1966), and the essay on the New Deal by Bernstein in Barton Bernstein, ed., *Towards a New Past* (New York, 1968).

Of the general histories of the New Deal, the second and third volumes of Arthur Schlesinger, Jr., *Age of Roosevelt* are partisan, but brilliantly written; however, they take the story only to 1936. James McGregor Burns, *Roosevelt: The Lion and the Fox* (New York, 1956), is critical and sometimes overly dramatic. Undoubtedly the best single-volume study is William E. Leuchtenberg, *Franklin D. Roosevelt and the New Deal* (New York, 1963). The most rewarding memoir for my purposes was Frances Perkins, *The Roosevelt I Knew* (New York, 1946); it is both sympathetic and clear-headed. Interesting as an impression written before F. D. R. became a hero is Ernest K. Lindley, *The Roosevelt Revolution* (New York, 1933). Some impressions have also been culled from *The Secret Diary of Harold L. Ickes* (3 vols., New York, 1953–54). *The Memoirs of Herbert Hoover* (3 vols., New York, 1951–2) are indispensable for putting the New Deal in some critical perspective. Hoover's wrestling with the depression is reevaluated in Carl N. Degler, "The Ordeal of Herbert Hoover," *Yale Review* (1963), pp. 563–83, and in Albert U. Romasco, *The Poverty of Abundance* (New York, 1965).

XIV. THE MAKING OF A WORLD POWER

The literature on foreign policy is not only voluminous, but highly specialized as well. Hence this survey of the literature concentrates only upon those works that I have used for the special and limited purposes of this book. There are a number of admirable surveys of American foreign policy; two of them I used a good deal: Richard W. Leopold, *The Growth of American Foreign Policy* (New York, 1962), which focuses on the twentieth century but has a helpful analysis of the early period, and Thomas A. Bailey, *A Diplomatic History of the American People* (7th ed., New York, 1964), which is unusual for its broad coverage of the literature, recent and remote. Bailey's *The Man in the Street. The Impact of American Public Opinion on Foreign Policy* (New York, 1948) assesses the role of public opinion in foreign affairs as no other work does. I have also found suggestive as well as sometimes irritating four works that attempt to draw broad conclusions about the nature of American foreign relations: Dexter Perkins, *Foreign Policy and the American Spirit* (Ithaca, 1957); Frank Tannenbaum, *The American Tradition in Foreign Policy* (Norman, Okla., 1955); R. W. Van Alstyne, *The Rising American Empire* (New York, 1960); William Appleman Williams, *The Tragedy of American Diplomacy* (rev. ed., New York, 1962). The last is the most critical and is by the leader of the economic interpretation school of diplomatic history.

For the history of American foreign relations prior to 1890 the literature is rich and complex, but for the purposes of this book, most of it was not relevant. I found helpful and convincing Felix Gilbert, *To the Farewell Address: Ideas of Early American Foreign Policy* (Princeton, 1961). I have followed Gilbert in my chapter, supplemented by Paul A.

Varg, *Foreign Policies of the Founding Fathers* (East Lansing, Mich., 1963), a much-neglected book. Max Savelle, "The Appearance of an American Attitude toward External Affairs, 1750–1775," *American Historical Review*, LII (July, 1947), 655–66 shows that before the Revolution Americans were already seeing themselves as worthy of a separate foreign policy. Alexander De Conde, *Entangling Alliance. Politics and Diplomacy under George Washington* (Durham, N.C., 1958), sees more partisanship than principle in the Farewell Address, but his case is not convincing. I have not attempted to canvass the works dealing with the diplomacy of westward expansion, but Norman Graebner, *Empire on the Pacific* (New York, 1955), deserves to be mentioned since his view of the motivation for Polk's desire for Oregon is the one I have followed. Frederick Merk, *Manifest Destiny and Mission in American History, A Reinterpretation* (New York, 1963) in a sense builds on Graebner, since Merk argues that *most* Americans were not really interested in expansion.

There are a number of works that take the 1890's as a starting point for an assessment of American foreign policy in subsequent years. A good survey is Foster Rhea Dulles, *America's Rise to World Power, 1898–1954* (New York, 1955). Written by a political scientist and deeply concerned with the conflict between idealism and realism in foreign policy formulation is Robert Endicott Osgood, *Ideals and Self-Interest in America's Foreign Relations. The Great Transformation of the Twentieth Century* (Chicago, 1953). This book has influenced my own thinking greatly. Perhaps the most influential book on the foreign policy of the twentieth century is George F. Kennan, *American Diplomacy, 1900–1950* (Chicago, 1951). Despite his reputation as a realist, Kennan is here more concerned with reforming American policies than he is in objectively analyzing them. Norman A. Graebner, ed., *An Uncertain Tradition* (New York, 1961) contains a number of good sketches of twentieth-century secretaries of state that I have drawn upon. Probably the fullest discussion of the coming of the Spanish-American War and imperialism is Ernest R. May, *Imperial Democracy* (New York, 1961), which is based upon research in a number of foreign archives. Less ambitious, but no less penetrating, is the briefer H. Wayne Morgan, *America's Road to Empire* (New York, 1965). I have used both with profit. Richard Hofstadter's conception of the "psychic crisis" of the 1890's is presented in his essay "Manifest Destiny and the Philippines," in Daniel Aaron, ed., *America in Crisis* (New York, 1952). One of the most provocative studies is Walter La Feber, *New Empire* (Ithaca, 1963), which stresses the economic concerns behind the imperialist thrust, especially the impact of the depression of 1893. I am much indebted to this book, as I am to Thomas J. McCormick, *China Market* (Chicago, 1967), which sees the interest in the economic potentialities of Asia as the prime source of American imperialism. Both these books place too heavy emphasis on economic motivation, but their evidence cannot be ignored. Further data on the economic background to the Open Door notes are provided in the earlier Charles S. Campbell, Jr., *Special Business Interests and Open Door Policy* (New Haven, Conn., 1951). Ernest May, *American Imperialism. A Speculative Essay* (New York, 1968), presents an eclectic explanation for imperialism that sidesteps the economic argument. The most recent and fullest study on the anti-imperialists is the well-written Robert L. Beisner, *Twelve Against Empire* (New York, 1968), which I have used. Important for Theodore Roosevelt, though his administration is peripheral to my interest, is Howard K. Beale, *Theodore Roosevelt and the Rise of America to World Power* (Baltimore, 1956).

The literature on American entrance into the First World War is large. It can best be approached through two highly competent and thorough review articles: Richard W. Leopold, "The Problem of American Intervention, 1917: An Historical Retrospect," *World Politics,* II (April, 1950), 405–25, and Daniel M. Smith, "National Interest and American Intervention, 1917: An Historiographical Appraisal," *Journal of American History,* LII (June, 1965), 5–24. Excellent as a summary of a great body of literature is the interpretive study, Daniel M. Smith, *The Great Departure* (New York, 1965), on which I have drawn. The classic statement of neutrality as the cause for United States entrance into war in 1917 is Charles Seymour, *American Diplomacy During the World War* (Baltimore, 1934). Charles C. Tansill, *America Goes to War* (Boston, 1938), makes the strongest case for economic interests being the primary cause. The most judicious statement in short compass of the role of economic interest is Paul Birdsall, "Neutrality and Economic Pressures," *Science and Society,* III (Spring, 1939), 217–28. I have been strongly influenced also by the fruit of a lifetime of work on Woodrow Wilson by Arthur S. Link, *Wilson the Diplomatist. A Look at His Major Foreign Policies* (Baltimore, 1957). Helpful also was the very full and thorough Ernest R. May, *The World War and American Isolation, 1914–1917* (Cambridge, Mass., 1959).

Perhaps most influential in my thinking about the 1920's on foreign policy has been William Appleman Williams, "The Legend of Isolationism in the 1920's," *Science and Society,* XVIII (Winter, 1954), 1–20, even though I have not followed his heavily economic views as far as he goes. I have also drawn a good deal from Herbert Feis, *The Diplomacy of the Dollar* (Baltimore, 1950), and from Joseph Brandes, *Herbert Hoover and Economic Diplomacy* (Pittsburgh, 1962). Albert K. Weinberg, "The Historical Meaning of the American Doctrine of Isolation," *American Political Science Review,* XXXIV (June, 1940), 539–47 is a good survey of the practice of isolation. Two fine studies of foreign poli-

cies in the 1920's from which I have learned much are John Chalmers
Vinson, *The Parchment Peace, The United States Senate and the Washington Conference, 1921–1922* (Athens, Ga., 1955), and Robert H. Fer-
rell, *Peace in Their Time, The Origins of the Kellogg-Briand Pact* (New
Haven, Conn., 1952), though I have not always followed their interpretations.

A good introduction to the diplomacy of the 1930's, with a splendid
annotated bibliography, is Robert A. Divine, *The Reluctant Belligerent*
(New York, 1965). The collection of articles in Alexander De Conde,
ed., *Isolation and Security* (Durham, N.C., 1957) helped to shape my
thinking on isolationism, especially the article by Richard Current. Warren I. Cohen, *The American Revisionists* (Chicago, 1967), dissects the
writings of five historians who prepared the ground for the isolationist
policies of the 1930's. Two of the best known of the revisionist books on
American entrance into the First World War, which had a profound
influence on isolationist thought in the 1930's, are: C. Hartley Grattan,
Why We Fought (New York, 1929), and Walter Millis, *The Road to
War, 1914–1917* (New York, 1935). The best general book on isolationism and one on which I drew heavily is Manfred Jonas, *Isolationism
in America, 1935–1941* (Ithaca, 1966). More traditional in approach
and somewhat charged with disdain toward the isolationists are the
two books of Selig Adler, *The Uncertain Giant: 1921–1941. American
Foreign Policy Between the Wars* (New York, 1965), and *The Isolationist Impulse: Its Twentieth Century Reaction* (New York, 1957). My
thinking about the coming of the war with Japan has been influenced by
Armin Rappaport, *Henry L. Stimson and Japan, 1931–1933* (Chicago,
1963), which emphasizes the role of the Stimson Doctrine in antagoniz-
ing Japan; Waldo H. Heinrich's superb biography of Joseph Grew, the
U.S. ambassador in Japan during the 1930's, *American Ambassador*
(Boston, 1966); Paul W. Schroeder, *The Axis Alliance and Japanese-
American Relations, 1941* (Ithaca, 1958), which is revisionist in its suggestion that not all responsibility for war rests upon Japan.

The number of works devoted to the foreign policy actions since 1945
has mounted rapidly. Among the oldest on the early years but still highly
useful is William H. McNeill, *America, Britain and Russia* (London,
1953). I have used it with profit. More stimulating than factual is John
Lukacs, *A History of the Cold War* (Garden City, N.Y., 1961). Hard-
line in outlook, but filled with solid information and analysis is John
Spanier, *American Foreign Policy Since World War II* (2nd rev. ed.,
1965). The fullest survey of the Cold War diplomacy, though somewhat
marred by an excessive attention to alleged domestic influences on foreign policy, is Walter LaFeber, *America, Russia, and the Cold War,
1945–1966* (New York, 1967). Highly stimulating and remarkably detached in places is the readable Louis J. Halle, *The Cold War as History*

(New York, 1967). This book has contributed a good deal to my own conception of the years since 1945. Two specialized books on the Cold War deserve to be mentioned. D. F. Fleming, *The Cold War and Its Origins* (2 vols., Garden City, N.Y., 1961) is one of the earliest books to question the standard view, though its documentation is weak. More powerful, though narrower in time span, is Gar Alperovitz, *Atomic Diplomacy* (rev. ed., New York, 1962), which stretches credulity in its depiction of Truman as a master diplomatist. Less one-sided in its presentation is the solid little work, William L. Neumann, *After Victory, Churchill, Roosevelt, Stalin and the Making of the Peace* (New York, 1967). Herbert Feis, *Between War and Peace: The Potsdam Conference* (Princeton, 1960) is the standard and "official" study.

I have also used the writings of contemporaries like A. H. Vandenberg, Jr., ed., *The Private Papers of Senator Vandenberg* (Boston, 1952), Walter Millis, ed., *The Forrestal Diaries* (New York, 1951), Henry L. Stimson and McGeorge Bundy, *On Active Service in Peace and War* (New York, 1948), and Truman's and Eisenhower's *Memoirs*. George F. Kennan, *Memoirs, 1925–1950* (Boston, 1967) is both informative and readable. The revolution in American foreign policy of 1947–48 is excitingly told by a minor participant in Joseph M. Jones, *The Fifteen Weeks* (New York, 1955). Harry Bayard Price, *The Marshall Plan and Its Meaning* (Ithaca, 1955) is the standard study. The best book on the Korean War is David Rees, *Korea: The Limited War* (New York, 1964). Of the many books on the Vietnam War the one that should not be overlooked is Bernard Fall, *The Two Vietnams: A Political and Military Analysis* (rev. ed., New York, 1965). Three specialized works that I found helpful on the question of Communist Russian and Chinese involvement in Korea and Vietnam are: Soon Sung Cho, *Korea in World Politics* (Berkeley, 1967); Allen S. Whiting, *China Crosses the Yalu* (New York, 1960); and Melvin Gurtov, *The First Vietnam Crisis: Chinese Communist Strategy and the United States Involvement, 1953–1954* (Cambridge, Mass., 1966).

Index

ABOUT THE AUTHOR

Born in Orange, New Jersey, Carl N. Degler served in the Army in World War II, graduated from Upsala College, received his M.A. and Ph.D. degrees at Columbia. He has taught at Hunter College, New York University, New York's City College, Adelphi, the Gradate School of Columbia University as a Visiting Professor and for fifteen years at Vassar College. With his wife and two children, he lives in Stanford, California, where he is now Professor of History at Stanford University.

THE PRESIDENT'S LADIES

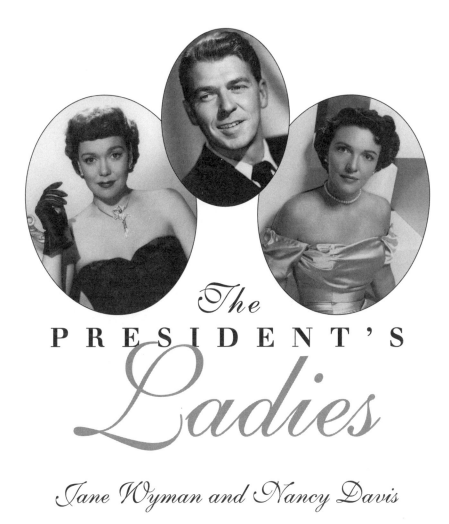

The
PRESIDENT'S
Ladies

Jane Wyman and Nancy Davis

BERNARD F. DICK

UNIVERSITY PRESS OF MISSISSIPPI • JACKSON

www.upress.state.ms.us

The University Press of Mississippi is a member of the Association of American
University Presses.

Copyright © 2014 by University Press of Mississippi
All rights reserved
Manufactured in the United States of America

First printing 2014

∞

Library of Congress Cataloging-in-Publication Data

Dick, Bernard F.
The president's ladies : Jane Wyman and Nancy Davis / Bernard F. Dick.
pages cm
Includes bibliographical references and index.
ISBN 978-1-61703-980-5 (hardback) — ISBN 978-1-61703-981-2 (ebook)
1. Motion picture actors and actresses—United States—Biography. 2. Presidents' spouses—United States—Biography. 3. Wyman, Jane, 1917–2007.
4. Reagan, Nancy, 1923– 5. Reagan, Ronald. I. Title.
PN1998.2.D4955 2014
791.4302'80922—dc23   2013039754

British Library Cataloging-in-Publication Data available

For Peter N. Chetta

CONTENTS

THE PRESIDENT'S LADIES

INTRODUCTION

HOLLYWOOD CANTEEN (1944) WAS ANOTHER WARNER BROS. MORALE-booster, following on the heels of *Thank Your Lucky Stars* (1943). The latter brought out the Warners pantheon: Humphrey Bogart, Olivia De Havilland, John Garfield, Ann Sheridan, Jack Carson—and, most memorably, Bette Davis, lamenting, "They're Either Too Young or Too Old," and hitting the double entendres as if they were typewriter keys. *Hollywood Canteen* was mellower. It also spotlighted the Warners regulars: John Garfield, Bette Davis, Jack Carson, Alexis Smith, Eleanor Parker, Paul Henreid, Dane Clark, Joan Leslie, Janis Paige (in her screen debut), and Jane Wyman, with guest appearances by the Andrews Sisters (Universal) and Roy Rogers, Trigger, and the Sons of the Pioneers (Republic). The movie paid tribute to the historic Hollywood Canteen on Cahuenga Boulevard, the inspiration of John Garfield and Bette Davis, which opened its doors shortly after Pearl Harbor to service men and women of all nations involved in the fight against fascism. The hostesses were actresses, and the bus boys and dishwashers, actors. This was democracy in action, as the deities came down to earth and mingled with mortals—at least for the space of an evening. For *Hollywood Canteen*, screenwriter-director Delmer Daves added a wisp of a plot: A corporal on leave (Robert Hutton) wanders into the Canteen, hoping to see his dream girl, Joan Leslie. Jack Carson befriends the lovesick corporal and jokingly remarks that he has been "Leslieized," and Jane Wyman, who had just done a musical number with Carson, interjects, "Stop. I've been Reaganized!"

How odd that a surname could become a verb used in the passive voice. Jane Wyman may have felt passive in 1944, but not after she was loaned out to Paramount for *The Lost Weekend* (1945) and to MGM for *The Yearling* (1945), which brought her an Oscar nomination—her first of four. Her Reaganization would soon be over, even though she and Reagan were considered Hollywood's ideal couple, one that would disprove the myth that movie star marriages are ephemeral. Jane and Reagan

3

were married in 1940, but the marriage started foundering in 1947. Then in 1948, Jane filed for divorce, which was granted in 1949, the year Nancy Davis entered Reagan's life. Reagan was Jane's third husband, she was his first wife, and Nancy was his second. A Hollywood triptych.

Ronald Reagan was unique among American presidents. He had been an actor, married an actress who divorced him, and then married another. As an actor, Reagan may have occasionally had star billing, but he was never really a star. He was low gloss, with an affinity for romantic comedy. If he was cast in a drama, and could identify with his character—as he did in *Kings Row*—he acquitted himself well. When he could not, as in *Night unto Night*, he went through the motions, never embarrassing himself but causing audiences to wonder why he was in the film in the first place.

Nancy Davis, on the other hand, worked within her limitations, never receiving a damning review and, in fact, getting favorable ones from the *New York Times*, the *Los Angeles Times*, the *Hollywood Reporter*, and *Variety*. But while Reagan was second tier, Nancy was a notch below: second tier minus. Still, she was a pro, despite her limited repertoire (wife, mother, widow, teacher, secretary, nurse). Talent was not the issue; stardom was. Nancy Davis was never meant for center stage—except at 1600 Pennsylvania Avenue.

The President's Ladies is primarily concerned with the screen and television careers of Jane Wyman and Nancy Davis. Jane naturally receives greater attention, since she had the longer and more important movie and TV career. She made her first film in 1932, her last in 1969. In the mid 1950s, she entered television and was so popular as host of *Fireside Theatre* that it became *Jane Wyman's Fireside Theatre*. In 1981, Reagan's first year as president, she became a prime time soap opera queen playing Angela Channing in *Falcon Crest*. The series ended in 1990, a year after Reagan and Nancy left the White House, on 20 January 1989.

To use movie language, Jane Wyman is the star of *The President's Ladies*, with Nancy Davis heading the supporting cast, and Ronald Reagan making a guest appearance. Their lives and careers are interconnected. Jane and Reagan appeared together in four movies, but never appeared together on television. Nancy made one film with Reagan and appeared in five television shows with him: once on *Ford Theatre* and four times on *General Electric Theater*, which he hosted. Both Jane and Nancy did their best work without Reagan, and Reagan did his best work without them.

The inspiration for *The President's Ladies* comes from the last scene in *All about Eve* (1950), when Barbara Bates bows before a three-mirrored cheval. I envisioned a similar cheval, with Jane in the center, Reagan on the left, and Nancy on the right. Each receives his and her due, regardless of image size.

Wherever possible, I have used material from archives and special collections. For background on Reagan, I have only used secondary sources with detailed information about his acting career. The Reagan White House does not fall under the scope of this book, nor does Nancy Reagan—only Nancy Davis. Kitty Kelly's *Nancy Reagan: The Unauthorized Biography* has come in for its share of criticism. However, Kelly is sound on Nancy's early years and her movie career, which alone matter. Her accounts of Nancy Davis's sexual escapades read like tabloid copy, some of which seems spiteful, if not vindictive. Nancy Davis was no prude. In her autobiography, *My Turn*, she all but admits that she and Reagan were lovers, and that their first child, Patricia "Patti" Ann, was born "a bit precipitously" seven months after their marriage. "Go ahead and count," she writes, apparently feeling no guilt about what, in Hollywood, would have been considered a nonevent. Nancy was in love with Reagan. She did not expect him to further her career—particularly since, in 1949, only Jane's career was in the ascendant. Reagan did not give Nancy her start, even though he may have used his influence as host of *General Electric Theater* to get her on the program. But Nancy did well on her own, as did Jane.

I have seen most of Jane's films and all of Nancy's, as well as whatever of their television work I could locate. To talk about their acting, I must place their performances within the context of their films. An actor's films are part of his or her life. Therefore, I summarize plots, especially of those films and TV shows that are not readily available, striving for brevity without shortchanging either the film or the actor. I do the same when discussing Reagan's better (and lesser) movies. I have also included performing credits that, even when scanned, give new meaning to the label "working actor." Jane, Nancy, and Reagan have few gaps in their résumés. When they were not in a movie, they were on television—and, in the case of Jane and Reagan, on radio as well.

Jane Wyman, Nancy Davis, and Ronald Reagan: three actors, each a pro in his or her own way, with intersecting lives and careers. This is the cast of *The President's Ladies*.

I am indebted to the following for their help:

Carol Almanza and Connie McCoy, Northwest Missouri Genealogical Society, St. Joseph, for supplying me with material to reconstruct Jane's early years and describe the milieu in which she grew up

Sandra Archer, Head of Reference Services, Margaret Herrick Library, for directing me to the right sources

Sidney Bloomberg, former studio publicist, for searching out DVDs of Jane's, Nancy's, and Reagan's television work

Jonathan Auxler, Curator, Warner Bros. Archives, University of Southern California (USC), for providing me with the production files I needed

Stacy Behlmer, Coordinator of Special Projects and Research, Margaret Herrick Library, for her invaluable assistance

Ned Comstock, Senior Library Assistant, Cinematic Arts Library, USC, and the ultimate archivist, for alerting me to collections that I did not know existed

Grover Crisp, Vice President, Asset Management & Film Preservation, Sony Pictures Entertainment, for sending me a DVD of *Let's Do It Again*

Arlene Dahl, actress and author, for sharing her memories of the Reagans with me

Janis Paige Gilbert, actress and cabaret artist, for her vivid recreation of the *Cheyenne* shoot

Anthony Greco, for locating Jane's and Nancy's films that were unavailable on DVD

Kristine Krueger, National Film Information Service, Margaret Herrick Library, for patiently and accurately answering questions that would have exasperated lesser beings

Barbara Hall, Research Archivist, Academy of Motion Picture Arts and Sciences, for making it possible for me to hear tapes of Jane's *Lux Radio Theatre* appearances

Sandra Joy Lee, Director, Warner Bros. Archives, USC, for running such a researcher-friendly facility

Brandon Massey, Forest Lawn Records Department, for verifying the burial place of Jane's first husband, Eugene Wyman

Thomas J. Pucher, President, German *Falcon Crest* Fan Club DFCF, for providing me with the text of Jane's monologue for the last episode, and for creating a website (www.falconcrest.org) that is a tribute to the series, its creator, and its star

Kathleen Stein-Smith and MaryAnn Sena, Giovatto Library, Fairleigh Dickinson University (Teaneck campus), for expediting my requests for interlibrary loans and articles

And special thanks to my wife, Katherine Restaino, the best colleague any writer could have.

Chapter 1

The Abandoned Child

DURING HOLLYWOOD'S HEYDAY, THE STAR MACHINE PROCESSED FODDER for the fan magazines, ingested by readers who believed what they read. To say that an actor was adopted posed questions that studios preferred not to answer and certainly would not include in their hagiographic bios. Mention of adoption meant disclosing a star's past, which could include implications of illegitimacy or abandonment, neither of which was good copy. And so, Jane Wyman was not adopted. But she was.

On 27 May 1916, Manning Jeffries Mayfield and Gladys Hope Christian were married by a justice of the peace in Kansas City, Missouri. The bride and groom were the same age, twenty-one, although Gladys was five months younger. They returned to the groom's birth place, St. Joseph, Missouri, about sixty miles from St. Louis, moving into the home of his parents, Pulaski and Mamie Mayfield, at 3121 Mitchell Avenue. Manning's two sisters, Martha and Sarah—the latter, a public school teacher— also resided there. Living with in-laws was not the most auspicious beginning for a marriage, and four years later, the marriage was over.

The Mitchell Avenue house was spacious enough. It was a large, two-story house on a residential street. There were only seven homes on the block, with neighbors ranging from an Aunt Jemima Mills employee, a carpenter, and a contractor, to a chauffeur and the deputy county treasurer. Residents had their choice of grocers and were within walking distance of an auto repair shop, a lumber and coal company, a doctor, an engine house, and Barlett Park with its distinctive pavilion. This was small-town America, not much different from the rotogravure Indianapolis of Booth Tarkington's *Seventeen*.

For Gladys, the problem was not St. Joseph, it was living in a house with her husband's parents and sisters—a house in which she felt like an intruder. Gladys's father-in-law, Pulaski Mayfield, then in his sixties, had held positions in various mercantile companies. Unlike his own father, Manning finished high school at St. Joseph Central and spent his brief life working for the railroad. Gladys, a former secretary, was a homemaker—except that she was in her in-laws' home when she gave birth to her and Manning's only child. Sarah Jane, the future Jane Wyman, was born on 5 January 1917, less than eight months after her parents' marriage.

Sarah Jane was either premature or the result of premarital sex. If the latter—given his short-lived marriage—Manning may have had second thoughts about "doing the honorable thing." Gladys, for her part, may have wondered about ever becoming involved with Manning in the first place.

Names had special significance for the Mayfields, who were originally Southerners. Pulaski was born in Georgia; his father, Manning, in Alabama. Jane's birth father, Manning Jeffries Mayfield, was given his grandfather's first name, Manning, and Jeffries, his mother's maiden name. Mayfield's sister and grandmother were both christened Sarah. His great-great-great-grandmother was named Jane. The idea of inclusion seemed alien to the Mayfields. That Gladys was not consulted about her own daughter's name may also have contributed to the brevity of her marriage to Manning. But there were other reasons, too. In addition to Gladys's sense of being an outsider, Manning seemed indifferent to fatherhood and was more devoted to his job than to his wife and daughter. Gladys realized that their marriage was based more on expediency than love—particularly if conception occurred prior to marriage. But once Gladys gave birth, expediency was no longer an issue.

The marriage ended in 1920, followed by divorce a year later. In 1920, Manning Jeffries Mayfield left St. Joseph to become secretary of the shipping company, the Southern Pacific Westbound Conference. He had no qualms about relocating in California, eventually settling in San Francisco, where he died unexpectedly of pneumonia on 21 January 1922 at the age of twenty-seven. His body was shipped to St. Joseph, where he was buried on 28 January. Obituaries stated that Manning was unmarried, mentioning only his parents and sisters as survivors.

Gladys may not have had a husband, but she did have a five-year-old daughter. However, Sarah Jane did not figure in Gladys's plans, sketchy though they were. One thing, however, was certain: Gladys did not want the responsibility of taking care of a five-year-old. She put her daughter up for adoption. Mother and daughter may have reconnected in the summer of 1933, but for all practical purposes, Gladys had disappeared from Sarah Jane's life, ending her days in New York, where she died in 1960 at sixty-five, outliving her former husband by almost forty years. Pulaski Mayfield outlived his son by seven.

Sarah Jane was adopted unofficially by Richard and Emma Fulks, both then in their sixties (Emma was sixty, Richard, sixty-five) and living at 1209 North 38th Street in a quiet, upper-middle class neighborhood that was a slight improvement over 3121 Mitchell Avenue. There were the usual businesses: grocers, tailor, cleaner, druggist, post office, gas station, and hospital. A block and a half away was Frederick Street, where trolleys ran downtown to the shopping district. Lake Contrary, with its amusement park, was accessible by trolley, as was Krug Park. It was the kind of neighborhood that was ideal for raising children, and, between them, the Fulkses had already raised four before Sarah Jane came into their lives.

Emma, born in Saarbrucken, Germany, had three children by her first marriage to Dr. Morris F. Weyman: a son, also named Morris, and two daughters, Elsie and Mora. Richard Fulks, a widower, had a son, Ray, by a previous marriage. Emma was also on her second marriage, having divorced Weyman before emigrating from Germany. By 1922, when Sarah Jane joined the Fulks household, Morris and Elsie, then in their twenties, had already relocated in Los Angeles, where Morris followed in his father's profession, specializing in eye and throat disorders. Ray, the oldest, had moved to Texas. Mora, twenty-two, was probably not living at home, but even if she were, she would not have been much of a companion to the five-year-old Sarah Jane.

The adoption was Emma's idea. At sixty, with grown children, Emma yearned to experience motherhood again, however vicariously. She had no children by her second marriage, and, despite its idyllic location, 1209 North 38th Street, was a lonely place—in part because her husband did little to make Sarah Jane feel welcome.

Studio bios usually described Richard Fulks as a local politician—sometimes even a major one. Actually, he started as a law enforcement officer with the St. Joseph police force, graduated to chief detective, and resigned in 1909 at the age of forty-six. Seven years later, Fulks was elected county collector, a position he held until 1918. A picture of Fulks as chief detective reveals a dour, semi-bald man with a bushy moustache and the half-closed eyes of someone either bored or sleep-deprived. It was not a friendly face.

Emma was quite the opposite. She wanted the best for Sarah Jane. In 1923, she enrolled the little girl in the first grade at the Noyes School, which was within walking distance of the Fulks home. Emma was a devotee of the performing arts, particularly theatre and ballet. Since she never pursued her dream of becoming an actress, she prepared Sarah Jane for the profession that might have been hers, taking her downtown for plays and movies. It was the movies that captivated Sarah Jane. Emma, believing that dance lessons would not hurt, enrolled her at the Edward A. Prinz Dancing Academy, at Tenth and Robidoux, where Sarah Jane was introduced to a world that offered a refuge from everyday life—particularly school, which held little interest for her. But Emma had already determined Sarah Jane's future.

According to Ronald Reagan's biographer, Anne Edwards, Emma brought Sarah Jane to Los Angeles in 1922, presumably to visit her children—but, more importantly, to continue on to San Francisco, where she hoped to persuade Mayfield to legalize Sarah Jane's adoption. There is no way of knowing when Emma and Sarah Jane left for the West Coast. Supposedly, they did so after Sarah Jane's fifth birthday. But that was less than a week before Mayfield died.

What took precedence over a visit with her children was Emma's obsession with making Sarah Jane into a star. If Baby Peggy could become a star at five, why not Sarah Jane? It was not to happen in 1922, but Emma tried again seven years later. In 1929, Baby Peggy's reign was over; Shirley Temple was not even on the cusp of stardom; Richard Fulks was dead; and Sarah Jane was twelve. There might be a market for tweens who could dance and act. Perhaps this time it would work out. But it didn't. Hollywood was not interested. To Emma, this rejection was a setback but not a defeat. Sarah Jane's time would come in a few years—as it did. Meanwhile, it was back to St. Joseph, where she finished grade school and perhaps received a diploma from the Edward A. Prinz Dancing Academy.

Sarah Jane's second exposure to Hollywood made her determined to succeed in the only profession that appealed to her. Prinz understood his student's desire to excel. Once Emma learned that his son, LeRoy, was working in Hollywood as a choreographer, she and Sarah Jane headed for Los Angeles. LeRoy proved an invaluable contact. He managed to get Sarah Jane into the chorus of *The Kid from Spain* (1932), a Samuel Goldwyn production starring Eddie Cantor, with Jane as one of the Goldwyn Girls, the producer's name for a chorus line that included future stars Betty Grable and Paulette Goddard. They were both older than Jane, but not by much—Goddard by six years, Grable by one. But none of this mattered. They were all Goldwyn, and eventually golden, girls.

Sarah Jane languished in extras' limbo for four years until she finally received billing as Jane Wyman. Then she was fed into the star machine.

...

MYTH: Jane Wyman was born in 1914.

FACT: January 5, 1914 is often given as Sarah Jane's birthday, but there is enough documentation at the Northwest Missouri Genealogical Society to prove that this date is off by three years. Anne Edwards, one of the first to solve the mystery of Jane's birth, found it odd that Jane would add three years to her age, since subtraction is more common with movie stars. Once Sarah Jane Fulks became Jane Wyman, Jane and the studios may have preferred the earlier date, since it would have meant that she entered the movies at eighteen, rather than fifteen, when she should have been in school. She was fifteen when she made her first (unbilled) appearance in *The Kid from Spain* (1932). By 1935, when she turned eighteen, she had been an extra in at least eight pictures.

MYTH: Emma envisioned Sarah Jane as the next Shirley Temple.

FACT: Hardly. In 1929, when Emma and Sarah Jane made their second trip to Los Angeles, Temple was one year old and Sarah Jane twelve.

MYTH: Sara Jane Fulks reinvented herself as Jane Durrell, an "itinerant radio singer," working the Middle West-South circuit and performing in such cities as Denver, Chicago, and New Orleans.

FACT: Jane had an attractive singing voice, as she revealed in such films as *Kid Nightingale, Hollywood Canteen, Night and Day, Here Comes the Groom, Just for You*, and *Let's Do It Again*. After the Lux Radio Theatre broadcast of *Nobody Lives Forever* (17 November 1947), in which she co-starred with her then husband Ronald Reagan, Jane admitted that she was no stranger to the microphone, having sung on local radio as a teenager, but not specifying where. "Jane Durrell" was a wise choice, evoking the image of a chanteuse rather than a kid in gingham.

MYTH: Jane's mother was an actress, who appeared under the surname Pechelle in Paris.

FACT: The press kit for *The Kid from Kokomo* (1939) contained more than the usual amount of fabrication, as did the kit for *Torchy Plays with Dynamite* (1939), which described Jane as "part French, her mother having been an actress in Paris." Gladys Hope Christian was a doctor's secretary who never set foot on a stage. The *Kid from Kokomo* press kit included a news release, "She's from Missouri," which had Jane playing soccer, tennis, basketball, and volleyball in school—and nicknamed "Just Folks" because of her real name, "Sarah Jane Folks" [*sic*].

MYTH: In summer 1933, Jane returned to St. Joseph and enrolled at the University of Missouri.

FACT: In summer 1933, Jane did return to St. Joseph, where she "shared a house on 913 North Second Street with Mrs. Gladys H. and Myrtle Johnson." Actually, it was the home of Gladys and Myrle Johnson, and the address was 913 1/2 North Second Street, which was owned by a bookkeeper, Charles Hauck. North Second Street was not that different from the other places Jane had lived, except that it was more working class, a mix of residences and businesses such as milling, packing, and glassworks. It was a neighborhood of accountants, salespersons, candy company workers, carpenters, teamsters, and grocers—the simple folk with whom Jane had lost touch.

The Johnsons seem to have been husband and wife, although they were not married in Buchanan Country. Most likely, Gladys H. was Gladys Hope Christian, Jane's birth mother—which would explain Jane's decision to spend the summer at the Johnson home. It is tempting to invoke the *Stella Dallas/White Banners/To Each His Own* syndrome: birth mother desiring some contact, even visual, with child—or the reverse: child seeking contact with birth mother either physically (*Our Very Own*) or preternaturally (*The Uninvited*). But at sixteen, Jane was hardly a romantic. It is one thing to visit Hollywood, another to work there as a bit player along with countless others dreaming of stardom. Jane needed time to reflect, and Hollywood was no place for introspection. Perhaps she believed St. Joseph held the "answers for personal roots, personal happiness, [and] the right man." But it didn't, and Jane returned to Los Angeles and the only life she knew: that of an extra.

There is no record of Jane having studied at the University of Missouri. Given her antipathy to the classroom, it is hard to imagine her embracing higher ed.

MYTH: While Sarah Jane Fulks (not yet Jane Wyman) was lunching at Sardi's with the wife of character actor Vince Barnett, William Demarest, "then in the agency business," joined them. Convinced that she had movie potential, Demarest handed her his card, offering to represent her.

FACT: The venerable Sardi's is on West 44th Street in the heart of New York's theatre district. Sarah Jane in New York at the age of seventeen or eighteen and lunching at Sardi's?

It is true that William Demarest had been an agent, but he had also worked in the theatre, coming to Hollywood in 1926 when the silent era was waning, and the following year appearing in ten Warner Bros. releases, the most important of which was *The Jazz Singer* (1927). Demarest took time off to appear on Broadway in *Earl Carroll's Vanities*, which ended an eight-month run in April 1932. When *The Kid from Spain* was released that November, he was back in Hollywood, where Sarah Jane Fulks was adjusting to the lot of the unbilled. Since she was shuttling from one film to another, it is hard to imagine her having the time or money to visit New York.

Demarest was, however, instrumental in Jane Wyman's career. He was then represented by a minor agency, Small and Landow, at 8272 Sunset Boulevard. Through some fast talking (at which he excelled), Demarest convinced the agency to take on Jane. Jane received billing in *Smart Blonde* (1936). The part was inconsequential, but she made the credits. Small and Landow was just the beginning. Soon Jane would switch to a more powerful agency.

LeRoy Prinz, a St. Joseph native like Jane and a friend of Demarest, was equally instrumental. In 1929, Prinz choreographed *Earl Carroll's Sketch Book* (1929), which enjoyed a run of 392 performances, and in which Demarest appeared as a member of the ensemble. That same year, Prinz made his film debut as the choreographer for Paramount's *Innocents of Paris*.

Prinz found Jane work as an extra in Paramount's *All the King's Horses* and *College Rhythm* (both 1934), which he choreographed. She appeared as a chorine in a number of films, two of which were Warner Bros. releases, *Gold Diggers of 1933* and *Cain and Mabel* (1936). Warners seemed the perfect studio for Jane: Demarest had connections there, and Prinz was a rising choreographer. Knowing that a Warners contract was a distinct possibility, Jane affected the look—or what she thought was the look—of a movie star: not too flashy, but with eyelashes applied individually to add a touch of glamour meant for close-ups. There was a method to her madness: She did not have to remove her eyelashes at night. Demarest and Prinz prescribed a less theatrical look, and Warners signed her up on 6 May 1936 at a salary of sixty-five dollars a week. Initially, Jane Wyman was another Hollywood brunette who could easily go blonde. But she was not star material, not in 1936. Yet in the coming years, Jane Wyman, in the words of the powerful gossip columnist Louella Parsons, blossomed into a "charming, sophisticated woman." "Charming" the studios understood, "sophisticated," they did not.

MYTH OR FACT? "Wyman" derives from Jane's short-lived marriage to Eugene Wyman, whom she met at Los Angeles High School in the early 1930s.

FACT: Once she was hired as a contract player at Warners, her name became Jane Wyman, which she herself may have suggested. Marriage gave her the surname by which she will always be known.

Her marriage to Eugene Wyman was neither a myth nor a secret. Reliable Hollywood insiders, including Ruth Waterbury, who wrote for *Photoplay*, the most popular of the fan magazines, insisted the marriage was fact. Others have noted the similarity between the names of Jane's stepbrother, Dr. Morris Weyman, and Eugene Wyman. The similarity, however, is purely coincidental. Each man had his own identity. Eugene was the son of Ernest F. and Mayme L. Wyman. His mother died in May 1933 at fifty-six; his father died on 28 October 1938 at sixty-one. The latter date is significant.

At the time of Ernest's death, Jane was on loan to Twentieth-Century Fox for *Tail Spin* (1939), a film about women flyers in which she had a minor role. *Tail Spin* began shooting in October 1938. After Ernest's death, Fox issued a press release stating that "in the tradition of the theatre that the show must go one, blonde Jane Wyman reported for work yesterday morning on the set of *Tail Spin* at 20th Century-Fox while funeral arrangements were being completed for her father at Forest Lawn Memorial Park," and that "in spite of her personal tragedy" and "in a state of near collapse," the magnanimous Jane did not want to deprive the extras of a day's wages.

The press release was churned out of the star machine. Ernest was not Jane's father, but Eugene's. Ernest Wyman, a Los Angeles native and sales manager at Ducommun, an aerospace company with several locations in Southern California, died suddenly of pneumonia. At least the burial site is correct. The Wymans—Ernest, his wife, and son—are interred at Forest Lawn Cemetery, Glendale, in lot 246 of the Vesperland section. Jane and Eugene were indeed married, presumably on 8 April 1933. Wherever they met, it was not at Los Angeles High School, where, if Jane ever was a student, she was probably enrolled under the name of Sarah Jane Fulks. (Attempts to verify name and dates of attendance proved fruitless.) When Eugene died in November 1970 at sixty-four, he was eleven years older than Jane; in April 1933, he would have been twenty-seven, while she was sixteen. Jane may have attended Los Angeles High School for a short time, but given that she began working as an extra in 1932, explaining how she ever could have graduated requires the imagination of a novelist—or what in Hollywood passes for one, a studio publicist. Jane could, understandably, have been attracted to an older man like Wyman, perhaps because he served as a father figure—or at least someone who could alleviate the burden of having to go it alone in a business where competition for secondary roles was as intense as campaigning for leads. Stars had to worry about maintaining their places in the firmament; the others had to fight to get there.

The news release was an attempt to generate advance publicity for *Tail Spin*, Darryl F. Zanuck's title, changed from the alliterative "Women with Wings." Since Jane had an insignificant role in a forgettable movie, the publicity—such as it was—did nothing for her or for *Tail Spin*, which opened to tepid reviews.

Jane Wyman's early life is a skein of fact and speculation, an enigma within a matrix of mysteries—some admitting of clarification, others enshrouded in darkness. Jane disclosed only what she wanted known. If the star machine mythologized her otherwise mundane life, why take out the blue pencil? At the end of John Ford's *The Man Who Shot Liberty Valance* (1962), a newspaper editor refuses to print the truth about the title character, delivering instead the director's credo: "This is the West, sir. When the legend becomes fact, print the legend." The star machine had been doing that long before 1962, although no one in the business would have expressed this practice so epigrammatically.

Chapter 2

The Name below the Title

THE 1932–36 MOVIES IN WHICH JANE APPEARED FLEETINGLY VARIED IN quality, but they at least paid the rent for her South Normandie apartment. For her uncredited role in *My Man Godfrey* (1936), Jane received either twenty-five dollars a day for three days if she was a "bit woman," or fifteen dollars a day for one to three days if she was a "dress extra." Jane was probably the latter. She could have appeared in any or all of the four crowd scenes in the film: the scavenger hunt party, a cocktail party at the Bullocks' mansion, a cocktail lounge, or the nightclub known as "The Dump" on the site of a former Hooverville. For *Cain and Mabel*, there were three categories of "girls." If Jane was one of the thirty-two in the "Coney Island Number," the pay was fifty dollars a week; if she was one of the forty in "1000 Love Songs," it was either fifty dollars a week for four weeks, or fifty dollars for one week. For additional income, Jane resorted to modeling, which taught her "poise" and helped rid her of "self consciousness."

Until Jane was signed by Warners, she was the chorus girl or the extra without a close up, working at various studios and waiting for her big break. But at least she was in some prestigious movies, like Fox's *King of Burlesque* (1936), in which a successful burlesque producer becomes infatuated with a socialite who persuades him to go legit. The result is a fiasco, prompting him to leave his trophy wife, return to his roots, and resume his former career with his star and true love. Fox, which excelled at recycling, refitted the plot for *Nob Hill* (1945), in which a Barbary Coast impresario is seduced into branching out into opera.

Although *King of Burlesque* had a stellar cast (Warner Baxter as the producer, Alice Faye as his star, Jack Oakie as his sidekick, Mona Barrie as the socialite), director Sidney Lanfield was no Busby Berkeley.

Lanfield's camera never panned the ladies of the chorus so as to permit the viewer to make out their faces. One can only speculate as to which numbers Jane appeared in—probably the early ones, "Alabama Bound" and "Whose Big Baby Are You?," but not the one that only required an extra to soar over the audience on a swing, looking perfectly composed. Jane had no intention of being another girl on a red velvet swing.

Billing came with *Smart Blonde* (1936), the first of the nine-part Torchy Blane series, most of which starred Glenda Farrell as the reporter sleuth. The series was Warners' attempt to cash in on the private citizen-as-private-eye movie, the most famous of which was MGM's *The Thin Man* (1934). Warners' approach was the reverse of MGM's: Instead of a married couple like Nick and Nora Charles, there was Torchy Blane and her lieutenant detective (played in all but two films by the blustery Barton MacLane). She had the brains, he had the badge.

The inspiration for Torchy Blane was "Kennedy" (no first name), a hard-drinking reporter in the "MacBride and Kennedy" stories by *Black Mask* writer Frederick Nebel. Warners changed Kennedy's gender, but kept MacBride—minus the *a*. In *Smart Blonde*, Jane, billed eighth, was Dixie, a hat check girl, and appeared in three scenes, only one of which indicated she had a flair for comedy. After a wild party, Dixie is lolling around in bed with an ice pack on her head and a St. Bernard at her feet. When she cannot remember how she wound up with the dog, Torchy reminds her that St. Bernards are rescue dogs that carry small barrels of whiskey around their necks. Jane did not go unnoticed. The *Variety* reviewer (18 November 1936) was impressed: "Jane Wyman is particularly vivid in a sparkling comedy role." Warners must have thought so, too. Her name appeared in 40 percent size type in the credits.

As a contract player, Jane learned that the "supporting cast" was aptly named. She provided support wherever she was needed, appearing in seven films in 1937, six in 1938, five in 1939. Although the roles varied—some were better (and bigger) than others—she faced the dilemma that confronted every contract player: how to convince audiences that her character was important, even if she was scurrying from one set to another, mastering lines on the run, and entrusting coherence to the director and editor.

After *Smart Blonde*, Jane was pegged as a light comedienne—sassy, fast-talking, quick-witted, but unsophisticated, non-drawing room, dumb when necessary, but always the reliable good sport or gal pal who pays her own way. Jane was a mere nineteen when she made *Public Wedding* (1937), which revealed an actress who had mastered the art of rapid-fire line readings that muted the witless dialogue. Jane did not so much toss off the lines as discard them like soiled linen—and fast enough to keep anyone from seeing the stains. After "Flip" (Jane) and a struggling artist (William Hopper, son of actress-columnist Hedda Hopper) agreed to pose as a young couple for a publicity stunt, they expected to go their respective ways. Then they learn that a real justice of the peace officiated at the ceremony. The "marriage" triggers a series of adventures, partly engineered by Flip, who turns the artist into a society painter until her con man stepfather attempts another scam that nearly gets all of them thrown in jail. Flip comes to the rescue, shooting off her lines like bullets, saving everyone's skin (including her own), and rewarding the audience with a happy ending.

This was the kind of farce that Jane could handle. Four years of extra work made wisecracks and sassiness natural. Occasionally, Jane would have a chance to display her brassy side, which as she knew was only one facet of her persona. Like so many comics, Jane wanted to be taken seriously as an actress, but this reevaluation would not take place until the middle of the next decade.

Jane also learned that the movie business did not observe the traditional working day. Despite her billing, the *Mr. Dodd Takes the Air* shoot, which lasted from 26 April–5 June 1937, required Jane to be at the studio for twelve days:

- 1 May, 9:00 a.m.–5:25 p.m.
- 3 May, 9:00 a.m.–6:25 p.m.
- 4 May, 9:00 a.m.–6:03 p.m.
- 5 May, 9:00 a.m.–6:30 p.m.
- 6 May, 10:00 a.m.–8:20 p.m.
- 21 May, 9:30 a.m.–5:30 p.m.
- 24 May, 7:00 p.m.–9:10 p.m.
- 27 May, 9:00 a.m.–6:00 p.m.
- 28 May, 9:00 a.m.–4:00 p.m.
- 2 June, 9:00 a.m.–6:05 p.m.
- 3 June, 10:00 a.m.–6:20 p.m.
- 4 June, 9:00 a.m.–3:45 p.m.

It made no difference that she only had to be on the set for a few scenes. The schedule went with the job.

This schedule also resulted in her hospitalization. "JANE WYMAN HOSPITALIZED FOR NERVOUS BREAKDOWN" read a *Variety* headline

(23 June 1937) that was printed on page sixty-seven. Clearly a starlet's breakdown was not front-page news. Jane's was more of a nervous collapse resulting from a schedule that had her going from one movie to another, something she had never experienced when she was an extra. Her condition was not serious. In less than a week, Jane was ready to say "I do" to Myron Futterman in New Orleans on 29 June.

Two of Jane's 1937 films have some significance: *Ready, Willing and Able* and *Mr. Dodd Takes the Air*. The former was a Ruby Keeler vehicle, memorable if only for the Johnny Mercer-Richard Whiting classic "Too Marvelous for Words," and Keeler's dancing on typewriter keys. Jane was ignored in the publicity material and the studio's campaign plan, as indicated by the print size in which her name appeared (20 percent as opposed to Keeler's 80) and her billing (eighth). In the latter, Jane was billed fifth, despite her plot-resolving role. The star was Kenny Baker, whom Warners was grooming as Dick Powell's successor. Powell's career as a crooner was waning, and Baker had the kind of crystalline voice that used to be called "dulcet" or "honeyed." You could experience synesthesia, tasting and hearing his rendition of Al Dubin and Harry Warren's "Here Comes the Sandman," which could put the most heavily caffeinated moviegoer to sleep. Baker played a small-town electrician whose voice brought him to New York and a short-lived radio career. His invention of a device to improve radio transmission makes him prey for swindlers, who would have succeeded had it not been for Jane's quick thinking. Baker and Jane were the reasons the film worked, even though they were nearly blown away by Alice Brady's whirlwind of a performance as a self-dramatizing opera diva. The couple—Baker with his small-town wholesomeness, and Jane with her merrymaking eyes—looked as if original sin had passed them by. Her eyes could register other emotions, but until she went dramatic, all she had to do was get them to sparkle.

Mervyn LeRoy directed both *Mr. Dodd* and *The King and the Chorus Girl* (also 1937), in which Jane was another chorine, this time a member of the Follies Bergère. In his notoriously flawed autobiography, LeRoy takes credit for Jane's stardom, claiming that one day he spotted her on the Warners lot in a yellow polo coat. Sensing a star in the making, he cast her in *Elmer the Great* (1933) with Joe E. Brown: "She did a beautiful job and her career was launched." Not really. Hers was a bit part that went uncredited. Strangely, LeRoy does not mention *Mr. Dodd Takes the Air*.

The Singing Marine (1937) was the companion piece to *Mr. Dodd*. The title character is an Arkansas marine (Dick Powell), whose sudden fame as a radio singer turns him into an insufferable snob. The entire cast, including Jane (eleventh billed in a superfluous role), was eclipsed by the brilliant harmonica solos of Larry Adler. In *Slim* (1937), which starred Henry Fonda and Margaret Lindsay, Jane's character didn't have a name, only "Stumpty's Girl." Still, her name was in 40 percent size print.

Although Jane was first billed in *Public Wedding*, this honor occurred only because she had no competition; by then, she was better known than her leading man, William Hopper. *Public Wedding* was a brainless farce. Still, it made Jane realize that she could land a lead—even if it was in a B movie. At least she was half way up the pyramid.

Hers was not an unbroken ascent. There was no rubric at Warners for the billing of contract players, no vertical progression from unbilled to billed, from B movie to A movie, from name below the title to name above it. The year 1937 was characteristic: Jane appeared in seven movies, with star billing in one, but fifth—and lower—billing in the others. Jane had no guarantee 1938 would be any better, but she could at least adjust to the routine. She knew that Kenny Baker had failed to live up to the studio's expectations, although he fared better on radio (*The Jack Benny Program* and *The Texaco Star Theater*) and played opposite Mary Martin on Broadway in the Kurt Weill-Ogden Nash musical, *One Touch of Venus* (1943). He at least had radio and the theatre, neither of which held any appeal for Jane. Movies were her medium.

But she also was familiar with the Hollywood revolving door scenario. Scene 1: Studio head reacting to news about X. "Who is X?" Scene 2: "Bring me X." Scene 3: "Bring me the new X." Scene 4: "Who is X?" Or in short, "You're only as good as your last picture." But Jane's last pictures were intended to supplement Warners showcase attractions for 1937: *Marked Woman, The Prince and the Pauper, The Life of Emile Zola, They Won't Forget,* and *Tovarich*. There was always room for what in vaudeville were called "the better cheaper acts," contract talent that did not warrant big bucks. These included Jane, Ronald Reagan, Wayne Morris, and Dennis Morgan. The actors were beta males, "boy next door" types, sunny and upbeat like Jane—or so Warner Bros. thought. Jane's variety was not infinite, but it surpassed that of most of her male co-stars—including Reagan.

Jane probably met Reagan when they were cast in *Brother Rat* (1938). Theirs was a combination of attraction and indifference—attraction on Reagan's part, initial indifference on Jane's. Reagan was understandably drawn to Jane. Even if he did not know that she was a Midwesterner like him, he sensed something refreshingly non-Hollywood about her; she was serious about her craft, but not publicity hungry. She may not have conjured up images of Labor Day picnics, church socials, and canned peaches, but she was not another tinsel queen—nor would she ever be one.

Reagan was attracted to Jane Wyman but knew nothing about Sarah Jane Fulks. Hardened by a childhood of desertion and indifference, with attention coming only from Emma Fulks—who set her adopted daughter on the career path that she envisioned for herself—Jane had developed the will to succeed and the resilience to persist when success eluded her, qualities that saved her from self-pity. If she projected an upbeat image, this was her way of warding off the darkness that seeps in from despair. June Allyson shrewdly observed that despite Jane's public image, there were times when "a sweet sadness radiated from her large soulful eyes." The underside of the cockeyed optimist was a wary pessimist. Even the most carefully crafted mask is subject to fissures. The sweet sadness, as Allyson described it, is often observable when a pause in a conversation produces a pensiveness that briefly exposes the person behind the persona. "Talking to [Wyman], one gets the impression she's wound up like a tight spring," an interviewer wrote in a 1940s fan magazine. Jane was well acquainted with the night, but her dark places were barred to the public. Fanzine writers had to rev up the hype to get a readable story from a wound-up spring that would not uncoil. Nancy Reagan may have been willing to publish her memoirs with all their lacunae, but Jane was content with her mask, determined to repair any crack as soon as it occurred.

Since Jane had experienced two disastrous marriages, the second worse than the first, she was averse to being courted— especially, perhaps, by a newcomer. Shortly after Reagan arrived at Warner Bros., Jane married for the second time. The groom was a New Orleans dress manufacturer, Myron Futterman, born in 1903 and thus fourteen years older than Jane. The age difference was part of a pattern. It may seem like a psychological cliché, but Jane clearly wanted an older man to compensate for her absentee father and her so-called adoptive father, whose pursuit of a dead-end career in local politics left no time for her. What Futterman wanted was a stay-at-home wife; what he got was an actress hell-bent on a movie career. The marriage was short-lived, lasting only 29 June 1937–6 December 1938.

Another failed marriage, another divorce. No time for tears. It was back to work. Jane had been loaned out to Universal for a ridiculous melodrama, *The Spy Ring* (1938). She may have been the female lead, but the character was simply a plot peg in a war preparedness film (spies working for an unnamed but readily identifiable—at least in 1938—country, determined to steal an anti-aircraft device). Jane did what she was required to do, which was the equivalent of the advice given to community theater newcomers: "Learn your lines and don't walk into the furniture."

The Spy Ring is one of those films whose importance, however minimal, derives from the director, Joseph H. Lewis, responsible for such film noir classics as *My Name Is Julia Ross* (1945) and *Gun Crazy* (1949). Lewis knew he was making a no-frills quickie. His rationale was simple: Make it as short as possible. "Wherever I could, I cut words out, and told it silently through the camera." Even at sixty minutes, *The Spy Ring* was not short enough.

In 1938, Jane may have wondered about her status at Warners. The new kid on the block was Priscilla Lane, whom the studio had elevated to high second tier. Priscilla would never make grand tier, where Bette Davis, Kay Francis, and Olivia De Havilland were ensconced. Jane would get there, but not for a decade. She had resigned herself to waiting—besides, she was only twenty-one.

From all the hoopla, one would think it was Priscilla's time. She was one of the three Lane sisters, a group that also included Rosemary and Lola. Rosemary may have been the most talented (she starred on Broadway in *Best Foot Forward*). Lola, with her sultry looks, could have joined the ranks of film noir's dark ladies. But Priscilla had a wholesomeness that audiences found refreshing. As Warners' resident virgin, she offset the studio's stereotyped tough dame, personified by Glenda Farrell, Ann Sheridan, Kay Francis, Ann Dvorak, and Joan Blondell.

Lane was cast as the female lead in *Brother Rat*, the first of four films in which Jane and Reagan appeared together. For Jane, the picture came at the right time. Now living on 3350 W. Ninth Street, she was valuable enough to Warners for her name to appear in 50 percent type size (the same as that used for the comparative newcomer Reagan). Still, she had to test for the part of Claire. When production head Hal Wallis was satisfied, Jane was put on salary, originally at two hundred dollars a day for five and a half days—which turned out to be eighteen days. Not bad for a secondary role, particularly for someone who had only been at the studio for two years.

Originally, the female lead was to have been Olivia De Havilland at a salary of ten thousand dollars. Either De Havilland passed on the role, or Warners thought she was better suited to *The Adventures of Robin Hood* (1938). The part went to Priscilla, who did not get ten thousand dollars.

Wallis's only criticism of Jane was not her acting, but her wardrobe, which was "too smart and too cute for the character she is playing . . . a plain, unattractive girl." He had to admit, though, that she looked "gorgeous," unlike Priscilla, who was "rather short and plump" and, in one outfit, "dumpy looking." Jane was playing a chemistry major, and her wardrobe was modified to suit the character. She may not have looked "gorgeous," but she certainly was not dumpy.

Brother Rat is set at the Virginia Military Institute, the title taken from the vernacular for a cadet. Although the film is dedicated to VMI, Warners played it safe by adding a disclaimer stating, in effect, that the cadets' antics were simply a way of letting off steam, in no way implying a relaxation of discipline. However, one would never know it from the frat house behavior in the dorm. The film was adapted from a hit play of the same name that ran on Broadway from December 1936 to May 1938, racking up 577 performances. The play's director was the legendary George Abbott, always addressed as "Mr. Abbott" and known for his ability to pace a production so that there would be no loss of momentum. To him, fluidity was all.

Comedy was not the forte of the film's director, William Keighley, who was better at melodrama, especially crime films (*G-Men*, *Bullets or Ballots*, *Each Dawn I Die*). While *Brother Rat* was a stage farce, the movie belonged somewhere between farce and romantic comedy. *Hamlet's* Polonius, who had names for such hybrids, might have called it "romantico-farcical"— in this case, more farcical than romantic. Eddie Albert reprised his stage role as the hayseed cadet, "Bing" Edwards, a mediocre student but an outstanding athlete. In the play, Albert was the lead, but in the film Priscilla Lane was top billed, followed by Wayne Morris as the VMI cadet in love with her; Jane Bryan, Albert, Reagan, and Jane. Albert, Bryan, Jane, and Reagan stole the film from the leads, waiting off camera until it was time to enter the movie. When the time came, they took over—not to upstage the stars, but to resolve the action. A tepid romance between a stolid Morris and a chirpy Lane—who sounded as if she believed the bluebird of happiness was in everyone's back yard—could not compete with a clandestine marriage (Albert and Bryan), a pregnancy (Bryan), and possible expulsion (Albert).

In the stage version, Jane's character was named Claire Ramm and played by Mary Mason, a versatile but now forgotten Broadway and radio actress, whose stage career lasted from 1927 to 1942. For the film,

"Ramm" became "Adams," which was more in keeping with Anglo-Saxon last names like Randolph, Edwards, Crawford, Andrews, and Scott.

Jane was still a blonde when she played Claire, a bespectacled, scholarly chemistry student bent on becoming a bacteriologist. As Claire and Dan (Reagan) discover each other, they glow with the innocence of first love, making their relationship more appealing than that between a child of privilege (Lane) and a brash cadet (Morris).

The *Brother Rat* subplot generated far more interest. The audience rooted for Albert, hoping he would be able to graduate—which he does after Jane preps him for a chemistry final. The audience also rooted for Jane and Reagan, who represented another kind of innocence: the awkwardness that comes when mutual attraction turns serious, and neither party is sure of the next move. In a sweetly seductive scene, Jane removes her glasses, causing Reagan to see her in a different light. When he does, Jane tosses the glasses on a cot. Perhaps that was the scene that inspired one critic to describe Jane as "cutely intriguing."

Reagan and Jane looked as if they enjoyed the farcical moments, particularly when Jane, in the dorm tutoring Albert, has to leap onto a bed, pulling the blanket over her to avoid detection. Jane and Reagan would have more opportunities to demonstrate their comedic skills—separately, for the most part. Initially, Reagan was pegged as a lightweight, and Jane as the quick-with-a-quip girl. Reagan would gain stardom before Jane did, showing his serious side in *Knute Rockne-All American* and *Kings Row*. Jane would have to wait until 1945, when she was loaned to Paramount for *The Lost Weekend*, and the following year to MGM for *The Yearling*, which brought her an Oscar nomination. Recognition came in 1949, when she won an Oscar for *Johnny Belinda*, after which came a rash of undemanding light comedies and a few dramatic surprises, until she entered the new mass medium of television as her friend Loretta Young had done.

Meanwhile, it was more of the same. *Brother Rat*'s success prompted a sequel, the labored *Brother Rat and a Baby* (1940), which was shot in four weeks (3 October–30 October 1939) and featured the same sextet: Lane, Morris, Bryan, Albert, Reagan, and Jane. The billing remained the same, except that this time Jane's name preceded Reagan's. Morris and Reagan are in New York, Albert and Bryan in Tennessee. When Albert becomes a serious candidate for the position of VMI coach, he and Bryan hop a bus to New York with their appallingly cute baby, Commencement (as in "graduation"). The child swallows quarters and wedding rings, causes a model ship to fall off a mantle, and mangles

Reagan's sketches (he's an illustrator). Morris is more abrasive than he was in the original, and Albert's cluelessness is less humorous. Lane's effervescence had lost its fizz, and for some reason the former Claire Adams became Claire Terry. The few scenes Jane and Reagan had together required her to make a play for him. Reagan resorted to his all-purpose reaction of biting his lip, which could indicate puzzlement, annoyance, or confusion. Jane had little to do, but poor Reagan, after discovering what Commencement has done to his illustrations, screams at the top of his lungs and collapses on a sofa—doing neither with much comic aplomb, perhaps owing to Ray Enright's direction. Enright, like Keighley, excelled at melodrama (*Angels Wash Their Faces*, *The Wagons Roll at Night*, *Thieves Fall Out*) and especially westerns (*Trail Street*, *Return of the Bad Men*, and the uncommonly brutal—for 1948—*Coroner Creek*). But *Brother Rat and a Baby* was an alien species. Enright was so exasperated by the script that he put it in overdrive, speeding through it, letting Reagan and Morris bellow their lines and allowing Commencement to take up too much screen time, perhaps hoping that the child's antics would make audiences forget what a mediocre film they were watching. Neither actors nor script mattered. The star was Commencement, who ends up as the sole human passenger (there is also a bull dog) on a plane to Peru, where, naturally, he warms the hearts of Peruvians and becomes a media figure.

Warners had already entered its boxing phase (e.g., *Winner Take All* [1932], *The Life of Jimmy Dolan* [1933], *The Irish In Us* [1935]) when it decided to make *Kid Galahad* (1937), with Wayne Morris as a bellhop turned boxer, Edward G. Robinson as a fight promoter, and Bette Davis as his mistress. The film ends tragically with a fight fix gone bad, resulting in Robinson's murder and Davis walking into the night as she did that same year in *Marked Woman*. The next two "Kid" films would be more upbeat: *The Kid from Kokomo* (1939), in which Morris once more donned boxing gloves, and *Kid Nightingale* (1939), with John Payne inheriting them. In *The Kid from Kokomo*, Jane was billed fifth after May Robson in another *Lady for a Day* (1933) makeover, this time as a petty thief hired by a fight manager (Pat O'Brien) to masquerade as the long-lost mother of the title character, a promising boxer (Wayne Morris). It was Robson's movie; the actress was in full gallop, charging through the film like a thoroughbred and leaving everyone else behind. Jane was a budding journalist, assigned to do a story on "The Kid," which naturally led to romance. This was another shoot that often required Jane, despite her billing, to be on the set for the entire day:

- 20 December 1938, 9:00 a.m.–5:30 p.m.
- 22 December, 9:00 a.m.–12:21 p.m.
- 23 December, 10:30 a.m.–6:00 p.m.
- 24 December, 9:00 a.m.–3:30 p.m.
- 29 December, 9:a.m.–4:30 p.m.
- 30 December and 3 January 1939, 9:00 a.m.–6:00 p.m.
- 6 January, 5:00 p.m.–9:00 p.m.

The Kid from Kokomo's significance derives primarily from Dalton Trumbo's script. Trumbo was the best known of the Hollywood Ten—eight writers (Samuel Ornitz, Albert Maltz, Herbert Biberman, Alvah Bessie, Ring Lardner Jr., Lester Cole, John Howard Lawson, and Trumbo), one director (Edward Dmytryk), and one writer-producer (Adrian Scott)—who stood by their First Amendment rights when they were subpoenaed to testify before the House Committee on Un-American Activities (HUAC) about the so-called communist subversion of the motion picture industry. Trumbo was cited for contempt, imprisoned, and blacklisted. He practiced his own form of subversion, using fronts and pseudonyms, until 1960, when Otto Preminger hired him to adapt Leon Uris's *Exodus* and Kirk Douglas to adapt Howard Fast's *Spartacus*.

If there is any leftist propaganda in *The Kid from Kokomo*, which netted Trumbo a mere $750, only a witch hunter could find it. Although Trumbo extols small town life and exposes the dark underside of professional boxing (hardly a revelation), he respects his characters, who emerge as decent people—some down on their luck and reduced to thievery, but eventually redeemed by Trumbo's humanistic vision.

Kid Nightingale was completely apolitical. John Payne and Jane co-starred—he as the title character, an aspiring opera singer; Jane as an aspiring pop singer. It's literally love at first sight, with the two using their eyes as semaphores—Jane enticingly and Payne abashedly, like a schoolboy seeing his first female nude in an art book. Suckered into the fight racket, Payne is touted as "Kid Nightingale, the Swinging Singer," at which point the plot became so porous that you could peer into its interstices. Payne wins the championship, but his future as an opera star and Jane's as a pop singer disappear beneath the wave of euphoria that the writers expected to sweep over the audience. THE END came on so abruptly that by the time everyone filed out of the theater, they forgot the unresolved subplot.

Jane had the dubious honor of bringing the Torchy Blane series to an end in *Torchy Plays with Dynamite* (1939), the weakest of the lot. Where

Glenda Farrell could project an image of a savvy reporter at home in a high testosterone newsroom— becoming one of the boys while remaining a girl—Jane sported a wardrobe that only a graduate of the Columbia School of Journalism with well-heeled parents could afford. Perhaps not feeling at home in the role, she conveyed cleverness through widened eyes, as if to suggest that she had just hatched a brilliant scheme—in this case, getting herself arrested so she could be incarcerated in the same prison as the girlfriend of a notorious bank robber. Reporters will go to extremes for a story, and Torchy is no exception—except that Jane's prison looks like a college dorm with bars. An unconvincing escape and a wrestling subplot constitute the climax, in which the robber is apprehended, and Tracy and her fiancé (Allen Jenkins) use the reward money for a down payment on a home.

Jenkins, a reliable character actor, looked as if he could be a garbage collector or repairman. But as a male lead opposite Jane? To fans of the Torchy Blanes, Jane and Jenkins were a mismatch. Glenda Farrell and Barton McLane were the anointed couple. When Lola Lane and Paul Kelly replaced them in *Torchy Blane in Panama* (1938), the intriguingly aggressive Lane and the tough talking, square-jawed Kelly made a believable pair, dressed as if they belonged to the working class. But Jane looked like she bought her clothes at a department store where there was no bargain basement. She could handle sequels and remakes, but not a series associated with another actress.

Warners thought there was still some life left in a Torchy Blane-type private eye. In *Private Detective* (1939), Jane, in the title role and blonde again, solved a complicated custody suit involving a couple whose five-year-old son is heir to a fortune. The villains wear tailored suits, Jane's police detective fiancé is charmingly clueless, and Jane barely escapes carbon monoxide poisoning. Jane acquitted herself professionally, sounding and acting as if she *could* work for a detective agency. Her no-frills wardrobe helped. But Warners did not see any future in a female detective series, and Jane went back to the contract player's bullpen. As a Warners recyclable, Jane could end up in any kind of a movie—original, remake, or series finale. She had no intention of going down in film history as the last of the Torchy Blanes, even though she was—and in a film that was the least memorable of the series.

When MGM showed no interest in making a sequel to *Tugboat Annie* (1933), Warners bought the rights. Tugboat Annie, the feisty lady of the Norman Reilly Raine's series that ran in the *Saturday Evening Post* in the late 1920s, was modeled on the Norwegian born Thea Christensen

Foss, founder of a tugboat company in Tacoma, Washington. The series inspired MGM's *Min and Bill* (1930), with Marie Dressler as the queen of the waterfront and Wallace Beery as her boozy consort and co-owner of their towing and salvage operation. With Dressler's death in 1934, MGM was no longer interested in Annie, and there was no one else on the lot with Dressler's earthiness. After buying the rights, Warners discovered that it also did not have an Annie. Wisely, the studio signed Marjorie Rambeau, who played an alcoholic in *Min and Bill*. Rambeau was an earth mother like Dressler—although Rambeau's Annie was more of a Mrs. Malaprop ("octoroon" for "octogenarian") and less of a dockside diva than Dressler, whose Annie was a grand dame in work clothes.

Tugboat Annie Sails Again (1940) finds Annie, now a widow, trying to run the business, with Reagan as her assistant engineer, while battling her competitor (Alan Hale, whom no one can hate). Reagan and Jane, who plays the spoiled brat of a shipping tycoon, were cloned from the characters played by Robert Young and Maureen O'Sullivan in the MGM original. The script provided Jane and Reagan with a "meet cute," with her backing into his car and sending it off a pier. Car fanciers need not worry. Jane has it dredged up and repainted, contritely returning it to Reagan, and then pushing him off the pier as punishment for the public spanking he gave her. Such a display of pettiness does not augur well for a romance, even though she jumps in to rescue him. But Jane makes amends by working as a swab on Annie's tugboat and learning how the other half lives. She matures, Reagan cools off, and Annie saves her towing company by citing an obscure article of maritime law, which keeps Hale from putting her out of business. Jane and Reagan squared off against each other effectively, but no one ever wins in this kind of agon because each is too exhausted to continue fighting—and so they marry and then resume the battle.

Tugboat Annie Sails Again made no demands on Jane. Reagan had a chance to strip off his shirt twice, in case a second look was needed. Good torso, forgettable movie, but first-rate Rambeau. It was not an easy shoot. Some of the actors had to work nights to bring the picture in on time. Jane's dive from the pier required four takes, ruining the same number of dresses. But the most telling information in the *Tugboat Annie* production file comes from the salary breakdown. Jane, Reagan, and Hale were contract talent. Rambeau was outside talent. Still, Hale—in what can only be considered a supporting role—made $10,000, while Jane, Reagan, and Rambeau netted $2,160, $3,330, and $8,333, respectively. Reagan's stock had risen at the studio, compared to Jane's. Hers would climb, but not for a few years.

Warners was a man's studio, unless you were Kay Francis. Olivia De Havilland, or Bette Davis. Occasionally, a production file will include the stars' salaries. There is often a disparity between contract talent and outside talent, and between actor and actress. Salaries were not always commensurate with either role or billing. In *Larceny, Inc.* (1942), Edward G. Robinson headed the cast, followed, in order, by Jane, Broderick Crawford, Jack Carson, and Harry Davenport. Robinson received $100,000; Jane and Harry Davenport each received $7,500, although hers was the bigger role; while Carson was paid $4,900. Crawford, on the other hand, made $20,000.

The highest salaries in *Casablanca* (1942) went to director Michael Curtiz ($73,400) and producer Hal Wallis ($52,000). The actors' salaries were not entirely determined by billing. Humphrey Bogart was followed by Ingrid Bergman, Paul Henreid, Claude Rains, and Conrad Veidt. Bogart and Henreid were contract talent receiving $36,667 and $25,000, respectively. The outside talent was Bergman, Rains (an odd designation for a Warners regular), and Veidt. Although Veidt's was a supporting role, he made the same as Bergman, $25,000, with Rains getting $22,000 for a much larger role. The ultimate irony is that Bergman was paid the same as third- and fifth-billed actors.

Chapter 3

Jane and Ronnie

ON 20 FEBRUARY 1948, MICHAEL DRAKE OF NEW HAVEN, CONNECTICUT, read that Jane and her third husband, Ronald Reagan, were divorcing. He immediately dashed off a letter to gossip columnist Hedda Hopper, who was so well known that a letter addressed to "Hedda Hopper, Hollywood Blvd., Los Angeles, Calif." managed to reach her. "Maureen and Michael will never have parents like Jane and Ronnie," Drake lamented.

It was "Jane and Ronnie," not to mention Maureen, born a year after their marriage, and Michael, adopted in 1945. To Drake, the Reagans were the model Hollywood family, personable and scandal-free. The parties were not Jane Wyman and Ronald Reagan, but Jane and Ronnie. The same held true with Elizabeth Taylor; regardless of who her husband was at the time, she was always "Liz." When she was married to Richard Burton, they were "Liz and Dick." Similarly, Rosalind Russell was always "Roz," Dean Martin "Dino," Dorothy Lamour "Dottie," Ann Sheridan "Annie," and Frank Sinatra "Frankie," "Ol' Blue Eyes," or, in the 1940s, "The Voice." On the other hand, neither Joan Crawford nor Joan Fontaine was a "Joanie," and Katharine Hepburn was never "Katie." To the press and the public, Jane and Ronnie were the perfect couple. Neither was Hollywood royalty, accorded the spotlight and red carpet treatment. They were working actors, leading a normal life by Hollywood standards. Warners did not have to cover up indiscretions or place them on suspension. If they had not gone into pictures, one could easily imagine Jane in Broadway musicals, and Reagan as a professional athlete, sportscaster, or rancher.

Although Reagan was born in Tampico, Illinois, about a two-hour drive from Chicago, this was only his birthplace. Jane had greater feeling for St. Joseph, having lived there for fourteen years. Reagan's memories of Tampico were understandably hazy. John Reagan, his father, was a combination shoe salesman and store manager. His mother, Nelle, the parent to whom Ronald felt closer, supplemented the family income with earnings from needlework and dressmaking. The Reagans were an itinerant family, eventually settling in Dixon, Illinois, some forty miles from Chicago, in 1920, when Ronald was going on ten. If Ronald felt an attachment to any town, it was Dixon. Compared to Tampico (technically a village), Dixon was a metropolis with a much larger population, theaters that he frequented, and a high school from which he graduated. Although he had attended various grade schools before the family settled in Dixon, Ronald was not aversely affected by his father's tendency to relocate.

Jane, on the other hand, understood desertion and privation, living briefly with her birth parents before she was deposited with another couple consisting of a coldly indifferent husband and a wife who was a stage mother. And yet the drive that Emma Fulks instilled in Jane brought her to the base of the pyramid that looms before every hopeful. Jane climbed doggedly until she reached the summit, where she was rewarded with four Oscar nominations and one Oscar.

Although Reagan worked in the same media as Jane—film and television—he never garnered any Oscar nominations, much less an Oscar, yet he went on to much greater fame. In 1940, one could hardly envision Ronald Reagan as governor of California or president of the United States. A local politician, perhaps, or a member of Congress—maybe even an Olympic swimmer. While still in grade school, he proved to be an excellent swimmer, eventually becoming a lifeguard. In high school and college, he played football. Like many young athletes, Reagan had a touch of the showman. He went out for dramatics at Dixon High School; at Eureka College, he did the same. At nineteen, he was cast as Thyrsis in Edna St. Vincent Millay's antiwar play, *Aria da Capo*. Thyrsis was a shepherd in Greek pastoral poetry, but Millay's Thyrsis does not have a drop of bucolic blood. A boundary dispute with Corydon, another shepherd, is decided in favor of Thyrsis, ceding him the water rights, which he refuses to share. But when Corydon discovers precious stones on his property, Thrysis's greed leads to a double murder: Thyrsis poisons Corydon, who in turn strangles Thyrsis. To Reagan, Thyrsis was just a lead in a weird play. Few nineteen-year-olds would think of water rights as a metaphor for the source of conflicts that have set countries against each other: land, natural resources, fuel lines, tribal dominance, self-determination, governance, and religion.

Ronald Reagan was also a natural politician. In 1928, his first year at Eureka, the college president, Bert Wilson, was disturbed by Eureka's declining enrollment and embarked on a radical reconfiguration of the college. These changes would have resulted in the cancellation of some courses the students needed for graduation. Reagan, then a liberal, received an ovation for his speech in support of a student strike. Wilson resigned, and no programs or courses were cancelled. Reagan discovered a form of celebrity more exciting than curtain call applause in the response of his fellow students, many of whom had never seen him on stage or even cared about theatre, but were impressed at the sight of one of their own stepping out of their midst—like Thespis, emerging from the chorus to become the first actor. Politics or acting? Reagan enjoyed both. Getting elected to the college senate, Eureka's equivalent of the more familiar student council, was just the beginning.

But graduation meant job-hunting. With a sociology major and an economics minor, Reagan was not exactly marketable, particularly during the Great Depression. Still, neither Jane nor Reagan stood in bread lines or went on relief. Jane began doing bit parts in 1932 and was a full-fledged lady of the chorus when Warners signed her in 1936, a year before Reagan made his film debut. After graduating from Eureka, Reagan had no trouble finding work in local radio, first in Davenport, Iowa, then at WHO in Des Moines, where he met Joy Hodges, a singer at the same station. In February 1937, Reagan persuaded WHO to send him to Catalina to report on the Chicago Cubs, who were in spring training there. The trip was a pretext; he really wanted a movie career.

Reagan's only contact was Hodges, who was then under contract to RKO. After advising him to remove his glasses, Hodges introduced Reagan to her agent at the Meiklejohn Agency, which, coincidentally, represented Jane. In 1937, at twenty-six, Ronald Reagan became a contract player at Warners. It took Jane four years to receive billing. Reagan got it in his first film, *Love Is on the Air* (1937), perhaps because as a former radio announcer he seemed right for a role that required him to unmask a gang of criminals during a broadcast. The *New York Times* (12 November 1937) ran a cursory review, mentioning no one by name—including the female lead, June Travis, who was not an unknown. Hal Wallis, Warners production chief, was also unimpressed, dismissing Reagan as "a hick radio announcer." Regardless, the studio made use of Reagan's broadcasting skills by using his voice for the radio announcer in *Hollywood Hotel* (1937), *The Amazing Dr. Clitterhouse* (1938), and *Boy Meets Girl* (1938).

Three years later, Wallis changed his mind after seeing Reagan as George Gipp in *Knute Rockne-All American* (1940). "Marvelous," Wallis wrote in his autobiography, *Starmaker*. From then on, the hick radio announcer was "my friend, Ronnie Reagan." Wallis does not mention Jane at all in *Starmaker*, even though he produced several of her films, including *Brother Rat*, *The Kid from Kokomo*, *My Love Came Back*, *Brother Rat and a Baby*, *Larceny Inc.*, and *Princess O'Rourke*. The omission was understandable; Wallis simply did not take her seriously as an actress, nor, for that matter, did Warners. And when *The Lost Weekend* (1945) converted the skeptics, it was a year after Wallis left Warners to become an independent producer at Paramount.

Marriage Is a Private Affair (1944) may have been the title of an MGM movie, but in Hollywood, little is private. Even when a version of the truth is offered, it rarely appears in unadulterated form. Did Ronnie propose to Jane, Jane to Ronnie, or did Jane resort to drastic means to wangle a proposal out of him? Shortly after the Reagans left the White House in January 1989, biographer Edmund Morris had lunch at the Bel-Air Hotel with Nancy (identified in the text as the "former first lady"), who provided him with a startling bit of news: Reagan married Jane out of sympathy after she tried to kill herself. Startling? Yes. Accurate? Undetermined. Morris consulted the *Brother Rat and a Baby* (1940) production file and discovered that on 4 October 1939, one day after filming began, Jane was hospitalized with "stomach cramps." "Cramps" was often used as a euphemism in the daily production reports to explain an actress's absence because of menstrual problems. Whether "stomach cramps" was also code for a drug overdose or a legitimate diagnosis is unknown. If it was an overdose, Warners knew how to keep such information from the public. If it was a gastrointestinal problem, it was short-lived; Jane finished the picture and went on to act in five more that were released the following year.

One could speculate indefinitely on Nancy's allegation. Was Jane so desperate to marry an actor whom she considered a superior that she attempted suicide to snare him? Was it merely a ruse? Was Nancy repeating an ancient rumor that she accepted as fact? Is there any connection between 1 October when Jane separated from Futterman and 4 October when she was hospitalized? Was it the aftereffects of a troubled marriage, perhaps, that caused acute colitis? As for Jane's desire to remarry, she may have decided that the columnists were right about Reagan and herself being an item. There was not as much of an age disparity (six years) as there had been in her first two marriages. Two stars, same studio was good press. One thing is certain: Reagan gave Jane a fifty-two carat amethyst engagement ring, which is not the sort of present a man gives a woman he is marrying out of sympathy. Although the truth will probably never be known, it is difficult to imagine Jane's resorting to such an extreme form of trickery—or to imagine Reagan's falling for it. Jane was too tough-minded and success-driven to endanger her life; Reagan, too image-conscious to turn stooge. Joy Hodges, who was herself attracted to Reagan, told Morris that when she discreetly suggested marriage, claiming that they would make a good team, Reagan replied, "Why, honey, I'm in love with Jane Wyman." And Jane was in love with him—for a time. Unfortunately, marriage was not her strong suit. There would be five in all: Eugene Wyman, Myron Futterman, Ronald Reagan, and Fred Karger— whom she married in 1952, divorced in 1954, and remarried in 1963, only to divorce again in 1965. This second time, however, Karger divorced *her*.

Jane hoped that her marriage to Reagan would be a "till death do us part" relationship. Warners hoped so, too. In fact, the studio played matchmaker once Jane and Reagan had become an item. When Louella Parsons heard the news, she added the two to her "Hollywood Stars of 1940 on Parade" for appearances in San Francisco, Philadelphia, and Washington, D.C. The two-month tour, mid-November 1939–January 1940, was conceived as a showcase for young performers such as Susan Hayward, Joy Hodges, Arlene Whelan, and June Preisser, a former vaudevillian and acrobat with an ebullient personality who proved to be an audience favorite. Jane got some laughs for one of her comic routines with Reagan, whom *Variety* described as "deft, and obviously at home on a stage." Audiences, however, were unimpressed. None of the troupe conformed to the image of a Hollywood star. The tour did not advance anyone's career. Other than Jane and Reagan, only Susan Hayward became a star—as well as an Oscar winner for *I Want to Live!* (1958). Although 1940s Paramount would have been a perfect fit for Preisser, the studio had its own "blonde bombshell" in Betty Hutton, whom it chose to promote, relegating Preisser to programmers like *Sweater Girl* (1942), which at least showed off her dancing ability.

Jane and Reagan were back in Los Angeles in time for their wedding on 28 January. Since Jane's previous marriages were civil, a church wedding meant little to her but much to Reagan, who had been raised in the Christian Church (Disciples of Christ), a form of Protestant Christianity that espouses the basic tenets of the faith: God as creator of heaven and earth, Jesus as Son of God, baptism, the Eucharist, evangelism, and the fellowship of man. Like other denominations, the Christian Church has its own hierarchy, but unlike Roman Catholicism, there is no pontiff or college of cardinals.

It was important to Nelle that her son be married in the faith. Thus Rev. Cleveland Kleihauer, the pastor of the Hollywood Beverly Christian Church, performed the ceremony at Wee Kirk O'Heather at Forest Lawn Cemetery in Glendale, a reconstruction of the church in Glencairan, Scotland, where the beloved Annie Laurie was said to have worshipped. If Jane was superstitious, she would have questioned the setting: a church located on the grounds of the final resting place of such Hollywood royalty as Marie Dressler, Lon Chaney, and Irving Thalberg (to be joined later by Joan Blondell, Spencer Tracy, Walt Disney, Humphrey Bogart, Robert Taylor, Clark Gable, and Carole Lombard, among others). This was the same cemetery from which her father-in-law, Ernest Wyman, had been buried a year earlier, and the same church that was the scene of Jean Harlow's funeral in 1937. Nelle Reagan may have chosen it because there was Scottish blood on her grandfather's side. But Jane was too happy for morbid thoughts. If others were married in such a setting, why not her and Ronald Reagan? Besides, she resolved, this would be the last time she would say "I do." But it wasn't.

Since Jane always referred to Emma Fulks as her mother, and to Emma's daughter, Elsie, as her sister, the press noted that Jane's "sister," Elsie Wyatt, was matron of honor. Jane, a mink hat resting gently on her blonde hair, wore a long-sleeved satin gown and carried a mink muff with an orchid corsage pinned to it. Reagan, his hair looking pomaded, wore a dark suit with a boutonniere. In the absence of a father, Louella Parsons's third husband, Harry Martin, gave Jane away. Convinced that her talent caravan brought the two together (which it did, physically), but not realizing that they needed no prodding from her, Parsons hosted the wedding reception at her Beverly Hills home on Maple Drive.

After a short honeymoon in Palm Springs that was marred by rain, the Reagans went back to work at Warners. Nineteen forty was not Jane's best year. Her releases were negligible and included *Brother Rat and a Baby*, *An Angel from Texas*, *Flight Angels*, *My Love Came Back*, *Gambling on the High Seas*, and *Tugboat Annie Sails Again*. Reagan's included two that turn up regularly on *Turner Classic Movies*: *Knute Rockne-All American*, in which he played Notre Dame football legend George "the Gipper" Gipp and had a death scene that was so restful it made dying seem like the answer to an insomniac's prayer, and *Santa Fe Trail*, in which he played a young George Custer, overshadowed, as was everyone in the film, by the towering presence of Raymond Massey as John Brown, looking as if he were Jeremiah incarnate.

In the *Los Angeles Examiner* (22 May 1949), Louella Parsons recalled Jane's vowing in 1940, "I'm going to be as good as Ronnie." If Jane considered Reagan a better actor than herself, it was because her deep insecurity caused her to doubt her talent, especially in view of the roles she had been given. After 1945, she thought differently—and so did the public.

Chapter 4

Slouching toward Stardom

BY 1952, JANE COULD COMMAND $150,000 A PICTURE, BUT IN 1940, she was just supporting cast or a B-movie female lead. In *An Angel from Texas* (1940), she and Reagan were supporting players; the leads were Eddie Albert, Rosemary Lane, and Wayne Morris. *Angel* was an adaptation of George S. Kaufman's 1925 comedy, *The Butter and Egg Man* (the title refers to the backer of a Broadway show). Since moviegoers were more familiar with "angel," which carried the same meaning, the title was changed to *An Angel from Texas*. But the plot remained the same: A Texan (Albert) is so desperate to further the career of an aspiring actress (Lane) that he invests in a play, "The Greater Glory," which is so mired in the excesses of nineteenth-century melodrama that it can only succeed if played as farce. As the producers, Morris and Reagan were such smooth talkers that hooking a rube like Albert took little effort. Morris delivered his lines staccato style with no loss of clarity; Reagan tried to do the same, but was less successful. Jane, who played Reagan's wife (as she was when the film came out in June 1940), was more comfortable with the pace and the character. She played the wise woman who bails out a Broadway neophyte and his fiancée as if she were performing a humanitarian gesture, when in reality she is educating her venal spouse in basic ethics. Still a blonde and becomingly costumed, Jane reveled in sparring with Reagan and rescuing him from the shady—and potentially dangerous—types that prey upon theatre novices. A surprise ending awaited those unfamiliar with the play. Although "The Greater Glory" turns out to be plagiarized, it proves such a hit that everyone makes a profit. So much for intellectual property.

In *My Love Came Back* (1940), it was Albert's turn to be demoted to supporting cast, with Jane elevated to fourth place. The stars were Olivia

De Havilland and Jeffrey Lynn, who was good-looking and virile yet sensitive—the perfect partner for the fair, but not ravishingly beautiful, Olivia. Despite the billing, no one was the star. *My Love Came Back* was a diversion with some attractive performers who looked upbeat enough to keep audiences interested in a plot that took so many detours it could never get back on the main road. The narrative kept bifurcating so often that it was impossible to isolate the main plot, which seemed to be the perennial debate about high vs. pop culture.

Olivia, Jane, and Albert are students at a music academy who decide that injecting a bit of jazz into the classics could prove lucrative. Olivia, the most talented of the trio, captures the fancy of the school's newly appointed president (Charles Winninger), who makes her his protégée, much to the resentment of his son and daughter. Unable to distinguish between paternalism and infidelity, the children assume the latter. Jane, blindingly blonde, has little to do other than to convince the audience she is a student of the violin. She succeeded admirably, as did Olivia, who had to work harder at the fingering because of her close-ups. As in most comedies, misunderstandings are clarified, couples resolve their differences, and a world turned upside down spins itself upright.

Jane may have had second billing in *Gambling on the High Seas* (1940), but her character existed solely as the love interest for Wayne Morris, an investigative reporter out to expose shipboard gambling, The movie is typical of the way Warners treated low-wattage contract players, and for a time Jane fell into that category. They were the equivalent of floaters who would sub for an executive secretary one day and be back in the secretarial pool the next.

Until *The Lost Weekend* established her as a true actress, Jane was in a state of billing arrhythmia, pushed back to fifth place in *Flight Angels* (1940). The title was a clever metaphor for what were then known as stewardesses. However, frequent flyers would have thought otherwise after sitting through a film that featured husband-hungry flight attendants and pilots with women at every airport. Romance eclipsed the more serious theme of perfecting aircraft to guarantee the safety of passengers and crew during periods of poor visibility. Warners apparently thought that a blonde Jane could be a brassy wisecracker like Glenda Farrell and Joan Blondell. She was indeed brassy, but likeably so—a tomboy in a uniform, making a play for Wayne Morris, whom she nearly topples off a ladder. She can also get down and dirty, even engaging in a realistic catfight with Margot Stevenson. Again, Jane and Morris provided the laughs, lightening up the main plot involving a pilot's (Dennis

Morgan) retinitis, which could spell the end of his career. Hint: Glasses do the trick.

Although not exactly a war preparedness film, *Flight Angels* was released in May 1940, eight months after World War II erupted in Europe. At the end, the film did a 180-degree plot spin, with Morgan planning to fly for China, then under siege by Japan. But then he is conscripted to train American flyers—but for what? Obviously, to become professional pilots like himself, or, should it be necessary, to serve their country in a war it would soon enter.

The roles did not get much better in 1941. In *Honeymoon for Three* (1941), Jane was fourth billed after Osa Massen. The Danish-born Massen was one of Hollywood's lesser lights, who appeared in a few respectable films (e.g., MGM's *A Woman's Face*, RKO's *Deadline at Dawn*) before moving over to television for the rest of her career, which ended in the early 1960s. The *Honeymoon* leads, Ann Sheridan and George Brent, were not marquee magnets, but their names counted for something at the box office. *Honeymoon* could not conceal its stage origins, Allan Scott and George Haight's Broadway hit *Goodbye Again* (1933), concerning a philandering novelist (Brent) and his secretary (Sheridan), who has to extricate him from his amours. Like Jane, Sheridan could handle repartee, while Brent simply delivered his lines. As Massen's cousin, Jane, in hats that Dashiell Hammett would have called "perky," did the "big brown eyes" bit, tossing off her lines like confetti—unlike Brent, who treated his as if they were excess baggage. Although Sheridan was the star, Charlie Ruggles, as Massen's befuddled husband, and Lee Patrick, as a mother who names her children after her favorite authors (one is called Booth Tarkington), walked off with the film.

Of all the inferior B movies Jane made at Warners, *The Body Disappears* (1941) is the nadir. Those expecting a thriller instead saw a travesty of James Whale's *The Invisible Man* (1933). The film, which should have aroused the ire of medical schools, begins with an ill-fated bachelor party, at which Jeffrey Lynn's behavior is so gross that his friends, all future doctors, decide to teach him a lesson. After he passes out, they deposit him in the lab. Edward Everett Horton, an eccentric scientist who has developed a serum to produce invisibility, assumes Lynn is a corpse and proceeds to render him headless, like Claude Rains in *The Invisible Man*. Jane played Horton's daughter, so smitten with Lynn, even in his headless state, that she takes the serum, too. "Dumb!" is the only plausible reaction to this oleo of science fiction, romance, mystery, and slapstick. Worse is the racially offensive portrayal of Horton's factotum, played by the African American Willie Best as the stereotypical witless, eyeball-popping black that was also the lot of Mantan Moreland in the Charlie Chan series. Naturally, Lynn and Jane regain their heads—as if there was any other alternative. However, in *The Body Disappears*, the special effects overshadowed everyone: Jane, Lynn, and even Horton, whose quirkiness, if used intelligently, might have resulted in a wacky comedy—but only if the headless scenes were kept to a minimum. But they weren't; they were the gimmick that sold the tickets.

The Body Disappears is atypical of the Warners B movie. Jane could have protested and gone on suspension, as De Havilland did when she turned down the female lead in *Flight Angels* (which went to Virginia Bruce), but Jane was not a big enough star, and other studios weren't knocking at her door. On the positive side, at least she had a chance to wear a stunning white backless gown. Although Warners released several movies in 1941 in both the A and B categories, for which she would have been suited (such as *Navy Blues*, *International Squadron*, and *Kisses for Breakfast*), the roles went, respectively, to Ann Sheridan, Julie Bishop, and Jane Wyatt. Jane could have also handled the leads in *Strange Alibi* and *Bullets for O'Hara*, both of which were played by Joan Perry, who shortly thereafter became Harry Cohn's second wife.

Another problem facing Jane was her status at the studio. She had been at Warners since 1936 and was still low second tier. Warners had other talent to promote—for example, Julie Bishop, Joan Leslie, Brenda Marshall, and Alexis Smith. Jane was the all-purpose actress, the perennial sidekick—girl friend—hoofer—reporter-private eye-bookworm-flight attendant-ingénue. You name it, Jane played it—except for femme fatales and high-end hookers.

Her next part was a poster girl for Uncle Sam. Once the Selective Training and Service Act was passed on 16 September 1940, the studios, always headline-conscious, added the draft to the list of short-term plots, which gave way to combat and home front films after Pearl Harbor. Of the few draft-themed films, Abbott and Costello's *Buck Privates* (1941) was the best, followed by the Bob Hope and Danny Kaye vehicles, respectively, *Caught in the Draft* (1941) and *Up in Arms* (1944). Although many men found little humor in conscription, Hollywood decided that grumbling about it was both unmanly and unpatriotic; instead, the studios mined the draft for whatever humor could be extracted. A hierarchy emerged, with enlistees at the top, followed by draftees and 4Fs. Draft dodgers were lumped with traitors until they redeemed themselves. Although *For Me and My Gal* (1942) was set during World

War I, its release coincided with another world war, which became the subtext. Similarly, *Sergeant York* came out shortly before Pearl Harbor, yet seemed to have little to do with the war in which Alvin York distinguished himself, and more to do with the one that America was about to enter. When Gene Kelly in *For Me and My Gal* brought the lid of a trunk down on his hand to avoid being drafted, one could imagine him being hissed in some quarters. But Judy Garland shames him into enlisting, and eventually the draft dodger turns hero. Alan Ladd as the title character of *Lucky Jordan* (1942) wanted nothing to do with the military, even cajoling an elderly woman into posing as his dependent mother so he could get a deferment. But he, too, turns patriotic when she is brutalized by Nazi thugs.

Although World War II had broken out in Europe eighteen months before *You're in the Army Now* went into production, America was still encased in an isolationist cocoon. But the county emerged on 7 December 1941, determined to avenge the "day that will live in infamy." When *You're in the Army Now* opened at New York's Strand Theatre on 20 December 1941, the day had already occurred. Perhaps some moviegoers found humor in the picture, but for wartime America, the film was a relic from another age. In fact, some may even have wondered how the Allies could ever win if the characters played by Jimmy Durante and Phil Silvers were representative of the US Army.

In *You're in the Army Now*, Jane had another phone-it-in role as a colonel's daughter in love with Regis Toomey, a relationship that has to be taken on faith, since virtually nothing is made of it. Even their kiss, at the time the longest ever seen on the screen, was as passionate as a peck on the cheek. The stars were Durante and Silvers, in that order, as bumbling vacuum cleaner salesmen. In 1941, Durante was better known than either Silvers or Jane. He was a popular radio (*The Chase and Sanborn Hour*) and Broadway (*Strike Me Pink, Jumbo, Red, Hot and Blue*) personality. But what really endeared him to the public was Rodgers and Hart's musical *Jumbo* (1935), an extravaganza produced by the great Broadway showman Billy Rose. Envisioning a mass audience for the show, Rose arranged for parts of it to be transmitted over NBC radio on Tuesday evenings.

In the 1930s, Durante was a familiar name in three media: stage, radio, and film, the last of which he entered in 1930, making his debut in *Roadside Nights* (1930). The real reason for Durante's star billing in *You're In the Army Now* was that he was also set to play the role of Banjo in *The Man Who Came to Dinner* (1941), a more prestigious Warners release. Durante would never get a part like Banjo again, or have access to screenwriters like the Epstein brothers, who adapted the Kaufman and Hart stage classic.

In 1941, Silvers's reputation was essentially that of a burlesque and vaudeville comic. He entered the movies in 1941 with *Tom, Dick and Harry* and *You're in the Army Now*, whose opening scene—a vacuum cleaner demonstration—plays like a vaudeville skit. Warners must have seen something in Silvers, perhaps as Durante's sidekick in a series that would rival Universal's Abbott and Costello comedies. Durante and Silvers, however, never teamed up again. Each went his own way. Durante appeared in MGM musicals and eventually on television with *The Jimmy Durante Show* (1954–57). Silvers stayed on at Warners for *All Through the Night* (1942), adding a touch of the zany to a Nazis-in-America movie. Then it was freelance time: Fox's *Orchestra Wives* (1942) and *Coney Island* (1943), and Columbia's *Cover Girl* (1944) and *A Thousand and One Nights* (1945). Next, he went to Broadway, where he earned a Tony for his performance in *Top Banana* (1952), in which he recreated some classic vaudeville and burlesque sketches. But it was Silvers's television series, *The Phil Silvers Show* (1955–59), in which he played the irrepressible Master Sergeant Ernie Bilko, which made him a household name.

For two years, 1955–57, both Durante's and Silvers's shows were on the air, Durante's on Saturdays, Silvers's on Tuesdays. Durante did vaudeville routines in a nightclub setting; Silvers did slapstick and wreaked havoc at Fort Baxter. Durante and Silvers did not need Cole Porter to tell them to "Be a Clown." Motley had long been their dress of choice.

By the time *You're in the Army Now* was released, the one song that was supposed to sell it, "I'm Glad My Number Was Called," sung lustily by men—with Jane chiming in—had become an anthem for some, a lament for others, and a shrug of the shoulders for the rest.

For Reagan, the war meant a hiatus in his movie career. He, too, had to serve his country, but not in combat—and not when his studio needed him to complete a movie. The week before Pearl Harbor, Jane and Reagan were winding up one picture and starting another. Reagan was completing *Juke Girl* with Ann Sheridan, scheduled for a May 1942 release. His next film, *Desperate Journey*, was set for a three-month shoot, January–April 1942. Jane was even busier. In December 1941, she was working in two films, finishing *Larceny, Inc.* at her home studio before reporting to RKO for *My Favorite Spy*. In January 1942, it was loan-out time again for a supporting role in the Fox musical *Footlight Serenade*. If the war seemed remote to Jane, the press of work was part of the reason; the other was that she was a new mother. Reagan would don the uniform; Jane, the costume.

If Jane thought she had had her fill of espionage in Universal's *The Spy Ring*, another cloak and dagger movie was awaiting her at RKO. *My Favorite Spy* (1942) exploited the country's fear in the months following Pearl Harbor of Nazi operatives, joining the ranks of Universal's *Saboteur*, Warners' *All Through the Night*, and Paramount's *Lucky Jordan* (all 1942 releases). All three portrayed an America infiltrated by enemy agents in the service of a foreign country that, although unspecified, was clearly Germany. The domestic Nazis looked like gangsters, dark-suited thugs with dour faces and merciless eyes. The ringleader was the exception, a stylish dresser with a continental accent.

In *My Favorite Spy*, Jane was third billed, after Ellen Drew (on loan from Paramount). Accorded the name-above-the-title treatment was the popular band leader Kay Kyser, whose befuddled expression suited his character: a similarly named band leader accidentally drafted and then recruited as a counter-espionage agent, with Jane (a blonde again) as his contact. The director was Tay Garnett, whose forte was high drama (*China Seas*, *Mrs. Parkington*, *Valley of Decision*, and especially *The Postman Always Rings Twice*). If *My Favorite Spy* did not seem like a Tay Garnett film, that was because it was a Harold Lloyd production. If Lloyd, one of Hollywood's great silent comics, had directed—or, ideally, starred in—*My Favorite Spy* (at forty-nine, he was only a few years older than Kyser), he might have gone lighter on the mayhem. There are just so many times Kyser can conk the spies on the head as they bob up and down under a stage curtain. Lloyd could—and did—perform sound comedy. But to RKO, he was just a producer, and *My Favorite Spy* became his last production.

The movie was by no means an embarrassment. There were a few good songs by Johnny Burke and Jimmy Van Heusen, and there was Jane, game as ever, first seen in a beret and trench coat, and then outfitted in a classier wardrobe. Unfortunately, the writers tossed her character into the discard bin. As long as Kyser was reunited with his wife (Drew), who cared about his more interesting partner in espionage? Drew was in the final scenes—not Jane, who was in character limbo.

Jane's sole 1942 Warners release was *Larceny, Inc.*, in which she was another plot catalyst in a movie dominated by a star who never received an Oscar nomination, yet who was one of the finest actors on the lot: Edward G. Robinson. Although the public perceived Robinson as a "tough guy" who could work both sides of the law (gangster, con artist, G-man, detective), he was actually a stage-trained actor, a 1913 graduate of the American Academy of Dramatic Arts, who enjoyed a successful career in the theatre before going to Hollywood, where he came to prominence in *Little Caesar* (1930). Rarely was Robinson able to show his comedic side. *Larceny, Inc.* was an exception, as was *The Amazing Dr. Clitterhouse* (1938), in which he played a physician writing a book intended to help criminologists understand the criminal mind. In order to lend the book credibility, Clitterhouse himself becomes a criminal and eventually a murderer, killing a gangster (Humphrey Bogart) who intended to lock Clitterhouse in a cold storage vault where he would have frozen to death. There is no jail time for Clitterhouse, who is acquitted for ridding society of a menace. *Clitterhouse* was atypical Robinson, who had never exhibited such theatricality before, brandishing a cigarette like a drawing room habitué, and looking delightfully effete with carefully lined eyes and shadowed eyelids.

Larceny, Inc. was another "crime does not pay, but sometimes neither does the criminal" movie. It was basically a caper film, with Robinson as an ex-con who plans to rob a bank next door to a luggage shop, first buying the store and then digging a tunnel from its basement to the bank vault. Jane's role was purely functional, a gangster's daughter who looks upon Robinson as a father figure because he befriended her own father. Although Jane was never teamed with Robinson again, they were an endearing surrogate father and daughter. Unaware of Robinson's intentions, Jane mounts a hugely successful sales campaign for the luggage store with the help of a salesman (Jack Carson, always a good comic foil). Robinson delivered some of the lines as if he were playing Noël Coward. Examining a wallet in the luggage store he plans to buy, Robinson inquires, "Crocodile?" "No, alligator," the owner says. "Oh, domestic," Robinson replies disdainfully, putting the wallet back as if his hands had been sullied. Robinson also knew how to deliver a double entendre without leering. When the owner of a lingerie shop (Barbara Jo Allen, better known as Vera Vague) flirts with him, purring, "I hope you drop in and look at my lingerie," Robinson, no stranger to hidden meanings, comes back with, "I hope you drop by and look at my trunks."

Larceny, Inc. began shooting on 3 November 1941. On Monday, 8 December, it was business as usual at Warners. Jane and Robinson were on the set from 9:00 a.m. to 5:00 p.m. That same day, a reader, Stephen Karnot, submitted a synopsis of an unproduced play, "Everybody Comes to Rick's," to Hal Wallis and Jack Warner. The film became *Casablanca*, Wallis's choice of title.

For Reagan, January 1942 meant *Desperate Journey*, followed by a stint in the service. For Jane, it meant another loan out, this time to Fox, where she had worked twice before: first as an unbilled lady of the chorus in *King of Burlesque* (1936), and then as a streetwise flier in *Tail Spin* (1939). Although Jane had little to do in *Footlight Serenade* (1942), a minor Betty Grable vehicle, she would not even have been in the picture if it had been filmed as planned.

In 1939, Kenneth Earl and Fidel LaBarba's treatment, "A Straight Left (1939)," was under serious consideration at Fox, whose head of production, Darryl Zanuck, had been, among other things, an amateur boxer. Zanuck was drawn to the main character, a supposedly washed-up fighter who makes a spectacular comeback and then disappears, presumably drowned under mysterious circumstances. If the treatment had continued to final screenplay stage, someone along the way would have realized that it had the makings of an effective melodrama, not a musical. LaBarba was the one who should have known; he was a professional boxer, as well as a Stanford University alumnus. His journey from the Bronx to Stanford to Hollywood was American Dream material. But in golden age Hollywood, one pair of writers was often shadowed by another working on the same project. The expectation was that, between them, a filmable script would emerge. The final credits attribute the screenplay, "based on a story by Fidel LaBarba and Kenneth Earl," to Robert Ellis, Helen Logan, and Lynn Starling, If anyone contributed to the authenticity of the fight sequences, it would have been LaBarba, whose life merited a movie of its own. All *Footlight Serenade* owed to the treatment was the boxing background.

Footlight Serenade was a tour de force for Victor Mature, playing a self-enraptured boxer recruited for a musical revue with a boxing match finale. It is hard to know if Jane appeared in the dance sequences. Since she wore the costumes, one would assume she did so—but without the identifying close up. Jane, however, was too good a dancer to need a double. As was common during the palmy days of the movie musical, the dance sequences were filmed in long shot, so it was obvious that a double was not being used. If a double were needed, a medium shot would be followed by an extreme long shot with similarly dressed performers, whose features were not delineated. Grable did not need a double, either; she was a talented dancer and a high kicker—not to mention having the best legs in Hollywood. Jane had some wise cracks and one good scene in which Mature needed money to foot a bill. Jane emptied her purse on a table, but realizing there was no money among the contents, discreetly pulled a bill from her bra.

Jane had one line that, in retrospect, appears quasi-prophetic. When Grable announces that she has become the star's understudy, the cynical Flo (Jane) replies, "You have as much of a chance being [the star's] understudy as I have of being the first lady." Jane might have become the first lady if she had remained married to Ronald Reagan, although it is doubtful that the White House would have been her kind of home.

Chapter 5

Reaganless for the Duration—and Beyond

IF JANE WAS EVER MEANT TO MARRY, IT WAS NOT TO ANY OF HER four husbands. As reductive as it sounds, she needed a man—if not older, then at least understanding and supportive—who could provide the security she lacked in both her youth and her profession. A mere sixteen when she married the twenty-seven-year old Eugene Wyman, Jane at least got a star's surname out of it. Myron Futterman was another older man, fourteen years older, to be exact. The couple married on 29 June 1937 and separated on 1 October 1938. Jane filed for divorce, citing as reasons Futterman's refusal to have children, his unflattering comparisons of her with his first wife, and his criticism of her behavior at parties, where, he claimed, she enjoyed dancing and flirting with other men. The *Los Angeles Times* (6 December 1938) reported that "Mrs. Futterman's testimony was corroborated by that of her maid, Margaret Johnson." That was enough for Superior Judge Caryl M. Sheldon, who granted the divorce.

What Futterman interpreted as flirtatiousness was effusiveness. Some of this was natural; some of it was a form of protective coloration to conceal Jane's frustration at being pegged as less-than-star-quality when she knew that there were reserves within her yet to be tapped. And so she put on a happy face, which was de rigueur in a business where a long face is the kiss of death. Dancing had been her childhood refuge; if she reveled in it (which Futterman did not)—particularly with men who could dance as well as she—she did so because dancing allowed her to lose herself in a world where nothing mattered but the music, the rhythm, and a partner who felt the same way. That was not the partner she would find in Ronald Reagan. In 1940, "[Jane] saw Reagan as a father figure and she admired his mind." In Reagan, she was not looking for a dancing partner—a father figure, perhaps. Since she had had no luck with her first two father figures, she may have wondered if the third would be the real thing. Jane Wyman did not understand that she had transcended the need for a surrogate of any sort. All she needed was a movie that would upgrade her to first class.

Years later, Futterman had no regrets about his short-lived marriage to Jane: "I knew that Jane would some day be a great actress. It meant everything in the world to her. She had such great determination . . . . Determined as she was to become a big Hollywood star, she vowed to let nothing stand in her way." And nothing did, including husbands.

When Jane married Ronald Reagan in 1940, his career was moving faster than hers. Reagan at least had appeared in two significant pictures, *Knute Rockne-All American* and *Santa Fe Trail*. In the former, as George Gipp, he had one of the most beatific death scenes in film history, ranking with the transfigured expirations ("death" is too crass) of Greta Garbo in *Camille* (1936) and Bette Davis in *Dark Victory* (1939). Looking serene and about to slip away into endless sleep, Reagan opened up the tear ducts of men who had steeled themselves against emotion. In the second film, he was a dashing George Custer, looking as if he was born to the uniform. Although his was a supporting role, he was in stellar company with Errol Flynn, Olivia De Havilland, and Raymond Massey.

None of Jane's 1940 movies could compare with Reagan's then modest achievements. Until 1943, the situation remained unchanged. In 1941, Jane languished in *Honeymoon for Three*, went headless in *The Body Disappears*, and was overshadowed by Jimmy Durante and Phil Silvers in *You're in the Army Now*. Meanwhile, Reagan had leads as a crusading journalist in *Nine Lives Are Not Enough* (1941), and as a brash Yank in the RAF who redeems himself by sacrificing his life in a suicide mission in *International Squadron* (1941), one of Warners' "war preparedness" films, released in October 1941. But in an America that was a few months away from war, *International Squadron* seemed almost prescient.

Nineteen forty-two was Reagan's year, not Jane's. She may have had the female lead in *Larceny, Inc.*, but there was only one true lead, Edward G. Robinson, who personalized the film. In *My Favorite Spy*, it was Kay Kyser's turn. If Jane felt she was not getting her due, she had some consolation in being a mother, which is what she wanted when she married Futterman. Maureen Reagan was born on 4 January 1941, which seemed almost like a birthday present for Jane, who was born on 5 January 1917. But Jane was disappointed, declaring, "I wanted a boy." Jane's letdown may explain why Maureen never thought of her as the paragon of motherhood. But motherhood alone would not satisfy Jane. She still yearned for a career—just not in the kinds of movies she was being given, which did not tap the well springs of her talent.

In 1942, Reagan was on a roll. The previous year, he had been considered for the important, but secondary, role of Drake McHugh in *Kings Row*, in addition to being the dark horse in the running for the lead, Parris Mitchell, which went to Robert Cummings. Remarkably, Cummings gave a Reagan-like performance: blazingly sincere and colorless. In retrospect, Reagan's landing his part was not that much of a coup. During the studio years, the casting director—in this case, Warners' Steve Trilling—would generate a list of every available contract player, as well as outside talent, who seemed suited to a role. The list could be long and varied. In Reagan's case, it meant being lumped together with Dennis Morgan, Eddie Albert, John Garfield, Arthur Kennedy, and Michael Ames. Interestingly, executive producer Hal Wallis chose Reagan on the basis of his performance in *International Squadron*, which revealed another side of the actor whom Wallis had previously dismissed as a lightweight. Drake was Reagan's most famous role, not so much because of his acting, but because a line in the film became the title of his autobiography, *Where's the Rest of Me?* (1965), a question he asks in *Kings Row* after realizing that his legs have been amputated. The title was fodder for satirists, but it did not keep Reagan from the White House.

That Reagan was a candidate for the Humphrey Bogart role in *Casablanca* might seem like Hollywood folklore, but it is true. On 8 December 1941, Warners story analyst Stephen Karnot was assigned to synopsize an unproduced play, "Everybody Comes to Rick's." Three days later, his synopsis was ready, along with a suggestion that it was "a box office natural" for Bogart, Cagney, or Raft as the lead, and possibly Mary Astor as the heroine. A few weeks later, the trades announced the cast: Ann Sheridan, Ronald Reagan, and Dennis Morgan, playing the characters that eventually became Ilsa Lund, Rick Blane, and Victor Laszlo. This was a common case of reckless publicity, typical of the times. Casting coups were often erroneous—and in this case the scoop was bizarre. As the script developed, it took on a more continental flavor, requiring European-accented actors for Ilsa and Laszlo, actors such as Michelle Morgan and Jean-Pierre Aumont. But that is the way casting lists were created: first inclusive, then exclusive, and finally decisive. Wallis created the perfect trio: Bogart, Bergman, and Henreid.

If Reagan had read the *Hollywood Reporter* on 5 January 1942 and learned that he was cast in *Casablanca*, along with Ann Sheridan and

Dennis Morgan, he would have shrugged. He knew both of his co-stars, and he had worked with Sheridan in *Kings Row* and *Juke Girl*. As for *Casablanca*, it was just another Warners melodrama. He had *Kings Row*; that was what mattered. But what mattered even more was his importance to Warners, which by 1940 was considerably more impressed with him than it had been when he arrived three years earlier. *Knute Rockne-All American* and *Santa Fe Trail* enhanced his public image, fortified by a face without guile that made him the quintessential American, although both films, particularly the latter, were historically flawed—but only to historians, not to the general public. And as America moved inexorably toward involvement in a world war that was already raging in Europe, two of Reagan's pre-Pearl Harbor movies, *Murder in the Air* and *International Squadron*, released in June 1940 and October 1941, respectively, would have seemed, in retrospect, no different than the kinds of movies that saturated the screen during the war years. Spies and saboteurs were featured in *Murder in the Air*, and deadly aerial warfare in *International Squadron*. Now Reagan was perceived as defender of his country and martyr for the cause, even though in *International Squadron* his character dies atoning for the deaths of two flyers caused by his recklessness. Still, to his squadron, he died a hero—if heroism is death as self-imposed penance.

On 7 December 1941, Reagan was a few months shy of thirty-one and still draftable. Regardless, Warners considered him valuable enough to obtain a temporary deferment for him through April. He still had to finish *Desperate Journey*, and eventually did. *Desperate Journey*, released in September 1942, was one of the few films of the period—such as *All through the Night, The Hitler Gang*, and *Once Upon a Honeymoon*—that portrayed the Nazis as dunderheads. As a result of Reagan's roles in *Secret Service of the Air, Murder in the Air*, and *International Squadron*, he had become the studio's flyer of choice. Thus it was natural for him to play another Yank in the RAF, who outwits his Nazi captors seeking information about his aircraft by making up names for airplane parts, such as "thermacockle" and "dermodyne." Reagan was more convincing in that sequence than he was in the remainder of the film, which was chiefly an action adventure, where combat noise was punctuated with periodic snippets of dialogue that today would pass for sound bytes. One of Reagan's most memorable lines occurs when the car the other flyers commandeered runs out of gas. It's a tense moment, because they are being pursued by a Nazi patrol. Reagan ruefully remarks that it's the first time he ever ran out of gas with a couple of guys. That one line presaged a "mission accomplished" ending for the desperate journey.

To many draftees, Reagan seemed to have an easy time. For the next three years, he was part of the First Motion Picture Unit of the Army Air Corps, narrating and appearing in propaganda films like *Rear Gunner*, released in theaters as short subjects. Although he never saw action and, in fact, never left the States, to the public, he was serving his country— as evidenced by the shorts made by the unit. Only a few would have wondered how he managed to star in *This Is the Army*, which came out in August 1943. But that, too, was a flag-waver and, in its own way, a recruitment film with an Irving Berlin score.

By the time Reagan was discharged in September 1945 with the rank of captain, Jane's career, which for the past two years had been in low gear, accelerated rapidly with *The Lost Weekend*, already in the theaters when Reagan returned to their home in the Hollywood Hills. His discharge was facilitated by William Guthrie, a former FBI agent and now location director at Warners, who convinced the military that the studio had several films planned for Reagan that were of "vital interest to the war effort"—an odd phrase, since the war was over, unless the military was expecting Hollywood to gird itself for the next. But whatever those films were, they never materialized. Reagan's name did not appear on the screen again until 1947.

Chapter 6

Angel in the Wings

WHEN JANE MADE *PRINCESS O'ROURKE* (1943), SHE HAD NO IDEA IT would represent a turning point in her career, nor did she give the movie any thought. Olivia De Havilland was the star, and she was only supporting cast. At least Jane had the female lead in *Crime by Night* (1944), a perfect example of the eccentric billing that existed during the studio years. Jane, now a brunette, was first billed under the title, followed by Jerome Cowan, Faye Emerson, and Eleanor Parker. Cowan was really the star. He was never a leading man, but he was a fine character actor. In 1944, Jane was better known, which explains the billing. Cowan played a smooth-talking detective, hired to solve an axe murder. All Jane had to do as Cowan's assistant was deliver snappy dialogue, come up with some smart deductions, and eventually give Cowan a kiss that will make her more than his amanuensis. Although *Crime by Night* was not a series film, it recalled the detective-secretary teams in Fox's Mike Shayne and Columbia's Ellery Queen movies.

Whether Warners knew it or not, it was following the repertory model, in which an actor could play a lead in one production and a supporting role in the next. Faye Emerson nabbed the lead in *Danger Signal* (1945), but Eleanor Parker had already co-starred with John Garfield in *Between Two Worlds* (1944) the same year she was cast in a throwaway role in *Crime by Night*. Jane may have enjoyed seeing her name at the head of the cast, even though it was below the title. All she did, however, was feed lines to Cowan, whom she had to kiss at the fade out to prove that love was possible between an employee and her boss, despite their age difference. At the time of the shoot, Cowan was forty-seven and not especially handsome; Jane was twenty years younger, and quite attractive. He looked his age; she didn't.

Jane had been in mind-numbing films before, but *Make Your Own Bed* (1944) was one of the worst. She was billed over Jack Carson, Warners' resident stooge-patsy-clown, in a role that had him running the gamut from befuddlement to self-assertion. Carson and Jane played an engaged couple—he, a detective, and she, his fiancée. The pair ends up posing as servants for a gunpowder manufacturer and his dithering wife. *Make Your Own Bed* was designed for anyone who finds humor in kitchen disasters, buzzers mistaken for phones, wrong doors, a standing joke about a double bed (the only clue to the title), and Nazi spies posing as radio actors. As if that weren't enough, the employer and his wife are so eager to keep the couple that they agree to take turns preparing the meals.

When *Make Your Own Bed* was released in spring 1944, Nazis had already been portrayed as buffoons, sadists, mass executioners, and rapists. They were never fully realized characters; investing them with the slightest bit of humanity would have been considered traitorous. They were either a source of menace (*Escape, Hitler's Children, Hostages, Till We Meet Again*) or ridicule (*All through the Night, Desperate Journey, The Hitler Gang,* and *Once Upon a Honeymoon*). In the Three Stooges shorts *You Nazty Spy* (1940) and *I'll Never Heil Again* (1941), the Stooges had the right idea: Make the Nazis look so cartoonish that fearing them would be like fearing a kid with a scary Halloween mask—particularly if the trick-or-treater came from next door. *Make Your Own Bed* operated according to the same premise, except that one had to sit through a tedious movie until the spies were unmasked.

Jane may have thought she had a better role in *The Doughgirls* (1944), except that it meant going back to fourth billing. First and fourth in the same year—and now with her name following Carson's. The cast was headed by Ann Sheridan, now low first tier, followed by Alexis Smith, Carson, and then Jane. It was strange casting, yet it illustrated Warners' ever-shifting hierarchy. Sheridan was adept at repartee, particularly zingers. She could also handle melodrama (*Nora Prentiss, The Unfaithful*). Jane was a more versatile actress, although she had yet to prove it. Warners was giving Alexis Smith the big build up. Smith could handle a song, as she proved in *San Antonio* (1945) when she delivered a memorable "One Sunday Morning," but for the most part she was the other woman or a high maintenance wife.

The Doughgirls was the movie version of Joseph Fields's play of the same name, which opened at the end of 1942 and ran for 688 performances. Fields, the brother of the great lyricist Dorothy Fields, was a highly successful playwright and director in the 1940s and 1950s. *The*

Doughgirls was Fields's third hit in a row, the others being *My Sister Eileen* (1940) and *Junior Miss* (1941), coauthored with his frequent collaborator, Edward Chodorov. However, Fields was the sole author of *The Doughgirls*, which, like his other two plays, became a successful movie.

The Doughgirls posed few problems for Warners, which knew, even before it bought the rights for $250,000, that the script had to pass muster with the Breen Office. The plot revolved around three couples, none of them legally married, who, for delightfully implausible reasons, find themselves in the same Washington, D.C., hotel suite. Both the play and the film were products of the war years and intended to have a limited shelf life. The play was studded with references that 1940s theatergoers would understand (Harry Hopkins, H. V. Kaltenborn, André Kostelanatz) but would go unrecognized in another era. The movie was less elitist, with references to the Roosevelts, meatless Tuesdays, Washington bureaucracy, rationing—and especially, the scarcity of hotel accommodations in the nation's capital.

Fields had a gift for topical humor and the twist-counter-twist plot (the couples finally are married, thanks to a Russian Orthodox priest). The James V. Kern-Sam Hellman screenplay reproduced Fields's plot, minus the swearing (mild as it was) and the implications of premarital sex (although only the women occupy the suite).

There was no way of disguising the fact that *The Doughgirls* was a single-set play with the action taking place in a Washington, D.C., hotel suite. Jack Carson and Jane have reserved the rooms, but discover that their suite has been usurped by two other couples, a Russian sergeant (played uproariously by Eve Arden with a smashing accent), and other sundry types, such as a sleep-deprived man, unable to get accommodations, who wanders into any room that is not locked.

The play was directed by George S. Kaufman, who moved it along for three acts without leaving the audience time to wonder why an impossible situation is resolved with a line or two of dialogue. The film's director, James V. Kern, who also coauthored the screenplay, was no Kaufman. He changed Jane's character, Vivian, from an ingénue to an airhead, whiny and witless, who has to deliver cringe-inducing lines that were never in the play, speaking them in a teenager's voice to suggest naiveté. Told she should record a statement verbatim, Jane replies that she recorded it word for word. The nadir of the action occurs at the end when Jane discovers that Alexis and her hero-husband have been invited to the White House for lunch with the Roosevelts. Jane affects a pixilated look, noting how much she enjoyed the president in *Princess*

O'Rourke. The line made her even more of a scatterbrain, since President Roosevelt does not appear in the film except as a presence. At least Jane got the last close up, her doll-like face filling the screen and looking quizzically at the audience, as if wondering how they could buy such silliness.

Although *The Doughgirls* turned a profit, it would have been a better film if it had retained the play's breeziness, or if Fields had adapted it himself. But at the time he was preparing to direct Arthur Miller's first play, *The Man Who Had the Luck,* which was a resounding flop. (Five years later, Arthur Miller won the Pulitzer Prize for *Death of a Salesman* [1949]). The reference to *Princess O'Rourke* was typical of Warners' self-promotion, a quality it shared with other studios that would toss in allusions to their earlier films. Rarely was the allusion as subtle as it was in Paramount's *Lady in the Dark* (1944), where Ray Milland whistled "Dream Lover" to Ginger Rogers, as if to remind her that two years earlier they made *The Major and the Minor,* in which the same song dominated the soundtrack. For the most part, such references did not require explication. Paramount's popular "Road movies" were known for their cross-references. At the end of *Road to Morocco* (1942), Dorothy Lamour remarks, "I have the strangest feeling that we've been through this before"—meaning the first two movies in the series, *Road to Singapore* (1940) and *Road to Zanzibar* (1941).

The Doughgirls was released in November 1944. Three months earlier, Jane had been loaned out to Paramount for a film that launched the second phase of her career: Jane Wyman as dramatic actress. When Jane was tapped to play Jack Carson's wife in *Princess O'Rourke,* she treated the job simply as a contractual obligation. By then she knew that despite having co-starred with Edward G. Robinson in *Larceny, Inc.,* there was no guarantee co-star status would continue. And, in fact, it didn't. Jane was relegated to fifth place in *Princess O'Rourke,* after Olivia De Havilland, Robert Cummings, Charles Coburn, and Jack Carson. For them, *Princess O'Rourke* was just another résumé entry. But not for Jane.

There never was any doubt that De Havilland would star as the European princess in exile (country unspecified) residing in a four-star hotel in New York with her uncle (Coburn), enjoying all the privileges of royalty except freedom. But Cummings was not Hal Wallis's first choice for De Havilland's deliverer, an air force pilot whose presence sets the princess-commoner plot in motion. Wallis would have preferred Reagan, Dennis Morgan, or even Franchot Tone. When none of them proved available, Cummings got the part. Wallis was not all that certain about

Jane, either; he was also considering Brenda Marshall, until he decided to go with Jane. Like Carson, she had her name in 50 percent type, as opposed to De Havilland's 90 percent, but it was still large enough to be noticed.

Princess O'Rourke is unusual in several respects. First, it employs the rich girl-poor boy plot, generally reserved for screwball comedy, where class poses no obstacle to true love. But *Princess O'Rourke* is not screwball. De Havilland could never compete with screwball heroines like Jean Arthur, Carole Lombard, Claudette Colbert, and Irene Dunne. She was a serious actress; comedy, unless it was romantic, was not her medium. And when she tried screwball in *The Well-Groomed Bride* (1946), she seemed to be slumming. Cummings, on the other hand, could do light comedy and lesser screwball (*It Started with Eve, The Bride Wore Boots, Tell It to the Judge, Marry Me Again*).

Princess O'Rourke was also a departure from royalty-commoner films like *The Student Prince, The Swan, Caravan,* and *Roman Holiday,* in which class is an insurmountable barrier. But this was wartime, and Hollywood had to keep up morale. Norman Krasna, who both wrote and directed the film, did not want a flag-waver finale, just a deus ex machina in the form of President Roosevelt. When Cummings is told that in order to marry the princess he must renounce his American citizenship, he declines, sounding not jingoistic but touchingly sincere in one of the film's quieter moments. But President Roosevelt solves everything, as if equalizing the classes is another form of lend lease.

Krasna's screenplay won the Oscar it deserved. His competition was four war-themed films, *So Proudly We Hail, The North Star, Air Force,* and *In Which We Serve,* none of which had that smooth blending of romance, poignancy, and optimism that 1943 audiences so desperately needed. *Princess O'Rourke* had its patriotic moments (few 1943 films did not), but one of them was uncommonly moving.

When writer-producer Charles Brackett and director Billy Wilder saw the film, what impressed them was the scene in which the two couples—De Havilland and Cummings, and Carson and Jane—are at a Chinese restaurant for what they hope will be a war-free evening. And it is, until Nan Wynn sings "Honorable Moon," a lament for a China valiantly resisting absorption into the Japanese Greater East Asia Co-Prosperity Sphere—a euphemism for becoming a satellite of imperial Japan. Jane is visibly moved by the song, which conjures up a war in which she could lose her husband (Carson), also an air force pilot. Carson, unaffected (or pretending to be) by the song, breaks the somber mood by asking Jane why she is wearing such a fancy dress. Fighting back tears, Jane quickly replies, "You know why, you big lug," and immediately suggests that they dance.

Brackett and Wilder were not the only ones impressed by Jane's performance. On 12 October 1943, Lt. James M. Wylie of the 705th Bomb Squad wrote to Jane, requesting a mascot for his crew. He wanted the dog in *Princess O'Rourke* who filled in for President Roosevelt's iconic Scottish terrier, Fala. Interestingly, Lt. Wylie did not write to De Havilland or Cummings, perhaps thinking that the down-to-earth Jane would not find the request presumptuous. Jane immediately had Prince O'Rourke, the offspring of Whiskers, Fala's stand-in, sent to the bomb squad, along with a message: "Very best wishes to you and crew. Jane Wyman."

Chapter 7

Highs and Lows

JANE HAD NO IDEA THAT THE RESTAURANT SEQUENCE IN *PRINCESS O'Rourke* would attract the attention of Wilder and Brackett. They were searching for an actress to play the female lead in *The Lost Weekend* (1945), which they were adapting from Charles Jackson's 1944 bestseller. Jane just did what the scene required. Realizing that the evening could be their last for the duration, she dressed elegantly, not expecting to hear a song about war-torn China. Even in a night on the town, she cannot escape the war that could leave her a widow. Her only solution is to steer her husband onto the dance floor so that she does not break down in tears.

The restraint Jane displayed in this role convinced Brackett and Wilder that they had found their Helen St. James. Brackett had a print of *Princess O'Rourke* screened for Paramount executives, who agreed that Jane was right for the part. She was not encumbered by the baggage of stardom; even better, she looked as if she could help a bedeviled man rid himself of his demons. Wilder and Brackett envisioned a woman of silent strength, who could reform a devious, self-destructive alcoholic by channeling her strength into him—not by commiserating with him or making light of his addiction, but just by being the still point of his boozy world. Thus they reworked the novel, so that the woman succeeds in her mission. Their ending was vastly different from that of the original, in which the man has no intention of abandoning the bottle. None of Paramount's contract players seemed right for the role. Claudette Colbert, then in her forties, was too old; Paulette Goddard's sexy image was at odds with the character; and Veronica Lake's signature peek-a-boo bang made her more of a pop icon than an actress. In *The Hurricane* and *Johnny Apollo*, Dorothy Lamour proved that she could handle serious drama, but

58

her plate was full with *Rainbow Island, And the Angels Sing* (both 1944); *Road to Utopia*, the underappreciated *A Medal for Benny*, based on a John Steinbeck story, and Mitchell Leisen's *Masquerade in Mexico* (all 1945), a remake of his 1939 masterpiece, *Midnight*.

On 21 August 1944, a Paramount loan out had been negotiated with co-star billing for Jane, whose name would appear under Ray Milland's in the same size print. Jane suspected that *The Lost Weekend* would be a career-booster. Although the film did not require an eye-catching wardrobe, she contacted William Meikelejohn, head of casting and talent, requesting her own makeup man and designer. When Meikelejohn refused, Jane persisted until Paramount's makeup artist, Wally Westmore, conceded. However, the studio's reigning costume designer, Edith Head, did not concede, having no intention of honoring a request from a loan out. The clothes did not matter; they were not designer label. Jane's character was a *Time* magazine researcher, whose only extravagance was a leopard skin coat, which became a major plot point when it brought her together with Don Birnam (Milland).

In the 1940s, strict fidelity to the novel would not only have been impossible, but would also have deprived Jane of a role that brought her to the attention of director Clarence Brown and the film that won her an Oscar nomination, *The Yearling*. Jackson's novel is told solely from Birnam's point of view, isolating the reader within his consciousness as he alternates between self-destructive lucidity and hallucinatory drunkenness. The ending is far from encouraging. After consuming two full glasses of whiskey, Birnam crawls into bed, pleased to have survived one more lost weekend. "No telling what might happen the next time but why worry about that?" An uncompromisingly faithful adaptation would have created a furor with Alcoholics Anonymous and other temperance groups. The film version had to give alcoholics—present, former, and recovering—something that offered them hope. Wilder and Brackett knew the novel could only be their point of departure.

Wilder and Raymond Chandler had just converted James M. Cain's *Double Indemnity* into a 1944 film noir, scuttling the ending in which a murderous couple—she dressed as a death goddess and he with an eventually lethal gunshot wound—prepare to take the big swim in an ocean where a shark eagerly awaits them. The film version ends with a love-death, in which the two shoot each other—she seriously wounding him, and he, the better shot, finishing her off.

Wilder and Brackett treated Jackson's novel the same way. The movie had to be geared to a mass audience and provide Jane with a more significant role than her character had in the novel—especially since she would be given co-star billing. Jackson's Helen was a stick figure, even lacking a last name. Unable to comprehend the extent of Birnam's condition, she can only offer sympathy and soothing clichés. The film's Helen has a last name, St. James. She does what Jackson's Helen cannot do, redeeming a man who defies redemption. Helen has a stature that she lacked in the novel, making it possible for Jane to show that she is truly Milland's co-star. Wilder and Brackett discarded the novel's finale, substituting a tripartite one that is completely original. First, Helen must talk Birnam out of committing suicide. Birnam had stolen her leopard coat and brought it to a pawnshop, where he intended to exchange it for the revolver he had previously hocked. Once Helen realizes he is serious, she tries to stall him. She locates a bottle of whiskey and persuades him to take a drink, even offering to join him. When that does not work, she argues with great conviction that if he had enough will power to reject her offer, he can cure himself by writing a novel based on the nightmarish events of the past weekend. Helen is not Don's sole redeemer; she shares credit with Nat the bartender, who arrives with Don's old typewriter. Now Don has no excuse. He sits down at the typewriter and begins a novel entitled "The Bottle." As the camera reverses the direction of the opening shot, panning right to left, from the back of the apartment building to the New York skyline, Don's voice is heard, pitying "the poor bedeviled guys on fire with thirst . . . as they struggle blindly toward another binge, another bender, another spree."

There was another reason a faithful film version of *The Lost Weekend* would have been impossible: its homoeroticism. In the novel, Don was expelled from the University of Pennsylvania for writing a love letter to another male student. One of the Greenwich Village bars Don frequents seems to cater to gays, although Jackson leaves the clientele to the reader's imagination. The closest the film comes to suggesting anything even vaguely homoerotic occurs in the alcoholic ward sequence. Don is attended by Bim, a male nurse (played with the right degree of sexual ambiguity by Frank Faylen), who calls him "baby." In the novel, when Don leaves the ward, Bim whispers, "Listen, baby . . . I know you." Jackson implies that there is another demon within him that needs to be exorcised, his repressed homosexuality, which others seem to sense. The joint combination of repression and alcoholism turned him into a failed writer, able to quote Shakespeare at length but not write anything of his own.

The screenplay, then, is a radical overhauling of the novel. For example, the coat check mix up at the opera does not occur in the novel, in which the reader never learns how Birnam and Helen met. In the film, they are both at a performance of *La Traviata*. The first act "Drinking Song" reminds Don of the bottle of rye in his raincoat pocket, as the swaying gowns of the women in the chorus dissolve to a shot of swaying raincoats in the coatroom. As Violetta and Alfred toast each other with champagne, Birnam envisions the bottle awaiting him. Rushing off after the first act, he hurries to the coatroom, expecting to claim his raincoat. When he is handed a leopard coat, he realizes that there has been a mix-up and he must wait until the opera is over for someone to be handed his raincoat. That someone is Helen. Don is the same crafty manipulator he was in the novel, but not the same pompous intellectual, lording it over the less educated who are unable to understand his allusions. Finally, there is the ending, the only one that a 1945 audience would find palatable—particularly after the hallucinatory scene in which Don, convulsed with DTs, sees a bat encircling the room as a mouse tries to wriggle out of a hole in the wall, but not quickly enough to escape the predatory bat that pulls it out and devours it.

Although Charles Jackson professed "to loathe & detest all that Hollywood represents," he seemed pleased with the film. Still, it saddened him when people congratulated him on his movie, rather than on the novel that inspired it. But the film was no more Jackson's than *Double Indemnity* was James M. Cain's. Both were Billy Wilder's recreations. *The Lost Weekend* won its share of Oscars: actor (Milland), director (Wilder), picture (Paramount), screenplay (Wilder and Brackett). Jane had a few more years to wait for hers.

After *The Lost Weekend*, Jane was scheduled for another loan out, MGM's *The Yearling*. But a production delay brought her back to Warners for a few scenes in *Night and Day* (1946), purportedly "based on the career of Cole Porter." "Career" was the right word; it had little to do with his life. His songs were treated as revue material, diversions for the watch checkers. *Night and Day* was a formula biopic. Throw in some familiar tunes, sexy chorines, a few specialty numbers, and sitting through a 134-minute movie won't be a total write-off. "Begin the Beguine" is given the Latin American treatment, the "tropical splendor" of the lyric translated into lush Technicolor, suggesting that the setting is a banana republic. The song is from *Jubilee* (1935), where it did not need kitsch to take its place among Porter's most sensuous ballads.

Naturally, liberties had to be taken with Porter's life. The average moviegoer would not suspect that Porter was gay. His marriage to Linda Lee Thomas led the public to assume he was heterosexual. It was a *marriage blanc*, one with no strings. Jane's character, Gracie, made little sense, but then, neither did the movie. Jane is first seen in a New Haven music hall, singing "I'm in Love Again" and looking like a real trouper. The voice was unmistakably hers, and the long shots proved that she did her own dancing. Her lessons at the Prinz Dancing Academy paid off. Since LeRoy Prinz staged the numbers, he went out of his way to showcase Jane's musical talent in her few scenes, which had nothing to do with the shows in which they were introduced. "I'm in Love Again" is sung early in the film when Porter was at Yale. The song is from *Greenwich Village Follies* (1924), which premiered a decade after Porter left Yale. There is no context for "Let's Do It," which is actually from *Paris* (1928). In the film, it becomes an impromptu piece that Jane virtually sight reads, gliding over the double meanings—the few that survived—and using her expressive eyes to show that she understood them.

The most flagrant violation of chronology occurs at the premiere of *See America First*. Jane is in the middle of "You Do Something to Me," performing it as if the musical stage were her natural habitat. Suddenly, men rush down the aisles handing out newspapers, whose headline, "LUSITANIA SUNK," sends the audience rushing out of the theater. Never mind that "You Do Something to Me" was from *Fifty Million Frenchmen* (1929). The headline responsible for the mass exodus implied that the show opened and closed the same fateful night. Actually, *See America First* ran for fifteen performances, opening on 28 March and closing on 6 April 1916; a German U-boat torpedoed the *Lusitania* on 7 May 1915. The character of Gracie was then downgraded, as if she were responsible for the show's failure. She is next seen as a member of the chorus, and finally as a gold-digger specializing in unsuspecting millionaires with European accents, each of whom she nicknames "Peaches," rather than attempt to learn their names.

Night and Day's significance has nothing to do with Porter or Jane, but with Mary Martin, who repeats her version of "My Heart Belongs to Daddy," which she introduced in Porter's *Leave It to Me!* (1938). On Broadway, Martin performed a genteel striptease while toying with Porter's discreetly risqué lyrics. In the film, she did more of a tease than a strip, but she still invested the lyrics with the same mock innocence that made her an overnight sensation in 1938.

One More Tomorrow was released in late spring 1946; *Night and Day*, two months later. Anyone who saw both films must have wondered if Warners had demoted Jane as punishment for her outstanding performance in *The Lost Weekend* at a rival studio. She had gone from co-star in *Weekend* to supporting cast, fifth billed, in *Night and Day* and *One More Tomorrow*. Her stint in *Night and Day* was LeRoy Prinz's inspiration. Since Jane had to wait until shooting began on *The Yearling* (and Warners had no intention of letting her remain idle), Prinz knew she was the only one at the studio who could give the musical numbers the verve and style they required. Jane did not consider Gracie *infra dig*; she responded to Prinz's staging as if she had always been a musical comedy star.

One More Tomorrow was another matter. It was finished two years before the release of *The Lost Weekend*, about the same time that *Princess O'Rourke* was nearing completion. Warners had no faith in the film, which was ready in June 1943 and sat on the shelf until the studio decided that it was 1946 or never. Warners chose June '46 for its release, making *One More Tomorrow* another of the summer's oubliette-ready movies, which included *Her Kind of Man, Janie Gets Married, Two Guys from Milwaukee*, and *Shadow of a Woman*. Warners expected all of them to break even, knowing at the same time that the reviews would range from lukewarm to negative. Those for *One More Tomorrow* were not even lukewarm; they were the equivalent of a cold shoulder.

As early as 1942, Warners, for some reason, was interested in remaking Philip Barry's play *The Animal Kingdom*, which RKO had filmed in 1932, with Leslie Howard recreating his stage role, Tom Collier, an idealistic publisher infatuated by the mercenary Cecilia Henry (Myrna Loy). But then the scales drop from his eyes, and he realizes that his true love is Daisy Sage (Ann Harding), his former lover. Both the play and the two film versions include the same third-act curtain line: Tom announces to Pat, his butler and drinking buddy (played engagingly by Jack Carson in the 1946 version), "I'm going back to my wife"—meaning not the gold digger but Daisy.

Why Warners wanted to remake *The Animal Kingdom* is hard to fathom. Ten years had elapsed since the RKO version was released back in the pre-code era. In 1942, the Production Code was in full force, making it impossible to replicate the ending of the original, which implied that cohabitation without a wedding band is preferable to marriage without love. In 1946, "I'm going back to my wife" could never be the fade-out line that it was in the 1932 version, which was far more faithful to the original. Instead, *One More Tomorrow* ends in anticlimax with a newspaper headline announcing Tom's divorce, clearing the way for his union with Daisy (now called Christie) to be legitimized.

Still, Warners forged ahead, perhaps because Hal Wallis, then production chief and a passionate theatergoer, was attracted to the play. He must have known that a remake along the lines of the original would raise the hackles of the Breen Office, unless Tom and Daisy/Christie were friends, not lovers. Nonetheless, a screenplay was ready by 26 September 1942. True to form, Joe Breen denounced it as "a violation of the provisions of the Production Code." The script was then purged of expressions such as "damn it," "damn right," "ravished" (as in "You look ravished"), and "Good Lord." Breen even found the line "We weren't hungry that morning" overly suggestive. Producer Henry Blanke complained to Jack Warner, now "Colonel" Warner, that the latest script by Helen Deutsch and Charles Hoffman was too faithful to the play, reflecting Barry's distinction between the two women in Tom's life: Daisy/Christie as more of a wife than a kept woman; and Cecilia more of a kept woman than a wife. The casting also reinforced this difference. Alexis Smith's Cecilia seemed more of a Park Avenue mistress than a publisher's wife with a home in the suburbs, while Ann Sheridan's Christie was more of a Connecticut homemaker than a back street lover.

Benjamin Glazer was brought in to ensure that the Tom-Christie relationship came off as purely platonic—as if there were any other possibility. The screenplay was ultimately credited to Charles Hoffman and Catherine Turney, with additional dialogue by Julius J. and Phillip G. Epstein, who were not at their best. *One More Tomorrow* was a lost cause, the victim of too many concessions that stripped the play of its urbanity and wisdom, until all that remained were the bare bones of Barry's triangular plot, minus the literary and musical allusions.

The time was advanced to 1939. En route to his Connecticut home, Tom (Dennis Morgan, who was no Leslie Howard) arrives to find it in darkness. Previously, an announcement came over the air about ominous events in Europe, which makes the darkness both a plot point (a surprise party) and a harbinger of things to come (World War II). After that, it was just a matter of democratizing Barry's play. Daisy, a fashion illustrator, became Christie, a magazine photographer and aspiring painter. Franc Schmidt, a concert violinist, was renamed Frankie Connors (Jane) and became Christie's assistant. Tom Collier went from a book publisher to the editor of a muckraking journal. Joe Fisk, Tom's novelist friend, was christened Jim Fisk (Reginald Gardiner, who looked more like a "Jim" than a "Joe"), one of the journal's writers and Frankie's fiancé-lover-significant other-whatever, who delivered his lines if he were in a Noël Coward or Frederick Lonsdale comedy. *One More Tomorrow* assumed audiences would accept a relationship between a perky Jane and a droll Gardiner. They didn't, the film sank, and *Princess O'Rourke, Make Your*

Own Bed, Crime by Night, The Doughgirls, and *The Lost Weekend* had already been released by the time *One More Tomorrow* arrived in summer 1946. Jane was then in Florida, completing a film that provided her with the most complex character she had yet played. Later came an even more demanding role, one in which she did not even speak. Why should she care about a movie she could barely remember?

Chapter 8

Going for the Gold

"JODY!" A WOMAN SHOUTS FROM THE PORCH OF A RAMSHACKLE house. The woman is Jane, barely recognizable at first. Her usually animated eyes are now those of a woman who has resigned herself to a life without prospects.

For the screen version of Marjorie Kinnan Rawlings's Pulitzer Prize winning novel, *The Yearling*, Jane was loaned out again, this time to MGM. Originally, MGM's own Spencer Tracy was slated for Penny Baxter, with Anne Revere, on loan from Twentieth Century-Fox, as Ma. Both could easily pass for salt-of-the-earth types. But although Tracy was box office, Revere, a fine actress who fell into oblivion during the period of the blacklist, was not. The director, Clarence Brown, happened to see *The Lost Weekend*. What he saw in Jane was similar to what Brackett and Wilder had seen in *Princess O'Rourke*. Brown never said so publicly, but that quality was obviously her ability to invest a role with truth and integrity, displaying a strength that her benign face belied. Jane always credited Brown with showing her how to play such a complex character as Ma Baxter. She did so not by resorting to emotional memory or improvisation, but by relaxing into the part: "He taught me that if you can relax before the camera, a character has a chance of getting through, becoming visible." Perhaps Jane gave too much credit to the director for teaching her something that she had been doing all along. On the other hand, in *The Yearling*, in which she was cast against type, Brown's advice might have alleviated Jane's anxiety about undertaking a role that was unlike any other that she had played.

The Baxters—Ma, her husband, Penny (Gregory Peck), and their son, Jody (Claude Jarman Jr. in his film debut)—live in the Florida scrub country. Ma is dressed like a frontier woman, who, even in an extreme

66

long shot, looked as if she had just arrived from John Ford country. And, in a sense, the Florida wilderness was a frontier, and the Baxters' twelve-acre farm, a clearing in the wilderness, lush and Edenic but populated by rattlesnakes and bears. Theirs was a community where men traded dogs for rifles—then resorted to hog stealing when the dog proved a disappointment—and where a trip to the general store was the highlight of the week.

Theirs was also an insular world in the literal sense. The Baxters regarded their farm as an island, a kind of jungle outpost, and venturing into the wilderness was neither an aesthetic experience nor a communion with nature. Nature was a force to be feared, particularly when the rains flooded the Baxters' cornfield and destroyed the crops. The natural world—the elements and the animals—were equivalent to the hostile tribes with which the settlers had to contend.

Naturally, Jane was both surprised and flattered by Brown's choice. By 1945, she had grown tired of her good friend-confidante, dutiful-but brighter-than-husband wife-ministering angel repertoire. Jane, always a character actress—even in a leading role—never was a prima donna like Bette Davis and Miriam Hopkins; when she cracked wise, she was genial and good natured, not biting or cynical. She sensed that there were other characters within her that the right script and director could bring forth, diversifying her mostly monochromatic portrait gallery. *The Yearling* provided the color and the recognition.

Unlike so many of Jane's other roles, Ma proved a challenge. Barely twenty-eight when shooting began, she looked forty, her hair lightened so she could be a convincing mother to the strikingly blond Claude Jarman Jr. Ma must behave as if she were sexually and emotionally frigid, incapable of showing affection to either her husband or son. Jane did not have to create her own backstory for the character. Clarence Brown did it for her, and all Jane had to do was to react—often with her face alone. Early in the film, we see the little cemetery on the Baxters' farm. The camera slowly pans the crudely inscribed gravestones, all with the Baxter name, stopping with a close up of Ma, who has come to visit the graves of the children she had lost. Hers is the face of a woman whose solution to grief is emotional detachment, and repressed maternalism is her way of masking her fear that the next grave could be Jody's.

Jane made audiences understand Ma, even though the character was hardly empathetic. When Jody adopts a fawn, it does not turn out to be another Bambi; rather, it leaps over the fence and devours the corn shoots, doing the same after the crop has been replanted. When Penny demands that Jody destroy the fawn, the boy cannot. When Ma pulls the trigger but only wounds the animal, Jody must put it out of its misery.

Jarman's was a spectacular debut. It was a great role for a ten-year-old from Tennessee with no acting experience. During *The Yearling* shoot, Jarman bonded with Peck so well that they acted as if they were father and son. If Peck seemed like a man of the wilderness, he did so partly because his father, a respected University of Michigan athlete, taught him to fly fish, shoot, and ride a horse. For Penny Baxter, Peck drew on his own boyhood, which became the character's as well. That Peck could play Lewt in *Duel in the Sun* (1946) and Jimmy Ringo in *The Gunfighter* (1950) so believably is a reflection of that mysterious process whereby an actor taps into his own experiences and transfers them to his character.

Jane, on the other hand, had no model for Ma Baxter except herself: a child abandoned and insecure, relegated to Extraville for four years, until she emerged as a supporting player and grew into an actress. The fleeting sadness that others had detected in Jane's eyes also appeared in Ma's. They were the eyes of someone who understood what Virgil meant by the *lacrimae rerum*: the tears at the heart of the human condition, which those inured to suffering, like Ma, can feel but cannot shed.

Ma's attitude towards Jody was not that of an affectionate mother, but an unsmiling monitor. Although she knew Jody had to become a man in the same way his father did, she wanted to preserve his innocence as long as she could. It is only when he runs away after killing the fawn and then makes his way back to the farm, that Jody can truly lay claim to manhood. He has undergone the traditional rite of passage from adolescence to adulthood, from innocence to experience. "He ain't a yearlin' no longer," his father proudly notes. And most fathers would have agreed.

The Yearling was an audience favorite, receiving Oscar nominations for best picture, actor, actress, director, cinematography, interior decoration, and editing. Jarman was awarded a miniature statuette as "outstanding child actor of 1946." The film received awards from *Redbook* and *Esquire* magazines (best picture) and *Parents* magazine and *Modern Screen* (picture of the month), plus accolades from the *Los Angeles Times*, *New York Times*, and *Daily News*. But what mattered to Jane, who had been in the business for more than a decade, was that she received her first Oscar nomination. Her competition was a quartet of actresses in dissimilar roles: a cosmetics queen who had been forced to give up her illegitimate child (Olivia De Havilland in *To Each His Own*); a woman of mixed race whose life ends in a love death with her ex-lover after they have mortally wounded each other (Jennifer Jones in *Duel in the Sun*); an Australian nurse who pioneers a treatment for polio (Rosalind Russell in *Sister Kenny*); and a married woman who nearly succumbs to adultery (Celia Johnson in *Brief Encounter*). The winner was De Havilland. *The Yearling* won for cinematography and interior decoration. Jane at least felt better about herself as an actress. And when *The Yearling* opened at New York's Radio City Music Hall on 23 January 1947, lines stretched around the 50th St. side of the theatre almost to Fifth Avenue.

Jane had had two box office hits in a row. There would be more—and not just a nomination next time.

Chapter 9

Frontier Gal

ALTHOUGH WARNERS RELEASED SOME RESPECTABLE WESTERNS (E.G., *They Died with Their Boots On, San Antonio, Silver River, Colorado Territory*) and one classic (*The Searchers*), the studio's reputation was founded on the crime film. Warners not only had actors who could work both sides of the law (James Cagney, Humphrey Bogart, Edward G. Robinson), but those who were at home on the range (Errol Flynn, Dennis Morgan, Ronald Reagan). The studio expected similar versatility of its female players. Actresses, too, were expected to take up residence in the Old West, if necessary. Bette Davis, the reigning diva, was the exception, but Olivia De Havilland, Ann Sheridan, Alexis Smith, Miriam Hopkins, and Virginia Mayo all had to relocate when the script required them to. Since Jane had played virtually every other type of character, it was only a matter of time before she made her first western.

Humphrey Bogart might have been her co-star in *Badmen of Missouri* (1941), but he felt it would be an anticlimax compared to his other 1941 pictures, *High Sierra* and *The Maltese Falcon*. The part went to Dennis Morgan, impressively cast against type as Cole Younger, a onetime member of Quantrill's Raiders, Confederate outlaws led by William C. Quantrill who wreaked havoc in Kansas in the early 1860s. Morgan, who was also an Irish tenor (he's given a ballad to prove it), is first seen puffing on a corncob pipe—as if it were as natural to him as a cigarette was to Bogart. Lean in 1941, Morgan looked as if he could rob a bank with a twinkle in his eye and honey in his voice. As the female lead, Jane would seem to be the romantic interest. She was—but for Cole's brother, Bob (Arthur Kennedy). Jane, still a blonde, but with long tresses and Reconstruction-era costumes, responded well to Kennedy. How could she resist a man with the sexiest jaw in film—until Kirk Douglas arrived on the scene a few years later?

With *Badmen*, Ray Enright was in his element, directing a gritty western, with dusty roads and bleak vistas, not the romanticized West of John Ford. Yet despite the film's sympathetic depiction of the Younger Brothers, it was an improvement over the beatification of the James boys in Fox's *Jesse James* (1939) and *The Return of Frank James* (1940), or the portrait of William Bonney in MGM's *Billy the Kid* (1941). The Greeks gave warriors heroic stature by converting their deeds into poetry that transcends any thing resembling human speech. In the *Poetics*, Aristotle argued that heightened language purges human actions of their baseness, which, if left intact and described without the idealizing power of poetry, would merely be a catalog of carnage. Instead, Homer turned Achilles, a vengeful neurotic, into a hero, destined for a brief but glorious life. Sophocles turned a boastful and arrogant Oedipus, and Antigone, his daughter with a death wish, into tragic figures. And Euripides made the infanticidal Medea into a wronged woman.

Hollywood had its own purgation process, which resembled a distillery. In the western, whatever would rob the outlaw-hero of his humanity was siphoned off like sediment, leaving only his essence, the common bond that links all humans together. The western villain was another matter; good riddance to the Clantons in *My Darling Clementine* and the gunmen in *High Noon*. The process often works the same way in the crime film. Most audiences can understand—and even empathize with—upwardly mobile gangsters, who start with small jobs (gas stations, diners), move on to nightclubs and fancy restaurants, and graduate to armored cars and banks. Each stage can be accompanied by an improvement in wardrobe.

In Arthur Penn's *Bonnie and Clyde* (1967), Clyde starts with a grocery story and advances to banks. After he and Bonnie rob their first bank, their getaway is orchestrated by banjo music, giving the scene a silent comedy quality, so that the robbery seems more quaint than criminal. After another robbery, when the bank manager jumps on the running-board of the getaway car, Clyde shoots him in the face—a momentary intrusion of reality into a folk tale that is slowly fading into myth, with all its terrible beauty. And yet we sympathize with the ill-starred couple, who are betrayed and die more violently than their victims. Bonnie Parker and Clyde Barrow have been put through the Hollywood purgation machine, entering as two thrill-seeking kids and emerging as anti-heroes.

The enormous success of *The Godfather*—first the novel, then the film, and then the sequel, *The Godfather Part II*—suggests that crime is perennially fascinating, as long as the criminals have panache. In the 1930s panache meant upward mobility, as evidenced by tailored suits, spats, shirts with cuff links, and cigars. In westerns, the wardrobe was limited, but if the outlaws had an integrity that showed on their faces (Tyrone Power in *Jesse James*, Jack Buetel in *The Outlaw*, Paul Newman in another Billy the Kid film, *The Left-Handed Gun*), and if the avenger looked like John Wayne (*The Searchers*) or Randolph Scott (*Comanche Territory*), it was, to amend scripture, a case of "Vengeance is theirs."

Similarly, *Badmen* turned Cole (Morgan), Jim (Morris), and Bob (Kennedy) Younger into Robin Hoods, coming to the aid of farmers facing eviction because carpetbagger lawyers schemed to foreclose on their properties. Historically, the brothers teamed up briefly with Jesse James, which the film fleetingly acknowledges; however, *Badmen* completely ignores the Youngers' bank and train robberies. And there is no suggestion that the Youngers may have wanted to keep fighting the Civil War because they could not adjust to civilian life, with all its ordinariness. The film ends with Jane informing Bob that a pardon is imminent. He smiles; she smiles. *The End*. Apparently theft, in the interest of the masses, is legal.

Historically, it was not so simple. Cole and Jim were paroled. Jim had adjustment problems and killed himself. Bob died of tuberculosis in prison. Since the after story is a downer, the writers, Charles E. Kent (story) and Charles Grayson (screenplay), preferred to have the audience file out of the theater in an upbeat mood. Historians, eager to take them to task for sweeping the dust of history under the celluloid carpet, might recall Hitchcock's famous words: "It's only a movie."

Eight years later, Warners brought the Youngers—this time all four of them—back for an encore in a film that bears their name. *The Younger Brothers* (1949) featured Wayne Morris (now playing Cole), Bruce Bennett as Jim, James Brown as Bob, and Robert Hutton as Johnny. Geraldine Brooks took on Jane's part, Mary Hathaway. Although in color, *The Younger Brothers* is inferior to the original, which is generally the case with remakes. But the brothers were always good for a return engagement; six other films followed, the most recent being *The Assassination of Jesse James by the Coward Robert Ford* (2007).

Jane had a chance to do one more western, Raoul Walsh's *Cheyenne* (1947). She was the studio's sole choice for the female lead, but according to an undated press release, Humphrey Bogart and Zachary Scott, respectively, were slated for the roles of a professional gambler and a Wells Fargo inspector who rips off his own company. Scott was a charmer, a bit too oily for the character, but there was no way Bogart could pass as a flashily dressed gambler. Neither made the cut. Billed above the title were Dennis Morgan as the gambler, Jane as the inspector's wife, Bruce Bennett as the inspector, and Janis Paige as a dance hall performer.

For some reason, Walsh and producer Robert Buckner were convinced that Jane should be a blonde. "We believe she is much more effective as a blonde," which would provide "a much better dramatic contrast with Janis Paige's black hair." Otherwise, "there is a strong possibility of Janis Paige taking this picture from under Miss Wyman's nose." Paige nearly did, because the script provided her with two musical numbers, one of which required her to strut across a bar in tights, the other, to sing while working the room and flirting with the patrons. Naturally, Paige's wardrobe was flashier than Jane's. Wives and mistresses rarely wear the same label. Fortunately, a blonde Jane failed to materialize. Instead, she was a brunette, with her hair styled differently than Paige's. Jane's was longer, and in one scene, cascaded down her back, making her look both ravishingly innocent and highly desirable.

John Huston was originally entrusted with the screenplay. When Huston withdrew, Alan Le May and Thomas Williamson took over, making it into a whodunit revolving around the identity of "The Poet," who robs in verse. The writers devised a clever meet cute, complete with double entendre, a rarity in westerns. Jane and Morgan are staying at the same hotel, in adjoining rooms with a common bath. Morgan slips into the tub, not knowing that it had been filled for Jane. Angrily, she knocks over the partition, leaving Morgan in his bath with his head poking out of the screen. The next morning, Morgan strikes up a conversation with Paige, assuming she was the one who knocked over the screen. Everything he says has a double meaning. His casual allusion to the tub incident ("After you knocked it over, I folded it up and put it in a corner") causes Paige to almost choke on her coffee. There's also a bit of sexy footwork in the movie. Since the Sundance gang believes Jane and Morgan are married, the pair has to prove it by sleeping alongside each other. Morgan gets frisky and starts playing footsie with Jane, who uses her feet to rebuff him. In the fadeout, as they are embracing in a stagecoach, the camera tilts down to their stocking feet, with their toes pressed snugly against each other. That passed for sex in 1947.

Although *Cheyenne* was not vintage Walsh, it still bore his signature. The credits appear against a towering mountain, a visual reminder of the peak from which Roy Earle (Bogart) plunged at the end of *High Sierra*. Walsh's West is not John Ford's (the *Cheyenne* exteriors were filmed in Flagstaff, Arizona, not Monument Valley). Walsh's landscape is primordial, not poetic. Mountains loom like giants, as if mocking Ford's mythic West, and suggesting an Eden turned to stone. Walsh's women are men's equals: Ida Lupino in *High Sierra*, Virginia Mayo in *Colorado Territory*, Ann Sheridan in *Silver River*—and Jane in *Cheyenne*, who looked as if she could survive in a West that was not prettified by majestic vistas and crimson sunsets.

Each of the four principals is play acting. Morgan is forced to masquerade as the "The Poet," the scourge of Wells Fargo. Bennett is the respectable Wells Fargo inspector who is really "The Poet," stealing from his own company and leaving doggerel behind in the empty valises. Jane is Bennett's wife, who knows he is a thief but has mixed feelings about exposing him. And Paige is the sexy entertainer who, unbeknownst to Jane, is also her husband's mistress.

Since none of the characters is what he or she seems, they all must react with their eyes when a situation arises that calls for quick thinking. Jane had already mastered the art of using her eyes expressively. She registered emotion with absolute calm, methodically plotting the next move and buying time by speaking each word slowly until the deception is complete. There is one scene in particular that illustrates Jane's mastery of the art of underplaying. When Morgan finds himself in a tight spot, Jane comes to his aid by claiming to be his wife, doing it so convincingly that the Sundance Kid (Arthur Kennedy) believes her. Close your eyes, and the experience is like hearing a sentence being forged—right down to the period.

If Jane gave such a realistic performance, it was partly because she understood her character. At the time of the shoot, she was playacting herself. Reagan had discovered politics, and a publicity release quoted Jane's description of herself as a "speech widow," because Reagan was "mixed up in politics and is out campaigning for the Democrats all the time." (He later shifted his allegiance to the other party.) Whoever thought such a disclosure would strengthen their marriage was sadly mistaken. The specter of divorce had not yet cast a shadow over the storybook marriage, but it soon would. Jane must have sensed that her marriage was in jeopardy; she insisted on flying home weekends to be with her family. But her gesture was only a stopgap measure.

As late as 2011, Janis Paige had vivid recollections of the *Cheyenne* shoot, her first on location. Jane knew the trials of location shooting, having endured them when she had to travel to Sonora, California, in the foothills of the Sierra Nevada, for the *Badmen of Missouri* exteriors. Paige not only had to rough it, she also had to wear period costumes, including laced boots. One day, she fell into a patch of poison oak, a mishap that doubled her discomfort. But the camaraderie she enjoyed with the cast and director, Raoul Walsh, more than made up for it. Although Paige had been warned that Walsh was a "man's director" and highly methodical, she also found him warm and caring.

Paige and Jane remained friends during the six years Paige was at the studio. When Paige was up for renewal in 1950, Jack Warner called her into his office and informed her that her contract would not be renewed. The reason for letting her go was that the studio did not know what to do with her. Janis Paige could enliven a movie with a song and dance, but she did not fit into any category—much less leading lady. What Warner failed to realize was that Paige was made for musicals, although, like Jane, she could also do other kinds of films. But, as Warner informed Paige, Virginia Mayo was the studio's new musical star. On her last day at Warners, Paige stopped by Jane's dressing room and told her the news. Jane took her hand tenderly and said, "Janis, remember: 'Talent will out.'" And it did—for both of them.

A year later, on 3 October 1951, Paige made her Broadway debut in Howard Lindsay and Russel Crouse's *Remains to Be Seen*, which ran for 199 performances. She was back on Broadway in May 1954 to star opposite John Raitt in *The Pajama Game*, followed by a return to Hollywood for *Silk Stockings* (1957), in which her ode to lingerie, "Satin and Silk," left a deeper impression than the dancing of the leads, Fred Astaire and Cyd Charisse. Broadway beckoned again in 1963 with Meredith Wilson's *Here's Love*, based on the Christmas classic, *The Miracle on 34th Street* (1947). But Janis Paige's greatest triumph occurred when she replaced Angela Lansbury in *Mame* in 1968. Paige and Jane disproved F. Scott Fitzgerald's adage, "There are no second acts in American lives." Paige found hers on the stage and later in cabaret; Jane, on television.

Chapter 10

Strange Interlude

AS A WARNERS CONTRACT PLAYER, JANE HAD BEEN LOANED OUT TO Universal (*The Spy Ring*), MGM (*The Crowd Roars, The Yearling*), Columbia (*Wide Open Faces*), Fox (*Tail Spin, Footlight Serenade*), RKO (*My Favorite Spy*), and Paramount (*The Lost Weekend*). But *Magic Town* (1947) was a new experience; she would be appearing in an independent production for a company created by Oscar-winning screenwriter Robert Riskin, with RKO as distributor. The result was the disappointing *Magic Town*, Robert Riskin Productions' only release.

It was understandable that Riskin would go independent. The year 1947 marked the close of Hollywood's boom years. In the late forties and throughout the fifties, older actresses found themselves paired with younger actors, as if the studios hoped that audiences would suspend disbelief when Rosalind Russell costarred with Robert Cummings in *Tell it to the Judge* (1949), Bette Davis with Sterling Hayden in *The Star* (1952), and Joan Crawford with Jeff Chandler in *Female on the Beach* (1955).

The 1950s did not bode well for Hollywood's contract talent. Stars, greater and lesser, defected to television, finding, for a time, a home on the tube. The dramatic shows and series were glad to get anyone with a name. NBC was honored to have Loretta Young in her own show, which ran for eight seasons. Jane, with nothing to lose, followed suit in *Fireside Theatre*, which later became *Jane Wyman's Fireside Theatre*.

There were those, like Henry Fonda, Joan Fontaine, Deborah Kerr, Shelley Winters, and Olivia De Havilland, who alternated between film and theatre. Undaunted by live television, despite limited stage experience, others moved on to *Studio One, Robert Montgomery Presents, Climax!*, and *Playhouse 90*, where Claudette Colbert, Jean Pierre Aumont, William Lundigan, Diana Lynn, and Michael Rennie prolonged their careers.

Some returned to the theatre, took supporting roles in movies, landed a television series or a soap if they were lucky (Fred MacMurray in *My Three Sons*; Robert Young and Jane Wyatt in *Father Knows Best*; Ruth Warrick in *All My Children*; Anna Lee in *General Hospital*), or left the business (Irene Dunne, Peggy Dow, Gloria Jean).

In 1946, television was not yet an option for stars of diminishing wattage, or directors tired of haggling with studio bosses and seeking greater control over their films. Independent production, however, was a possibility. Independent production companies had existed since the movies began, and included such organizations as Carl Laemmle's Independent Moving Pictures Company (IMP), the precursor of Universal, and long forgotten studios with classical names like Rex, Centaur, Phoenix, and Capitol. Later came such notable independent producers as D. W. Griffith, Samuel Goldwyn, Hal Roach, David Selznick, Edward Small, Sol Lesser, and Hunt Stromberg. All distributed frequently through United Artists, of which Griffith was a co-founder.

The 5 May 1946 *New York Times* included an open letter from Frank Capra, "Breaking Hollywood's Pattern of Sameness," in which he wrote a bit exaggeratedly about a "revolution" in the movie business that would cause audiences to take note of the "unusual number of good pictures . . . different from the typical Hollywood product." The letter was really an advertisement for Liberty Productions, which he, director William Wyler, and former Columbia executive Sam Briskin formed in 1946, a boom year that seemed to augur well for the movies. It was not a good year, however, for Liberty Productions, whose sole release was *It's a Wonderful Life* (1946), a failure in its day but now a television perennial. That same year, Rosalind Russell discovered that after seven years as an MGM contract player and then a multipicture deal with Columbia, it was the right time to go independent. In July 1946, Russell and her producer-husband, Fred Brisson, formed Independent Artists, with RKO as distributor. Independent Artists' initial release was *The Velvet Touch* (1948), a great vehicle for Russell as a stage actress who murders her producer. Although the film was a hit, the next, a labored comedy, *Never Wave at a WAC* (1952), was not, extinguishing the Olympic torch that was Independent Artists' logo.

Russell was not the only star to go the indie route. Rita Hayworth formed Beckworth Productions, based at her home studio, Columbia. But Beckworth's films (*The Loves of Carmen*, *Affair in Trinidad*, and *Salome*) were no match for *You Were Never Lovelier*, *Cover Girl*, *Gilda*, and *The Lady from Shanghai*, for which Hayworth is best remembered. Humphrey

Bogart's Santana, also releasing through Columbia, came up with the film noir masterpiece *In a Lonely Place*. But the company's other productions—*Knock on Any Door, Tokyo Joe*, and *Sirocco* (a *Casablanca* clone)—would never blot out memories of *The Petrified Forest, High Sierra, The Maltese Falcon, Casablanca*, and *Treasure of the Sierra Madre*. Going independent, for those willing to take the risk, was a way of warding off the encroaching conglomeratization of Hollywood. And it was a risk, as Capra warned at the end of his letter: "The way of the independents is hard. It is strewn with failures." Capra would know such failures.

Anyone planning to go indie in 1946 was a dreamer. And yet dreamers founded the movie industry. These were immigrants and their sons, for the most part, who divined the public's taste and catered to it, enriching themselves and their studios by their prescience. Theirs was a vision built on business acumen, instinct, and guts—all of which Frank Capra had. But he never expected that *It's a Wonderful Life*—which went on to become his best loved film—would fail so abysmally and be ignored at Oscar time. It is now considered the end of his classic period, although he would go on directing until 1961.

Screenwriter Robert Riskin, Capra's best collaborator (*American Madness, Platinum Blonde, Lady for a Day, It Happened One Night, Mr. Deeds Goes to Town, Lost Horizon, You Can't Take It With You, Meet John Doe*) should have reconsidered after the failure of Frank Capra Productions, which he and Capra founded and which they dissolved after the disappointing reception of *Meet John Doe* (1941). Riskin knew he had to go his own way. The most logical explanation for Riskin's setting up his own production company was his desire to compete with Capra, who had supposedly asked him to join Liberty. The two were briefly quartered at—where else?—RKO, their distributor. The fact that Robert Riskin Productions' sole release was *Magic Town* proved that the writer had not yet disassociated himself from the Capraesque plot or the Capraesque hero personified by James Stewart (*You Can't Take It with You, Mr. Smith Goes to Washington, It's a Wonderful Life*).

Although Jane would work with Capra in *Here Comes the Groom* (1951), she was as close as Riskin could get to Jean Arthur, Stewart's leading lady in *You Can't Take It with You* and *Mr. Smith Goes to Washington*. Stewart was freelancing at the time, and apparently liked the script. Jane was still at Warners and loanable. Stewart embraced the challenge that *Magic Town* offered. The script was the reverse of *Mr. Smith Goes to Washington*. He would not be playing an idealist like Jefferson Smith, but another Smith, "Rip," a failed pollster hoping to jumpstart his career by locating a "mathematically perfect" town to act as a barometer of America's views on everything—national and international. Smith finds such a microcosm in Grandview, somewhere in small-town America. Masquerading as an insurance broker eager to relocate, Smith charms the residents, even the high-principled Mary Peterman (Jane), the acting editor of the local paper, who becomes part of the woo-her-lose-her-reclaim- her subplot. Stewart generated more erotic heat with Katharine Hepburn in *The Philadelphia Story* than he did with Jane. Her no-nonsense hairdo and demure wardrobe were deterrents to passion—except for one scene, in which Smith teaches Mary how to shoot a basket. When the ball gets caught in the net, Rip hoists her up to retrieve it. As she slowly slides down his body, her skirt rides up and then slowly returns to its proper length. Sexy? For 1947, yes—and still provocative.

Smith's scheme backfires. Hordes of Americans descend on Grandview, as if it were a utopia. But the Capra triad (victory-defeat-comeback) prevails. Rip convinces the residents to back a new civic center, even if doing so means higher taxes, so that Grandview will become a "magic town," whose citizens wrought the magic.

Magic Town was a Capraesque film without the Capra touch, a Democratic film with a Republican solution that did not offend members of either party. But that was part of Capra's genius: perfecting the politically ambiguous film that champions the constitutionally unrecognized Party of Humankind. William Wellman (*Wings, Call of the Wild, The Ox-Bow Incident, The Story of G. I. Joe*) was hardly the ideal director, resorting to such commonplace Capra touches as collapsing time with a montage of newspaper headlines. Wellman, who worked best with men, was not meant for the populist film. And the extent of his contribution has been contested. Did Wellman direct all of *Magic Town*, or just some of it? Or did Riskin himself direct the film—except for the last few weeks, when Capra prevailed upon Wellman to finish it? Wellman claimed he was the sole director, and Riskin's widow, Fay Wray, concurred. One thing is certain: *Magic Town* is atypical Wellman. If Capra had directed it, there might have been some magic in *Magic Town*.

Chapter 11

And the Winner Is . . .

ALTHOUGH WARNERS WAS CHIEFLY NOTED FOR GANGSTER-TOUGH guy-fresh headlines movies, it also distinguished itself with adaptations of novels: *Penrod and Sam, Captain Blood, The White Cockatoo, Anthony Adverse, Oil for the Lamps of China, The Maltese Falcon, Kings Row, Now, Voyager, Treasure of the Sierra Madre,* for example. But stage adaptations predominated: *First Lady* (1937), *Tovarich* (1937), *Jezebel* (1938), *Boy Meets Girl* (1938), *Brother Rat* (1938), *The Old Maid* (1939), *Dark Victory* (1939), *No Time for Comedy* (1940), *The Man Who Came to Dinner* (1941), *George Washington Slept Here* (1942), *The Male Animal* (1942), *Watch on the Rhine* (1943), *Old Acquaintance* (1943), *Between Two Worlds* (based on *Outward Bound,* 1944), *Janie* (1944), *Arsenic and Old Lace* (1944), *Pillow to Post* (1945), *The Corn Is Green* (1945), *Deception* (1946), *Life with Father* (1947), *The Voice of the Turtle* (1947), *Wallflower* (1948), *Key Largo* (1948), *Rope* (1948), *The Decision of Christopher Blake* (1948).

And *Johnny Belinda* (1948). Although in the early 1930s Elmer Harris had originally written *Johnny Belinda* as a play, he first tried to interest MGM in his drama, thinking it might work better as a film. MGM toyed with the possibility but questioned the commercial value of a movie with a non-speaking heroine, whose rape by a local fisherman had to comply with the Production Code's mandate that "rape should never be more than suggested." However, rape by suggestion can be even more frightening than a reenactment, since the details are left to the viewer's imagination. When MGM passed on the project, Harris tried Broadway, which proved far more receptive. *Johnny Belinda* ran there from 18 September 1940 to 21 June 1941, chalking up 321 performances.

A movie version seemed unlikely. Since the main character, Belinda McDonald, is both hearing and speech-impaired, the actress playing her does not utter a single line of dialogue. On Broadway, the role was played by Helen Craig, the wife of actor John Beal. Craig was a highly respected actress who never attained stardom but worked in the theatre from 1936 to 1967. Despite glowing reviews, *Johnny Belinda* did not lead to another challenging part for Craig. However, in 1946 she appeared in the Mary Martin musical *Lute Song*, in which a newcomer in her first and only Broadway show played a lady in waiting. She was Nancy Davis, who six years later became the second wife of Ronald Reagan.

The Chicago-born Harris began his playwriting career in 1908, having worked briefly as a journalist. That same year, he had a summer home built for himself and his wife on Prince Edward Island, the setting of *Johnny Belinda*, whose main character was inspired by a local woman. Structurally, the play is a three-act melodrama, with the exposition relegated to the first scene, which introduces everyone but Belinda. We meet the local doctor, who becomes Belinda's teacher; the God-fearing inhabitants; the fisherman-villain; and the young woman who loves him. Belinda appears in the second scene, set in her father's gristmill, where she encounters the doctor. In act 1, scene 3, also set in the mill, Belinda is raped by the fisherman. Then the plot escalates into a series of events, climaxing in the birth of Belinda's son, followed by Belinda's shooting of the rapist who tries to claim him, and her trial and vindication. Belinda is paroled for five years in the custody of the doctor, the equivalent of announcing their engagement.

Jerry Wald, one of the best (and sadly unrecognized) producers in Hollywood, convinced Warners to buy the rights for $50,000, arguing that Paramount and RKO had both made films about hearing- and speech-impaired women. In *And Now Tomorrow* (Paramount, 1944), Loretta Young awakens one morning to discover that she cannot hear the rain beating against the window. A traumatic experience rendered Dorothy McGuire incapable of speaking until the last scene of *The Spiral Staircase* (RKO, 1946). By 1948, audiences knew that there were service men and women who returned to civilian life with missing limbs and sightless eyes, and they were ready for films about paraplegics (*The Best Years of Our Lives* and *Till the End of Time*), as well as blind (*Pride of the Marines*) and emotionally disturbed veterans (*Daisy Kenyon*). The public was also ready for *Johnny Belinda*.

The film could not proceed without the right director and star, and Jerry Wald made inspired choices on both counts. When Errol Flynn vetoed the studio's choice of Jean Negulesco as director of his next epic, *The Adventures of Don Juan* (1948), which turned out to be a low point in the actor's career, the assignment fell to Vincent Sherman. Realizing that Negulesco was meant for better projects, Wald sent him the *Johnny Belinda* script, which Negulesco eagerly agreed to direct. The Production Code did not pose a problem for Warners, which had learned to circumvent it by converting hookers into hostesses (*Marked Woman*), unwed mothers into spinsters (*The Old Maid*), and gangsters into anti-heroes—despite the "crime does not pay" finale (*Little Caesar, The Public Enemy, High Sierra*). Negulesco knew how to film Belinda's rape: It would be rape by suggestion, but so shocking in light of her helplessness that many can still recall the scene's impact.

The next hurdle was the star. There were few actresses at Warners who could handle the role. Certainly not Bette Davis, the resident drama queen. Perhaps the highly versatile Eleanor Parker. But Parker had just finished *Of Human Bondage* and *Never Say Goodbye* (both 1946), and was slated for *Escape Me Never* and *The Voice of the Turtle* (both 1947). Wald, who had seen Jane in *The Yearling*, convinced her that she could play Belinda. Jane knew the part would not be easy, but her Oscar nomination for *The Yearling* was the deciding factor. She could—and would—play Belinda. Since the script called for Dr. Jack (Lew Ayres) to teach Belinda sign language, Jane had to master it, too. That was the easy part. The real challenge was playing a woman relegated to a silent world on the windswept island where she lives with her father (Charles Bickford) and aunt (Agnes Moorehead).

As soon as filming began, Negulesco and Wald noticed that Jane's facial expression suggested she could hear what was being said. She was then fitted with plastic ears and cotton earplugs. Jane and Negulesco worked out their own sign language, quite different from the kind taught at schools for the deaf. Star, director, and crew then began communicating through the "Wyman-Negulesco" method. Jane devised a special way of walking, starting not with the right, but with the left foot, to show Belinda's alienation from a world so unlike her own. Once Jane learned to inhabit her character, she did not pick up a cue as she ordinarily would, but delayed her reaction by a beat.

Belinda might be hearing-impaired, but she could absorb rhythm in her own way. There is an exquisite scene in which Belinda attends a dance where she is unable to hear the fiddler's music. But she knows it comes from his violin, which she regards as a talisman, a mysterious instrument prompting people to move in a way she has never witnessed before. Locky, a loutish fisherman (Stephen McNally, who, as Horace McNally, had played the sympathetic doctor on Broadway) begins leering at Belinda's moving feet. Sensing that she would be easy prey, he takes advantage of her father and aunt's absence, and brandishing the violin he has stolen, he strides into the barn where Belinda is sewing a torn sack. Her reaction to the violin, which she associates with an unusual kind of movement, is one of joyful innocence. Locky attempts to play it, producing grating sounds that, naturally, Belinda cannot hear. But she responds to what she recalls from the dance. Tired of the preliminaries, Locky kisses her passionately. He then backs her against the barn wall, approaching her menacingly and casting a shadow over her pleading face.

Not satisfied with taking advantage of Belinda, Locky returns to claim their child, forcing her to kill him. At her trial, Belinda does not understand why she is being judged, as Jane's uncomprehending and anxious (but not fearful) face reveals. Just when it seems that Belinda will lose her child, Locky's wife (convincingly played by Jan Sterling) admits that she knew what her husband had done after he made an incriminating slip of the tongue.

Negulesco was the right director for *Johnny Belinda*. He had a unique way of guiding actresses cast against type toward performances that revealed a depth that had never been fully exploited (Geraldine Fitzgerald in *Three Strangers* and *Nobody Lives Forever*, Irene Dunne in *The Mudlark*, Claudette Colbert in *Three Came Home*). After the rape, he cuts to a shot of the bleak seacoast, followed by a dissolve to Belinda—her face a mask of shame and demoralization—pushing a wheelbarrow filled with potatoes and moving like a weary pack animal. When her father discovers the rapist's identity, the ensuing altercation leads to the father's death, resulting in another profoundly moving sequence, in which Belinda delivers the Lord's Prayer in sign language over his body.

In every way, *Johnny Belinda* was a Jerry Wald production. Wald never failed to congratulate Jane on the dailies. He courted Negulesco ("very good shot," "excellent"), even though Delmer Daves had been his first choice as director. Realizing that Negulesco and *Johnny Belinda* were a better fit, he championed the director when the studio criticized him for the preponderance of "pictorial shots," not understanding how these can enhance mood. Wald came to his director's defense: "If Negulesco leaves the picture I leave the studio."

Since Ayres had been a conscientious objector during World War II, Wald had second thoughts about casting him in a leading role, preferring Robert Donat or Ronald Colman. But remembering how persuasive Ayres was as Dr. Kildare in the eponymous MGM series, Wald decided he would make the perfect rural doctor. Negulesco also had his preferences:

Brian Aherne as the doctor, and either Anne Revere or Judith Anderson as the aunt. At one point Rory Calhoun and Janis Paige were being considered for Locky and his wife. Either would have been effective, except that Paige was going through the Warners "spin cycle": *Cheyenne* and *Love and Learn* (1947); *Winter Meeting, Wallflower, Romance on the High Seas, One Sunday Afternoon* (1948). Fortunately, choices and preferences were discarded in favor of a cast that shed every vestige of their screen personas and became the characters they were playing.

After Jack Warner saw the final cut, he rose abruptly declaring, "Sorry boys, I have to take a leak." Returning, he explained that he got his best ideas in the men's room and proceeded to chastise Wald and Negulesco for making "a picture about a deaf and dumb girl." He believed that the film's salvation lay in "narration over her silent close-ups to tell the public what she was thinking." So much for urinary inspiration. Since Wald and Negulesco were adamant about not adding voiceover narration, Warner was forced to back off.

When the 1948 Academy Awards were announced, *Johnny Belinda* was nominated for best picture, actor (Lew Ayres), actress, supporting actor (Charles Bickford), supporting actress (Agnes Moorehead), director (Negulesco), screenplay, cinematography, art/set direction, sound recording, scoring (Max Steiner), and editing. Jane was up against Ingrid Bergman as a warrior saint (*Joan of Arc*), Olivia De Havilland as a mental patient (*The Snake Pit*), Barbara Stanwyck as a bed-ridden wife who overhears her own murder being planned (*Sorry, Wrong Number*), and Irene Dunne as a Norwegian matriarch in turn-of-the-twentieth century San Francisco (*I Remember Mama*). Bergman and De Havilland had already won Oscars for *Gaslight* (1944) and *To Each His Own* (1946), respectively. Perhaps this time the gold would go to one of the others. On 14 March 1949, the awards ceremony took place at the Academy Theater in Hollywood. When it was time for Ronald Colman to present the best actress award, he opened the envelope and simply announced, "Jane Wyman for *Johnny Belinda*." It was an honor Jane had not expected. She dropped her purse, and as the contents spilled out on the floor, she rushed to the stage and delivered the evening's shortest acceptance speech: "I accept this very gratefully for keeping my mouth shut for once. I think I'll do it again." Hers was the only Oscar *Johnny Belinda* received that evening.

Knowing how Hedda Hopper championed the film, Wald thanked her for "the many nice things you did for Wyman, Negulesco, and myself in getting the picture off to a flying start." Jerry Wald died at fifty-one. No doubt working for moguls like Warner and Harry Cohn contributed to his early death. But his legacy is secure, and *Johnny Belinda* is part of it.

The Non-Marrying Kind

WHEN REAGAN WAS DISCHARGED IN FALL 1945, HE RETURNED TO A changed household and a different wife. Jane went on location to Florida for *The Yearling*. When she had to return to MGM for the interiors, the sets weren't ready. As soon as she wound up work on *The Yearling* in mid-January 1946, Warners wasted no time squeezing her into a few scenes in *Night and Day*, which revealed her underutilized flair for musical comedy—a flair she had exhibited earlier when she sang "What Are You Doing the Rest of Your Life?" with Jack Carson in *Hollywood Canteen*. But Jane had already been pegged: comedy, yes; musical comedy, no. Jane seemed to enjoy playing the bubbly Gracie, even though the part was superfluous. At least she had a chance to show off her dancing and to sing some of the mildly risqué lyrics of "Let's Do It." Then, it was over to RKO for *Magic Town* (1947) with James Stewart; Flagstaff, Arizona, for *Cheyenne*; and Fort Bragg, some 180 miles north of San Francisco, for *Johnny Belinda*, starting on 3 September 1947 and wrapping up six weeks later.

Meanwhile, Reagan had discovered his true calling: politics. When Robert Montgomery resigned from the presidency of the Screen Actors Guild (SAG), having decided to direct, star in, and occasionally produce his own films (*Ride the Pink Horse*, star and director; *Once More, My Darling*, star, director, producer; *Eye Witness*, star and director; *The Gallant Hours*, director), Reagan finished out his term. Reagan was so effective that the members elected him president in November 1947, a position he held for the next five years. The SAG presidency compensated for Jane's absence and the lusterless films that had been planned for him. When Jane returned from Fort Bragg, Reagan talked constantly about politics, which she found unendurable. It was bad enough that when there was a ballgame on the radio, he not only kept the radio on, but called the game—as if to prove that he had not lost his sports casting skills. Perhaps a few of the guests were impressed. Jane was not.

Reagan may not have lorded it over Jane that he was a college graduate, but he loved to hold forth—to the point of dominating a conversation. On one occasion, when Reagan was in an unusually expansive mood, Jane learned over and told June Allyson, "Don't ask Ronnie what time it is because he will tell you how a watch is made." Although Jane was an avid reader, she felt inferior to her politically savvy, college-educated husband. She knew he had the upper hand when it came to discussing contemporary affairs.

She also knew the pitfalls of a dual-career marriage, but made light of them. When Louella Parsons posed the question, "How have you two avoided that two careers-in-the family jinx?" (*Los Angeles Examiner*, 14 July 1946), Jane dismissed the idea that her marriage could ever be in jeopardy, noting that "young couples all over the country have two jobs . . . and do all right. There's no reason why two actors can't do the same if they're in love and don't start taking themselves big." But after *The Yearling*, Jane *was* taking herself big. She was an Oscar nominee, something Reagan never was. Before *The Yearling*, she measured her success against Reagan's, developing the habit of downplaying her native intelligence. Twice in one interview she told columnist Erskine Johnson (*Daily News*, 18 June 1948) "I'm not very bright." When she discussed learning that Reagan's friends wanted him to run for Congress, she said, "He's very politically minded. I'm not. I'm not very bright." Then, as if providing further evidence, she recalled the time she asked the minister at their wedding reception if he would like a drink: "I'm not very bright—and I'll stand on that." "Bright" is not the right word to describe Jane Wyman. She possessed creative intuition, the kind that enables an actor to locate points of contact between self and character, fusing them into a filament that lights up aspects of the role only suggested by the script and revealed without the actor's even knowing how the process took place. This was Jane's method—as opposed to The Method. Perhaps it came down to the same thing. Regardless, Jane did not have to attend Actors Studio to know how to find her way into a character. She simply did it.

Jane had been cast in supporting roles so often that when Reagan took center stage, she waited in the wings, preferring self-deprecation to inarticulateness. Nineteen forty-seven seemed to augur well for Reagan, who was oblivious to signs that their marriage was in trouble. *Stallion Road* (1947) was scheduled for an April release, followed by the disastrous

That Hagen Girl (1947) in the fall. In the latter Shirley Temple played a troubled teenager whose illegitimacy and adoption sparked rumors that Reagan's character is her birth father. The film proved that prodigiously talented child stars do not always mature into actors. In Temple's case, the uniqueness she once possessed dissipated in adolescence, leaving behind a distinctly ordinary performer.

Reagan had better luck with *The Voice of the Turtle* (1947), a sanitized version of John Van Druten's wartime hit, which made it clear that Reagan had not lost the knack of wooing a woman with disarming sincerity and a melting smile. Since Sally Middleton (Eleanor Parker in the Margaret Sullavan role, wearing her hair in the same page boy style) is recovering from a failed relationship, any display of aggressive masculinity on Reagan's part would have clashed with the gradual way her defenses drop until she can put the past behind her. Reagan behaved like a gentleman, while at the same time projecting a cool self-confidence. The best scene in the film, which is also in the play, requires Reagan to help Parker with the zipper on the back of her dress. The zipper does not cooperate, and his fumbling causes the dress to fall to the floor in a heap, leaving an embarrassed Parker in her slip, while the impish Reagan, looking mildly apologetic, clearly enjoys the view.

Reagan may not have been the first choice for the male lead in *The Voice of the Turtle* (Cary Grant was), but his ingenuousness worked to the film's advantage. To moviegoers, Reagan was not a screen icon like Grant, but an occasional romantic lead in a B movie with a flimsy plot. Since he was playing a sergeant on leave in New York, his military image, forged by *International Squadron, Desperate Journey*, and especially *This Is the Army*, brought an authenticity to the film—not to mention his ingratiating naiveté, a characteristic that was not Grant's trademark.

Jane was similarly occupied. *The Yearling* was doing record business, with her performance netting her an Oscar nomination. *Magic Town* proved a disappointment, although James Stewart, impressed by Jane's perfectionism, voiced his admiration: "She was painstaking, she insisted on perfection. It was an honor to work with her." Although she knew her next Warners film would be the demanding *Johnny Belinda*, she was more concerned about her pregnancy, which she hoped would shore up her shaky marriage. The press had no idea that the marriage, ideal by Hollywood standards, was in jeopardy.

On 2 June 1947, the *New York Times* reported that the Reagans would be contributing $75,000 for the construction of the Wyman-Reagan School of Speech and Dramatic Art on the campus of Reagan's alma

mater, Eureka College. Then on 28 June, tragedy struck. Jane gave birth
to a daughter, three months premature, at Queen of Angels Hospital.
Reagan was not present. He, too, was hospitalized, but at Cedars of Lebanon with viral pneumonia that put his life in jeopardy. He recovered, but
Jane had a harder time. When she went into labor, she suspected something was wrong. She gave birth to a baby girl, whom she named Christine. The infant lived for nine hours and eleven minutes. Jane would
have no more children. Reagan would, but not by her.

Jane could not afford to be depressed. She threw herself into preparing for *Johnny Belinda*, learning sign language so she could enter the
world of a young woman who could neither hear nor speak, branded by
the community as "The Dummy." Six months after the death of Christine Reagan, the marriage was virtually over. Meanwhile, in October
1947, anti-communism, Reagan's latest crusade, took on special meaning in Hollywood when the House Committee on Un-American Activities (HUAC) began hearings on communist subversion of the movie
industry.

Although Reagan was a friendly witness, he did not advocate the abolition of the Communist Party, admitting that he "would hesitate to see
any political party outlawed on the basis of its political ideology." He
was not asked to name names. Six months earlier, he did—but in his
own way. According to his biographer, "Reagan and Wyman met with
FBI agents on April 10, 1947." Newly released files, however, indicate
that he also met with them the previous year. Aware of Reagan's anti-
communist orientation, agents dropped by his home in 1946, arguing
that the Hollywood communists were both a threat to his profession and
the country. The April date is the crucial one; it was a month after his
election as SAG president. In his autobiography, *Where's the Rest of Me?*,
Reagan wrote that he was visited by "three men from a well known
government agency," obviously FBI agents, whose names he could not
divulge. More likely there were two, Richard Auerbach and Fred Dupuis,
armed with enough evidence to justify his becoming an informant, who
would "report secretly to the F. B. I. about people whom he suspected of
Communist activity."

Reagan did not exactly name names, although he admitted that two
actresses, Anne Revere, Oscar winner for Best Supporting Actress in *National Velvet*, and Karen Morley, frequently named by HUAC informants,
"follow the Communist Party line." He then added the names of eight
others, including Howard da Silva and Dorothy Tree, who appeared in a
couple of his films; Larry Parks, who received an Oscar nomination for

his portrayal of Al Jolson in *The Jolson Story*; and Karen Morley's husband, actor Lloyd Gough. Reagan carefully refrained from calling anyone a communist, stating only that they adhered to the party line. It was not much of a distinction, but it may have salved Reagan's conscience. But observing the distinction did nothing for Revere and Morley, who ended up being blacklisted.

Ironically, around 1938, Reagan, "carried away by stories of the Communist Party helping the dispossessed, the unemployed, and the homeless," seriously considered joining. Such a change would not have been surprising. To many New Deal Democrats, the Great Depression signaled the failure of capitalism, which, if it were to survive, needed an infusion of socialism. To the radicals, change meant communism, the answer to an economically polarized America. Reagan's concern for the marginalized was the equivalent of first fervor; when it abated, he went back to making movies—until, in 1947, he realized that, as SAG president, he could be a leader, and as a friend of the FBI, a patriot. What he failed to consider was that he had been elected to help SAG members keep their jobs, not lose them because of politics.

Reagan's crusade against communism continued beyond the blacklist. Twenty years later, in January 1967, two weeks after he was sworn in as governor of California, he was obsessing over Mario Savio's Free Speech Movement at the University of California at Berkeley, which had devolved into the filthy speech movement. A notorious dance replete with drugs and sex gave Reagan more ammunition to use against a cause that was originally a plea for due process and respect for students' First Amendment rights. Convinced that the student protests were communist instigated, Reagan sought out the FBI, which had a similar agenda. Although Berkeley's president, Clark Kerr, was anti-communist, he did not believe in banning communist speakers from campus. To the FBI, Kerr's stance made him suspect. He could not withstand the combined forces of J. Edgar Hoover and Governor Reagan, both of whom wanted him fired.

Even with Kerr's dismissal, Reagan's paranoia did not abate. He fervently believed that communists were behind the widespread opposition to the Vietnam War and the military draft, burning issues on college campuses in the late 1960s and early 1970s that resulted in sit-ins, teach-ins, and in some instances, the occupation of buildings. He was committed to exposing communism as an aberration and never abandoned his crusade, which culminated at Berlin's Brandenburg Gate in June 1987, when he challenged General Secretary Mikhail Gorbachev to "tear down this wall." Two years later, the Berlin Wall came tumbling down. After another two years, in December 1991, the Soviet Union imploded, ending up, as Reagan predicated, on the ash heap of history. The crusade that began in 1946 ended in triumph for Reagan forty-five years later. Although the demise of the Soviet Union was not entirely his doing, many Americans credit him with it.

Jane was not as staunch an anti-communist as Reagan, even though she attended SAG meetings and heard radicals like John Howard Lawson and Dalton Trumbo denounce her husband as a "fascist" and "capitalist scum." She simply wanted to work—as did Reagan, who believed he could serve his profession as both actor and activist. Reagan seriously believed the strikes that came close to paralyzing moviemaking in postwar Hollywood were the work of communists. He was also convinced that the movie business—his business—was in danger of falling into the hands of communists who would use the medium to determine screen content, limiting it to explorations of the human condition with an emphasis on universal brotherhood. In retrospect, we know this fear was unfounded. First, Hollywood communists were a minority; more importantly, movies need audiences. With the end of World War II, moviegoers, having been fed a diet of propaganda and flag-waving, preferred a change of menu. Film was the great unifier during the war, building morale and promising a brighter tomorrow. Other wars—Korea, Vietnam, Iraq, Afghanistan—did not have the same effect, since none were—to use the name the Russians gave the Second World War—"The Great Patriotic War."

But in 1946, Reagan believed that "godless, atheistic" communism, redundantly denounced in pulpits throughout the land, threatened not only his country, but also his profession. Reagan and Jane were given confidential agent code numbers T-10 and T-9, respectively. "T" meant "temporary, suggesting that he was not on the FBI payroll, but rather that "his motives were . . . personal and political." A visit by FBI agents meant nothing to Jane, who told them what little she knew. Politics were Reagan's forte, not hers. Besides, she was pregnant, her due date in September (it turned out to be in June). Although the loss of the baby was devastating, Jane could not afford prolonged grieving; she had to immerse herself in a script without dialogue. The communist scare may have seemed real to Reagan, but it was quite remote to her. As the months passed, and talk of communist infiltration of the industry became widespread, Reagan's anti-communism became so consuming that he started preaching about it. Jane, utterly exasperated, "whispered to a friend, 'I'm so bored with him, I'll either kill him or kill myself.'" In late September 1947, Reagan received a subpoena to appear before HUAC, testifying on 25 October. Two months later, the marriage made in heaven had moved down—if not to hell, at least to purgatory.

The 5 December 1947 columns of Hedda Hopper and Louella Parsons, the two most powerful purveyors of Hollywood gossip, were ominous: "Ronald Reagan Scouts Idea of Marital Break" (Hopper), and "Jane Wyman, Mate in Rift" (Parsons). Reagan made light of the matter to Hopper, noting that it was just a "tiff" and that they had had tiffs in the past. Jane, meanwhile, had gone to New York, to visit a friend who had recently given birth, Reagan claimed. When she returned, he said, he was confident that they would solve their problems and enjoy a "happy life . . . for as long as we live." Jane was less sanguine. Interviewed in New York, she described herself as "not the happiest girl in the world." A legal separation was a possibility, she suggested. She tried to sound upbeat, but all she could do was express the hope that "we can solve our problems."

But the "tiff" was really a rift that widened into a rupture. Parsons, who was quite close to Jane, was informative. The New York trip was really an attempt to avoid reporters' prying questions, which Jane could answer—but not with Reagan's euphemisms. New York was not the diversion she expected; in fact, she remained in her hotel room for most of the trip. She also confessed that "things hadn't been right with them for a long time." Parsons was not optimistic: "I wish I could say with Ronnie that I believe in 50 years they will be together, but after talking, with Jane I am not so sure." Two months later, the headline of Parsons's column (9 February 1948) made it official: "Jane Wyman to Sue Reagan for Divorce."

The fan magazines portrayed a totally obfuscated Reagan and a career-driven Jane. Reagan was so "well liked" that the problem had to be Jane, who was "physically and emotionally strained" and—worse—Janus-faced. Jane Wyman was "cute and flip" on the outside, but "cynical" within. She "viewed the world through lemon-colored glasses, feigning warmth and affection, to all appearances outgoing, but deeply distrustful of strangers." Since the writer knew nothing about Jane's childhood of abandonment, privation, and loneliness, it is not surprising that Jane was accused of cynicism and being "torn by inner conflicts she couldn't even seem to solve." It took Jane a decade to admit to herself that she was not just an actress but an artist, with greater talent than her husband. Naturally, she would resent his politicizing every discussion or ignoring her to talk politics with his cronies.

Reagan emerged as a husband more sinned against than sinning. "I don't know what made her do it. I can't understand why she wanted a divorce in the first place," he told one writer. Reagan was still in love with Jane, who could no longer reciprocate. When Reagan was in London filming *The Hasty Heart* in 1949, his co-star Patricia Neal admitted to enjoying his company, but realized that "he was still in love with Jane Wyman." The rumor mill began to turn: a dual-career marriage, a love affair with her *Johnny Belinda* co-star, Lew Ayres (which Jane denied), the loss of Christine, post-*Johnny Belinda* depression were all blamed— anything other than Reagan's politics, which left no room for a wife who did not share them and could not abide his grandstanding. One had to become a member of Reagan's audience, a role that was not in Jane's repertoire. Once, when Reagan was holding forth at a SAG meeting, Jane had had enough of his verbosity and, according to actress Rosemary DeCamp, shouted, " Oh, for God's sake, Ronnie, shut up and go shit in your hat."

Jane originally intended to establish residency in Las Vegas to qualify for a quick divorce. That was all the optimists had to hear; six weeks might give the couple time to kiss and make up. The *Los Angeles Examiner* (27 February 1948) reported that after Jane checked into the Flamingo Hotel, word began circulating that a reconciliation was in the offing. Reagan denied the rumors. Jane only stayed a week in Vegas, claiming she could not tolerate the wind.

But divorce was inevitable. Jane charged mental cruelty, informing the *Daily News* (28 June 1948) that she and Reagan had "continual arguments as to certain political views," and that she "came to realize that we just did not have enough in common to sustain a happy married life." Jane hired one of Hollywood's best lawyers, the University of California-educated Loyd Wright, who had represented some of Hollywood's biggest names, including Mary Pickford, Charlie Chaplin, Jack Benny, Mae West, Hal Wallis, and D. W. Griffith. On 18 July 1949, the divorce became official. Jane got the house on Cordell Drive and custody of Maureen and Michael, whom Reagan could visit whenever he wished. But, for the time being, such visits would be in Malibu, as Jane had decided to sell the Cordell Drive home. Reagan agreed to pay five hundred dollars monthly in child support and the same in alimony, if Jane was unable to work.

But Jane *was* able to work, and so was Reagan. Each had a full plate for the next few years. For Reagan, it was another movie version of a Broadway comedy, *John Loves Mary* (1949). Jane would be off to London for *Stage Fright* after completing *A Kiss in the Dark* and *The Lady Takes a Sailor* (both 1949).

In his autobiography, *An American Life*, Reagan mentions Jane once: "The . . . year I made the Knute Rockne movie, I married Jane Wyman . . . but it didn't work out, and in 1948 we were divorced." Although an autobiography would have been the ideal place to air his version of the break-up, Reagan chose silence. It just "didn't work out." Reagan did not adjust well to bachelorhood; even SAG was no substitute. Celebrity biographer Kitty Kelly has documented his relationships, platonic and otherwise, drawing on personal interviews with women who had no reason to tarnish Reagan's reputation (not that pre-presidential dalliances could) but nonetheless willing to divulge what they knew. Reagan was democratic when it came to dating; one didn't have to be a major star. Minor ones like Adele Jergens, Penny Edwards, Peggy Stewart, and Piper Laurie would do, as long as they were younger than he was and attractive. Most of the women eventually realized they were merely diversions meant to fill the void left by Jane.

Gossip columnist and author Doris Lilly, best known for *How to Marry a Millionaire*, recalled a post-divorce "delightful little romance" with Reagan, who took her to nightclubs where he talked, she listened, and they both drank. Reagan also sent her risqué billets doux, in which he fantasized about "tossing off a short one" with her and, in the same letter spelled "damn" and "hell" d—n" and "h—l." Two of the letters were eventually auctioned off and purchased for $4,400 by Malcolm Forbes, who gave them to Nancy Reagan, infuriating Lilly, who believed that Nancy would destroy them. To Lilly, the letters were historically important. Most presidential historians, however, would be more curious about Reagan's reluctance to spell out innocuous expletives than in his "tossing off a short one."

One woman to whom Reagan is known to have proposed was the actress Christine Larson, whom fans of B westerns might remember from such movies as *Belle Starr's Daughter*, *Silver Trails* (both 1948), and *Brave Warrior* (1952), and from appearances on early 1950s television series like *The Lone Ranger* and *The Cisco Kid*. Reagan, however, was only one of several men (including John Howard, Lew Ayres, and Mickey Rooney) with whom she was romantically involved. Reagan presented her with a diamond watch instead of the traditional ring, and Lawson "decided to keep the watch and rejected the offer." Reagan made no attempt to date Virginia Mayo during *The Girl from Jones Beach* shoot, perhaps because she was happily married to actor Michael O'Shea. Mayo, for her part, found Reagan's charm "overwhelming," believing "it was the basis of his career as an actor"—and, one might add, as a politician. But Mayo noticed that "he did have, occasionally, young ladies on the set."

There was nothing unusual about Reagan's new bachelorhood. Like many divorced men, he was playing the field, and in Hollywood, the field was burgeoning. Jane was not sitting home at nights, either. They were two attractive and available people. The difference between them lay only in the protocols of the mating ritual: The male is the agent and the female the object. Reagan had many objects, and Jane had many agents. Reagan remarried before Jane. His second wife was born Anne Frances Robbins, but she became known to moviegoers in the 1950s as Nancy Davis and to the world as First Lady Nancy Reagan.

Chapter 13

These Three

IT IS NOT UNCOMMON FOR DIVORCED MOVIE STARS TO REMARRY within their profession. Tyrone Power seemed happy with Annabella, until World War II intervened. Afterward, Power was a changed man, ready for a second go around with Linda Christian. When Humphrey Bogart's stormy marriage to Mayo Methot ended, he found a soul mate in Lauren Bacall. Tom Cruise's three marriages were all to actresses: Mimi Rogers, Nicole Kidman, and Katie Holmes. "Stick to your own kind," Anita advised Maria in *West Side Story*. And Reagan did. Nor was there anything unusual about Reagan's marriage to Nancy. Movie history is replete with such marriages: between actresses and producers (Norma Shearer and Irving Thalberg, Hal Wallis and Martha Hyer, David Selznick and Jennifer Jones); actresses and directors (Charles David and Deanna Durbin, Joseph L. Mankiewicz and Rosa Stradner, Charles Vidor and Evelyn Keyes, John Huston and Evelyn Keyes); screenwriters and actresses (Robert Riskin and Fay Wray, Robert Anderson and Teresa Wright).

Jane would also remarry, although her next husband, Fred Karger, was a musician on the periphery of the movie business. Reagan married an actress who aspired to be a star but proved to be, at best, a supporting cast stalwart who could play leads if they were ordinary women. Nancy Davis continued in the business even after she married Reagan on 4 March 1952. She went on making movies until 1958, using television as a safety net until 1962, when she retired from the business four years before Reagan was elected governor of California. By then, she had spent almost a decade in the movies (1949–58) and another appearing sporadically on TV (1953–62).

Nancy must have sensed that stardom would always elude her and that she would be just another character actress playing mothers, aunts,

95

and next door neighbors—or, if she were lucky, a recurring role in a sit-com. At any rate, once Reagan became governor, she had her work cut out for her making the governor's mansion habitable, redecorating his office, and preparing him for his next change of address to 1600 Penn-sylvania Avenue—which was more suited to her tastes, although it, too, needed redecorating.

In the 1950s, Reagan, Jane, and Nancy shared a common bond: tele-vision, which could jump-start a career when movie roles were few or nonexistent. In 1958, Jane, Nancy, and Reagan were all on the tube within a few months of each other. Nancy co-starred with Reagan on *General Electric Theater* in "Turkey for the President" (23 November). Jane had her own show. She was such a successful host on *Fireside Theatre* that the program was renamed *Jane Wyman's Fireside Theatre*. In Spring 1958, Reagan starred on *General Electric Theater* in "The Coward of Fort Bennett" with Neville Brand and John Dall (26 March) and "No Hiding Place" with Geraldine Page (6 April). During that period, Jane appeared five times on her own show: "The Doctor Was a Lady" (27 March 1958), "The Bravado Touch" (17 April), "Man of Taste" (24 April), "The Last Test" (8 May), and "Hide and Seek" (22 May).

None of them would have thought that their lives would become as interleaved as they did. But once Reagan the actor yielded to Reagan the politician, then to Reagan the governor, and finally to Reagan the president, his movies—known to subsequent generations from televi-sion broadcast—became a mirror reflecting his persona. To see Reagan flash his folksy smile is to see a montage of Reagan smiles. When Reagan stood at Berlin's Brandenburg Gate on 11 June 1987 demanding, "Mr. Gorbachev, tear down this wall," there was a distant echo of "Win one for the Gipper." "Time present and time past / Are both perhaps present in time future," T. S. Eliot wrote in "Burnt Norton," the first of the *Four Quartets*. Reagan's past was his present—and future.

But with Reagan's ascendency and Nancy's transition from actress to First Lady, Jane was, except for film buffs, Angela Channing of *Falcon Crest*, cunning and imperious, qualities that she rarely displayed on the big screen. Jane was "button nose," as Reagan called her, until it was time for her second self to emerge. Jane Wyman may have won an Oscar and a Golden Globe, but to the press, she was Ronald Reagan's first wife, sought out only for statements about her ex, which she refused to make.

Jane, Reagan, and Nancy were three actors in the same profession; Jane and Nancy were two women with the same husband. That much is a given. But to think of them as a trinity downgrades their achievements.

Jane would have been ill at ease as the housewife in *The Next Voice You Hear* (1950), a role that Nancy played memorably. However, Nancy could never have accomplished what Jane did in *Johnny Belinda*, performing as if she were in a silent movie in which everyone else spoke. It is hard to imagine Nancy in the scene in which Belinda, proud of her mastery of signing and desperate for recognition from her father, makes the "father" sign with her hands, her eyes glowing with pride and at the same time eager for approval. Yet Nancy's film and television work was perfectly respectable—in a few instances, better than respectable—as was Reagan's. Reagan and Nancy were professionals—not in Jane's league, but not little league, either. On the other hand, Jane had her limitations. She was uncomfortable in comedies that blurred into screwball. When her role in *The Doughgirls* was downgraded from ingénue to ditz, she played it in the only way she knew how: as a bubblehead. Jane could not do deadpan; Jean Arthur could, and with an innocence too pure for life to sully. Jane could use her doll-like face to convey innocence for a particular scene, such as the one in *Johnny Belinda* where Stephen McNally entices her with the violin. But madcaps were alien to her, probably because she had a disdain for that type, having come up the hard way in a business with a low survival rate. Fortunately, screwball was not one of Warners' specialties, so Jane only had to don the motley in *The Body Disappears*, *Make Your Own Bed*, and *The Doughgirls*.

When an actor switches professions, embracing one that seems radically different from the first, the public is initially taken aback. Eventually, however, people become accustomed to such change, whether it is Ron Howard shedding his *Happy Days* image for the director's chair, or Glenda Jackson abandoning movies for a seat in the British parliament. As the years go by, *Happy Days* ends up on *TV Land* or *Nickelodeon*, while Howard's reputation as a director keeps growing (*Splash, Cocoon, Apollo 13, A Beautiful Mind*). Jackson's movies appear on cable channels, but not with much regularity. Jackson is a cultivated taste; her mesmerizing performances in Ken Russell's *Women in Love* and *The Music Lovers* are things of beauty for those who seek them out.

Reagan and Nancy underwent a more radical transition, moving from the sound stage to the world stage. As they changed spotlights, their former professions mattered only to film historians. They were considered "fading stars" who had lost their standing in corporate Hollywood, but not among their colleagues from the studio era. Claudette Colbert remained a close friend. When Reagan was president, she was a frequent visitor at the White House, as he was at her home on Barbados, where he knew he would get gourmet cooking. When Reagan was making movies, he and Nancy socialized with Arlene Dahl and Fernando Lamas, their neighbors on the Pacific Palisades. Dahl was a close friend of the Reagans. She came to Warner Bros. in late 1946 to co-star with Dennis Morgan in the musical *My Wild Irish Rose* (1947). Two of the first actors she met were Jane and Reagan. She found Jane "delightful, funny, warm, and outgoing"—qualities that endeared Jane to others as well. Reagan struck her differently, as "cordial but standoffish." Jane and Reagan's marriage was on the verge of unraveling in December 1946, but the two (Jane especially) acted as if they were still very much in love. But such was not the case. Jane, who was never much for introspection except when it came to interpreting a complex character, had all she could do to divest herself of Ma Baxter, and prepare for a contemporary film like *Magic Town* and a period one like *Cheyenne* without becoming copy for stories about another Hollywood marriage on the rocks. That was for the scouts, who haunt restaurants and nightclubs, garnering bald facts or mere conjectures that could be gussied up as gossip.

Of all the studios where Dahl worked, MGM is the one most associated with her. It was also Nancy Davis's first studio. Arlene met Nancy in 1949. They immediately became friends; after Nancy married Reagan, they became neighbors. When Nancy expressed her desire to have a son (she already had a daughter, Patti), Dahl, who believed in folklore and astrology, explained that when *she* wanted a son, she was advised to place a blue light near her bed—perhaps because of the blue for boys, pink for girls tradition. She gave Nancy a blue light, and Nancy had a son, Ronald Prescott Reagan, born on 20 May 1958. Dahl, Nancy, Cyd Charisse, and Doris Day patronized the same hairdresser. After a session at the salon, the four would have tea. Dahl, also an astrologist, would read the leaves. When Nancy asked for a reading, Dahl complied. The leaves, she explained, suggest California, not for moviemaking, but something of a radically different nature. Reagan was elected governor of California in 1966. Whether Arlene Dahl's readings were the source of Nancy's interest in the stars is unknown, but Nancy had an early introduction to the art of prognostication. Dahl was so convinced that Reagan would be president that, although she was living in Bordeaux at the time, she voted for him by absentee ballot. She picked a winner. The stars? The man? The people? All three?

Clearly, Reagan and Nancy were not Hollywood has-beens, although neither of their movie careers was comparable to Jane's, which spanned almost four decades. Reagan's was limited to two, Nancy's to almost one.

Television broadened their fan base, but it was never as big as Jane's, which included *Fireside Theatre* regulars and later *Falcon Crest* devotees. Reagan was, to use an old-fashioned term, a journeyman actor. Nancy, if she continued in the business, would have fallen into the category of supporting actress/occasional lead/sitcom regular or series guest, any of which would have added a few more lumens to her wattage—but not enough to light up the screen, big or small.

Chapter 14

The Rest—and Best—of Reagan

REAGAN MADE OVER FIFTY FILMS OF VARYING QUALITY. THE BEST ATTEST to a talent that served him as well on the screen as it did in politics. He had his strengths and weaknesses. His strengths were evident in dramas like *Tennessee's Partner* and *Kings Row*, and in comedies like *The Girl from Jones Beach* and *Bedtime for Bonzo*. During the studio era, producers were savvy enough to know that actors must play to their strengths, and Reagan's lay in comedy, melodrama, westerns, and war films. Although he appeared in two musicals, *This Is the Army* and *She's Working Her Way through College*, he was never a song and dance man. Only once was he given a part that was beyond him, with results that were not disastrous, just disconcerting.

Night unto Night (1949) was the only film that revealed Reagan's limitations as a serious actor. He could manage any kind of drama but psychological. Warners should have known as much, yet even before Reagan returned to civilian life, the studio had selected his next film, *Night unto Night*, in which he would play an epileptic biochemist. Reagan could have gone on suspension, arguing that he was wrong for the part. But he had no intention of jeopardizing his thirty-five hundred dollar a week contract. *Night unto Night* began production on 20 September 1946 and should have been ready for an early 1947 release. Instead, it arrived in theaters in spring 1949.

It is difficult to know why Warners bought the rights to Philip Wylie's novel without having the right actor to play the tortured scientist, saved from suicide by a widow haunted by her husband's ghost. The widow was not the problem; she was the studio's new discovery, the Swedish born Viveca Lindfors, Warners' answer to Ingrid Bergman. Lindfors was a talented actress, better equipped for the stage than the screen—but no Bergman. The problem, however, was the male lead. There were few actors at Warners in 1946 who could convey the character's mental anguish, except perhaps John Garfield or Dane Clark, either of whom would have been more effective than Reagan, whose idea of angst was a granite-like face.

Don Siegel had just graduated from the montage unit to the director's chair, when he was handed *Night unto Night*, his second film. He did the best he could with a self-defeating script. The opening title, "The east coast of Florida," is followed by an intricate tracking shot from the beach to the house facing it. The front door is strangely ajar, so that the camera can enter just as a woman (Lindfors) rushes down the staircase and on to the grounds, throwing desperate glances at an upstairs window as if someone were there, and then coming face to face with a man (Reagan), who has come by to rent the house. The spectacular opening shot suggested a brooding melodrama with shocking revelations. Instead, it became an apologia for the spirit world, with a Wagnerian redemption by love finale.

The film chugged along toward the climax, a dinner party during a hurricane. The widow's sister (Osa Massen) drinks too much and divulges the scientist's dark secret, as if epilepsy were a communicable disease. Silently, he leaves the table and goes upstairs with a revolver. A power failure provides the right atmosphere for the denouement, in which the widow offers him the love he needs to stay alive. The winds howl, the rain lashes the windows, the redeemer and the redeemed embrace—and the film is shelved for three years, until the studio decided to release it in May 1949, a few months before another and better Reagan movie, *The Girl from Jones Beach*, hit the theaters. The latter was a commercial success; *Night unto Night* found favor with neither critics nor audiences. Siegel could not generate any heat between Reagan and Lindfors because the script made it impossible for a scientist who does not believe in a hereafter to fall in love with a woman who does. Lindfors tried to make their romance believable, but she was saddled with Reagan, who delivered his lines as if he were trying to remember something more important. Although Reagan was supposed to be an epileptic, he was spared an on-camera seizure, blacking out instead.

Ironically, in his last film for Warners, *The Winning Team* (1952), Reagan played another epileptic, the great pitcher and Baseball Hall of Famer Grover Cleveland Alexander. The script reduced Alexander's epilepsy to seizures, which would only make sense to the knowledgeable. At least Reagan was in his element and fared better as a ballplayer than he did as a marine biologist. Since Reagan's co-star was Doris Day, billed first, a few musical numbers were thrown in to lighten the mood, "Take Me Out to the Ball Game" being one of them. Alexander's is an inspiring story, but there was little inspiration in *The Winning Team*.

Night unto Night was planned as Lindfors's American debut, but by the time it was released, she had already appeared in two other films, *To the Victor* and *The Adventures of Don Juan* (both 1948). Her English had improved considerably, so much so that anyone who saw *Night unto Night* might have wondered about her occasionally faulty enunciation. Reagan, meanwhile, was on a roll. He had starred in four movies by the time *Night unto Night* opened nationwide: *Stallion Road*, *That Hagen Girl*, and *The Voice of the Turtle* in 1947; and *John Loves Mary* in February 1949, three months before the release of *Night unto Night*.

During the filming, Reagan would engage Lindfors in conversation, although all she ever remembered was his claim that sex is best following an afternoon shower. Reagan must have been programmed in high testosterone mode that day, since most actresses used words like "charming" and "paternal" to describe him. Virginia Mayo found him especially helpful when they were making *The Girl from Jones Beach*; he would explain the studio hierarchy to her and "point out the important people, giving me the correct names and titles, before I was officially introduced."

The Girl from Jones Beach enabled Reagan to do what he did best, romantic comedy. He had no competition in his pursuit of the title character (Virginia Mayo), who spends her mornings sunning herself at Jones Beach in a white strapless bathing suit and her evenings teaching English to international students. I. A. L. "Izzy" Diamond, Billy Wilder's second great collaborator (the first was Charles Brackett), was well versed in the "meet cute" tradition and devised a neat one for Reagan and Mayo. Reagan, a commercial artist eager for Mayo to pose for him and convinced that his cool virility will win her over, enrolls in her class. When she inquires about his origins, he replies in an accent that sounds vaguely Czech—or so Mayo assumes. Reagan reveled in the role, slipping in and out of various accents and explaining the variety by invoking his family's peripatetic background. He turns courtship into a game that proves unwinnable. He flirts; she's coy. He's attracted to her body; she wants to be admired for her mind. In lieu of love talk, they quote poetry at each other as if they were participants in a literary competition. Eventually, the artist is unmasked, but by that time, mutual attraction has set in, signaling a happy ending.

Diamond tacked on a coda that had nothing to do with the "will they or won't they" romance (we know they will), but rather with the bathing suit. When the teacher's picture in 1949's hottest bathing suit appears in the papers, the school board demands her resignation. She refuses, the case goes to court, and the artist and the teacher's lawyer (Jerome Cowan) present the jury with an illustrated history of the bathing suit, proving that what shocks one generation strikes another as innocuous. Anyone, especially teachers, seeing the film today would roll their eyes at the thought of one of their own being dismissed because of a swim suit. But this was a time when women were designated as either Miss or Mrs., depending on marital status ("Ms" did not exist), and the classifieds carried dual listings: "Help Wanted—Male" and "Help Wanted—Female." Never the twain shall meet—at least not in the 1949 job listings.

Reagan's best films of the 1950s were *Bedtime for Bonzo* (UI, 1951) and *Tennessee's Partner* (RKO, 1955). Any actor playing opposite a chimpanzee who can drink milk from a glass, ride a bike down a city street, and steal a necklace from a jewelry store knows who the star is—and it is not himself, despite what the credits say. But Reagan was a good sport and gave a winning performance in *Bedtime for Bonzo* as Dr. Peter Boyd, a psychology professor convinced that he can teach moral reasoning to Bonzo, a chimpanzee, by providing a nurturing environment. The professor and Jane (Diana Lynn), a young woman in his employ, would play father and mother to Bonzo, treating him as if he were their own child.

The premise derives from the familiar heredity vs. environment debate, with Boyd's dean espousing the former. The dean knows that Boyd's father was a con man who died in prison. Since Boyd is engaged to his daughter, the dean is concerned that his future son-in-law may have inherited criminal tendencies. The Bonzo experiment is Boyd's attempt to illustrate the connection between a sound home environment and character development. If a chimp can be taught the difference between right and wrong and return a necklace to the display window from which he has taken it, there is hope for humankind. In the 1930s, Hollywood promoted the "environment as a determinant of character" theory—but usually in a negative way, emphasizing the connection between crime and the environment that produced it in such films as *Dead End* (1937), *Angels with Dirty Faces* (1938), *Crime School* (1938), *Girls on Probation* (1938), and *Dust Be My Destiny* (1939). *Bedtime for Bonzo* was the opposite, the equivalent of a chimpanzee's Boys Town.

Reagan and Lynn took on the challenge of playing surrogate parents to Bonzo, doing it so artfully that the audience warmed to this unorthodox family and regarded the chimp as a precocious but mischievous child. Even the director, Fred de Cordova, found himself addressing Bonzo as if he were one of the actors—which, of course, he was. Reagan felt similarly. At the beginning of the film, Bonzo escapes from the college lab, refusing to be treated like a scientific experiment. He climbs on to an ivy-encrusted ledge, as if contemplating suicide. A colleague (Walter Sleazak) prevails on Boyd to reason with Bonzo. "Good morning. Bad as all that?" Boyd asks, carefully working his way along the ledge. Reagan behaved like a seasoned politician, using a combination of charm and tact to rescue Bonzo, as if he were a sulking child in need of affection. The gentle approach works, and Bonzo is ready for a different experiment that will prove even a chimp can benefit from a home in which he is treated as a family member, not as a specimen.

Although Reagan played the title character in *Tennessee's Partner* (1955), he was not the star. Top billed was John Payne as Tennessee, followed by Reagan, Rhonda Fleming, and Coleen Gray. The actresses played characters that do not exist in Bret Harte's classic short story, although Gray's Goldie Slater was suggested by the trashy waitress in the original who betrays both Tennessee and his nameless partner. In terms of film history, *Tennessee's Partner* is significant, not for Reagan— although he does well as the partner, renamed "Cowpoke"—but for the director, the venerable Allan Dwan, who spent half a century in the business, racking up a staggering total of some four hundred movies between 1911 and 1961; the producer, Benedict Bogeaus, who specialized in bringing minor classics of fiction to the screen (Thornton Wilder's *The Bridge of San Luis Rey*; Ernest Hemingway's "The Short Happy Life of Francis Macomber"; and James M. Cain's *Love's Lovely Counterfeit*, filmed as *The Macomber Affair* and *Slightly Scarlet*, respectively); and the director of photography, John Alton, renowned for his meticulously calibrated monochrome, but also capable of working in color, as he proved in this and other Dwan-Bogeaus productions (*Silver Lode*, *Cattle Queen of Montana*, in which Reagan co-starred with Barbara Stanwyck, *Escape to Burma*, *Pearl of the South Pacific*, and *Slightly Scarlet*).

Although the film claims to be "based on Bret Harte's Tennessee's Partner," all it owes to the source are the title and the two main characters, neither of whom has a real name. "Tennessee" is a nickname, and the Partner doesn't even have that. "I do not think we ever knew his real name," the story's narrator states at the beginning. But the same is true of Tennessee. These are men without given names or identities, without pasts or futures, but only the present. Tennessee and his partner bond together in a strangely beautiful relationship, personifying the pure love between men that, according to Leslie Fiedler's *Love and Death in the American Novel*, lies at the heart of the American wilderness novel, in which women, like the nameless waitress in the story, are intruders in a male microcosm.

"Tennessee's Partner" is written with such emotional restraint and controlled poignancy that the tears that would ordinarily spill out at the end, in which the Partner follows Tennessee in death, do not materialize. If they did, they would be antithetical to Harte's spare form of storytelling, which asks the reader to enter the consciousness of men whose emotions have been stunted by the overriding need to survive in a world where deep feelings are a liability. "Tennessee's Partner" is almost like a folk tale about two men, who, like the loners in the movie western, arrive from nowhere without pasts to burden them. The Partner, then living with Tennessee, decides to head out to San Francisco for a wife, stopping at Stockton where his crude proposal to a waitress gets him smacked in the face with a plate of toast. But he persists, the waitress consents, and a short-lived marriage results. But once Tennessee meets the new bride, the marriage is over. The two run off together, leaving the Partner confused but not vengeful. When the bride sets her sights on another and dumps Tennessee, he returns to live with the Partner as if nothing had happened.

Harte's Tennessee is an outlaw, who is eventually apprehended and sentenced to death by hanging. The guileless Partner, thinking that compensating the victims for their losses would satisfy the jury, offers his savings to return for Tennessee's life—but to no avail. Tennessee is hanged, and the Partner buries him, dying shortly thereafter. "It's time to go for Tennessee" are the Partner's last words. "And so they met" are the narrator's. Ideally, the reader should just pause and reflect, perhaps ruefully, about a friendship too pure to be sullied by adultery or terminated by death.

No screenwriter could do much with such a dispassionate text, in which the sole woman is just a plot point. Fleshing her out into Goldie, a demure-looking vamp, made her even more of an unwelcome presence. Goldie provides the love interest for Cowpoke; the Duchess (Rhonda Fleming), a madam, does the same for Tennessee. Both actresses played their roles to the hilt, with Fleming looking every bit as if she could run a classy whore house, and Coleen Gray alternating between virgin and whore, capable of being either at a moment's notice.

When Tennessee discovers that Goldie is really a "tramp," he packs her off to San Francisco to spare Cowpoke from learning the truth. But Cowpoke, believing that the two have run off together, seeks revenge.

Reagan played the later scenes well, switching from naïf to avenger and confronting Tennessee in a violent brawl. Once Cowpoke and Tennessee are reconciled, the plot moves toward its climax, with Cowpoke dying in an attempt to save Tennessee's life, and Tennessee and the Duchess lighting out for another territory.

Reagan only did a handful of westerns in his career (*Santa Fe Trail, The Last Outpost, Cattle Queen of Montana, Tennessee's Partner, Law and Order*), yet it was a genre at which he excelled. He was very much at home on the range, where he did not have to run the limited gamut from a grin and a smile to an embrace and a fade out. Reagan could do serious drama, but only if he were playing someone with whom he could empathize. He was not the type to resort to emotional memory, plumbing the depths of his psyche to wriggle into the skin of a suicidal epileptic. But cast him as a lawyer who takes on the KKK (*Storm Warning*), or a Korean War POW (*Prisoner of War*), and he could deliver. These were roles within his range, which was not much different from that of most of Warners' contract actors—except Cagney, Robinson, and Bogart, who had more opportunities to demonstrate their versatility.

Reagan reached his dramatic peak in *Kings Row* (1942) as the dapper Drake McHugh, an orphan hoping to make his fortune in real estate, until a conscienceless doctor needlessly amputates his legs to prevent Drake from marrying his daughter. *Kings Row* was Reagan's most prestigious film. It was based on the controversial 1940 novel of the same name written by Henry Bellamann. The novel depicted small-town America as a pre-Peyton Place, darker and more class conscious, where incest, nymphomania, insanity, homosexuality, anti-Catholicism, racism, murder, suicide, medical malpractice, and euthanasia were masked by a veneer of righteousness and gentility. It was a town festering with suppression and shame. Dr. Alexander Tower's daughter is a victim of incest and as mentally unstable as her mother, and whom the doctor poisons before taking his own life. Dr. Henry Gordon, a surgeon, refuses to give anesthetics to patients he considers morally unworthy and performs an unnecessary amputation on his daughter's suitor because he does not come from her class. His daughter Louise knows about her father's lack of medical ethics and threatens to expose him, only to have him threaten her with institutionalization. Louise then disappears from the plot, but from the way Nancy Coleman played her in the film, it was evident that Coleman had either read the novel or been informed about Louise's fate: commitment to an asylum after her father's death. Kings Row is the kind of town in which the Tower house is so forbidding that children boycott a birthday party held there, and where the mad woman is not in the attic but at an upstairs window.

Reagan had the perfect team in *Kings Row*. The director was Sam Wood, one of the most versatile in the business, who could handle farce (the Marx Brothers films, *A Night at the Opera* and *A Day at the Races*), romantic comedy (*Guest Wife, Good Sam*), literary and stage adaptations (*Goodbye, Mr. Chips, Kitty Foyle, Kings Row, For Whom the Bell Tolls, Saratoga Trunk, Our Town, Command Decision*), and biopics (*Pride of the Yankees, The Stratton Story*). The western was alien to him, yet he attempted one, *Ambush*, his final film, completed a week before his fatal heart attack on 22 September 1949. Wood's daughter, actress K. T. Stevens, attributed his early death at sixty-five to the rigors of location shooting, as well as his virulent anti-communism, which also took its toll on his health.

The screenwriter was Casey Robinson, who also adapted *Dark Victory* as a vehicle for Bette Davis, with Reagan in the supporting cast as one of F. Scott Fitzgerald's sad young men, who drink their lives away. Robinson knew how to adapt *Kings Row* without eviscerating it, creating a version that would conform to the Production Code. He dispensed with the clergymen and Jamie Wakefield, whose effeminacy ("too pretty for a boy") is established early in the novel and whose attempted seduction of Parris could never be depicted, even though in the book it is described with great delicacy. Gone, too, was the affair between the white Peyton and the African American Melissa, neither of whom even appears as a character in the film. Since Peyton eventually shoots himself, Robinson reasoned that one suicide was enough. The score for *Kings Row* was composed by the eminent Erich Wolfgang Korngold. The producer was Hal Wallis. The production designer was William Cameron Menzies. And James Wong Howe was the director of photography. Reagan would never again work with such a distinguished group.

Warners knew there would be problems with *Kings Row* once America entered the war. February 1942 was not an ideal release date, but the alternative was to shelve the film for a few years, as the studio did with *Arsenic and Old Lace*, which was shot in December 1941 and released in 1944 after the play had ended its Broadway run. But it would not have mattered when *Kings Row* was released during the war. There were those who believed, like *New York Times* critic Bosley Crowther, that such a negative portrait of American life was hardly a morale booster. In his review (3 February 1942), Crowther labeled the film "gloomy and ponderous," and wondered "just why the Warners attempted a picture of this sort in these times." It was as if a movie depicting a community of misfits was unpatriotic, and only an America with white picket fences and rambling roses was the proper image for a nation at war. But Wallis believed in the film.

Casting, however, was another matter. Reagan's role, Drake McHugh, was not the lead; he was third billed after Ann Sheridan and Robert Cummings. Sheridan was Randy Monaghan, the daughter of a railroad worker in love with Drake. Cummings was eventually cast as the idealistic Parris Mitchell, who is hopelessly in love with the aptly named Cassandra "Cassie" Tower (Betty Field), the mentally disturbed daughter of the reclusive Dr. Tower (Claude Rains). When Parris chooses medicine as a profession, Tower agrees to mentor him, leaving him the house after he poisons his daughter and commits suicide as a way of rewarding Parris for not pursuing a relationship with Cassie. Having no reason to remain in Kings Row. Parris resumes his medical studies in Vienna, developing a specialty in psychiatry.

Wood wanted Cummings for Parris, even though the actor had to commute between Universal in the San Fernando Valley, where he was completing *It Started with Eve* (1941) with Deanna Durbin and Charles Laughton, and Warners in Burbank. Sheridan was also doubly committed, but at least both jobs were at her home studio, where she could go from *The Man Who Came to Dinner* sound stage to the *Kings Row* set. Cummings was not the ideal Parris. Crowther thought that "he looks and acts like a musical comedy juvenile trying to find his bearings in a heavy Ibsenesque plot." But at least Cummings projected an air of integrity, which made the character believable. Cassie was the problem. Wood campaigned for Ida Lupino, but neither she nor her agent felt the role was right for her, believing that appearing in a secondary role with Ann Sheridan in the lead would look like a demotion. Jack Warner, whose idea of casting was staying within the shallow pool of contract talent before looking elsewhere, preferred his own actresses, Joan Leslie and Priscilla Lane—or Susan Peters, if MGM would loan her out.

The actress who really wanted to play Cassie was Bette Davis, hoping for a mad scene that would top the one she had in *Juarez*. If Davis had been given the role, she would have done a star turn, taking over the film by sheer force of personality and deflecting attention from every one else. Betty Field inherited the role. Initially a stage actress and married to playwright Elmer Rice, Field proved she knew the difference between theatre and film when she played Curley's wife in *Of Mice and Men* (1939) with the right blend of provocation and sensuality. She worked the same combination into her characterization of Cassie, portraying her as both mentally unstable and sexually available, so that audiences could easily infer that she saw Parris as her liberator. Those familiar with the novel would have appreciated the subtlety with which Field used her quivering body and tremulous voice to convey Cassie's sexual longing.

In the novel, Parris and his childhood love, Renée, often went swimming after school. Robinson eliminated Renée as a character but retained the swimming scene, with Cassie and Parris. Thus Cassie's lack of inhibition is evident in the prologue, in which Parris, Drake, Randy, and Cassie appear as children. Cassie and Parris meet near a lake, where they innocently strip off their clothes and go skinny-dipping. Wood ignored Joe Breen's mandate that "there is no suggestion of nude bathing." The young Cassie (Mary Thomas) may not have been in the altogether, but she certainly looked it. How anyone could have objected to a moment of such prelapsarian innocence is hard to fathom. In view of what was going on in Kings Row, two grade school children swimming in the nude was a welcome moment of normalcy.

Reagan knew that the scene in which Drake discovers he is legless would be the hardest he had ever had to play. He rehearsed it repeatedly, consulting surgeons and paraplegics, until he realized that, as an actor, he had to find his own way into the scene. Realizing what has happened, Drake calls out, "Randy!" When she rushes into the room, we see a close up of Reagan's face, tightened into a mask of fear and incomprehension, as he makes the tragic discovery. In a voice both questioning and demanding, he cries, "Where's the rest of me?" The close up of a face marked by helplessness and despair is not enough. Wood cuts to a shot of Sheridan hovering over Reagan, his facial muscles so taut that they too seem grief-stricken.

Casey Robinson realized that Drake had suffered enough to be spared his fate in the novel, cancer of the hip. Instead, Parris reveals the truth about the needless amputation, causing Drake to let out an "As if that's going to stop me" laugh. With Reagan's life-affirming face, the storm clouds dispersed, a broken world was made whole, and amputees—of whom there would be many more by the end of the war—were given hope. If Ronald Reagan could do business from his bed, so could they from a wheelchair.

Kings Row may have been Reagan's finest hour, but it was not Jane's. And she did not appreciate his frequent screenings of the film. His obsession with it might have been a contributing factor to the divorce, but it was not the cause. Reagan's obsession with the film may have gotten the better of him, but he had every reason to be proud of his performance.

For the first time in his career, he realized what an actor has to do to prepare for a role in which a close up and a single line of dialogue convey a state of mind. That Reagan managed magnificently. Reagan could envision himself as immobile, but not suicidal.

Although neither Jane nor Reagan realized it at the time, the divorce was mutual. Jane could no longer remain in the shadow of her husband, playing helpmeet, when she had a career that was moving faster than his. And he could no longer bear to be eclipsed by a wife who could not stand by him as he eased his way out of Hollywood and into national, and soon, international politics. But Nancy Davis could.

Chapter 15

Stars in Her Eyes

IN NEW YORK, THE EVENING OF 6 FEBRUARY 1946 WAS RELATIVELY mild. The temperature reached a high of 48, and it was in the 40s at 8:00 p.m., when audiences started filing into the theaters. Broadway was at its zenith. *Oklahoma!* was in its third season and *Carousel* in its second. Other musicals included the revival of Victor Herbert's *The Red Mill*, *Bloomer Girl*, *Billion Dollar Baby*, *Song of Norway*, *Up in Central Park*, and *Follow the Girls*, with Gertrude Niesen lamenting the plight of the single female in "I Wanna Get Married," whose unexpurgated lyrics could only be heard on the stage of the Broadhurst Theatre. For theatergoers preferring straight plays, there was *Life with Father*, now in its seventh year, and *The Voice of the Turtle* in its third. Among the newer plays were *I Remember Mama* at the Music Box and *The Magnificent Yankee* at the Royale (now the Bernard B. Jacobs) Theatre.

That evening, a new musical was opening at the Plymouth (now the Gerald Schoenfeld), right next to the Royale. Actually, it was a musical version of an ancient Chinese play, *Pi-Pa-Ki*, adapted by Sidney Howard and Will Irwin, with a score by Raymond Scott and lyrics by Bernard Hanighen. The star was Mary Martin, who had scored a great success three years earlier in Kurt Weill's *One Touch of Venus*. *Lute Song* was a departure for Martin, who was used to a traditional book musical with a score by a well-known composer like Cole Porter or Kurt Weill. Martin accepted the challenge of playing the wife of a Chinese student (Yul Brynner), who is forced to marry a princess (Helen Craig). Eventually, the couple is reunited, but only after the wife's parents die from famine. The score had some lovely moments, including an imperial march grand enough for Puccini's *Turandot*, and Martin's "Mountain High, Valley

Low," plaintive and tonally spare, but haunting in the way a melody can be when stripped of embellishments and reduced to a pure vocal line.

Martin looked elegant as Tchao-Ou-Niang in her Valentina costumes, which she wore even when she was reduced to begging. The critics agreed it was an exquisite production, chinoiserie at its finest. Martin could do no wrong, but her co-star Yul Brynner only gave a "satisfactory performance," according to the *New York Times* (7 February 1946). Martin believed so much in the show that she accepted a salary cut, which had no effect on the box office. *Lute Song* closed after 126 performances. Assuming London's West End would be more receptive to the musical, the producers dispatched Dolly Haas, Martin's understudy and wife of the caricaturist Al Hirschfeld, and Brynner to London. But the British were unimpressed, and the show barely lasted three weeks. Anyone lucky enough to have seen the two-week revival at the New York City Center in 1959, with Dolly Haas as the wife, experienced an uncut gem of musical theatre awaiting a setting. *Lute Song* required stylized acting devoid of affectation—theatre without theatrics.

The original cast included such stalwarts as Clarence Derwent, and Mildred Dunnock. Playing a lady in waiting was the twenty-five-year-old Nancy Davis, in her first and only Broadway show. Ironically, a few blocks north of the Plymouth was the Rivoli, where *The Lost Weekend* was still playing. One would like to think that Nancy knew who Jane Wyman was; if she did, she probably thought of Jane as just another movie star, hardly on a par with artists of the legitimate theatre.

Nancy might never have been in the show. Director John Houseman thought that she lacked authenticity. To Houseman, she was nothing but "a pink-cheeked, attractive but awkward and amateurish virgin." What he didn't know was that the virgin, whose status would soon change—if it hadn't already—was bent on an acting career. When Nancy was living in Chicago, she sought out Martin during the *One Touch of Venus* tour. Martin was less interested in Nancy's future than she was in repaying a debt to Nancy's stepfather, neurosurgeon Loyal Davis, who was always on call when Martin had back problems. Nancy went unnoticed by the critics; hers was a role that was only intended to lend an air of authenticity to the production. Replacing her would not have saved *Lute Song*.

The key members of the cast did well for themselves: Martin went on to *South Pacific*; Dunnock to Arthur Miller's *Death of a Salesman*; Derwent to Jean Giraudoux's *The Madwoman of Chaillot*; and Brynner to his signature role in *The King and I*. In a few years, Nancy would be westward bound.

Unlike Jane, who had to serve a grueling apprenticeship among the unbilled until she graduated to B movies and eventually stardom, Nancy was born for the stage. It made no difference if it were in a theater, a sound stage, a television studio, a dais, a dance floor, or a platform—Nancy usurped the spotlight whenever she could. Jane relied on the director of photography's ability to determine the right ratio of key to fill light, with back lighting for depth, to show her to advantage. As governor's wife and first lady, Nancy received star treatment from approved photographers. Jane always dressed like the movie star she was, tastefully but not ostentatiously. Nancy dressed like an ad for The Tailored Woman, which once occupied the corner of Fifth Avenue and 57th Street, known for clothes with "good style, good lines, good quality, and quiet colors." That was Nancy Davis—and Nancy Reagan.

Nancy always claimed she was born in New York. That was stretching it a bit. According to her birth certificate, she was born in the borough of Queens to Mrs. Edith P. Robbins, "housewife," and Kenneth Seymour Robbins, who gave as his profession the "automobile business." In Edith's case, "actress" would have been more accurate than "housewife," a role for which Edith was ill suited. She was a married actress.

Edith began her stage career in 1907. When it ended in 1929, her résumé consisted of at least forty credits in such perennials as *Charley's Aunt*, *The Little Minister*, *The Royal Family*, and *Seven Keys to Baldpate*. She began with bit roles in plays at the Columbia Theatre in Washington, DC, which was managed by her brother, Joseph Luckett. She performed mainly in stock and on tour, at one point serving as the leading lady of E. H. Hurley's stock company in Dallas. Broadway was another matter. Edith appeared six times in New York in productions that rarely lasted more than two weeks. She did not impress the critics; in fact, the *New York Times* (16 February 1926) thought that *The Right to Kill*—a melodrama about a woman who murders her blackmailing lover, with Edith as the district attorney's wife—was "badly cast," except for the leads. She also had no luck with movies, making only three: *The Spirit of the Poppy* (1914), *The Coming Power* (1914), and *The Other Girl* (1916). Since the films were shot in New York (*The Other Girl* was shot in both Manhattan and Staten Island), traveling from Washington, DC, to New York was not a problem. She had already appeared in two New York productions, *The Crisis* (1908) and *Drifting* (1910), the latter at Nazimova's 39th Street theatre, named after the great Russian actress, who became a close friend and Nancy's godmother. Since *The Right to Kill* was based on a Russian melodrama, and the *New York Times* described the lead as giving a

Nazimova-like performance, Nazimova probably used her influence to get Edith a part in the "badly cast" production. Regardless, it was an opportunity to play New York.

Nancy was very much her mother's daughter. Edith considered age a number to be changed at will. It was bad enough that she was twenty-seven when she married Robbins, who was five years younger. There was no way Edith could pass for twenty, but twenty-four might work. And so, she would only be two years older than her husband. Nancy felt similarly about age: "Mother used to say, 'A woman who will tell her age will tell *anything*.'" Nancy, born in 1921, preferred 1923, so she could claim she made her Broadway debut at twenty-three rather than at twenty-five. Jane, on the other hand, at first added to her age, preferring a 1914 birth date to 1917, so it would seem that she was eighteen when she started in pictures, not fifteen. When she became an established star, the deception ended, and publicity releases always gave her birth date as 1917.

"Some are born great, some achieve greatness, and some have greatness thrust upon 'em," as Malvolio was seduced into believing in *Twelfth Night*. Edith was meant to marry a man whom she could thrust into greatness, not a man who sold cars. Two years after Nancy's birth, Edith's marriage to Robbins was over, and it was on to Chicago to join the company of George M. Cohan's *The Baby Cyclone*. It was there that she met her next husband, neurosurgeon Loyal Davis. Edith had no intention of either of them being stranded on the road to fame. If she were to marry Davis, her acting days would be over. But that did not matter. She would simply change venues, and make her living room a stage, sashaying her way into Chicago society, gaining acceptance for herself and patients for Davis, whom she married on 21 May 1929. The bride was forty-one, the groom thirty-three. Marrying younger men had a rejuvenating effect on Edith, who came off looking younger than her husbands. Nancy was more traditional: When she married Reagan, he was ten years older than she.

Edith was determined that Nancy should be an actress and marry well. Although Edith did not complete high school, she sent her daughter to the best, the Chicago Girls Latin School, after which Nancy went east to Smith. But to Nancy, college, even a prestigious one like Smith, was less important than succeeding in a business where her mother only enjoyed modest success.

When she was fifteen, Nancy decided to consign Anne Frances Robbins to New York's Bureau of Vital Records. She replaced "Anne Frances" with Nancy, her mother's nickname for her, and "Robbins" with

Davis, her stepfather's surname. And so, in 1936, Nancy Davis emerged from the wings to occupy a stage that grew increasingly larger, eventually becoming international. It was a wise choice. "Anne Frances Robbins" sounded like a debutante in a frilly white gown with a high bodice. "Nancy Davis" was dissyllabic and pure Anglo-Saxon, like Ronald Reagan. It also sounded wholesomely Protestant.

In her last year at Girls Latin, Nancy played the lead in Katharine Dayton and George S. Kaufman's *First Lady*. The role, created by Jane Cowl, required the high style that would have been beyond the capacity of a high school senior. How well Nancy did in the part must be left to the imagination, although it was certainly the best primer on Washington politics that a future first lady could have: lunching with the right crowd in the right places, agonizing over seating arrangements at dinner parties, cultivating allies without empowering them, destabilizing the opposition, and resorting to chicanery and blackmail if necessary. After playing Lucy Chase Wayne in *First Lady*, Nancy did not have to read Machiavelli.

The play, which ran for 246 performances, arrived at the right time, 26 November 1935. Nineteen thirty-six was an election year, and there already was speculation about Franklin D. Roosevelt's being reelected. (He was, overwhelmingly.) Meanwhile, to dissipate the miasma of the Great Depression, Dayton and Kaufman offered audiences a wicked comedy of manners, in which manners were discarded as two women battled to get their husbands into the White House. Nancy probably never saw the play on Broadway, but if she saw the 1937 movie version with Kay Francis in Cowl's role, she would have found inspiration in Lucy, the granddaughter of a president and the wife of Secretary of State Stephen Wayne, whom Lucy intends to make the next president. Her social rival, Irene Hibbard, the wife of Supreme Court Justice Carter Hibbard, has a candidate of her own: a handsome senator, whom she is planning to marry after divorcing Carter. Lucy launches a campaign to nominate Hibbard, knowing he doesn't stand a chance against her husband. The scheme backfires when a newspaper tycoon courts Hibbard, forcing Irene to remain with her husband, if it means becoming First Lady. When Lucy learns that because of a treaty the United States does not recognize Irene's divorce from an Eastern European prince, she confronts her rival, reminding her that, technically, she and Hibbard are not married. Lucy then threatens to inform the press. Irene accuses her of being a "dirty politician" like her grandfather, to which Lucy replies, "You bet I am. Because if I weren't, you'd be in the White House." Even if Nancy did not keep her copy of the play, she had learned enough about Washington protocol—scrupulously observed as often as it was flagrantly discarded—to survive as First Lady herself.

Nancy had two role models: her mother and her godmother, Alla Nazimova, one of the most respected actresses in the theatre. Edith first met Nazimova when she took on a small part in the touring company of 'Ception Shoals (1917), in which Nazimova was an orphan whose uncle sequestered her in a lighthouse, hoping to isolate her from a world that he has rejected. Edith played a woman in labor who gives birth with such harrowing realism that it traumatizes the orphan, who leaps from the lighthouse to her death.

Nazimova was a well-known lesbian who had come out at a time when it was more fashionable to remain closeted. There is no proof of any sort of relationship between Edith and Nazimova. Edith was more like a combination fan and social secretary. In 1929, when Nazimova was in Chicago, appearing in Turgenev's A Month in the Country, Edith arranged for her to be guest of honor at the Dramatic League luncheon. In 1938, when Nazimova was playing one of her most famous roles, Mrs. Alving, in Ibsen's Ghosts, Edith staged a reception for her.

Since none of Nazimova's stage performances have been captured on film, one has to look to her movies for evidence of her talent. Two films in particular reveal her ability to play an almost tragic heroine, as well as a minor character in a memorable scene. In Escape (1940), she played Robert Taylor's mother whom he rescues from a concentration camp, presumably Dachau, with Nazimova looking so regal that incarceration seemed like a mistake. But the reunion with her son had a poignancy that came from the heart. She was equally touching in a small role in Since You Went Away (1944), explaining to Claudette Colbert that, as an immigrant, she grew to love America and believed every word of Emma Lazarus's "The New Colossus," from which she quotes as if it were holy writ.

But Nazimova could do nothing for Nancy when she was trying to break into the theatre. She died in 1945, two years after Nancy graduated from Smith. Nancy could never have reached Nazimova's heights; one can hardly imagine her as an Ibsen or Turgenev heroine. She could not affect the high style or court the tragic muse, and she lacked the stage voice of those who could, like Katharine Cornell and Judith Anderson. Fortunately, there were touring companies and summer stock.

Shortly after graduation, Nancy joined the touring company of George Batson's Ramshackle Inn prior to its New York opening on 5 January 1944. Batson had written the comic melodrama for Zasu Pitts, who made a career out of playing fluttery women with fluttery hands. Pitts was quite capable of serious drama, as she revealed in Erich von Stroheim's *Greed* (1924). But her pixilated expression was meant for comedy—much to the delight of the public, who preferred the zany Zasu to the tragedienne.

Although *Ramshackle Inn* was intended as Pitts's Broadway debut, it soon became her calling card. After the play closed, she toured extensively with it, turning it into a summer stock perennial. The play is an "old dark house" melodrama about a retired librarian, Belinda Pride (Pitts), who buys a colonial inn for three thousand dollars, assuming it will be on the order of the one in *Grand Hotel*—complete with a revolving door. The price alone should have prepared her for a classic case of deferred maintenance, with a leaky roof and a cellar full of contraband liquor. None of the guests are what they seem to be: Patton, the porter, is head of a bootlegging operation; Joyce Rogers is an undercover FBI agent; Dr. Russell and his wife, Gail, are also involved in liquor smuggling; and Russell's alleged sister-in-law, Alice Fisher (Nancy), is a gangster's moll, whom they have sedated and kidnapped so that she can serve as a pawn if they need one.

Alice Fisher is the smallest part in the play. In fact, it could have been cut without altering the plot. Alice had three scenes: In the first and third, she does not speak; in the second, she does. Rushing into the lobby, she frantically asks Pitts, "Are you my friend? Oh, you've *got* to be my friend." Pitts's reply was bound to get a laugh: "I'm everybody's friend." Alice tries to call the police, only to be prevented by her bogus brother-in-law, who threatens her with another injection. In the third act, once the culprits have been caught— thanks, in part, to Belinda's powers of deduction—the still sedated Alice is carried out of her room, presumably for questioning. There was little any actress could do with a role that was never mentioned in a review. *Ramshackle Inn* had a decent run of 216 performances, closing in early July and then going on to Washington, DC, and Chicago. Nancy, for some reason, was not in the show when it reached New York. Alice was played there by Maurine Alexander, in her one and only appearance on the New York stage—which may say something about a role too insignificant to leave an impression.

Fortunately, Edith had worked with several major stars, notably Spencer Tracy, who could provide Nancy with companionship whenever he was in New York—the best he could offer a dreamer with an impossible dream. "Nancy was one of those girls whose phone number got handed around a lot." Nancy was networking before the term was even coined. But how could it be otherwise? Her mother and godmother were actresses, and she grew up in a home where movie and stage stars like Walter Huston and Spencer Tracy were frequent guests. Although Nancy lacked Nazimova's bravura, she still thought of herself as a stage actress in need of a stage to command. But that only happened when she did *First Lady* at Girls Latin and played a few leads in summer stock. She was not discouraged by her failure to appear in the Broadway production of *Ramshackle Inn*. Thanks to Mary Martin's intercession, Nancy got the role of Si-Tchun in *Lute Song*, which kept her employed until June 1946.

By then, George Batson had written another vehicle for Zasu Pitts, *Cordelia*, which included a part for Nancy. The play was set in the early 1900s, with Pitts as the title character, a combination do-gooder, problem solver, and matchmaker, whose latest act of charity is raising two sisters whose mother deserted them. For additional income, Cordelia rents a room to a gambler, shocking the community, which tries to declare her unfit to raise the girls. But the situation changes when the gambler suddenly dies, leaving Cordelia with enough money to send the older sister to finishing school so she can marry into society. Nancy played Millicent, a young upper class woman in love with the gambler and the perfect candidate for Cordelia's advice to the lovelorn.

Cordelia was set for a fall 1946 opening in New York, following tryouts in Boston, Hartford, New Haven, and Scranton. Except for *Variety*, the out-of-town reviews were respectful, hinting that the play was purely for fans of the star. But it was clearly not meant for Broadway. Even changing the title to *A Dangerous Woman* and bringing in a play doctor, Jack Kirkland (best known for his dramatization of Erskine Caldwell's *Tobacco Road*), could not salvage it.

Nancy did not despair. Pitts made her part of the touring company of Sidney Howard's *The Late Christopher Bean*. Guy Kibbee appeared as a country doctor with a discovery: Christopher Bean, who once stayed with the doctor's family, left behind paintings, once dismissed as worthless but now considered masterpieces. Nancy played the doctor's older daughter, Susan, in love with a paperhanger who is really a talented artist. Pitts had the plum role of the domestic, Abby, created by Pauline Lord, and later interpreted by Edith Evans, Marie Dressler, and Lillian Gish. Abby has to be underplayed, which Pitts could do easily. At the end of the third act, she must reveal that she and Bean were secretly married, and therefore the paintings are hers. As Susan, Nancy had more lines than she did in *Ramshackle Inn*, but with two seasoned performers like Pitts and Kibbee in the leads, Nancy could not hope for more than a brief mention in a review.

In 1948, live television drama was in its infancy, and Nancy was present at its birth. She played the lead in *Broken Dishes*, the play that brought Bette Davis to Hollywood, on *Kraft Television Theatre* (12 May 1948). When *Ramshackle Inn* and *The Late Christopher Bean* were aired live on *Philco Television Playhouse* on 2 January 1949 and 6 February 1949, respectively, Nancy was in the cast, presumably in the roles she had played on tour. Pitts starred in *Ramshackle Inn*, and Lillian Gish made her television debut as Abby in *The Late Christopher Bean*.

Live television was only a substitute for theatre; while Nancy could have done well in the new medium, she knew she would never become a star like Nazimova. Yet she could surpass Nazimova and even her mother in one respect: She would make her name in the movies, doing what Nazimova did—but in reverse. Nazimova made her reputation on the stage, with movies as a default. If Nancy had a default mode, it was television.

Nancy would continue to do television, but for the time being, she set her sights on film. If Broadway was not beckoning, why not try Hollywood?

Chapter 16

Twinkle, Twinkle, Little Starlet

ON 2 MARCH 1949, MGM SIGNED NANCY AT THREE HUNDRED DOLLARS a week, starting on 7 March when her first film, *Shadow on the Wall*, would begin shooting. MGM, the "Tiffany of studios," was the right one for her. Tracy and Gable were both MGM contract players. Dory Schary, who produced Nancy's best-known film, *The Next Voice You Hear*, credited Loyal Davis for alleviating his back pain. Benjamin "Benny" Thau became infatuated with her.

Thau, born in 1898, was old enough to be Nancy's father; in fact, he was two years older than Loyal Davis and four years older than Nancy's birth father, Kenneth Robbins. Before he arrived at MGM in 1929, Thau booked vaudeville acts for the theater circuit owned by Loew's, Inc., MGM's parent company. Louis B. Mayer, impressed by Thau's ability to spot talent, made him MGM's casting director and later his assistant. Thau's penchant for nubile starlets was common knowledge, although what they saw in a "cold, detached man, who spoke in an almost inaudible whisper" can only be explained by their ambitiousness. If they opted for the casting couch, it was available by appointment: "Thau's casting couch was the busiest in Hollywood."

Exactly what Thau's casting couch looked like is impossible to know. Harry Cohn's, on the second floor of Columbia Pictures, was a divan. Cohn's office was a study in white—chairs, piano, couch. The desk was on an eight-inch riser, so that when Harry rose to greet someone, he would seem taller than his visitor. Behind the desk were Columbia's Oscars, fittingly spotlighted. Behind them were shelves filled with nylon stockings, a rarity in wartime, and expensive perfumes, for those who would accommodate him—which happened often—on the white divan. To Paul Lazarus, Columbia's vice president of publicity, the divan was a

Jane, eyes filled with longing, and camera-ready Reagan in *Brother Rat* publicity shot (WB, 1938). Margaret Herrick Library.

Jane with Reagan and cadets in *Brother Rat* (WB, 1938). Margaret Herrick Library.

Jane and Reagan on their wedding day, 28 January 1940. Margaret Herrick Library.

The couple seated on the Wishing Chair at Forest Lawn, 28 January 1940. Margaret Herrick Library.

Jane, still blonde, and Reagan smiling for their fans. Margaret Herrick Library.

Reagan, columnist Louella Parsons, and Jane. Margaret Herrick Library.

Jane, looking less upbeat and perhaps more like her real self. Margaret Herrick Library.

Jane and Jack Carson in *Princess O'Rourke* (WB, 1943), the picture that got her the part of Helen in *The Lost Weekend*. Margaret Herrick Library.

Jane in the leopard coat, an important plot element in *The Lost Weekend* (Paramount, 1945). Margaret Herrick Library.

Jane going over a song with Cary Grant as Cole Porter, with Monty Woolley looking on, in *Night and Day* (WB, 1946). Margaret Herrick Library.

Jane and Gregory Peck as the Baxters in *The Yearling* (MGM, 1946). Margaret Herrick Library.

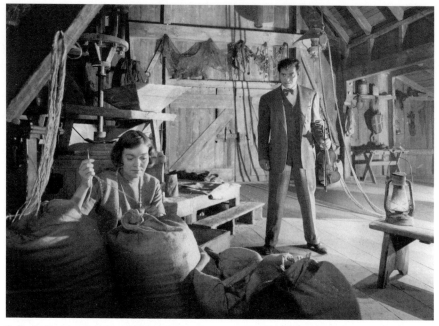

Belinda (Jane), unaware of the presence of Locky (Stephen McNally), with rape on his mind in *Johnny Belinda* (WB, 1948). Margaret Herrick Library.

Jane, David Niven, Victor Moore, and the keyboard Niven will not be using on their honeymoon in *A Kiss in the Dark* (WB, 1949). Margaret Herrick Library.

The anticipated gentleman caller (Kirk Douglas) giving Laura (Jane) a lesson in self-confidence by candlelight in *The Glass Menagerie* (WB, 1950). Margaret Herrick Library.

An aspiring actress (Jane) and a deadly killer (Richard Todd) in *Stage Fright* (WB, 1950). Margaret Herrick Library.

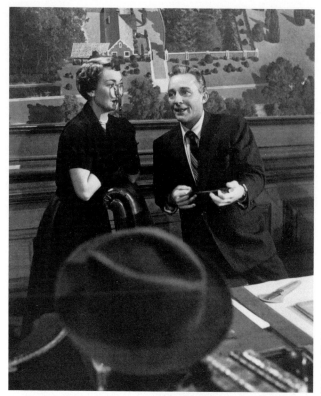

Jane and Bing Crosby romping through "In the Cool, Cool, Cool of the Evening" in *Here Comes the Groom* (Paramount, 1951). Margaret Herrick Library.

Jane as a former governess, eligible for only menial jobs because of her age in *The Blue Veil* (RKO, 1951). Margaret Herrick Library.

Jane, showing some leg in *Just for You* (Paramount, 1952). Margaret Herrick Library.

Jane, making contact with Rock Hudson, who will restore her vision in *Magnificent Obsession* (UI, 1954). Margaret Herrick Library.

Jane and Fred Karger, husband #4 and #5. Margaret Herrick Library.

Leon Ames, ogling Jane as she goes into her dance in *Let's Do It Again* (Columbia, 1953). Margaret Herrick Library.

A psychiatrist (Nancy), a troubled child (Gigi Perreau), and her murderous aunt (Ann Sothern) in *Shadow on the Wall* (MGM, 1950). Margaret Herrick Library.

Nancy reconstructing the murder scene in *Shadow on the Wall* (MGM, 1950). Margaret Herrick Library.

The Smiths (James Whitmore, Gary Gray, and Nancy) in *The Next Voice You Hear* (MGM, 1950). Margaret Herrick Library.

Nancy and John Hodiak in *Night into Morning* (MGM, 1951), Reagan's favorite among her films. Margaret Herrick Library.

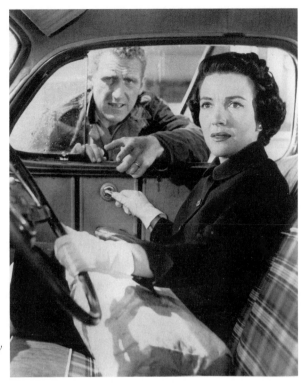

James Whitmore and Nancy as a conflicted couple in *Shadow in the Sky* (MGM, 1952). Margaret Herrick Library.

Nancy and Reagan in their only film together, *Hellcats of the Navy* (Columbia, 1957). Margaret Herrick Library.

"Where's the rest of me?" Reagan and Ann Sheridan in that devastating moment in *Kings Row* (WB, 1942). Margaret Herrick Library.

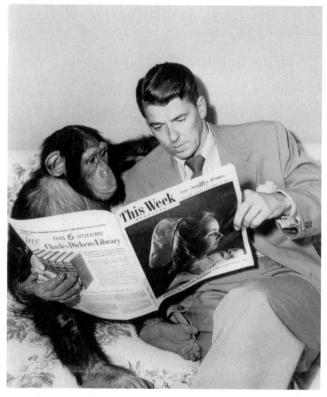

Reagan and the title character in *Bedtime for Bonzo* (UI, 1951). Margaret Herrick Library.

The blissfully wedded Reagans.
Margaret Herrick Library.

Jane and Hayley Mills, the strict aunt and the joyful niece, in *Pollyanna* (Buena Vista, 1960).
Margaret Herrick Library.

Jane the artist.
Margaret Herrick Library.

Jane as the "Wine Lady" in a
1981 *Falcon Crest* publicity release. Margaret Herrick Library.

prototype of the proverbial casting couch—not meant for grand amore, best enjoyed in a king-size bed, but for fellatio, which some of the moguls preferred, since they could experience a release of tension without having to perform and perhaps compromise their manhood. Small wonder that one of the first questions Cohn posed to a young actress was whether it was true that she was Hollywood's foremost practitioner of fellatio. Harry used the vernacular, probably unaware of the technical term.

Whatever relationship Nancy had with Thau had little, if anything, to do with her quest for stardom. Stories about Nancy's sleeping her way to the top are baseless because, for her, there was no top. There was no way she would achieve parity with such MGM stars as Katharine Hepburn, Greer Garson, Elizabeth Taylor, Ava Gardner, and Deborah Kerr. And if, for some reason, she thought she could compete with them, she would have bypassed Thau and set her sights on Mayer, whose indifference to monogamy was well known. "Rumors about [Nancy's] association with Benny Thau shadowed Nancy's happiness during her first months at the studio." Rumors were all they were. MGM was like an extended family: When one member sees another in the company of a third—and not just once—speculation is inevitable, especially if the third party is a vice president like Thau.

Nancy may not have known it at the time, but she was Greer Garson's replacement. That Mrs. Miniver was Benny Thau's mistress may seem to be at odds with Garson's ladylike persona, but Thau preferred cool, patrician types to bosomy blondes. When Garson won the Oscar for *Mrs. Miniver* (1942), she had no further need of a protector and embarked upon an affair with Richard Ney, who played her older son in the film. Garson and Ney were married on 24 July 1943. She was thirty-nine, and he twenty-six. The marriage ended in divorce three years later.

Thau would have been a more traditional choice. He was five years older than Garson, and able to separate his attraction to her from his desire to further her career. Thau found the artist in Garson, worshipping the woman and nurturing her art. He knew that unless Garson developed a less theatrical way of delivering her lines, the studio would drop her. He persuaded MGM drama coach Lillian Burns to help Garson make the transition from stage to screen acting, so she would look and sound natural on camera. Starting with Tennyson and Browning, Burns taught Garson how to recite poetry as if it were rhythmical prose. The technique worked. Garson was nominated six times for Best Actress: *Goodbye, Mr. Chips* (1939), *Blossoms in the Dust* (1941), *Mrs. Miniver* (1942),

Madame Curie (1943), *Mrs. Parkington* (1944*)*, and *Valley of Decision* (1945), winning for *Mrs. Miniver*. But Thau paled alongside the strikingly handsome Ney in his naval uniform, which Garson found irresistible—at least for a time.

Nancy was the closest substitute for Garson that Thau could find. "He was head over heels in love with her," according to MGM contract actress Audrey Totter. Although Nancy lacked Garson's imperial air, she was well bred and college-educated, attractive but not glamorous. To Thau, she was a fascinating anomaly, capable of either observing decorum or ignoring it. What may have begun as fatherly affection quickly changed to passion, more on Thau's part than on Nancy's.

There was little that Thau could do for Nancy. Despite her stage background, she did not have to learn line delivery for the movies. She had a natural way with dialogue, treating it as if it were ordinary speech. But Nancy never had roles that were as challenging as Garson's. One could hardly imagine Nancy's aging fifty years as Garson had to in *Mrs. Parkington*. Most actresses could have handled the kind of dialogue Nancy was given; it was the language of everyday life, devoid of complexity and subtext.

Although Kitty Kelly's *Nancy Reagan* is the result of prodigious research, the stories it contains about Nancy's sexual exploits are so lurid they appear spiteful. Nancy was no prude. Noting in her autobiography *My Turn* that her daughter, Patricia Ann (Patti Davis), was born on 22 October 1952, and that she and Reagan were married on 4 March 1952, she challenged the reader to "go ahead and count," having no intention of doing the math for them.

Nancy Davis was not Nancy Reagan. And Nancy Reagan is no more to be judged by Nancy Davis's actions than Ronald Reagan's presidency is to be judged by his films. As Farebrother wisely notes in George Eliot's *Middlemarch*, "Character is not cut in marble—It is not something solid and unalterable. It is something living and changing."

If Nancy table-hopped at the MGM commissary like a restaurant hostess, she did so because she was Edith Luckett's daughter. After Edith married Loyal Davis, she started signing her letters "Lucky" Davis. To some, it might have seemed like a self-created nickname, derived from her former surname. But lucky she was to be Loyal Davis's wife. Davis was twice blessed: He had a wife who transformed him into a celebrity neurosurgeon who profited from Edith's show business contacts. Edith's circle was limited, but she knew how to widen the pool of contacts. Her connection with Spencer Tracy, with whom she worked in *The Baby*

Cyclone, gave her access to Katharine Hepburn, the woman beyond his reach but available as a companion—but more important, as a contact for Nancy, now at MGM, Hepburn's studio.

Edith started cultivating Hepburn as early as 1944. Ignoring the fact that she had not heard from Tracy and Hepburn for two weeks, she wrote that she, Loyal, and Nancy attended a special screening of *Dragon Seed*, a film Hepburn might have preferred to forget. (She played a Chinese woman—one who sounded as if she had been educated at Bryn Mar—who poisons a hall full of Japanese soldiers.) The same letter also included the non sequitur that Edith's neck tumor had been removed, and that Nancy broke her engagement to "a darn nice kid" because "she's seen a lot of unhappy marriages." Hepburn's response is unknown, although from the chatty tone of Edith's letters, which span the period from 1944 to 1948, one could assume that Hepburn replied. At least she sent Edith a Christmas card in 1948, acknowledging her present of a letterbox.

And Loyal Davis decided to make use of Edith's contacts. Davis reminded Tracy about "Doctor of the Old School," a novel he had written specifically for the movies, noting that Tracy "agreed to produce it within the term of [his] new contract." When Tracy proved ineffectual, Edith moved on to John Huston, recalling that Walter, his father, "used to act out the old doctor" and begging him to read the manuscript because "it's very close to [Loyal's] heart." Huston read it and gave her an honest appraisal: "It is certainly a deeply sincere and moving book . . . but I am not sure about its being a natural for a picture." "Doctor of the Old School" never reached the screen.

Edith's contacts were more personal than professional; Nancy's were the opposite. Nancy luxuriated in the presence of stars, realizing at the same time that they became what they were because others helped them achieve their potential. The problem was that Nancy had already achieved hers and could go no further, at least in pictures. If she thought she had made an impression on Mary Martin, she might have realized that all Martin did was get her an insignificant role in a short-lived musical. Tracy, feeling indebted to Loyal Davis for his concern for Tracy's hearing-impaired son and perhaps embarrassed by his failure to get "Doctor of the Old School" produced, arranged for Nancy's screen test. The rest was up to Nancy.

Chapter 17

Nancy at Tiffany's

WHEN JANE RECEIVED BILLING FOR THE FIRST TIME IN *SMART BLONDE*, she did not head the supporting cast. But Nancy held that position in *Shadow on the Wall* (1950), filmed in 1949. It should have been Nancy's debut, except that it was not released until May 1950, when audiences had already seen her in smaller roles in two other films: *The Doctor and the Girl*, with Glenn Ford, Charles Coburn, Gloria De Haven, and Janet Leigh, released in September 1949; and *East Side, West Side* with Barbara Stanwyck, James Mason, Ava Gardner, Van Heflin, and Cyd Charisse, released three months later.

Neither film impressed the *New York Times*. The reviewer for the *Hollywood Reporter* (8 September 1949), on the other hand, noted that Nancy played the older sister in *Doctor* "with real charm," and that in *East Side, West Side* "Nancy Davis makes her few moments as a friend count conspicuously" (13 December 1949). *The Doctor and the Girl* was the better of the two. It captured the disparity between New York's upper- and underclass in a variety of ways, such as the Gilded Age elegance of Dr. Michael Corday's (Glenn Ford) home and the third-floor walkup in the shadow of the Third Avenue El, where Evelyn Helden (Janet Leigh) lives. Background is all-important to Michael, whose father (Charles Coburn), an eminent surgeon, is intent on keeping his children—Michael, Fabienne (Gloria DeHaven) and Mariette (Nancy)—at home, expecting each to marry within his or her class and at a time that he will determine. Evelyn lives alone and works in a candy store, making taffy. "Sticky background," as she informs the class-conscious Michael when she becomes his patient. The girl humanizes the doctor, giving him the courage to defy his father, who assumed his son would become a neurosurgeon, only to discover that Michael intends to serve the urban poor. Estrangement results when Michael and Evelyn marry and settle in the Third Avenue walkup, where he sets up his practice, with his wife as receptionist.

Nancy did well as the dutiful daughter, allowing her father to dictate her future as the wife of a pediatrician (Warner Anderson). In her first scene, Nancy greets her brother effusively with the right combination of love and admiration, stopping short of a less-than-sisterly display of affection, while at the same time implying that he is more than her hero. After Fabienne rebels, takes up with a married man, gets pregnant, and dies after a botched abortion, Mariette realizes that she is all her father has. She and her pediatrician husband will remain in the ancestral home, with Mariette playing the triple role of wife, daughter, and caretaker. Nancy understood that Mariette was not the defiant type and played her last scene with an air of selfless resignation.

There was one scene that showed what a sensitive actress Nancy could be when she had the right material. Mariette and her husband are visiting Michael and Evelyn in their dingy apartment. It is a cold winter day, and Mariette is wearing a mink coat. When Michael leaves the room, Mariette, knowing that Evelyn only has a cloth coat, persuades her to accept the mink. They devise a scenario, in which Evelyn will make some innocuous comments about the coat in the presence of her husband, prompting Mariette to offer it to her. To the men, a conversation about a coat was girl talk; they had more important matters to discuss. After a coatless Mariette leaves, Evelyn reminds Michael of his sister's generosity, only to hear him dismiss it, informing her that Mariette has other coats in her closet. The coat incident only emphasized the disparity between his sister's lifestyle and his own, which he must learn to accept if he is to be true to his calling. It is only when the elder Dr. Corday observes his son performing an operation on a child of immigrant parents that he is convinced Michael has found his mission. Father and son are reconciled, weekly family dinners will continue, and Mariette will not age well, given the burdens she must shoulder.

To MGM, *Shadow on the Wall* was just an eighty-four-minute low-budget thriller, and the studio was in no hurry to release it. Far more important were *The Doctor and the Girl* and *East Side, West Side*, with their impressive casts and box office potential. But the later release date for *Shadow* proved advantageous. To moviegoers, *Shadow on the Wall*, in which Nancy's role was integral to the plot, seemed like MGM's way of rewarding her for serving her apprenticeship in the two earlier films.

East Side, West Side was a glossier version of *The Doctor and the Girl*. Both acknowledged that there was a line of demarcation in New York that was not on the city's grid, but in the minds of the privileged, who devised their own grid on the basis of address. *The Doctor and the Girl* was more open about its existence. *East Side, West Side*, however, did not emphasize the income- and class-based disparity between the two worlds; rather, it concentrated on life among the affluent, with their spacious apartments and terraces offering spectacular views of the New York skyline. Theirs was a world that moviegoers wanted to see, especially those on the other side of the divide: a world of dinner parties, elegantly gowned women, and men in tuxedos, where adultery is grand amore, not sweaty sex. It is also a world where Jessie (Barbara Stanwyck) suffers nobly, while Brandon (James Mason), her investment banker husband, has his fling with home-wrecker Isabel Morrison (Ava Gardner), surname Allen in the novel, whose uninhibited earthiness is her only selling point. Although Brandon explains his lapses as an addiction, it is nothing other than adultery raised to the level of cheating in style, not in pay-by-the-hour motels.

Nancy, second billed in the supporting cast, played Helen Lee, Jessie's close friend. Nancy fared better in the screen version than she would have if screenwriter Isobel Lennart had been more faithful to the original, in which Helen had some dialogue but was essentially faceless. Lennart added a scene that was not in the novel, in which Helen visits Jessie after reading about the brawl between Bran and one of Isabel's thuggish lovers. It was not an easy scene; Helen had to act as if she were paying a social call, but really hoping to get Jessie to face a situation that she had been avoiding. It was a subtle bit of acting in a film that was decidedly lacking in nuance.

Although Nancy had only two scenes, she made the most of them. In the first, she was dressed as if she were a spokeswoman for Christian Dior's "New Look," with its tailored jackets, long skirts, and tapered waists. Nancy played the scene with the right kind of probing and concern. Cautiously, she wonders why women are so reticent about sharing confidences, thus giving Jessie an opportunity to initiate a conversation. When Jessie is elusive, Helen comes to the point: "Is everything all right between you and Bran?" Since Helen knows about Bran's infatuation with Isabel, who has returned to New York, she asks, "What would you do if she came back?" But Isabel has come back— to reclaim Bran. Nancy had one more scene, in which she appeared fashionably dressed as the hostess of a reception she and her husband are giving for foreign correspondent Mark Dwyer (Van Heflin), on the occasion of his first book. She circulates among the guests, moving gracefully from one group to another and engaging in animated conversation, as if hostessing were second nature to her, as it would soon become.

When Isabel is murdered, Brandon becomes a suspect. Dwyer, an ex-cop, finds a piece of a fingernail at the murder scene and through some wildly improbable sleuthing, discovers that it belongs to a jealous rival (Beverly Michaels). No longer under suspicion and free of his addiction, Brandon expects Jessie to forgive and forget. Instead, she does what women in the audience hoped she would do: she packs a suitcase and walks out.

The film was based on Marcia Davenport's 1947 novel of the same name. In her memoir, Davenport claimed she never saw the movie but was told it was a "horror." But it was not so much a horror as a disembowelment. Davenport's carefully demarcated New York became an urban cliché, with the affluent given a disproportionate amount of screen time, on the assumption that moviegoers are fascinated by a lifestyle that few of them enjoy. The novel was Edith Wharton for Book of the Month Club subscribers, written in a semi-literary but descriptive style that suggests high art but is really high gloss. Davenport did not conceal her disdain for a world in which women are pampered in beauty parlors, enjoying facials and pedicures, and leaving with their toenails painted green. She revels in describing apartments with damask upholstery and baroque chairs, alabaster jars and crystal clocks. But that was not the people's New York, which Davenport intimately knew, as did Jessie during the period when her mother, Rosa Landau, was trying to establish herself as a stage actress. Jessie had never forgotten Auntie Esther's dressmaker's shop in the Garment District, where, as a child, she sat fascinated, watching Esther at her cutting table. But that was in the past. When Rosa became a star, it was time to relocate. And when Jessie became Mrs. Brandon Bourne and an heiress, only the Upper East Side would do.

The affair between Jessie and Dwyer, delicately portrayed in the novel, became a platonic relationship in the film, in contrast to the physical one between Brandon and Isabel. Oddly, Brandon and Isabel are secondary characters in the novel. In fact, Isabel is constantly mentioned, but she never appears as a character. Even her death is reported, not dramatized. And unlike the film, in which Lennart created a new character—the trashy Fabrice, who kills Isabel—Davenport's Isabel is not murdered. In a violent altercation with her low-life lover, she falls and hits her head against the fireplace. But that was not the kind of death that MGM wanted for Ava Gardner, the studio's temptress-femme fatale-lady with a checkered past. Since Gardner was now a MGM star, she was given the star treatment, and Davenport's words became flesh—and smoldering flesh, at that. One could easily see how the arrogant but weak Brandon—especially as played by James Mason—could become enthralled by her. In their scenes together, it was not Bran and Isabel, but James Mason and Ava Gardner—he, struggling against the tug of the flesh, and she subverting his efforts.

Shadow on the Wall proved that Nancy was indeed an actress. The film is an unusual thriller, in which the sole witness to a murder is a child (Gigi Perreau), who never saw her stepmother's killer except as a shadow on the bedroom wall. The murderer is the child's aunt (Ann Sothern), who discovers that her married sister (Kristine Miller) has been engaging in afternoon trysts with her fiancé. Since the murder weapon belonged to the girl's father (Zachary Scott), he is charged with his wife's murder. However, a psychiatrist (Nancy) develops a special interest in the case when the girl, morose and uncommunicative, is placed under her care. Nancy seemed to have a visceral connection with the character, behaving as if she really headed the psychiatric unit of a children's hospital, giving orders, and even berating a cafeteria worker for making noise while she is trying to make contact with the troubled child.

As the psychiatrist begins to make progress, the aunt, suspecting her niece can identify her, tries to do away with the girl, first by poisoning her milk (which, fortunately, falls off the table) and then by attempting to steam her to death during hydrotherapy. When both attempts fail, she demands custody of her niece, who is brought to her Connecticut home. It is evening, and when the child walks up the steps to the house, the aunt appears, casting a shadow on the wall. The result is pure cinema, with a single image resolving the plot. The niece screams, the aunt confesses, the father is acquitted, and the psychiatrist is ready for a new role as stepmother of her former patient.

By 1949, Nancy had acquired enough stage and television experience to ease into movie acting. Speaking in a doctor's crisp tones when necessary, she succeeded in making contact with the child by using a dollhouse to pinpoint the scene of the murder. Next she brings her patient to the apartment where the murder was committed, so that she and the father's lawyer can reenact it. Nancy was in full control of her character; it was as if the white coat were part of her wardrobe.

Nancy and the nine-year-old Perreau were outstanding. The *New York Times* (19 May 1950) described Nancy as "beautiful and convincing" and called Perreau "excellent," an epithet that *Box Office* (15 March 1950)

bestowed on Nancy. The problem was Sothern. It was difficult to accept the same actress who endeared herself to 1940s audiences as the
wisecracking showgirl in the *Maisie* series, as a woman who murders
her sister and plans the same fate for her niece. Sothern was meant for
comedies and musicals.

The film with which Nancy will always be associated is *The Next Voice
Your Hear* (1950), her only film to play Radio City Music Hall (albeit for
a very short time). The producer was Dore Schary, who left RKO after Howard Hughes gained control of the studio, rendering it extinct in
1957 and thus making it the first of the majors to shut its doors. MGM
did not have great expectations for the film, which was budgeted at
$460,000 with an eighteen-day shooting schedule, excluding four days
for rehearsals.

Schary was a believer in the message picture, particularly in 1949,
when the Cold War generated its own big chill, and communism was
perceived as a threat to America's internal security. Once the Soviet
Union became a nuclear power, the old believers were convinced that
judgment day was imminent. Only God could save the planet, and so the
deity took to the air in *The Next Voice You Hear*.

The film originated as a short story by the same name published in the
August 1948 *Cosmopolitan*. Schary felt it had the makings of his kind of
movie, except that the plot had to be streamlined. Screenwriter Charles
Schnee accomplished as much by limiting the action to a six-day period
in which God usurped prime time on radio, speaking in a heavenly Es-
peranto that enabled everyone throughout the world to hear his words.
On the first day, the deity paraphrased the opening of Genesis, enumerating the miracles he had wrought, and reminding listeners that they
can do the same by bringing the gift of "peace and loving kindness" to
each other and thus to the world. Significantly, God does not deliver a
jeremiad, only a homily.

By contemporary standards, *The Next Voice Your Hear* is an artifact,
harking back to an age when radio was a mass medium, with families
tuning in after dinner to listen to their favorite programs. The film begins with a familiar sight: the Smiths—husband (James Whitmore), wife
(Nancy), and young son (Gary Gray)—about to have breakfast on the
morning of the first day. Whitmore and Nancy played the scene with
a disarming naturalness, he squeezing oranges and she cutting off box
tops, the 1950s equivalent of discount coupons, before making the toast
and pouring the cereal. It is an eat and run breakfast, as usual, with
father rushing off to work, son to school, and mother to her chores.

One can hardly imagine the real Nancy Davis preparing breakfast in a cramped kitchen—much less cutting off box tops—but Nancy the actress was amazingly believable as a homemaker, living in a working class neighborhood and pregnant with her second child. She understood the character, the wife of a short-tempered, underpaid plant worker, trying to hide her fear of going into false labor, which had proved fatal to the women in her family.

Although *The Next Voice You Hear* seemed uncharacteristic of director William Wellman, whose last MGM movie was *Battleground* (1949), he lavished great care on the opening scene, portrayed so naturally that audiences would not suspect that everyone's life would be changed by bedtime. Wellman also worked in some business that, with less skilled actors, might seem precious. When Nancy butters her toast, Whitmore takes it from her, reminding her of her diet, but allowing her to take one bite. Such playfulness would not continue beyond the first day.

At 8:30 that evening, the Smiths turn on the radio, expecting to hear their favorite program. But it is evident from their puzzled expressions that they are hearing something that we cannot hear. They are hearing the voice of God, who even has dominion over broadcasting. Each evening brings a new message. Those who made the connection between the six broadcasts and the six days of creation must have wondered what lay in store on the seventh day. The community assembles in a local church to hear the seventh broadcast, but there is none. Apparently, no one remembered Genesis 2:3: "So God blessed the seventh day and made it holy, because on it he rested from all the work he had done in creation." The Smiths experience their own moment of creation, when Mrs. Smith goes into labor and gives birth to a baby girl. Life continues, and Nancy gets a close-up when she is wheeled out of the delivery room, her eyes peacefully closed and her face transfigured. And for anyone who missed the message, the end title summed it up: "In the beginning was the Word, and the Word was with God, and the Word was God"—John 1:1.

Schary never considered anyone other than Whitmore for Joe Smith, who proved in *Battleground* that he could play tough and tender. Nancy was another matter. She had previously been up for the female lead in the Cary Grant political melodrama *Crisis* (1950) and even tested for the part. Although Shary described her test as "excellent, " the role went to the sexier Paula Raymond. Nancy would never be a pinup, but put her in a designer gown and she had a glamour that would have been appreciated in the Gilded Age. Nancy Davis was the wrong co-star for Cary

Grant, but the right one for James Whitmore. It was only after Nancy and Whitmore read through the entire script, with Shary playing the other parts, that he and Wellman knew they had their Mr. and Mrs. Joe Smith. Schary did not even ask for a test, which "would be a waste of everybody's time."

Although Bosley Crowther did not exactly warm to the film, his *New York Times* review (30 June 1950) was not unfavorable. Admitting that the film was "reverent whimsy" and by no means "intellectual," he could not help but express his admiration for the cast, complimenting Whitmore on a "grand job" and Nancy for being "delightful as his gentle, plain, and understanding wife." *Variety* (7 June 1950) was ecstatic: "The screen has never had a better example of husband-wife affection and understanding than that which Wellman builds between James Whitmore and Nancy Davis, the Mr. and Mrs. Joe Smith, Americans." But the *Hollywood Reporter* (7 June 1950) came close to describing Nancy's style of acting: understated and deceptively ordinary. She may have been playing a typical American homemaker, but "being typical is no small art, as one can see in the sweet, unaffected playing of the role by Miss Davis." "Unaffected" is the right word. Her performance was an illustration of the Latin maxim, *ars artem celare* ("It is an art to conceal an art").

MGM thought that Whitmore and Nancy made the perfect middle-class couple and reteamed them in *Shadow in the Sky* (1951), which had a taut script by Ben Maddow. The plot detailed the dilemma that families face when they must decide whether or not to bring a disturbed relative into their home. In *Shadow*, the relative is Burt (Ralph Meeker), a psychiatric patient suffering from post-traumatic stress disorder. Betty (Nancy), his married sister, is reluctant to make him part of her household. Her husband (Whitmore) is also conflicted, since Burt saved his life when they were both in the Marines during World War II. The couple finally agrees to take in Burt, and for a while tension abates—but not for long.

MGM was giving Meeker the star treatment after his impressive screen debut in Fred Zinnemann's *Teresa* (1951), in which his rough-hewn virility and blue-collar diction recalled Marlon Brando. And in fact Meeker replaced Brando during the Broadway run of *A Streetcar Named Desire*. Like Brando, Meeker was a Method actor, who brought a bruising realism to his roles, with moods of gentleness alternating with explosions of anger. The *Shadow in the Sky* credits did not list the actors vertically, but horizontally: Meeker and Nancy first, and under them, Whitmore and Jean Hagan, who played a sympathetic nurse. MGM was also grooming Hagen for possible stardom. Hagen, who made her stage debut in Lillian

Hellman's *Another Part of the Forest* (1946), which brought Patricia Neal to Hollywood, proved in *Adams's Rib* and *The Asphalt Jungle* (both 1949) that she could handle comedy as well as drama. But she never lived up to the studio's expectations, despite her flawless performance in *Singin' in the Rain* (1952) as a silent star with a voice that would only appeal to a grackle.

Just as Nancy was typecast as wife-sister-widow, Meeker found himself stuck in tough guy mode (villain in *Jeopardy*, fugitive in *The Naked Spur*). When Broadway beckoned with the lead in William Inge's *Picnic* (1953), he left MGM, returning to the studio for only two more films, the more memorable being *The Dirty Dozen* (1967). But the film for which he will be remembered is *Kiss Me, Deadly* (1955), in which he appeared as Mickey Spillane's Mike Hammer.

Forsaking Hollywood for Broadway may have given Meeker the lead in a Pulitzer Prize-winning play, but it also proved to be a dead end. Although he would work in the theatre until 1965, he never had another role like Hal Carter in *Picnic*, which must have been disillusioning to someone who won the 1948 Theatre World award for *Mister Roberts*. Few knew Meeker was a Northwestern University alumnus, like Charlton Heston and Patricia Neal. As the vagrant Hal in *Picnic*, whom he played with the right combination of aggressiveness, bravado, and poignancy, Meeker proved he could handle a leading role—if the character was a wrong-side-of-the-tracks alpha male.

It was the same with Nancy, who was cast as loving mother, all-suffering wife, resilient widow, compassionate teacher, and perfect confidante. It was a repertoire limited by the taxonomy that existed during the time of the studio system, when performers were stamped, labeled, and classified. Since the studio saw nothing alluring about Nancy, a romantic lead was out of the question. She could never pass for a femme fatale or "the other woman," only the wife whose husband is under another's thrall. *The Next Voice You Hear* may have had more cachet than her other films, but Nancy played Mrs. Smith so well that she would be playing Mrs. Smiths indefinitely. No more glamorous wardrobes like those she wore in *East Side, West Side*, or even *The Doctor and the Girl*. Her wardrobe in *Shadow* was bargain basement austere. For some reason, her hair glistened, as if pomaded into a metallic sheen, hardening her features. But then again, *Shadow* was not her film. Meeker was the star, with everyone else in his shadow.

The critics generally disliked the film. The *Hollywood Reporter* (18 December 1951) admitted that while Nancy's role was "stupidly written," she played it with "some aplomb." The *New York Times* (19 July 1952) reviewer termed *Shadow in the Sky* "a modest little drama" with "natural sounding dialogue, "quiet acting," and "sympathetic direction." The problem was the script: "[T]he performances themselves . . . are so natural that the predominant artificiality . . . just doesn't stand a chance."

Neither did Nancy at MGM. Although Nancy received favorable, and at times laudatory reviews in the trades, the studio was on the verge of dropping her. But she was still good for a few more simpatico parts, such as that of a widow in *Night into Morning* (1951). This was Reagan's favorite among her films, the one he claimed "not enough people saw . . . but all who did loved it."

"Loved" is an exaggeration, but in terms of production values and casting, *Night into Morning* was superior to *Next Voice*, although in its attempt to make personal tragedy redemptive, the former was a companion piece. In *Night into Morning*, it is not God's voice but his presence that is felt when an English professor (Ray Milland) plans to throw himself out of a window after losing his wife and son in a freak fire. The film captured academe in the early 1950s, when professors wore jackets and ties and reigned supreme in the classroom. Dr. Philip Ainley (Milland) does not lose his hauteur even after he loses his family. His support group consists of Tom Lawry (John Hodiak), a junior colleague, and Katherine (Nancy), the department secretary, a widow who understands Ainley, having gone through a similar dark night of the soul when her husband was killed in action.

The script artfully tip-toed around the familiar "two men-one woman" plot, with Katherine all but engaged to Lawry but drawn to Ainley, whose suffering is close to the kind she once knew. In fact, Nancy has the film's best scene when she tracks down Ainley, suspecting that he plans to take his life. When she finds him, the writers, Karl Tunberg and Leonard Spiegelgass, gave her a speech which she delivered magnificently, arguing that Ainley's wife and son can only remain alive spiritually if he goes on living. Delicately, she convinces him that he is the key to their immortality; live and they live on in him. It was Nancy's finest moment on the screen. The speech, admittedly, was not on the order of a Tennessee Williams monologue, but compared to what she was usually given, it was a showpiece.

Milland played the final scene as if Ainley always knew Katherine was meant for Lawry. He may have lost Katherine, but he found God. On the last day of the semester, he not only wishes the class well, but also asks that they go with God, using his basic Spanish to say "Vaya con Dios."

Newsweek (25 June 1951) described Nancy's performance as "honest," and *Daily Variety* (17 May 1951) singled her out for infusing her character with "warmth and understanding." Bosley Crowther preferred the first half of the film to the second, "a morbid swirl of sentiment and self-pity" (11 June 1951). That judgment may be too harsh. Milland did not so much wallow as wade in self-pity, playing the self-destructive drunk as if his personal tragedy entitled him to behave boorishly. But that was Philip Ainley: hotshot scholar wooed by Yale and now wearer of the mask of tragedy while expecting others to don it as well. Jean Hagen, as the Girl Next Door, was misused. Although her character was extraneous, Hagen played her as another lost soul, trying to strike a spark of humanity in a fellow sufferer, but getting a blast of frigid air instead. Hagen, like Nancy, was not what MGM was looking for.

In 1951, Schary decided that hearing the voice of God was not enough. Moviegoers also had to hear the voice of America—not the red, white, and blue America, but rainbow America, with its richly diverse palette. He planned an eight-episode film, appropriately entitled *It's a Big Country* (1951). Audiences were used to flag wavers, particularly during the war, but never one in which Old Glory was wrapped around every frame. One would think that an exacting critic like Bosley Crowther would have damned the movie as jingoism, but in his *New York Times* review (9 January 1952), he wrote that "except for the shallow chauvinism of the narration, this would be an easy film to watch and generally enjoy." MGM had no illusions about the film, which did not even open in a Broadway movie theater, but at the Trans-Lux on Lexington Avenue and 52nd Street. Nancy was fourth billed after Gary Cooper, not because of the significance of her role, but rather because of the alphabetical order of the cast, democratized as "citizens" in keeping with the film's egalitarianism.

The studio brought out its stalwarts—Ethel Barrymore, Janet Leigh, Gene Kelly, Van Johnson, Marjorie Main, James Whitmore, Keenan Wynn, and Lewis Stone—featuring them and others in a series of vignettes about the privilege of being American. The opening sequence, a conversation between two train passengers, William Powell and James Whitmore, triggers a debate on the definition of "American" that becomes the prologue to an eight-episode movie about the nation's rich diversity, proving that a simple definition is impossible. The mini-panorama ranges from the poignant (an elderly woman, played exquisitely by Ethel Barrymore, registering her objection that she was not included in the 1950 census) to the self-congratulatory (a montage featuring African

American icons of popular culture, such as Joe Louis, Jesse Owens, Sugar Ray Robinson, Lena Horne, Ethel Waters, and Marian Anderson—but not Paul Robeson, whose politics were too far to the left for him to be included).

The eighth episode, in which Nancy appeared, was such an anticlimax that Schary tacked on a rousing finale so the film could come full circle, glorifying a country in which nothing is insignificant. Compared to a widow ignored by a census taker, a mother who lost her son in the war, and a daughter in love with a man of a different ethnicity, a schoolboy getting a pair of glasses over his father's objections seemed trivial. Yet the final episode is presented as if debates about spectacles occurred regularly in American households. The boy is the son of Italian immigrants, whose father (a hammy Fredric March) believes that glasses will make him an object of ridicule among his peers.

Strange as it may seem, that was the climax of *It's a Big Country*. Nancy is a grade school teacher, looking very much at home in the classroom. During a class in long division, she notices that one of her pupils has trouble seeing the blackboard. Gently, she recommends glasses, even giving him a note for his parents, but not expecting to be challenged by his father. Gradually, the father backs down, even getting a pair for himself so his son will not feel self-conscious. That something as commonplace as corrective lenses was chosen as the coda is hard to explain, except perhaps that to some grade schoolers, glasses were an impediment to acceptance. If Schary wanted an upbeat ending, he had one, with Nancy, the boy, and his parents celebrating over red wine and lasagna.

Reagan was proud that Nancy held her own with March, whose *papa italiano* went beyond caricature into stereotype, prompting Crowther to remark charitably that "Fredric March is not at his best." Nancy, on the other hand, acted like a classroom veteran. Significantly, Schary does not discuss *It's a Big Country* in his autobiography, but only lists it among the films made "under my executive supervision"—which is one way of accepting responsibility without having to explain.

Chapter 18

The Empress of Ice Cream

"SHE PROJECTED ALL THE PASSION OF A GOOD HUMOR ICE CREAM." That was Spencer Tracy's summation of Nancy, whom he dated occasionally when he was in New York. The truth is that Nancy did not have star quality, whatever that elusive je ne sais quoi is. When Katharine Hepburn was asked to define it, she replied, "I don't know what it is, but whatever it is, I have it." Indeed she did.

MGM tried to give Nancy the star buildup. The photo collection at the Margaret Herrick Library includes a trove of glossies featuring Nancy in a swimsuit, Nancy with a tennis racquet, Nancy in a cocktail dress, Nancy in a suit, and Nancy moving into her first apartment. These are photos of an attractive woman, devoid of glamour, but with a sincerity that was refreshingly unfeigned. Even when fashionably dressed, Nancy looked like a woman going out for the evening, not a model in a provocative pose. Nancy's problem was that she wanted to be a star without having the equipment to become one. There was certainly a place for her in the business, but assuming it would mean joining the ranks of the non-stars, working actresses who alternated between movies and television and sometimes theatre. Their number was legion. Nancy's generation included Jeff Donnell, Ella Raines, Nancy Coleman, Ann Doran, Gloria Henry, Piper Laurie, Gloria Talbot, June Lockhart, and Marjorie Lord, for starters. In the theatre there were actresses whose names never appeared above the title, but who had no trouble finding work on and off Broadway and in television: Lenka Peterson, Neva Patterson, Nita Talbot, Audra Lindley (James Whitmore's wife), Polly Rowles, Luella Gear, Betty Miller, Phyllis Love, and a host of others memorialized in playbills. But Nancy, who was supporting cast material even when she had second billing, was loath to join a line that extended beyond the horizon.

By 1952, MGM realized that Nancy was not meant for stardom. In her last film for the studio, *Talk about a Stranger* (1952), released two months before *Shadow in the Sky*, she was second billed after George Murphy, an MGM stalwart about to become an MGM retiree. The film was a bitter-sweet experience for both of them—more so for Murphy, who had been at the studio for fifteen years. His tenure as SAG president gave him a taste for politics, and in 1964, he was elected to the United States Senate, where he served from 1965 to 1971. Even after her marriage, Nancy was intent on an acting career. She free-lanced until 1958 and continued in television until 1962, when she settled for being Nancy Reagan.

Despite her billing in *Talk about a Stranger*, neither she nor Murphy was the main character. That was Billy Gray as Bud, their son, whose childish prank alienates a reclusive neighbor (Kurt Kasznar) and sets the slight plot in motion. For Nancy, *Talk about a Stranger* was MGM's version of a pink slip. Her billing was a bon voyage, and her performance was like that of an employee on her last day on the job. As another pregnant wife, she had a few scenes, some dialogue, and no effect on the plot. In fact, Murphy could have been a widower for all it mattered. John Alton's chiaroscuro lighting added some noirish overtones to what was essentially a movie about profiling. An antisocial man, living in a house worthy of *Psycho*'s Norman Bates, is so creepy that Bud assumes he must be the one who poisoned his dog. He isn't. The recluse turns out to be a doctor, who performed an operation on his own son that caused the boy's death. Guilt-ridden, he retreats to a house that in a Hitchcock film would have harbored deeper secrets. But this is a family movie, and the presumed villain turns out to be human after all, even providing Bud with another dog. At least the *Hollywood Reporter* (26 February 1952) found Nancy "appealing" as the mother.

Talk about a Stranger was not intended as a subtle criticism of McCarthyism, but in retrospect, the theme—people are not always what they seem, and false assumptions can tarnish reputations—was very much in keeping with the times, when signing the wrong petition, subscribing to the wrong journals, and supporting the wrong cause could result in the charge of being a "Red," a "Commie," or a "Pinko." And if the unfortunate liberal were in film or television, such actions could render him or her unemployable.

Nancy knew from experience the consequences of being confused with another. Another Nancy Davis's name was included in the 28 October 1949 *Hollywood Reporter* among those supporting the Hollywood Ten, who were facing prison sentences because they stood by their First

Amendment rights and refused to answer the burning question of the age: "Are you now, or have you ever been, a member of the Communist Party?" Nancy was aware of the paranoia that spread throughout Hollywood after the HUAC hearings began in 1947, when progressives were shunned by their onetime friends, who feared guilt by association. She had just started in the business and had no intention of seeing her career jeopardized because she had the same name as a leftwing sympathizer. Nancy, who had just completed *East Side, West Side,* sought out Mervyn LeRoy, who directed the film and was always gracious to her. In his autobiography, LeRoy offers a slightly different version. Nancy told him, "Someone is shoving Communist literature under my door." If true, this incident would have made her apprehensive about her future.

The real confusion between her and the other Nancy Davis did not become an issue until 1953, however, when she was married to Reagan and no longer at MGM. There was a Nancy Lee Davis, a movie extra and the person who supported the Hollywood Ten. However, she did not work in the business between 1945 and 1952, and "could not have been on any studio blacklist" or confused with the Nancy Davis at MGM. If Nancy sought out LeRoy in 1949, it was probably to put in a good word for her with Reagan. As LeRoy tells it, after Nancy left, he phoned Reagan to say, "You're single and she's kind of cute and you should meet her." An alternate version has Nancy persuading LeRoy to have Reagan call *her,* which he did a month later. A third version has Nancy, her mind set on Reagan as a husband, hinting to Dore Schary that she would like to meet him. This would have been in early fall 1949. Schary's wife, Miriam, arranged a dinner party, at which Reagan held forth. This time he had an attentive listener in Nancy. Theirs may not have been an arranged marriage, but it was a marriage by arrangement.

Like the stories in *Rashomon,* all three versions contain elements of truth. The nature of the "Communist literature" was never clarified, but there *was* a Nancy Lee Davis, Reagan did call Nancy for a date, and the Scharys gave a dinner party at which Reagan and Nancy were present. The upshot was that Nancy met Reagan in the fall of 1949, was his lover by 1951, and became his wife in 1952. Theirs was a fairy tale romance featuring a damsel in distress, a Red Cross Knight, and a dragon with hammer and sickle. Even an accomplished screenwriter could not have manipulated history to work so well in Nancy's favor.

Chapter 19

Post-Oscar Blues

IN 1948, NANCY WAS ON THE EVE OF HER BRIEF, GAUDY HOUR AS AN MGM contract player. That year, Jane Wyman made the film that would net her an Oscar. But Oscars are a blessing and a curse. Except for something extraordinary on Oscar night—Greer Garson's seemingly interminable acceptance speech for *Mrs. Miniver*, or Louise Fletcher's for *One Flew over the Cuckoo's Nest*, which she delivered in sign language for her hearing-impaired parents—one can hardly remember who won what a year later, much less who said what. Rarely is the winner on a roll for the next few years. Kim Hunter's Oscar for *A Streetcar Named Desire* (1951) never led to stardom. Hunter was a superb stage actress, destined for an occasional major role in a minor film (*Deadline USA, The Young Stranger*) but otherwise relegated to the supporting cast. Gloria Swanson's Oscar-nominated comeback in *Sunset Boulevard* was never followed by anything worthy of her. The same was true of Shirley Booth after she won her *Come Back, Little Sheba* Oscar. *Johnny Belinda* provided the occasion for Jane's only Oscar. She would be nominated two more times.

Jane deserved better than her next two films. Fortunately, they did not derail her career, which moved smoothly into the next decade. Meanwhile, it was business as usual. Three months after *Johnny Belinda* was released in fall 1948, *A Kiss in the Dark* (1949) premiered. Oddly, the film was planned as a vehicle for Joan Crawford, who had the sense to pass on it, once she realized it was a frothy romantic comedy co-starring the urbane David Niven. Jane took over as a tenant in an apartment house owned by a neurotic concert pianist (Niven). Theirs is another meet cute: she, in shorts, backing out of her apartment while vacuuming and bumping into Niven, whose discreet ogling of her extremities prompts her to ask if he is inspecting the premises.

The writers' next challenge was to make Niven one of the people, which Jane accomplishes as if she were a specialist in the art of humanizing stuffed shirts. *A Kiss in the Dark* is the kind of film that could only work if the humanizing were treated with a feather-light touch and gentle humor, much like Monty Woolley's transformation from a crusty boarder to a genuine member of the household in *Since You Went Away*. Director Delmer Daves, who was better suited to melodrama (*Dark Passage, To the Victor*), did not trust Harry Kurnitz's script, and instead of downplaying the farcical elements, exaggerated them, with Niven as a klutz who steps into an animal trap and ends up dangling from a tree.

For a movie about a world-famous pianist, *A Kiss in the Dark* took a condescending, even mocking, view of classical music. Jane prefers jazz and tries to introduce Niven to it, making no effort to enter his world. At the end, Jane and Niven, now married, are about to head to the West Coast for a concert, when Niven's manager arrives with a keyboard, assuming that he will use it for practice. Jane looks warily at it, as if it were her rival, and then at Niven, whose sly smile suggests that he knows a better way to pass the time.

Jane anticipated the public's confusion about how she could go from *Johnny Belinda* to *A Kiss in the Dark*. Her answer was simple: "It's a test of versatility for me. Comedy is as exacting as drama. It demands more of a performer technically, although audiences aren't as apt to give a good comedy performance the recognition it deserves." Jane knew that *A Kiss in the Dark* would not showcase her versatility, but only her comedic skills, which had been on view for a decade. She did what the script called for. She was charming, cunning, but never exploitative—even when corralling Niven into leading a troupe of boys on an outing, where he encounters only indifference and hostility. But then, classical music is longhair, and the boys wear their hair short.

Except for one day when she was suffering from "cramps" Jane had a much easier time than Niven, who, in addition to suffering through a throat infection, was having difficulty mastering the piano. He also had trouble fitting into his wardrobe, especially the dress coat he wears on stage. Shirts were another problem: A heavy perspirer, he needed two of each. Still, the picture was finished in forty-eight days and came in under budget.

If implemented in real life, the premise of Jane's next film, *The Lady Takes a Sailor* (1949), would have reduced women to underlings. Jane was the head of a nonprofit organization committed to truth in advertising. A squall on Long Island Sound causes a collision between her sailboat and a surfacing submarine. She is rescued by the captain (Dennis Morgan), a marine biologist conducting top-secret underwater research. When he deposits her on land, no one believes her story, which the captain cannot corroborate because of the nature of his mission. Chauvinistically, the film assumes that when two careers are at stake, the male's comes first, and that when national security is an issue, the scales of justice are imbalanced.

The writers had to exhaust their creative powers to generate a romance between a man so committed to his (never explained) research that he abandons the woman he rescued to deal with the tabloid press, which turns the rescue into an underwater romance, complete with an ornery octopus. The plot then veers off into low-grade screwball, with the career woman and the biologist engaged in a win some/lose some contest, with the biologist doing most of winning. Then the message-bearer arrives in the person of Jane's friend, Warners' resident big sister, Eve Arden, announcing that a career is no substitute for a man in your bed on a cold winter's night. The script gave Jane no other choice than to agree. All that matters, the film seems to say, is that his mission was not compromised, even though her rights as an individual were. It was hard work convincing audiences that a woman would give up a career for a man who placed his before hers. Jane did it, looking as if she had been seduced by Morgan's devilish eyes. In December 1949, the Cold War was heating up, the Soviet Union had become a nuclear power, Hollywood was under investigation by HUAC, and atomic espionage was a growing threat to internal security. Perhaps *The Lady Takes a Sailor* is more of a footnote to an age than a Jane Wyman film.

In 1951, it was loan out time again to MGM. Jane took the change as a good sign. It was at MGM that the interiors for *The Yearling*, which produced her first Oscar nomination, were filmed. But that was in 1946, when MGM was "the Tiffany of studios," on whose stationery was printed, "More Stars Than There Are In The Heavens." That was not an idle boast. MGM was home to Spencer Tracy, Jean Harlow, William Powell, Myrna Loy, Judy Garland, Mickey Rooney, Lana Turner, Katharine Hepburn, Robert Taylor, and the incomparable Greta Garbo. By 1951, some of the stars had left the heavens, others were not shining as brightly as they once did, and the studio was no longer Hollywood's Tiffany.

In the 1930s, Jane appeared in about thirty films; in the 1940s, twenty-seven; in the 1950s, fourteen. The glory days were coming to an end, but that did not mean the end of Jane Wyman, only the end of one phase of her career and the beginning of another. Most of her 1950s films were worthy of her, but *Three Guys Named Mike* (MGM, 1951) was not one of them. Jane was thirty-four, looking perhaps thirty and playing an aspiring American Airlines flight attendant. But the time was 1951, when there were no flight attendants, just stewardesses, who, when they married, were expected to retire and do the wifely thing and raise a family. It was also a time when horny males tried to score with the attendants, meals were free, and civilized flying meant sitting two abreast. At least the title is accurate: there are three Mikes from which to choose: a flyer (Howard Keel), an advertising executive (Barry Sullivan), and a graduate student who gives every indication of being a future Nobel Prize winner (Van Johnson). Of course, Jane picks Van Johnson, still looking like the barefoot boy with cheek of tan. Jane and Johnson would work together again, but in a much better movie.

Chapter 20

The Last Picture Shows

BY 1952, NANCY'S MOVIE CAREER WAS DRAWING TO A CLOSE. WHEN she had the opportunity to co-star with Lew Ayres in *Donovan's Brain* (United Artists, 1953), she signed on immediately. Although it was a low-budget film (which netted Nancy $18,000 and second billing), it had a respectable lineage, originating as a novel of the same name by the prolific Curt Siodmak, the brother of director Robert Siodmak and a well-known screenwriter in his own right (*The Wolf Man, Frankenstein Meets the Wolf Man, I Walked with a Zombie*). For a work of science fiction, *Donovan's Brain* (1943)—in which a scientist tries to keep a dead man's brain alive, only to discover that it has telepathic powers—was favorably reviewed. Writing in the *New York Times* (21 February 1943), Sally Benson found the novel so compelling that "only skeptics will not believe."

Donovan's Brain was meant for the movies—or rather, the book's basic premise was. Any filmmaker who remained faithful to the original ran the risk of censure from moralists incensed by the scientist's amorality. The novel is formatted as a series of journal entries written by Dr. Patrick Cory, who details his experiments keeping a brain alive, beginning with a monkey's and then, when an opportunity presents itself, with a human brain. Cory is interested in science for its own sake, not for what it can do for humankind. A plane crash provides Cory with exactly what he wants: a dead man, Warren H. Donovan, whose brain is still functional. Donovan was a billionaire, whose life unfolds gradually as Cory embarks on a dark odyssey to learn more about the man whose brain is gradually taking possession of him. Cory concludes that the brain is like a radio station, in which a "thought created in the mind of person number one can be received by person number two." Soon Donovan's brain assumes control of Cory's motor responses, causing him to lead a dual existence.

Toward the end of the novel, Cory merges with Donovan, a transformation Siodmak indicates by substituting "Donovan" for "Cory" in the text.

Since *Donovan's Brain* is cast as a thriller, with Cory functioning as both a scientist and a private eye trying to learn about the enigmatic W. H., suspense is generated incrementally, as Cory encounters those who were part of Donovan's life. Their memories, when pieced together, add up to a portrait of the Czech-born William Dvorak, who, after changing his surname to Donovan, became the embodiment of the American dream—along with its nightmare corollary. He grew more amoral as his fortune increased, impregnating his wife so often that only two children (both of whom loathe him) survived, and driving a rival for his wife's affection to suicide. An alcoholic, he would have died of liver failure if his plane had not crashed.

Ironically, the brain can do what Donovan could not while he was alive: make amends by paying back some of the victims of his inhumanity. But when the brain is threatened, it retaliates, killing Cory's close friend, Dr. Schratt, who at least succeeds in killing it first. The novel ends without Cory being held accountable for the deaths his experiment has caused, Schratt's and that of a blackmailing photographer. For those who believe that science fiction should be didactic, Siodmak added a moralistic coda: "The brain's constructive imagination for mechanical devices and chemical exploitations is limitless, but to create kindness, honesty, love, humanity itself must first grow into that shape. Man can engender what he is himself. Nothing more."

Those may have been inspiring words in 1943, the bleakest year of World War II, and Cory may have learned that "Nature has set limits which we cannot pass." But Cory passed them with impunity and is even offered a new job. Crime indeed can pay. Small wonder *Donovan's Brain* was never filmed as written. Although it inspired three movies, none of them captured the original's unique blend of horror and science fiction. The first (1944) and third (1962) were the weakest.

The year after the novel was published, the Poverty Row studio, Republic, came out with a version called *The Lady and the Monster* (1944), with an additional character, Franz Mueller (Erich von Stroheim). Stroheim conformed to moviegoers' image of a mad scientist—but with a twist: Instead of robbing graves like Dr. Frankenstein, Dr. Mueller put a dead man's body to use by removing his brain to see if its thoughts can be transmitted to the living. When the brain takes possession of his assistant, Patrick Cory (Richard Arlen), the plot veers off into mad ghoul territory—but not for long. At the end, a voice tells us that Cory was sent to prison for his role in the experiment and will emerge to find his beloved (Vera Hruba Ralston, wife of Republic's president, Herbert J. Yates) waiting for him. What might have been an engrossing thriller became a moralistic warning against organ preservation, which, if heeded, would have meant the end of transplants. The third was a German-made film released in the United States as *The Brain* (1962), with Siodmak's intricate plot recast as a whodunit with Donovan as murder victim.

The best of the lot was the second, appropriately entitled *Donovan's Brain* (1953) and closer to the novel, focusing exclusively on Cory's (Lew Ayres) attempt to keep the brain alive after the fatal plane crash. In this version, Cory is conducting an experiment not for its own sake, but to benefit humanity. If there are blood banks and eye banks, why not a brain bank for the neurologically impaired? When the brain hijacks Cory's personality, he becomes a version of Mr. Hyde, the widely detested plutocrat W. H. Donovan, who built a financial empire on fraud and intimidation. The film's Donovan is quite different from Siodmak's self-made man, who carved out his empire as methodically as America's oil and railroad tycoons did theirs. If Donovan recalls any character in American cinema, it is Charles Foster Kane in Orson Welles's *Citizen Kane* (1941), who, even in death, left his mark on the living. Like the novel, the movie ends with the destruction of the brain, which Schratt (in the film, called Schrott) accomplishes with a bullet while remaining unharmed himself, which was not the case in the original. Whether Cory will serve time, as his counterpart did in *The Lady and the Monster*, is left unresolved. He and his wife (Nancy) are convinced that the jury will realize that what he did was motivated by humanitarian concerns.

There was nothing Nancy could do with the role of the stand-by-your-man wife. Janice, her character in the novel, was in a bind. Cory ignored her, treating her as his assistant (she had been a nurse). Neither the novel nor the film allowed Janice/Nancy to assert her independence or even challenge her husband. Instead, she dutifully assists him, and she does not question his periodic absences from their desert home, during which he conducts his affairs as W. H. Donovan. In short, her character makes no sense. Nancy's only decent scene occurs at the end when Cory, still possessed by the brain, tries to strangle her, returning to his senses at the moment the brain is destroyed. It is a brief scene, but at least it showed that Nancy could register terror on cue.

The film was not well reviewed. The *Hollywood Reporter* critic (30 September 1953) filed a minority report, calling *Donovan's Brain* "one of the best pieces of science fiction to hit the screen," and describing Nancy as "charming and competent as the wife." "Competent," yes. "Charming" depends on one's idea of a wife who participates in an experiment that is illegal and possibly unethical.

Nancy did not appear on the screen again until 1956, and then it was not in a feature, but in a twenty-three-minute short, one of Twentieth Century-Fox's CinemaScope specials. *The Dark Wave* (1956) dramatized the social and psychological problems of an epileptic child. Directed by Jean Negulesco and starring Nancy and Charles Bickford, the film received Oscar nominations in two categories: short subjects (two-reel) and documentary/short subjects.

In 1953, Nancy was a new mother. However, Patti's birth did not alter Nancy's career plans any more than Maureen's birth or Michael's adoption altered Jane's. What Nancy wanted in 1953 was essentially what Jane wanted in 1947: another child along with a career. Jane had a baby girl who died the day she was born. Nancy miscarried twice before Ronald Prescott Reagan was born in 1958. Meanwhile, there was television and a two-picture deal with Columbia. One of the films starred Reagan, with Nancy, as usual, second billed in a role that amounted to about fifteen minutes of screen time. As for her career: A better one lay in the future. It is impossible to imagine Reagan becoming governor, much less president, without Nancy. Their marriage may not have been made in heaven, but it was made with 1600 Pennsylvania Avenue in mind.

Submarine movies were too few to constitute a genre, but the best of a meager lot were *Destination Tokyo* (1944) and the German film, *Das Boot* (1981). *Hellcats of the Navy* (1957), unlike *Destination Tokyo*, did not have an all-male cast, and except for the close quarters sequences suggesting an absence of personal space, it did not induce claustrophobia—except in Reagan, who suffered from claustrophobia to begin with. The Hellcats, a submarine squadron put into operation by Admiral Chester W. Nimitz, commander in chief of the Pacific Fleet, was part of an ongoing naval buildup after Pearl Harbor. In 1944, in preparation for an attack on the Sea of Japan that would isolate Japan from the Asian mainland, one such submarine, the *Starfish*, was assigned the task of bringing back a chart of the Japanese minefields, which thus far were undetectable by radar. Reagan played the go-by-the books *Starfish* commander, Casey Abbott, who tightens his jaw, narrows his eyes, and furrows his brow when he has to make a life or death decision—such as letting one of his men drown rather than wait and risk an attack by a Japanese destroyer. His dilemma is complicated by the fact that the diver was his rival for navy nurse Helen Blair (Nancy). Later, Casey finds himself in a similar situation when he is unable to extricate himself from a cable. Lieutenant Commander Landon (an unsmiling Arthur Franz) has to decide whether or not to abandon Abbott for the sake of the ship. Landon, who always believed that Casey sacrificed the diver because he wanted Helen for himself, does what the second in command must do. But Casey is Ronald Reagan, who must survive to marry Helen and bask in the glow of postwar peace, such as it was.

Neither Reagan nor Nancy knew that the screenplay was rewritten by a blacklisted screenwriter, Bernard Gordon. On 27 November 1986, Gordon wrote to the Academy of Motion Picture Arts and Sciences, stating that he rewrote David Lang's script under the name of Raymond T. Marcus, resulting in co-screenplay credit for the two of them. Gordon used the same pseudonym for the science fiction films *Earth vs. the Flying Saucers* (1956) and *The Man Who Turned to Stone* (1957). And, as John T. Castle, he wrote the screenplay for *The Lawless Breed* (1952), in which Rock Hudson proved that he could play a western outlaw, the historical John Wesley Hardin, as well as romantic leads. If there was anything subversive in *Hellcats*, only an exegete could find it. *Variety* (1 May 1957) commiserated with Nancy, who was stuck with "a thankless role."

Whatever role Nancy had to play—daughter, homemaker, teacher, secretary, widow, lab assistant, confidante, or nurse—she played it convincingly. The problem was that the scripts gave her little to work with. A few scenes and a few lines do not add up to a character, unless the lines and the scenes are equally potent—which they were not in *Hellcats*. Nancy had more chemistry with James Whitmore in *The Next Voice You Hear* and with Ray Milland in *Night into Morning* than she did with Reagan, who was unhappy with his part and acted as if Nancy were an appendage. Nancy looked every inch a nurse. But that was the problem: She fit every kind of role she was given, looking the part, acting the part, but handicapped by sketchy lineaments no actress could flesh out. Another problem was her voice. It was warm and homey, with the soothing intonation of a mother dishing out oatmeal to her family on a cold winter morning. It was a voice that could have served her well as a character actress. Nancy, however, was willing to share the spotlight but not step out of it—until it was no longer shining on her.

Many movie careers end neither with a bang nor a whimper, but a thud. Nancy's was one that ended just that way. Although she was billed as Gary Merrill's co-star (and wife) in Columbia's *Crash Landing* (1958), she was on the screen even less than in *Hellcats*. In *Crash Landing*, she had a grand total of three scenes, one of which only required her to look anxious after hearing that her pilot-husband's plane developed engine trouble over the Atlantic. Nancy appears first in a flashback, doing her wife-mother bit, upset that her martinet husband is punishing their son for telling an untruth. So much for Nancy. Most of the action takes place aboard the plane, with the usual assortment of characters, including a Portuguese couple, an American family with an infant, a husband with a terrified wife, two executives at odds with each other, a school teacher and a widower, and a psalm-reciting Greek Orthodox priest. The ocean landing is the only exciting part of the film, but once we know a destroyer is nearby to assist in the evacuation, there is no suspense. No one dies, no one is critically injured, and the passengers and crew get to New York by sea rather than air.

Four years earlier, the definitive plane-in-trouble movie, *The High and the Mighty* (1954), had been released, dwarfing later clones like *Crash Landing*. The former offered some unforgettable vignettes, including Jan Sterling's decision to remove her elaborate makeup before landing, hoping that the man waiting for her will accept her as she is—which he does. And Merrill is no John Wayne, who walks into the night in a memorable fade out. Merrill comes home to a champagne reception and an elegantly dressed Nancy. Humanized by the experience, he is now able to be a father rather than a disciplinarian. Why Nancy accepted a role that was little more than a walk-on is hard to fathom.

The best part in the film is that of the high school teacher, sensitively played by Irene Hervey, who was third billed. In her few brief scenes Hervey conveyed the loneliness of a woman who has remained unmarried because no one ever proposed to her. Nancy would have been perfect as the teacher. She had the kind of angular body that suggested spinsterhood, and eyes that revealed a desire to avoid it. Hervey was touchingly genteel, but the part needed an actress who could convey the banked bitterness of a woman tired of being labeled the school's innovator, praised for introducing visual aids into the classroom (this was 1958, remember), but signaling to those who could decode her body language that she would rather be a wife.

After *Hellcats*, Reagan did not plan on making another feature film, only a made-for-TV movie, *The Killers* (1964), directed by Don Siegel, who directed the film that Reagan preferred to forget, *Night unto Night* (1949). In the interim, Siegel had become a master of violence, as evidenced in *Riot in Cell Block 11* (1954), the classic *Invasion of the Body Snatchers* (1956), *Baby Face Nelson* (1957), and later, *Dirty Harry* (1971). If *The Killers* evokes Hemingway's short story of the same name, it does so simply because Universal had made a similarly titled movie in 1946 with Burt Lancaster that at least bore some semblance to Hemingway's classic. Universal felt the title was good for another go-around, perhaps hoping that audiences might associate it with Hemingway or regard it as a remake of Robert Siodmak's 1946 film noir. What they got instead was a ninety-five-minute crime movie with Reagan, heavier than he was in *Night unto Night*, as a conscienceless gangster who kills in cold blood. Although Reagan had never played a villain before, he was surprisingly effective. But the film was deemed too violent for television and ended up in theaters, where it attracted little attention. In time, though, it developed a cult following. But none of this mattered to Reagan. Two years later, on 8 November 1966, Ronald Reagan was elected governor of California.

Chapter 21

A Cathedral and a Conversion

WHEN JANE WAS PREPARING TO SAIL FOR ENGLAND TO STAR IN AL-
fred Hitchcock's *Stage Fright* (1950), converting to Catholicism was the
furthest thing from her mind. Soon, it became an obsession.

Her reputation preceded her. In January 1949, the *London Daily Express* named Jane best actress and Laurence Olivier best actor of 1948,
Jane for *Johnny Belinda* and Olivier for *Hamlet*. It was an odd juxtapo-
sition: an actress who delivered no lines, and an actor who delivered
Shakespeare's. But the honor carried a cash award of $4,000, which Jane
in turn gave to London's Royal Academy of Dramatic Art (RADA).

Jane was a bona fide star; her billing attested to her status. But first
billing was Warners' way of capitalizing on her Oscar-winning performance in *Johnny Belinda*. She was one of four stars whose names were
above the title, the others being Marlene Dietrich, Michael Wilding, and
Richard Todd. None of the four dominated the film, although to many
critics and moviegoers, Dietrich was the main attraction. Initially, Hitchcock did not want an American for Jane's part. He preferred a British
actress, so that there would be no need to explain why an American
like Eve Gill (Jane) would be a student at RADA four years after the
end of World War II. Yet by casting the venerable Alistair Sim and Dame
Sybil Thorndike as Eve's British parents, and establishing such a warm
relationship between father and daughter, family background receded
into the wings while a cunning plot unfolded on center stage. The main
characters are role-playing. Eve thinks she's studying theatre, but she is
really the lead in a whodunit, in which she must unmask the murderer,
who cannot possibly be the dashing Jonathan Cooper (Todd), whom she
befriends. When Jonathan protests his innocence, he fools both Eve and
the audience—the latter through a notoriously misleading flashback. The

stage actress Charlotte Inwood (Dietrich) is not only starring in a West End revue, but is also playing a role in the whodunit—the "it" being her husband's murder. She swears she is innocent, despite her bloodstained dress, and Inspector Wilfred Smith (Wilding) becomes the romantic lead in the murder case he is investigating.

Regardless of what has been written about her unhappiness during the shoot (with Hitchcock's aloofness and Dietrich's outshining her), Jane called Hitchcock a "pussy cat" in one of those sound byte interviews on *Turner Classic Movies* (TCM) and spoke warmly of Dietrich, who had all but adopted her. But that was in the 1990s. In 1949, she believed Dietrich usurped the spotlight, which she did—but only once, lolling around while singing Cole Porter's "The Laziest Gal in Town." Dietrich reduced every double entendre to a single meaning, the one Porter intended, as she languidly affirmed her prowess while at the same time admitting her sloth. The lyrics were the problem:

> *It's not 'cause I wouldn't,*
> *It's not 'cause I shouldn't,*
> *And, Lord knows, it's not 'cause I couldn't.*
> *It's simply because I'm the laziest gal in town.*

Audiences, no matter how unsophisticated, understood exactly what she meant. Even in 1950, moviegoers could interpret body language and inflections. After much wrangling with the Breen Office, "Lord knows" became "You know." In another verse, "proposition" ("Ev'ry proposition I turn down") was changed to "invitation," as if that word were less suggestive. How could Jane compete with such lyrics—or with Dietrich's self-fabricated glamour?

Todd made his American debut earlier, co-starring in *The Hasty Heart* (1949) with Reagan and Patricia Neal. Todd was not a box-office draw, nor was Wilding, better known in Britain than America at the time—although that would change when he went Hollywood and became Elizabeth Taylor's second husband. That left Dietrich, a cult figure with her glittering pedigree.

Jane must also have sensed Hitchcock's indifference toward her and her character. He later told François Truffaut, "I ran into great difficulties with Jane," referring to the scene in which Eve impersonates Charlotte's maid in order to find evidence that would clear Jonathan. Eve treats the impersonation as an acting exercise. She experiments with facial expressions and hairstyles, first trying the dowdy look, with glasses perched on the rim of her nose and a cigarette between her lips. Discarding that guise, she chooses another: the maid so in awe of the star that she speaks haltingly, almost obsequiously. Regardless of what Hitchcock may have thought, it was an ingenious conceit: an Oscar-winning actress playing a theatre novice playing a maid. Jane knew, despite her billing, Hitchcock considered Dietrich the star, making sure that she was flatteringly lighted and elegantly costumed. But the role called for it; Dietrich played a stage actress. According to Hitchcock, in order to keep from being upstaged by Dietrich, Jane kept improving her appearance and, as a result, "failed to sustain the character." That was not true. Hitchcock may have forgotten that Eve abandoned the charwoman look in favor of one befitting a star's maid. If he felt that a more radical transformation was necessary he should have convinced Jane, as he had other actresses, that she had to affect a plainer look, so that a narcissistic star would be convinced she had a maid from London's East End. But narcissists like Charlotte are only interested in being waited on, and Jane does so convincingly until the moment of truth arrives. The problem was that Hitchcock did not care about Eve Gill. Besides, Jane was not a blonde, his favorite type. Dietrich was.

Hitchcock was frequently off target when he spoke of his films. He told Peter Bogdanovich that he disliked *Stage Fright* because of "the lack of reality in one of the characters"—specifically Jane's. "[The character] should have been a pimply faced girl. Wyman just refused to be that and I stuck with her." Hitchcock was unfairly blaming Jane for the film's tepid reception. If Jane refused to look pimply, who could blame her? To do so would be totally inconsistent with the character. If Eve's skin were an issue, she would have consulted a dermatologist before applying to RADA.

Hitchcock's dismissal of *Stage Fright* belied the careful planning that he lavished on it. *Stage Fright* begins with the credits appearing against a safety curtain, introducing the film-as-play metaphor that runs throughout. It ends with a literal *coup de théâtre*: with the safety curtain coming down on Jonathan as he is trying to escape from the police. Also to his credit, Hitchcock made admirable use of Jane's and Todd's eyes when Eve and Jonathan are in the prop room beneath the stage. Hitchcock alternates between extreme close ups of their eyes—Jane's cautious but not fearful, Todd's bulging and maniacal. As Jonathan speaks, his eyes widen into pools of menace, forcing Eve to realize she has been shielding a murderer. Until she can ease him out of the room and lock the door, Jane uses the same technique she employed in *Cheyenne*. Playing for time, she syllabified each word as if she were speaking to a child—which, in a sense, she was, albeit a deadly one. She and Todd played the scene brilliantly, and Hitchcock, always fascinated by eyes, caught the revealing interplay of theirs.

Since Jane had a chauffeured car at her disposal, she used Sundays for sightseeing. When the car was proceeding along Victoria Street, Jane caught sight of a neo-Byzantine edifice with an imposing bell tower. Instinctively, she asked the driver to stop, not knowing what it was. Her curiosity was piqued, and she decided to enter. She was about to undergo a transformative experience. She had come upon Westminster Cathedral, England's largest Catholic church. At first, Jane confused the cathedral with the better known Westminster Abbey, which was Church of England, the scene of royal weddings and coronations, and the burial place of such distinguished writers as Chaucer, Blake, Dickens, T. S. Eliot, and Gerard Manley Hopkins. She soon learned the difference. As she told a magazine writer, "I'd never seen such a sight in my life. "

As if drawn to something mysterious, she kept returning to Westminster Cathedral, learning about the Catholic mass, genuflection, and rosaries—which at first she thought were the equivalent of admission tickets, after seeing them on sale in the gift shop. She bought two, one for herself, and one for her best friend Betty Kaplan, who had been a bridesmaid at her wedding. "Now we can go in," she said confidently. "That started the whole thing."

When Jane was at MGM in 1946, she was unaware of the Catholic church on Jasmine Avenue, a block away from the studio. It was St. Augustine's, a former mission church rebuilt in the Gothic style, and a favorite with MGM employees, including non-Catholics like Joan Crawford, who would stop by simply to meditate or collect their thoughts. The parish had many pastors over the years, but none more popular than the Irish-born Father John O'Donnell, who was stationed there from 1923 to 1938. The charismatic priest even became part of MGM's extended family, so much so that the studio sponsored a barbeque each summer to support St. Augustine's. His contacts with the film community led to his being hired as a consultant for films with religious themes. Fr. O'Donnell's popularity may have been the reason for his transfer (some considered it banishment) to Immaculate Heart of Mary on Santa Monica Boulevard, a world away from MGM. Parishioners rallied to his support, petitioning Archbishop Cantwell to keep him at St. Augustine's. But Fr. O'Donnell, faithful to his vow of obedience, would not oppose the archbishop's decision, saddened as he was by it. The archbishop moved quickly; within a few days, St. Augustine's had a new pastor. Eight years later, the widow of a Culver City businessman left a hundred thousand dollars in her will to Fr. O'Donnell, "the Irish priest who won the hearts of many a movie mogul"—and also Jane Wyman's.

On her return to America in October 1949, Jane vowed to become a Catholic. Friends introduced her to Fr. O'Donnell, who gave her a Latin missal, which she cherished. "I'm going to become a Catholic if it kills me," she announced. Fr. O'Donnell assured her it wouldn't, and five years later, on 8 December 1954, the feast of the Immaculate Conception, Jane and her children, Maureen and Michael, were received into the faith at the Church of the Good Shepherd in Beverly Hills.

Jane was a full-fledged Catholic, if not as rigid as her friend Loretta Young, whom she dubbed "Mother Superior." Sunday now meant not just mass, but also vespers, and during the second week of Lent, a religious retreat with Loretta and Irene Dunne. If Jane had not experienced the peace that passeth understanding, she came close: "There's a serenity, a gaiety in these friends of mine. If we have problems, as Loretta has said so many times, 'Give them to the Lord.' I'll add one line to that, 'Give them to the Lord and go for broke.'"

Chapter 22

Zinging with Bing

IN 1951, IT WAS LOAN OUT TIME AGAIN: MGM FOR *THREE GUYS Named Mike*, RKO for *The Blue Veil*, and Paramount for *Here Comes the Groom* and *Just for You*, both with Bing Crosby. *Groom* gave Jane an opportunity to work with both Crosby and director Frank Capra, whose best work was behind him. Jane was not a screwball heroine like Claudette Colbert and Jean Arthur. And the public did not associate her with Crosby, whose most frequent co-star was Dorothy Lamour, who made a cameo appearance in *Groom*, whose plot was pure Capra—or as his detractors would say, "Capracorn."

Pete Garvey (Crosby), a journalist covering the plight of war orphans, is flying back to the United States with two of them. Since *Groom*, like the *Road* movies, is a comedy interspersed with musical numbers, the action stops periodically for musical sequences, the first of which takes the form of a history lesson. The passengers include Lamour, Louis Armstrong, Phil Harris, and the studio's resident clown, Cass Daley, who would cross her eyes and reconfigure her body to get a laugh. Using the rear of the plane as if it were a sound stage (which it was), they launch into "Misto Cristofo Columbo," simplifying the discovery of America for the orphans.

When Crosby was not in a *Road* movie with Lamour and Bob Hope, he was paired with actresses who would not commandeer the spotlight (Joan Caulfield in *Welcome, Stranger*, Coleen Gray in *Riding High*, Rhonda Fleming in *A Connecticut Yankee in King Arthur's Court*). In Jane, he met his match. *Groom* derived from a treatment by Robert Riskin and Liam O'Brien, the latter the brother of actor Edmond O'Brien and a writer-television producer, whose play, *The Remarkable Mr. Pennypacker*, was made into a 1959 movie. Riskin was more than Capra's best screenwriter;

he was the director's other self, his inner voice. Even when Riskin tried to emerge from Capra's shadow, he could not escape Capra's influence. *Magic Town* was a Capra script with an alien director.

The treatment, entitled "You Belong to Me," provided the template: Garvey (Crosby); his longtime fiancée Emmadel Jones (Jane); romantic entanglements (Emmadel's patrician fiancé, Wilbur Stanley [Franchot Tone]); the orphans who bring out Emmadel's maternal instincts; a wedding with one groom present (Wilbur) and another in reserve (Garvey); a nervous bride (Emmadel); and the groom's fourth cousin, Winifred (Alexis Smith), secretly in love with Wilbur and eager to take Emmadel's place at the altar. In *Groom*, Garvey knows what Emmadel wants—and it is not Wilbur. "You Belong to Me" would have been a perfect title, except that it had been used for a 1941 movie with Barbara Stanwyck and Henry Fonda.

Groom is a hybrid; it is neither screwball nor comedy of remarriage. In *The Awful Truth* (1937), the classic comedy of remarriage, the exes try to undermine each other's prospects. The result is a duel of wits, which no one wins, because each is really trying to woo back the other. In *Groom*, there is neither a battle of the sexes nor real verbal sparring. Garvey is only interested in regaining Emmadel; if he succeeds, his orphans will have a mother, and he, a wife and kids. Garvey is a trickster, using every stratagem in his repertoire to induce Emmadel to dump Wilbur. *Groom* is a pastiche of romantic comedy, screwball, farce, and comedy of remarriage (with an ex-fianceé in lieu of an ex-wife), yet without a center to hold all these plot threads together. This defect is evident at the beginning, when Garvey has a blind orphan (Anna Maria Alberghetti, in her movie debut) sing "Caro Nome" from *Rigoletto* for a conductor and his wife, who are so charmed that they adopt her—after which the three of them vanish from the plot.

The ending is pure Riskin, who recycled the finale of his best screenplay, *It Happened One Night*—but without the runaway bride. Garvey pretends the FBI is after him because he lacks a wife to make the adoption legal. Actually, he talked a fellow reporter into posing as an FBI agent about to arrest him. Unable to bear the thought of the children being deported, Emmadel has second thoughts about marrying Wilbur, who gallantly bows out and yields to Garvey. Thus the guests are not deprived of a wedding (compare *The Philadelphia Story*) and can even look forward to another with Wilbur and Winifred (again, compare *The Philadelphia Story*, in which James Stewart and Ruth Hussey follow in the footsteps of Cary Grant and Katharine Hepburn).

Saddled with a disjointed script, Capra reduced it to set pieces, as if he were staging a revue and ensuring that each of the principals has a solo or a duet. As the star, Crosby had both, but the others, except for Jane, shared a low-intensity spotlight. The best-acted scene, however, is non-musical. It takes place in the back of a chauffeured car in which Crosby and Tone engage in civilized banter, each trying to outdo the other in asserting his claim to Emmadel's affections. Tone, relaxed and unthreatened, is convinced that that social status and wealth mean more to her than marriage to a peripatetic reporter who lacks both. Garvey, unruffled and confident, rebuts each of Tone's claims like a laid-back debater. Crosby and Tone, confined to a space with minimal movement, bring off the scene with facial expression and intonation, even though the well-bred Wilbur doesn't stand a chance against the wily Garvey.

Jane's musical comedy skills had been displayed briefly in *Hollywood Canteen* and a bit more in *Night and Day*. Her dance lessons at the Edward A. Prinz Dancing Academy in St. Joseph and those unbilled appearances in 1930s musicals paid off royally in *Here Comes the Groom*—so much so that audiences may have wondered why Jane never developed into another Alice Faye or Betty Grable. The answer is simple: Except for a few classics like *42nd St.*, *Gold Diggers of 1933*, and *Gold Diggers of 1935*, Warners never took musicals as seriously as did MGM, Fox, and even Universal. Since the studio did not cultivate musical talent, no one thought of Jane as a musical comedy star. She was an actress, at first supporting cast, and finally a lead, but strictly comedy or drama. But give her a song and dance routine, and it seemed as if she had spent her entire career in musicals.

The one number that she and Crosby perform in *Groom* flows directly from the action. Garvey and Emmadel have a special song, Johnny Mercer and Hoagy Carmichael's "In the Cool, Cool, Cool of the Evening," which is technically a duet but structured in such a way that each has a chance to go solo and then rejoin the other. Desperate to find accommodations for his orphans, Garvey persuades Emmadel to bring him to the real estate office where she works. Flipping through the files of available homes, he finds a cottage and removes the "Sold" sticker. Pleased with himself, he starts warbling the song. Emmadel joins in, as if it were a familiar tune from their courtship—which apparently it is. Jane is game, Crosby is slick, and just when he seems to be running away with the song, she ropes him in, as if to remind him that they are equals. It's essentially a reunion song, not a courtship ritual, although there are times when Crosby is on the verge of turning it into one. But Jane, faithful to her character, prevents him from rekindling their romance by artfully steering him back for the finale, which they perform like two vaudevillians giving their all to get a hand.

"Evening" is not just a duet, but a dance number. Capra used long shots so that the audience knew there were no doubles. Crosby and Jane shared a similar rhythm: hers, a bit more polished; his, easygoing but stopping short of blasé. Each respected the other's art, making "Evening" the movie's highlight. The number does not end in the office. It continues into the hallway and on to the elevator, ending when Crosby and Jane leave the building as if making an exit. "Evening" is more than a musical interlude; it's a musical truce between a man and a woman at odds with each other. But the truce does not last beyond the song. Ever the con artist, Garvey succeeds in settling the children in the cottage, even though it has a new owner.

"In the Cool, Cool, Cool of the Evening" won an Oscar for best song. The Jane-Crosby rendition also became a hit single on the Decca label.

Groom was a three-month shoot, costing $2.07 million with Crosby receiving $150,000 and Jane $125,000. Capra made out best: $176,000. But Tone and Smith didn't do badly, earning $27,500 and $25,009, respectively.

Jane and Crosby's next (and last) movie together, *Just for You* (1952), was a real musical, not a comedy with music like *Groom*. The production data is misleading; the shoot was a little over two months (24 October–17 December 1951). Because of the musical numbers—particularly Jane's big one, "Checkin' My Heart"—she started earlier, working from 4 September to 10 December, for a total of ten weeks with four weeks free. Crosby received his usual $150,000, while Jane earned $133,333. It was a difficult shoot for the thirty-four-year-old Jane. A kidney stone kept her off the set for two days. Jane, however, was determined to get her one big production number right, knowing that, if she did, she would convince the skeptics that she could handle a musical—and perhaps cause them to wonder why she was so underutilized.

Jane would often arrive at the studio at 7:30 a.m. and leave at 5:00 p.m. Even when she had a 10:00 a.m. call, she would stay until 6:00 p.m. She could not rely on the memory of those who saw her in *Night and Day*; that was five years in the past, and her character meandered through the film, showing up for a musical number or comic relief.

That Paramount intended *Just for You* to be the companion piece to *Here Comes the Groom*—but in color—was evident from the opening shot of Broadway at W. 45th Street, where *Here Comes the Groom* was emblazoned on the marquee of the Astor theater. This composition also served as an establishing shot of the Great White Way, the turf of Broadway producer Jordan Blake (Crosby). Jane is Carolina Hill, the leading lady of his new musical. Blake is a widower, whose teenage son Jerry (Robert Arthur) is in love with Carolina. The only problem is that Carolina is in love with Jordan, who is in love with Broadway.

Crosby's most memorable screen priest was Father O'Malley in *Going My Way* and *The Bells of St. Mary's*. Whenever he had to interact with children as a priest, parent, or layperson, he was warm and compassionate, an orphan's dream father. His scenes with Robert Arthur in *Just for You* had an unfeigned naturalness, as if the two were actually father and son. That Crosby, however, was the actor. In real life, he was cold and aloof to his first wife, Dixie Lee, and to his sons, one of whom, Gary, did a *Mommie Dearest* and wrote an exposé, *Going My Own Way*, in which he catalogued the indignities he was subjected to for the slightest infraction. Crosby's other two sons, Dennis and Lindsay, committed suicide. To Paramount's founder, Adolph Zukor, Crosby was a loner who preferred the adulation of his fans to the love of his wife and children: "Many who knew Crosby think of him, despite his affability, as a lonely man. He will be found late at night at some little hamburger joint, reading his paper, sipping coffee. For a man with a famous face he has the amazing ability to conceal himself."

Despite the discrepancy between the person and the persona, it was the persona that was on view in *Just for You*, with Crosby doing what he always did best: singing, dancing, and acting with his characteristically unflappable style. He establishes Jordan Blake's take-over personality early in the film, when a lavish production number isn't generating the same heat that it did out of town. Crosby steps onto the stage, showing how it should be performed, leaving no doubt in anyone's mind that he was a song-and-dance man before turning to producing. Crosby tears into "I'll Si-Si Ya in Bahia," his limber body responding to the Latin beat as if it were his own rhythm. Crosby knew how to respond to the music—including music for a square dance, a type hardly associated with him. Yet in *Welcome, Stranger* (1947), he not only calls the dance from the stage, but then moves onto the floor, turning the square dance into a courtship ritual, as he woos Joan Caulfield with his own brand of cool sexiness.

Crosby was at home in a musical, but so was Jane. Unlike her part in *Groom*, in which she only had a duet with Crosby, she now had a chance both to harmonize with him and to do a star turn on her own, as befits a Broadway diva like Carolina. Choreographer Helen Tamaris, better known for her work in the theatre (*Annie Get Your Gun, Fanny, Plain and Fancy*), staged Jane's big number, "Checkin' My Heart," which on Broadway would have been a showstopper. Dressed in an elegant wedding gown, Jane angrily plucks the flowers from her bouquet, implying that the groom abandoned her before they even reached the altar. After heeding the advice of her alter ego, who pops up in each panel of her three-way mirror, she resolves to pay more attention to a man's bank account than to her emotions, proclaiming, "I'm not exactly hapless/in a strapless gown," as she turns her bridal outfit into one.

Tamaris's choreography was so precise, with movements synchronized with the music, that vamping was impossible. Jane responded well to Tamaris's Broadway-style staging, which complemented the skills she had acquired—and never lost—as a student of dance and her years as an unbilled lady of the chorus. Tamaris had formerly been a dancer, and all Jane needed was guidance, which Tamaris provided.

Jane's other number, apart from her duet with Crosby, was a semi-solo, "The Maiden of Guadalupe," a bit of exotica by Harry Warren and Leo Robin, in which Jane sang while dancers sensuously enacted a tragic love story. But for audiences, particularly record buyers and radio listeners, the musical highlight was the Warren-Robin duet, "Zing a Little Zong." At the opening night party, Jane and Bing (it's impossible to think of them as Carolina and Jordan) break into "Zing," a specialty number, lively but witless, in which the *s* in words like "song," "season," and "sing" is pronounced as if it were *z*. The space is far more confined than the one in *Groom*, which encompassed three playing areas: the office, the elevator, and the doorway. Here, movement is limited, but Jane and Crosby treat the living room as if it were a stage, and "Zing" as if it were a duet that neither could make into a solo. Since Paramount believed it had the makings of a hit song (it was nominated for a best song Oscar, but lost to "Do Not Forsake Me" from *High Noon*), Jane and Bing reprised it at the end.

Jane looked ageless. Her figure was that of a twenty-something. Not too many actresses her age could appear in tights and a bathing suit, looking as if they had not gained a pound since they were eighteen. But Jane and Crosby were a mid-career team, destined for only two movies. Except for a few forays into comedy, Jane went back to drama, further solidifying her reputation as a serious actress and winning two more Oscar nominations. Crosby's next leading lady was Grace Kelly, first in

The Country Girl (1954), for which he and Kelly both were nominated for Oscars. Kelly won hers, but Crosby lost to Marlon Brando in *On the Waterfront*. His last film with Kelly was *High Society* (1956), a musical adaptation of *The Philadelphia Story* with a score by Cole Porter that was so well integrated with the script that the songs seemed like dialogue set to music. Then there were concerts, television appearances, and finally death in 1977, the same year that two other icons, each representing a different kind of music, passed away: Elvis Presley and Maria Callas.

Chapter 23

Glass Animals and Blue Veils, Cabbages and Couture

EVER SINCE *JOHNNY BELINDA*, JERRY WALD FELT A SPECIAL AFFECTION for Jane, who would star in two more of his productions. She had just returned from England after winding up *Stage Fright* when she was back before the cameras in *The Glass Menagerie* (1950), which Wald and Charles K. Feldman were producing for Warners. Feldman was one of the few agents who could boast of a bachelor's degree from the University of Michigan, a law degree from University of Southern California, and an affection for Henry James, whom he allegedly read each morning. As president of Famous Artists Corporation, Feldman represented such stars as Marlene Dietrich, Lauren Bacall, Tyrone Power, Ingrid Bergman, and Claudette Colbert, to name some of the more prominent of his three hundred clients, which also included directors and writers. Feldman then turned to producing; he was especially interested in bringing two of Tennessee Williams's greatest plays, *The Glass Menagerie* and *A Streetcar Named Desire*, to the screen. The latter proved to be not only an example of great filmmaking, but also a triumph over the parochialism of the Breen Office—despite a revised ending that was a sop to the righteous.

Menagerie was as fragile as the glass animals that Laura Wingfield (Jane) collects, speaking of them as if they were human. Laura is the embodiment of "passive gentility," to borrow Henry James's phrase from *The Portrait of a Lady*. Afflicted with a disability that makes her limp, Laura has created her own world in the St. Louis tenement where she lives with her brother, Tom (Arthur Kennedy), a would-be writer reduced to working in a warehouse, and her mother Amanda (Gertrude Lawrence),

162

who ignores Laura's handicap, expecting it to go unnoticed by any "gentleman caller." *Menagerie* was not like *Streetcar*, with the action moving inexorably toward a tragic denouement. Although Laura is not institutionalized like Blanche du Bois, once her gentleman caller (Kirk Douglas) arrives and activates her long dormant self-confidence, he confesses that he will not be returning because he is engaged. *Menagerie* ends on a note of sober resignation. Tom joins the Merchant Marines (and presumably morphs into Tennessee Williams), but Laura and Amanda are doomed to a life of passive gentility. The play is a series of prismatic moments, delicately wrought in language that suddenly soars into poetry and then drops down to prose.

To be reasonably faithful to the original, a film transfer should respect the text, no matter how modified. But *Menagerie* was more complicated. Strict fidelity would demand that whenever the language turned poetic, the shift would be natural, neither a deviation from ordinary speech nor an ascent to the ether. What *Menagerie* needed behind the camera was Elia Kazan, who directed both the stage and screen versions of *Streetcar*, complete with most of the original's haunting language. Blanche's dialogue, delivered by Vivien Leigh with a dreamy delicacy so gossamer that it could easily tear, ran in counterpoint to Marlon Brando's sweaty vernacular.

But Irving Rapper was no Kazan. A thoroughly competent Warners contract director, Rapper could not reproduce Williams's art of poeticizing the plight of lost souls. All he could do was gently stir the hidden springs of unfulfilled dreams and false expectations that lay below the surface. After reading the script, Williams knew what was wrong: "A good deal of the truth, dignity, poetry and pathos has gone out the window."

Jane affected the voice of someone who had resigned herself to life's vicissitudes, which, in Laura's case, had left her fatherless and crippled (a word her mother detests), living in a glass world, with glass animals as her only friends. She conveyed Laura's vulnerability through a rueful smile and eyes that resigned themselves to a life devoid of event, except for an intrusion of reality that would send her back to her glass menagerie. Unknowingly, the audience was watching Jane as Sarah Jane Fulks—if she had never left St. Joseph and perhaps opened "Miss Sarah Jane's Dance Studio," living vicariously through her students. Jane understood Laura, who was the self she had left behind.

Arthur Kennedy had the dual task of playing Tom and supplying the voiceover narration, making the film the "memory play" that Williams intended. Although Lawrence was cast against type (the following year she starred on Broadway as Anna in *The King and I*), she was a surprisingly effective Amanda, striving desperately to maintain an air of Southern graciousness in a cramped midwestern apartment. Kirk Douglas as the gentleman caller, Jim O'Connor, had the most difficult role. Screenwriter Peter Berneis added a scene in the warehouse where Jim and Tom work, and where Jim charms the boss with the skills he acquired from his speech class, while Tom, embittered by his lot in life, behaves like a sullen worker overqualified for his job. Even though he is engaged, Jim accepts Tom's invitation to dinner, ignoring or oblivious to the fact that he has been invited to be the fairy tale prince who rescues Laura from her tenement tower. Knowing that his engagement precludes the possibility of ever seeing Laura again, Jim makes the most of the evening, trying to do for her what his public speaking class did for him. In Laura, he has the perfect pupil. Jane plays the scene with a bittersweet docility, as if she were being given a demonstration of a skill she will never use. Jim's attempt to build up Laura's self-esteem comes off as ego gratification, as if his life-changing speech course qualifies him to play therapist to the shy and diffident.

When Amanda learns that Jim is engaged, a shadow of disappointment momentarily crosses Lawrence's face and then disappears as she wishes him happiness. Amanda is still a Southern belle, now middle-aged, but always observant of the amenities. There is a flashback in which Amanda entertains seventeen gentleman callers on the family plantation. From the way Lawrence moved among them, discreetly flirtatious but with an air of ladylike superiority, one could believe that Amanda was not fantasizing about her popularity. The studio's first choice for Amanda, however, was not Lawrence, but the Alabama-born Tallulah Bankhead, who could have brought the affectations of the Deep South to an urban apartment overlooking an alley. But Bankhead's behavior, exacerbated by her heavy drinking, was so "disgraceful" that Warners had no choice but to look elsewhere.

Berneis, whose screenplay of *Portrait of Jennie* preserved the mysterious parallel universe of Robert Nathan's novel, where a struggling artist encounters a dream child from another era, could not work the same magic with *Menagerie*. The play can either be performed as poetry moored to earth until it is unfettered so it can take flight, or as a Clifford Odets-like drama where three people live out their lives of quiet desperation in a tenement across from the Paradise Dance Hall, whose name mocks the fallen world they inhabit.

Audiences were no more ready for a downbeat ending in *Menagerie* than they were for *Streetcar* the following year. The film does not end with the play's final lines, spoken by Tom: "For nowadays the world is lit by lightning. Blow out your candles, Laura—and so goodbye." Rather, the film version ends with the arrival of a new gentleman caller, thus inspiring hope where little exists. (Williams preferred "the sound of approaching footsteps" or at best a "shadow.") On the stage, *Streetcar*'s devastating conclusion was the institutionalization of Blanche after her rape by Stanley severs her last remaining thread of sanity. Stella remains with her husband, knowing what he has done but needing his brand of lovemaking. In the film, after Blanche departs with the doctor, speaking the famous line, "Whoever you are, I have always depended upon the kindness of strangers," Stella takes up her baby and rushes upstairs to her neighbor Eunice, vowing never to return to Stanley.

And another type of change occurred in the movie version of Williams's *Sweet Bird of Youth*: Instead of being castrated, Chance Wayne (Paul Newman) gets his nose broken. Other versions of Williams's plays preserved the integrity of the original: *Summer and Smoke, Suddenly Last Summer, The Fugitive Kind* (based on *Orpheus Descending*), and *Night of the Iguana*. *The Glass Menagerie* will always pose a challenge to adapters trying to retain the original's fragility without breaking it like Laura's unicorn, which loses its horn and thus its uniqueness.

The Blue Veil (1951) was Jane's final film for Wald, who had now found a producing partner in the versatile playwright-screenwriter-movie director Norman Krasna. The team produced two films for RKO, the first of which was *The Blue Veil*. Wald knew *Veil* would be perfect for Jane as Louise Mason, a young woman who entered what in the nineteenth century was called the "governess trade" after losing her husband in battle during World War I and her newborn shortly thereafter. Robbed of motherhood, Louise decides to mother other women's children. Louise was one of those youth-to-old age roles that test an actor's ability to traverse the years, particularly in a film where time is collapsed and one needs more than a white wig and makeup to be convincing. Jane met the challenge superbly and, in fact, received an Oscar nomination for her work, only to lose to Vivien Leigh for *A Streetcar Named Desire*.

The celebrated radio writer, Norman Corwin, wrote the script for *The Blue Veil*, which is very much in the tradition of radio drama, with its short scenes, telescoped action, and rapid passage of time. Jane had never played a role requiring her to age over such a short period of time, yet in each stage of her character's development, she adopted the right voice,

posture, and walk. Since a governess did not have a fashionable wardrobe, Jane looked properly spinsterish in funereal dresses and prim hats.
Even when Louise is supposed to be in her twenties, Jane behaved like
an old maid when a young professor proposes to her. Given Jane's appearance and clothes, it seemed as if he regarded her as more of a mother
figure than a future wife. Louise soon realizes as much and returns to her
beloved profession, where she can give and receive the only love she will
ever know: her love for children and their love for her.

The climactic moment occurs when Louise raises a young boy whose
British father enlists in the RAF, and whose mother (Audrey Totter), joins
her husband in England. When the husband is killed, the wife remarries,
leaving Louise to raise her son, Tony. After five years, the mother and
her new husband return to America to reclaim Tony, prompting Louise
to flee with him to Florida. When the case reaches the district attorney
(a compassionate Everett Sloane), Jane, her voice quietly tremulous, and
looking even older and frailer than her years, forcefully declares herself Tony's real mother, arguing that birth does not make a mother, and
abandonment precludes separating a child from the only mother he has
known.

The Blue Veil had the makings of a three-hankie movie, but director
Curtis Bernhardt kept it from turning lachrymose by letting Jane find
the core of the character in Louise's sense of quiet resignation, until injustice drives her to abscond with Tony and risk a kidnapping charge.
When Louise pleads her case, Jane did not play the scene so that the
audience would pity her character, but only see her as a woman claiming
her rights. Although Jane did not have to learn sign language or have
her ears blocked, *The Blue Veil* was as difficult as *Johnny Belinda*. Here
she had to sustain the same character through three decades reduced
to two hours, with the passage of time conveyed through montage and
scrapbook-like scenes. *The Blue Veil* was another personal triumph. She
would have one more cavalcade film, *So Big*.

Some degree of versatility was expected of contract players during the
studio years, the bottom line being the ability to deliver dialogue intelligently and wear period clothes as if they came out of one's own closet.
With Jane, the operative word was not "versatility," but art. She had
proved earlier that she could play practically anything except call girls
and gun molls. What was expected of her was not merely adjusting to
the exit-one-film-enter-another policy, with which she was already familiar, but following one film with another in a genre that was radically
different from the previous one. Her achievement in *The Blue Veil* is even

more impressive when measured against *Just for You*, which she made the following year. There, she was a musical comedy star, who looked as if her world was Broadway. Similarly, her performance in *So Big* (1953) only confirmed her mastery of the art of seamless role shifting. There is not a vestige of the chic Carolina of *Just for You* in Jane's portrayal of Selena Peake DeJong.

Anyone who thought that the aging process in *The Blue Veil* was the result of artfully applied makeup and a maiden aunt wardrobe could no longer advance that argument after seeing Jane in *So Big*. Like *The Blue Veil*, *So Big*, based on Edna Ferber's Pulitzer Prize winning novel, is a decade-spanner (three in the film, at least four in the novel)in which only Jane ages. Richard Beymer and Tommy Rettig, respectively, play Selena's son, Dirk, and her prize pupil, Roelf, as boys. Steve Forrest and Walter Coy play the same characters as men. Director Robert Wise allowed the action to glide gracefully through the years, and Jane to age at the same pace, even more imperceptibly and less dramatically than she did in *The Blue Veil*. In both films, she aged not just in appearance and deportment, but also in her eyes, which reflected knowledge accumulated over the same period and brightened slightly by the glint of triumph over life's disappointments and hardships. These were not eyes bespeaking self-pity, an emotion alien to both Louise and Selena, who could accept life's slings and arrows without asking why.

John Twist's screenplay consisted of interconnected highlights from Ferber's novel, sometimes modified, but always faithful to the spirit of the original, with additions that provided a new perspective on some of Ferber's characterizations. Twist followed the character arc that Ferber had created for Selena, bringing her from a charmed childhood that ended with her father's death, to the Illinois farm country where she taught the children of Dutch truck farmers. Ferber's Selena is not quite the ebullient teenager (Jane at her transformative best) seen at the beginning of the film. In the novel, Selena's father was a professional gambler who was shot to death. In the film, he is a failed businessman who dies of a heart attack.

But Twist followed Ferber's structure, explaining the meaning of the title (Selena's nickname for her son) and reproducing the novel's main episodes, such as Selena meeting her future husband, Purvis DeJong (Sterling Hayden), after he bids an unheard of ten dollars for her basket at a church social, knowing that its contents are meager. Twist also includes Purvis's death, which leaves Selena with a son to raise and a farm that she eventually turns into an income-producing property. Imbued with a pioneer's determination, she endures the sexist taunts of the men who believe that a woman who sells her vegetables in the Chicago Haymarket is one step above a woman who sells herself.

Selena prospers, proud that her asparagus is on the menu at the Drake Hotel. But Dirk has forsaken architecture, his intended career, because sales pays better. Twist fashioned the script as a frame narrative, opening and closing with Dirk and Roelf, well into their thirties, and the artist Dallas O' Hara (Nancy Olson) at Selena's farm, with their reminiscences constituting the bulk of the film. Early in life, Selena's father taught her that there were two kinds of people: "wheat," the business-savvy kind that drives the economy, and "emeralds," the creative kind that endows a country with a lasting legacy. Roelf turned out to be an emerald. Dirk, a would-be emerald, devolved into wheat. But the film ends on a joyous note: Even though Selena knows her son has embraced the corporate world, she delights in his sweeping her up in his arms and waltzing around the living room to Max Steiner's wistful music.

Jane's performance was at least worthy of an Oscar nomination, but none was forthcoming. Best Actress went to Hollywood's new golden girl, Audrey Hepburn, for *Roman Holiday*.

The vagaries of the studio system continued even into its prolonged sunset in the 1950s—or until the stars from the golden age faced the inevitable and either retired from the screen, changed careers, reinvented themselves, or found outlets for their talent in television, summer stock, and Broadway, if they could master an entire script and commit to eight shows a week. Jane may have been encouraged by her Oscar nomination for *The Blue Veil*, but she knew that when she was cast as Betty Rogers, Will Rogers's wife, in *The Story of Will Rogers* (1952), it would not be as the star—especially with Will Rogers Jr. in the title role. She had gone a similar route several times before, notably after winning an Oscar for *Johnny Belinda* and then treading water in *A Kiss in the Dark* and *Three Guys Named Mike*, competing with David Niven in the former and all the Mikes—especially Van Johnson—in the latter. But, as she told the press, her respect for Will Rogers motivated her to take the role. Besides, Jane's was only a supporting role in a film in which her wardrobe consisted of period costumes designed to reflect the changing fashions of the first decades of the twentieth century.

As a biopic, *The Story of Will Rogers* scrolls, sometimes ploddingly, through the highlights of Rogers's life: performer in Wild West shows, Hollywood actor, media icon, columnist, radio commentator, and much-in-demand public speaker, whose homespun philosophy, genial political satire, and blazing humanity endeared him to the public. If anyone personified the average American of the post-World War I era, it was Will Rogers. In 1952, many would have known about his death in 1935 when a plane, piloted by his close friend Wiley Post, crashed while flying from Fairbanks, Alaska, to Point Barrow, killing both of them. In the film, Rogers tells Betty that he had always wanted to visit Alaska after he failed geography, because he could not identify the location of Point Barrow. It was one of those prefigurative lines for the knowledgeable; for the others, a fatal airplane crash was all that mattered.

As the plane takes off at the end of the film, the somber soundtrack and Jane's face, a mix of apprehension and resignation, are worthy metaphors for impending death. Although Jane never worked in the silents, she could have succeeded simply because of her ability to register moods without widening her eyes (nature had done that) or resorting to hokey alarm. Like many artists, Jane could never explain the art of acting, except in reference to her body of work.

In August 1954, Jane was loaned to Paramount for the Pine-Thomas production of *Lucy Gallant* (1955). Pine-Thomas, a production company based at Paramount, was formed by William H. Pine and William C. Thomas, two enterprising graduates of Columbia and the University of Southern California, respectively. They were known in the industry as the "Dollar Bills," not merely because they shared the same first name but because they produced a string of commercially successful B movies in the 1940s (*Aerial Gunner*, *Submarine Alert*, *Wildcat*, *Tornado*, etc.) as well as a few B+ ones like *El Paso* (1949) and *Jamaica Run* (1953). The team decided to try for an "A" with *Lucy Gallant*, which, despite its elaborate production, was a B movie in disguise. Jane's salary, however, was definitely in the A range: $163,000 for ten weeks, with an additional $16,300 per week thereafter, if necessary.

In 1954, Jane was thirty-seven; her co-star, Charlton Heston, was thirty. In some scenes, Jane could pass for a woman Heston's age; in others, she looked like a woman her own age. Heston looked a strapping twenty-five. This was the dilemma faced by actresses who achieved fame in the 1930s and 1940s and were still active in the 1950s: How to play opposite younger co-stars without looking like the September part of a May-September romance, unless the age difference was part of the script. In *Magnificent Obsession* and *All That Heaven Allows*, Rock Hudson was eight years younger than Jane. However, in both films the age difference was dictated by the plot. In the former, Jane was the second wife of a doctor who died when the only available resuscitator was being used to save the life of a reckless playboy (Hudson). In the latter, she played a widow in love with her gardener (Hudson), who was not only younger but not of her class.

The age difference between Jane and Heston mattered less than *Lucy Gallant*'s tired marriage vs. career story line. The title character is a would-be bride, abandoned by her fiancé, who could not bear the ignominy of marrying a woman whose father had committed suicide. Finding herself stranded in a Texas oil town with her elaborate trousseau, Lucy refuses to let her designer wardrobe go unworn and sells it off to the locals, who have only known gingham and calico. Flush with success, Lucy opens a dress shop, not expecting a lanky rancher, Casey Cole (Heston), to complicate her life. Jane and Heston tried their best in the love scenes, but Jane was defeated by unflattering lighting and a lacquered appearance, which did not make her look younger, only made up. Unfortunately, Jane's character had no backstory. One has to assume that Lucy was always a potential entrepreneur who had delayed marriage until middle age, which would explain why she first appears in the kind of tailored suits favored by 1950s career women.

When Casey turns oil tycoon, and Lucy's shop burns to the ground, the film poses a perennial question: Will Lucy give up her dream of bringing haute couture to Texas and marry Casey, or will she build an even bigger Gallant's? The answer is "Yes" to both. When Casey bails Lucy out after her unscrupulous business manager tries to supplant her, Lucy repays his generosity by agreeing to marriage. When Casey asks, "What about the store?" Lucy replies, "What store?" For the fade out, they go into a decorous clinch appropriate to a woman of Jane's (and Lucy's) age.

The film's only historical value lies in the appearance of designer Edith Head as herself at a fashion show that inaugurates the opening of the new Gallant's. The show itself is a marvel of elegance and grace, making it bearable to sit through a film that reiterates the clichéd argument that a woman is incomplete without a man. Or, to summarize the philosophy of the salty Molly Basserman (Thelma Ritter), having a man is better than ending up a rich old maid with a monogrammed hot water bottle.

Chapter 24

Addio del passato

THE YEAR 1956 MARKED THE END OF JANE'S TWENTY YEARS AT WAR-
ners, where she received her first screen credit. It was fitting that *Miracle
in the Rain*, her last film for the studio, reflected her newfound faith and
religion. She was not as embittered as Reagan was when he left Warners
in 1952. Jack Warner did not even say goodbye, and no sooner had Reagan gone than his name was removed from his parking space. Jane had
been doing television since 1952 and sensed that would be her medium
for the duration, with an occasional return to film if a tempting offer
came her way. *Miracle* was a graceful exit from the studio that made her
a star who would shine just as brightly on the small screen.

Miracle in the Rain (1956) began as a *Saturday Evening Post* (3 April
1943) short story by Ben Hecht that Warners bought for seventy-five
thousand dollars but never got around to filming until 1955. Hecht was
Hollywood's premier man of letters: newspaper reporter, fiction and
nonfiction writer, playwright, memoirist, and screenwriter. He and his
close friend Charles MacArthur authored the stage classic *The Front Page*
(1928), adapted three times for the screen—twice under the original title
in 1931 and 1974, and most memorably as *His Girl Friday* (1940), which
retained the same plot, but with a female Hildy Johnson (Rosalind Russell). Hecht was also a prolific screenwriter, known for, among other
films, the Oscar-winning *Underworld* (1927), *Scarface* (1932), *Nothing
Sacred* (1937), *Wuthering Heights* (1939, with MacArthur), and *Notorious*
(1946). As a reporter for the *Chicago Daily News*, Hecht heard his share
of human interest stories, some of which may have crossed the borders
of credibility into the preternatural: "I encountered many things in the
city . . . . I met the torrents that spun me around, tides that drowned me

171

and comets that pulled me against the sky. I have had many adventures." And one of those adventures was the basis of "Miracle in the Rain," perhaps a story that the teller believed was true and passed on to Hecht. This ill-starred romance of a typist and a GI in the early days of World War II ends in their deaths—the soldier in the war, the typist in New York's St. Patrick's Cathedral, clutching in her hand the soldier's talisman, the one he was wearing when he was killed in the Pacific and which, except for a miracle, she could not have had in her possession. Hecht was familiar with the layout of St. Patrick's. In his sprawling autobiography, *Child of the Century* (1954), he writes fondly of Gertie, a German cook dying of cancer, who wanted a high mass said for her at St. Patrick's. A priest waived the usual fee and celebrated a mass at the side altar of her favorite saint, St. Anne. In both the story and the film, the typist is drawn to the altar of St. Andrew.

Miracle in the Rain reunited Jane and Van Johnson—she as Ruth Wood, a typist; he, as army private Art Hugenon on leave in New York where he meets her on a rainy afternoon in spring 1943. Ruth becomes her mother's sole provider after her songwriter father abandoned them. Jane played her as a woman in her late twenties, guileless and refreshingly unsophisticated, without pretensions and aspirations. Her face bore the imprints of time and stress. Rudolph Maté, a more sensitive director than *Lucy Gallant*'s Robert Parrish, as well as a former cinematographer, made certain that Jane was flatteringly lighted. Jane responded by drawing on her own brand of incandescence to invest Ruth with a spiritual aura.

Miracle recalls *The Clock* (1945), another World War II film, in which a similar pair meets, falls in love, and manages to marry in one weekend. Ruth and Art are not so fortunate; both are dead at the end—he in battle; she of pneumonia. But, as Art's spirit reminds Ruth, "Nobody ever dies." *Miracle* is a film of such deep faith that, while it might not have convinced skeptics to accept a hereafter, it certainly made one seem possible.

Hecht wrote the screenplay himself, retaining the main characters (Ruth, her neurotic mother, Grace, her co-worker, Art) and the plot points (the auction; the Roman coin; Art's death in the Pacific; Ruth's discovery of the cathedral, clearly St. Patrick's; her attraction to the side altar of St. Andrew; Art's spectral appearance; Ruth's death; and Grace's discovery of the coin in Ruth's hand). Hecht also softened Ruth's character, so that it would conform to Jane's talent for projecting an image of transcendent innocence that could be calibrated but not downgraded to despair. Such was not the case in the original, in which Ruth became so bitter after Art's death that she turns on her mother. For the film, Hecht had Ruth withdraw into herself, not comprehending how the only happiness she had ever known could be taken from her. Jane's Ruth has not lost hope. She is awaiting some sign, perhaps from St. Andrew, whose statue she feels she must illuminate, if only with candles.

In addition to giving Ruth a depth she lacked in the original, Hecht brought the action full circle, from a meeting in the rain to an apparition and death—or rather, a death and transfiguration in the rain. Art's death inspires Grace (Eileen Heckart) to bring Ruth to St. Patrick's Cathedral, where Ruth dies, but not in front of St. Andrew's altar, as she did in the story. Dying in the rain at the cathedral's entrance is more dramatic than expiring at a side altar. Having Grace find the coin at the entrance is spiritually more uplifting than finding it in the morgue, as happened in the story. A miracle is a spiritual phenomenon, and what better setting for one than a cathedral? Hecht knew what movie audiences wanted: a coda with an image of purification, as if the past had been washed away, leaving eternity in its place.

Miracle marked the first time St. Patrick's interior was used for a movie. The New York archdiocese was obviously impressed by the intensely spiritual nature of the script, and perhaps by the fact that the Polish-born Rudolph Maté was Catholic, as were Jane and Eileen Heckart. The city and the archdiocese cooperated to the fullest—the city for location shooting at 32nd St. and Eighth Avenue, 50th St. and Broadway, the *New York Times* building, and Central Park; the archdiocese for access to St. Patrick's, whose administrator, Father Joseph Francis Flannelly, met with producer Frank Rosenberg and Maté.

Fr. Flannelly was one of the best-known clergymen in New York. A native New Yorker, he was ordained at twenty-three in 1928 and elevated to the rank of auxiliary bishop at fifty-four. He was the celebrant at Babe Ruth's funeral mass in 1948, and he supervised the completion of the famous bronze doors at the cathedral's Fifth Avenue entrance. His congeniality dispelled any doubts that Rosenberg and Maté might have had about intractable priests. Knowing that some compensation was warranted, Rosenberg arranged for a donation, not realizing that the studio was unfamiliar with church protocol and treated the matter as if it were payment for services rendered. Rosenberg was mortified, apologizing profusely for "the less than attractive way in which the donation was made by an individual who should not have handled the matter in the first place." Fr. Flannelly probably smiled; he was used to a different form of bureaucracy, which can sound just as coldly formal. But he was also a man of great benevolence, well known for his Saturday morning masses at the side altar of St. Joseph during the 1960s.

During location shooting, which lasted from 17 May to 7 June 1955, Jane resided at the elegant St. Moritz on Central Park South, her one compensation for getting soaked in a climactic downpour supplied by the city's hydrants. Near the end of the film, Ruth has developed a bad cough. While she and Grace are passing St. Patrick's, Grace suggests that they drop in. Ruth, awestruck, wanders along the side altars, stopping at St. Andrew's, illuminated solely by the few lighted candles on the stand before it. Not knowing what votive candles are, Ruth took two and placed them in front of the statue. Even though Art is dead, Ruth senses that there may be some connection between a statue that needs light and herself. Later, seriously ill with pneumonia, Ruth leaves her sick bed and sets out for St. Patrick's, determined to brighten a statue that she associates with Art. Delirious, she stands at the entrance, where Art appears in a vision, reminding her that death is not the end. Ruth collapses in the rain as a priest emerges and carries her inside. Grace arrives and, kneeling at Ruth's side, notices something in her hand: a Roman coin that Ruth had given to Art, who made it into a pendant that he was wearing when he died. Is the story a fable, or a reminder that "there are more things in heaven and earth, Horatio, / Than are dreamt of in your philosophy (*Hamlet*, 1,5)"? Hamlet may have been right.

There were no Oscar nominations for Jane or the film. Jane was probably grateful that she did not contract pneumonia herself after being bombarded with so much water. She had other plans: a television series, for one thing.

I Do, I Don't, I Do, I Don't

THERE WAS NO MORE REASON FOR COLUMBIA TO TURN ITS ARGUABLY definitive comedy of remarriage, *The Awful Truth* (1937), into the musical *Let's Do It Again* (1953) than there was to remake *It Happened One Night* (1935) as *You Can't Run Away from It* (1957). All a remake does is invite comparison with the original, which usually emerges in a better light. If the argument was that the remake was intended for moviegoers who never saw the original and preferred the stars of their generation to those of their parents', the solution might be to re-release the original with the expectation that audiences who loved it then would love it even more—and hope that the original would convert a younger generation to the glories of golden age Hollywood.

In *Let's Do It Again*, Lucy and Jerry Warriner are now Constance (Jane) and Gary (Ray Milland) Stuart. Constance is a former musical comedy star, whose composer-husband habitually lies about his whereabouts (he's drumming away in basement night clubs), prompting Constance to go on the town with the suave Courtney Craig (the impeccably groomed Tom Helmore). More of a comedy with musical sequences than a full-fledged musical, *Let's Do It Again* at least gave Jane one last chance, albeit in a minor film, to show what she might have been if her flair for musical comedy had been recognized, or if she had tried Broadway. Doing so would have meant taking a chance, as Rosalind Russell did in *Wonderful Town* (1953), winning a Tony in the bargain; or as Bette Davis did, less successfully but nonetheless valiantly in the musical revue *Two's Company* (1952). Lucille Ball did better in *Wildcat* (1960), which at least produced a hit song, Cy Coleman and Carolyn Leigh's "Hey, Look Me Over."

Jane had been tempted. She was perfectly relaxed on live television—for example, when she co-hosted the *Merv Griffith Show* and appeared on

Perry Como's Kraft Musical Hall in 1958. But doing a Broadway play would be a completely different experience. It was a surprise, then, to read in the *New York Times* (8 May 1966) that director-playwright Reginald Denham had persuaded Jane to star in a new play that he and his wife Mary Orr (author of the short story, "The Wisdom of Eve," on which *All about Eve* was based) had written, called "Wonderful Us." The play, later renamed *Minor Murder*, was inspired by an actual incident in Australia involving the murder of a widow resulting from her attempt to terminate her adolescent daughter's close friendship with another girl. When the girls tried to pass off the murder as an accident, the press became involved, with a reporter (Jane's role) covering the case. Why Jane even considered a grisly melodrama, a genre totally unsuited to her, is impossible to understand. She may have been influenced by the team's credentials. Denham had directed *Janus*, *The Bad Seed*, and *Dial "M" for Murder* on Broadway and had written the hit plays *Ladies in Retirement* and *Wallflower*, the latter with his wife. Jane wisely passed on *Minor Murder* (a pun on the murderers' ages), which never reached Broadway, but is available through Dramatists Play Service for fifty dollars a performance.

It would have made sense for Jane to choose a musical. What she could have brought to the musical stage is on display in *Let's Do It Again*, in which Jane's musical numbers are the movie's raison d'être. Jane's costumes were created by Jean Louis, whose name was his calling card. Columbia's resident couturier, Jean Louis designed the black strapless gown and arm-length gloves that gave Rita Hayworth iconic status as she bumped her way through "Put the Blame on Mame" in *Gilda* (1946). But he did not restrict his services to Columbia. He was responsible for the nude gown that Marlene Dietrich wore in her Las Vegas debut, and the beaded one into which Marilyn Monroe was stitched before she purred "Happy Birthday" to John F. Kennedy.

Although Jane was not the glamorous type, Jean Louis's gowns gave her the semblance of glamour, providing the aura of sophistication expected of a onetime Broadway star living in a Park Avenue apartment with a sunken living room, a grand piano, and a bar. Jane makes her first appearance in a low cut (as were all of her costumes) silvery blue gown after a night on the town with Courtney Craig, who has been keeping her company while her husband pretends to be in Chicago. Next comes *The Awful Truth* kind of divorce in which each party attempts to sabotage the other's marital prospects, with, naturally, the ex-wife gaining the upper hand—but just before the divorce becomes final. And of course there is a bed around where they can resume their conjugal activities.

The songs, for the most part, are integrated with the plot, but each is really an opportunity for Jane to emerge in another Jean Louis creation and give moviegoers a taste of what they had been missing while she was toiling away in B movies at Warners. As Jane performs "It Was Great Fun While It Lasted," she strips down to a black lace slip, stepping discreetly into the shower before retiring. When Courtney asks her to substitute for the out-of-town Lucy Warriner (an inside reference to *The Awful Truth*) at a backers' audition, Jane arrives in a pink gown with a rhinestone-studded bodice, swiveling her hips while singing the torchy "Slow Burn over a Fast Man," working the living room as if it were a club and getting Courtney the funding he needs.

Later, in a bright red gown with a peplum, she dances a mean mambo with Frank McGraw (Aldo Ray), an Alaska millionaire willing to invest in the show if he can enjoy her company. Every scene is a veritable fashion show: Jane in a lavender negligee; a purple suit with a white fur collar and cuffs; and in a white lace negligee with pants. The film's highlight derives from *The Awful Truth*, in which Lucy Warriner (Irene Dunne) passes herself off as her husband's flashy sister, shocking her would-be in-laws with her relatively tame (but not for their patrician taste) bump-and-grind version of the song "Gone with the Wind," implying that when she performed it, a wind machine blew up her dress. In the remake, Constance masquerades as her husband's anthropologist sister, shocking the guests (but not Gary's fiancée, played unpretentiously by Karen Booth, wearing another of Jean Louis's strapless creations with a black lace bodice) with her rendition of a Zambezi puberty ritual. Dressed in a slinky gown discreetly slit to reveal legs that were clearly made for dancing, Jane goes into her act. When Gary's inebriated brother (Leon Ames) yells, "Go, girl, go," Jane does, gyrating as if she was born to shake, rattle, and roll—and, best of all, looking as if she were enjoying every minute of it.

Columbia wisely released *Let's Do It Again* in July 1953; it was a summer movie, forgotten in autumn, with little meaning for anyone but Jane. The film's musical supervisor was Fred Karger, who became her fourth husband on 2 November 1952. The ceremony took place at the El Montecito Presbyterian Church in Santa Barbara. Jane filed for divorce two years later.

In 1954, Jane had still not given up on marriage. She was not exactly on the town, but the gossips had her moonstruck over ladies' man Greg Bautzer, then known as Hollywood's most eligible bachelor. Then came Travis Kleefeld, who reinvented himself as singer Tony Travis, "ten years younger . . . very handsome, very charming, able and willing to take Jane to the best places and openly smitten with her." Jane felt similarly, and in record time they were engaged. Their relationship prefigured the one between herself and Rock Hudson in *All That Heaven Allows* (1955), in which she played a middle-aged woman in love with a younger man (Hudson). In 1954, Jane was thirty-seven, and Travis was ten years younger.

Age was the problem. Jane had not anticipated Hollywood's reaction to their engagement. It was as if she were robbing the cradle. Some wags claimed that Travis's wealthy parents objected to their son marrying an actress (as if his profession were superior to hers). Criticism from the press was bad enough, but "when her own acquaintances tore her to bits, she couldn't take it any longer." For a brief period, Travis gave Jane what she never had in her youth: the onrush of young love, when nothing else matters except the ecstasy of the moment. Jane never had that experience. When other fifteen-year-olds were dating and sipping milk shakes at the soda fountain, Jane was working as an extra in the movies, supplementing her meager income by taking whatever job she could get, from manicurist to telephone operator. A childhood of deprivation and indifference left a void in her life that none of her husbands could fill. Eugene Wyman was a stopgap measure. Myron Futterman was a father figure who shunned the nightlife that she craved. Reagan, like herself, was too preoccupied with a career to be the kind of lover she envisioned. Adolescent fantasies can linger into adulthood, but in Jane's case, they were never realized, because they were unattainable. Jane wanted what some women, if they are lucky, achieve in their twenties: the perfect combination of husband, lover, father, and friend. Jane would have settled for a husband-lover. She had all the children she would ever have, but midway in the journey of her life, she craved the youth she had never known, as if the latest love of her life could recreate it for her.

Travis would not have been the one, even if they ignored the frowns of friends and family. He was star struck, attracted to young actresses like Elaine Stewart and Cleo Moore, as well as Mona Freeman, not particularly glamorous but able to understand his need to connect with an industry that was not putting out the welcome mat for him. Jane was a STAR. He was as much attracted to her persona as he was to her, but it was impossible to separate the two. He was engaged to a woman who, along with Gregory Peck, was voted "the world's favorite screen actor and actress," according to an international popularity poll conducted by the Foreign Press Association. How could he compete with a world favorite?

Interestingly, Jane was attracted to two men who were musicians, the other being Frederick Maxwell Karger Jr., known professionally as Fred Karger, a conductor, band leader, composer, and vocal coach who was musical supervisor at Columbia when he met Jane at a party. The attraction was mutual. Jane did not play an instrument, but she had music in her soul, as was evident in her duets with Crosby in *Here Comes the Groom* and *Just for You*. Freed from the strictures of the script, she responded to the call of the music, as if she and Crosby were doing a specialty act. To watch Crosby and Jane perform "In The Cool, Cool, Cool of the Evening" is to watch a couple on a night out, singing and dancing their cares away before tomorrow turns the evening into a memory. What Jane wanted only the movies could give her. Travis thought he could, too, until midnight struck, and Cinderella had to go back to work.

Externally, Karger exuded a fatherly concern that attracted women beset with insecurities. When Marilyn Monroe, then virtually unknown in Hollywood, came to Columbia for the quickie musical *Ladies of the Chorus* (1949), she was assigned to Karger, who helped her through her two musical numbers, one of which was "Every Baby Needs a Da-da-Daddy," in which she had to strut across a burlesque runway in an iridescent black gown, slit up the side. Marilyn was instinctively drawn to him; Karger, now divorced, took pity on the young starlet and even brought her to live in the home he shared with his mother, daughter, and sister. But he soon realized that no one could help Marilyn, and the relationship ended.

Jane saw the same warmth and compassion in Karger that Marilyn had, not knowing that his reserves were limited. Karger and Jane were both in the business, but her name appeared above the title, while his was near the end of the credits. Karger also had too many problems, health-related and otherwise, to be the right match for Jane. He had a heart condition, which contributed to his death at sixty-three. But at the time Jane was desperate for one more walk down the aisle with someone who could fill the void in her life before it got any wider. Karger, a mere thirteen months younger than Jane, seemed eminently qualified. Since they shared the same taste in music, Jane envisioned movie work interspersed with nightclubbing and dancing. After they married, she had an even shorter honeymoon than she did with Reagan. The couple had a day to themselves before reporting to Columbia for what was then known as "Love Song," but later retitled *Let's Do It Again*.

Unfortunately, this was another dual-career marriage, exacerbated by the fact that Karger was still paying alimony to his ex-wife, a Hollywood attorney. Still, Jane tried, even dismissing the servants and doing the cooking herself. But they were living in Jane's house; she made more money than he. Jane could not afford to be without servants. She had a two-picture commitment with UI to fulfill before returning to Warners. A fan magazine writer summed the marriage up accurately: "Karger might have had a better chance if he could have married Sarah Jane Fulks." But Sarah Jane no longer existed; there was only Jane Wyman, the unattainable. The marriage lasted for two years. On 10 November 1954, Jane filed for divorce, charging mental cruelty. The divorce was granted on 7 December, the day before Jane was received into the Roman Catholic faith. Soon, she began to think differently about Karger, who was a Catholic, but not a practicing one. Once he returned to the faith, there seemed to be hope. They remarried on 11 March 1961. But again, it did not work. This time, Karger divorced Jane, telling the Los Angeles Superior Court on 10 March 1965 that she had walked out on him.

Karger remarried in 1968, dying eleven years later. Jane never remarried and outlived him by twenty-eight years. Sarah Jane Fulks was meant to be a wife and mother; Jane Wyman was meant to be an actress.

Chapter 26

The Actress and the Octopus

IN *THE LADY TAKES A SAILOR* (1949), JANE ENCOUNTERED A REAL OCTOPUS in her underwater adventure with Dennis Morgan. Three years earlier, the *Saturday Evening Post* ran a four-part series, dubbing the agency that represented Jane, the Music Corporation of America (MCA), the "star-spangled octopus." The agency had tentacles reaching out to every medium: music, radio, theatre, film, literature, and soon television. In the 1950s, MCA was in the market for a studio, one in particular, Universal-International. It was not accidental that Jane made two of her best films at UI during the same decade.

Jane had not been in a Universal movie since she was loaned out for *The Spy Ring* (1938). Between 1938 and 1953, the year Jane returned for *Magnificent Obsession* (1954), there had been significant changes. The films had improved in quality, and even the corporate name was different. It was no longer Universal, but Universal-International, a result of the union of old and (comparatively) new Hollywood. Old timers, however, still thought of it as Universal;, and eventually it reverted to its original name.

When William Goetz and Leo Spitz formed International Pictures in 1944, they had no intention of merging with Universal. Their goal was to create an independent production company, with Spitz's old studio, RKO, as distributor. They chose "International" to attract a global market by offering star-driven movies: Gary Cooper in *Casanova Brown* and *Along Came Jones*; Loretta Young in *Along Came Jones* and *The Stranger*; Edward G. Robinson in *The Woman in the Window* and *The Stranger*; Orson Welles in *Tomorrow Is Forever* and *The Stranger*; and Claudette Colbert in *Tomorrow Is Forever*. These were quality films, but lackluster box office.

Between 1944 and 1946, moviegoers preferred fare like MGM's *Gaslight*, *Meet Me in St. Louis*, and *They Were Expendable*; Warners' *To Have and Have Not* and *The Big Sleep*; and Goldwyn's *The Best Years of Our Lives*.

International was only two years old when Goetz and Spitz realized it could no longer be a freestanding studio. A merger was inevitable, and Universal was the right match. It had the global appeal that Goetz and Spitz were seeking: 37 percent of its 1944 profits came from abroad. It also had the right logo—a revolving globe announcing "A Universal Picture." And so, in 1946, Universal-International (UI) became the corporate name. The logo changed from a revolving globe to a stationary one, over which was superimposed "Universal," with "International" under it.

Soon UI was gaining the prestige that Universal lacked in the early 1940s. Lillian Hellman's *Another Part of the Forest*, Arthur Miller's *All My Sons*, and the Sigmund Romberg-Dorothy Fields musical *Up in Central Park* reached the screen in 1948. Ernest Hemingway's much-anthologized short story, "The Killers," was the point of departure for the 1946 movie of the same name that was more film noir than *echt* Hemingway, but a classic in its own right. The film version of Betty McDonald's best seller, *The Egg and I* (1947), was immensely popular (and profitable), and new stars like Jeff Chandler, Tony Curtis, and Rock Hudson were to movie audiences of the 1950s what Clark Gable, Tyrone Power, and Errol Flynn were to those of the previous decade. Older stars, too, found a place at UI—some briefly (Joan Crawford, June Allyson, Ronald Colman, Errol Flynn, Gregory Peck), and others, like James Stewart, for a longer period. Between 1948 and 1955, Stewart made seven films for the studio, five of which were with Anthony Mann, who was responsible for his transformation from the lanky idealist of *Mr. Smith Goes to Washington* to the avenging antihero of *Winchester '73* (1950).

The sale of UI to Decca Records in 1952 only meant a new owner. UI came under the Decca label, as if it were another form of vinyl. Universal-International was especially attractive to Lew Wasserman, Jane's and Reagan's agent and president of MCA, which represented artists from virtually every form of entertainment. Wasserman came up the hard way, from Chicago's burlesque theaters and movie houses, to Jules Stein's MCA. By 1947, MCA was representing Hollywood royalty such as Bette Davis, James Stewart, Betty Grable, Gregory Peck, Ginger Rogers, Shirley Temple, and John Garfield. And Jane and Reagan.

Wasserman had a special interest in each of them. He knew that Jane was the more talented, although Reagan could be useful in other capacities. He had a homespun bonhomie, malleable enough for whatever persona Wasserman devised for him: announcer, spokesperson, and especially, facilitator. In 1940, Jane was languishing at Warners with a paltry salary of five hundred dollars a week, and without any possibility of graduating to high—or even middle—drama. Wasserman came to her aid with a three-year contract starting at fifteen hundred dollars and increasing to twenty-five hundred dollars a week. She had to wait until 1945 to go dramatic, and then it was not at Warners but at Paramount with *The Lost Weekend*. Jane's situation continued to improve. After receiving an Oscar nomination for *The Blue Veil* (1951), she "signed a multimillion-dollar contract" that included loan-outs to Paramount, Columbia, and UI.

By contrast, in 1952, Reagan made his last picture at Warners, which had been his home studio since 1937. In 1949, Wasserman negotiated a five-year, five-picture contract for Reagan at UI at seventy-five thousand dollars a picture. When Reagan balked at making two movies that he deemed inferior, UI exercised its right to terminate the contract after three films, reducing Reagan's UI output to *Louisa* (1950), *Bedtime for Bonzo* (1951), and *Law and Order* (1953). *Louisa* was a late love movie with old school charm liberally dispensed by senior citizens Spring Byington, Edmund Gwenn, and Charles Coburn, with Reagan and the rest of the cast on standby. *Bedtime for Bonzo* had Reagan upstaged by a chimpanzee. And *Law and Order* left him stranded on the frontier with only Dorothy Malone in lieu of a decent script. But Wasserman had another role for Reagan—and it was not on the movie screen.

Jane was always one of Wasserman's favorites. Although she had no complaints about the 1940 Warners contract, it only led to more money, not better roles. In 1944, Jane sought Wasserman's help. She was desperate for a break-through part that would convince the industry that she was a dramatic actress as well as a comedienne. After Paramount bought the rights to *The Lost Weekend*, Wasserman supposedly talked Billy Wilder into testing Jane for the role of Helen St. James, a far cry from the ditz she played in her previous film, *The Doughgirls*. Since Wilder was planning to test Jane anyway (and was under no obligation to Wasserman, who was not his agent), he had no problem acceding to Wasserman's request. However, Wasserman did not get her the role. Instead, it was the favorable impression she made on Wilder and Brackett in *Princess O'Rourke* that did it. Jane always credited them with getting her the role, as she told Hedda Hopper in a *Chicago Sunday Tribune* interview (3 October 1948): "I had done just one little sequence in 'Princess O'Rourke' and thru an accident Charles Brackett and Billy Wilder saw it when they were casting 'Lost Weekend.' . . . It was my small miracle."

Wasserman and Jane were more than agent and client, they were also friends who had something in common. Each came up through the ranks; Wasserman through the nether world of Chicago's entertainment scene, Jane, through the labyrinth of unbilled hoofers and party scene extras. Reagan had it easy by comparison, with a college degree, experience as a radio announcer, a pop singer contact in Hollywood, and a lead in his first movie. What Wasserman saw in Jane was an unusually versatile actress in a business where bravura was often mistaken for talent. Jane had the talent, but not the panache. Flamboyance was not her style. In Reagan, Wasserman saw a lightweight whose rising importance in the Screen Actors Guild (SAG), of which he was president, would prove valuable in expanding MCA's boundaries. Jane was the artist; Reagan was the politician who understood that the art of the deal is the art of persuasion, or, under certain circumstances, of equivocation—especially when a technicality could derail the process.

In 1952 Reagan was completing his last year as SAG president when MCA decided to branch out into television production with Revue Productions. The timing was right. Wasserman knew that television was rapidly eclipsing film as a mass medium, although he did not discount film's continued appeal. If one of MCA's tentacles could wrap itself around television, another could do the same with film, which meant acquiring a studio. These were forbidden thoughts, implying a revival of vertical integration, with a talent agency owning a television production company and a movie studio, each of which could employ MCA talent. Forbidden thoughts—but not for Lew Wasserman.

Originally, MCA created Revue Productions in 1943 for live radio programming. Then, MCA represented the biggest names in radio entertainment, some with their own shows (*The Jack Benny Program*, *The Frank Sinatra Show*, *The Edgar Bergen and Charlie McCarthy Show*, *The Eddie Cantor Show*), and a superabundance of movie stars such as Jane, Reagan, James Stewart, Donna Reed, Fred MacMurray, Bette Davis, Gregory Peck, Ginger Rogers, Joan Crawford, and John Garfield, who could star on such dramatic programs as *Lux Radio Theatre* and *Suspense*. By 1951, radio's heyday was ending, soon to be retired with emeritus status and eulogized as "The Golden Age of Radio" or "Old Time Radio." But Revue could continue as an MCA subsidiary, producing television series, the first of which was *The Adventures of Kit Carson* (1951).

When Wasserman realized that it might have been premature to enter television production without securing special permission from SAG, he turned to his client, Ronald Reagan. It was now time for Reagan to repay his agent for brokering so many deals for him, the latest being the seventy-five thousand dollar per picture contract that he negotiated at UI. Reagan did not fail Wasserman. He argued convincingly that, in view of the precarious state of the movie business, actors could at least find work on the small screen. And so, on 23 July 1952, a special waiver went into effect for seven years, giving Wasserman time to add other shows to Revue's ever-growing list of series, such as *Wagon Train*, *Schlitz Playhouse of Stars*, and *Alfred Hitchcock Presents*. In fact, Wasserman needed more time, not for Revue, but for UI, MCA's next conquest. And he managed to obtain another waiver that carried him through 1960.

Jane and Reagan did not realize that they were part of a carefully or-chestrated series of events, not a concatenation of isolated incidents. The timeline tells the story:

1. In 1949, Wasserman arranges a five-year, five-picture contract for Reagan at UI.
2. In 1951, Revue enters television production, sanctioned the following year by a waiver and good for seven years, allowing MCA to engage in television production. Revue, true to its octopus origins, draws in a number of series, including *Lux Playhouse*, *State Trooper*, *Mike Hammer*, *Studio 57*, *Pepsi-Cola Playhouse*, and in 1954, one of the most popular, *General Electric Theater*, with Reagan as host and frequent star, and on which Jane appeared in 1955 as the title character in "Amelia."
3. In 1951, Wasserman studies Decca Records' progress in its attempt to take over UI, which it accomplished with considerable help from Serge Semenenko, the *eminence gris* of Boston's First National Bank, known for his deep pockets, and perhaps also from Sidney Korshak, the Mob's favorite lawyer. Wasserman was familiar with the infernal circles in which both moved, having traversed Chicago's dark streets and darker alleys.
4. Decca completes the UI purchase in 1952, the same year that Wasserman sought the blanket waiver for MCA to enter television production.
5. In 1953, Jane arrives at UI for *Magnificent Obsession* (1954) at a salary of $150,000, thanks to Wasserman. A year later, she receives the same for another UI release, *All That Heaven Allows*(1955), again courtesy of Wasserman. When John F.

Kennedy was elected president in 1960, Wasserman, a lifelong Democrat, assumed the White House would sanction MCA's acquisition of UI. The year before, tired of renting space at Eagle-Lion Studios and Republic Pictures for Revue's series, Wasserman bought the UI lot for $11.25 million, so that Revue could have a permanent home. Today, the lot; tomorrow, the studio. Then MCA's empire would be complete. He did not count on Attorney General Robert Kennedy invoking the Sherman Act against MCA, whose envisioned conglomerate—talent agency, television production company, and movie studio—would have constituted a flagrant violation. Forced to choose between the talent agency and the studio, Wasserman chose the latter. On 16 September 1962, MCA Artists passed out of existence, with Revue eventually becoming Universal Television.

6. Jane and Reagan profit from Revue. Jane appeared twice on *Wagon Train* in 1958 and 1962, respectively, once on *Lux Playhouse* in 1959, and once on *General Electric Theater* in 1955. By 1955, she had taken over as host and frequent performer on *Fireside Theatre*, which, because of her popularity, was renamed *Jane Wyman's Fireside Theatre*, produced in cooperation with her own company, Lewman Productions (a combination of "Lew" for Lew Wasserman and "man" for Wyman along the lines of Desi Arnaz and Lucille Ball's Desilu). To a great extent, Jane owed the beginning of her television career to MCA, and particularly to Lew Wasserman.

7. Revue Productions benefited Reagan even more. He appeared three times on *Schlitz Playhouse of Stars*, and once on *Wagon Train*, forty-three times on *General Electric Theater* (thirty-four times as a performer) from 1954 to 1962, endearing himself to viewers with the folksy style that helped him win the governorship of California and the presidency of the United States. Reagan understood the difference between the big and the small screen. He scaled down his persona for the latter, turning it into his personal sound stage. Film gave Reagan his first audience. Television gave him his second and biggest, which would extend far beyond *General Electric Theater*.

Chapter 27

The Actress and the Auteur

UNIVERSAL WAS NEVER A DIRECTOR'S STUDIO. THERE WERE ONLY A few directors at Universal in the 1930s and 1940s who could qualify as auteurs, able to sign their films as if they were paintings: James Whale (*Frankenstein, Bride of Frankenstein, The Old Dark House*), who raised horror to the level of gothic; Robert Siodmak, who could manipulate light and shadow to create a sunless milieu (*Phantom Lady*); and Jules Dassin, who could pace a film, moving it steadily and inexorably toward a harrowing finale (*Brute Force*). In the 1950s, Universal, then Universal International, was blessed with two extraordinary directors: Anthony Mann, who de-mythologized John Ford's West, and Douglas Sirk, art historian, Shakespeare translator, and man of the theatre, with a range that extended from psychological melodrama to romantic comedy—the former often pictorially ironic, with a glossy surface concealing the rot within.

In 1953, Jane probably had little, if any, knowledge of Douglas Sirk, who would be responsible for her fourth and last Oscar nomination (*Magnificent Obsession*), as well as the movie that followed it, *All That Heaven Allows*, now included among the culturally and historically significant films that constitute the National Film Registry. She probably saw some of his movies starring actors that she knew (Linda Darnell in *Summer Storm*, Charles Boyer in *The First Legion*, Claudette Colbert and Don Ameche in *Sleep, My Love*, Colbert and Ann Blyth in *Thunder on the Hill*, Ann Sheridan in *Take Me to Town*). Most likely, Jane would have associated the films with the performers, not the director. To her, a director was someone like Billy Wilder, Jean Negulesco, Raoul Walsh, or Clarence Brown, who worked at the Big Five (RKO, MGM, Fox, Warners, Paramount), not at the Little Three (Universal, Columbia, United Artists).

Sirk was the perfect director both for actors whose glory days were drawing to a close and for those for whom such days were yet to come. He could even make lesser vehicles seem more significant than they were: *Slightly French*, in which Dorothy Lamour took a leave from being the female appendage in the *Road* movies, to play a sideshow performer whom a washed-up director turns into a French *artiste*; *Thunder on the Hill*, which allowed Ann Blyth to give her vocal chords a rest and reactivate her dramatic side, as she did so ably in *Mildred Pierce*; and most impressively, Lana Turner in his last American film, the remake of *Imitation of Life* (1958), as a single mother who discovers a world within a world in postwar America, where light-skinned blacks pass for white.

After arriving in Hollywood in 1938, Sirk had no difficulty finding work. There was a colony of émigrés, forced out of Nazi Germany for religious—or, in Sirk's case, artistic—reasons, who often sensed that something worse than a pogrom was imminent. Or, as was the case with Sirk (and also Fritz Lang), they sensed that they would be expected to make films glorifying the Third Reich. Sirk was first offered contracts at Warners and Columbia, neither of which panned out, although he returned to Columbia a decade later for *Slightly French* and *Shockproof* (both 1949).

One powerful member of the émigré community was Seymour Nebenzhal, the New York-born independent producer who began his career in Germany with such films as G. W. Pabst's *Pandora's Box* (1928) and Fritz Lang's *M* (1931). Nebenzahl launched Sirk's American career with *Hitler's Madman* (1943), originally conceived as a Poverty Row production, which ended up being distributed by MGM. The title character was Reinhard Heydrich, "the beast of Prague," an epithet he acquired when Hitler named him deputy reich protector of Bohemia and Moravia after the 1938 annexation of the Sudetenland, the German-speaking part of the former Czechoslovakia. Heydrich's assassination in 1942 triggered a series of reprisals, starting with the liquidation of the entire male population of the mining village of Lidice, a few miles from Prague, and the deportation of the women to concentration camps, culminating in the destruction of Lidice itself.

For a decidedly low-budget film, *Hitler's Madman* was well acted, especially by John Carradine, whose Heydrich evoked a third-rate actor in a ratty touring company. One scene in particular conveys the Third Reich's inhumanity more than any other. Girls at a local high school are lined up to be inspected by Heydrich for service as sex slaves for German soldiers at the Russian front. Realizing that there is a doctor waiting to examine each of them, one of the girls (a young Ava Gardner) cries out, "Don't go in there. We'll all be examined as if we were cattle and sent to the Russian front." She then leaps out of the window to her death. *Hitler's Madman* was Sirk's response to the regime that had cost him one career, and yet prepared him for another, far more illustrious, one. It was also Nebenzahl's indictment of the man who implemented the Final Solution.

Summer Storm (1944), Sirk's second American film, was another Nebenzahl production, released by United Artists, and one of the few Sirk made that have a genuine literary pedigree, the others being *The Tarnished Angels* (1957) from William Faulkner's *Pylon*, and *A Time to Love and a Time to Die* (1958) from Erich Maria Remarque's novel of the same name. Not every one of his films was high art. There were also adaptations of well-crafted but ephemeral plays (*The First Legion, Thunder on the Hill*, produced in London as *Bonaventure*) and best sellers (*Magnificent Obsession, Written on the Wind, Imitation of Life*). Yet Sirk did not discriminate between the literary and the popular. In fact, he worked even harder to raise the latter to the level of art, as a comparison of *Summer Storm* and *Magnificent Obsession* reveals.

Sirk had wanted to film Anton Chekhov's only novel, *The Shooting Party*, when he was working at UFA studios in the 1930s, but he had to wait until he came to Hollywood, where a faithful adaption would have been impossible. *The Shooting Party* was too psychologically complex and layered with symbolism to transfer smoothly to the American screen. More important, *The Shooting Party* is meta fiction, with traces of its creation in the form of footnotes and references to illustrations and deleted passages. *Summer Storm* retains the novel's point of departure—a crime of passion—but deviates from it in so many ways that it is almost an original screenplay. It is also a Douglas Sirk film, adapted and directed by him.

Chekhov conceived the novel as a whodunit in the form of a frame narrative, beginning and ending in a publishing house, where a former judge offers an editor a manuscript entitled "The Shooting Party." Reluctantly, the editor agrees to read it, but decides it cannot be published as written (it is eventually brought out with significant changes), for reasons that later become clear. The opening line, "A husband has murdered his wife," is the hook, enticing the reader to continue, just as "Some kids found her," the opening sentence of James Ellroy's *My Dark Places*, piques one's curiosity about "her," Ellroy's mother, whose murder remains unsolved. All one knows at the start of *The Shooting Party* is that a husband has committed a murder. But the source is suspect: The line is spoken by the judge's parrot, which the judge later kills. And the "husband" is not really a husband, and the "wife" is the judge's lover, Olga, a child of nature, whose mother was killed by lighting, "heavenly electricity." Olga knows that she will die the same way—in a storm during a shooting party—not by lightning, but by a knife through her heart.

Sirk had to cut a swath through the literary overgrowth to clear a path for a screenplay, which is also a frame narrative, but set at a different time. The novel ends in the 1870s, when there was still a gulf between the peasants and the privileged. *Summer Storm* begins in 1912 and ends shortly after the Russian Revolution has made everyone a comrade, and the great estates, such as the count's, have been confiscated. There is also a manuscript, but the judge is not the one who brings it to the publisher. The count does, and the publisher is now a woman (Anna Lee), whose reading of it provides a smooth segue into the film.

Summer Storm is a model of streamlining, a case of *amour fatal*, in which an upper class male becomes infatuated with a lower class female and kills her. Then, as a sop to the Legion of Decency and the Production Code, he is reduced to performing menial labor after the Revolution levels distinctions between the classes. But by itself loss of privilege would not satisfy moralists. The judge has to die—and he does, from a policeman's bullet. A dagger for Olga, a bullet for the judge—different forms of heavenly electricity. Chekhov would not have approved of the ending. Men like the judge either become alcoholics or suicides. But the Legion of Decency frowned upon suicide, and cirrhosis of the liver is not as dramatic as a street killing. *Summer Storm* was critically and commercially successful, with the *New York Times* (23 October 1944) commending the film for its "finely etched mood of the decaying mores of pre-revolutionary Russia," and Linda Darnell for her "surprisingly adept" performance as Olga.

Olga was a peasant-class Emma Bovary, an unreconstructed dreamer, who died as she lived. Sirk knew that Darnell's dark beauty pointed to a sinister side that could not surface in the demure types she played in *Chad Hanna*, *The Mark of Zorro*, and *Blood and Sand*. With the right script, however, she could be a femme fatale or a *femme noire*. What Sirk brought out in Darnell Otto Preminger deepened in *Fallen Angel*, where her allure proved fatal to her character. As Darnell's career progressed, she revealed other aspects of her talent: a flair for wise cracks in *A Letter to Three Wives*; sophisticated comedy in Preston Sturges's *Unfaithfully Yours* and Edmund Goulding's *Everybody Does It*; and searing melodrama in *No Way Out*.

Sirk did the same with Jane in *Magnificent Obsession*, finding similarities between her and the character, Helen Phillips, and monitoring Helen's emotional trajectory, which takes her from marriage to widowhood, blindness, and the restoration of her sight by the man who inadvertently caused her to lose it. Helen's was the kind of emotional arc in which a portentous line reading, an ominous chord, or a manipulative close up could cause the film to slip into bathos. Sirk knew that, under his direction, Jane could keep a firm grip on the character. He sensed, as did others, that Jane had her own dark places that were barred from entry even by herself: "People who know Jane Wyman attest to the fact that she is . . . a *very* private person, and might even be described as introverted." Sirk would agree. He saw the same kind of sadness in her eyes that June Allyson did, but he also saw that Jane masked it with a cheery façade, her "face to meet the faces that you meet," as T.S. Eliot described the public self in "The Love Song of J. Alfred Prufrock."

In "From UFA to Hollywood," the documentary accompanying the DVD of the 1935 and 1953 versions of *Magnificent Obsession*, Sirk speaks about his discovery, Zarah Leander, who became a sensation in one of his last UFA films, known in America as *Life Begins Anew* (1937), or sometimes as *To New Shores* (*Zu Neuen Ufern*). In Leander, he saw an actress capable of adopting a masculine persona, with the voice of a chanteuse that seemed to emanate from the depths of her being—something quite different from the executives, who only saw an extremely tall woman with a big behind. To Sirk, Leander was the perfect choice to play a woman who keeps her British lover out of prison by assuming responsibility for his debts, even though doing so means deportation to Australia.

Similarly, in Jane, Sirk saw something he had perceived in other actors, insecurity, which in Jane's case stemmed from the childhood she lost when her father deserted his family, leaving her with the sole pleasures of dance lessons, stage plays, and movies. Jane learned resignation at an early age, and it was that acceptance of life's inequities that Sirk drew upon for her character, who, within a brief period, loses her husband and her sight but never asks why. *Magnificent Obsession* (1954) was based on Lloyd C. Douglas's 1929 bestseller of the same name. The script called for Jane to play Helen, the wife of a famed neurosurgeon, who dies unexpectedly after the only available resuscitator is used to save the life of playboy Bob Merrick (Rock Hudson). Sirk and Jane had their work cut out for them. Sirk had to upgrade the movie from a "weepie" or "three-hanky movie" to romantic melodrama. Jane had an equally difficult task, imparting credibility to a woman who under ordinary circumstances would never have fallen in love with the man others blamed for her husband's death. But the deeply Christian message of the novel (Douglas was a former Lutheran minister who changed denominations and became a Congregationalist) was intensified by Sirk's blue and white color scheme and Jane's ability to bring her character to the height of forgiveness.

The adaptation was the work of veteran screenwriter Robert Blees, who had coauthored the script of Sirk's *All I Desire* (1952), a Ross Hunter production and one of Barbara Stanwyck's better mid-career roles. Blees could not ignore the first version of *Magnificent Obsession*, which Sarah Y. Mason and Victor Heerman adapted, with Irene Dunne as Helen and Robert Taylor as Merrick. Neither the 1935 nor the 1954 version adhered strictly to the novel, although Blees's script and Sirk's direction came close to capturing the novel's spirit and tone. The book was structurally imperfect, with explanations or statements of fact serving as exposition. But it presented a compelling story, one in need of an editor/screenwriter who could cut away the excrescences and get to the core of the narrative. That core was simply the regeneration of a profligate who atones for a death he did not intentionally cause, and whose way of atoning is embracing philanthropy. Or, as Douglas puts it, he is implementing the message that brought "the man who discovered it to a cross at the age of thirty-three." The screenplay's emphasis on the spiritual renewal of a wastrel required an actor who could negotiate the rocky ascent from prodigal son to Christian prototype without evoking groans from audiences who assumed they were in a theater, not a church. Although Robert Taylor could not handle the transition, his matinee idol looks compensated for his shortcomings. Rock Hudson could handle it—and did.

Mason and Heerman knew that *Magnificent Obsession* would have to be pitched to a predominately female audience. The novel did not center around Helen, but rather Merrick and his conversion. The film had to do the reverse. For it to work, Helen had to become the main character. Hers was a transformation to which more audiences could relate than to Merrick's spiritual awakening. Helen is put through a cycle of suffering that moviegoers, especially women, would understand. Hers is a triple tragedy: loss of husband, loss of income, loss of vision. Her vision is restored by a man who went through a different transformation, internal rather than external. The writers knew that the only way to bring Helen to the fore was to demote everyone else, except Merrick, to supporting cast, stripping them of any negative character traits that would clash with Helen's nobility and Merrick's metamorphosis. Neither actress playing Helen's stepdaughter, Joyce (Betty Furness in the original, Barbara Rush in the remake), was the "silly little ass" of the novel. Nor could Tommy Masterson, Joyce's suitor and later her husband, be the alcoholic that Douglas made him, although in the 1935 film version he is not averse to imbibing. In the remake, he is played by the clean-cut Gregg Palmer.

The novel posed other problems. Douglas's Dr. Hudson is a forty-six-year-old widower who had lost his wife seventeen years earlier. Although Helen is supposed to be younger than her husband, Irene Dunne was thirty-seven with a matronly air, and Jane looked as if she were easing into middle age. Jane was also playing opposite the twenty-eight-year-old Rock Hudson, whose studio-bestowed last name required the doctor's surname to be changed to Phillips. Both Dunne and Jane played opposite younger actors. Taylor was thirteen years younger than Dunne. With Dunne programmed into high noble mode and Taylor playing the rake until epiphany time, the two seemed more like suffering mother and errant son. Any kind of sexual chemistry was absent in both versions. Jane and Hudson found different facets of the characters to emphasize. Hudson was moving in his attempt to right the wrongs he had done, both because of his conversion to the doctor's mystical brand of Christianity, and because of his deep devotion to a woman whose blindness occurred because he was so eager to proclaim the good news that he prevented her from entering a cab, causing her to be hit by an oncoming car. Merrick undergoes the cycle of remorse-atonement-redemption, becoming a successful neurosurgeon who saves Helen's sight. As played by Jane and Hudson, Helen and Merrick are neither mother and son figures, nor passionate lovers. Their love scenes are so chaste that one tends to smile at such innocence between adults. Helen and Merrick evolve into a higher state of being, transcending anything as limiting as physical passion. They become the forgiver and the forgiven, the restorer and the restored, the redeemer and the redeemed.

Instead of debating the superiority of one version over another, one would do better to contrast them. Wisely, neither includes the doctor's secret journal, written in code and embodying his philosophy, which, simply put, consists of helping those in need but swearing them to secrecy and encouraging them to do the same for others. In the novel, Merrick and Nancy Ashford manage to decipher the journal, becoming the equivalent of code breakers. Adding the journal would have burdened the film with an unnecessary subplot, making it more melodramatic than it is. Each version makes use of classical music. Stahl's lacks a real score, except for Tchaikovsky's *Romeo and Juliet Fantasy*, played during the credits and promising an unashamedly romantic movie. Sirk relied on UI's Frank Skinner and music supervisor Joseph Gershenson to

fashion a score less sweeping than the Tchaikovsky: a muted Romanticism blending Chopin and Johann Strauss, and at transformative moments—such as Merrick's operation on Helen—the "Ode to Joy" from
Beethoven's Ninth Symphony. In each film, Helen has an accident, inadvertently caused by Merrick, that leaves her blind. Douglas, a stranger
in the house of fiction, simply informs us that Helen, now an Italian tour
guide, was "fatally hurt" in a train wreck. The writers realized they could
not retain the train wreck without explaining why Helen was in Italy in
the first place. Italy is discarded, a car replaces the train, and the accident
occurs locally.

The films, separated by almost twenty years, differ not only in physical production, but also in acting style. Douglas's Helen is an orphan
who persuades Joyce Hudson to give up the high life for serious study,
thereby endearing herself to Joyce's father, who proposes marriage. One
could hardly imagine Dunne mentoring a wayward girl. Her Helen is
courtly; Jane's is egalitarian. Jane's Helen bonds so well with her stepdaughter that they act like sisters, as opposed to Dunne's lady of the
manor and Betty Furness's ingénue, who seem like guardian and ward.
Taylor's Merrick was a cocky playboy, making passes at everyone from a
nurse to Helen herself. In the 1930s, he possessed a handsomeness that
verged on male beauty, something that Plato might have appreciated,
but that hardened in the 1940s and 1950s as he moved out of the lover
boy suite into the men's club, with a repertoire that ranged from gangster (*Johnny Eager*), outlaw (*Billy the Kid*), and murder-minded husband
(*Undercurrent*), to Communist agent (*Conspirator*) and buffalo hunter (*The
Last Hunt*). Rock Hudson's Merrick was cut from a different cloth. His
recklessness is depicted in the first scene, as he cuts through the water in
his speedboat, caring only about the thrill it brings, and heedless of the
consequences. He is an unapologetic chauvinist, treating women as if
they were hors d'oeuvres at his private banquet. Hudson had the kind of
face that could go from granite to clay, molded into whatever the scene
required. At courting time, it softened into boyishness. When the plot
turned serious, so did Hudson, with an intensity that never turned his
face marmoreal, but gave it a gravitas that translated into deep concern.

Neither Sirk nor Blees made any attempt to disguise the fact that Hudson was younger than Jane. The novel implies that there was an age difference, but not as much as the one between Helen and the doctor. Still,
Jane and Hudson played their love scenes with a purity that banished
any thoughts of carnality. In fact, Hudson's determination to become
a successful neurosurgeon makes him more of a savior than a lover.

Naturally, audiences will think of the two as future wife and husband, but from the way they played their roles, it would be a marriage made in heaven—which, if it were to be consummated, would take place there.

When it came to visual style, Sirk had the upper hand. Universal did not make a color film until 1942. Stahl was limited to black and white, with their gradations, resulting in a movie that was commercially successful but visually undistinguished. Sirk, however, was a former stage director and art historian. By 1953, Universal was alternating between films in color and monochrome. Of Sirk's twenty-two UI films, thirteen were in color: *Has Anybody Seen My Gal?*, *Meet Me at the Fair*, *Take Me to Town*, *Taza*, *Son of Cochise*, *Magnificent Obsession*, *Sign of the Pagan*, *Captain Lightfoot*, *All That Heaven Allows*, *Written on the Wind*, *Battle Hymn*, *Interlude*, *A Time to Love and a Time to Die*, and *Imitation of Life*. Except for *Has Anybody Seen My Gal?*, *Sign of the Pagan*, *Written on the Wind*, *The Tarnished Angels*, and *A Time to Love and a Time to Die*, all were Ross Hunter Productions.

To cite the current form of cinematic authorship, *Magnificent Obsession* is "A Douglas Sirk Film" and "A Ross Hunter Production." Sirk was fortunate in his producers. Nebenzahl, Hunter, and Albert Zugsmith, whom Sirk affectionately called "Zug," and who produced *Written on the Wind* (1956) and *The Tarnished Angels* (1957). "We got along great," Sirk claimed, and indeed they did. Although Zugsmith's attraction to the sensational (*Platinum High School*, *College Confidential*, *The Private Lives of Adam and Eve*) seemed at odds with Sirk's aesthetic, the two films they made together had sensational elements of their own, not as blatant as Zugsmith's exploitation flicks, but perhaps even more daring in their subtlety—at least for those who could fill in the ellipses in *Written on the Wind*, with its nymphomania, impotence, and sterility, and *The Tarnished Angels* with its phallic symbolism in the form of pylons of "totemic sexuality." There is one shot in *The Tarnished Angels* that suggests that something of Zug had rubbed off on Sirk. The film, photographed in CinemaScope, opens spectacularly with Dorothy Malone standing alongside a plane, with the wind from the propeller rippling her dress and revealing a panty line, an effect that has never been duplicated.

Ross Hunter was the antithesis of Zugsmith and more Sirk's type of producer. Before there was a Ross Hunter, there was a Martin Fuss, Cleveland-born and star-struck, who acquired some stage experience at the Cleveland Playhouse before moving to Hollywood. His good looks necessitated a change of name, and Columbia's casting director conjured up "Ross Hunter." After some decent roles in forgettable films (e.g., *Ever Since Venus*, *Louisiana Hayride* [both 1944], *She's a Sweetheart* [1945], *Hit the Hay* [1946]), he moved over to Universal-International, graduating from associate producer to producer. "Find a good story and dress it up . . . with beautiful settings and smart clothes" was Hunter's credo, and Sirk concurred. When Sirk learned that Hunter wanted him to direct *Magnificent Obsession,* his first reaction was bewilderment. He wondered how he could make "trashy stuff" into art. Then he reflected on the theme: one man's dying so that another might live, which reminded him of Euripides' *Alcestis,* in which a wife agrees to die in place of her husband. The theme of blindness in both the literal and metaphorical senses also intrigued him. He believed, then, that the film could work, as he explained: "There is a very short distance between high art and trash, and trash that contains the element of craziness is by this very quality nearer to art." Sirk knew the distance he had to traverse to bring *Magnificent Obsession* to the threshold of art; he had to "dress it up."

For Sirk, a painter as well as an art historian, there was little distinction between style and meaning, as seen in the palette he chose, which consisted of various gradations of blue, white, and occasionally, pink and grey. Blue connoted serenity, purity, and with white, constituted the colors of the Virgin: "Blue and white, the colors of Our Lady, express a detachment from the things of the world and the flight of the liberated soul to God . . . ." Blue predominates in the scene following the capsizing of Merrick's sailboat: blue sky, blue lake, and blue-suited officers. Nancy Ashford (Agnes Moorehead), the hospital superintendent, first appears in a blue sweater and skirt. For variety's sake, Jane wears pink and gray before switching to blue suits, and later, a white blouse and purple skirt. When Helen learns that her condition is hopeless, Sirk darkens the frame until it turns bluish white, as Helen slowly makes her way to the terrace and accidently knocks over a plant. Before performing the crucial surgery, Merrick looks out at the blue sky. The operating room itself is bathed in blue, with white supplied by the scrubs, the sheets, and Helen's bandaged head.

Magnificent Obsession was UI's moneymaker of the year. Budgeted at $780,000, it grossed $8 million and netted Jane an Oscar nomination. But Grace Kelly deservedly won for shedding her cool blonde look to play the wife of an alcoholic actor (Bing Crosby, also cast against type) in *The Country Girl.*

Exactly how Jane became involved in *Magnificent Obsession* is open to speculation. According to Sirk, Hunter told him that he had Jane Wyman for the lead. That was all Sirk needed to hear: "She was still a real star then—and I was terribly impressed." Whenever he could,

Hunter preferred to use actresses from Hollywood's golden age, such as Ann Sheridan, Barbara Stanwyck, Lana Turner, Virginia Grey, and June Allyson, and so it was natural that he would seek out Jane. On the other hand, Jane was represented by Lew Wasserman, who by now was a close friend. He and his wife Edie attended Jane's wedding to Fred Karger. Hunter's eagerness to have Jane star in *Magnificent Obsession* would have fit in nicely then with Wasserman's agenda. Today, Jane at UI; tomorrow, UI.

Wasserman wanted the best deal for Jane, and he got it: ten weeks at $15,000 a week for a total of $150,000. Hudson, however, was contract talent, as opposed to Jane, who was "outside talent"; thus, he only received $12,500. The film came in at $884,857, a mere $766 over budget, although it had the look of a more expensive production. Since *Magnificent Obsession* did not call for high fashion, the wardrobe was bottom line. Jane's cost $6,090, Hudson's $2,670. The actors wore clothes appropriate to their characters. Jane could do low cut, and Hudson could bare his chest, but not in *Magnificent Obsession*.

For Jane, it was a demanding ten weeks. She usually arrived at the studio around 6:30 a.m., with a call set for 8:30 a.m. Her day would end at 4:45 p.m., except when the company was filming at Arrowhead. Then, she would arrive at 6:15 a.m., working until 3:30 p.m. unless she had to return to the studio, in which case she would have dinner there. To prepare for the scenes in which Helen was blind, Jane worked with a sight-impaired woman. Sensing that *Magnificent Obsession* would be one of the high points of her career, Jane made radio appearances, gave interviews, and even traveled to New York with Karger. When it came to money, Jane had a Depression mentality: Get what you can now, since the sky might fall tomorrow. Edie Wasserman planned to be in New York at the same time as Jane and Karger, and she invited the couple to share her suite at the Waldorf. Since the studio had already booked a hotel for them, Jane made what she thought was a simple request: UI should give her what it would have spent on their accommodations for "pocket money," and also pay any room service charges incurred during their stay. Jane not only got a free trip to New York, but spending money as well. But it was worth it to the studio: the film had great box office, Jane got an Oscar nomination, and Rock Hudson became the new star in the pantheon.

But when Jane reported at UI in late September 1953, it was simply for another movie with a director with whom she had never worked. She need not have worried. Sirk wanted a Helen divested of Irene Dunne's *noblesse*, who was neither a madonna of the sorrows nor the saint of the sightless, but a woman who loses a husband, then her sight, before a concatenation of events, fortuitous and ordained, results in the restoration of her vision.

Once the film wrapped up on 27 October, Jane headed over to Paramount for the title role in *Lucy Gallant*, a real haute couture movie. By 7 January 1955, she was back at UI for *All That Heaven Allows*, which was completed in mid-February, at which time she returned to Warners for *Miracle in the Rain*, her last film for the studio. Clearly, her game was going into extra innings.

The success of *Magnificent Obsession* encouraged UI to make a similarly themed movie, *All That Heaven Allows*, uniting the same quartet (Sirk, Jane, Hudson, Moorehead) and key crew members (director of photography Russell Metty, color consultant William Fritsche, wardrobe designer Bill Thomas, composer Frank Skinner, and music supervisor Joseph Gershenson, all of whom had worked with Sirk before). Jane was paid the same amount, $150,000, she received for *Magnificent Obsession*. Hudson, who was paid twenty-seven thousand dollars, fared better than he had previously, proof of his growing popularity and importance to the studio. This time, the screenwriter was newcomer Peg Fenwick, who was working from an original story and not burdened by the additional weight of a novel and its first screen incarnation. She recycled the plot points of *Magnificent Obsession*, with Jane as another widow, Hudson as her gardener, Moorehead as her close friend, and a supporting cast consisting of Gloria Talbot and William Reynolds as the self-righteous children, Jacqueline de Wit as the town gossip, Donald Curtis as the town lecher, and—for contrast—a couple (Charles Drake and Virginia Grey) living far from the madding crowd in their personal Walden.

In *All That Heaven Allows*, the age factor is significant. Jane's character, Carey Scott, must not only be older than Ron Kirby (Hudson), but also come from a different social milieu. In their class-conscious community, a romance between an older woman and a younger man would raise eyebrows, but if the younger man raked her leaves and pruned her trees, jaws would drop. Hudson played Kirby with such disarming openness, and with such unaggressive masculinity, that he would have been a godsend to women tired of "Me Tarzan, You Jane" males. Since he was an uncommonly handsome man, his physical deterioration from AIDS in the early 1980s reduced him to a wraith with a haunted look, a spectral Rock Hudson. But until then—and certainly in the 1950s—he projected a rare form of heterosexual appeal: virility as a comfort zone, where a woman would never feel compromised as long as she entrusted herself to his care. It was this quiet, confident, and unassuming masculinity that Hudson's Ron Kirby projected and that drew Carey to him. And there was that smile, warm and inviting, that seemed to emanate not so much from open lips as from a strong jaw that bespoke sincerity, and from eyes that did not so much twinkle as dance to a beat of their own. He found his "different drummer" in himself without ever having read *Walden*. What Kirby can offer Carey is a world without desperation, quiet or otherwise. Alida (the underappreciated Virginia Grey), the wife of Kirby's best friend, Mick (Charles Drake), explains to Carey that while her husband has read and absorbed *Walden* (Sirk has Carey read two passages from the text), Kirby never did. He didn't have to, Alida explains; he lives it. And he wanted Carey to live it also.

The shoot was not an easy one for Jane. It was not the hours. She was used to schedules that varied from 7:30 a.m. to 3:15 p.m., 7:00 a.m. to 4:50 p.m., 7:30 a.m. to 3:15 p.m. or even 6:30 a.m. to 4:15 p.m. and 10:40 a.m. to 6:10 p.m. But there was another, more personal matter that was disturbing her. When filming began, Jane and Karger had been divorced for a year. The marriage was unraveling when she was making *Magnificent Obsession*. The disillusionment that Jane felt—four marriages, four failures—combined with her character's dilemma as a widow in love with a younger man from a different world seeped into her interpretation. She was playing a woman who gets pawed by a lothario at a party, admonished by her children—who could accept her remarriage but not to Kirby—and shunned by a community that considers her a traitor to her class. Jane's ability to inhabit such a conflicted character resulted in a performance that peels away the layers of Carey's protective insulation as if they were Salome's veils. When she relaxes in the warmth of Hudson's embrace or dances uninhibitedly at Alida and Mick's rustic home, with its heterogeneous mix of whites and persons of color, enjoying the freedom that a class-free environment can offer, she behaves like a girl on a date, introduced to her boyfriend's circle and reveling in the experience of otherness.

Then there were the times when Jane had to look bewildered, her eyes uncomprehending and her face immobile, as if she were metamorphosing into stone. Jane was bearing two weights: her own and Carey's. She embodied the fears of any older woman involved with a younger man who is not interested in her money, but only in offering her a lifestyle that can bring her the peace she seeks. Interwoven with Carey's fears was Jane's own worry that after four failed marriages, the solitary life might be all that is left for her. For Jane Wyman, there might not be a Ron Kirby. (And as it turned out, there wasn't.) By amalgamating the inner life of her character and her own, Jane gave a performance that was even more impressive than her Helen in *Magnificent Obsession*, in which each plot point generated its own emotion. In *All That Heaven Allows*, Jane used the plot points to connect Cary Scott with herself. In *Magnificent Obsession*, Helen was the patient. In *All That Heaven Allows*, it is Kirby's turn to play that role after a fall leaves him with a serious concussion. But when he opens his eyes, and a deer passes in front of the picture window before him, we know that Cary and Kirby will thumb their noses at convention and retire to a place where "the sun is but a morning star."

Sirk revived his favorite color scheme, with bluish bedrooms, walls, and windows. It was only coincidental that UI's color films opened with the familiar globe in a blue sky. The logo was UI's, but the palette was Sirk's. Blue was his way of sanctifying a relationship that, if it ever turned physical, would have made sex a sacrament. Frank Skinner provided his own brand of spirituality with a soundtrack consisting of Liszt's *Consolation #3* for reflective moments such as the credits, which provide an aerial view of the town square, and the last movement of Brahms's First Symphony, which—like the "Ode to Joy" in *Magnificent Obsession*—does double duty as a love/regeneration theme, underscoring those sacred moments when love is expressed without passion and renewal occurs without guilt.

Jane and Hudson were not destined to be reunited a third time. They had great rapport, as was evident in their two movies. Hudson acknowledged the "help" that Jane gave him, praising her for being "a wonderful girl." Jane was even more enthusiastic: "After working with Rock Hudson, I say he's got to be the biggest thing to hit the industry." When Hudson told Jane, "You really went out of your way to be nice to me when you didn't have to, " Jane's replied, "Let me tell you something. It was handed to me by someone. And I handed it down to you. And now it's your turn to hand it to somebody else." Jane had apparently adopted the philosophy of the doctor in *Magnificent Obsession*, giving back to another what someone has given to you—except that in Jane's case, there was no one person who brought her to the pinnacle of her profession, only a few individuals who eased the ascent, such as William Demarest, LeRoy Prinz, Lew Wasserman, Charles Brackett, and Billy Wilder. Now a devout Catholic, she would doubtless have attributed her success to a divine source, but there is no denying that her perseverance and quest for perfection played a major—if not the most significant—role.

Chapter 28

The Beginning of the End

WHEN JANE WAS FIRST STARTING OUT IN THE MOVIE BUSINESS, DISNEY was not a studio, but a company known for its early cartoons, distributed by United Artists, and for animated features like *Snow White and the Seven Dwarfs* and *Pinocchio*, distributed by RKO. But by the 1960s, Disney was a player. As the studio system receded into the past, the Disney Company filled the void, eventually creating its own cable network and film division. Jane, now in the twilight of her movie career, found herself working for Disney twice.

Pollyanna (1960), based on Eleanor H. Franklin's beloved children's classic of the same name, and faithfully adapted and directed by David Swift, proved a boon to character actors from golden age Hollywood— Adolphe Menjou, Donald Crisp, and Agnes Moorehead—who had the chance to engage in some scene-stealing, despite the brevity of their roles. It was also a chance for Jane to attempt a new role as a matriarch/boss lady, not knowing that she would be playing a similar type for nine years on *Falcon Crest*. Anyone who wondered how the loveable "Janie" Wyman could play the steel-willed Angela Channing might study her Polly Harrington, the titular head of Harrington Park, named for her father, whose memory she is determined to preserve, keeping the town exactly as it was in his day. Into her life comes her orphaned niece, Pollyanna (Hayley Mills), who democratizes her aunt's autocracy, encouraging the locals to think for themselves and adopt her message of "gladness"(her favorite word).

Jane was first billed, but the credits ended with "Introducing Hayley Mills," who had earlier appeared in the British film *Tiger Bay* (1959). *Pollyanna* was Mills's American debut. She did not project the image of an animated doll as Shirley Temple did, neither did she display the vulnerability of Natalie Wood. But she did have a feistiness that set her apart from other child stars and made her the perfect foil for Jane's Polly.

The plot, in its simplest form, charted the transformation of a town, as the silent majority found its voice, the curmudgeons reclaimed their humanity, a fire-and-brimstone minister (brilliantly played by Karl Malden) abandoned rhetoric for plain speech, and a glacial matriarch melted into a loving aunt. All of these things happened because an orphaned minister's daughter brought the good news to people who only heard it in its transmogrified form.

Jane looked elegant in picture hats and period costumes, seeming younger than she was at the time (early forties). The makeup and hairstyle helped, especially since her love interest was the local doctor, played by Richard Egan, her junior by a few years but looking as if he and Jane were contemporaries. Their romance, derailed when she was loath to relinquish the power she wielded over Harrington Park, got back on track when a bazaar designed to raise money for a new orphanage—a project Polly had vetoed—brought out the entire community in defiance. The bazaar, the film's visual highlight, is as authentic a piece of Americana as the Labor Day sequence in Joshua Logan's *Picnic* (1956).

Pollyanna may have tugged at a few heart strings and sent a tear or two trickling down the cheeks of moviegoers when Pollyanna's fall from a tree threatens her mobility. But the good doctor has connections with a Baltimore hospital, and the smiling locals give Pollyanna a grand send off, a sure sign that she will soon be skipping about, climbing trees and spreading her gospel of gladness.

Oddly, *Pollyanna* was not nominated for any Oscars, although it certainly deserved consideration for art direction and costume design. Hayley Mills did, however, receive a miniature Oscar for "the most outstanding performance during 1960." Hers would not be a spectacular career, although her work in *Whistle down the Wind*, *The Parent Trap*, and *The Trouble with Angels* suggested that, with better scripts, things could have been otherwise.

Unfortunately, for Jane, *Pollyanna* was preceded by *Holiday for Lovers* (1959) and followed by *Bon Voyage!* (1962) and *How to Commit Marriage* (1969). Ronald Alexander's *Holiday for Lovers*, which starred Don Ameche and Carmen Mathews, previously had a respectable Broadway run. There was nothing unique about it, only that it was the kind of well-crafted family play that the theatre needs periodically. No one could predict how this kind of play would fare: profanity-free, slightly risqué (with references that would pass over the heads of the kiddies and even some of the tourists), a clash of wills (parent vs. child), a winning victory for the younger generation, and a happy ending for all.

The movie version was an excuse to use Twentieth Century-Fox's back lot as a stand-in for São Paulo, Rio de Janeiro, and Lima, all of which the cast visited courtesy of stock footage and rear projection. In 1959, the film was another by-the-books comedy, in which a psychologist father (Clifton Webb) learns to accept the fact that his two daughters are old enough to live their own lives. When Meg (Jill St. John), the older daughter, goes off to tour South America (where she meets her idol, a suave Brazilian architect [Paul Henreid]), the complications pile up. Some are mildly amusing, others are tedious and badly played. Each plot point is telegraphed before it occurs. Meg's decision to stay in Brazil prompts her stuffy father, eager mother (Jane), and younger sister to fly to São Paulo, where they experience a modified form of culture shock. The younger daughter, an underutilized Carol Lynley, is wooed by an oafish air force sergeant (Gary Crosby), who is so desperate to wed her (but on his terms) that when she wavers, he spanks her—with her mother's approval. Jane, smartly dressed, played the scene as if she couldn't wait for it to end so she could get on to the next one.

Meanwhile, Meg falls in love with the architect's adoptive son, a high-testosterone painter committed to art and disdainful of filthy lucre. Despite a script that suggests otherwise, the parents let go, and the children make their own decisions. It is hard to imagine either daughter wedding the ideal husband, and if a sequel were ever made (it never was), it should open with a double divorce.

Clifton Webb, first-billed, was less effete than usual and at times genuinely moving in his scenes with Jill St. John. But he was given a protracted drunk scene that represented a low point in cinematic inebriation. Two musical diversions eased the tedium: a Portuguese rendition of "Chattanooga Choo Choo" and José Greco and his company demonstrating the art of flamenco. In an earlier era, Jane would have been a member of the supporting cast, using her charm to rein in Webb before he succumbed to self-parody.

If *Bon Voyage!* (1962), Jane's second film for Disney, had been her last, instead of her penultimate, one could imagine the puns that would have been made. The movie is another family travelogue on the order of *Holiday for Lovers*, with the Willard family from Terre Haute (Fred MacMurray and Jane as the parents; Deborah Walley, Tommy Kirk, and Kevin Corcoran as their children) embarking on a much-anticipated vacation to Paris and the French Riviera. MacMurray was top billed, reprising his harried and befuddled dad character familiar to viewers of his television series, *My Three Sons* (1960–72), in its second year when the film was released. Jane was the voice of reason, whose wardrobe, designed by Bill Thomas, was hardly the kind that the wife of a plumbing company owner could afford. No matter. A trip to Paris requires a Paris wardrobe. Besides, Jane deserved whatever perks the Walt Disney Company could afford, if for no other reason than to compensate for a role that came down to a costume change per scene.

The daughter is wooed by the son of a contessa (played with the right mix of vulgarity and disdain by Jesse Royce Landis), who holds the purse strings. The older son engages in a random sampling of eligible and not so eligible females, and the younger wanders off during a tour of the Paris sewers, leaving his father stranded and forced to get attention by wiggling his finger through a manhole cover. But the children are not the only ones to find, or think they have found, romance. MacMurray is approached by a chic hooker (played with touching restraint by Françoise Prévost), who ruefully nods when she learns that her potential client is happy married. Jane, meanwhile, is wooed by a Hungarian lothario, whom the irate MacMurray socks in the jaw. Eventually, the family returns to Terre Haute, sadder but wiser—but not until Jane does a brief jitterbug, proving that she could still rule the dance floor. At 130 minutes, *Bon Voyage!* was even more tedious than *Holiday for Lovers*, but at least Jane did not disgrace herself. She was a middle-aged actress playing a middle-aged wife whose allure was still very much in evidence.

Rarely does a last film measure up to a star's best work. Jean Arthur was fortunate; *Shane* is a classic western, with Arthur giving a beautifully understated performance. Then it was two abortive returns to Broadway, an unsuccessful sitcom, and retirement. For the others, it was Hollywood leftovers, which at least Greta Garbo raised to haute cuisine in *Two Faced Woman* (1941), acting with abandon and dancing a sexy "Chica Choca." Bette Davis was less fortunate with her cameo in *Wicked Stepmother* (1989), a far cry from *Jezebel* and *Dark Victory*. And Joan Crawford should be forgiven for *Trog* (1970), which ended another distinguished career. *How to Commit Marriage* (1969), Jane's farewell to the big screen, was similarly unworthy of her—as well as of her co-stars, Bob Hope and Jackie Gleason.

Perhaps it was the prospect of working with Hope and Gleason that induced Jane to sign on for the movie, not realizing that she would be third billed. Jane and Hope were good friends. She appeared several times as a guest on his radio show, and on one occasion (11 February

1953), joined him for a rendition of "Down by the Old Mill Stream." They sounded like seasoned vaudevillians, clowning around at first and then performing the song straight, with Jane and Hope singing different lyrics that meshed in a kind of contrapuntal two-part harmony. Then, Hope could turn a one-liner into a zinger. In one skit, Jane's agent vetoes her decision to appear with Hope in a nightclub act, instructing her to say nothing when Hope arrives. Hope reacted to Jane's silence by cracking a joke about *Johnny Belinda*: "She's already got an Oscar for this kind of thing, so let's not overdo it." That was the old Bob Hope. *How to Commit Marriage* featured a Hope at odds with an age that was alien to him, and looking as if he would rather be back on the road to wherever with Crosby and Lamour—but knowing that the road was now closed. Although Jane had been off the big screen for six years, television viewers, who may not have seen her in her glory days, knew who she was if they watched *Jane Wyman's Fireside Theatre*. Television was the medium that gave Hope longevity when his movie career was ebbing, one droplet after another. And Gleason had already achieved immortality with *The Honeymooners*, one of the most beloved of television series.

Except for the wacky word bending of Irwin Corey, as an Indian guru preaching "peace through protein," *How to Commit Marriage* is a tedious and often painful comedy of remarriage. Jane and Hope are the Bensons, whose marriage unravels in the opening sequence, as shot by shot the events leading to their breakup—sex reduced to cuddling, coffee cups used as ash trays, shaving cream where the shampoo should be—are interspersed with the credits. Jane's opening line, "I want a divorce," seems like the punch line of a visual set up that specified the grounds for divorce.

Complications arise when their daughter decides to quit college and marry a pianist, whose classical tastes are at odds with those of his father, Oliver Poe (Gleason), a rock n' roll impresario representing such groups as the Frozen Fish Sticks and the Mothergrabbers. Rather than tell their daughter that they have filed for divorce, the Bensons pretend to be the loving couple their daughter imagines them to be. Learning the truth, Poe interrupts the wedding, but eventually sanity is restored. The three couples merge into one unharmonious family: Poe and his significant other (the ravishing Tina Louise); his son and the Bensons' daughter, and the Bensons themselves—parents, children, and in-laws.

The writers, Michael Kanin and Ben Starr, filled the hollows of the script with topical references familiar to 1969 audiences (flower children, the peace movement, Hare Krishna hippies, Indian gurus) and a succession of farcical scenes that diverted attention from the escalation of the Vietnam War, the anti-draft movement, sit-ins, teach-ins, and student unrest that were more characteristic of the era (and dramatized the same year in *Medium Cool* [1969]). *How to Commit Marriage* was America sunny side up—no runny eggs or burned hash browns, straddling the gap between a comedy of remarriage and a dumbed down farce when Hope loses a game of golf to a skirt-wearing chimpanzee named Mildred.

At fifty-two, Jane looked matronly but elegant, and Hope was fit for a man pushing seventy. Unfortunately, the once great comic was now unloading his one-liners instead of firing them off. Director Norman Panama could not harmonize the stars' different performing styles: Hope cracked jokes that were flat and witless, Gleason offered a big screen version of Ralph Kramden, and Jane stuck to the script, trapped in a movie that weaved in and out of romantic comedy, farce, and satire. *How to Commit Marriage* is the kind of film in which an early reference to a mudslide is followed by a real one at the fadeout. The clever credits sequence and the split screen effects proved only to be distractions from a joyless domestic comedy.

Chapter 29

Worlds Elsewhere

NANCY ENTERED THE BUSINESS TOO LATE TO BE PART OF RADIO'S golden age, when stars appeared on such shows as *Lux Radio Theatre* and *Screen Directors' Playhouse*, reprising their film roles or taking on roles created by others. For movie buffs, the closest equivalent to the neighborhood theater was *Lux Radio Theatre*, which aired from 1934 to 1955. For diehard fans, Monday evenings at 10:00 p.m. were sacred. This was the time they tuned in to CBS for an hour-long version of a movie, frequently with the original stars. Some could act with voice alone. Loretta Young, Fred MacMurray, and Claudette Colbert were among the best, racking up twenty-six, twenty-five, and twenty-four performances, respectively, on *Lux Radio Theatre*. Jane's appearances numbered fourteen, eight of which were films in which she had starred: *Magic Town, The Yearling, The Lady Takes a Sailor, Here Comes the Groom* (with Fred MacMurray in Bing Crosby's part), *The Blue Veil, The Story of Will Rogers, Just for You* (with Dick Haymes in lieu of Crosby), and *The Glass Menagerie* (with Fay Bainter as Amanda and Frank Lovejoy as Tom).

Radio drama was not a natural medium for Jane, except when she felt some rapport with her character. Then, she would throw herself into the role, channeling the character into her voice as if she were on a sound stage where the camera had been replaced by a microphone. Since Jane did not have a radio voice, she had to work harder than Reagan, who did. Reagan began in radio and had the right kind of voice for the medium: clear, authoritative, and resonant. In her teens, Jane sang on radio, but the ability to carry a tune is not the same as creating a character in front of a mic. But stars were expected to do radio, and Jane and Reagan obliged. Jane had no problem recreating a role from one of her movies. In *Magic Town,* (15 December 1947), she was reunited with her original co-star, James Stewart, whose natural delivery inspired Jane to relax into the part, as the two worked their own brand of magic on the air.

Listeners were also fortunate to hear Jane and Gregory Peck reprise their roles in *The Yearling* (19 January 1948). Jane resurrected her Ma Baxter voice, sounding uneducated but not ignorant. She spoke in the vernacular of the Florida scrub country ("heered" for "heard," "them" for "their," "growd up" for "grown up"), using its idioms ("What's he seed?" "I were lucky," "They all gone") as if she were a native. *The Yearling* was one of *Lux Radio Theatre*'s best presentations. The bear hunt was a brilliant combination of human and nonhuman sounds, and the musical bridges between the scenes had a true regional flavor.

Ordinarily, Jane had no problem taking on another actress's role. For the *Body and Soul* broadcast (15 November 1948), John Garfield repeated one of his best characterizations: Charlie Davis, torn between professional boxing and self-improvement. Although his mother urges him to continue his education by attending night school, Charlie's fear of poverty thrusts him into a profession in which fights are fixed, and someone is expected to take the fall. Garfield knew how to suppress anger while suggesting that it could flare up at any moment. And yet there were times when his tough guy voice turned tender, as it did in his scenes with Jane (in the Lilli Palmer role). Garfield's acting inspired Jane to become every bit his equal, as she urged him to quit the business, calibrating her voice without raising it. Refusing to participate in a fixed fight, Charlie goes into the ring and wins. "Come on, let's go home," he tells Jane. That evening, Garfield was the draw, but even he was nearly upstaged by the boxing match that sounded as if it were being broadcast live.

Lilli Palmer was not a major star, but Doris Day was. Still, Jane had no qualms about playing Day's role in *On Moonlight Bay* (5 May 1952), that of a baseball-loving teenager, who grows increasingly feminine as Gordon MacRea discovers the woman inside the tomboy. Jane succeeded in sounding eighteen; at thirty-five, she could take on the voice of a teenager even though she could no longer play one on the screen. *On Moonlight Bay* also gave Jane a chance to sing. She had a solo ("Tell Me") and two duets with MacRea ("On Moonlight Bay" and "Cuddle Up A Little Closer"). A Christmas sequence included "Silent Night," which MacRea sang with such feeling that it seemed as if the season had arrived. *On Moonlight Bay*, based on Booth Tarkington's Penrod stories, was an hour of nostalgia and a distraction from the war being fought in Korea.

It may have been William Keighley's idea to co-star Jane and Reagan in the 17 November 1947 broadcast of *Nobody Lives Forever* in the roles that Geraldine Fitzgerald and John Garfield originated in the 1946 film. Keighley, then host of *Lux Radio Theatre*, introduced Jane and Reagan as "happily married people" (married, but at the time not happily) and noted that he had directed them in *Brother Rat*—as if farce prepared them for hardboiled melodrama. Reagan came off better than Jane, although neither was particularly convincing: he, as a professional con man recently discharged from the army and ready to return to his old ways; she, as the wealthy widow he plans to fleece, until love intervenes. If Jane was less effective than she might have been with another actor, it was because Reagan gave her nothing to work from except his literal line readings. At the end of the broadcast, Keighley commended them for their performances. Jane admitted that she had worked in radio as a singer, and Reagan demonstrated his expertise as a sportscaster by illustrating how he would call a football game. At the time, listeners had no idea that his habit of playing sportscaster when company was present contributed to Jane's gradual disenchantment and eventual divorce.

Jane was also not at her best in *One More Tomorrow* (1 June 1947) and *Flamingo Road* (2 October 1950). Although she had a minor role in the film version of the former, she was now playing Ann Sheridan's role on *Lux*: the mistress of a magazine publisher (Dennis Morgan), who had also been his conscience until he married a gold digger (Alexis Smith). With Morgan and Smith in their original roles, Jane did not stand a chance. Her performance was not embarrassing, just underpowered.

Why Jane agreed to play Lane Bellamy, Joan Crawford's role in *Flamingo Road* (1949), is hard to fathom. No actress could surpass Crawford at playing hard-bitten women who conceal their vulnerability behind a façade that is more of a carapace. On *Lux Radio Theatre* (6 June 1949), Rosalind Russell offered her take on the title character in *Mildred Pierce*, for which Crawford won her only Oscar. Although Russell was Warners' and director Michael Curtiz's first choice for *Mildred Pierce*, Crawford was made for the part of a woman who rose from waitress to entrepreneur. When Crawford cleared tables and picked up tips, it seemed as if she had been waitressing all her life. Russell was a fine actress, but there was never a Mildred Pierce like Joan Crawford.

And who, except Crawford, could play a carnival performer when she was in her forties and the character at least fifteen years younger? Age did not matter to Crawford; she made the character's age her own. Jane, much younger than Crawford, had no problem with Lane Bellamy's voice. It was the character, a hooch dancer, that eluded her. Jane sounded like a kid from the wrong side of the tracks who stumbled onto a carnival and found a job. Lane is befriended by Fielding Carlisle (Zachary Scott in the film), the deputy of the corrupt Sheriff Titus Semple (Herbert Butterfield, sounding uncannily like Sidney Greenstreet from the movie). Believing her presence will undermine his plan to run Carlisle for state senator, Semple has her carted off to jail for vagrancy. Lane becomes Semple's bête noire. In a foreshadowing line, Lane tells the corpulent Semple about a destructive elephant that had to be shot: "You don't know how hard it is to get rid of a dead elephant." Jane turned the line into a wisecrack without coating it with venom, as Crawford did. When Lane accidentally kills Semple, it is the same as ridding the community of a dead elephant. If Crawford tuned in that evening, she may have smiled, knowing that there was only one Lane Bellamy—and it was not Jane Wyman.

Nancy may not have done radio drama, but she made her television debut earlier than either Jane or Reagan. Since Nancy was based in New York in the late 1940s, it was only natural that she would be among the first actors to venture into live television. The opportunities were multiplying, with *Kraft Television Theatre, Studio One, Robert Montgomery Presents, Playhouse 90, Climax!* For an actor between plays, live TV drama was the next best thing. One such program was NBC's *Kraft Television Theatre* (1947–58), which specialized in hour-long adaptations and original teleplays aired on Wednesday evenings from 7:30 p.m. to 8:30 p.m. Nancy appeared in Martin Flavin's *Broken Dishes* (12 May 1948), the play that brought Bette Davis to Hollywood after she impressed the critics with her performance as the outspoken daughter of a milquetoast father and an overbearing mother.

What was unique about live drama was that each presentation was the equivalent of an opening night, and the one million Americans who owned television sets in 1949 were first-nighters. If Nancy had not gone on dates with Spencer Tracy and Clark Gable and played tennis with Katharine Hepburn, she might have done more during television's golden age. But after *Broken Dishes,* she merely reprised her roles in *Ramshackle Inn* (2 January 1949) and *The Late Christopher Bean* (6 February 1949) on NBC's *Philco TV Playhouse,* which aired Sunday evenings from 9:00 p.m. to 10:00 p.m. *Philco TV Playhouse* would have been ideal for Nancy. It specialized in adaptations of plays (*Dinner at Eight, Street Scene, Camille*) and novels (*Rebecca, Dinner at Antoine's*). But a month after the telecast of *The Late Christopher Bean,* Nancy Davis was an MGM contract player.

Even so, Nancy did not abandon television, appearing fourteen more times in various series before ending her acting career in 1962. One such performance was in *Climax!*, the only available record of her work in live television drama. *Climax!*, CBS's hour-long dramatic series (Thursday, 8:30 p.m.–9:30p.m.) started out live, before switching to film and tape. Nancy appeared during the second season in *Bailout at 43,000* (29 December 1955). Since *Climax!* sometimes originated from Los Angeles, as was the case with *Bailout*, Nancy did not have to travel to New York, where she learned the rudiments of television acting in a cramped studio. Paul Monash's engrossing script dramatized the life-risking decisions air force personnel make when they volunteer to test ejection seats for high-altitude bailouts. Director John Frankenheimer artfully integrated live drama with filmed segments, including a climactic bailout with the parachute opening majestically like a silken dome. *Bailout at 43,000* was one of the few television dramas of the period that seemed like a feature film, mainly because of the director. In 1959, Frankenheimer moved on to film, bringing with him some of his specialties (tight framing, scenes as set pieces), which he used to advantage in *All Fall Down* (1961), *Birdman of Alcatraz* (1962), and especially *The Manchurian Candidate* (1962). Frankenheimer's intense close-ups kept dialogue to a minimum, with inner conflicts and fears expressed facially. Nor did he discriminate; all the actors were subjected to this soul—baring process, which, in live television, did not allow for retakes.

Charlton Heston starred as a captain trying to compete with younger men. Lee Marvin was a major who suffered a broken back because of a faulty ripcord. And Richard Boone appeared as a colonel who volunteered and ended up disabled. Nancy was Heston's wife, forced to deal with a brooding husband who volunteered for the bailout but was rejected because of age. When he is later deemed eligible, Nancy confronts Boone in a powerful scene, voicing her concern about her husband falling six miles just to test a device and urging Boone to remove his name from the list. Although Boone reluctantly agrees to go in his place, Heston intervenes and bails out successfully.

Nancy did a creditable job, never going up on lines and playing her few scenes with conviction. This was a man's show, and few actresses could compete with Heston, Boone, and Marvin. Nancy, to her credit, held her own. *Bailout* offers a glimpse of what Nancy Davis might have been like on the stage; she made a secondary role count by taking on her husband's anxiety without letting him know it. Nancy played the good wife, as she always would, even after leaving the business.

After her brief MGM period was over, Nancy, uncertain about her movie career, returned to television. By 1953, CBS's *Schlitz Playhouse of*

Stars, which premiered the previous year, had switched from live hour-long programs to filmed thirty-minute ones. This was ideal for a new mother like Nancy, who went back to television in 1953, appearing in "22 Sycamore Road" (5 June 1953) on *Schlitz*, and in "First Born" on *Ford Theatre* (5 February 1953). When *Ford Theatre* joined the ranks of dramatic programs in 1949, it had a lofty goal: showing live hour-long versions of novels (*Little Women*) and plays (*Twentieth Century*), generally with New York actors. But rather than compete with *Kraft Television Theatre*, *Ford Theatre* soon changed its format to filmed, half-hour presentations.

"First Born" marked the first time Reagan and Nancy co-starred in a television drama. By 1953, *Ford Theatre* had moved from CBS to NBC, ending its eight-year run in 1957 on ABC. Nancy played the second wife of a widower (Reagan) with a son (Tommy Rettig), who is still devoted to the memory of his mother (Paula Corday). Nancy's was the most difficult role; she had to win over the hostile son without trying to compete with his mother. Her pregnancy aggravates the situation, making the boy more sullen than ever. The real acting chores fell to Nancy and Rettig. Anyone could have played Reagan's role; the soignée Corday appeared in a few flashbacks, lending a continental air to the proceedings—while at the same time making one wonder why a sophisticated woman would marry such a dull man. Nancy and Rettig worked off each other effectively, he rejecting her ministrations, and she trying new approaches, until rapport grew out of their interplay.

Television, even more than film, confirmed Nancy's talent. The television screen can be heartless. In 1950s television, the intricate lighting to which movie actors were accustomed—the transfiguring kind that rendered faces opalescent, robbing them of character in the process—did not exist. The medium favored non-divas like Donna Reed, Jane Wyatt, Lucille Ball, Marjorie Lord, and Barbara Stanwyck. For audiences craving the glamour of yesteryear, there was *The Loretta Young Show* (1953–61), which brought Hollywood to the small screen. For performers like Young, it was not a matter of adopting a television persona, but rather of adjusting the filmic one so that it would fit the dimensions of a smaller screen. Since Nancy never acquired a persona, she did not have an image to alter. She played her limited repertory of wives, mothers, and widows with conviction, endowing them with character and integrity. Even when she was in the movies, she did not have to be elaborately lit. The camera caught her sincerity, which manifested itself in honest performances, even in mediocre productions.

Reagan's television appearances on *General Electric Theater* were mostly unimpressive. Although he could still flash his trademark smile, folksy and inviting, his face had hardened, and his brow was furrowed. To look pensive, he sealed his lips and screwed up his eyes. His range of expressions was even more limited on television than in film. By the late 1950s, he had put on weight, which ill-fitting costumes—particularly army uniforms and suits—only emphasized. If he looked uncomfortable, it was partly because what he was wearing was a size too small. Three of his better *General Electric Theater* performances were in "Bargain Bride" (7 April 1957), "The Castaway" (12 October 1958)," and "The Iron Silence" (24 September 1961). For "Bride," Reagan had to adopt a Scottish accent, which sometimes sounded Irish and at other times midwestern. His character was a confirmed bachelor with whom a minister (Edgar Buchanan) strikes a bargain: a pair of mules in exchange for looking after a carnival performer (Eva Bartok) who has defected from her troupe. Feminists would have been appalled, but this was television in 1957, and the idea of frontier-style barter was not considered sexist—particularly since the performer gains the upper hand, providing the Scot with exotic dishes and instructing him in the art of kissing, so that each profited from the bargain. He found a mate who could cook, and she a husband who learned to bathe and kiss. Reagan may have been the star, but it was Eva Bartok's show. Reagan's changing from chauvinist to lover was a shift, not a transformation, but at least he looked endearingly naughty when he asked for another lesson in osculation. That evening, however, Bartok did the real acting.

Reagan was much better in "The Castaway," based on a story by Ernest Haycox, whose "Stage to Lordsburg" provided the plot for John Ford's *Stagecoach* (1939). Reagan was a wagon master accompanying settlers to Oregon in the 1880s. When Indians express their wish to buy one of the women, a young jokester offers one up, setting off an attack that leaves a few dead on both sides—but no sale. Reagan could handle this kind of role: an army captain who could mount a horse without effort and ride tall in the saddle. While Reagan turned in a respectable performance, he was overshadowed by some of the lesser players, particularly Jim Davis, then a veteran of B movie westerns and soon to become a television star playing Jock Ewing in *Dallas*.

One of the best and oddest *General Electric Theater* presentations was "The Iron Silence," in which the anti-communist Reagan was cast as a major in the Soviet army, stationed in Hungary after the 1957 uprising. Reagan did not attempt an accent, nor did many of the others, American

English being the great leveler. The director was former actress Ida Lupino, one of the first women in postwar Hollywood to occupy the director's chair, joining the ranks of such trailblazers as Alice Guy Blaché, Lois Webber, and Dorothy Arzner.

"The Iron Silence" was freely adapted from two Guy de Maupassant stories, "Mademoiselle Fifi" and "Boule de Suif," set during the Franco-Prussian War. Writer Ken Kolb updated them, changing the occupiers from German to Russian. Reagan was a conflicted member of the Soviet military, who cannot bring himself to deal harshly with the locals who resist the occupation. As an act of protest, the parish priest refuses to toll the church bell; hence the title. When the occupiers learn they can return to Mother Russia, they celebrate by inviting some prostitutes to dinner, and one of the women inadvertently causes a soldier's death. In reprisal, the other prostitutes are executed, except for the one accused of the murder (a fiery Carol Lawrence), who takes refuge in the tower. The major, never a committed communist (and with Reagan in the role, how could he be?), turns into a spokesman for democracy, American style, and simply asks that she toll the bell not just for the Russian soldier (which would please the Soviets), but for the women. The bell tolls, the Soviets leave, and, ideally, the disaffected major should seek asylum in the West. But that would mean another episode.

There was little Lupino could do with Reagan, who delivered his panegyric to democracy as if he were at a lectern. Instead, she concentrated on three of the others: Carol Lawrence, primarily a musical theatre performer (she created the role of Maria in *West Side Story*), but giving every indication that, with the right script and director, she could be a first-rate dramatic actress; Vic Morrow, as the sadistic officer whose accidental death leads to the murder charge; and Abraham Sofaer as the priest, who is the embodiment of passive resistance. But as was generally the case with *General Electric Theater* episodes featuring Reagan, he was upstaged by his co-stars and even some of the supporting cast. They were the actors; he was the personality.

Between 1953 and 1961, Nancy and Reagan appeared together in five television shows: "First Born" on *Ford Theatre*; "A Turkey for the President" (23 November 1958), "The Other Wise Man" (25 December 1960), and "Money and the Minister" (26 November 1961) on *General Electric Theater*; and "The Long Shadow" on *Dick Powell's Zane Grey Theatre* (19 January 1961). Nancy was at her best in "First Born" and "The Long Shadow." In the latter, she played an army widow in the post-bellum West. Reagan played a cavalry officer, who must inform her that her son has been killed, supposedly in an Indian ambush (this turns out to be untrue). When Reagan presents her with her son's saber, Nancy accepts it as if it were a talisman, maintaining her dignity despite her disappointment with the man in whose care she had entrusted her son.

For a half-hour episode, "The Long Shadow" was unusually complex, a web spun out of deception and equivocation that untangles when Reagan, transmitting his customized semaphores of concern (ridged brow, pursed lips, pained eyes), divulges the truth: The son was neither a model soldier nor the victim of an ambush; he was killed by his supposed best friend (a creepy Scott Marlowe, intent on killing Reagan). Marlowe and Nancy gave the best performances, Marlowe passing himself off as an avenger to assuage his guilt, and Nancy registering emotions from grief to disillusionment, and finally acceptance, enhanced by the distinct possibility that her widowhood was coming to an end. "The Long Shadow" was impressively directed by Budd Boetticher, a once underrated movie director now admired for his Randolph Scott westerns, such as *The Tall T*, *Decision at Sundown*, *Buchanan Rides Alone*, and *Comanche Station*.

Nancy made the most of her role in "Money and the Minster" as the wife of a clergyman (Reagan, in another tight-fitting suit), whose devotion to an elderly woman has made him heir to her estate. When the woman's nephew (Gary Merrill) challenges the will, arguing that his aunt changed it because she had become infatuated with the minister, his wife urges her husband to relinquish his claim to the estate. Reagan, putting on his principled expression (the same as his concerned/perplexed/determined one), refuses, knowing the money could be used for church improvements. When the aunt's diary is produced as evidence, the nephew relents after reading the unflattering statements she had written about him. Nancy played her helpmate role well, but Merrill ran the gamut from belligerent to repentant, outshining Reagan, who pontificated in lieu of acting. Ellen Corby as the nurse, Connie Gilchrest as the housekeeper, and the pop singer Jaye P. Morgan as the nephew's flashy wife did more with their roles than Reagan did with his.

Television would have embraced Nancy if she continued in the medium. She had developed the art of playing wives and mothers with the right degree of realism, projecting a winning naturalness that made audiences accept her character even if they rejected the plot. She was not a sitcom mom who knew what was best when father didn't. In "Obituary for Mr. X," (*Dick Powell Theatre*, 23 January 1962) Nancy was part of a formidable ensemble. The star was Steve Cochran, playing Nancy's husband, a deputy sheriff involved in an affair with the secretary (Dina

Merrill) of a newspaper editor (John Ireland). Cochran's supervisor (a sympathetic Gary Merrill) is concerned that his deputy is justifying his job by picking up vagrants, one of whom is the title character (memorably played by Eduard Franz), whom he accidentally kills in a hit-and-run accident.

It was an evening of flawless performances. Cochran conveyed the deputy's emotional turmoil perfectly, giving a better performance than he ever did in film. Dina Merrill played against type, acting as if her character were meant for something other than pounding typewriter keys. Gary Merrill was especially moving in his attempt to save his deputy from self-destruction. John Ireland registered the zeal of a truth-seeker who discovers the identity of "Mr. X" and writes up his story.

Nancy had only a few scenes, but she made them count. In her best, she phones Cochran to remind him of his promise to attend a reception that evening, while suspecting that he has probably forgotten the commitment or else will come up with an excuse. To the wife of a (mostly) absentee husband, being elected president of a card club is a coup, and a reception in her honor an inauguration. The way Nancy used her face and voice was a lesson in the art of looking doubtful while sounding confident. It was a heartbreaking scene, ending with Cochran begging off to attend a traffic seminar and Nancy stoically accepting the fabrication.

Nancy ended her television, as well as her acting, career with appearances on *87th Precinct* and *Wagon Train*. The former was a short-lived but well-reviewed NBC series (September 1961–September 1962), inspired by the novels and short stories of Ed McBain (*né* Salvatore A. Lombino), the man of many pseudonyms—including the most famous, Evan Hunter (*The Blackboard Jungle, The Birds* screenplay). The star was Robert Lansing as Detective Steve Carella, with regulars Ron Harper, Norman Fell, and Gregory Walcott as his colleagues. The scripts played like police procedurals, intricately plotted until the wind-up that was too quick for a dénouement but long enough to solve the case. The program's failure to go beyond a season was partially due to its hour-long format, 9:00 p.m.–10:00 p.m. on Mondays, which placed it in competition with the popular CBS sitcoms *The Danny Thomas Show* (9:00 p.m.–9:30 p.m.) and *The Andy Griffith Show* (9:30 p.m.–10:00 p.m.). For crime buffs, there were other shows in which the plot was resolved in thirty minutes, such as *Dragnet*, *77 Sunset Strip*, and *Robert Taylor's Detectives*.

"The King's Ransom " (19 February 1962), based on McBain's 1959 novel of the same name (but without "The"), was a typical example of the series. The title was a pun on the surname of the main character, a successful shoe manufacturer who receives a call that his son had been kidnapped and that the price for his return is $250,000. However, the victim is not King's son, but his chauffeur's. Despite the mix up, the kidnappers still demand the ransom, posing a dilemma for King, who needs the money to take over another shoe company. McBain's script was as high tech as the era allowed, involving traced calls and intercepted radio messages interwoven in a narrative of ever-mounting suspense until the mastermind is apprehended and the boy is freed. Of special interest is the script's humanizing of two characters who would ordinarily be considered villains: a bank robber and his wife, suckered into the kidnapping scheme by a ruthless hood, who plans to kill the boy after the ransom is paid. Both the robber and his wife, lured by the prospect of easy money, are decent people gone astray. The wife (Virginia Vincent) even takes pity on the boy, whom she unsuccessfully tries to free. When the police finally arrive, the boy is unwilling to implicate the pair, knowing that they were only accomplices in a scheme that spiraled out of control.

Looking chic in a basic black dress and pearls, Nancy was an attractive but unnecessary presence as King's wife. King could have been a widower for all it mattered. At least Nancy had one good scene, in which she tried unsuccessfully to convince her husband to pay the ransom, even though it is not for their son. But she could not compete with the real drama, which did not involve her character.

At least she wound up her acting career with a decent role in "The Sam Darland Story" on *Wagon Train* (26 December 1962). By then, the series that originated on NBC in 1957 had moved to ABC in the same 7:30 p.m.–8:30 p.m. Monday time slot—although that, too, would change as the program came to an end in 1965. The star that evening was Art Linkletter, on leave from his job as emcee of *People Are Funny*, and cast as the visionary leader of a group of homeless boys hoping to establish a settlement in a ghost town abandoned for lack of water. Nancy received special billing: "With Nancy Davis as Mrs. Baxter." She played a member of the wagon train, a war widow without a family, whose chief concern, after realizing that their leader is an ex-con, is the boys' welfare. The man's conviction, however, revived him spiritually and made him the precursor of Boys Town's Father Flanagan. When Nancy is captured by Indians and witnesses Linkletter's genius in negotiating for her release, she acknowledges his integrity and joins his community. The town's water is restored with an explosion that activates the wells in a climax similar to the one in the Humphrey Bogart film *Sahara* (1943), in which shelling accomplished the same effect. The biblical parallels were the same, with Linkletter and Bogart acting as Moses figures, and dynamite and artillery taking the place of a rod and a stone.

Nancy could look back at her career knowing that she never received a damning review and, in fact, enjoyed her share of favorable ones. She remained within her repertory, which included various kinds of women—except for femme fatales, mistresses, call girls, and murderesses. She could have continued with her repertory, but that was not what she wanted. Nancy was her mother's daughter. Edith Luckett relinquished her career after marrying Loyal Davis—whom she believed was meant for something better than performing prefrontal lobotomies—and groomed him into a surgeon to the stars. Nancy would do the same for Reagan. Once she played her last role, she took on Reagan's vision of himself as presidential material. The SAG presidency was just the beginning of a journey to the White House, and Nancy intended to accompany her husband on every leg of it.

Nineteen sixty-two may have signaled the end of Nancy's acting career, but not Jane's. That year, she made her penultimate feature film, *Bon Voyage!*, and appeared on *Wagon Train* in "The Wagon Train Mutiny." In 1966, when Reagan was elected governor of California, Jane starred in "When Hell Froze" on *Bob Hope Presents the Chrysler Theatre*. When Reagan took office the following year, she made her second appearance on *Insight*, a syndicated program produced by the Paulist Fathers, in "Why Does God Allow Men to Suffer?" When Reagan was elected fortieth president of the United States in 1980, Jane was featured on both *The Love Boat* and *Charlie's Angels*. And in Reagan's first year as president, Jane starred in a series that revitalized her career, *Falcon Crest*. She would continue to act until arthritis and diabetes made it impossible for her to continue. But that would not be until 1995, by which time Reagan and Nancy had become subjects for biographers and historians. They had acquitted themselves well in the media they embraced—although Nancy fared better in television drama than Reagan, who gave his best performances during his presidency, when he charmed the camera into projecting the image of a true American, devoid of guile and artifice, who differed from other Americans only in his street address. For Reagan and Nancy, there was no graceful transition from the sound stage to the White House, only a first act, followed by a second and a third. They disproved F. Scott Fitzgerald's maxim that there are no second acts in American lives. The Reagans had three: actor and actress, governor and wife, and president and first lady. Jane did likewise while staying in the same profession, appearing in movies, in television, and as the star of a nighttime soap that brought her a generation of fans who had never seen *Johnny Belinda*.

In retrospect, it is apparent that Nancy—equally at home in the governor's mansion and in the White House—was the perfect wife for Reagan. Although she wrote, somewhat ingenuously, in *My Turn* that she thought she married an actor, only to discover that he was a politician, she must have sensed, as others did, that for Reagan movies were only the prologue to a drama that would eventually be played out on a world stage. Once on the set of *Kings Row*, Robert Cummings jokingly remarked that Reagan should run for president. Reagan's one-word reply, "Yes"— spoken with utter seriousness—suggested loftier ambitions. Jane could never have been a politician's wife. It was politics, after all, that led to their divorce. Eventually, Nancy saw the politician within the actor, who needed only a sympathetic mate to bring it to the fore. That Nancy could do. When their acting careers came to a close, Nancy knew that both she and her husband were on the threshold of something unsettlingly new, which they embraced for different reasons—Reagan, because he believed he was destined for something higher; Nancy, because she believed she was, too. And they were both right.

In Ayn Rand's *Atlas Shrugged*, John Galt sums up his philosophy with a dizzying radio speech: "I swear by my life—and love of it—that I will never live for the sake of another man, nor ask another man to live for mine." To understand Jane's position, change the text to read, "I will not sacrifice my career for another or expect another to sacrifice his for me." Jane would never have given up her career for Reagan, whether he was struggling to stay in the business or entering politics. She was an Oscar winner, who had miles to go before the big sleep. Nancy, on the other hand, had come to the end of the bifurcating road in the yellow wood: She knew which path to take.

Nineteen sixty-two was also a crucial year for both America and Reagan. The Cuban Missile Crisis in October seemed to presage the dreaded confrontation between the United States and the Soviet Union, which, thanks to hard line diplomacy, never occurred. Reagan lost his beloved mother, Nelle, earlier that year. His acting career was at low ebb. *General Electric Theater* went off the air, and Nancy made her last appearance as an actress on *Wagon Train* the day after Christmas. Lew Wasserman broke the news to Reagan that, at fifty-one and looking more like a rancher than an actor, he was not on any producer's short list. Reagan's days as a leading man were over, but another career loomed large.

Reagan's conservatism, coupled with his anti-communism, which intensified after the Bay of Pigs fiasco and the Cuban Missile Crisis, convinced him that the Red Scare was as real in 1962 as it had been in the late 1940s. It also convinced him that he belonged to the wrong party. To Reagan, communism was a cancer that had metastasized to the point of invading the cells of the media—film, television, and theatre. He espoused these sentiments in an address to the Phoenix Chamber of Commerce (30 March 1961), warning the audience that unless the communist threat were averted, "[W]e will be spending our sunset years telling our children . . . what it was like in the United States when men were free." He went on to deliver a rough draft of what might serve as his platform speech if he ever ran for office. Considering himself a veteran—which, of course, he was—he questioned, but wisely did not inveigh against the presence of veterans with non-military illnesses and injuries in VA hospital beds. He insisted that there was no justification for federal aid to education and argued against government regulation of farm production. His bottom line was reduced taxes and spending, which would include cuts to entitlement programs like Medicare and Social Security. Without conjuring up the specter of socialism, he implied that it was casting a dark shadow on the land. This was Reagan in the process of shedding every vestige of his Democratic past. The process was completed the following year when he became a registered Republican.

Loyal Davis, who was in the audience, was so taken with the speech that he exhorted his son-in-law to give up acting and pursue a career in politics. Barry Goldwater, a Republican senator from Arizona and the embodiment of conservatism, was also impressed—so much so that he sought Reagan's support in his bid for the presidency. Goldwater lost to Lyndon Johnson, but Reagan had seen the light. If Goldwater could run for president, why couldn't he? However, a group of powerful Republicans knew that the path to the White House needed a stopover in the governor's mansion and persuaded Reagan to run against Edmund "Pat" Brown for governor of California. On 4 January 1966, Reagan announced his candidacy. Ten months later, he defeated the incumbent, winning by almost a million votes.

Reagan's odyssey to the White House began when he was a student leader at Eureka College, and was marked by detours into broadcasting and acting, until a confluence of events—historical, personal, and providential—brought him to the point of no return. If he is known as the "Great Communicator," it is because he learned how to work an audience in three media: radio, film, and television. No other president could make that claim.

Chapter 30

From the Hearth to the Vineyards

IN THE LATE 1940S, MANY STARS OF A CERTAIN AGE SENSED THAT THE studio system was not what it had been when they entered the business. Some may even have realized that the safety net the system provided would soon drop, leaving them in free fall. But there was an alternative to hanging on and wondering when the end would come. They could take a break from the big screen and try the small one, crossing the Hollywood bridge but not burning it. In 1948, this meant New York and live television drama.

Although Margaret Sullavan was a luminous screen presence (*The Good Fairy, Three Comrades, The Mortal Storm, No Sad Songs for Me*), she saw herself primarily as a stage actress, for whom film was another medium for displaying her art. Live television did not intimidate her; it only required a more intimate acting style. When *Studio One* premiered on CBS, 7 November 1948, the play was "The Storm," starring Margaret Sullavan. When *Philco TV Playhouse* went on the air in 1948, Oscar-winner Paul Muni (*The Story of Louis Pasteur*) appeared in Elmer Rice's *Counselor-at-Law* in the role he had originated on Broadway. Muni was also more at home on the stage than the screen, to which he brought a rich theatricality, detailed and at times fussy, that set him apart from his peers. He was not the only movie actor to appear on *Philco TV Playhouse*. Others soon followed, such as David Wayne, Marsha Hunt, Jessica Tandy, Ralph Bellamy, Betty Field, and Kim Hunter. When someone of Claudette Colbert's stature decided it was not beneath her dignity to do a comedy sketch on *The Jack Benny Show* (1 April 1951), it was as if she were expunging the stigma attached to the new medium and issuing an "all clear" to her colleagues.

When filmed television arrived in 1949, actors with little or no stage experience had ample opportunities. There were sitcoms, series, and dramatic shows like *Ford Theatre* and *Schlitz Playhouse of Stars*, which originally aired live before switching to film. And beginning in 1949, there was *Fireside Theatre*, filmed at Hal Roach Studios in Culver City. *Fireside Theatre* was not the first example of filmed television. That was NBC's *Your Show Time*, half-hour dramatizations of famous short stories, which lasted a mere six months (January–July 1949). *Fireside Theatre*, a half-hour anthology series, debuted on NBC on 5 April 1949. Jane had no idea that six years later she would be hosting *Fireside Theatre* and that it would be renamed *Jane Wyman's Fireside Theatre*.

Fireside Theatre was the brainchild of Lithuanian-born Frank Wisbar, *né* Franz Wyzbar, who mastered the art of the low-budget movie at the quintessential Poverty Row studio, PRC, grinding out movies like *Strangler of the Swamp*, *Secrets of a Sorority Girl*, and *Devil Bat's Daughter*. That skill stood him in good stead when he had to produce—and often write and direct—a half-hour episode each week, stinting on budget but not on quality. *Variety* was impressed; Wisbar's achievement "could match in production quality, story . . . any Hollywood-produced two-reeler." Wisbar envisioned a series that made no pretense at art and was intended only "to entertain a tired audience." For the most part, the scripts were original, with an occasional public domain classic like Chaucer's "The Pardoner's Tale" and Edward Everett Hale's "The Man without a Country" to diversify the fare. The casts were a mix of unknowns—many of whom (George Nader, Wally Cox, Shirley Jones, Rita Moreno, Marjorie Lord) would not remain so for long—and recognizable names from the past that still registered with viewers (Geraldine Fitzgerald, Richard Greene, Ann Savage, John Agar, Harry Davenport, Douglas Dumbrille, Gene Raymond, Trudy Marshall).

Although *Fireside Theatre* fell under the rubric of "filmed television," for the first three months of its existence some of the shows were live, including the inaugural one, "Friend of the Family," starring Yul Brynner and Virginia Gilmore (then Brynner's wife). Gilmore was the better known, at least to moviegoers who remembered her from *Swamp Water*, *Berlin Correspondent*, *The Loves of Edgar Allan Poe*, and the Danny Kaye musical *Wonder Man*. Two years later, Brynner became a Broadway star when he appeared opposite Gertrude Lawrence in *The King and I*, winning an Oscar for his performance in the 1956 film version. The prospect of seeing the early work of future stars like Brynner made *Fireside Theatre* watchable—in addition to the swiftly unfolding plots.

Wisbar was the first host of *Fireside Theatre* (1949–53), followed by golden-haired Gene Raymond (1953–55). On 20 September 1953, an unusual event occurred in television: *The Loretta Young Show* premiered on NBC and lasted until 10 September 1961. The Oscar-winning Young was one of the biggest Hollywood stars to make a successful transition to television. Hers was an anthology show—but with a difference. Instead of a different story with a different star each Sunday evening, it was a different story with the same star—herself. Young was also a close friend of Jane, and when Jane converted to Catholicism in 1954, their bond became closer. It was not coincidental that, in 1955, Jane became the host of *Fireside Theatre*.

Young entered the business as an extra when she was four; that was in 1917, the year of Jane's birth. In 1952, Young realized the roles she was being handed were not worthy of the actress who surprised Hollywood when she won an Oscar for *The Farmer's Daughter*. Television in 1953 was the new frontier, and Young was ready to settle in with a show that would allow her to expand her range, creating characters more varied than those she had played in the movies. When *The Loretta Young Show* premiered, Jane had no intention of joining her friend on the tube. Her film career was far from over. She received a nomination for *The Blue Veil* and had no dearth of movie offers. She and Young were never rivals or up for the same roles; they were not even from the same studio. Still, Jane was intrigued by Young's phenomenal success in such an intimate medium. Lew Wasserman, who entered television even earlier than Loretta with Revue Productions, was also intrigued. If *The Loretta Young Show*, why not *The Jane Wyman Show*—or something similar? While Loretta provided the inspiration, Wasserman provided the means through Lewman, the production company he and Jane created. Jane's *Fireside Theatre* debut took place on 30 August 1955, with Jane as host and star of "Technical Charge of Murder," in which she played a recluse befriended by a cab driver, who accidentally runs over a man. On 20 September she again acted as host and starred in "Holiday in Autumn," with Fay Wray. Jane chose the scripts, occasionally passing some on to Young that would work better on her show. Young, who was only interested in scripts with a moral, reciprocated when she came upon one whose sole purpose was entertainment.

Jane's television debut, however, did not take place on *Fireside Theatre*; it had occurred eight months earlier on *General Electric Theater* on 2 January 1955. Reagan, naturally, was the host, but she was the star, playing Dr. Amelia Morrow in "Amelia." Since Reagan's introductions were filmed separately, the two probably never met on the set. And if they did, they would have exchanged a curt nod. In a sense, both Jane and Reagan were working for Wasserman. *General Electric Theater* was produced by Revue; *Jane Wyman's Fireside Theatre* was produced by Lewman, Inc., in association with Revue. Each episode of the latter included the Lewman, Inc. and Revue Productions copyrights. But for the three seasons (1955–58) Jane was associated with the show, it was treated as a Revue production. The end credits read "Filmed at Revue Productions in Hollywood."

Because of her film commitments, Jane could not appear in every episode. Unlike Loretta Young, she had not yet retired from the movies. Her film schedule determined her availability. Still, of the eighty-two episodes aired during her three years on the show, she appeared in forty-seven. Jane continued Wisbar's tradition of using a mix of unknowns and established stars. Since she had better contacts in the business than he, she was able to recruit more recognizable names, such as William Bendix, Virginia Grey, Fernando Lamas, Margaret O'Brien, Linda Darnell, Jan Sterling, Joseph Cotten, Lee Marvin, and Peter Lawford.

"Two Sides to Everything" (23 October 1956) was typical of *Jane Wyman's Fireside Theatre*. It opened with Jane and co-star Simon Scott, their backs to the camera, waiting for an elevator. Before the doors open, they kiss quickly, move apart, enter the elevator like two strangers, get off at the same floor, and go to their respective offices. They are Peg and Jim, reporters at rival newspapers—she for the *Morning Bulletin*, he for the *Evening Herald*. Peg's editor forbids fraternization between his employees and those of the *Herald* except in the lobby, at the elevator, and on stairways—hence the furtive kiss.

"Two Sides to Everything" is a swift-moving battle of the sexes, in which Peg scoops Jim when she gets a call to cover a fire at a state prison. One of the convicts behaves so heroically that Peg slants the story in his favor, angling for an early parole by arguing that through his heroism he has paid his debt to society. It was good rhetoric, but not good enough. She did not count on the convict's preference for jail, which causes her to lose her job. Jim's failure to cover the fire had already cost him his. "Two Sides to Everything" recalls *The Awful Truth* and *Adam's Rib*, in which the female emerges as wilier than the male. Earlier, Peg and Jim had appeared on a local talk show in which they traded insults, much to the annoyance of the moderator. However, audiences warmed to the idea of a feuding couple, and Peg and Jim were hired at (for 1956) the handsome salary of three hundred dollars a week for on-air exchanges of nastiness from a man and a woman who would not allow love to interfere with one-upmanship.

Fireside Theatre alternated between quiet, thoughtful dramas and those with a real arc, with action that mounted in intensity until it is resolved. "Birthright" (5 February 1957) represented the first type. The action moved horizontally, stopping periodically for a new revelation, but never rising to a peak. Jane, a nurse in a maternity ward, is in love with a doctor (Tom Tryon), whose parents cannot wait for them to marry so they can have grandchildren. However, the nurse has had a hysterectomy, which, while it will not impede true love, will disappoint her in-laws. Adoption is obviously the solution, but until the plot reaches that stage, vignettes take up the slack: one patient, abandoned by her husband, does not even want to look at her baby (Jane wins her over); another hopes for a son after bearing five daughters (she gets her wish).

"A Widow's Kiss" (9 January 1958) illustrates the second type of drama, in addition to being one of the best. It was a taut melodrama of the eleventh hour school, in which the cavalry/serum/eleventh hour rescue/governor's pardon arrives in time to ensure a happy ending. The first image is that of a spider on a child's bed. Then Jane walks into the frame, noting that widows have been known to spoil a vacation. But she does not mean a woman who has lost her husband; she means a black widow spider. A Mexico vacation comes to an abrupt end when Jane's daughter is bitten by a black widow. Since the local hospital cannot treat the child, Jane drives to San Diego, where she learns that her daughter needs blood from someone bitten by a black widow within the past year. There is only one such person, a woman living in a seedy boarding house. Jane must endure the landlady's suspicions and the husband's advances until she locates the woman, who, after a little intimidation from a police officer, agrees to be a donor.

"Swindler's Inn" (10 April 1958) could have stood on its own without the laugh track and applause grafted on to it. The plot was a version of a "get rich quick scheme" that backfires, sparing the con men and their accomplice jail time and leaving everyone chastened and wiser. Jane, using a Cockney accent that would have fooled Hitchcock, is the housekeeper at a hotel catering to retirees ripe for a scam. One of the con men attempts to pass off a bag lady (Connie Gilchrist) as his mother, in need of a room, so he can bilk the residents of their savings by convincing them that their money would go to disadvantaged children. Jane held her own with Gilchrist, who had the showier part, but since it was Jane's show, she made certain that she would appear in all the important scenes, especially the unmasking.

If Jane seemed like a natural character actress, it was because she was never a leading lady, but a female lead. "Swindler's Inn" affords an opportunity to reevaluate Jane's career, seeing her as a character actress from the beginning, whether in a minor role or a lead. She and Nancy Davis had one thing in common: neither could trade on her beauty. The proof was in the performance. While Nancy remained within her limitations, Jane kept stretching herself.

The end of *Jane Wyman's Fireside Theatre* in May 1958 marked the end of the series. ABC aired reruns in the summer of 1963 under the name *Jane Wyman Presents*. The ratings began to fall in 1956, despite the new audiences that Jane's presence attracted. Still, *Fireside Theatre* enjoyed a decade-long run, earning a place in television history as the first successful anthology series.

Fireside Theatre was not the only Revue production in which Jane appeared. She guest-starred in two episodes of *Wagon Train*, a long-running (1957–65) one-hour series. The hour-long format made *Wagon Train* seem like a feature film. Jane, who made two westerns, was surprisingly at home in the Old West, looking as if she could easily pass for a pioneer woman. In "The Story of Dr. Willoughby" (5 November 1958) she played the title character, a doctor, whom the men dismiss as a "female sawbones." When she identifies herself as "Doctor," one of them jeers, "If you're a doctor, I'm the stork." Snide remarks are the prelude to a story about the perennial need to prove oneself, which Dr. Willoughby does. As a doctor, she is used to issuing orders. She all but commands the wagon master, Major Adams (Ward Bond), to find her a place on the wagon train, which causes the story to veer off in another direction, as the crusty geezer is humanized by a woman, whose devotion to her profession wins him over. She even restores an alcoholic's faith in women by not repulsing him when he kisses her.

Like many westerns, *Wagon Train* was an odyssey, in this case from St. Joseph, Missouri (Jane's birth place) to California. The route never varied, but the encounters did. The theme of male chauvinism was woven throughout "The Story of Dr. Willoughby." Even Indians practice it. When Dr. Willoughby and Major Adams are tending to a wounded Indian chief, the doctor is forbidden to remove the bullet because she is a woman. In a stunningly acted scene, Jane, lowering her voice, carefully explains what Bond must do. Although the viewer suspects they will not be killed, there is still the possibility of a cliffhanger. Suspense is generated through Jane's sotto voce instructions, given slowly so that Bond can execute them. Despite her fears, the doctor is in total control, and despite his inexperience, the wagon master proves an apt pupil. The bullet is removed, but ever the physician. Dr. Willoughby chooses to remain with her patient until he makes a full recovery. Although she is no longer part of the wagon train, one has no doubt that Dr. Willoughby will reach her destination, and that the men who scoffed at the idea of female doctor will now think differently.

Hannah, Jane's character in "The Wagon Train Mutiny" (19 September 1962) was the antithesis of Carol Willoughby. Self-righteous and defiantly racist, Hannah refuses to believe a wounded Comanchero, who warns that there will be a second attack on the wagon train in three days. Because the Comacheroes were New Mexican traders, many of mixed blood, whose best clientele were Comanches, the settlers viewed them with suspicion. Distrust increased after the Civil War, when it became known that some Comancheros supplied Comanches with firearms during the Indian wars.

"The Wagon Train Mutiny" would have played better as a half-hour teleplay. There is just so much drama that can be generated from a script that poses a series of questions together with an answer key. Will Hannah mend her racist ways? Yes. Can the wounded Comanchero be trusted? Yes. And what will Hannah do with the knife she is holding? Probably cut up vegetables. She cannot bring herself to use it on the wounded boy, even though she holds him responsible for her son's death. If she killed him, it would send the script off in another direction—in addition to infuriating Latinos. In fact, Hannah practically adopts the boy at the end. But as a character Hannah, despite her regeneration, was all cardboard.

Jane worked regularly in television, appearing on series (*The Red Skelton Hour, My Three Sons, The Love Boat, Charlie's Angels*) and in TV movies (*The Failing of Raymond, Amanda Fallon, The Incredible Journey of Doctor Meg Laurel*), never expecting to become a primetime soap opera queen. Capitalizing on the success of *Dallas*, the popular Friday nighttime soap, CBS followed up with another, *Falcon Crest*, after *Dallas* moved from 10:00 p.m.–11:00 p.m. to 9:00 p.m.–10:00 p.m. in December 1981. What oil was to *Dallas*, wine was to *Falcon Crest*, which moved into the vacant 10:00 p.m.–11:00 p.m. slot. And what J. R. Ewing (Larry Hagman) was to *Dallas*, Angela Channing (Jane) was to *Falcon Crest*.

Falcon Crest was the creation of Earl Hamner, who was responsible for one of television's best-loved shows, *The Waltons* (1972–81). The inspiration for the former was a story he heard about an Italian woman who ran a winery from her kitchen, which she treated as an office. *Falcon Crest* would feature an Italian matriarch who ran her business from an office in her home. The show would also be the antithesis of *The Waltons*, with a family that acted as if ethical behavior was intended for everyone else.

Jane owed the role to her agent, Robert Raison, who thought she would be the ideal Angela Channing. Jane thought so, too. Her decision to play a matriarch who will do anything—mislead, deceive, coerce, cajole, intimidate, scheme, blackmail, even remarry—to maintain control of the Falcon Crest vineyards was not surprising. She had played assertive women before both in film (*The Lost Weekend, The Yearling, So Big, Lucy Gallant*) and on television—women, like Dr. Willoughby, who, when they wanted something, made certain they got it, stopping short of murder. Others would murder in *Falcon Crest,* including Angela's older daughter, Julia, but not Angela. When Angela was engaged in a power play, all Jane had to do was give her voice an edge, raising it a notch from authoritative to domineering. Otherwise, she would use her normal voice, cunningly self-assured, but more businesslike, as if a discussion were a transaction and a conversation a one-sided dialogue.

To prevent viewers from switching channels after *Dallas,* the inaugural show, "In My Father's House" (4 December 1981), needed a hook. So the first episode of *Falcon Crest* opened with an amorous boy and a flighty girl on the verge of making love in a winery, only to be interrupted by a loutish drunk, whose death the girl accidentally causes after he pursues the boy up a flight of stairs to a catwalk. Trying to separate them, the girl knocks the drunk over the railing to his death. The dialogue is minimal. All we know is that the boy (later identified as Turner Bates) is a field hand, the drunk is "Uncle Jason," and the girl responsible for his death is his niece.

The format would be the same as *Dallas*. Main plots and subplots are intercut, so that at times they seem to be unfolding concurrently. The second scene seems totally unrelated to the first: a pilot learns that his plane will be delayed. The third returns to the fatal accident. We see Angela for the first time and learn that the girl is Emma, her younger daughter, making Jason Angela's brother. Angela, showing no emotion, has Jason's corpse placed in his truck, which her faithful manservant, Chao-Li, sends over a cliff, making it seem that Jason had an accident while driving under the influence. But why not simply call the police and have Emma explain the circumstances? Angela has her reasons. Strange as it may seem, before she married newspaper tycoon Douglas Channing, she was Angela Gioberti, from an illustrious winemaking family. Although Jane played Angela Channing to perfection, it was best that we never saw her as a Gioberti. Jane neither looked nor acted Italian. Ethnicity disappeared with her marriage to Channing.

In scene four, the pilot is identified as Chase Gioberti (Robert Foxworth), Angela's nephew and Jason's son, who lives in New York with his wife, Maggie (Susan Sullivan), and their two children, Cole (William R. Moses) and Vickie (Jamie Rose). Until their potential has been exhausted, all of them become recurring characters. The family heads out to Falcon Crest for Jason's funeral, at which Angela delivers the eulogy. In a voice firm but unfeeling, she refers to her brother as "my friend, my dearest friend," and then asserts with total candor that she is now the sole owner of Falcon Crest. The eulogy was characteristic of Jane's line readings throughout the series, dispassionate and fearlessly regal. And Angela's "dearest friend" was really her mortal enemy, as Cole discovered during a trip to Italy ("Lord of the Manor," 22 January 1982).

Once the will is read, the reasons for the cover up become clear. Chase will receive his grandfather's original fifty acres, the balance—about five hundred acres—going to Jason and Angela. In the event of the "natural" death of one of the survivors, the other is the sole heir. Thus, since Jason died a "natural" death by driving off a cliff in a drunken state, Falcon Crest is Angela's. She plans to buy out her nephew, assuming that, as a New Yorker, he would have no interest in the property. But Chase believes a move to Falcon Crest will bring his family closer together. Angela's face registers no sign of disappointment; in fact, she welcomes him. And at the end of the opening episode, she stands on the porch, a falcon in hand. CBS had a winner.

Angela will do anything in her power to get Chase to leave Tuscany Valley. When Paul Salinger, a Vietnam vet like Chase, fails to enlist Chase's support in setting up a charter aircraft operation, he seeks out Angela, who is more than willing to bankroll him, if he can get Chase to leave Falcon Crest so that she can buy up his property ("A Time for Saboteurs," 11 December 1981). Taking Angela at her word, Salinger resorts to sabotage, turning on the irrigation pump, flooding the vineyards, and endangering the harvest. Expecting payment for what he has done, Salinger is confronted by an enraged Angela. It would not have mattered if only Chase's vineyards were affected, but hers were, too. Self above all, and to thine own self be true. Angela knew herself; Salinger did not know Angela Channing.

Angela is even willing to drive a wedge between Chase and Maggie. When Maggie writes a screenplay, Angela bribes an opportunistic producer to encourage her, hoping that his presence will subvert their marriage. By the sixth season, the marriage starts unraveling without help from anyone. And Angela is not above using her own grandson, Lance Cumson (Lorenzo Lamas), to achieve her ends. Setting her sights on the Agretti Vineyards, she forces Lance to marry Melissa Agretti. It becomes a marriage in name only, since Melissa is pregnant with Cole Gioberti's child. And why pay a smooth-talking lawyer like Phillip Erikson (Mel Ferrer) for his counsel, if you could marry him and get it for free? Like Lance's marriage to Melissa, Angela's marriage to Erikson is based purely on expediency.

Jason's death—and the will with the curious codicil that if one of the children dies "under mysterious circumstances," the victim's heirs would inherit what is rightfully theirs—became a plot point during the first season. Although the victim is Jason, and his only heir is Chase, Angela remains unperturbed. She made certain that there was nothing "mysterious" about Jason's death, suggesting that she had already seen the will. The traumatized Emma has not forgotten the incident, referring to it as her uncle's "two deaths." And there is her lover, Turner Bates, who knows what happened that night and expects to be compensated for his silence. But before he can extort ten thousand dollars from Angela ("The Extortionist," 15 January 1982), he dies in a car accident. Although Bates's death is similar to Jason's, Angela had nothing to do with it. But she has no regrets. It's just one more obstacle out of the way.

Like *Dallas*, *Falcon Crest* featured guest stars such as Cliff Robertson, Gina Lollobrigida, Celeste Holm, Kim Novak, Anne Jeffreys, Jane Greer, Eve Arden, Morgan Fairchild, Leslie Caron, Robert Stack—and the best known of them all, the quintessential movie star, the "Sweater Girl" herself, Lana Turner, as the French-born, British-educated millionairess Jacqueline Perrault. Improbable as it seems, Jacqueline was Jason's wife and Chase's mother. After divorcing Jason, she remarried twice, with each husband wealthier than the last. Like Angela, Jacqueline owns vineyards, and like Angela, she is accustomed to playing the diva and has no intention of conceding the title to an American—particularly one who bottles California wine. In "Family Reunion" (19 February 1982), Jacqueline decides to visit her son, ostensibly to reconnect, but ultimately to lure him back to France to manage her vineyards.

When Jane learned that Lana would be appearing on the show, she summoned Earl Hamner to her dressing room and asked if it were true. When told it was, Jane fumed: "She is not a lady." She may not have been a lady by Jane's standards, but on *Falcon Crest* Turner behaved as if she were Lady Lana. Jane could get along with practically everyone on the show except Lana, who was constantly late, often as much as five hours. Jane refused to sit next to her on the set. Jane did her own makeup, but Lana needed a makeup artist, who provided her with a face unlined and masklike, evenly textured and creamily smooth. She behaved like a queen whose kingdom was wherever she resided, even if it were at another's estate—or on another's series. Lana was a movie star and onetime sex symbol; Jane was a first-rate actress. The two are not synonymous. Lana could act when the script gave her a chance, as it did in *The Postman Always Rings Twice*, *The Bad and the Beautiful*, *Peyton Place*, and *Imitation of Life*. But Lana's past clung to her. She was always the glamorous screen star and lover of gangster Johnny Stompanato, whom her fourteen-year-old daughter, Cheryl, stabbed to death with a kitchen knife, presumably to protect her mother. The charge was justifiable homicide; the publicity did not blacken Lana's reputation, only empurpled it.

Lana's image suited her character in "Family Reunion." As Jacqueline, she makes her first appearance, goddess-like, with no sign of jet lag and with luggage that looks as if it had just been purchased at Neiman Marcus. Her mink coat is partially open, revealing a shimmering white dress. She is, in fact, a study in white, with finely spun platinum hair that makes a crown superfluous. Royalty has arrived, and the California wine country has never seen anything like Jacqueline Perrault—or Lana Turner. Inevitably, Jacqueline and Angela will meet, but in the inverse of the classic meet cute. Jacqueline visits Jason's grave, to which Emma has also come. When Emma, in an Ophelia-like state of sweet delirium, starts babbling about Jason's "fall," Jacqueline, who had been fed the accident version, begins to question her. Angela's arrival prevents further questioning. Facing each other, with Jason's grave between them, they exchange greetings—or rather, names. "Jacqueline?" Angela asks, to which Jacqueline replies, "Angela?" Cut to commercial.

When Angela invites Jacqueline to dinner at Falcon Crest, Jacqueline, who is staying with Chase and his family, suggests that Angela dine with *them*. Angela has no choice but to accept. Jacqueline's is a catered affair, formal and pretentious, which Angela finds irksome. She is also unaccustomed to hearing California wines described as inferior to French ones, an opinion Jacqueline proclaims as if it were the first principle of oenology. Having had enough, Angela bolts from the table and returns to Falcon Crest, smarting from what may have been her first defeat—made easier by downing a few glasses of her own vintage. But *Falcon Crest* had not seen the last of Lana Turner. At the end of "Family Reunion," Chase is so pleased to be reunited with his mother that he invites her back.

The death of Jason subplot was still not resolved. It was good for a few more episodes, including a two-part, first season cliffhanger. In the first, "Penultimate Questions " (9 April 1982), Chase, now county supervisor (much to Angela's chagrin), has heard enough conflicting accounts of his father's death to demand an inquest. Angela is unfazed, confident that her slick lawyer, Phillip Erikson, will defend her if it can be proved that she has committed perjury and obstructed justice. But her perfidy was all for a good cause: hers and Falcon Crest, which were identical. Furthermore, she could not afford to besmirch the family name with a death caused by a hired hand's lust for her daughter.

Angela assumed that Emma, who behaves as if she were mentally unstable (and is, somewhat), would never be called to testify. But Emma has reconnected with her father, Douglas Channing, who, after a heart attack, has returned to Falcon Crest, hoping for a reconciliation with Angela and his daughters. When Emma and Channing arrive at the inquest, Angela interrupts the proceedings, insisting that her daughter is too distraught to testify. Meanwhile, Channing has another heart attack, this time fatal.

Throughout the episode, Jane played Angela as a woman who had no qualms about what she did. Angela is not some kind of sulfurous villain. She considers herself a "vineyardist," who made Tuscany Valley the touchstone of American winemaking and therefore should enjoy privileges denied lesser folk. She had originally testified that when she and Emma were returning from San Francisco, she noticed Jason's truck zigzagging along the road, and that, when she arrived at Falcon Crest, she learned that the truck plunged over a cliff and burst into flames. There was no trip to San Francisco, as anyone who recalled the *Falcon Crest* premiere knew. Angela's justification for perjury was simple: Since Jason was dead, the manner of his death was unimportant. The manner in which he died matters only in terms of the publicity it would generate. Driving off a cliff is less damaging than the truth, as it would not involve Emma or reflect unfavorably on Falcon Crest.

Angela's sang froid heats up in "Ultimate Answers" (16 April 1982). Emma eludes her captors and appears at the hearing. In a moment of rare (and implausible) lucidity, she accurately describes what happened on the night of Jason's death, including the cover up. Flash cuts are inserted for those who missed the inaugural episode or had forgotten it. Angela, believing in her own pragmatic way that she did nothing wrong, is not even concerned about the charges that could be brought against her. Her only concern is losing half of Falcon Crest to Chase, now that the "mysterious death" codicil has been resolved in his favor. Despite the will, Angela will not settle for half. "I'll fight you all the way" are her parting words to Chase, who offers her his hand. Angela accepts it, but unlike his, hers is gloved.

Jane created a thoroughly consistent character devoid of contradictions and incongruities, which was not the case with some of the other characters. *Falcon Crest* suffered the fate of all soap operas, daytime or primetime. To sustain audience interest, the villains become more lethal, the virtuous develop a dark side, and characters considered expendable either die or relocate. Plausibility buckles under the weight of coincidence, incongruity, disappearance, reappearance, marriage, remarriage, death, and disasters. But it was these violations of verisimilitude that made the series so fascinating. Who knew what bizarre disclosure would occur next? What virgin would turn whore? And what character would do a 180-degree turn?

Cole Gioberti, for one. Once the epitome of the All-American Boy, he is on the verge of becoming the All-American Stud, even impregnating Melissa's cousin. Assuming audiences had seen enough of Cole's hormonal side, the writers decided his days at Falcon Crest were over and banished him to Australia. His parents, who seemed like a monogamous couple, prove otherwise—particularly Maggie with Richard Channing, who leaves a bouquet of roses on the bed in appreciation of a night of good sex.

It was precisely such character transformations that made the series addictive. "Chain Reaction" (8 May 1987) took courtroom melodrama to a level beyond *The Paradine Case* and *Witness for the Prosecution*. Angela's son-in-law, Tony Cumson, has been accused of murdering the sadistic gangster, Roland Saunders (Robert Stack), whose mistress was Kit Marlowe, Cumson's former lover. Kit, played by the glamorous Kim Novak, interrupts the trial by admitting that *she* killed Saunders, at one point even poisoning his cigars (a technique that did not work). In the middle of the cross-examination, Peter Stavros (Angela's third husband) jumps up and admits that *he* killed Saunders in retaliation for his stepdaughter's murder. It was jaw-droppers like "Chain Reaction" that made spending an hour with Angela and company worthwhile. *Falcon Crest* made the improbable possible, once you accepted two basic premises: anything can happen to anyone, and anyone can be whatever the writers decide. Except for Angela and a few others like Chao-Li, stability of character is nonexistent. Angela works out of her study, devising ways to secure her ever-tottering throne. Saddled with a basket case like Melissa, Lance's ex-wife, Angela encourages Melissa's singing career, even financing her LP, which makes Melissa even more neurotic when she hears the poorly reproduced album. But as Angela calmly reminds her, she at least has an album. Jane reveled in playing the merry Machiavel. It was like a family game: Who screws whom, who does whom out of what, and who emerges on top.

Season two introduced two major subplots: the identity of both Richard Channing's mother and the murderer of Carlo Agretti. In "The Challenge" (1 October 1982), we learn that Richard Channing (David Selby), supposedly Douglas Channing's illegitimate son and now publisher of the *New San Francisco Globe*, has spent considerable amounts of money trying to learn the identity of his mother. Angela, believing he was the product of a liaison between her husband and his (unknown) mistress, wants satisfaction: "There is a woman responsible for all of my pain, and someone has to pay for it." In retrospect, the line is as ironic as Oedipus cursing himself in *Oedipus Rex*. The woman, as we learn later, is Angela herself, Richard Channing's birth mother. (Spoiler alert: the baby was taken from Angela at birth). Meanwhile, another woman will claim to be Richard's mother: Jacqueline.

It was bad enough that the silvery Jacqueline/Lana was revealed to be not only the mistress of Douglas Channing, but also part of a Mafia-like organization called the Cartel. In "United We Stand" (17 December 1982), Jacqueline interrupts an altercation between Chase and Richard Channing by thrusting a birth certificate in front of them: "Here. It's your birth certificate. You are both my sons." Lana delivers the news as if it were a curtain line in a hoary melodrama. Jacqueline knows that Richard is not her son, but Angela's. Although Richard's illegitimacy was a red herring, it was good for a few more episodes. In "Pas de Deux" (7 January 1983), Richard, unable to forgive Jacqueline for having him placed in an orphanage and later adopted, blurts out publicly that he is Jacqueline's son. It's now square-off time for Jacqueline and Angela— Jacqueline in her signature white, and Angela in red blouse and dark skirt. Jane, adopting a superior tone and relishing the opportunity to lord it over a woman "who abandoned her bastard son," practically forces Lana to sound repentant. But Jacqueline is playacting. The tale she fabricates is so bizarre that it could even be believable. Jacqueline has the upper hand; she knows who Richard Channing's mother is, but the writers are withholding the information. Let the revelation age a bit, like wine.

Lana's days on *Falcon Crest* were numbered. In "Climax" (11 March 1983), the Agretti murder subplot is finally resolved. Earlier in the series, Cole was the chief suspect ("Murder One," 22 October 1982). At Vickie Gioberti's wedding to Nick Hogan (like most marriages in the series, theirs is short-lived), Chase unmasks the real murderer, who also made an attempt on his and Maggie's life in the winery. The culprit is, of all people, Angela's daughter Julia, who bludgeoned Agretti to death to prevent his taking over Falcon Crest, and who tried to kill off Chase and Maggie for the same reason. Trapped, Julia pulls out a revolver and fires into the crowd. "Climax" marked the end of the second season. All we see is a casket lowered into the grave. It would not be until the fall that viewers learned that the victim was Jacqueline Perrault. So much for Lana.

Who would have thought that Julia (Abby Dalton of the beatific smile) harbored such a deadly alter ego, much less become so unhinged that she would be institutionalized in a facility staffed by nuns and eventually become one herself? Characters deemed non-recyclable were relegated to the discard bin, marked for disappearance or death. Death is simpler; just diversify—plane crash, heart attack, murder, drowning, fire, earthquake, fall, childbirth. Protatic characters are, by their very nature, disposable. Others disappear, relocate, or are institutionalized. Revelations abound. Julia had an illegitimate child whom she thought had died at birth, but who grew up to become a priest, giving Angela another grandson besides Lance—and a member of the clergy, to boot. Richard Channing, supposedly Douglas's illegitimate son, whose mother was reputedly Jacqueline, is actually Angela's son, who, as soon as he was born, was spirited away by his father and Jacqueline to prevent his becoming a male version of Angela (which he becomes, anyway). Placed in a French orphanage, he is later adopted by a business tycoon (E.G. Marshall). Since Richard Channing has designs on Falcon Crest, Angela's competitor and possible nemesis is her own son. She also has another grandson, Michael Channing, Richard's son by Cassandra Wilder, who died in childbirth.

Maggie, who had previously been stalked, kidnapped, and raped, was written out of the series after drowning in a swimming pool while trying to retrieve a ring. Meanwhile, Falcon Crest kept changing hands, until the end of the ninth season when it reverted to Angela, bringing the series full circle. But there were seven more seasons to go, each with its share of disclosures, reversals, betrayals, deceptions, and violence that increased exponentially.

The first two seasons were the least outrageous. By the third, *Falcon Crest* began to resemble a kaleidoscope with flashing colors, one gaudier than the next, until the spectrum was exhausted and all that remained was monochrome. One could write a dissertation on the intertwining genealogies, illegitimate births, fornications, adulteries, divorces, remarriages, murders, disappearances, and kidnappings. The writers had adopted the "all in the family" approach, stopping short of incest. If one character can sleep with or marry another, so much the better. That tack is preferable to inventing a new character who might have to be written out after an episode or two. For example, after Chase's death, Maggie marries Richard Channing, neither of them knowing that he is Angela's son—which makes Maggie, Angela's niece by her marriage to Chase, also her daughter-in-law. Angela's grandson Lance at one point marries Richard's stepdaughter, Lorraine, making him Richard's son-in-law and nephew. Richard Channing is the most consistent of them all. At least he stays with Maggie's side of the family. Before marrying Maggie, he had, under duress, married her sister. After Maggie's death, he marries her second cousin.

Family Theatre's maxim, "The family that prays together stays together," could apply to *Falcon Crest* if "prays" were changed to "preys." "The family that sleeps together keeps together" is another possibility. At least the intermarrying is not as bizarre as it is in Wagner's *The Ring of the Nibelungs*, in which Siegmund commits both incest and adultery with his married sister, Sieglinde, and their son Siegfried takes his aunt Brünhilde as his wife. *Falcon Crest* is middlebrow Oedipalism. Instead of a man's inadvertently marrying his mother and siring sons and daughters who are also his brothers and sisters, there is a family tree whose limbs sprout branches and whose roots keep bifurcating until there are no further dendrites. *Falcon Crest* suffered from the same plot template syndrome as *Dallas*. When the central character is a constant, the others become variables. They can change, revealing other aspects of themselves, but Angela is impervious to change. For her, there can only be further machinations. She has one love, Falcon Crest, which takes precedence over her own children. She has proprietary rights, which are inviolable. All Angela wants is for Falcon Crest to pass on to her heirs, while remaining hers for the duration of her life.

Angela was a unique character, and Jane played her as such. There is something childlike about Angela's methods, which, diabolical as they may seem, are in sync with her logic. To Angela, Chase Gioberti is an interloper with no right to Falcon Crest, despite the terms of the will. She will therefore use any means in her power to keep him—or anyone else—from treading on her turf. The end justifies the means. And if the end is good or at least morally neutral—and keeping Falcon Crest out of alien hands could qualify as either—the means are uncontestable. Jane's Angela Channing was delightfully Jesuitical. Expediency was all, and the way Jane widened her eyes as if to underscore the reasonableness of her actions made it seem that whatever she did was perfectly natural.

One only wishes that Angela had fared better in the last season. When Jane granted her first interview in eight years to Dominick Dunne, he asked, "It is true that you are going to be smothered with a pillow in the third episode [of the ninth series] and the audience won't know whether you are alive or dead?" After a pause, Jane said pointedly, "I *am* going into a coma for a while." End of discussion. Actually, someone does try to smother Angela with a pillow, and she does go into a coma—and into a mental hospital. Dunne had a good source.

In "Charley" (6 October 1989), Emma, cursed with a history of smarmy lovers, is wooed by Charley St. James. When Angela disapproves, Charley attempts to smother her with a pillow, sending her into a coma and Jane into her physician's care for dramatic weight loss (she had dropped to one hundred pounds), severe arthritis, and diabetes. When Jane returned to the series for the final three episodes, her character was thrown into plot purgatory. It was as if the writers wanted Angela to pay for her sins, which, compared to those of some of the other characters, were peccadillos. Angela is kidnapped, escapes, and is then subjected to a mental competency hearing, initiated by Richard Channing. Like mother, like son. To maintain control of Falcon Crest, one could imagine Angela doing the same to Richard. It's all in the family. Once the truth comes out about Angela's relationship to Richard, the narrative arc sags to ground level, and no amount of tightening could restore the original tautness. It was windup time. In the final episode, "Home Again"(17 May 1990), Angela and Richard agree that after her death each of Richard's sons—Michael, from his marriage to Cassandra Wilder, and Kevin, his adoptive son—will receive 25 percent of the estate, with the remainder going to Lance.

For the finale, Jane wrote her own coda, an interior monologue accompanied by a montage of familiar scenes, in which she paid tribute to both the series and its creator. At the reception following the wedding of Richard and Lauren, Angela steps out on the veranda and muses on the past:

> Grandfather, how long has it been since you came to the valley and planted your first vine from Italy? . . . Seems like only yesterday. I think of all the people who've passed through these vineyards . . . . Yes, the past has its place, but I'll keep looking to the future. After all, there's a wedding today. Children are playing, more children are on the way, and, of course, the land. Always the land. People come and go, but the land endures. I toast to you Falcon Crest, and long may you live.

Jane gave Angela the last word, vindicating her by emphasizing what was always apparent: Angela's primary goal was to keep Falcon Crest within the family and out the hands of opportunists like Michael Sharpe, who would turn it into an industrial park. Jane may not have gone out in a blaze of glory, but it was still a lovely light.

Chapter 31

Unholy Families

SOME EX-WIVES CAN MAINTAIN A FRIENDLY RELATIONSHIP, BUT NOT Jane and Nancy. Each felt the other was usurping the spotlight, which was never known to be impartial. How could Jane Wyman, even though she was an Oscar-winner and a television star, compete with the First Lady? If Jane was mentioned in the same context with Nancy, it was as Ronald Reagan's first or ex-wife, neither of which was a welcome epithet for someone who considered herself first and foremost an actress. As Reagan eased his way out of performing and into politics, Nancy accompanied him, until both had shed their performing past—except when writers insisted on revisiting it. But the tension between Jane and Nancy persisted, even though their paths did not cross.

They all shared a common bond: Maureen and Michael. Nancy was no more meant to be a stepmother than Jane was meant to be a stay-at-home mom. Jane was incapable of putting her children before herself. Although in her autobiography Maureen had more to say about Reagan than Jane, she summed up her mother in a single, thought-provoking sentence: "There was very little of Jane Wyman in any of her screen performances, and at the same time there was all of Jane Wyman in each and every role." One might also add that there are traces of Sarah Jane Fulks in the young Selena in *So Big*, the emotionally fragile Laura in *The Glass Menagerie*, the childlike Belinda in *Johnny Belinda*, the trusting Eve in *Stage Fright*, and the tragic Ruth in *Miracle in the Rain*. The effervescent Jane Wyman of the high spirits and sparkling eyes was one of many emanations. Jane immersed herself so thoroughly in each role that she carried the character home with her. When she was working, there was no time for Jane the mother. She was so determined to succeed that she believed she could only give a credible performance by making the character part of her. It worked—at least for her.

Maureen was her father's daughter. Her memoir, *First Father, First Daughter*, is dedicated to "Ronald Wilson Reagan, who made it all possible and to Dennis Cormac Revell (her third husband) who makes it all fun." Michael was not exactly his mother's son, but more of a chronicler of her moods and obsessions, which in time he understood were those of an artist. At the beginning of his spiritual autobiography, *Twice Adopted*, Michael distinguishes between those in whose memory it was written—his birth mother, his sister Maureen, "and, of course, my dad, Ronald Wilson Reagan"—and those to whom it is dedicated: his wife, Jane, and their two children. Michael is more understanding of Jane than Maureen is, even though he and his mother went through a period of estrangement. Although Michael had every reason to resent Jane, who shipped him off to boarding school at five and a half, he confesses to remembering two women on Mother's Day: his birth mother, Irene Flaugher, and Jane, "the mother who brought me home from Queen of Angels Hospital, the mother who raised me and taught me some of the most important lessons of my life." His picture of Jane is quite different from the one he drew of her in *On the Outside Looking In* (1987), in which he painted her in shades darker than the Wicked Witch of the West. The balm of time healed the wound; seventeen years later, he saw Jane trying to be a mother but succeeding as an actress, a woman who was better at playing mothers like Selena in *So Big* than being one.

It is natural for anyone with actor parents to consider pursuing their parents' profession. Maureen was drawn to both performing and politics—the former first. She tried theatre, a medium that her mother had avoided, working regionally in such shows as *Guys and Dolls, Any Wednesday*, and *Last of the Red Hot Lovers*. Broadway did not beckon, and television and movies offered no hope of stardom. Maureen played clubs and even entertained troops in Vietnam. Soon she realized that she was drawn to a much larger stage, her father's, and to the Republican Party, which she proudly admitted she joined before Reagan did. An unsuccessful bid for the Senate in 1982 did not lessen Maureen's enthusiasm for politics or her admiration for her father, even though their divergent views on abortion and the Equal Rights Amendment cost her his endorsement. Regardless, "he is a unique human being, my father; the White House hasn't taken that away from him."

Maureen was less troubled emotionally than Michael, who, in *Twice Adopted*, described the sexual abuse he suffered over a period of time at the hands of a man who ran an after-school day camp. Learning that he was adopted and wondering if he was illegitimate (he was) was difficult enough. Loss of self-worth and doubts about his own sexuality plagued him until he finally accepted a Christ quite unlike the one taught in the schools he was forced to attend. His Christ can heal even the deepest of wounds, including those caused by childhood molestation.

Since Jane was too immersed in her career to play mother, it was boarding school for both Maureen and Michael. Fortunately Michael, not yet six, ended up in the same school as Maureen, the Chadwick School in Palos Verdes. It was difficult for one so young to be separated from his parents, but Maureen, four years older, played mother and, despite the siblings' separate dormitories, frequently looked in on him. Maureen disliked boarding school as much as Michael, but she was more resilient. She went from Chadwick to Immaculate Heart High School in Los Angeles to the Marymount School in Tarrytown, New York. Jane apparently liked the name "Marymount"; instead of next enrolling her daughter at Marymount College, which is also in Tarrytown, she chose another Marymount, a junior college in Arlington, Virginia, where Maureen lasted a year. At eighteen Maureen declared her independence.

For Michael, the strain of living at home while Maureen was away in Tarrytown was compounded by Jane's tendency to move, which cost him his friends. His resentment turned to anger, followed by a violent confrontation with Jane, who hit him with a riding crop. He retaliated by slapping her in the face and addressing her as "Miss Wyman," lowering her status from mother to the woman who adopted him. What really gnawed at Michael was being separated from his father. Jane's decision to have Michael psychoanalyzed backfired when the psychiatrist suggested that the two of them "take a break from each other," and that Michael stay for a while with the Reagans in their Pacific Palisades home.

Michael had become familiar with the divorce scenario, playing parent against stepparent, until he realized that Nancy was no substitute for Jane—even though he cajoled Nancy into using her contacts to find out the identity of his birth mother. Living in Nancy's house made him appreciate Jane more, despite her faults: "Had my mother tried to be a full-time mom while being a full-time actress, she probably would have failed at both careers." Jane Wyman may not have been a dream mother, but she did not fail as an actress.

Death is tragic enough, but doubly so when a child predeceases her parents. Maureen was diagnosed with melanoma in 1996 and died from it on 8 August 2001, predeceasing her father by three years and her mother by six. The funeral mass took place ten days later at the Cathedral of the Sacred Heart in Sacramento. It was an impressive ceremony with several speakers, the most prominent of whom were Senator John McCain, a fellow Republican and, unlike Maureen, a skin cancer survivor, and Christine Todd Whitman, former governor of New Jersey and head of the Environmental Protection Agency (EPA). Two actors, with a special commitment to the Alzheimer's Foundation, a cause that Maureen embraced after her father went public about having the disease, also spoke: David Hyde Pierce and Shelley Fabares, who lost a grandfather and a mother, respectively, to Alzheimer's.

Jane, Michael, and Maureen's husband and adopted daughter, Dennis and Rita, sat on one side of the cathedral; Nancy, Patti, and Ron sat on the other. Jane placed a cross on the casket, Nancy a text of the Gospels. This was probably the first time Jane and Nancy occupied the same space, albeit in different sections. After the ceremony, Jane, eighty-four and forced to use a cane because of arthritis, and Nancy, eighty and still mobile, encountered each other on the cathedral steps. What transpired between them is known only to Nancy. Most likely, Nancy expressed her condolences, which Jane accepted. Each woman had known her share of tragedy. Jane had lost a daughter, and Nancy, for all practical purposes, had lost a husband, who no longer recognized her. When Nancy got in bed beside him, he asked, "Who are you?"

Even earlier, Nancy had lost her parents. Her stepfather, Loyal Davis, died in 1982; her mother, Edith, died five years later. Patti, who changed her name from Reagan to Davis in 1974, had become so estranged from her family that she did not attend her grandmother's funeral, prompting Nancy to write: "As for Patti—she said she couldn't come to the funeral, that she had travel plans that couldn't be changed." While not a Catholic, Edith was buried from the Church of St. Thomas the Apostle in Phoenix. Drawn to the congregation, she realized the parishioners needed a real church, not the barracks in which mass was being offered. Thus she embarked on a fund-raising campaign to construct a true place of worship. Maureen attended Edith's funeral. Unlike Patti and Ron, Maureen enjoyed a special relationship with her grandmother, partly because of their shared penchant for raunchy humor. Although Maureen's paternal grandmother, Nelle Reagan, had been a "steadying influence" in her earlier years, Maureen's true grandmother was "Deedee" Davis.

If there is such a thing as a creative gene, the Reagan children have it. Maureen was an actress, singer, activist, and memoirist. Michael worked as a widely published author and longtime radio talk show host

(1992–2010). Patti and Ron became celebrities in different way. Like Maureen, Patti tried theatre and television, leaving no impact on either. Posing nude in *Playboy* gave Patti notoriety while causing embarrassment to her parents, who should have been used to her ways by then. Reagan must have known that Patti did not march to the beat of a different drummer, because she was her own drummer. Her pro-choice, antinuclear, and environmental positions polarized father and daughter to the extent that Reagan was forced to admit, "She is against everything I stand for." At least Michael was not a disappointment; he succeeded in the same medium in which his father began his career, radio.

What Reagan and Nancy never realized about Patti was that she was a gifted writer. All they saw in *Home Front* (1986), her novel about the daughter of a California governor who became president, was a Dorian Gray-like portrait of themselves, which was not the case. *Home Front* is a roman à clef coauthored with Los Angeles writer Maureen Strange Foster, who polished each chapter as it was submitted. But the narrative is entirely Patti's, and it is her voice that resonates throughout. You do not have to read more than a few pages to realize that the Canfields are the Reagans: father Robert (Ronald), mother Harriet (Nancy), daughter Elizabeth "Beth" (Patti), and son Brian (Ron). And when Harriet, speaking of the White House, exclaims, "I just can't wait to redecorate," she is echoing Nancy's well-known reaction to 1600 Pennsylvania Avenue. The narrative is bookended by a prologue, in which the family is en route to Canfield's inauguration, and an epilogue, in which Beth receives a call from a former lover, a radicalized Vietnam vet, telling her that the victims of agent orange will be demonstrating in front of the White House the next day. Enclosed within prologue and epilogue is the story of Canfield's rise from spokesman for the fictitious National Motors (General Electric) to governor of California and ultimately the United States presidency.

Patti interweaves Canfield's story with Beth's, which, to a great extent, is her own. Like other autobiographical novelists, she changed names but created decipherable equivalents, like the Canfields. For example, Patti attended the Orme School in Mayer, Arizona, while Beth is sent to Devon, also in Arizona, where "everybody's parents were somebody." Unlike the author, who attended Northwestern University for a year, Beth enrolls at another fictitious school, Montclaire College, outside of Chicago. Patti did the same with Robert and Harriet Canfield, who are like Reagan and Nancy in some ways, and unlike them in others. There is no mention of their ever having been in the movies. Harriet was a department store salesperson when she met her husband—a far cry from a MGM contract actress. Nancy's favorite color, red, is limited to the rosebud motif on the dinnerware. Harriet's lineage is totally unlike Nancy's. Harriet, "a short, fleshy woman," is half Swedish, frustrated by her inability to shed ten pounds. (Nancy was constantly dieting but was never short and fleshy.) Harriet and Nancy, however, have one thing in common: an unswerving devotion to their husbands.

Home Front is a coming of age story, politically at least, in which Beth's disaffection grows into rebellion, as she distances herself from her father's anti-communism, which has led him to believe that communist agitators are behind the student protests against the Vietnam War (as Reagan believed). Beth knew that when her father decided to run for governor, the family dynamic would change. As she matured, she saw herself on the other side of the divide, a liberal with conservative parents, who could no longer abide their politics. She threw herself into the fray, allying herself with the antiwar movement. Since Beth is the president's daughter, her peers find her motives suspect. She has to fight to gain a place in the movement, which she eventually does, despite the obstacles that the Canfield White House placed in her path. "Home front" is a phrase usually associated with World War II, when the nation was united. The home front in the novel is America during the Vietnam War, when the nation was divided. Canfield could not appreciate the difference. For him, war is war, and whenever one's country is involved, choice ceases to exist. It was like a one-party system. Vote "yes" to war, any war. There is no alternative.

Home Front is an extraordinary debut novel, which Patti never surpassed. Few novels about the 1960s captured the period as well as *Home Front*, which portrays the panic caused by the draft lottery that led some men to flee to Canada, feign homosexuality, and behave so outrageously at their pre-induction physicals that they were classified as undesirable. Worst of all was the effect the war had on students, who at one time would have advocated passive resistance but now embraced radicalism, even at the cost of innocent lives. She created a memorable character in Greg, Beth's first lover, who enlisted in the marines, went to 'Nam, and came back disaffected and asocial, living reclusively in the Oregon woods. When Beth asks Greg what happened, his reply echoes that of a generation: "Vietnam happened."

If Reagan and Nancy were displeased with *Home Front*, it could not have been because of their portraits in it. Since Patti did not resort to caricature, they could not claim that they were reduced to cartoon figures.

The novel was not about them. It was about the narrator, Beth, whose initiation into sex, discreetly rendered, may have shocked her parents. But at least Patti does not make Beth the result of premarital sex. What should have impressed the Reagans was their daughter's gift for poetry. The novel is studded with Beth's poems, one of which, "A Marriage," is a grim parody of a ceremony in which the groom is a soldier and the bride, his rifle:

> *before the altar*
> *the old-enough-to-know youth and his gun*
> *trembled in holy wedlock,*
> *and sealed their union with salute,*
> *but beyond the altar*
> *death's blood blurted out the half-mast truth.*

It is as fine an antiwar poem as Wilfred Owen's "Dulce et Decorum Est."

Like his sister, Ron Reagan was a liberal. In fact, he was so liberal that on *Saturday Night Live* he re-created the scene in *Risky Business* in which Tom Cruise danced in his shirt and briefs. One would like to think his parents were amused, but they probably were appalled. Still, Ron Reagan was more than an exhibitionist; he was a talented dancer, who won a scholarship to the Joffrey Ballet School in 1979 and performed with the company until January 1983, when he asked for a release from his contract. Like his siblings, he published a memoir, *My Father at 100* (2011), written with a candor that could not mask his deep feelings, in which he speculated that his father began showing symptoms of Alzheimer's in 1986 at the time of the Iran-Contra Affair, in which a covert arms sale to Iran was authorized in exchange for the American hostages being held in Lebanon, with some of the money diverted to the anti-communist Nicaraguan contras. The disclosure of what was essentially an illegal action caused many to question Reagan's credibility, but it did not blacken his reputation. More likely, Reagan did not have Alzheimer's in 1986 (he went public about it in 1994), but was simply forgetful, as he often was. Still, Reagan left office in 1989 with one of the highest approval ratings of any president in American history.

The Reagans were not a dysfunctional family. It was just that Reagan, Jane, and Nancy functioned at a level that only those who have occupied that or a similar level would understand. If, as Michael Reagan observed, Jane could never have doubled as actress and mother, no president and first lady could fulfill their obligations to their country and to their children equally well. The children did not do badly; they enjoyed their own degree of celebrity.

Jane was a celebrity to the end, changing residences regularly—not with the idea of finding something better, but something simpler. When she was filming *Falcon Crest*, she had a condo in Santa Monica, overlooking the Pacific. She did not consider moving even after the series was cancelled in 1990. She worked occasionally thereafter, playing Jane Seymour's mother in "The Visitor" on *Dr. Quinn, Medicine Woman* (1993) and appearing as herself in the documentaries *Wild Bill: Hollywood Maverick—The Life and Times of William A. Wellman* (1995), and *Off the Menu: Last Days of Chasen's* (1997), a valedictory to the fabled restaurant. Jane and Nancy were both interviewees in *Hollywood Maverick*, having worked with Wellman in *Magic Town* and *The Next Voice Your Hear*, respectively. In *Last Days of Chasen's* Jane appeared as herself, but Nancy was listed as "Nancy Davis (uncredited)." These were the only times Jane and Nancy appeared together on film, albeit in different segments.

Jane seemed at home in Santa Monica, where she was a regular at the Bob Burns Restaurant, the closest she could find to Chasen's, which used to be *her* place, until the former president and first lady made it theirs. Still, it was a good life—but to Jane, it was just life.

When Loretta Young married Jean Louis in 1993 (she was eighty; he, eighty-four) and moved to Palm Springs, Jane felt the urge to relocate as well. There was nothing to keep her in Los Angeles, only memories that would never see a memoir. Jane decided on Rancho Mirage, a resort community in Riverside County, 120 miles southeast of Los Angeles. Once Jane settled there, Loretta enlisted her support in making improvements to St. Louis Catholic Church in Cathedral City, which needed new carpeting. The first thing Loretta noticed about the church was that the carpeting had become so frayed that a heel—particularly a high heel—could get caught in the threads and cause an accident. Loretta had no intention of landing on her backside in a house of God. When Loretta died in 2000, Jane devoted her philanthropic efforts to Sacred Heart Catholic Church in Palm Desert, which she endowed with padded pews, kneelers, and an improved sound system.

Loretta Young was a public Catholic, known for her visits to the stigmatists Padre Pio and Theresa Neuman, her friendship with Bishop Fulton J. Sheen, her private audience with Pope Pius XII, and her pilgrimages to Lourdes and Medjugorje, the village in the former Yugoslavia where the Virgin supposedly appeared in 1981. Jane was as private a Catholic as she was a person. She was reluctant to grant interviews, and when she did, she revealed nothing about her private life, walking out when the topic changed to Ronald Reagan. "I never discuss the gentleman," Jane coolly informed Earl Hamner when he brought up the subject. She broke her silence after Reagan's death: "America has lost a great president and a great, kind and lovely man."

Jane lived in semi-seclusion during the last years of her life. Catholicism was not enough. She sought the kind of mystical union with God known to cloistered nuns and monks. Thus Jane became a member of the Third Order Dominicans, known simply as lay Dominicans, and was buried in the Dominican habit. The requirements—such as following *The Rules of the Third Order*, spiritual readings, mass and communion (daily, if possible), and fasting on Fridays—were not onerous. Jane was serious about the faith that gave her life meaning and asked little of her in return. As an actress, she knew that she had not embraced a profession, but a vocation, a calling that came not from within but from outside of herself.

Jane died, presumably in her sleep, on Monday, 10 September 2007. A funeral mass was held two days later at Sacred Heart Catholic Church at 10:30 a.m., preceded by a recitation of the rosary. Internment followed at Forest Lawn Memorial Park in nearby Cathedral City. Her fans, who expected a grand send-off, with the *Falcon Crest* regulars in attendance, were disappointed. But Jane died as she lived, avoiding the limelight unless it was necessary to sell a picture or receive an award.

The service was brief. Michael, too overcome with emotion to speak at length, delivered a short eulogy, concluding with, "She built men, not boys. I am lucky to be her son." The pastor, Rev. Howard Lincoln, praised Jane for her generosity: "I saw my first $100,000 check because of Jane Wyman." "Her new home is in heaven," Rev. Lincoln concluded. Michael should be pleased. Jane now had a permanent address. She was home at last.

EPILOGUE

In summer 2012, the Weinstein Company announced that it would be distributing *The Butler* (retitled *Lee Daniels' The Butler* prior to its August 2013 release to avoid confusion with a similarly named 1916 silent film), inspired by the life of the African American Eugene Allen (called Cecil Gaines in the film and played by Forest Whitaker), who served as the White House butler for thirty-four years under eight administrations. The film limited the presidents to Dwight D. Eisenhower (Robin Williams), Lyndon B. Johnson (Liev Schreiber), Richard M. Nixon (John Cusak), John F. Kennedy (James Marsden), and Ronald Reagan (Alan Rickman).

And Jane Fonda played Nancy. The casting of Fonda occasioned some controversy. To many, the political activist and one of most strident opponents of the Vietnam War is still "Hanoi Jane" because of her 1972 trip to the North Vietnamese capital. Although there is a slight physical resemblance between the two women, Fonda's public image is so at odds with Nancy's that unless a viewer has a sense of the ironic, the disparity could politicize the film, detracting from the title character, who should be the dominant figure. On the other hand, Reaganites would not take umbrage if their hero was impersonated by the same actor who played Severus Snape in *Harry Potter and the Deathly Hallows—Part Two*.

Nancy Reagan—not Nancy Davis—can be portrayed in a movie, but not Jane Wyman. That is, unless the movie is about Ronald Reagan, in which case her role will be as secondary as it was in real life. Jane will be remembered as an outstanding actress, whose films crop up on *Turner Classic Movies* and other cable outlets specializing in films of the past. And if Warner Home Video releases the rest of *Falcon Crest*, her legacy will be secure. While *TCM* commemorates Jane's birthday on 5 January, it does not acknowledge Nancy's on 6 July. Nancy was not a movie star, only an actress who made some movies.

Nancy will always be controversial. There will be historians who will agree with Kitty Kelly that she was her husband's shadow self, or as

Kelly phrased it, "the puppet master pulling Ronald Reagan's strings." Nancy was really the answer to the question posed by the title of Reagan's first autobiography, *Where's the Rest of Me?* Nancy was the rest of him; she was his complement, the woman who was as much a friend as a wife. Hers was a dual role, the toughest she ever had, which, if played properly, would relegate her children to the supporting cast—as it did. Jane was just Reagan's wife—and not even for a decade. She did nothing for his career, nor did he do anything for hers. Jane could never be a politician's wife. As her marital record shows, she was not meant to be anyone's wife for long. Most important of all, Nancy accepted Reagan's obsession with communism, even though she may not have shared it. To Jane, it was grounds for divorce.

Reagan and Nancy were actors, who understood the art of performance, both in front of the camera and in public. They knew the importance of rehearsals and appreciated the transformative effects of makeup and lighting. Nancy might have functioned as assistant director-dialogue coach-script supervisor, reading drafts of Reagan's speeches, suggesting revisions, critiquing his delivery, and, in general, being an extension of him. But she was no female Pygmalion. As with any actor, once Reagan rehearsed the script and mastered it, he was on his own. The public never saw the rehearsals, only the performance, which was pure Reagan.

It was not really Jane who was Reaganized. It was Nancy—and for eight years, so was the nation.

NOTES

ABBREVIATIONS

AHC-MHL	Alfred Hitchcock Collection, Margaret Herrick Library
BRC-NYPLPA	Billy Rose Collection, New York Public Library for Performing Arts
HHC-MHL	Hedda Hopper Collection, Margaret Herrick Library
JAC-MHL	Jane Ardmore Collection, Margaret Herrick Library
JHP-MHL	John Huston Papers, Margaret Herrick Library
KHP-MHL	Katharine Hepburn Papers, Margaret Herrick Library
NWMOGS	Northwest Missouri Genealogical Society, St. Joseph
PC-MHL	Paramount Collection, Margaret Herrick Library
TCFC-USC-CAL	Twentieth Century-Fox Collection, University of Southern California, Cinematic Arts Library
UC-USC-CAL	Universal Collection, University of Southern California, Cinematic Arts Library
WBA-USC	Warner Bros. Archives, University of Southern California

CHAPTER 1

7   "On 27 May 1916": Information about Jane's birth and years in St. Joseph, MO, derive from material at NWMOGS and from emails from staff members Connie McCoy and Carol Almanza

8   "Names had special significance": William Addams Reitwiessner, http://www.wargs.com/political/wyman.html, accessed 19 September 2010

10 "Since she never pursued her dream": Cliff Jahr, "Great Hollywood Comebacks," *Ladies Home Journal*, June 1985, 58; Richard G. Hubler, "Calamity Jane Wyman," *Coronet*, January 1956, 92–96

11 "found it odd": Anne Edwards, *Early Reagan: The Rise to Power* (New York: William Morrow, 1987), 189

11 "itinerant radio singer": studio bio, *Lucy Gallant*, PC-MHL

11 "The press kit": "She's from Missouri," *The Kid from Kokomo*, WBA-USC, #80071, f. 688B, 16

11 "part French": *Torchy Plays with Dynamite*, WBA-USC #5, *Current Publicity Layout*, f. 1854B

12 "she shared a house": Edwards, *Early Reagan*, 190

12 "it was the home": email from Carol Almanza, NWMOGS, to author, 28 June 2011

12 "Perhaps St. Joseph held": Lawrence J. Quirk, *Jane Wyman: The Actress and the Woman* (New York: Dembner Books, 1986), 19

12 "then in the agency business": Jane Wyman, studio bio, PC-MHL

13 "eyelashes applied individually": Jane Ardmore, "The Lady Goes for Broke," 4, JAC-MHL, #2810

13 "charming, sophisticated woman": Jane Wyman, studio bio, PC-MHL

14 "Reliable Hollywood insiders": Quirk, *Jane Wyman*, 16

14 "Others have noted": Reitwiessner, "The Ancestors of Jane Wyman"

14 "press release": Jane Wyman, UC-USC-CAL

14 "burial site": email from Brandon Massey, Forest Lawn Records Dept., to author, 2 Feb. 2011

14 "were indeed married": Edmund Morris, *Dutch: A Memoir of Ronald Reagan* (New York: Modern Library, 1999), 153; *see also* Notes, 717

CHAPTER 2

16 "Jane received": *My Man Godfrey*, UC-USC-CAL

16 "For *Cain and Mabel*": *Cain and Mabel*, WBA-USC, #B00057. f. 1787

16 "poise," "self-consciousness": *Mr. Dodd Takes the Air*, press kit, WBA-USC, #1494A

17 "Her name": *Smart Blonde*, WBA-USC, #2879B, f. 115

18 "the *Mr. Dodd Takes the Air* shoot": *Mr. Dodd Takes the Air*, WBA-USC, *Daily Production Report*, # S1494A

19 "as indicated by print size": *Ready, Willing and Able*, WBA-USC, #2878B, f. 1484A

19 "She did a beautiful job": Mervyn LeRoy, as told to Dick Kleiner, *Take One* (New York: Hawthorn, 1974), 115

20 "Still, her name": *Slim*, WBA-USC, #00390, f. 691B

21 "a sweet sadness": June Allyson, with Frances Spatz, *June Allyson* (New York: Putnam's, 1982), 96

21 "an interviewer wrote": quoted by Dominick Dunne, "Jane's Turn," *Vanity Fair*, November 1989, 233

22 "Wherever I could": Peter Bogdanovich, *Who the Devil Made It* (New York: Knopf, 1997), 650

22 "Still, she had to test": *Brother Rat*, WBA-USC, #00051, f. 1748

22 "Originally, the female lead": ibid., Budget Sheet

23 "too smart," "gorgeous, " "dumpy looking": ibid., memo from Hal Wallis to Robert Lord and William Keighley, 28 June 1938

24 "cutely intriguing": ibid., *National Box Office Digest*, 18 Oct. 1938, 6

24 "shot in four weeks": *Brother Rat and a Baby*, WBA-USC, #1485A, f. 281

28 "After buying the rights": *Tugboat Annie Sails Again*, WBA- USC, #800453, f. 12759A

28 "the most telling information": ibid., #800452, f. 2203

29 "Robinson received": *Larceny, Inc.*, WBA-USC, #1486A. Salary Information, f. N-27, 2123A

29 "The highest salaries": *Inside Warner Bros. (1935–1951)* selected, edited and annotated by Rudy Behlmer (New York: Simon and Schuster, 1985), 209–11

CHAPTER 3

30 "Maureen and Michael": HHC-MHL, "Jane Wyman," f. 3610

30 Information about Ronald Reagan's early years derives from a variety of sources, the most informative being Edwards, *Early Reagan: The Rise to Power*, and Morris, *Dutch: A Memoir of Ronald Reagan.*

32 "student strike": Morris, *Dutch*, 24

32 "a hick radio announcer": Stephen Vaughn, *Ronald Reagan in Hollywood: Movies and Politics* (New York: Cambridge UP, 1994), 28

33 "marvelous," "my friend, Ronnie Reagan": Hal Wallis and Charles Higham, *Star-maker* (New York: Macmillan, 1980), 68, 78

33 "married Jane," "stomach cramps": Morris, *Dutch*, 162

34 "an amethyst engagement ring": Joseph Morella and Edward Z. Epstein. "The Jane Wyman Story," *Good Housekeeping*, July 1985, 182

34 "Why, honey": Morris, *Dutch*, 720, n. 162

34 "When Louella Parsons heard the news": Edwards, *Early Reagan*, 198–200

34 "deft": ibid., 199

35 "Scottish blood": ibid., 29

CHAPTER 4

45 "if it had been filmed as planned": *Footlight Serenade* , TCFC-USC-CAL

CHAPTER 5

47 "[Jane] saw Reagan": Edwards, *Early Reagan*, 205

48 "I knew that Jane": Jack Burton, "Why Can't Jane Wyman Stay Married?" *Filmland*, June 1954, 60

48 "I wanted a boy": Edwards, *Early Reagan*, 230

49 "lumped together": ibid., 239–40

49 "a box office natural": Rudy Behlmer, *America's Favorite Movies: Behind the Scenes* (New York: Ungar, 1982), 155

49 "Wallis created": ibid., 162

51 "vital interest": Vaughn, *Ronald Reagan in Hollywood*, 117

CHAPTER 6

55 "Wallis would have preferred": *Princess O'Rourke*, WBA-USC. #800335, f. 2173, memo from Wallis to Trilling, 30 March 1942

57 "Very best wishes": HHC-MHL, "Jane Wyman," f. 3610

CHAPTER 7

59 "On 21 August 1944": *The Lost Weekend*, PC-MHL, #125, f. 1

59 "conceded": ibid., #128, f. 5, memo from Wally Westmore to George Bertholm, 11 September 1944

59 "No telling": Charles Jackson, *The Lost Weekend* (Syracuse: Syracuse UP, 1996), 244

60 "Listen, baby": ibid., 139

61 "to loathe & detest": Blake Bailey, "Weekend in the Sun," *Vanity Fair*, March 2013, 251

64 "a screenplay was ready:" *One More Tomorrow*, WBA-USC, #800316, f. 1750

64 "a violation": ibid., letter from Joseph Breen to Jack Warner, 7 October 1942

64 "Henry Blanke complained": ibid., memo to Warner, 18 May 1943

CHAPTER 8

66 "He taught me": Ardmore, "The Lady Goes for Broke," 6, JAC-MHL, #2810

67 "flattered by Brown's choice": "The Yearling," *Lion's Roar*, 6, 1, Spring 1947, 24

68 "taught him": ibid.

CHAPTER 9

73 "We believe": *Cheyenne*, WBA-USC, #B0327, f. 1813B, memo from Steve Trilling to Robert Buchner, 6 March 1946

74 "speech widow": ibid., f. 648B

74 "had vivid recollections": phone interview, 18 August 2011

CHAPTER 10

77 "revolution": Frank Capra, "Breaking Hollywood's 'Pattern of Sameness,'" *Hollywood Directors 1941–1976*, ed. Richard Koszarski (New York: Oxford UP, 1977), 83

79 "Did Wellman": Ian Scott, *In Capra's Shadow: The Life and Career of Robert Riskin* (Lexington: UP of Kentucky, 2006), 207

CHAPTER 11

80 "work better as a film": Rudy Behlmer, "The Making of *Johnny Belinda* (Against All Odds), 2," *Johnny Belinda: Original Motion Picture Score*, Brigham Young University Film Music Archives, Provo, UT

80 "rape should never": Leonard J. Leff and Jerold L. Simmons, *The Dame in the Kimono: Hollywood Censorship and the Production Code from the 1920s to the 1960s* (New York: Grove Weidenfeld, 1990), 285

82 "Negulesco eagerly agreed": Behlmer, *Inside Warner Bros.* 300–1

82 "Wyman-Negulesco method": Behlmer, "The Making of *Johnny Belinda*," 6

83 "He courted Negulesco": *Johnny Belinda*, WBA-USC, #800227, f. 2016

83 "If Negulesco leaves the picture": Jean Negulesco, *Things I Did . . . and Things I Think I Did* (New York: Linden Press/Simon & Schuster, 1984), 127

83 "Negulesco also had his preferences": *Johnny Belinda*, WBA-USC. #800227, story memos, 9 September 1946–30 August 1947

84 "Sorry, boys": Negulesco, *Things I Said*, 127–28

84 "I accept this": Mason Wiley and Damien Bona, *Inside Oscar: The Unofficial History of the Academy Awards*, ed. Gail McColl (New York: Ballantine, 1987), 189

84   "Wald thanked her": letter to Hedda Hopper, 23 March 1949, "Jerry Wald 1940–
     1962," #59, f. 2615, HHC-MHL

CHAPTER 12

86   "sports casting skills": Kitty Kelly, *Nancy Reagan: The Unauthorized Biography* (New
     York: Simon & Schuster, 1991), 84
86   "Don't ask Ronnie": Allyson, *June Allyson*, 96
87   "She was painstaking": Arno Johansen, "What Price Career?" *Movieland*, May 1948,
     92
88   "the infant lived": Morris, *Dutch*, 252
88   "would hesitate": *Thirty Years of Treason: Excerpts from Hearings before the House Com-
     mittee on Un-American Activities, 1938–1968*, ed. Eric Bentley (New York: Viking,
     1971), 146
88   "Reagan and Wyman met": Edwards, *Early Reagan*, 305
88   "newly released files," "report secretly": *New York Times*, 2 September 2012, Sunday
     Review, 4
88   "three men": Ronald Reagan, with Richard G. Hubler, *Where's the Rest of Me?* (New
     York: Duell, Sloane and Pearce, 1965), 169
88   "their names," "follow the Communist Party line," "eight others": Seth Rosenfeld,
     Subversives: The FBI's War on Student Radicals, and Reagan's Rise to Power (New York:
     Farrar, Straus, Giroux, 2012), 127–28
89   "carried away by stories": Morris, *Dutch*, 158
90   "Fascist": Reagan, *Where's the Rest of Me?*, 167
90   "Reagan and Jane": Edwards, *Early Reagan*, 306; Kelly, *Nancy Reagan*, 540
90   "his motives": Rosenfeld, *Subversives*, 138
91   "I'm so bored": Morris, *Dutch*, 237
91   "things hadn't been right": *Los Angeles Examiner*, 5 December 1947, 1
91   "I wish I could say": ibid., 1,3
91   "physically and emotionally strained," "cute and flip," "cynical," "viewed the
     world," Laura Pomeroy, "What's Ahead for Jane Wyman?" *Motion Picture*, July
     1948, 34–35
91   "torn by inner conflicts": ibid., 34
92   "I don't know why": Johansen, "What Price Career?" *Movieland*, May 1948, 51
92   "he was still in love": Edwards, *Early Reagan*, 364
92   "according to actress Rosemary DeCamp": Kelly, *Nancy Reagan*, 84
92   "Jane only stayed a week": *Los Angeles Examiner*, 6 May 1948, 1, 3
92   "would be in Malibu": Edwards, *Early Reagan*, 355
93   "In his autobiography": Ronald Reagan, *An American Life: The Autobiography* (New
     York: Simon & Schuster, 1990), 92
93   "delightful little romance," "Two of the letters": Kelly, *Nancy Reagan*, 86, 553
93   "decided to keep the watch," "overwhelming," "he did have": ibid., 90, 357

CHAPTER 13

97   "fading stars": Kelly, *Nancy Reagan*, 122
98   "delightful," "cordial," "tea leaves," phone interview with Arlene Dahl, 18 Septem-
     ber 2011

CHAPTER 14

102 "sex is best": Edwards, *Early Reagan*, 319

102 "point out": ibid., 356–57

104 "Even the director": Reagan, *Where's the Rest of Me?* 217

104 "four hundred movies": Peter Bogdanovich, *Allan Dwan: The Last Pioneer* (New York: Praeger, 1971), 6

107 "attributed his death": Tony Thomas, "Sam Wood," *The Hollywood Professionals*, vol. 2 (New York: A. S. Barnes, 1974), 172–73

107 "too pretty for a boy": Henry Bellamann, *Kings Row* (Garden City, NY: Sun Dial Press, 1940), 4

108 "Wood wanted Cummings": Behlmer, *Inside Warner Bros.*, 144

108 "a demotion": ibid., 140

108 "preferred his own actresses": ibid., 139

109 "there is no suggestion": ibid., 138

CHAPTER 15

112 "pink-cheeked": Ronald L. Davis, *Mary Martin: Hollywood Legend* (Norman, OK: U of Oklahoma P, 2008), 97

113 "forty credits": Edith Luckett, clippings file, BRC-NYPLPA, which contains a handwritten list, presumably by Luckett, of the plays in which she appeared.

114 "Mother used to say": Nancy Reagan, with Michael Novak, *My Turn: The Memoirs of Nancy Reagan* (New York: Random House, 1989), 67

115 "You bet I am": Katharine Dayton and George S. Kaufman, *First Lady* (New York: Dramatists Play Service, 1935), 81–82

116 "In 1929": Kelly, *Nancy Reagan*, 320

117 "Are you my friend?": George Batson, *Ramshackle Inn* (New York: Dramatists Play Service, 1971), 44–45

117 "Nancy was one of those girls": Edwards, *Early Reagan*, 393

118 "George Batson had written": *Cordelia*, clippings file, BRC-NYPLPA

CHAPTER 16

120 "Thau's penchant," "cold, detached man": Charles Higham, *Merchant of Dreams: Louis B. Mayer, M.G.M., and the Secret Hollywood* (New York: Dell/Laurel, 1994), 220

120 "Thau's casting couch": ibid., 149

120 "white divan": Bernard F. Dick, *The Merchant Prince of Poverty Row: Harry Cohn of Columbia Pictures* (Lexington: UP of Kentucky, 1993), 72

121 "foremost exponent": ibid., 6

121 "Rumors": Edwards, *Early Reagan*, 394

121 "Greer Garson's replacement": Scott Eyman, *Lion of Hollywood: The Life and Legend of Louis B. Mayer* (New York: Simon & Schuster, 2005), 398.

121 "He persuaded": Michael Troyan, *A Rose for Mrs. Miniver: The Life of Greer Garson* (Lexington: UP of Kentucky, 1999), 78

122 "head over heels in love": Kelly, *Nancy Reagan*, 458

122 "go ahead and count": Nancy Reagan, *My Turn*, 103

122 "Character is not cut in marble": George Eliot, *Middlemarch*, ed. with introduction and notes by Rosemary Ashton (New York: Penguin, 1994), 734–35

123 "a darn nice kid": KHP-MHL, #62, f 800, Davis, Loyal and Edith, 1944–48, letter from "Lucky" Davis to Katharine Hepburn, 24 August 1944

123 "agreed to produce": ibid., Loyal Davis to Spencer Tracy, 26 July 1944

123 "used to act out": JHP-MHL, #98, f. 987, Davis, Loyal and Edith, 1948–72, Edith Davis to John Huston, n.d. (probably 1955)

123 "It is certainly": ibid., Huston to Edith, 10 June 1955

CHAPTER 17

127 "horror": Marcia Davenport, *Too Strong for Fantasy* (New York: Scribner's, 1967), 370

130 "excellent": Dore Schary, as told to Charles Palmer, *Case History of a Movie* (New York: Random House, 1950), 4

131 "waste of everybody's time": ibid., 45

133 "not enough people": Reagan, *Where's the Rest of Me?* 238

135 "Schary does not discuss": Dore Schary, *Heyday: An Autobiography* (Boston: Little, Brown, 1970), 373, 374

CHAPTER 18

136 "She projected": Kelly, *Nancy Reagan*, 83

136 "I don't know what it is": Anthony Hopkins on Hepburn, "Word of Mouth," *A Lion in Winter, Turner Classic Movies*

138 "could not have been": Edwards, *Early Reagan*, 402

138 "someone is shoving": LeRoy, *Take One*, 192

138 "you're single": ibid.

138 "An alternate version": Kelly, *Nancy Reagan*, 79

138 "A third version": Edwards, *Early Reagan*, 394

CHAPTER 19

139 "vehicle for Joan Crawford": *New York Times*, 5 March 1948, 17

140 "It's a test": "Jane Wyman Returns to Romantic Comedy," *Showtime*, March 1949, 7

140 "cramps": *A Kiss in the Dark*, WBA-USC, #80350, f. 1275B, Eric Stacy to T. C. Wright, 22 April 1948

140 "Shirts were another problem": ibid., f. 1489A. Stacy to Wright, 5 March 1948

CHAPTER 20

143 "like a radio station": Curt Siodmak, *Donovan's Brain* (Mill Valley, CA: Pulplesspress.com, 1999), 50

144 "the brain's constructive imagination": ibid., 182

147 "On 27 November 1956": *Hellcats of the Navy* file, MHL

147 "Gordon used the same pseudonym": Paul Buhle and Dave Wagner, *Blacklisted: The Film Lover's Guide to the Hollywood Blacklist* (New York: Palgrave, 2003), 93, 125

CHAPTER 21

151 "After much wrangling": *Stage Fright*, AHC-MHL
151 "I ran into great difficulties": François Truffaut, *Hitchcock* (New York: Simon & Schuster, 1967), 140
152 "failed to sustain": 141
152 "a pimply faced girl": Bogdanovich, *Who the Devil Made It*, 518
153 "I'd never seen": Ardmore, "The Lady Goes for Broke," JAC-MHL, #2810, 7
153 "Now we can go in": ibid., 8
153 "Parishoners rallied": *Los Angeles Times*, 6 November 1936, 6
154 "the Irish priest": ibid., 7 July 1946, 1
154 "There's a serenity": Ardmore, "The Lady Goes for Broke," 9

CHAPTER 22

156 "The treatment": Scott, *In Capra's Shadow*, 219
158 "*Groom* was a three-month shoot": *Here Comes the Groom*, PC-MHL
158 "Crosby received": *Just for You*, PC-MHL
159 "Many who knew Crosby": Adolph Zukor, *The Public Is Never Wrong: My Life in Motion Pictures* (New York: Putnam's, 1952), 2

CHAPTER 23

163 "A good deal": Behlmer, *Inside Warner Bros.*, 318
164 "disgraceful": ibid., 320
165 "Williams preferred": ibid., 321
169 "Jane's salary": *Lucy Gallant*, PC-MHL, #1581, Paramount contract summaries, Wyman, Jane

CHAPTER 24

171 "Warners bought": *Miracle in the Rain*, WBA-USC, #800531, f. 2098B
171 "I encountered many things": Ben Hecht, *A Child of the Century* (New York: Simon & Schuster, 1954), 111
172 "A priest waived": ibid., 502
173 "apologizing profusely": *Miracle in the Rain*, WBA-USC, letter from Frank Rosenberg to Father Flannelly, 11 June 1955

CHAPTER 25

177 "ten years younger": *Movie Stars Parade*, March 1956, 62
178 "when her own acquaintances": ibid., 63
178 "the world's favorite": *New York Times*, 28 January 1951, X5
179 "took pity": Donald Spoto, *Marilyn Monroe: The Biography* (New York: Harper Paperbacks, 1994), 174
180 "Karger may have had": *Modern Screen*, April 1954, 100

CHAPTER 26

181 "four-part series": David G. Wittels, "Star-Spangled Octopus," *Saturday Evening Post*, 10, 17, 24, 31 August 1946

183 "Wasserman came to her aid": Edwards, *Early Reagan*, 213

183 "signed": ibid., 433

183 "Wasserman supposedly talked": ibid., 280

185 "a special waiver": Bernard F. Dick, *City of Dreams: The Making and Remaking of Universal Pictures* (Lexington: UP of Kentucky, 1997), 157

185 "Decca Records" ibid., 143–45

186 "Wasserman bought the UI lot": Clive Hirshorn, *The Universal Story* (New York: Crown, 1983), 159

CHAPTER 27

191 "The people who know": Joseph Morella and Edward Z. Epstein, *Jane Wyman: A Biography* (London: Robert Hale, 1985), 37

191 "the documentary": *Magnificent Obsession*, Criterion Collection, Universal Studios Home Entertainment

192 "the man who discovered it": Lloyd C. Douglas, *Magnificent Obsession* (New York: Mariner/Houghton Mifflin, 1999), 144

192 "silly little ass": ibid., 7

194 "fatally hurt": ibid., 308

195 "We got along great": Jon Halliday, *Sirk on Sirk* (New York: Viking, 1972), 114

195 "totemic sexuality": Michael Stern, *Douglas Sirk* (Boston: Twayne, 1979), 158

196 "Find a good story": Publicity release in *Pillow Talk* file, UC-USC-CAL

196 "trashy stuff": Halliday, *Sirk on Sirk*, 96

196 "Euripides' *Alcestis*": ibid., 95

196 "a very short distance": ibid., 96

196 "Blue and white": Jean Chevalier and Alain Gheerbrant, trans. John Buchanan-Brown, *A Dictionary of Symbols* (New York: Penguin, 1996), 104

196 "She was still a real star": Halliday, *Sirk on Sirk*, 93

197 "the best deal": *Magnificent Obsession*, UC-USC-CAL, #1749, box 136

197 "the wardrobe": ibid.

197 "arrive at 6:15 a.m.": ibid., *Daily Production Reports*

197 "pocket money": ibid., correspondence, letter from Clark Ramsay to Charlie Simonelli, 25 June 1954

198 "Hudson fared better": *All That Heaven Allows*, UC-USC-CAL, #226, Production Budget

200 "the sun": Henry Thoreau, *Walden and 'Civil Disobedience'* (New York: Signet, 1960), 221

200 "a wonderful girl": Mark Bego, *Rock Hudson: Public and Private* (New York: New American Library, 1986), 60

200 "After working with Rock": ibid., 59–60

200 "Let me tell you something": Rock Hudson and Sara Davidson, *Rock Hudson: His Story* (New York: William Morrow, 1986), 71

CHAPTER 29

210 *"Broken Dishes"*: William Hawes, *Live Television Drama: 1946–1951* (Jefferson, NC: Mc-Farland, 2001), 242

218 "Nineteen sixty-two": Edwards, *Early Reagan*, 477–86

219 "Yes": ibid., 361

CHAPTER 30

222 William Lafferty, "Frank Wisbar": "'No Attempt at Artiness': *Fireside Theater* and the Rise of Filmed Television Programming," *Cinema Journal*, 27, 1 (Fall 1987), 34

222 *"Variety* was impressed": ibid.

222 "to entertain a tired audience": ibid., 35

230 "She is not a lady": *"Falcon Crest*: A Look Back," Paley Center for Media

237 "Jane wrote her own coda": Episode 227, http://www/falconcrest.org/english/master.php?path=show/episodes/ai/bts/9

CHAPTER 31

239 "There was very little of Jane Wyman": Maureen Reagan, *First Father, First Daughter: A Memoir* (Boston: Little, Brown, 1989), 44

240 "the mother who brought me home": Michael Reagan, with Jim Denney, *Twice Adopted* (Nashville: Boardman & Holman, 2004), 4–5

240 "he is a unique human being": Maureen Reagan, *First Father, First Daughter*, 401

241 "Miss Wyman": Michael Reagan, *Twice Adopted*, 187

241 "take a break": ibid., 173

241 "Had my mother": 61

242 "Who are you?" Arlene Dahl interview, 18 September 2011

242 "As for Patti": Nancy Reagan, *My Turn*, 305

242 "a steadying influence": Maureen Reagan, *First Father, First Daughter*, 59

243 "she is against everything": *Ronald Reagan: An American Life*, 566

243 "I just can't": Patti Davis, with Maureen Strange Foster, *Home Front* (New York: Crown, 1986), 2

243 "everybody's parents": ibid., 15

244 "a short, fleshy woman": ibid., 66

244 "Vietnam happened": ibid., 204

245 "before the altar": ibid., 77

247 "Third Order Dominicans": "About St. Dominic and the Third Order of St. Dominic," rosarychapel.net, accessed 19 June 2012

247 "I never discuss the gentleman": *"Falcon Crest*: A Look Back"

247 "She built men": "Jane Wyman buried in a habit," posted by Deacon Greg Kanda, Beliefnet.com, accessed 18 June 2012

250 "puppet master": Kelly, *Nancy Reagan*, 528

APPENDIX

JANE WYMAN

GOLDWYN/UNITED ARTISTS
The Kid from Spain (1932)

WARNER BROS.
Elmer the Great (1933)
Gold Diggers of 1933 (1933)
Bengal Tiger (1936)
Cain and Mabel (1936)
Freshman Love (1936)
Here Comes Carter (1936)
Polo Joe (1936)
Smart Blonde (1936)
Stage Struck (1936)
Gold Diggers of 1937 (1937)
Public Wedding (1937)
Ready, Willing and Able (1937)
Slim (1937)
The King and the Chorus Girl (1937)
The Singing Marine (1937)
Brother Rat (1938)
Fools for Scandal (1938)
He Couldn't Say No (1938)
Mr. Dodd Takes the Air (1938)
Kid Nightingale (1939)
Private Detective (1939)
The Kid from Kokomo (1939)
Torchy Plays with Dynamite (1939)
An Angel from Texas (1940)
Brother Rat and a Baby (1940)
Flight Angels (1940)
Gambling on the High Seas (1940)
My Love Came Back (1940)   Feature Films (*= unbilled)

Tugboat Annie Sails Again (1940)
Bad Men of Missouri (1941)
Honeymoon for Three (1941)
The Body Disappears (1941)
You're in the Army Now (1941)
Larceny, Inc. (1942)
Princess O'Rourke (1943)
Crime by Night (1944)
Hollywood Canteen (1944)
Make Your Own Bed (1944)
The Doughgirls (1944)
Night and Day (1946)
One More Tomorrow (1946)
Cheyenne (1947)
Johnny Belinda (1948)
A Kiss in the Dark (1949)
The Lady Takes a Sailor (1949)
Stage Fright (1950)
The Glass Menagerie (1950)
The Story of Will Rogers (1952)
So Big (1953)
Miracle in the Rain (1956)

PARAMOUNT
Bolero (1934)
College Rhythm (1934)
Rumba (1935)
Stolen Harmony (1935)
Anything Goes (1936)
The Lost Weekend (1945)
Here Comes the Groom (1951)
Just for You (1952)
Lucy Gallant (1955)

FOX FILM CORPORATION
George White's 1935 Scandals (1935)

UNIVERSAL
My Man Godfrey (1936)
The Spy Ring (1938)

TWENTIETH CENTURY-FOX
King of Burlesque (1936)
Tail Spin (1939)
Footlight Serenade (1942)
Holiday for Lovers (1959)

MGM
> *The Crowd Roars* (1938)
> *The Yearling* (1946)
> *Three Guys Named Mike* (1951)

COLUMBIA
> *Wide Open Faces* (1938)
> *Let's Do It Again* (1953)

RKO
> *My Favorite Spy* (1942)
> *Magic Town* (1947)
> *The Blue Veil* (1951)

UNIVERSAL-INTERNATIONAL
> *Magnificent Obsession* (1954)
> *All That Heaven Allows* (1955)

WALT DISNEY PRODUCTIONS/BUENA VISTA
> *Pollyanna* (1960)
> *Bon Voyage!* (1962)

CINERAMA RELEASING CORPORATION
> *How to Commit Marriage* (1969)

TV MOVIES

> *The Failing of Raymond* (ABC, 27 November 1971)
> *Amanda Fallon* (NBC, 4 May 1973)
> *The Incredible Journey of Doctor Meg Laurel* (CBS, 2 January 1979)

RADIO (*= SPECIAL COLLECTIONS, MARGARET HERRICK LIBRARY)

THEATRE GUILD ON THE AIR
> *The Willow and I*, 29 January 1950

THE BOB HOPE SHOW
> 11 February 1953, 1 July 1953
> Available from Radio Memories, 370 38th Sq SW, Vero Beach, FL 32968-3933

LUX RADIO THEATRE
> *Devotion*, 17 February 1947
> **One More Tomorrow*, 9 June 1947
> **Nobody Lives Forever*, 17 November 1947
> **Magic Town*, 15 December 1947
> **The Yearling*, 19 January 1948

Body and Soul, 15 November 1948
The Lady Takes a Sailor, 15 May 1950
Flamingo Road, 2 October 1950
On Moonlight Bay, 5 May 1952
Here Comes the Groom, 15 September 1952
The Blue Veil, 24 November 1952
The Story of Will Rogers, 12 January 1953
Just for You, 13 April 1953
The Glass Menagerie, 8 March 1954

RECORDINGS

"In the Cool, Cool, Cool of the Evening" and "Misto Cristofo Columbo" with Bing
Crosby, *Decca Records Catalogue* #27678

TELEVISION (*= PALEY CENTER FOR MEDIA, NEW YORK AND BEVERLY HILLS)

JANE WYMAN'S FIRESIDE THEATRE (AS PERFORMER)
"Technical Charge of Murder," 30 August 1955
"Gusher City,"6 September 1955
"Holiday in Autumn," 20 September 1955
"One Last September," 18 October 1955
"Ride with the Executioner," 8 November 1955
"The Key," 15 November 1955
"Bamboo Cross," 6 December 1955
"Along Came a Bachelor," 20 December 1955
"Once upon a Nightmare,"3 January 1956
*"The House on Elm Street," 17 January 1956
"Not What She Pretended," 7 February 1956
"Kristi,"14 February 1956
"The Thread," 21 February 1956
"An Echo out of the Past," 6 March 1956
"Scent of Roses," 13 March 1956
"In a Different Life," 3 April 1956
"The Past Is Always Present,"17 April 1956
*"The Hidden People," 24 April 1956
"Ten Percent,"28 August 1956
"Dirty Face," 4 September 1956
"Approved by Censor," 11 September 1956
"Let Yesterday Die," 25 September 1956
"Assignment Champ," 2 October 1956
"No More Tears," 16 October 1956
"Two Sides to Everything," 23 October 1956
"Father Forgets," 13 November 1956
"The Marked Bullet," 20 November 1956
"While There's Life," 11 December 1956
"A Point of Law," 18 December 1956

"Twenty Dollar Bride," 8 January 1957
"Portrait in Fear," 15 January 1957
"The Golden Door," 22 January 1957
"Birthright,"5 February 1957
"Small Talk," 12 February 1957
"Farmer's Wife," 19 February 1957
"Married to a Stranger,"5 March 1957
"The Pendulum," 12 March 1957
"Mama Bufano's," 9 April 1957
"Not for Publication," 16 April 1957
"The Man in the Car," 30 April 1957
"Night of Terror," 14 May 1957
"The Way Home," 26 September 1957
"The Animal Instinct," 31 October 1957
"Death Rides the 12:15,"5 December 1957
"A Widow's Kiss," 9 January 1958
"My Sister Susan," 6 February 1958
"Swindler's Inn," 10 April 1958

WAGON TRAIN
"The Story of Dr. Willoughby," 5 November 1958
*"The Wagon Train Mutiny," 19 September 1962

FALCON CREST (1981–90)
Seasons 1, 2, and 3, Warner Home Video
*"In His father's House" (premiere, 4 December 1981)
*"Family Reunion" (19 February 1982)
**Falcon* Crest: A Look Back," 12 October 2010, Paley Center for Media. Reminiscences by Robert Foxworth, Susan Sullivan, Margaret Ladd, Ana Alicia, Lorenzo Lamas, David Selby, Abby Dalton, and the show's creator, Earl Hamner.

TELEVISION DOCUMENTARIES

Wild Bill: Hollywood Maverick—The Life and Times of William A. Wellman (1995), as herself, Warner Home Video
Off the Menu: Last Days of Chasen's (1997), as herself, Northern Arts Entertainment
For Jane Wyman's other television appearances, see: http://www.imdb.com.

NANCY DAVIS

THEATRE

Ramshackle Inn (tour), 1943
Cordelia (tour), 1946
Lute Song (Broadway), 1946
The Late Christopher Bean (tour), 1947

FEATURE FILMS

MGM

> *East Side, West Side* (1949)
> *The Doctor and the Girl* (1949)
> *Shadow on the Wall* (1950)
> *The Next Voice You Hear* (1950)
> *It's a Big Country* (1951)
> *Night into Morning* (1951)
> *Shadow in the Sky* (1952)
> *Talk about a Stranger* (1952)

UNITED ARTISTS

> *Donovan's Brain* (1953)

COLUMBIA

> *Hellcats of the Navy* (1957)
> *Crash Landing* (1958)

SHORT SUBJECT

> *The Dark Wave* (1956) Fox

TELEVISION (*=PALEY CENTER FOR MEDIA, NEW YORK AND BEVERLY HILLS)

LIVE

> *Broken Dishes, Kraft Television Theatre* (12 May 1948)
> *Ramshackle Inn, Philco Television Playhouse* (2 January 1949)
> *The Late Christopher* Bean, *Philco Television Playhouse* (6 February 1949)
> *"Bailout at 43,000," *Climax!* (29 December 1955)

FILMED

> *"First Born," *Ford Theatre* (5 February 1953)
> "Twenty-two Sycamore Road," *Schlitz Playhouse of Stars* (5 June 1953)
> "The Pearl Street Incident," *Schlitz Playhouse of Stars* (14 May 1954)
> "That's the Man," *General Electric Theater* (15 April 1956)
> "Turkey for the President," *General Electric Theater* (23 November 1958)
> "The Payoff," *General Electric Theater* (20 November 1960)
> "The Long Shadow," *Dick Powell's Zane Grey Theater* (19 January 1961)
> "Shadow of the Past," *The Tall Man* (7 October 1961)
> "Money and the Minister," *General Electric Theater* (26 November 1961)
> "Obituary for Mr. X," *Dick Powell Show* (23 January 1962)
> "King's Ransom," *87th Precinct* (19 February 1962)
> "The Sam Darland Story," *Wagon Train* (26 December 1962)

TELEVISION DOCUMENTARIES

Wild Bill: Hollywood Maverick—The Life and Times of William A. Wellman (1995), as herself, Warner Home Video (DVD)
Off the Menu: Last Days of Chasen's (1997), unbilled, archive footage, Northern Arts Entertainment

RONALD REAGAN

FEATURE FILMS

WARNER BROS.
  Love Is on the Air (1937)
  Accidents Will Happen (1938)
  Brother Rat (1938)
  Cowboy from Brooklyn (1938)
  Girls on Probation (1938)
  Sergeant Murphy (1938)
  Swing Your Lady (1938)
  Angels Wash Their Faces (1939)
  Code of the Secret Service (1939)
  Dark Victory (1939)
  Hell's Kitchen (1939)
  Going Places (1939)
  Naughty but Nice (1939)
  Secret Service of the Air (1939)
  Smashing the Money Ring (1939)
  An Angel from Texas (1940)
  Brother Rat and a Baby (1940)
  Knute Rockne-All American (1940)
  Murder in the Air (1940)
  Santa Fe Trail (1940)
  Tugboat Annie Sails Again (1940)
  International Squadron (1941)
  Million Dollar Baby (1941)
  Nine Lives Are Not Enough (1941)
  Desperate Journey (1942)
  Juke Girl (1942)
  Kings Row (1942)
  This Is the Army (1943)
  Stallion Road (1947)
  That Hagen Girl (1947)
  The Voice of the Turtle (1947)
  John Loves Mary (1949)
  Night unto Night (1949)

The Girl from Jones Beach (1949)
The Hasty Heart (1950)
Storm Warning (1951)
She's Working Her Way through College (1952)
The Winning Team (1952)

UNIVERSAL-INTERNATIONAL
Louisa (1950)
Bedtime for Bonzo (1951)
Law and Order (1953)

PARAMOUNT
The Last Outpost (1951)
Hong Kong (1952)
Tropic Zone (1953)

RKO
Cattle Queen of Montana (1954)
Tennessee's Partner (1955)

MGM
The Bad Man (1941)
Prisoner of War (1954)

COLUMBIA
Hellcats of the Navy (1957)

UNIVERSAL
The Killers (1964)

ARMY AIR CORPS SHORTS IN THE FIRST MOTION PICTURE UNIT (1942–44)

Beyond the Line of Duty (Narrator)
Cadet Classification (Narrator)
Fight for the Sky (Narrator)
For God and Country (Actor)
Rear Gunner (Actor)
Target Tokyo (Narrator)
Westward Bataan (Narrator)

RADIO (*=PALEY CENTER FOR MEDIA; **=MARGARET HERRICK LIBRARY)

*HOLLYWOOD PROFILE #1. A 1961 FIVE-PART PROGRAM ON CBS RADIO
Part 1: Reagan on his California Ranch
Part 2: Reagan on his days as a college athlete and sports announcer
Part 3: Reagan on breaking into the movies

Part 4: Reagan on the differences between film and television acting

Part 5: Reagan on the future of the movies

HOLLYWOOD PROFILE #2. A 1961 FIVE-PART SERIES ON CBS RADIO WITH REAGAN
INTERVIEWING NANCY

24 November: Nancy on marriage and career

25 November: Nancy on the role of a wife in furthering a husband's career

26 November: Nancy on her childhood

26 November: Nancy on her stage and screen work

26 November: Nancy on her children

HOLLYWOOD PROFILE #3. A SPECIAL 24 DECEMBER 1961 FIVE-PART CHRISTMAS
SERIES ON CBS RADIO WITH REAGAN AND NANCY

"The Lore of Christmas"

"The Traditions of Christmas"

"Early Christmas Memories"

"Christmas at the Reagans"

"Words about Christmas"

LUX RADIO THEATRE

** *Knute Rockne-All American* (2 December 1940)

**Nobody Lives Forever* (17 November 1947)

**Cloak and Dagger* (3 May 1948)

**Stallion Road* (4 October 1948)

**John Loves Mary* (19 June 1950)

**Louisa* (5 February 1951)

Carbine Williams (22 March 1954)

TELEVISION

For a list of Reagan's numerous television credits as performer, see Edwards, *Early Reagan*, 526—31 and imdb.com.

The following are part of the Paley Center for Media's Collection:

"First Born" (5 February 1953), "And Suddenly You Know" (10 December 1953), *Ford Theatre*

"The Long Shadow" (19 January 1961), *Zane Grey Theater*

"The Last of the Private Detectives" (n.d.), and "Who Killed Julie Greer?" (26 September 1961), *The Dick Powell Show*

"The Fort Pierce Story" (23 September 1963), *Wagon Train*